Insider Histories of the Vietnam Era Underground Press, Part 2

Voices from the Underground series, edited by Ken Wachsberger

Insider Histories of the Vietnam Era Underground Press, Part 1

Insider Histories of the Vietnam Era Underground Press, Part 2

My Odyssey through the Underground Press, by Michael Kindman

Stop the Presses! I Want to Get Off! A Brief History of the Prisoners'
Digest International, by Joseph W. Grant

Voices
from the
Underground

*

Insider Histories of the Vietnam Era Underground Press, Part 2

EDITED BY KEN WACHSBERGER

Michigan State University Press · East Lansing

⊛ The paper used in this publication meets the minimum requirements of ANSI/NISO Z39.48-1992 (R 1997) (Permanence of Paper).

Michigan State University Press
East Lansing, Michigan 48823-5245

Printed and bound in the United States of America.

18 17 16 15 14 13 12   1 2 3 4 5 6 7 8 9 10

LIBRARY OF CONGRESS CATALOGING-IN-PUBLICATION DATA
Insider histories of the Vietnam era underground press / [edited by Ken Wachsberger ; foreword by Markos Moulitsas].
p. cm.— (Voices from the underground series ; pt. 2)
Includes bibliographical references and index.
ISBN 978-1-61186-031-3 (pbk. : alk. paper) 1. Underground press publications—United States. 2. Human rights—United States—History—20th century. 3. Vietnam War, 1961–1975—Protest movements—United States. I. Wachsberger, Ken.
PN4888.U5I65 2011
070.4'49331880973—dc22
2010003522

Cover design by Erin Kirk New
Book design by Sharp Des!gns, Lansing, Michigan

green press initiative Michigan State University Press is a member of the Green Press Initiative and is committed to developing and encouraging ecologically responsible publishing practices. For more information about the Green Press Initiative and the use of recycled paper in book publishing, please visit *www.greenpressinitiative.org*.

Visit Michigan State University Press at *www.msupress.msu.org*

Contents

Foreword by Susan Brownmiller   xi

Preface by Ken Wachsberger   xiii

Soldiers Against the Vietnam War: *Aboveground*
and *The Ally* Harry W. Haines, with appendices
by Harry W. Haines and James Lewes   1

"Tell us about the plan to burn down barracks buildings at Fort Carson." The army intelligence officer wasn't keeping notes during the interrogation, so I figured the gray room had a microphone somewhere, recording my answers. My cover was blown, and here I sat in my dress uniform, summoned to explain my role in the publication of *Aboveground*, an antiwar paper directed at soldiers stationed at Fort Carson, Colorado. Harry Haines looks back at the widespread GI antiwar movement, that largely hidden, secret part of the war's history that embarrasses and threatens the regime that rules America today. Two appendices, by Haines and James Lewes, identify nearly 500 underground antiwar newspapers produced by, or aimed at, members of the U.S. armed forces during the Vietnam War.

Fast Times in the Motor City: The First Ten Years
of the *Fifth Estate*, 1965-1975 Bob Hippler, with
an appendix by Patrick Halley   47

Harvey Ovshinsky wasn't happy when his mother moved to Los Angeles in 1965 and dragged along the popular senior from Detroit's Mumford High School. Wandering around town in a funk, Ovshinsky happened upon the Sunset Strip. There he saw two sights that piqued his interest: a gathering place called the Fifth Estate Coffeehouse and Art Kunkin's *Los Angeles Free Press*. Ovshinsky began hanging out at the coffeehouse and working on the *Free Press*. He was captivated by its antiwar politics, its concern for developing a radical Los Angeles community, and its coverage of the local music scene. Before the year was over, he returned to Detroit and founded *Fifth Estate*. Over forty years later, writes alumnus Bob Hippler, the snake oil of Reagan and the two Bushes has bankrupted the country, most workers do not have a union, and countries still suffer under the yoke of neocolonialism; but the public has rejected Bush II's bogus "war on terror" and illegal occupation of Iraq, and *Fifth Estate* is the nation's longest-lived underground paper to emerge from the Vietnam era. In an appendix, Patrick Halley tells how he infiltrated the "Divine Light Mission," a religious cult started in India; how he pied the Guru Maharaj Ji, the fifteen-year-old perfect master, during the kid's visit to Detroit to receive the key to the city; and about the steel plate he wore in his head as a reminder until he died.

Fag Rag: The Most Loathsome Publication in the English Language   Charley Shively   97

On Friday evening, June 27, 1969, New York City police raided the Stonewall Bar on Sheridan Square. Instead of going quietly into the waiting vans, the motley crowd of queers and queens attacked the police. Stonewall was closed, but sporadic street rioting continued in Greenwich Village for the next few days. The event quickly became the Bastille Day of an emergent, nationwide gay and lesbian liberation movement, and the inspiration for a whole network of Gay Liberation Front papers, including Boston's *Fag Rag*. All of them offered a brisk brew of sexual liberation, anarchism, hippie love, drugs, peace, Maoism, Marxism, cultural separatism, feminism, effeminism, tofu/brown rice, urban junkie, rural purism, nudism, leather, high camp drag, poetry, essays, pictures, and more. In this article, *Fag Rag* collective member Charley Shively gives context to the paper's history into the present by tracing the history of the gay press back to Paris and Chicago in the twenties.

The Kudzu: Birth and Death in Underground Mississippi
David Doggett   121

Yes, there was an underground press in Mississippi in the sixties. How could there not be writers in the land of Faulkner, Tennessee Williams, Richard Wright, and Eudora Welty? The paper was called *The Kudzu* after the notorious vine that grows over old sheds, trees, and telephone poles throughout the South. How did it come about that a bunch of Mississippi white kids, descended from rednecks, slave owners, and Bible-thumpers, published for four years in the state's capital a running diatribe of social, economic, and political revolution, a proclamation of sexual liberation, illegal drugs, and heretical mysticism? How does anyone, anywhere, rise above the overpowering flow of one's native culture, the suffocating vise-like grip of the familial and communal, birth-to-death universe view? David Doggett tackles these questions and more in his fascinating history of *The Kudzu*.

The Wong Truth Conspiracy: A History of Madison Alternative Journalism Tim Wong

153

No Midwest city is as closely associated with the antiwar movement and counterculture of the Vietnam era as Madison, Wisconsin. At the University of Wisconsin, thousands took part in antiwar marches. The Army Math Research Center was bombed and one researcher was killed. Off campus, the Mifflin-Bassett neighborhood declared "independence" from Madison and the United States. Energy flowed into creating a wide variety of alternative economic institutions. In this article, the history of the alternative press from March 1967 to the present is told by Tim Wong, whose own 8½ years of alternative journalism in Madison chronicled the transition from the sixties to the eighties.

New Age: Worker Organizing from the Bottom Up Paul Krehbiel

189

Paul Krehbiel's first day on the job at Standard Mirror Company in South Buffalo in the spring of 1968 is still emblazoned in his mind. "When I walked into the factory I was assaulted by loud crashing and banging sounds. Black and green pipes and hoses crisscrossed everywhere, hissing like coiled cobras. The once-white walls looked like old teeth, coated in a yellowish-brown film after years of smoking. My nostrils sucked in the stink of sickening smells. A gray mist hung in the air, like fog in a Hollywood movie. But it wasn't romantic or intriguing. The mist was deadly. It had ground-up glass in it. After four hours in the foggy room, I felt like someone had rubbed sandpaper over my throat." This was not a torture chamber. It was one room in the auto-parts factory where he worked, eight hours a day, five days a week. It was also his first step on the way to becoming a founder of the progressive rank-and-file workers' newspaper *New Age.*

Ain't No Party Like the One We Got: The Young Lords Party and *Palante* Pablo "Yorúba" Guzmán

233

When Paul Guzman went to Mexico for a semester of study in early 1969, he was already an experienced political activist and aspiring "black militant." After 3½ months in a country where everyone was a Latino and proud of that heritage, he returned to New York as Pablo "Yorúba" Guzmán, ready to learn about Puerto Rico's militant history. In May 1969, he joined a group of college-age Latino males who would later merge with two similar groups to become the New York Young Lords Organization. His days of identifying with black or white North Americans, even radicals, were over, he writes in this history of the group's newspaper, *Palante*; it was time to look within and without and begin organizing in the barrios, creating a Puerto Rican, even a pan-Latino, movement.

Let a Hundred Flowers Blossom, Let a Hundred Schools of Thought Contend: The Story of *Hundred Flowers*
Ed Felien   255

The year 1970 was a turning point for America. Resistance to the war in Vietnam had matured into a permanent institution, a persistent and articulate counterculture. A new consciousness was being developed about capitalism, racism, and sexism. And in the last eight months of the year, Minneapolis's *Hundred Flowers* blossomed, flourished, and withered. In this article, former staff member Ed Felien discusses his involvement in the paper and tells why he is neither repentant nor nostalgic about his involvement.

The Furies: Goddesses of Vengeance   Ginny Z. Berson, with appendices by Ginny Z. Berson and Charlotte Bunch   269

Women's liberation in the nation's capital in the early 1970s was thriving. With consciousness-raising groups enabling hundreds of women to understand that the personal is political, women established rape counseling, child care, and other services; began researching the Pill and testifying in Congress; and created their own forms of media. In the winter and spring of 1972, while Richard Nixon and his minions were preparing to bug Democratic National Headquarters at the Watergate Building, twelve self-proclaimed revolutionary lesbian feminists—who were known collectively as the Furies—began putting out the first issues of what would almost instantly become *The* "legendary" *Furies*. Former collective member Ginny Berson tells her story here for the first time.

At This End of the Oregon Trail: The Eugene *AUGUR*, 1969–1974   Peter Jensen   289

An alien force had taken over our country. It talked peace and made vicious war; it owned both political parties. We were all that was left of the opposition. Above all, the media had caved in and was reporting inflated daily body counts for generals in Saigon and Washington. The press was just another chain of corporations acting like a line of skimpily dressed cheerleaders for the boys in grunt green. In such a setting, writes Peter Jensen, the Eugene *AUGUR* began publication in 1969.

Karl and Groucho's Marxist Dance: The *Columbus Free Press* and Its Predecessors in the Columbus Underground
Steve Abbott   303

The writings of Malcolm X and Martin Luther King bump up against the poetry of Allen Ginsberg and Walt Whitman on a bookcase in Steve Abbott's house in Old North Columbus. Political extremes coexist comfortably here, from Tom Wolfe and Abbie Hoffman to Marxist and anarchist treatises, from texts on drugs and sensual massage to analyses of racism and community organizing. What may appear to be a library tour, writes Abbott, is evidence of a personal odyssey that represents the myriad influences and contending philosophies that typified the alternative/underground press during its heyday in the late 1960s and early 1970s. The *Columbus Free Press*, in its content and its internal struggles, reflected both its community and its time—a time filled with days of agony and days of wonder as the ideals of mystical transformation and principled political struggle contended for the lives of those involved.

"Raising the Consciousness of the People": The Black Panther Intercommunal News Service, 1967–1980
JoNina M. Abron   335

On Tuesday, August 22, 1989, Huey P. Newton was murdered. The man who had been an international symbol of black resistance to white oppression was found dead on a street in Oakland, California, the same city where he had cofounded the Black Panther Party twenty-three years before. Six days later, over 2,000 people, including ex-Panthers from all over the country, mourned Huey's death and celebrated the enduring contributions that he and the party made to the political empowerment of black and other disenfranchised people in the United States. JoNina Abron was one of the speakers that day, along with Bobby Seale, Elaine Brown, Ericka Huggins, David Hilliard, and Emory Douglas. As she looked into the faces of her Panther comrades in the front pews, she writes, she thought about the good and hard times they had shared "serving the people body and soul," and about her experiences as the last editor of the Black Panther newspaper.

Both Sides Now Remembered: Or, The Once and Future Journal   Elihu Edelson   369

Jacksonville, Florida, was not the most fertile ground for an underground paper in late 1969. The city was ruled like a feudal fiefdom by a local machine that included the Florida Publishing Company, a monopoly that put out both the morning and evening papers. Three nearby military bases contributed to the ultraconservative atmosphere. New Leftists could be counted on the fingers of one hand; a handful of blacks put together the Florida Black Front, a local version of the Black Panthers. Some good rock bands—like the Allman Brothers and Lynyrd Skynyrd—were to come out of Jax, but they had to make their names in Atlanta. Because none of the local hippies had any journalistic experience, they went, naively, to an editor of FPC's *Florida Times-Union* for advice. Elihu Edelson, a public-school art teacher and part-time newspaper art critic, was about to get "sucked in" to the story of *Both Sides Now*.

It Aint Me Babe: From Feminist Radicals to Radical
Feminists Bonnie Eisenberg, with help from Laura X,
Trina Robbins, Starr Goode, and Alta, with appendices
by Laura X and Trina Robbins   385

The 1960s were a tumultuous time in Berkeley, California, where the spark of student rebellion in the U.S. was born with the nonviolent free speech movement in 1964. As the Vietnam War escalated and students faced the threat of being drafted, the U.C. Berkeley campus and surrounding residential communities became the site of major student protests. By the spring of 1969, Governor Reagan was determined to "reestablish order." When an innocuous group of students and local counterculture activists turned a university-owned vacant block into a park, they were met with an astounding show of force. During the resulting protest rallies, one bystander was shot and killed by police, scores were shot and beaten, and thousands suffered from tear gas dropped by low-flying helicopters. When the Independent Socialists suggested that Bonnie Eisenberg go to Boston for the summer to participate in a printing apprenticeship program at the New England Free Press, she was ready for a new adventure. At the time, she had no idea that it would lead to her starting *It Aint Me Babe*, the first national newspaper of the emerging women's liberation movement in the United States.

About the Authors   417

Index   421

Foreword

SUSAN BROWNMILLER

As Ken Wachsberger continues to collect memoirs from the founders and insiders of the alternative press, the story gets wider and deeper—there is so much to tell! Now we have volume 3 in front of us, but readers should not expect an orderly chronological sequence. If you are familiar with volumes 1 and 2, you know that "orderly" was not a concept with much traction in the counterculture, while in-your-face audacity was a governing rule. So many political issues and lifestyle changes were exploding simultaneously in so many cities. You had to have been there, and luckily for future historians, these contributors were at the heart of the scene.

Pride of place in this volume is given, quite rightly, to Harry Haines's account of several papers that grew out of the GI coffeehouse movement and the general dissatisfactions and unrest on U.S. military bases at home and abroad during the Vietnam War. I was particularly engaged by "We Demand" from a 1971 issue of *The Bond* that called for "election of officers by vote of rank and file," "an end to saluting and sir-ing of officers," and "the right of collective bargaining." Truly seditious stuff. Distribution—getting their labor of love into the hands of readers—was a problem for all the alternative papers of the era as hawkers frequently were harassed by cops on the street, but the distribution of the GI antiwar papers to soldiers on military bases required some highly creative methods. Bundles sent through the mail were camouflaged to look like care packages from families or church groups back home.

Bob Hippler's narrative of the first ten years of *Fifth Estate* in Detroit reenters the swirling political currents of the era as Stalinists, Trotskyists, and Maoists fought to influence the paper. External forces, like Lyndon LaRouche and the rise of the mystical religious cults, needed outright debunking, and got it. In an addendum, Patrick Halley recalls the time when Guru Maharaj Ji, the fifteen-year-old "perfect master" from India, set up shop in Motor City and Detroit's city fathers gave him their symbolic key to the city. Halley personally dealt with the guru at a city council meeting in a pie-throwing action. Another problem identified by Halley afflicted most of the alternative papers: whether or not to achieve financial solvency by running sexploitation ads. Many papers of the era seem to have capitulated, but *Fifth Estate* did not.

The many evolutions of "Freep," the *Free Press* of Columbus, Ohio, are thoughtfully parsed by Steve Abbott, who gracefully admits to guilty-as-charged when the staff women confronted the sexist behavior of the staff men in a purge. Abbott asserts that drugs are underplayed in most accounts of the alternative press, and wishes to correct the record. Weed and hallucinogens were integral to the lifestyle and creative process at "Freep," but Quaaludes, called "sopors" for soporifics, were regularly denounced in print because their tranquilizing effect on the hippie community undercut the urge for political action. Abbott does a charming riff on the colorful aliases used by "Freep" writers, to make the contributors' list seem larger, to protect anonymity on a sensitive story, or just for fun. "Ultimately," he writes, "little of this mattered." When staff members requested and received their FBI files under the Freedom of Information Act, they were astonished by how much the feds knew. They also learned that the guy who handled their advertising and distribution was an informant.

White males who essentially ran the papers always understood that some political reporting and opinion required a voice separate from theirs (see Pablo Guzmán on *Palante*, the Young Lords paper, and JoNina Abron on the *Black Panther Intercommunal News Service*), but their collective feelings were hurt when the women they worked with—and lived with and slept with—began expounding on women's liberation. A special one-time "Women's Issue" or a "Women's Caucus" did not stem the rising tide. During the seventies, independent feminist papers sprang up across the country. In this volume, Wachsberger includes accounts of Berkeley's *It Aint Me Babe* (extraordinarily influential on the national level despite its short life) and *The Furies* in Washington, DC. Bob Hippler quietly notes that the *Fifth Estate* "had no openly gay staffer until I rejoined it in January 1973, having 'come out' as a gay person in 1972."

Yes, the times they were a-changing in ways the founders and insiders of the alternative press could not have imagined when they started their journeys. Hang on—it's quite a ride.

Preface

KEN WACHSBERGER

few weeks after volume 1 of the four-volume Voices from the Underground Series came out in January 2011, I was interviewed by Marc Stern, host of "Radio with a View," the Sunday-morning talk show on Boston's WMBR 88.1 FM. He asked me why I had chosen to devote so much time to the subject of the underground press, which was the independent, dissident press of the Vietnam era. I thought about it for a few seconds. It's an existential issue, I told him, and it's more than the underground press.

The Voices from the Underground Series is about the antiwar movement and about reclaiming our history. One day we're everywhere, in communities all across the country, uniting as patriots to rescue our country from a corporate government run amuck. We were heroes. We ended the war. But by the war's end, even though the majority of citizens knew our government's actions were wrong and they wanted out, our citizens were more divided than at any time since the Civil War, in no small part because of the social issues that continue to divide us today even though the nuances have changed. Collectively we freaked out and swung to the right. Far to the right. Here comes Ronald Reagan. Veterans of the antiwar movement, now entering the work force and starting to raise families, began the horrifying process of self-censoring out of fear of "guilt by association."

Their own kids would grow up having no idea that their parents were part of the heroic antiwar movement. I know that because I was teaching at Eastern Michigan University. Their children were my students. They didn't have a clue.

But, as I told Marc, I never stopped speaking about the period. I told my kids, I told my students, and I continued to write about what we had done. My fellow conspirators in the Voices from the Underground Series did the same. Friend, reader, you're in for another treat.

And if your parents or grandparents came of age during the Vietnam era, ask them what they did during the war. Chances are, you'll hear some good stories.

* * *

Books published by academic presses have notorious lag times between the time the text is finalized and the time the books make their public appearance. In the long, ongoing process of updating stories from the first edition of *Voices from the Underground*—which appeared in 1993 during the George Bush I years—and adding stories that are new to this expanded series of insider histories of underground papers from the Vietnam era, specific stories were finished long before their respective volumes appeared in print. Stories that appear in volume 1 of this new series were finished between 2007 and 2010. Volume 1 came out in 2011. This is no reflection against Michigan State University Press, the publisher of the Voices from the Underground Series; it is a condition that is endemic to the system of book publishing.

As contributors were updating their stories, the George Bush II years were coming to an ignominious end, the economy was devastated, and the Republicans were in disarray as they faced well-deserved public scorn. Barack Obama was now president-elect and we were looking forward to at least some breathing space with his upcoming presidency. The country in general was feeling hopeful again, with a few glaring exceptions, most notably those bigots who couldn't get used to a black guy running the show. But even for the optimists, there was a fear of believing. The revised stories reflect those mixed feelings.

The contributions to this third volume were revised and written at the same time as the stories that you've already read from the first volume, so they also conclude with reflections on the upcoming Obama years. A lot has changed since then.

By the time volume 1 actually appeared in print, two years of the Obama administration had gone by. The taxpayer-financed bank bailout—conceived during the Bush years but carried out during the Obama years—had succeeded in improving the financial statistics that determine the general state of our economy, but the only actual beneficiaries were the banks and other financial managers who had executed the decisions encouraged by Bush that brought the ruin in the first place. The rest of the economy had tanked and wasn't going anywhere, housing values were way down, and the job market was still shrinking.

The Republicans, now out of power in all three branches of government, voted against every idea the Democrats proposed to improve conditions for the average citizen, and then blamed Obama because conditions worsened for the average citizen. The Democrats, as usual, failed to connect the current devastation to the Republican reign of corruption (Obama wanted to "look forward") or their continued obstruction; ran from their modest achievements; and let the Republicans define the terms of debate. So in the midterm elections, the Tea Party wing of the Republican Party bought its way into the public eye largely on the bank account of two anti-government billionaire brothers and the Republican Party cheerleaders at Fox TV, who convinced middle-class Tea Party members that their interests lay in opposing their own interests and instead supporting large corporations.

With Democrats still controlling the executive branch and the Senate, but Republicans now controlling the House, the two parties' priorities for fixing the economy clashed. The Democrats fought to retain the social programs that benefited regular folks, and proposed paying for them with tax increases for the rich. The Republicans fought to slash and burn the social programs so they could give tax breaks to the rich. The Democrats argued that investment in government programs was needed to jump-start the economy and repair our deteriorating infrastructure. The Republicans argued that no mission was more important than that of decreasing the deficit. Every respectable economist supported the Democrats' position; so did most of the polls. The two sides fought for their respective sides and arrived at their usual compromise: tax breaks for the rich; social programs slashed and burned to close the deficit!

Who said *Alice in Wonderland* was fiction?

As I sit down to write this preface to volume 3, legislators in Republican-held states, including my beloved Michigan (current home) and Ohio (childhood home), are trying to obliterate unions and the middle class through coordinated attacks against the labor movement. Unions are fighting back in what hopefully will be a rebirth of union militancy. Democrats, including at the state level, are finding their voice: Dennis Kucinich and Bernie Sanders, of course, remain steady working-class heroes. But the Wisconsin state Democrats—their surprise show of courage was breathtaking. May they remain true to progressive principles. The polls continue to show support for the best of liberal and progressive intentions, but Democrats continue to give the dictionary to Republicans. During the health-care debates, they go limp in support of "end-of-life care," so the minority Republican argument against "death panels" carries the day. Now, "invest in jobs" loses out to "balance the budget—middle class be damned."

And Obama—still embroiled in Iraq and Afghanistan—joins NATO in enforcing a no-fly zone over Libya. Is this the first step to all-out war? As of this writing, he's doing his best to insist that no troops will be involved, but we know pressure is building to get rid of Moammar Gadhafi, and it would be politically damaging for him to stop at less—on a par with Bush I invading Iraq and not getting rid of Saddam Hussein. The CIA is already talking to the rebels, whoever they are, while Congress is voting whether or not we should send them arms. Can troops be far behind? Stay tuned.

Meanwhile, where is Obama on support for the workers in this country? Eerie silence as he prepares to launch his bid for a second term.

We learned during the Vietnam era that you could trust a conservative more than you could a liberal because you always knew where a conservative stood—against the middle class, education, the elderly, the poor, women, students, the environment, peace, privacy in the home, the First Amendment, voter registration, affordable insurance, and other issues that treated America as a home for real people, not patriotic slogans and religious crusades; and for tax breaks for the rich and the myth of American omnipotence. You knew basically where a liberal stood also, but you could never trust them to stick to their beliefs. Put another way, you could always trust them—to sell you out.

The stories in *Insider Histories of the Vietnam Era Underground Press, Part 2* remind us again that the lessons of the Vietnam era remain relevant today. "By God, we've kicked the Vietnam syndrome once and for all!" George Bush I exclaimed at the end of the first Iraq War. Wishful thinking, George. We've just begun to fight.

*　*　*

I am delighted that Susan Brownmiller agreed to write a foreword to this volume. Susan is one of the pioneer leaders of the second wave of the feminist movement that burst forth in the sixties and seventies and is still changing the world. Her first book, the groundbreaking *Against Our Will: Men, Women, and Rape*, redefined rape forever as a feminist issue. She has been a supporter of the Voices from the Underground Series since it first came out in its earlier iteration in 1993.

Not long after the first edition went out of print, long before it had reached its sales potential (a story for another time), I received a phone call from Susan. She was at the time in the process of writing her history of the feminist movement, *In Our Time: Memoir of a Revolution*, and she needed a copy of *Voices* for her research. She said, "Hi, Ken, this is Susan Brownmiller." I thought to myself, "Susan Brownmiller!" Honestly I can't remember if I expressed my surprise out loud. Okay, I admit it, I felt like a groupie because she was an important figure in a movement that I at times followed and at other times led (I'm talking about the general antiwar/countercultural movement, not the feminist movement) but at all times respected highly and loved being a part of. Sadly I wasn't able to help her—my personal supply of books to sell was already gone. Fortunately Marilyn Webb, whose story of the founding of *off our backs*, the first major feminist paper to emerge on the East Coast, appears in volume 1 of the Voices from the Underground Series, was able to help Susan. Marilyn's story is footnoted several times in Susan's book.

I never forgot that incident, so while I was working on this new edition I contacted Susan and asked her for a testimonial quote. Generously, she came through. Her quote appeared on the back cover of volume 1, along with quotes from Bill Ayers, Tom Hayden, and Chris Atton, professor of media and culture at Scotland's Edinburgh Napier University. Here's what Susan wrote:

> What a boon to historians! Ken Wachsberger's *Voices from the Underground* is crucial to an understanding of the literary and political history of the 1960s counterculture movement. This valuable resource must stay in print, if only for academics who wish to study the amazing phenomenon of the alternative newspapers, put together by amateurs, that sprang up across the country in those fervent years. Wachsberger's material, largely in the form of "how we did it" memoirs, is rich in personal histories and anecdotal details that are collected nowhere else.

So when I visited her on my next trip to New York and met her for the first time, I expected her to tell me how much she loved the book. Instead she said, "You don't have enough on the feminist press. You need to include *It Aint Me Babe*." I tried to explain to her that I already had *off our backs* in the first volume and *The Furies*, the radical lesbian paper put out by the legendary Furies collective, which appears in this volume, and that while the series contained representative writings of the different genres of underground papers, it didn't pretend to be comprehensive. But she insisted the feminist papers deserved more. She told me to contact Laura X, whose interview with a rape victim in Berkeley had inspired Susan to write *Against Our Will*.

Laura X is legendary in feminist lore as the premier archivist of the feminist movement. She embraced my invitation and pulled together other key figures from Berkeley's *It Aint Me Babe*, the first major feminist underground paper, to tell their story for the first time. The lead author is Bonnie Eisenberg, founder of *Babe*, but she received critical help from Laura, Trina Robbins, Starr Goode, and Alta. Appendices are by Laura, who writes about her archives, and Trina, one of the pioneer feminist comix artists, who helped to break through the men-only barrier.

The story of *It Aint Me Babe* appears, for the first time ever, in this volume, so it was only natural for me to invite Susan. I am truly honored that she accepted my invitation.

And, incidentally, she was right. I needed to include *It Aint Me Babe.* You'll see why when you read their story.

* * *

While I'm talking about stories that didn't appear in the first edition of *Voices from the Underground*, I want to point out that for over a quarter of a century I've been a proud member of the National Writers Union, which has been affiliated with the UAW since 1981. If you are a writer, I urge you to join also, especially if you are looking at a book, journalism, or agent contract and don't understand what the legalese means, or if you've already been screwed by your publisher and need help filing a complaint. Go to www.nwu.org and join online. (*Now! You can finish this preface after you join!*) But in the sixties and seventies, when I thought about union workers I thought about hard hats, those right-wing, pro-war, hippie haters. So admittedly I didn't even know there were rank-and-file underground papers. I never even considered including one in the first edition of *Voices* because I didn't know there were any to include. The first edition came out. Then it went out of print. Some years later I created my first Web site to promote my books. Ever the optimist and student of self-hypnosis, instead of writing "no longer available" by *Voices*, I wrote "temporarily out of print."

One day I received an e-mail from Paul Krehbiel noting the status of *Voices* and asking when it would be back in print, and if I would be interested in the story of a paper that was directed at union workers at the factories in upstate New York. As it turned out, his timing was impeccable because his e-mail arrived at the time when I was in the early stages of pulling together my resources and energy to start creating this second edition. I'm always interested in looking, I thought to myself, but I won't take it unless it's up to the quality of the stories that I've already got. I wrote back to Paul that I would be happy to look at it, but that I wasn't looking for mere 2,000-word snapshots; I wanted the whole story, with the quotes, anecdotes, analyses, head-trips, and character descriptions of the current collection. Paul accepted the challenge and came through. His story begins on his first day of work, when, upon walking into the factory, "I was assaulted by loud crashing and banging sounds. Black and green pipes and hoses crisscrossed everywhere, hissing like coiled cobras. The once-white walls looked like old teeth, coated in a yellowish-brown film after years of smoking. My nostrils sucked in the stink of sickening smells." It was there that he began to develop the consciousness that led to his role in the founding of *New Age.* Welcome, Paul.

Finally, in the first edition to *Voices from the Underground*, Harry Haines's story of *Aboveground* included an appendix that listed military underground papers written by or directed at members of the military. At the time it was the most extensive such listing in existence. But Harry always knew that it was nowhere near complete. Along came James Lewes. James got his PhD from the University of Iowa in 2000. His doctoral thesis was on the GI-produced underground newspapers. In 2003 it was published by the Praeger imprint of Greenwood

Press. He was a researcher and Web designer for the groundbreaking film *Sir! No Sir!*, about the military resistance movement during the war. His principal contribution was the creation of the largest repository of Vietnam-era GI movement materials on the Internet. He is now working through the GI Press Project to digitize all surviving copies of GI newspapers before the poor quality of the paper used to produce them crumbles to dust.

While reading his book, I found a listing of GI underground papers. I compared it to Harry's and discovered many that we didn't have, so I contacted James and asked him if he could write an appendix to Harry's appendix. His positive answer now brings the list of papers in the Voices from the Underground Series to nearly 500, more than double what we had. It is safe to say the list still isn't complete—but I am confident that nowhere will there ever appear a list that is more comprehensive than the two combined appendices that follow Harry's story, unless it reproduces our list completely and then merely adds to it. As Country Joe McDonald, of "and the Fish" fame as well as a former military man and a longtime supporter of families of veterans, was inspired to write to me, the Voices from the Underground Series is "an important project. That information needs to be available. I liked the list of GI newspapers and was not aware there were so many." Harry's story, with his and James's appendices, is the lead piece in this latest volume. Welcome, James.

Soldiers Against the Vietnam War: *Aboveground* and *The Ally*

HARRY W. HAINES

"Tell us about the plan to burn down barracks buildings at Fort Carson." The army intelligence officer wasn't keeping notes during the interrogation, so I figured the gray room had a microphone hidden somewhere, recording my answers. My cover was blown, and here I sat in my dress uniform, summoned to explain my role in the publication of *Aboveground*, an antiwar paper directed at soldiers stationed at Fort Carson, Colorado.

Aboveground was the brainchild of my buddies Tom Roberts and Curt Stocker. Intelligence officers had already questioned Roberts and Stocker, and now it was my turn. A couple of my articles, written under the name "A Fort Carson GI," rested on the table. The intelligence officer sat directly across from me, and the articles were spotlighted by a single bulb that hung from the ceiling. "I need to know about the plan to set fire to the barracks," he repeated.

"I don't know anything about setting fire to barracks," I said.

"I understand how you feel about the war, but these barracks buildings are tinder boxes—do you realize that men could die?"

"I know the buildings are very unsafe, sir."

"But you won't cooperate."

"As far as I know, there is no plan to set fire to anything at Fort Carson, sir." I wondered how much he knew. A few weeks earlier, somebody actually suggested that we do just that—torch a few barracks. The suggestion came from a GI during a meeting at the Home Front, the GI coffeehouse in nearby Colorado Springs. The Home Front, one of many coffeehouses operated by the United States Servicemen's Fund (USSF) and located near army posts across the country, served as a base for all kinds of antiwar activities, including the publication of *Aboveground*. We'd gather each month at the Home Front to talk about articles for the coming issue of the paper. Sometimes the meetings would develop into lengthy discussions about the war and what we should do to end it. The suggestion to torch a barracks came at one of these meetings.

The GI who proposed the idea seemed especially weird to me. No one at the coffeehouse

A complete collection of *Aboveground* is deposited with the William Joiner Center for the Study of War and Social Consequences at the University of Massachusetts Harbor Campus, Boston.

knew him, and he didn't seem to know much about Fort Carson or Colorado Springs. More important, his suggestion was truly reckless. The Fort Carson barracks were World War II structures, and their estimated burn time was about ten minutes, max. Burning a barracks meant more than arson. It meant murder. It meant killing GIs, guys like us. We ignored the suggestion and went on with the meeting. And here, a couple of months later, an army intelligence officer alluded to the same bad idea.

What I didn't know was this: At the precise moment I was being questioned, an anonymous clerk in Fort Carson's headquarters company was passing an envelope to Roberts and Stocker. The envelope contained the identifications of military intelligence agents who worked undercover. The guy at the meeting—the guy who tried to get us to set fire to barracks buildings—was an agent. Our little band of dissidents was so potentially threatening that military intelligence actually risked the incineration of U.S. soldiers in order to discredit us! This incident provided some insight into the nature of political power in the United States.

"Well, if you don't know anything about the plan to burn down barracks, tell me about the money. Where does *Aboveground*'s money come from?"

"You mean the money to finance the paper?" I asked.

"Yes. How much support comes from the Communists?"

My fear was turning to anger. I was just out of college. I had majored in communication and I was on my way to a radio news job when the draft got me. Back in school, I decided on a career in broadcast news the day I saw the tape of Edward R. Murrow's famous "See It Now" program about the dangers of Joe McCarthy. The interrogator's question revealed the same kind of contempt that McCarthy and his supporters shared for their opponents, or so it seemed to me.

"I don't know what you mean about Communists, sir." I said.

"We know there are Communists in *Aboveground*'s organization," he said. "Why don't you help the country by identifying them? You'd also be helping your buddies Roberts and Stocker. We don't think they know what they're getting themselves into."

I smiled at the thought of "*Aboveground*'s organization" and was tempted to say, "*What* organization?" Roberts and Stocker operated *Aboveground* on the principle of democratic participation. If you contributed to the content or distribution of the paper, you had a say about how things were done. Staff volunteers discussed and voted on the content of most of the nine issues of *Aboveground.* Although Roberts and Stocker maintained editorial leadership, they often published opinions with which they strongly disagreed, and these opinions often came from the civilian antiwar activists at the Home Front. The newspaper's volunteer staff had a core group of five or six, plus several others who came and went according to military reassignments and the transient nature of the Colorado counterculture in 1969 and 1970. To talk about "organization" was to miss altogether the amorphous nature of "the Movement" and the broad spectrum of political viewpoints that swirled around *Aboveground* and became represented in its pages.

Four political factions were involved in the paper's operation, and all of them were based at the Home Front. First, there were the civil libertarians. Like me, these were dissident GIs who agreed that the Vietnam War was essentially illegal and immoral. We doubted that the war was even constitutional, and we were certain that it violated our country's values. Our experience in the army led us to distrust the military hierarchy. This political viewpoint was strongly influenced by men like Roberts and Stocker, soldiers who had already pulled tours of duty in Vietnam and who were now reassigned to stateside posts.

Ironically, the army had trained Roberts and Stocker to do journalistic work! They had both been assigned to the Tenth Psychological Operations Battalion in South Vietnam. Based on their war experience, they concluded that the corruption and brutality of the South Vietnamese government precluded victory, because the vast majority of the South Vietnamese didn't support the Saigon regime. Simply, GIs were fighting and dying for a government that wasn't worth the sacrifice of *one* American life. Roberts and Stocker—and other soldiers who had already been to 'Nam—were potentially dangerous, and the army made a mistake by reassigning them to stateside posts where they could talk about the war to recently drafted troops. Stories of corruption and atrocities spread throughout the army as the returning GIs tried to warn the rest of us about the war's realities. *Aboveground* and the other two hundred or so GI underground papers helped spread the word to soldiers who were headed to Vietnam. So the civil libertarians wrote articles for the paper that stressed the history and nature of American involvement and how the war violated the Constitution and traditional American values.

The second political faction was called the "radicals," a very imprecise term that covered a variety of viewpoints and that seemed to change daily. The antiwar movement was composed of numerous political groups that sometimes cooperated and often competed for political leadership. The term "radical" was used at the Home Front to identify a wide assortment of these groups, all of which shared a generally Marxist orientation. The "radical" faction included members of the Weatherman group of Students for a Democratic Society, the Young Socialists, and the New York-based American Servicemen's Union (ASU).

The term was by no means negative. On the contrary, much of the Home Front's continuing debate focused on the meaning of "radical," and on the best "radical" strategy—including violence—to help end the war. One radical plan involved the organization of U.S. troops as the vanguard army of an armed revolution in the United States. The idea was to turn the guns around. This plan made more sense to some of the civilian volunteers than to those of us in the army. In 1969, most GIs simply wanted to be liberated from the army, not involved in armed revolution. It was also very difficult to organize GIs in an effective way. Once the military command identified a GI organizer, that person would be imprisoned, roughed up, or reassigned to some other post. What many of us hoped for was simply an increasing unwillingness by soldiers to comply with the war effort. And gradually, that's what happened throughout the ranks.

The biggest difference between the radicals and the civil libertarians was the radicals' emphasis on what they viewed as class distinctions in the military social structure. For example, the ASU viewed the military caste system as analogous to the system of exploitation in civilian life. The officers were the bosses, while the enlisted men were the workers. This particular position didn't make much sense to me, because many of the officers were themselves from lower-middle-class and working-class families. More important, many of the officers had already turned against the war and were actually participating in the antiwar movement. Officers were potential allies in the movement to end the war. As a draftee, I was less interested in union-like organizing than I was in simply ending the war and getting out of the army.

The ASU attempted to establish a local chapter at the Home Front, but this attempt failed to generate interest among more than a few soldiers. Nevertheless, the radicals' emphasis on class analysis profoundly influenced *Aboveground* because the analysis introduced considerations of social structure and the distribution of power. The faction compelled the rest of us to start linking the destruction of Vietnam to patterns of repression at home and in other parts of the world.

The third political faction that influenced *Aboveground* was a group of United States Servicemen's Fund (USSF) organizers who were also activists in the emerging women's liberation movement. This group, which included persons sent to Colorado Springs by the USSF to establish and operate the Home Front, began to influence the newspaper when Roberts and Stocker agreed to base *Aboveground* at the coffeehouse. These women were the first feminists I had met, although the term "feminist" was hardly in widespread use at this time. This faction attempted to link U.S. policy in Vietnam to women's oppression. They took on the difficult task of attempting to educate men (young GIs) about feminist issues.

Because the editorial decision making of *Aboveground* was based upon group consensus, these three factions exercised varying degrees of influence upon the newspaper's political orientation and content. The fourth group, less well defined than the others, shared a countercultural orientation with interests in Eastern spiritualism, the development of a communal society, and the use of hallucinogens as religious sacraments. This countercultural influence was a product of the social environment existing in the mountains of Colorado and was sometimes viewed by the other factions as anarchistic and politically unproductive.

What we had at the Home Front was a microcosm of the antiwar movement. So when my interrogator asked me to identify the "Communists," I was understandably amused.

"We have at least one of everything at the Home Front, sir," I said, "so there's probably a Communist there somewhere. I think Stocker is a Republican."

"So you don't care about the possibility of Communists taking over the newspaper and using Roberts and Stocker to spread anti-American sentiment at Fort Carson?"

"It's not anti-American sentiment that's getting spread," I said. "It's antiwar sentiment. And the troops don't need Communists to tell them that the war is wrong. The troops already know that it's wrong, and very soon you—the command, that is—will have to come to grips with the fact that a lot of us know that you've already lost the war. We *know* that guys are dying for no reason, sir."

"Uh huh," he said. "If you won't identify the Communists, at least tell me where the money comes from. We know that USSF is supplying cash for the newspaper. What are the other sources?"

From August 1969 to May 1970, Roberts and Stocker produced nine issues of *Aboveground*. Most of the issues were between four and eight pages, and the press runs ranged between 3,500 and 10,000 copies, distributed at Fort Carson and in Colorado Springs. The USSF support began in November 1969 (starting with issue number 4; see figure 1), and other sources of support included limited donations and subscriptions. Roberts and Stocker paid for the first two or three issues out of their own pockets. What made the October 1969 issue (number 3; see figure 2) unique was its partial funding by a Vietnam War widow who donated a portion of her husband's $10,000 military life insurance payment (GI "blood money") to the paper's operation. I decided to elaborate on this unusual one-time source of revenue.

"War widows, sir."

"What?"

"The paper is supported by donations from war widows throughout Colorado and a few

aboveground

VOLUME 1, NUMBER 4   THE COLORADO UNDERGROUND   NOVEMBER 1969

THIS PUBLICATION IS YOUR PROPERTY—IT CANNOT LEGALLY BE TAKEN FROM YOU

UCMJ
Page Three

ESSAY ON VIOLENCE
Page Two

Schedule For
Peace
Page Four

Moratorium
By Susan P. Clifton

All of you who shivered through the October Moratorium in Colorado Springs, thank you very much for your support. The war continues; your support is needed again on November 13 and 14 and until this war ends. Colorado College will have a teach-in—Symposium on Thursday, November 13th. Friday, following the all night reading of the war dead, there will be a Rally in Acacia Park or Shove Chapel, depending on the weather.

Despite attempts by Agnew, Laird, Rogers, etc. to discredit the Moratorium on war, we hope support will grow and grow. Only in this way will our government realize the concern of the American people to have the war end. Those of you who demonstrate your support of the Moratorium understand the injustice of this war. You have a constitutional right to dissent.

The times have changed dramatically since the war began. It is no longer a matter of innocent involvement; the so called "credibility gap" is shrinking rapidly. People are learning what this war is all about. They have learned that the government in Saigon is run by corrupt and oppressive cliques who serve only themselves. They have learned that the common people of Vietnam have grown to hate Americans who are supposed to be there to defend them. America cannot reverse the losses of these people but we can stop further losses by withdrawing as soon as possible.

(Continued on page six.)

FIGURE 1: Cover of *Aboveground* issue 4 (November 1969), the first issue supported by United States Servicemen's Fund. From *Aboveground* archives.

aboveground

VOLUME 1, NUMBER 3   BY SOLDIERS—FOR ALL   OCTOBER 1969

THIS PUBLICATION IS YOUR PROPERTY—IT CANNOT LEGALLY BE TAKEN FROM YOU

The Death

"This is Sergeant Menninger from First Army Headquarters . . . I'd like to come up and speak with you . . . Is it important? . . . Yes, it's very important . . . Kathie, there's some men from the Army coming up . . . I'm scared . . .

"This is Sergeant Menninger and this is Sergeant Ortiz . . . it is my duty to inform you that your husband, Private First Class Robert F. Nichols, RA11857896, died from wounds suffered in a mortar explosion.

(I can picture him laughing . . . he can't be dead.)

A little blue room with little grey chairs and the coffin—the silver, flag-draped coffin. (It hit me, it was all so cold.) (I wonder what's in there . . . is he all there . . . what does that body look like?)

WESTERN UNION. "THIS CONCERNS YOUR HUSBAND. PFC. ROBERT F. NICH-OLS. THE ARMY WILL RETURN YOUR LOVED ONE TO A PORT IN THE UNITED STATES BY FIRST AVAILABLE MILITARY AIRLIFT. AT THE PORT REMAINS WILL BE PLACED IN A METAL CASKET AND DELIVERED (ACCOMPANIED BY A MIL-ITARY ESCORT) BY THE MOST EXPEDI-TIOUS MEANS TO ANY FUNERAL DI-RECTOR . . . .

Cloudy day . . . cool outside . . . the hole was already dug . . . (I wanted to tell the man to keep his stupid flag, but I knew it wasn't his fault—he didn't do it.) (I wished everybody would go away . . . just wanted to touch the coffin . . . to make sure . . . if there was some way to know that it was my husband in there.)

"Didn't the escort give you the death certificate? . . . It was supposed to come with the body . . . There will be a presenta-tion for the medals . . . I don't want the medals . . . you can keep your medals and tell the Army what to do with them . . . They didn't mean anything to my husband and me anyway . . . ."

Dear Mrs. Nichols: The enclosed mail, addressed to Robert F. Nichols, RA118-57896, bears your return address. Official records of the Department of the Army, as of 1 August 1969, indicate that he was re-ported deceased on 23 July 1969.

"We are proud of his military accom-plishments and grateful to his contribution to our Nation's strength."—Stanley R. Resor, Secretary of the Army.

"I know that the loss of a loved one is one of the most difficult things a person has to face, but perhaps you may find some

measure of comfort in knowing that he served his Nation with courage and honor at a time of great need. The memory of his service will be treasured by a grateful Nation because he has joined . . . —William C. Westmoreland, Chief of Staff, US Army.

"Private Robert F. Nichols has given his life for his country and our country. Your husband's name will live always in the history of this Nation, and be revered with our other American heroes. He has left his family a sacred heritage . . ."—Ralph W. Yarborough, Senator from Texas.

(How phony . . . he was just in the Army to get his time done . . . first they took his freedom, then his life.)

"We were thinking about splitting when he got his orders" (I wish we would've).

(I was very angry . . . very bitter . . . more and more as the days went by . . . I want to strike out at something . . . I don't know what yet.)

"He must have know he was going to die . . . strange . . . he used to write on his letters 'FREE, SOMEDAY, MAYBE.' "

When he died he was not free . . . he died chained to a sick nation's fear, to its hate, to its stupidity. He died without the freedom they said he was fighting for.

other places. Their husbands get wasted in Vietnam, and they turn over the blood money to *Aboveground."*

"You mean these women give up a portion of the money that's supposed to be used to bury their husbands?"

"They go easy on the funeral expenses and donate what's left to *Aboveground* and to the Home Front," I lied.

"That's the most disgusting thing . . ."

"They feel very strongly about the war."

"They're disgusting. All of you are disgusting. And you're . . . confused. You're confused about what the war is all about."

"What *is* the war all about, sir?"

"It's about democracy. The Vietnamese don't know the difference between communism and democracy. We're in Vietnam to help give them the opportunity to decide for themselves, without being forced. If they decide to go Communist, well, that's okay. That's up to them. We just want to give them the chance to make up their mind. We're not trying to force anything on them. That's what the other side is trying to do, to force something on them. And you people are using the insurance money of the war dead to . . ."

"All of the war widows tell us that their husbands would approve of it."

"How much money has been . . . how much has been donated in this way?"

"Thousands," I lied. My interrogator left the room for about twenty minutes, and I had the feeling I was being observed by lenses embedded in the walls. Paranoia washed over me, and I imagined electrical currents running through the bars on the window. It was total vulnerability, the kind of vulnerability that the Home Front civilians never quite understood. To be in the army was to be totally vulnerable, observable at all times. And they could do things to you that they couldn't do to regular human beings outside the Green Machine. Once you stepped forward and took the oath, your "ass was grass" (just like the boot camp saying pointed out) and the army was "the lawnmower." The United States Constitution didn't mean much here. The interrogator returned and sat again, facing me at the small table with the light bulb hanging overhead.

"I suppose people at the Home Front have sex. I mean, who do they have sex with? Do they have sex with each other?"

"I don't know, sir. I don't have sex with Home Front people."

"Who do Roberts and Stocker have sex with? Do they have girlfriends at the Home Front?"

"They have girlfriends, of course. They date. I don't know about their sex lives. It's none of my business."

"Do they have sex with any of the war widows?"

"I have no idea."

"Do any of the GIs at the coffeehouse have sex with each other?"

"Not to my knowledge."

"How about the women's libbers? Are any of them lesbians?"

"I don't know, sir."

"I'm only asking these questions so I can help Roberts and Stocker. They're in over their heads. You can help them by cooperating. If you're their friend, you'll cooperate."

"I don't know anything about sex."

"Who uses drugs at the Home Front?"

"Nobody. There're no drugs at the Home Front."

"There are drugs all over Colorado Springs. You mean the Home Front is the one place in town where there are no drugs?"

"We police the area. The Home Front staff keeps out drug users. We know that the police could use drugs as a way of closing down the coffeehouse. The military could put the place off limits. Nobody uses drugs at the Home Front."

"Nobody?"

"The only way that drugs will get into the Home Front will be if the police plant some there, sir."

"I understand that *Aboveground* has a new printer. Who's the new printer?"

The paper's initial printer, a company in Colorado Springs, was discouraged by agents and police officers and halted production of issue five (December 1969–January 1970) following a visit by agents from the Federal Bureau of Investigation, Military Intelligence, and local Colorado Springs police officers. The company broke its agreement to print *Aboveground* as a result of the visit, and no other printer in Colorado Springs would agree to print the paper.

Roberts and Stocker eventually found a printer outside Colorado Springs who, although he favored U.S. policy in Vietnam, was willing to print *Aboveground* at about half of the original cost. The name of this printer was kept secret.

Roberts believed that action was taken to suppress issue five (see figure 3) because it contained a story potentially damaging to a former commanding general of Fort Carson. The story resulted from materials passed to Roberts and Stocker by another serviceman with access to the general's flight records. These materials indicated that the general may have violated army regulations by piloting helicopters at Fort Carson. Roberts assumed that Military Intelligence learned of the decision to print the story from undercover agents assigned to the Home Front coffeehouse.

"Not many people know who the printer is."

"You must have some idea, though."

"Well, I know that they ship the photo-ready stuff to Omaha, so maybe the printer is there," I lied. "Why do you want to know who the printer is, sir?"

"In case we have to protect him. These antiwar groups have falling-outs, you know. Which is one thing you might keep in mind. Communists will do anything to reach their goals, anything. You probably think you're doing the right thing, and I certainly respect that. But even if your heart is in the right place, I have to say that you may be hurting the interests of the United States, and you may be jeopardizing the lives of your fellow soldiers."

"I don't think so, sir."

"Maybe you'll change your mind . . . later."

The interrogation was over, and I returned to my unit. By anybody's estimation, I had lucked out in the army. My duty assignment was a closed-circuit radio station established during World War II at the Fort Carson army hospital. Back in the forties, there were few radio stations in the Colorado Springs area, so the army operated the closed-circuit station as a morale booster for patients. The station had its original control board, a beautiful mahogany and brass Stromberg-Carlson board and turntables big enough to play the huge hour-long transcriptions that used to be the mainstay of network radio drama. The station also had a great collection of

aboveground

VOLUME 1, NUMBER 5   THE COLORADO UNDERGROUND   DEC. 1969—JAN. 1970

THIS PUBLICATION IS YOUR PROPERTY—IT CANNOT LEGALLY BE TAKEN FROM YOU

"Villagers Must Die"

Page 2

GI Rights

Page 4

FBI/MI Pressure

The December issue of ABOVEGROUND was to be printed December 12 by Peerless Graphics of Colorado Springs. On December 11, at approximately 3 P.M., agents of the FBI, Military Intelligence and local police visited their print shop, intimidated the printers and consequently halted production of the paper.

Representatives of Peerless Graphics admitted the joint police visit took place, but denied their last minute refusal to print ABOVEGROUND had anything to do with it.

Peerless, who had accepted the ABOVEGROUND contract verbally two weeks before the refusal, had completed all but the final step in the printing process.

The FBI/MI/Local Police induced refusal caused a delay of at least one week in ABOVEGROUND finding another printer. None contacted in Colorado Springs, strangely enough, would have anything to do with the paper.

For example, a Mr. Bernheim of Gowdy Printcraft (the people who print the Mountaineer) said when asked if his firm would print ABOVEGROUND, "I wouldn't touch it with a 10-foot pole."

The First Amendment to the U. S. Constitution says: "Congress shall pass no law abridging freedom of speech or of the press or of the right of the people to peaceable assemble and petition the government for a redress of grievances."

It has now come to a point in America when passing laws against such rights is not a necessary step in controlling them. As in certain other countries a police squad investigates the exercise of First Amendment Rights — giving the appearance that something done was illegal.

This is not the case. ABOVEGROUND is legal.

But despite this fact the police intimidation continues.

FIGURE 3: Cover of *Aboveground* issue 5 (December 1969–January 1970), with help from a new printer after the original one was visited by FBI agents. From *Aboveground* archives.

1950s Cold War propaganda dramas aimed at soldiers. One dramatic series was about life in the U.S. after a Communist coup! Commissars were fixing Little League baseball games, and the party decided who married whom and when. I and the other GIs assigned to the station would sit for hours, howling with laughter at Cold War plays.

By 1969, many commercial stations were on the air, so no one—*no one*—listened to the closed-circuit station, not even the aged civilian manager who nominally ran it. Nevertheless, the army was concerned that I might pump the *wrong* propaganda into the closed circuits, so I was removed from the radio station and sent into army limbo. For a time, I was reassigned to the hospital admissions office, where I worked as a clerk. And a few weeks after my interrogation, orders for Vietnam came down.

The conflict between Roberts and Stocker and the so-called "radical" faction at the Home Front eventually split *Aboveground*'s volunteer staff. Roberts and Stocker decided to move the paper out of the coffeehouse, and the final issue (number nine; see figure 4) was published in May 1970. By that time, I was in Vietnam, assigned to a medical unit at Cam Ranh Bay. Stocker told me that, from his point of view, the "radicals" alienated many GIs who might have gotten involved in the movement, which by that time was called the GI Resistance. The feminists increasingly challenged young enlisted men unaware of the political basis of feminism and unconvinced of its relationship to their own situation in the army. And there was a serious ideological split among those who argued in favor of armed revolution and those (including Roberts and Stocker) who saw no indication that soldiers would take part in a widespread armed insurrection. Roberts said, "Some of the Home Front people couldn't understand why GIs wouldn't turn the guns around, because they were never in the army themselves. We knew what was going down in Vietnam, and we didn't wish the same hell on the United States. We just wanted to end the war, get out of the army, and get on with our lives."

Despite the factional split, *Aboveground*'s short-lived operation (August 1969 to May 1970) was successful. Like the other two hundred–plus antiwar papers published by service personnel throughout the United States and overseas, *Aboveground* signaled a willingness of soldiers to take responsibility for the ill-conceived and disastrous policy that brought so much misery to the people of Vietnam and the United States. At the Home Front, and at the other GI coffeehouses sponsored by the USSF, coalitions developed between civilian and military groups, and strategies were developed to stop the war. The coffeehouses and the GI undergrounds introduced many of us to the methods of political organizing that sustained us through the mean-spirited years of the Reagan-Bush regime.

The GI underground papers, along with publicized acts of civil disobedience committed by individual soldiers, encouraged other service personnel to act in varying degrees against the war effort. Passive resistance eroded military discipline. The generals and politicians could no longer depend upon American troops to carry out orders, requiring Nixon to shift the burden to the beleaguered South Vietnamese Army under the euphemistic banner of "Vietnamization."

Ironically, the brass viewed this process as a deterioration of morale, when actually our morale was increasingly strengthened by what we read in the papers. The GI papers were the tip of an iceberg that went very deep into the structure of the American soldier's experience of the Vietnam War. Antiwar soldiers had allies throughout the ranks and among the officer corps, but these allies had to be quiet and anonymous, something that our civilian comrades could not fully appreciate.

aboveground

FINAL ISSUE   FROM THE HOME FRONT   MAY 1970

THIS PUBLICATION IS YOUR PROPERTY—IT CANNOT LEGALLY BE TAKEN FROM YOU

CIVILIANS—25c   BY GIS—FOR GIS   GIS—FREE

REVOLUTION—THE AMERICAN WAY

Kent State and Cambodia both mean alot to GIs.

As long as America continues with its present foreign policy you will be fighting . . . fighting in Cambodia or doing some "GARDEN PLOT-TING" against civilians on a campus or in a city.

The campus and city demonstrations will grow more massive, more militant unless America changes. But these demonstrators are not "commies," not "un-American." Protest, even revolution, is an American tradition. What is American heritage? — The Boston Tea Party; Boston Massacre; The Revolutionary War; The Declaration of Independence:

"We hold these truths to be self-evident; that all men are created equal; that they are endowed by their Creator with inherent and inalienable rights; that among these are life, liberty and the pursuit of happiness; that to secure these rights, governments are instituted among men, deriving their just powers from the consent of the governed; that whenever any form of government becomes destructive of these ends, **it is the right of the people to alter or abolish it,** and to institute new government laying its foundation on such principles, and organizing its powers in such form as to them shall seem most likely to effect their safety and happiness." — Declaration of Independence, 1776.

Our form of government is destructive of those ends — life, liberty and the pursuit of happiness.

Where is **happiness** amid strife? Where is **liberty** in the draft, or in our school systems? Where are the lives of over 40,000 GIs?

The time has come to "alter or abolish" the American government.

If we don't Cambodias, Kent States, ABMs, Nerve Gases, Nuclear Submarines, racism, pollution, hunger, poverty, (et al.) will abolish US!

After the first American Revolution Thomas Paine said, "As revolutions have begun, it is natural to expect that other revolutions will follow."

"The tree of liberty must be refreshed from time to time with blood of patriots and tyrants, it is their natural manure," said good old Thomas Jefferson in 1787. Endless famous Americans have advocated revolution in times such as these.

NIXON! Remember what happened to George III. We will make Kent State our Boston Massacre. The Continuing American Revolution is growing. The American Empire is falling.

But, like George III, Nixon will use force to stop the revolution. The force is you — the GI. When the time comes will you be a Tory or a Patriot?

Ex-Army "EM" Tom Roberts

FIGURE 4: Cover of *Aboveground* issue 9 (May 1970), the final issue. From *Aboveground* archives.

Our power was in our anonymity, and in our willingness to act when specific opportunities developed. Acts of sabotage and fragging have received attention in the histories of the war, but the written record has necessarily avoided the more difficult subject of a generalized noncompliance among the troops to follow orders, a more challenging topic to pin down because its significance is not readily quantifiable.

Additionally, many antiwar Vietnam vets remained quiet about their activities. Like people in any organizational structure, antiwar GIs learned how to stand in place, as it were—to give the minimal effort to the war, except when the effort was a matter of life or death for a fellow soldier. In this way, the Green Machine slowly ground down. The papers fed the process. Papers like *Aboveground* contributed to this generalized noncompliance by letting antiwar GIs know that they were not alone, that there were many of us throughout the ranks, and that we were not crazy or un-American. The papers gave us a sense of solidarity and purpose, a way to focus the anger and profound sadness we shared as victims of the same policy that turned much of Vietnam into moonscape.

To my knowledge, only one group fully conceptualized the role of the GI underground papers in this particular way, a result of their early incorporation of Vietnam veterans into their operation. The group was based in Berkeley, California, and published *The Ally* from 1968 to 1974 (perhaps the longest run of any of the GI papers). *The Ally* was distributed among GIs throughout Vietnam. The group's initial objective was to encourage widespread desertion. To this end, they published addresses throughout the world where deserters might be expected to find help. As the group expanded its membership to include Vietnam veterans, they gradually understood that no widespread desertion would occur, so they redefined their role as one of competing with another information source—the military—for the mind of the individual soldier.

The Ally was probably unique among the GI papers in that it consciously focused on the soldier's position in a war that questioned traditional American values. *The Ally* gave legitimacy to the antiwar soldier's sense of ideological contradiction and isolation. *The Ally*'s editor, Clark Smith, explained to me that staff members gradually discovered that the paper represented a kind of comfort to some readers who "received *The Ally* as a kind of blessing . . . which made them feel better about themselves and about where they were." By attempting to undermine military morale, Smith said, the staff came to feel they were inadvertently helping some soldiers cope with the peculiar emotional stress of the war's ideological crisis. After shifting away from the desertion objective, the paper focused on ways that GIs could legally slow up the war effort from within the military. By late 1969, *The Ally*'s circulation varied between 20,000 and 25,000 copies a month, most of them distributed in Vietnam. The distribution method itself fed the soldiers' growing sense of power.

Initially, *The Ally* staff planned to ship portable printing presses to dissident soldiers in Vietnam so they could publish their own antiwar papers in the war zone! The staff soon figured out that this plan was not workable because conditions in Vietnam precluded underground printing operations among the troops. (Roberts and Stocker, who met in Vietnam, considered the publication of antiwar material in the combat zone, but concluded the operation would be too difficult.) Combat troops, because of their fairly constant movement, would not have time to use the presses, and troops in the rear areas were subject to observation by commanders and South Vietnamese police. In addition, for troops in the rear, the operation of a printing press would be a one-way ticket to the war zone. *The Ally* staff soon shifted to a method of clandestine distribution, which challenged the ability of commanders to control their men.

At first, building *The Ally*'s Vietnam circulation was a slow and difficult task, because the staff had to depend upon making contact with potential readers and distributors through the newspaper itself. Subscription coupons were published in each issue. By returning a coupon, an individual subscriber decided for himself whether or not he would receive the paper through the mail. Subscribers were, of course, subject to harassment if their commanders found copies in their possession, despite army regulations that allegedly protected GIs from such abuses. By checking the appropriate box on the subscription coupon, a reader could also indicate his willingness to distribute *The Ally* to other servicemen. Bundles containing up to 100 copies of *The Ally* would then be mailed each month to these distributors. The bundles were disguised as care packages from home. Gradually, a distribution system developed among troops in Vietnam, and the paper encouraged soldiers to pass along individual copies to other readers. Dated subscription coupons indicated that some copies of *The Ally* were still being circulated hand to hand as much as six months after publication.

The covert distribution was an important part of the newspaper's function as a political tool. Attempts by military commanders to limit the distribution of *The Ally* and other GI papers resulted in conflict, tension, and the gradual erosion of military morale and authority. Attempts by commanders to seize copies of *The Ally* added to dissatisfaction among the paper's readership and aroused curiosity about the paper's contents.

Clandestine distribution also afforded GIs the chance to fight the system of which they were an unwilling part. The contents of the paper sometimes prompted discussion between dissident lower-ranking soldiers and their potentially sympathetic commanding officers. The distribution method "was a form of counter-harassment," Smith told me. "In a sense, *The Ally* was an organizational weapon."

Distribution of *Aboveground* probably functioned in a similar way. Volunteers, acting in violation of military regulations, distributed copies throughout Fort Carson. Roberts and Stocker handed out copies to motorists entering and leaving the main gate of the post. They could usually distribute the paper for about twenty minutes before military police would arrive and pack them off for interrogation sessions. The reaction of the military, of course, would spark interest in the paper by the straight media concerned about First Amendment protection. In turn, this interest gave the paper a higher profile, even among soldiers who had never read a copy. Mere distribution of antiwar papers challenged the military's authority and helped strengthen the morale and solidarity of antiwar GIs.

And it was very satisfying to tweak the brass! As Stocker said, "I didn't start having fun in the army until we began publishing *Aboveground.* I came back from Vietnam with the intention of declaring myself a conscientious objector, so I could get the chance to tell people about what was actually happening to the Vietnamese. Roberts convinced me that it would be more effective to put out a paper, to spread the word among troops who hadn't gone to Vietnam yet . . . and to fuck with the commanders' minds a bit." On one occasion, Roberts folded copies of *Aboveground* into paper airplanes and sailed them over the stockade fence to inmates.

As the new millennium dawned, our country was at war again, this time led by one of the many privileged sons whose family connections kept him out of Vietnam. The same political forces that brought us the failed war of attrition in Southeast Asia embarked in the early 2000s on a crusade to control the remaining oil reserves in the Mideast, a key strategy in maintaining the American Empire in what is called the Second American Century. These same forces, corrupt and incompetent in so many ways, have spent decades reworking the memory of the Vietnam War to their own advantage. They've also slandered veterans like presidential hopefuls John Kerry and John McCain, and they've condemned another generation of vets to inadequate health care. As we enter our sixties, Curt Stocker and I mourn the loss of Tom Roberts, murdered in his Colorado home by a man for whom he did pro bono legal work. There's a lot of grief to go around.

I look back on my brief experience as an antiwar GI, and I recognize that Tom and Curt and my other antiwar comrades taught me bravery, and how to keep a smile on my face while fighting the forces of oppression. I see a new generation of antiwar soldiers, men and women dressed in different fatigues than the ones we wore, but bearing the same kind of witness that we bore so long ago. They're our replacements. They need our support.

The GI Resistance was part of a cultural revolution that envisioned a future that would require significant structural changes in the distribution of power in the United States. That vision is far from fulfilled, but we should know by now that we signed up for the duration.

APPENDIX 1

THE GI RESISTANCE: MILITARY UNDERGROUNDS DURING THE VIETNAM WAR (by Harry W. Haines)

The following list identifies 217 GI underground antiwar newspapers aimed at members of the U.S. Armed Forces during the Vietnam War. The list is divided into two groups: (a) 208 newspapers with distribution limited to specific military posts, bases, or ships; and (b) nine newspapers with national or international distribution, including U.S. military units in South Vietnam. The list is a compilation of GI undergrounds identified by James R. Hayes in his 1975 doctoral dissertation, *The War within a War: Dissent in the Military with an Emphasis on Vietnam* (Department of Sociology, University of Connecticut), and in my master's thesis, *The GI Underground Press: Two Case Studies of Alternative Military Newspapers* (Department of Communication, University of Utah). Additionally, several newspapers and their organizational affiliations were identified in two government documents: the *Annual Report for the Year 1972* of the House Internal Security Committee, and *Organized Subversion in the U.S. Armed Forces* (September 25, 1975), based on hearings conducted by the Senate Subcommittee to Investigate the Administration of the Internal Security Act and Other Internal Security Laws.

These newspapers were ephemeral publications. Only a few of them maintained continuity over extended periods of time. The normal turnover in military personnel and the systematic reassignment of malcontents by commanders made it difficult to sustain the papers. Some papers were published anonymously with only the name of a disbanded activist coalition and an expired post office box as clues to the mystery of their origins. The political and organizational complexities of the antiwar movement also made it difficult to identify the papers' affiliations.

Hayes's sources included the Chicago Area Military Project; volumes 1, 2, and 3 of the U.S. House Committee on Internal Security reports (1972); and the archives of the Wisconsin State Historical Society at Madison.

My work relied heavily on Clark Smith's private collection at Berkeley, and the Contemporary Issues Collection (organized by Russell G. Benedict) at the University of Nevada Library at Reno. In most cases, information included in the list was gathered by Hayes or myself directly from copies of the newspapers. The list identifies each paper's place of publication and distribution and, in the case of locally distributed papers, service branch and organizational and coffeehouse affiliations.

During the Vietnam War, several antiwar organizations used off-post coffeehouses as centers of operation. Most sources agree that the first GI coffeehouse was founded in January 1968 by United States Servicemen's Fund (USSF) activist Fred Gardner. Called the UFO, it was located in Columbia, South Carolina, and was operated by a coalition of dissident GIs from nearby Fort Jackson, USSF organizers, and University of South Carolina students. Gardner later moved on to help establish USSF-sponsored coffeehouses in other towns near military installations. GI newspapers sometimes evolved out of the organizations responsible for operating the local coffeehouses.

The newspapers were seen as part of the educational or propaganda function of the coffeehouses. Often, the newspaper was the prime factor around which several organizational functions rallied for a time. The role of the coffeehouse is described in the literature of the Nonprofit Service Corporation (NPSC), an incorporated arm of GIs United, a group that operated both Quaker House and Haymarket Square in Fayetteville, near Fort Bragg, North Carolina. The NPSC saw the coffeehouse as "an educational center where GIs and students can rap about common problems" and as "an alternative to downtown Fayetteville and Fort Bragg which exploit the isolation and depression of GIs."

The NPSC also purported to create in their coffeehouse "an atmosphere in which we can all begin to understand what this country is all about, and out of which a sense of solidarity, struggle and understanding will develop." Weekend rock concerts were provided, along with "cheap thrills, relevant entertainment, and raps about the problems we face in society, and how we together can deal with those problems: the war, the army, racism, sexism."

Like most other GI coffeehouses, the Quaker House and Haymarket Square provided reading material including *Bragg Briefs*, the underground paper produced by the local members of GIs United. The *FTA Show*, a celebrated variety program critical of the Vietnam War and starring Jane Fonda and Donald Sutherland, was first performed at the Haymarket Square on March 14, 1971.

The emergence of coffeehouses near military posts and bases was a significant development in the history of the general antiwar movement. Until the USSF began channeling funds to sponsor coffeehouses and thus provide a nationwide base for organizing antiwar soldiers, members of the armed services were essentially ignored or denounced by many campus-based antiwar organizations. Fred Gardner, a former army draftee, played a major role in the antiwar movement by recognizing and tapping potential dissent within the younger enlisted ranks of the military itself. As centers of dissident political activity and strong objection to the Vietnam War, the GI coffeehouses were likely places for underground papers to flourish.

The titles listed here require an explanatory note. The GI press embodied an imaginative use of ambiguity in its selection of titles whose meanings may be quite obscure to readers unfamiliar with military life during the Vietnam War. Reflecting the radical political consciousness of the 1960s, these titles often combined contemporary hip slang with military jargon in the creation of hybrids unique to the American military experience of Vietnam.

GI papers were often named by placing in a new context slang phrases and military jargon familiar to the intended readership: younger, lower-ranking enlisted personnel. For example, military commands such as "About face," "As you were," "Eyes left," "Left face," "Open ranks," "Open sights," "Head-on," "Forward," and "All hands abandon ship" were used as underground titles. The use of these typical military commands as titles of anti-military newspapers was an element of irony and ambiguity in the GI press, identifying the general nature of the papers to prospective readers and capitalizing upon possible anti-military dissidence already experienced by alienated or otherwise dissatisfied members of the armed services.

Hence, new connotations were given to military jargon. In the process, the phrase "about face" refers both to the command shouted at basic trainees as well as to a change in direction of United States policy in Southeast Asia, an "about face" promoted by most GI undergrounds. "As you were," a command given to lower-ranking military personnel to resume activity following their coming to attention at the arrival in their work area of a high-ranking officer, became a reference to the reader's prior status as a civilian. "Eyes left" and "left face," when used as underground titles, referred to the generally leftist political orientation of the papers.

All Ready on the Left, the title of a GI paper produced by Marine corpsmen at Camp Pendleton, took its name from an important response in a structured series of commands and responses shouted during weapons practice on a rifle range. The response denotes the readiness of soldiers located to the left of the range's commanding officer in anticipation of firing at targets.

"Your military left," a phrase used as the title of a paper published at Fort Sam Houston, Texas, originated from military slang that recognizes qualitative differences between civilian and military society. In its original context, the phrase is used to elicit a desired behavior: physical movement to the left by a basic trainee who has difficulty identifying left from right. Used by a drill sergeant, the phrase denotes desired movement in a particular direction and connotes a difference in reality between military and civilian life, as if one's *military* left or right were somehow different from one's *civilian* left or right. It is not a question of one's political orientation, but rather an acute observation of the military social milieu. Although the connotation may at first seem obscure to a reader inexperienced with the peculiar social context in which it operates, the slang phrase perceptively captures qualitative differences between military and civilian life and communicates that understanding among the troops, for whom it is essential information. Used as the title of the Fort Sam Houston underground paper, the phrase became more ambiguous. In one sense, it suggested that the paper represented a leftist political sentiment within the military. In another sense, it suggested the prospect of desertion, as if the word "left" were a verb rather than a noun.

Similar wordplay existed throughout the GI underground phenomenon. Camp

Pendleton's *Attitude Check* got its title from a military slang phrase meaning to examine one's current state of mind regarding motivation and acceptable behavior within the service. A recalcitrant soldier, or one who exhibits an "attitude problem," might be encouraged to undergo such an "attitude check" or self-examination. *Gigline*, published at Fort Bliss, Texas, borrowed its name from the military term identifying the line extending down the front of a soldier's uniform. This line, formed by the edge of the uniform's belt buckle and the uniform's fly, is required to be kept straight under threat of "gigs" or demerits. As an underground title, the term "gig" suggested the more hip interpretation of an event or happening, while "line" referred to the communication function.

Shakedown, the title of an underground paper published at Fort Dix, New Jersey, was a reference to the "shakedown inspection" of enlisted men's personal belongings. "Shake-downs" are often performed without notice by commanders in search of contraband. The title suggested the possibility that the paper would reverse the process: that is, it would investigate the military command, or at least give it a difficult time. *The Ultimate Weapon*, another Fort Dix paper, took its name from a large road sign located at the main entrance to the basic-training facility. Bearing the same words, the sign shows an infantryman in combat gear, complete with extended bayonet and threatening snarl. Adopted as the title of one of the most vehemently antiwar underground papers of the late 1960s, the epithet, while suggesting the pen is mightier than the sword, openly ridiculed an image of the American infantryman promoted virtually everywhere at Fort Dix, from road sign to post-exchange stationery. The title functioned to subvert or co-opt a symbol of military authority and esprit. The combat experience of some GI underground publishers was suggested in such titles as *Strategic Hamlet* and *The Last Incursion*, co-optations of official euphemisms.

The titles of *The Ally* and *The Bond*, two internationally distributed papers that eventually came to disagree on tactical and political matters, originated from the consensus of the Vietnam Day Committee of Berkeley, California. In 1967, this committee made the important decision to attempt the direction of antiwar propaganda at military personnel. Both titles reflect the interest of dissident civilians in building a cooperative antiwar effort between themselves and dissident service personnel, according to Clark Smith, *The Ally*'s publisher. *Aboveground* was named by publishers who hoped to communicate a sense of honesty and reliability. "We had nothing to hide," co-publisher Curtis Stocker said.

Fort Jackson's *Short Times* combined a traditional newspaper title with the term "short timer," meaning a member of the military who is about to be discharged from active duty and returned to civilian life. The title *Right On Post*, used by a California-based underground paper, performed a similar function by combining a traditional newspaper title with the slang phrase "right on," meaning "correct." The title is made more ambiguous by its reference to "post" as a military installation.

Plain Rapper, the name of a military paper published in Palo Alto, California, was a refer-ence to the necessity of receiving underground subscriptions in the mail in plain, unmarked envelopes to avoid overt or covert retaliation from military authorities. In another sense, the title connoted reliability and ease of understanding, with the term "rapper" meaning "speaker" or "communicator."

Originally a reference to the part of a ship above waterline, the term "broadside" was used as the title of an antiwar paper published in Los Angeles and distributed among navy personnel in the Southern California area. Since the term can also be used to describe a denunciation, it was a likely choice for use as an underground title.

As was *Aerospaced*, the name of a paper published at Grissom Air Force Base. Without the "d," aerospace is a useful word, describing both the Earth's atmosphere and the space beyond. With the addition of the "d," the term "aerospaced" described the state of mind represented in the paper. Those responsible for the paper suggest in the title that they are not simply "spaced," or somewhat out of touch with conventional reality; they are specifically *aero*spaced, or somewhat traumatized by their experience in the military social environment. Thus, the title (a hybrid of military-scientific terminology and hip slang) described a particular state of mind experienced by those who published the paper, and perhaps shared by readers.

Sacstrated, another Air Force underground, combined the acronym of the Strategic Air Command (SAC) with the word "castrated," the resulting title referring to the proposed effect of the paper upon the military, or to the metaphorical condition of intended readers as perceived by the paper's publishers. *The Fort Polk Puke*, while not at all ambiguous, is similarly evocative.

We Got the brASS, published by dissident GIs stationed in West Germany, derived its title from "we got the ass," a somewhat esoteric military phrase meaning "we are very angry." The original phrase, of which "we got the ass" is but a variant, would be "we got a *case* of the ass," an angry or dissatisfied condition. Used as the title of a GI underground, the phrase immediately communicated the paper's orientation and added yet another twist with the placement of the lower-case letters "br" in front of the upper-case "ASS." The term "brASS," of course, referred to commissioned officers.

Slang was also incorporated into the title of an underground paper published at Chanute Air Force Base in Rantoul, Illinois. The title, *A Four-Year Bummer*, suggested that the four-year period of active duty service in the military was similar to a bad drug-related or other unpleasant experience. *Green Machine*, a slang phrase describing the army and its predominant hue, and *Marine Blues*, a reference to both the dress uniform of Marine corpsmen as well as their possible state of mind, were used as GI underground titles.

FTA, published at Fort Knox and possibly the first GI underground produced by active duty army personnel, made use of the military slogan "F-T-A." This series of letters, when spoken by an army draftee in the late 1960s, meant something quite different than the paper's subtitle, *Fun, Travel, and Adventure* (derived from an army enlistment poster) might indicate. Although the publisher of *FTA* wisely chose his subtitle to avoid a possible charge of obscenity from a responsible military commander, the letters "FTA" on the masthead communicated the more common meaning among the troops: "Fuck the army."

Papers with Local Distribution

These antiwar papers, listed alphabetically, were produced and distributed by armed service personnel (often in cooperation with civilian dissidents) at military installations throughout the United States and abroad during the Vietnam War. A few were produced and distributed aboard United States war ships, including the USS *Enterprise* and the USS *Forrestal*. At least one paper, *OM*, was distributed at the Pentagon.

Many of the papers were produced by local groups affiliated with national organizations such as Movement for a Democratic Military, Pacific Counseling Service, and Vietnam Veterans Against the War. Where known, these organizational affiliations are specified in the list, along with known GI coffeehouse affiliations. Many of the papers may have had organizational and coffeehouse affiliations that remain unknown and go unlisted here.

Some listings identify both a military installation and a nearby city as a paper's base of production and distribution (as, for example, the listings for *Aboveground* and *All Ready on the Left*). Dissident GIs often found it necessary to conceal their publishing operations from military commanders and intelligence agents who attempted to suppress publication and distribution in accordance with Department of the Army memoranda and Department of Defense Directives 1325.6 (issued on September 12, 1969) and 1344.10 (issued on September 23, 1969). As a result, many of the papers developed an off-post/off-base operation in a nearby city. These off-post/off-base operations may have included affiliations with coffeehouses that, in some cases, remain unidentified here.

Because these papers were ephemeral publications, both Hayes (1975) and Haines (1976) had difficulty discovering dates of publication. The military's transient nature, as well as many successful attempts by commanders to suppress publication and distribution, often limited the papers to brief or sporadic operation. The absence of a full chronology is a weakness of the listing, and *Aboveground*'s nine-issue run (from August 1969 to May 1970) may not be typical of the GI undergrounds.

In my original 1993 version of the 217 GI papers published between 1967 and 1975 that appear below in two groups, I used five main designations: US Army (USA), US Air Force (USAF), US Navy (USN), Marine Corps (USMC), and service branch unknown. In this updated version, the original service branches remain the same. Thanks to the extensive and ongoing research of James Lewes, who has had access to a great many of the original publications I listed, as well as the work of a number of collectors and scholars not available to me when I created this list, we are now able to identify the producers of most papers I listed as "service branch unknown," as well as provide dates and addresses for many of the papers I originally listed by military installation alone.

In the first group, 88 papers were produced by Army personnel, 38 by Air Force personnel, 43 by Navy personnel, and 15 by Marine Corpsmen. Coalitions of Army and Air Force personnel produced six papers, Army and Navy personnel produced two papers, and Army Reservists and National Guardsmen produced three papers. The remaining papers were produced by a variety of different groups and organizations, whose members were drawn from all branches of the armed services, including one that was published by Vietnam Veterans and is designated with the acronym VET. Two papers were published by active duty resisters, including members of the Concerned Officer's Movement; these are identified by the acronym RITM (Resistors In The Military). Five papers were published by American GIs in exile: two in Canada, two in Paris, and one in Stockholm. These are identified by the acronym AMEX. The organizational and service branches of the remaining five papers published in Japan and Okinawa are unfortunately untraceable as no public collection has copies of these publications. These are identified by the original designation I applied to them: "service branch unknown."

1. *Abandon Ship* (USN), Boston, Massachusetts: 1969
2. *The Abolitionist* (USN), Okinawa: 1971, Pacific Counseling Service
3. *About Face* (USAF), Bergstrom Air Force Base: ca. 1971
4. *About Face: The EM News* (USMC), Camp Pendleton and Los Angeles, California: 1969 ("EM": enlisted men)
5. *Aboveground* (USA), Fort Carson, Colorado: 1969–70, "Home Front" Coffeehouse, Colorado Springs, Colorado
6. *ACT: The RITA's Newsletter* (AMEX), Resisters Inside the Army, Paris, France: 1968–71
7. *Aerospaced* (USAF) Grissom Air Force Base and Kokomo, Indiana: 1969–70
8. *Air Fowl* (USAF), Vandenberg Air Force Base: 1971–72
9. *All Hands Abandon Ship* (USN), Newport (Rhode Island) Naval Base: 1970–72
10. *All Ready on the Left* (USMC), Camp Pendleton and Oceanside-Vista, California: 1970–71
11. *Always Alert* (USA), Fort Lewis and Tacoma, Washington: n.d.
12. *Anchorage Troop* (USA-USAF), Fort Richardson, Elmendorf Air Force Base, and Anchorage, Alaska: 1970
13. *Anti*Brass* (USA), Los Angeles, California: 1970–71
14. *Arctic Arsenal* (USA), Fort Greely and Delta, Alaska: 1971, Socialist Workers and GIs United at Fort Greely
15. *As You Were* (USA), Fort Ord and Monterey, California: 1969–71
16. *Attitude Check* (USMC), Camp Pendleton and Oceanside-Vista, California: 1969–70, Movement for a Democratic Military, "The Green Machine" Coffeehouse, Vista, California
17. *AWOL Press* (USA), Fort Riley and Manhattan, Kansas: 1969–70
18. *Bacon* (USAF), March Air Force Base and Edgemont, California: 1972
19. *Barrage* (USA), Fort Sill and Lawton, Oklahoma: 1971–72
20. *Baumholder Gig Sheet* (USA), Paris, France: 1971
21. *Bayonet* (USA), The Presidio and San Francisco, California: 1969
22. *BCT Newsletter* (USA), Fort Ord: 1970, ("BCT": basic combat training)
23. *Bergstrom Bennies* (USA), Bergstrom Air Force Base: 1971–72, ("Bennies": benefits)
24. *Black Unity* (USMC), Vista, California: 1970–71
25. *Black Voice* (USA), Fort McClellan and Anniston, Alabama: 1971–72
26. *Blue Screw* (USAF), Aurora, Colorado: 1973–74
27. *Bolling Other* (USAF), Bolling Air Force Base and Washington, DC: 1971–72
28. *Bragg Briefs* (USA), Fort Bragg, Fayetteville, and Spring Lake, North Carolina: 1969–74, GIs United to End the War in Indochina, "Quaker House," "Haymarket Square," and "Mbari Cultural Center" coffeehouses, Fayetteville, North Carolina
29. *Brass Needle* (USA), Fort Lee and Petersburg, Virginia: 1971
30. *Broadside* (USN), Los Angeles, California: 1968
31. *Broken Arrow* (USAF), Selfridge Air Force Base and Mount Clemens, Michigan: 1969–71

32. *The Chessman* (USMC), Fort Beaufort and Frogmore, South Carolina: 1969
33. *Chessman II* (USMC), Fort Beaufort and Frogmore, South Carolina: 1971–72
34. *The coalition: Sacto area GI paper* (USAF), Mather Air Force Base and Sacramento, California: 1972
35. *Co-Ambulation* (USAF), Fairchild Air Force Base: 1971–72
36. *Come-Unity Press* (USAF), Yokota Air Force Base, Japan: n.d., Pacific Counseling Service
37. *COM MON Sense* (RITM), Washington, DC: 1970–72
38. *Counter-Attack* (USA), Fort Carson and Colorado Springs, Colorado: 1970–71
39. *Counter-Military Iwakuni* (USMC), Iwakuni, Japan: n.d., Pacific Counseling Service and Beheiren
40. *Counterpoint* (USA-USAF), Fort Lewis, McChord Air Force Base, and Seattle, Washington: 1968–69
41. *Cry Out* (USAF), Clark Air Force Base and Angeles City, Philippines: 1972, Pacific Counseling Service and National Lawyers Guild
42. *Custer's Last Stand* (USA), Fort Riley and Manhattan, Kansas: 1972
43. *Dare to Struggle* (USN), San Diego, California: 1972
44. *Demand for Freedom* (USN), Okinawa: 1970, Pacific Counseling Service and Beheiren
45. *The Destroyer* (USN), Philadelphia Naval Yard: 1970–71, "Liberty Hall" Coffeehouse, Philadelphia, Pennsylvania
46. *Different Drummer* (USA), Fort Polk: 1971
47. *Do It Loud* (USA), Fort Bragg and Spring Lake, North Carolina: 1970
48. *Drum* (USA), Fort Hamilton: n.d., Brooklyn, New York
49. *Duck Power* (USN), San Diego Naval Training Center and San Diego, California: 1969–70
50. *Dull Brass* (USA), Fort Sheridan and Chicago, Illinois: 1969–70
51. *EM-16* (USA), Fort Knox, Fort Campbell, and Radcliffe, Kentucky: 1970, ("EM": enlisted men)
52. *Eyes Left* (USAF), Travis Air Force Base and San Francisco, California: 1969
53. *Fall In At Ease* (USN), Iwakuni and Tokyo, Japan: 1970–73, "Hobbit" Coffeehouse
54. *Fat Albert's Death Ship Times* (USN), Charleston Naval Base and Charleston, South Carolina: 1973
55. *Fatigue Press* (USA), Fort Hood: 1968–72, "Oleo Strut" Coffeehouse, Killeen, Texas
56. *Fed Up!* (USA), Fort Lewis, "Shelter Half" Coffeehouse, Tacoma, Washington: 1969–73
57. *FID Amchitka* (USN), Kodiak Island Naval Base and Kodiak, Alaska: 1971–72
58. *FighT bAck* (USA), Heidelberg, Germany: 1972–78
59. *Final Flight* (USAF), Hamilton Air Force Base and San Francisco, California: 1969–71
60. *1st Amendment* (USAF), Yokota Air Force Base and Fussa, Japan: 1971–72
61. *1st Casualty* (USA), New York City [Vietnam Veterans Against the War]: 1971
62. *Flag-In Action* (USA), Fort Campbell, Kentucky: 1968–69
63. *Fort Polk Puke* (USA), Fort Polk, Texas: 1971
64. *The Forum* (USA), Fort Sill and Lawton, Oklahoma: 1971
65. *Fort Lewis Free Press* (USA-USAF), Fort Lewis, McChord Air Force Base, and Seattle, Washington: 1970

66. *Forward* (USA), West Berlin, Germany: 1970–78
67. *Forward March* (USN), Annapolis, Maryland: 1969–70
68. *A Four-Year Bummer* (USAF), Chanute Air Force Base and Champaign, Illinois: 1969–72
69. *Fragging Action* (USA-USAF), Fort Dix and McGuire Air Force Base: 1971–72
70. *Free Fire Zone* (USAF), Hanscom Air Force Base: 1971–72
71. *Freedom of the Press* (USN), Yokosuka, Japan: 1973–74, Pacific Counseling Service, National Lawyers Guild, Vietnam Veterans Against the War/Winter Soldier Organization
72. *Freedom Rings* (USA), Tokyo, Japan: 1970–71, Produced by GIs inside Tokyo Area
73. *FTA: Fun, Travel, and Adventure* (USA), Fort Knox and Louisville, Kentucky: 1968–73, "Fort Knox" Coffeehouse, Muldraugh, Kentucky
74. *FTA With Pride* (USA), Heidelberg, Germany: 1971–73
75. *GAF* (USAF), Barksdale Air Force Base and Shreveport, Louisiana: 1969–71
76. *Getting Late* (USN), Okinawa: n.d., Pacific Counseling Service
77. *Getting Together* (USAF), Lowry Air Force Base: 1971–72
78. *GI Movement in Yokosuka (GIMY)* (USN), Yokosuka, Japan: n.d., Pacific Counseling Service, "Yokosuka David" Coffeehouse
79. *GI Organizer* (USA), Fort Hood, Killeen, and Austin, Texas: 1969
80. *GI Voice* (USA), Fort Lewis and Tacoma, Washington: 1974
81. *Gig Line* (USA), Fort Bliss, El Paso, Texas: 1969–72, GIs for Peace, "GIs for Peace House," El Paso, Texas
82. *Graffiti* (USA), Heidelberg, Germany: 1969–71, Produced by GIs for GIs
83. *Grapes of Wrath* (USN), Norfolk, Virginia: 1972–75
84. *The Great Lakes Torpedo* (USN), Great Lakes Naval Training Station: 1970–71, Movement for a Democratic Military, "People's Place" Coffeehouse, Chicago, Illinois
85. *Green Machine* (USA), Fort Greely and Fairbanks, Alaska: 1969–70
86. *Hair* (USA), "Owl" Coffeehouse, Misawa, Japan: 1969, Pacific Counseling Service, National Lawyers Guild, and American Servicemen's Union Beheiren
87. *HanSen Free Press* (USN), Camp Hansen and Camp Schwab: 1972–73, "People's House" and "United Front" coffeehouses, Kin-Son, Okinawa
88. *Harass the Brass: The Airman's Voice* (USAF), Chanute Air Force Base and Champaign, Illinois: 1969
89. *Head-On* (USMC), Camp Lejeune and Jacksonville, North Carolina: 1968–69
90. *Helping Hand* (USAF), Mountain Home Air Force Base: 1971–74, "Covered Wagon" Coffeehouse, Mountain Home, Idaho
91. *Heresy II* (USA), Fort Leonard Wood: 1969
92. *Highway 13* (USA), Fort Meade Military Law Project: 1972–75, Baltimore, Maryland, and Washington, DC
93. *HOA Binh* (Vet), Denver, Colorado: 1971–72
94. *Huachuca Hard Times* (USA), Fort Huachuca and Sierra Vista, Arizona: 1969–70
95. *Hunley Hemorrhoid* (USN), San Francisco, California: 1972
96. *In Formation* (USA), Fort Knox and Louisville, Kentucky: 1970
97. *In the Belly of the Monster* (service branch unknown), Iwakuni, Japan: n.d., Pacific Counseling Service, International Counter-Military Collective and Beheiren

98. *Kill for Peace* (USA), Tokyo, Japan: 1969–71, Pacific Counseling Service
99. *Kitty Litter* (USN), San Diego, California: 1971–72
100. *Lackland Tailfeather* (USAF), Lackland Air Force Base and San Antonio, Texas: n.d.
101. *Last Harass* (USA), Augusta, Georgia: 1968–71, "Home in the South" Coffeehouse, Augusta, Georgia
102. *The Last Incursion* (USA), Fort Bragg and Fayetteville, North Carolina: 1971
103. *Left Face* (USA), Washington, DC: 1969
104. *Left Face* (USA), Anniston, Alabama: 1969–72, GIs United Against the War in Indochina, "GIs and WACs United" Coffeehouse, Anniston, Alabama
105. *Left Flank* (USMC), Koza, Okinawa: 1971, Pacific Counseling Service
106. *Lewis-McChord Free Press* (USA-USAF), Tacoma, Washington: 1970–74, "Shelter Half" Coffeehouse, Tacoma, Washington
107. *Liberated Barracks* (USMC), Kailua, Hawaii: 1971–75
108. *Liberated Castle* (USA), Fort Belvoir and Washington, DC: 1971
109. *Liberty Call* (USN), San Diego, California: 1971, San Diego Concerned Officer Movement
110. *Logistic* (USA), Fort Sheridan and Chicago, Illinois: 1968–69
111. *The Looper* (Army Reserve and National Guard), San Francisco, California: 1969–70
112. *Marine Blues* (USMC), Treasure Island Naval Station and San Francisco, California: 1969–70
113. *MacDill Freek Press* (USAF), MacDill Air Force Base and Tampa, Florida: 1971–72
114. *The Militant* (USA), Fort Greely: n.d.
115. *Military Intelligence* (USA), Santa Monica and Venice, California: 1970–71
116. *Morning Report* (USA-USN), Fort Devens and Groton, Massachusetts: 1970–72, "Common Sense" Bookstore, Ayer, Massachusetts
117. *My Knot* (USAF), Minot Air Force Base and Minot, North Dakota: ca. 1970
118. *Napalm* (USA), Fort Campbell: 1969–71, "People's House" Coffeehouse, Clarksville, Tennessee
119. *Navy Times Are Changin'* (USN), Great Lakes Naval Training Station: 1970–73, Movement for a Democratic Military, "People's House" Coffeehouse, Chicago, Illinois
120. *New England Military News* (RITM), Boston, Massachusetts: 1973
121. *New GI* (USA), Fort Hood and Killeen, Texas: n.d.
122. *New Salute* (USA), Baltimore, Maryland: 1969
123. *The Next Step* (USA), Heidelberg, Germany: 1970–71
124. *99th Bummer* (USAF), Westover Air Force Base: 1971–72, "Off the Runway" Coffeehouse, Holyoke, Massachusetts
125. *Obligore* (USMC), New York City: 1969–70
126. *The O.D.* (USA), Honolulu, Hawaii: 1969–70
127. *Off the Brass* (USAF), Pease Air Force Base and Portsmouth, New Hampshire: 1971–72
128. *Off the Bridge* (USN), "New People's Center" Coffeehouse, Yokosuka, Japan: 1973, Pacific Counseling Service, National Lawyers Guild
129. *Offul Times* (USAF), Offutt Air Force Base and Omaha, Nebraska: 1972–73
130. *Okinawa Ampo* (service branch unknown), Tokyo, Japan: n.d., Pacific Counseling Service, Ampo Collective

131. *Okinawa Strikes* (service branch unknown), "Freedom Family" Coffeehouse, Koza, Okinawa: n.d., Pacific Counseling Service, National Lawyers Guild

132. *Olive Branch* (USAF), MacDill Air Force Base and Jacksonville, Florida: 1970–72

133. *OM: The Servicemen's Newsletter* (USN), The Pentagon and Washington, DC: 1969–70

134. *Omega Press* (USN), "Omega House" and "People's House," Koza, Okinawa: 1971–75, Pacific Counseling Service, National Lawyers Guild

135. *On the Beach* (USN), Norfolk, Virginia: 1970–71

136. *Open Ranks* (USA-USN), Fort Holabird, Bainbridge Naval Training Center, and Baltimore, Maryland: 1969–70, "The DMZ" Coffeehouse, Washington, DC

137. *Open Sights* (USA), Fort Belvoir and Washington, DC: 1969–72

138. *Other Half* (USN), Glenview Naval Air Station and Glenview, Illinois: 1972–73

139. *Other Voice* (USAF), Richards-Gebaur Air Force Base and Kansas City, Missouri: 1972

140. *Our Thing* (USA), Huntsville, Alabama: 1970–71

141. *Out Now!* (USA), Long Beach, California: 1971, Movement for a Democratic Military

142. *The Paper* (USMC), Morehead City, North Carolina: 1971–72

143. *Patriots for Peace* (USA), Fort Benning and Columbus, Georgia: n.d.

144. *The Pawn* (USA), Fort Detrick and Frederick, Maryland: 1969–71

145. *Pay Back* (USA), Santa Ana, California: 1970–72, Movement for a Democratic Military

146. *People's Press* (USA), Fort Campbell and Clarksville, Tennessee: 1971–72

147. *Plain Rapper* (USA), Palo Alto, California: n.d.

148. *Potemkin* (USN), New York City: 1970–71

149. *P.O.W.* (USA), Fort Ord and Monterey, California: 1971–72, Pacific Counseling Service, Vietnam Veterans Against the War, Revolutionary Union, and American Servicemen's Union

150. *Puget Sound Sound Off* (USN), Puget Sound Naval Station and Bremerton, Washington: 1971

151. *Rag* (Army Reserve and National Guard), Chicago, Illinois: 1972–73

152. *Rage* (USMC), Camp Lejeune and New River Air Station, North Carolina: 1971–75

153. *Rap!* (USA), Fort Benning and Columbus, Georgia: 1969–71

154. *Rebel* (AMEX), Montreal, Canada: 1968, Exiled GIs

155. *Reconnaissance* (USAF), Forbes Air Force Base and Topeka, Kansas: 1972

156. *Redline: a newsletter for anti-war Reservists and National Guardsmen* (Army Reserve and National Guard), Boston, Massachusetts: 1970–71

157. *Right On Post* (USA), Fort Ord, Seaside, and Monterey, California: 1970, Movement for a Democratic Military

158. *Rough Draft* (USN), Norfolk Naval Air Station and Norfolk, Virginia: 1969

159. *Sacstrated* (USAF), Fairchild Air Force Base, Washington: 1971

160. *Seasick* (USN), "GI Center," Olongapo, Philippines: 1972, Pacific Counseling Service, National Lawyers Guild

161. *Second Front* (AMEX), Paris, France: 1968

162. *2nd Front International* (AMEX), Stockholm, Sweden: n.d.

163. *Seize the Time* (USN), Iwakuni, Japan: n.d., Pacific Counseling Service, International Counter-Military Collective

164. *Semper Fi* (USMC), "Hobbit" Coffeehouse, Iwakuni, Japan, Pacific Counseling Service, Beheiren
165. *1776–Right to Revolution* (service branch unknown), Okinawa: 1972
166. *Short Times* (USA), Columbia, South Carolina: 1969–72, "The UFO" Coffeehouse, Columbia, South Carolina
167. *Skydove* (USAF), Rickenbocker Air Force Base and Columbus, Ohio: 1972
168. *sNorton Bird* (USAF), Norton Air Force Base, California: 1970
169. *S.O.S.: Stop Our Ship Newsletter* (USN), California: 1972
170. *Spaced Sentinel* (USAF), Beale Air Force Base and Marysville, California: 1971
171. *SPD News* (USA), Fort Dix and New York City: 1969–71, ("SPD": Special Processing Detachment)
172. *Special Weapon* (USAF), Albuquerque, New Mexico: 1972
173. *Spread Eagle* (USA), Fort Campbell and Clarksville, Tennessee: 1969
174. *Square Wheel* (USA), Lee Hall, Virginia: 1971–72
175. *Star Spangled Bummer* (USAF), Wright Patterson Air Force Base and Dayton, Ohio: 1971–72, GIs United Against the War in Indochina
176. *Stars 'N Bars* (USN), Iwakuni, Japan: 1970, Pacific Counseling Service, Beheiren
177. *Straight Sheet* (USAF), Duluth Air Force Base and Duluth, Minnesota: n.d.
178. *Strike Back* (USA), Fort Bragg and Fayetteville, North Carolina: 1969–70
179. *Stuffed Puffin* (USN), Keflavik, Iceland: 1970
180. *Task Force* (USA), San Francisco, California: 1968–69
181. *The Time Has Come for a Much Needed Shakedown* (USA), Wrightstown, New Jersey: 1969–71, GIs United Against the War in Indochina, "Coffeehouse," Wrightstown, New Jersey
182. *This Is Life* (USN), San Diego, California: 1972
183. *Top Secret* (USA), Fort Devens and Cambridge, Massachusetts: 1969
184. *Travisty* (USAF), Travis Air Force Base and Suisun City, California: 1971–72
185. *Truth Instead* (USN), Treasure Island Naval Station and San Francisco, California: 1969
186. *Twin Cities Protester* (USA), Fort Snelling and Minneapolis, Minnesota: 1970
187. *The Ultimate Weapon* (USA), Philadelphia, Pennsylvania: 1968–70
188. *Underground Oak* (USN), Oakland, California: 1968
189. *Underwood* (USA), Fort Leonard Wood, Missouri: 1970
190. *Unity Now* (USA), Fort Ord and Monterey, California: 1969–70, Movement for a Democratic Military
191. *Up Against the Bulkhead* (USN), San Francisco, California: 1970–75
192. *Up Against the Wall* (USA), West Berlin, Germany: 1970
193. *Up from the Bottom* (USN), "Enlisted People's Place" and "EM Club," San Diego, California: 1971–73, Pacific Counseling Service, Movement for a Democratic Military
194. *Up Front* (USA), Los Angeles, California: 1969
195. *USAF News* (USAF), Wright Patterson Air Force Base and Dayton, Ohio: 1969
196. *Voice of the Lumpen* (USA), Frankfurt, Germany: 1970–71
197. *VS & SP* (USA), Fort Lewis: n.d.

198. *We Got the brASS: Journal of the Second Front International* (USA), Frankfurt, Germany: 1969

199. *We Got the brASS: Journal of the Second Front International Asian Edition* (USN), Tokyo, Japan: 1969–70, Pacific Counseling Service, Beheiren

200. *We the People* (service branch unknown), Iwakuni, Japan: n.d., Pacific Counseling Service

201. *Whack!* (USA), Fort McClellan: 1971, GIs United Against the War in Indochina, "GIs and WACs United" Coffeehouse, Anniston, Alabama

202. *Where Are We?* (USA-USAF), Sierra Vista, Arizona: 1971–72

203. *Where It's At* (USA), West Berlin, Germany: 1968–69

204. *The Whig* (USN), Quezon City, Philippines: 1970–71, Pacific Counseling Service

205. *Woodpecker* (USA), Fort Leonard Wood: 1972

206. *Yankee Refugee* (AMEX), Vancouver, Canada: 1968–69, Exiled GIs

207. *Yokosuka David* (USN), "Yokosuka David" Coffeehouse, Yokosuka, Japan: 1970, Beheiren

208. *Your Military Left* Series 1 (USA), Fort Sam Houston and San Antonio, Texas: 1969–70

Papers with National or International Distribution

The ten papers listed here had national or international distribution. The list identifies the papers, their places of publication, and their organizational affiliations. Some of the publications may have had affiliations that were not discovered by Hayes (1975) and Haines (1976). Additionally, the list does not identify dates of operation. *The Ally*'s lengthy publication life (1968 to 1974) was probably atypical, although Vietnam Veterans Against the War (Chicago) and Vietnam Veterans Against the War, Anti-Imperialist (New York City and Seattle) continue to publish sporadically, linking local chapters of politically active Vietnam veterans throughout the United States.

These papers were based in major cities and were often produced by coalitions of dissident civilians, active duty service personnel, and Vietnam veterans. At least three of the papers (*The Bond*, *GI News*, and *Winter Soldier*) functioned as organs for major organizations that provided, in varying degrees, leadership and influence in the antiwar movement. *The Bond*, established at Berkeley in 1967 by draft resister William Callison and a group of friends, was the first nationally distributed underground paper aimed exclusively at military personnel during the war. The paper promoted the organization of the American Servicemen's Union (ASU) as a collective bargaining agent, demanding the following ("We Demand," *The Bond*, July 24, 1971, pp. 4–5):

1. The right to refuse to obey illegal orders—like orders to fight in the illegal, imperialist war in Southeast Asia.

2. Election of officers by vote of rank and file.

3. An end to saluting and sir-ing of officers.

4. The right of black, Latin, and other national minority servicemen and women to

determine their own lives, free from the oppression of racist whites. No troops to be sent into black, Latin, or other national minority communities.

5. No troops to be used against antiwar demonstrators.
6. No troops to be used against workers on strike.
7. Rank and file control of court-martial boards.
8. The right of free political association.
9. Federal minimum wages [for service personnel].
10. The right of collective bargaining.

After raising *The Bond*'s circulation to about 1,000 copies a month, Callison turned over the editorship to Andrew Stapp, founder of the ASU. Stapp had been court-martialed three times at Fort Sill, Oklahoma, for offenses related to his attempts at organizing the ASU, and he eventually received a dishonorable discharge, which was subsequently overruled as illegal. Under Stapp's leadership, *The Bond* was moved to the ASU's New York City headquarters and its circulation rose to about 20,000.

The Bond pioneered the system of distribution that *The Ally* and other internationally distributed papers would modify to reach soldiers throughout the world, including units in West Germany and South Vietnam. *The Bond* encouraged dissident soldiers to provide the paper with unit rosters listing the names and military addresses of service personnel. The paper would then "bond" entire units, often generating conflict between lower-ranking personnel and commanders who attempted to confiscate copies of the paper. Other papers, including *The Ally*, relied on soldiers who volunteered to distribute copies that they received through the mail in bundles camouflaged to look like "care packages" from families or church groups back home.

The GI Press Service deserves a special note for archivists and researchers. Operated by the Student Mobilization to End the War, this service functioned as a clearinghouse for articles, photographs, and political cartoons submitted by locally produced GI papers throughout the United States. The service made these materials and other features available to subscribers, including many of the 208 locally produced papers identified above. The GI Press Service acted like a "wire service," linking many of the otherwise isolated GI papers and serving their needs with packets of material that the papers received through the mail. A complete collection of the GI Press Service packets would provide a good sampling of materials characteristic of the GI underground press.

1. *The Ally*, Berkeley, California
2. *The Bond: The Serviceman's Newspaper*, Berkeley, California, and New York City, GIs United Against the War in Indochina, American Servicemen's Union
3. *CAMP News*, Chicago, Illinois, Chicago Area Military Project
4. *GI News*, Chicago, Illinois, Vietnam Veterans Against the War/Winter Soldier Organization, Revolutionary Union
5. *GI Press Service*, New York City, Student Mobilization to End the War
6. *GI Voice*, New York City
7. *Veterans Stars and Stripes for Peace*, Chicago, Illinois

8. *Vietnam GI*, Chicago, Illinois
9. *Winter Soldier*, Vietnam Veterans Against the War/Winter Soldier Organization, Revolutionary Union

---

CONSTRUCTING THE LIST OF GI PAPERS (by James Lewes)

This listing of GI papers is meant to supplement the list of GI Papers prepared for the Voices from the Underground Series by Harry Haines. My list is grounded in the work I have done digitizing existing GI papers for the GI Press Project. In preparing for this work, I performed an extensive search of existing GI press collections in archives and special collections across the United States. The notes regarding the paper series below are drawn from the work of librarians and archivists at the Historical Society of Wisconsin, New York University, Northwestern University, Swarthmore College, Wayne State University, the University of Kansas at Lawrence, and Temple University, where the most important collections of GI papers are held.

The listing below includes a number of papers that changed their titles as staffs rotated in and out and new editors were found. Each variant of the paper is treated as a different publication. This is not done to pad out the number of papers. Rather, it fits with the treatment of the GI press by scholars and archivists who treat each title as a separate publication. If an organization can be identified, it is listed below the publication.

While I am not familiar with all of the different publications labeled as underground by the various contributors to the Voices from the Underground Series, I am familiar with enough of them to observe that the GI press news workers faced unique obstacles encountered by few other staffs. While it is true that alternative press publishers, staffs, and distributors going back to the Abolitionist press in the mid-1830s have been accused by opponents of exploiting that aspect of the First Amendment that guarantees their rights to publish, nevertheless they have been protected by the First Amendment.

This was not the case for the GI press, whose active-duty writers and readers–because they swore the Oath of Enlistment when they entered the armed services–were considered by the courts to have voluntarily suspended the privileges and protections afforded them by the Constitution. In an effort to bypass this delimitation, few contributors signed their work and their audiences were advised to cover their asses by withholding their names and addresses when they wrote letters and requested subscriptions to these publications. And yet editors and news workers still found themselves with little notice being punitively transferred to new bases, shipped overseas to Vietnam, or forced out of the military. As a result, a great many of the papers listed by Harry Haines and me only appeared for a few issues and a number that survived for more than a few issues changed their names as new writers and editors picked up the baton of resistance. The following notes track these changes:

Alconbury Raps. This paper was variously titled *Alconbury Raps*, *Alkonbury Raps*, and *Oinkenbury Raps*.

The American Exile in Britain. This paper was published by the Union of American Exiles in Britain and staffed mainly by draft resisters and veterans based in Oxford and London. Unlike Canada, France, Sweden, and Holland, the United Kingdom did not provide sanctuary to active-duty exiles. The first issue, vol. 1, no. 1, was published in 1969 and the final issue, vol. 3, no. 1, in 1974. It was renamed *The American Exile* in 1973. The first issue of *The American Exile* was numbered vol. 2, no. 5.

The American Exile in Canada. The group of publications collectively known as *The American Exile in Canada* was published continuously from 1968 through 1976. It was originally published by the Union of American Exiles. In 1971 the publication decoupled itself from the organization and was published from 1971–77 by Amex-Canada Enterprises. In the eight years it was published it changed its name four times. Each new edition picked up where the previous edition ended and each issue was numbered by both volume and issue number as well as consecutively, beginning with issue no. 1 and ending with issue no. 45, as follows: Issues 1 through 5 (vol. 1, no. 1–5) were titled *The Union of American Exiles Newsletter*; issues 6 through 15 (vol. 1, no. 6–15) were titled *The American Exile in Canada*; issue no. 16 (vol. 1, no. 16) was titled *AMEX—Canada: The American Expatriate in Canada*; issues 17 through 25 (vol. 2, no. 1–9) were titled *AMEX → Canada: The American Expatriate in Canada*; issues 26 through 45 (vol. 3, no. 1–vol. 5, no. 6) were titled *Amex-Canada: Published by Americans Exiled in Canada*.

Attitude Check (Vista, California) was published from 1969–70 by the San Diego chapter of Movement for a Democratic Military. In 1970, ideological and racial tensions between black and white GIs split the chapter in half. Each faction then published its own newspaper, *All Ready on the Left* and *Black Unity*. In the first issue of each the following note was published:

> The reason why MDM is divided and *Attitude Check* won't be around anymore is because we weren't getting the full support of the people. Third World people (black, brown, red, yellow) couldn't relate to it because they thought it was a white organization. White people couldn't relate to it because they thought it was a black organization. We are all struggling to reach the same goals but we have to organize our own people first. Once we organize among ourselves, then we can unite. Until all of us are free none will be free.

The first issue of *All Ready on the Left* was published with the *Pigleton Snout*.

Below Decks. No information is known about the paper *Below Decks*, except that it was first referenced as being published in Subic Bay in *GI Press Service* vol. 2, no. 9 (September 21, 1970) and continued to be listed through April 1971.

Dig It! was founded by former staff members of the *Baumholder Gig Sheet* who remained in Baumholder after the paper folded. It survived for a single issue and was then renamed *The Road*. The first issue of *The Road* was published May 31, 1971.[1]

Fat Albert's Death Ship Times (Charleston) was published for one issue and then renamed the *Death Ship Times* for vol. 1, no. 2.

Fort Lewis Free Press (Tacoma, Washington) came out for a single issue and then was renamed the *Lewis-McChord Free Press* for vol. 1, no. 2. It was later renamed *GI Voice* starting with vol. 6, no. 11.

Fort Polk Puke (Fort Polk, Louisiana) was published for two issues and then renamed *Different Drummer* for vol. 1, no. 3.

FTA With Pride (Tri-Cities Chapter) (Weisbaden, West Germany). Most collections with copies of *FTA With Pride* and *FTA With Pride Tri-Cities Chapter* treat them as different editions of the same publication. I disagree for two reasons: They were produced in different cities and the first issue of each publication is numbered vol. 1, no. 1. *FTA With Pride* is included in Harry Haines' list, *FTA With Pride Tri-Cities Chapter* is included in this supplemental list.

The GI Civil Liberties Defense Committee (New York City). Founded in 1968, the GI Civil Liberties Defense Committee provided pro-bono legal services to GIs being court-martialed for speech crimes. While the organization relied on press releases, many of which are listed in the section below on pamphlets and project reports, to draw attention to their legal work, from 1969–71 they distributed a series of newsletters to interested donors and GI movement organizations. Originally titled the *GI C.L.D.C. Newsletter* (1969), it was renamed first the *GI Defender* (1970) and then the *GI CLDC Newsletter* (1971).

GI News/VVAW/WSO (Chicago, Illinois) was renamed *GI News: A Publication of Vietnam Veterans Against the War/Winter Soldier Organization* for vol. 1, no. 9.

GI News and Discussion Bulletin (New York City). In the appendix to *Soldiers in Revolt*, David Cortright describes the *GI News and Discussion Bulletin* as a "political-analysis journal circulated among a select group of several hundred GI organizers and counselors . . . started by USSF in New York in January 1971 . . . since late 1973 [it has been] published by the GI Project Alliance."[2] Once the GI Project Alliance assumed responsibility for its publication, the organization renamed it *GIPA News and Discussion Bulletin* for issue 17.

The Great Lakes Torpedo (Chicago, Illinois). It is not clear whether this paper was a subset of *Navy Times Are Changin'*, as was claimed by the House Committee on Internal Security, or a different publication. It was published by the same organization–Great Lakes Movement for a Democratic Military–and had *Navy Times Are Changin'* printed below the masthead. Because neither the State Historical Society of Wisconsin nor the Deering Library, whose listings of GI papers are the most informative of the online collections, mentions a relationship between the two publications, they are treated here as distinct.

Hair (Misawa, Japan). No known copies of the original three issues of *Hair* are preserved in public collections. Unfortunately, what is listed in most collections as the fourth issue of *Hair* is actually the first issue of *Hair (Revived)*, which began publishing at issue 3+1.[3] By issue 3+2 the editors had dropped *(Revived)* from the title. However, it is important to view these later printings as issues of *Hair (Revived)* to avoid confusing the two publications.

Harass the Brass (Chanute AFB, Illinois). This paper, which was founded by airmen at Chanute AFB in 1969, lasted for one issue. It was renamed *A Four Year Bummer* for vol. 1, no. 2 and published through 1971.

The kNot (Minot AFB, North Dakota). Unfortunately no known copies of this paper are preserved in public collections, so it is difficult to trace its history. What is known is that this paper was founded in 1971 and that by June 1972 the paper had been renamed *My Knot.* What is not clear is how many issues were produced and whether it continued publishing through 1973.[4]

The Liberty Call (Portsmouth, New Hampshire). This paper seems to have been printed in two editions. This first, published in 1971, merged with *Off the Brass* shortly after it was founded. The second was produced by airmen at Pease AFB and published in Portsmouth in 1973. Unfortunately no known copies of either edition are preserved in any public collection.

The Liberty Call (San Diego). This paper was published in two editions, each of which is treated by me as a distinct paper. The first appeared four times between May and September 1971, the second only once, in May 1973.

New England Military News (Boston, Massachusetts). The first issue of this paper was published in February 1973, after the staffs of *99th Bummer, All Hands Abandon Ship, Free Fire Zone, Morning Report, Off the Brass,* and *Undertow* merged their papers.

Out Now (Long Beach, California). The paper *Out Now* was published by the Long Beach Chapter of the Great Lakes Movement for a Democratic Military from May through October 1970. It was renamed *Now Hear This!* and the first issue of *Now Hear This!* was published in December 1970. At some point in 1971 the paper was renamed *Out Now!* It continued publishing through February 1972.

P.E.A.C.E. (Mildenhall, England) was renamed *People Emerging Against Corrupt Establishments* for vol. 1, no. 8.

Second Front (Canada and Sweden). During my research, I have compiled an exhaustive listing of the surviving GI papers. In an effort to create the definitive listing, I have compared it to listings published in the GI press. Unfortunately, of all the titles included by Harry Haines and myself for the Voices from the Underground Series, *Second Front* has turned out to be one of the more problematic. In the GI press, I have found listings for two papers, *The 2nd Front International* published in Stockholm and *The Second Front* published in Boulogne. Neither title is found in the published catalogs of the collections. There are two editions of *The Second Front* preserved in the collections known to me, one published in Montreal and one in Stockholm; unfortunately neither version can be found in any listing published in the GI press. Because both sources agree a paper with *Second Front* in its title was being published in Stockholm in 1968, I am tempted to conclude that what is listed in the GI press as *The 2nd Front International* and what is listed in the holdings of the Tamiment Library as *The Second Front* are the same publication. Unfortunately, because these holdings are incomplete and the publisher listed by the Tamiment is different from that listed in the GI press,[5] this is probably not the case and I have decided to treat the four papers as distinct publications.

Shakedown (Wrightstown, New Jersey). While this paper is listed by the Historical Society of Wisconsin, Northwestern University, Swarthmore College, and Temple University as *Shakedown,* it was alternately titled, and listed in a number of GI newspapers, as *The Time Has Come for a Long-needed Shakedown.* This is the version of the title used in Harry Haines' list.

Skydove (Columbus, Ohio) was published by airmen from Lockbourne Air Force Base in 1972. After one issue it was renamed *Lockbourne Skydove.*

SOS News (Oakland, California) was published by the organization Support Our Soldiers, from April 1971 through 1973. In 1973, the paper was transferred to the GI Project Alliance and renamed *GIPA News*. The organization SOS, Support Our Soldiers, should not be confused with the similarly named organization S.O.S.–Stop Our Ship, which emerged from the efforts to halt the passage of the aircraft carriers *Constellation* and *Coral Sea*.

Stripes and Stars (London, England). Six issues of *Stripes and Stars* were published in London between February and November 1973. It was then renamed *Separated From Life*.

The Underground Oak (Oakland, California) was renamed *The Oak* in 1969. *The Underground Oak* is included in Harry Haines' list.

Veteran's Voice (Oakland, California). From May 1971 to January 1973, *Veteran's Voice* was published by Kansas City Veterans for Peace. In January 1973, publication was taken over by Vietnam Veterans Against the War. This publication should not be confused with the similarly titled *Veterans' Voice* that was published in Minneapolis from 1973–74 by Primetime Publishers, Inc.

We Got the brASS: Journal of the Second Front International (Frankfurt and Tokyo). There were two editions of *We Got the brASS: Journal of the Second Front International*, one published in Tokyo (subtitled "Asian edition") and one published in Frankfurt. There was a third edition published (in Tokyo) as *We Got the brASS, the Vietnam Edition*. The second issue of the German edition was alternately titled *We Got the Brass (again)*.[6] After three issues, the German edition of *We Got the Brass* was renamed *The Next Step*. The German and Asian editions are included in Harry Haines' list. The Vietnam edition is listed below.

Your Military Left (El Paso, Texas) was originally published from 1969 to 1970. In 1971, the paper was restarted. As both the first and second series begin with vol. 1, no. 1, they are treated below as separate publications. *Your Military Left* series 1 includes those papers published from 1969 to 1970. *Your Military Left* series 2 includes those papers published between 1971 and 1973. Series 1 is included in Harry Haines' list; series 2 is listed below.

Newspaper Titles

The 279 papers listed below include the following classifications: 20 papers produced by GIs in Exile [AMEX]; 6 papers produced by GIs in military prisons [CONF]; 28 papers produced by and for Draft Resistors [DRAFRES]; and 44 papers produced by Friends of Resistors Inside The Military [FRITM].[7] In addition, there are 5 nationally distributed papers [NATL] and 2 pro-war/anti-communist GI papers [PRO]; 6 papers produced by Reservists and National Guardsmen [RESV]; 24 papers produced by Resistors In The Military [RITM]; 77 produced by U.S. Army and Marine Corps [USA/MC] units; 39 produced by sailors and airmen [USAF/USN]; and 14 produced by veterans' organizations [VET]. Lastly, affiliations of 14 papers could not be traced. The designations USA/MC and USAF/USN are borrowed from David Cortright's *Soldiers in Revolt*. The designation RITM includes papers produced by the Concerned Officers Movement and Vietnam Veterans Against the War, both of which attracted active-duty personnel from all branches of the U.S. military. I have also included the titles of 120 pamphlets and GI project reports.

1st of the Worst (Tacoma, Washington [USA/MC]: 1970)

04B Notes (Heidelberg, West Germany [USA/MC]: 1976). Affiliated with the Augsburg Soldiers Committee

"A" Company Underground (Tillicum, Washington [USA/MC]: 1972)

a'Bout Face (Heidelberg, West Germany [USA/MC]: 1970–71).[8] Affiliated with Unsatisfied Black Soldiers

a'Bout Face (Heidelberg, West Germany [USA/MC]: 1971)[9]. Affiliated with the Black Disciple Party

About Face! The US Servicemen's Fund Newsletter (New York, New York [NATL]: 1971–73). Affiliated with the United States Servicemen's Fund

AFA Notes (New York, New York [FRITM]: 1975)

Alconbury Raps (Girton, Cambridge, England [USAF/USN]: 1971)

Alkonbury Raps (Girton, Cambridge, England [USAF/USN]: 1971)

Alliance (San Francisco, California [VET]: 1969). Affiliated with Veterans for Peace in Vietnam

Alliance for Conscientious Objectors Newsletter (Seattle, Washington [RITM]: 1972–74)

The Alternative (Fort Meade, Maryland [USA/MC]: 1971)

Ambush (Ottawa, Ontario [AMEX]: 1970). Affiliated with the American Deserters Committee

The American Deserter's Committee Newsletter (Montreal, Quebec [AMEX]: 1970)

The American Exile (London, England [AMEX]: 1974). Affiliated with the Union of American Exiles in Britain

The American Exile in Britain (London, England [AMEX]: 1969–73). Affiliated with the Union of American Exiles in Britain

The American Exile in Canada (Toronto, Canada [AMEX]: 1968–69). Affiliated with the Union of American Exiles

The American Exile Newsletter (Stockholm, Sweden [AMEX]: 1972–77). Affiliated with the Center for American Exiles

Amex-Canada: Published by Americans Exiled in Canada (Toronto, Canada [AMEX]: 1971–77)

AMEX-Canada: The American Expatriate in Canada (Toronto, Canada [AMEX]: 1969–71)

AMEX → Canada: The American Expatriate in Canada (Toronto, Canada [AMEX]: 1969–71). Affiliated with the Union of American Exiles

Amnesty News (New York, New York [FRITM]: 1974)

AntiWarrior (Washington, D.C. [DRAFRES]: 1969–69). Affiliated with the Student Mobilization Committee Against the War in Vietnam

Antithesis: Forum of the American Deserters Committee (Montreal, Quebec [AMEX]: 1970)

The Ash (Kaiserslautern, Germany [USA/MC]: 1969)

"B" Company Unbridled Voice (Tillicum, Washington [USA/MC]: 1972)

B-Troop News (Fort Lewis, Washington [USA/MC]: 1970)

Baltimore GIs United (Baltimore, Maryland [USA/MC]: 1969). Affiliated with GIs United

Battle Acts (New York, New York [FRITM]: 1970). Affiliated with Women of Youth Against War & Fascism

Battlefront (Jackson, Mississippi [PRO]: ca. 1968–71)[10]

Below Decks (Subic Bay, The Philippines [USAF/USN]: 1970–71). No copies of this paper exist in public collections.

Black Tribunal for Awareness and Progress (Karlsruhe, Germany [USA/MC]: 1971). Affiliated with the Black Dissent Group

Blows Against the Empire (Kirkland AFB, New Mexico [USAF/USN]: 1973)

Boston Draft Resistance Group Newsletter (Cambridge, Massachusetts [DRAFRES]: 1967–69)

The Bridge: The Butzbach Prison Journal of the American Group (Butzbach, West Germany [CONF]: 1972–73)

The California Veteran (Santa Monica, California [VET]: n.d.)

Call Up (Milwaukee, Wisconsin [RESV]: 1972). No copies of this paper exist in public collections.

Call Up! SDA (Patton Barracks, Heidelberg, West Germany [USA/MC]: 1970). Affiliated with Soldiers for Democratic Action

Can You Bear McNair (West Berlin, Germany [USA/MC]: 1970–71). No copies of this paper exist in public collections.

Catharsis (Boston, Massachusetts [USAF/USN]: 1970). Affiliated with Quonset-Davisville GI's for Peace

Challenge Bulletin (San Francisco, California [USA/MC]: 1972)

Chicago Action Committee Newsletter (Chicago, Illinois [DRAFRES]: 1969)

Chickenshit Weekly (El Paso, Texas [USA/MC]: 1972)

Cleveland Area Veterans for Peace Newsletter (Cleveland, Ohio [VET]: 1970)

Cockroach (Minot AFB, North Dakota [USAF/USN]: 1971). No copies of this paper exist in public collections.

Coffeehouse News (San Francisco, California [FRITM]: 1969). Affiliated with Support Our Soldiers

Column Left (Buffalo, New York [VET]: 1972)

COM Newsletter (Pearl City, Hawaii [RITM]: 1971). Affiliated with the Concerned Officers Movement. No copies of this paper exist in public collections.

Combat Ethnic Weapons (San Francisco, California [FRITM]: 1971)

Committee to Defend Fort Hamilton GIs (no address given [FRITM]: 1970)

Concerned Officers Movement Newsletter (Washington, D.C. [RITM]: 1970). Affiliated with the Concerned Officers Movement

Confinee Says (Camp Pendleton, California [CONF]: 1971). Affiliated with the Movement for a Democratic Military

Conscientious Objectors for Service Benefits Newsletter (Boston, Massachusetts [FRITM]: 1968)

Counterdraft (Los Angeles, California [DRAFRES]: 1968–72)

Cracked (MacDill AFB, Florida [USAF/USN]: 1970–71). No copies of this paper exist in public collections.

Death Ship Times (North Charleston, South Carolina [USAF/USN]: 1973–74)

Defense Committee Newsletter (Gainesville, Florida [RITM]: 1973). Affiliated with Vietnam Veterans Against the War

Dig It! (Baumholder, West Germany [USA/MC]: 1971). Affiliated with the American Servicemen's Union

The DIS Newsletter (Worcester, Massachusetts [DRAFRES]: 1969)

DMZ (Washington, D.C. [USA/MC]: ca. 1969)

Draft Action News (New York, New York [DRAFRES]: 1967)

The Draft Call (Madison, Wisconsin [DRAFRES]: 1968)

Draft Refusers Support Group Newsletter (Chicago, Illinois [DRAFRES]: 1970–73)

Draft Resistance Clearing House Memorandum (Madison, Wisconsin [DRAFRES]: 1967)

Draft Resistance Seattle Newsletter (Seattle, Washington [DRAFRES]: 1968)

Eat The Apple (Quebec, Canada [AMEX]: 1971)

El camina de justicia (Boulder, Colorado [FRITM]: 1970)

Equity Newsletter (New York City, New York [FRITM]: 1971–72)

Exile Report (Detroit, Michigan [AMEX]: 1971)

Exposure (Stuttgart, West Germany [service branch unknown]: 1970). No copies of this paper exist in public collections.

Eyes Right (Radcliffe, Kentucky [PRO]: 1969)[11]

Favorite Sons (San Bernardino, California [RITM]: 1973). Affiliated with Vietnam Veterans Against the War/Winter Soldier Organization

Fight Back! (Chicago, Illinois [RESV]: n.d.)

Fight Back (Long Beach, California [USAF/USN]: 1971)

Fight Back! (Long Beach, California [USAF/USN]: 1974)

Final Draft (Cambridge, Massachusetts [DRAFRES]: 1970–72)

First Amendment (Detroit, Michigan [USA/MC]: 1970)

First Amendment (Indianapolis, Indiana [USA/MC]: 1970).[12] No copies of this paper exist in public collections.

Fort Bragg Free Press (Spring Lake, North Carolina [USA/MC]: 1969). No copies of this paper exist in public collections.

Fort Bragg GI Center Newsletter (Spring Lake, North Carolina [USA/MC]: 1972)

Fort Bragg Rag (Fort Bragg, North Carolina [USA/MC]: ca. 1969). No copies of this paper exist in public collections.

Fort Dix 38 Speak Out (Fort Dix, New Jersey [CONF]: 1969)

Fort Polk GI Voice (Houston, Texas [USA/MC]: 1971)

Fort Polk Puke (Fort Polk, Louisiana [USA/MC]: 1971)

Fort Riley Chapter (Fort Riley, Kansas [USA/MC] 1971). Affiliated with the American Servicemen's Union

Forward (West Berlin, Germany [USA/MC]: 1970–78)

Forward March of American Idealism (Washington, D.C. [USA/MC]: 1969–71)

Free The Duluth (San Diego, California [USAF/USN]: 1973). No copies of this paper exist in public collections.

Freedom for Lt Howe Newsletter (Denver, Colorado [FRITM]: 1966)

FTA (Heidelberg, West Germany [service branch unknown]: n.d.)

FTA With Pride—TriCities Chapter (Wiesbaden-Biebrich, West Germany [USA/MC]: 1972–73)

The Gargoyle (Camp LeJeune, North Carolina [USA/MC]: 1966). This paper is referenced in the publication *Kauri*, which produced a joint issue with it, as being self-published by an active-duty Marine. No copies of this paper exist in public collections.

The Gazette (Eglin Air Force Base, Florida [CONF]: 1971–75)

Gazoo (Salem, Oregon [service branch unknown]: 1971). No copies of this paper exist in public collections.

Getting Late (no address [service branch unknown]: 1967)

GI Alliance Newsletter (Washington, D.C. [FRITM]: 1969)

GI C.L.D.C. Newsletter (New York, New York[FRITM]: 1969)

GI Civil Liberties Defense Committee Newsletter (New York, New York [FRITM]: 1968)

GI CLDC Newsletter (New York, New York [FRITM]: 1971)

GI Counseling Service Newsletter (New York City, New York [FRITM]: 1970)

GI Defender (New York, New York [FRITM]: 1970)

GI Fight Back (Long Beach, California [USA/MC]: 1974–76). Affiliated with the Movement for a Democratic Military

GI News and Discussion Bulletin (San Diego, California [NATL]: 1971–73)

GI Office Newsletter (no address given [service branch unknown]: 1970)

GI Says (Vietnam [USA/MC]: 1969). According to a report filed by Liberation News Service, the staff of this paper, who had survived the battle of Hamburger Hill, posted a $10,000 hit upon their commanding officer. No copies of this paper exist in public collections.

GI-SAC Anti-war Bulletin (Berkeley, California [FRITM]: 1969)

GIA (San Francisco, California [USA/MC]: 1969)

The Giessen Eagle (Marburg, West Germany [USA/MC]: 1970). No copies of this paper exist in public collections.

GIPA News (San Diego, California [NATL]: 1973–78)

GIPA News and Discussion Bulletin (San Diego, California [NATL]: 1973–78)

GIs Are Fighting (Fort Lewis, Washington [USA/MC]: 1971)[13]

GIs Fight Back (Fort Riley, Kansas [USA/MC]: 1971)

Hair (Revived) (Misawa-shi, Japan [USA/MC]: 1970–72)

Head-On Wish (Jacksonville, North Carolina [USA/MC]: 1968–69)

The Hogarm (Gainesville, Florida [VET]: 1971). Affiliated with Veterans For Peace

Hollow Man (Holloman AFB, New Mexico [USAF/USN]: 1972). No copies of this paper exist in public collections.

How Btry Times and Post Toastie Review News (Fort Lewis, Washington [RESV]: 1968)

Huachuca Hard Times (Dry Gulch, Arizona [USA/MC]: 1969)

I Will Fear No Evil (Kirtland AFB, New Mexico [USAF/USN]: 1973)

Inside-out: VVAW-WSO Newsletter for Prisoners / VVAW/SWO National Office (Chicago, Illinois [RITM]: 1974–77)

Jingo (Heidelberg, West Germany [service branch unknown]: 1975)

Kauri (New York, New York [FRITM]: 1966)

The kNot (Minot AFB, North Dakota [USAF/USN]: 1971–72)

Korea Free Press (Elmhurst, Illinois [USA/MC]: 1970–72)[14]

Lamboy Times (Heidelberg, West Germany [USA/MC]: 1975)

The Leavenworth Brothers (no address given [CONF]: 1974)

Liberty Call (Pease AFB, New Hampshire [USAF/USN]: 1971)

Liberty Call (Portsmouth, New Hampshire [USAF/USN]: 1973)

Liberty Call (San Diego, California [RITM]: 1973). Affiliated with the Concerned Officers Movement

Link News (Washington, D.C. [FRITM]: 1969–70)

Lock 'n' Load: A Publication of Vietnam Veterans Against the War/WSO (New York, New York [RITM]: 1973)

Lockbourne Skydove (Columbus, Ohio [USAF/USN]: 1972)

Longbitch (USS *Long Beach* [USAF/USN]: 1972). No copies of this paper exist in public collections.

Lukewarm (Luke AFB, Arizona [RITM]: 1971). Affiliated with the Concerned Officers Movement. No copies of this paper exist in public collections.

Madison Veterans for Peace Newsletter (Madison, Wisconsin [VET]: 1970–72)

The Man Can't Win if You Grin (Okinawa [service branch unknown]: 1971). No copies of this paper exist in public collections.

MDM Broadsheet (San Francisco, California [USA/MC]: 1970). Affiliated with Movement for a Democratic Military

MDM Torpedo / Movement for a Democratic Military (Chicago, Illinois [USAF/USN]: 1970–71). Affiliated with Movement for a Democratic Military

Memorandum/L.A. Veterans and Reservists Organizing Project (Los Angeles, California [VET]: n.d.)

Mennonite Draft Resistance Newsletter (Goshen, Indiana [DRAFRES]: 1970–71)

Military Issues (New York, New York [FRITM]: 1969)

Minnesota homefront sniper (Minneapolis, Minnesota [VET]: 1971)

Minnesota Veteran for Peace (Minneapolis, Minnesota [VET]: 1970)

Miss Rita (Paris, France [AMEX]: 1971). No copies of this paper exist in public collections.

Mordor News (Norfolk, Virginia [USA/MC]: ca. 1971)

Mothball Blues (Philadelphia, Pennsylvania [USAF/USN]: 1973)

Mother Country (Elmhurst, Illinois [FRITM]: 1970). Affiliated with the Revolutionary Youth Movement

National Steering Committee Meeting / Vietnam Veterans Against the War, Winter Soldier Organization (Chicago, Illinois [RITM]: 1974)

The New England Resistance Newsletter (Cambridge, Massachusetts [DRAFRES]: 1967–69)

The New Mobilizer (Washington, D.C. [FRITM]: 1969–70)

New SOS News (San Francisco, California [FRITM]: 1969)

The New Testament (Schweinfurt, West Germany [USA/MC]: 1972)

News/Center for Servicemen's Rights (San Diego, California [FRITM]: 1972)

News-Notes/Military Law Project (Baltimore, Maryland [FRITM]: 1975)

Newsletter for the GI Coffee Houses (Oakland, California [FRITM]: 1969). Affiliated with USSF and S.O.S.

The Nose (Fort Ord, California [USA/MC]: ca. 1970–71). Paper identified as one of a group of publications published by MDM, by Terence Mangan (a pseudonym) in testimony before the House Committee on Internal Security in October 1971.. No copies of this paper exist in public collections.

Now Hear This! (Long Beach, California [USAF/USN]: 1970). Affiliated with the Movement for a Democratic Military

The Oak (San Francisco, California [USAF/USN]: 1969). No copies of this paper exist in public collections.

Oinkenbury Raps (Girton, Cambridge, England [USAF/USN]: 1971)

On Korps (Camp Lejeune, North Carolina [USA/MC]: 1970). No copies of this paper exist in public collections.

OPAC Newsletter (Yellow Springs, Ohio [FRITM]: 1969)

Operation County Fair Newsletter (Chicago, Illinois [RITM]: 1973–74). Affiliated with Vietnam Veterans Against the War

The Oppressed (Washington, D.C. [USA/MC]: 1971)

The Other Half (Glenview NAS, Illinois [USAF/USN]: 1972–73)

The Other Side (Newport, Rhode Island [USAF/USN]: 1972) 15

The Other Side (Okinawa [FRITM]: 1971)

The Other Side: A Newsletter of the Concerned Officers Movement (Fayetteville, North Carolina [Fort Bragg Concerned Officers Movement]: 1970)

Out Now (Long Beach, California [USA/MC]: 1970). Affiliated with the Movement for a Democratic Military

P.E.A.C.E. (Mildenhall, England [USAF/USN]: 1970–71)

Pacific Stars and Gripes (Koza, Okinawa [FRITM]: 1975–76)

Palo Alto Times They Are a' Changin' (Palo Alto, California [DRAFRES]: 1969)

The Paper Bag (Petersburg, Virginia [USA/MC]: 1968–1970)

The Paper Grenade (Stockholm, Sweden [AMEX]: 1969–71)

Pawn's Pawn (Fort Leonard Wood, Missouri [USA /MC]: 1968–69). No copies of this paper exist in public collections.

Peace and Justice (Los Angeles, California [FRITM]: 1972)

Peace Exchange (St. Catharines, Ontario [AMEX]: 1970)

Peace Feeler (Media, Pennsylvania [FRITM]: 1968–69)

Peace Treaty News (New York, New York [FRITM]: 1971)

Peace Treaty News (Palo Alto, California [FRITM]: 1971)

Peace of Mind (Vietnam [service branch unknown]: 1970). No copies of this paper exist in public collections.

Pentagon GI Coffeehouse Newsletter (Oakland, California [FRITM]: 1970)

People Emerging Against Corrupt Establishments (Mildenhall, England [USAF/USN]: 1971)

The Philadelphia Resistance (Philadelphia, Pennsylvania [DRAFRES]: 1968)

The Pickle Press (El Toro and L.T.A., California [USA/MC]: 1972). Affiliated with Movement for a Democratic Military

Pig Boat Blues (U.S.S. *Chicago* [USAF/USN]: 1974). No copies of this paper exist in public collections.

The Pig Pen (Oberlin, Ohio [DRAFRES]: 1968)

The Pigleton Snout (Camp Pendleton, California [USA/MC]: 1970)

Polylogue (Augusta, Georgia [FRITM]: 1969)

Prisoners Strike for Peace (New York, New York [CONF]: 1973)

Proper Gander (Heidelberg, West Germany [USA/MC]: 1970–71)

The Raw Truth (Cambridge, Massachusetts [RESV—Reservists Against the War]: 1970–71)

Regional Newsletter (Cincinnati, Ohio [RITM]: 1973). Affiliated with Vietnam Veterans Against the War

The Representative (Koaz, Okinawa [USA/MC]: 1971)

Reservists Committee to Stop the War Newsletter (Cambridge, Massachusetts [RESV]: 1970)

Resist (East Palo Alto, California [DRAFRES]: 1967–68)

The Resistance (Boston, Massachusetts [DRAFRES]: 1968)

The Resistance National Edition (Boston, Massachusetts [DRAFRES]: 1967)

The Resistance Newsletter (Berkeley, California [DRAFRES]: 1967)

Resistance Notes (Honolulu, Hawaii [DRAFRES]: 1969)

Resister (Los Angeles, California [DRAFRES]: 1968)

Resister (Philadelphia, Pennsylvania [DRAFRES]: 1969–71)

Reveille (Monterey, California [RESV]: 1968)

Right On (Asaka-shi, Japan [USA/MC]: 1970)

Rip Off (Kyoto, Japan [Amherst House]: 1971)

Rise Up and Fight Back! (Norfolk, Virginia [NATL]: 1974). No copies of this paper exist in public collections.

RITA Notes (Paris, France, and Heidelberg, West Germany [FRITM] 1966–2010)

The Road (Mainz, Germany [FRITM—RITA Acts]: 1971)

Rose Garden (Twentynine Palms Marine Base, California [USA/MC]: 1971). No copies of this paper exist in public collections.

S.O.S.: Stop Our Ship (San Francisco, California [FRITM]: 1972)

Scaggie Aggie Review (USS *Agerholm* [USAF/USN]: 1974). No copies of this paper exist in public collections.

The Second Front (Montreal, Quebec [AMEX]: 1967–68)

The Second Front (Stockholm, Sweden [AMEX]: 1968)

Separated From Life (London, England [USAF]: 1974)

The Shitlifter (Tillicum, Washington [USAF/USN]: 1972)

Shrapnel (Fort Ord, California [USA/MC]: 1970). Paper identified as one of a group of publications published by MDM, by Terence Mangan (a pseudonym) in testimony before the House Committee on Internal Security in October 1971.

Sick Slip (Spring Lake, North Carolina [USA/MC]: 1969). No copies of this paper exist in public collections.[16]

SLAM (New Orleans, Louisiana [FRITM]: 1969)

SOS Enterprises Ledger (USS *Enterprise* [USAF/USN]: 1972). No copies of this paper exist in public collections.

SOS News (Oakland, California [FRITM]: 1971–72)

Spartacus (Petersburg, Virginia [USA/MC]: 1968–69)

Speak Out (Hanau, West Germany [USA/MC]: 1969). No copies of this paper exist in public collections.

Spirits Rebellious (Newport, North Carolina [USA/MC]: 1974). No copies of this paper exist in public collections.

Squadron Scandal: Voice of the Fulda Soldiers' Committee! (Heidelberg, West Germany [USA/MC]: 1976)

The Squeak (Jonesville, Michigan [FRITM]: n.d.)

The Star Bungled Beggar (Misawa, Japan [service branch unknown]: n.d.)

Stars and Strikes (San Francisco, California [FRITM]: 1975–76)

Stripes and Stars (London, England [USAF/USN]: 1973)

Summer Camp '69 (Fort Lewis, Washington [RESV]: 1969)

Sydney FTA (Sydney, Australia [USA/MC]: 1969)[17]. No copies of this paper exist in public collections.

TDIC (Minneapolis, Minnesota [DRAFRES]: 1969–70)

The Tidewater African (Virginia Beach, Virginia [USAF/USN]: 1973)

Together (MacDill AFB, Florida [USAF/USN]: 1972)

Toronto American Deserters' Committee Newsletter (Toronto, Canada [AMEX]: 1970)

Tricky Dix Law and Orders (New York, New York [FRITM]: 1971)

The Truth (Butzbach, West Germany [USA/MC]: 1973)

Tryin' Times: Milwaukee Area Draft Information Center Newsletter (Milwaukee, Wisconsin [DRAFRES]: 1970)

UAE Newsletter (Toronto, Canada [AMEX]: 1968)

The UCMJ: United Colorado Military for Justice (Aurora, Colorado [USA/MC]: 1974)

Undertow (Boston, Massachusetts [USAF/USN]: 1972). No copies of this paper exist in public collections.

UNDO News (Princeton, New Jersey [DRAFRES]: 1970)

United Front (Yokosuka, Japan [USAF/USN]: 1973)

Up-Tight (El Paso, Texas [USA/MC]: 1969)

Update—Southeast Asia: A News-Bulletin of Vietnam Veterans Against the War/Winter Soldier Organization. (Chicago, Illinois [RITM]: 1974)

USS Duluth Free Press (San Diego, California [USAF/USN]: 1973–74)

Venceremos (Frankfurt/Main, West Germany [USA/MC]: 1969–70)

Vet Cong (Chicago, Illinois [RITM]: 1972). Affiliated with Vietnam Veterans Against the War

The Veteran (Chicago, Illinois [RITM]: 1975–2010). Affiliated with Vietnam Veterans Against the War

The Veteran (San Francisco, California [VET]: 1972)

Veterans Peace Offensive (Detroit, Michigan [VET]: 1969). Affiliated with GIs & Veterans Against the War in Vietnam

Veteran's Voice (Kansas City, Missouri [RITM]: 1971). Affiliated with Vietnam Veterans Against the War

Veterans' Voice (Minneapolis, Minnesota [VET]: 1973–74)

Vets for Peace Newsletter (Berkeley, California [VET]: 1968–71)

Vietnam Grunt (Honolulu, Hawaii [service branch unknown]: 1968)

Vietnam Summer News (Cambridge, Massachusetts [DRAFRES]: 1967)

Vietnam Vet (Portland, Oregon [RITM]: 1972). Affiliated with the N.W. Caucus of Vietnam Veterans Against the War

Vietnam Veterans Against the War/Winter Soldier Organization (Chicago, Illinois [RITM]: 1973–77)

Vietnam Veterans Against the War/Winter Soldier Organization National Prison Project (Chicago, Illinois [RITM]: 1974)

Vietnam Veterans Against the War/Winter Soldier Organization, New York-Northern New Jersey Regional Office (New York, New York [RITM]: 1974)

Vietnam Veterans Against the War/Winter Soldier Organization Cincinnati Regional Branch (Cincinnati, Ohio [RITM]: 1973)

VVAW Newsletter (Detroit, Michigan [RITM]: 1972)

VVAW Newsletter (New York, New York [RITM]: 1971)

VVAW-WSO East Bay Chapter Newsletter (Oakland, California [RITM]: 1974)

The War Bulletin (Berkeley, California [FRITM]: 1972–73)

The War Resister (San Francisco, California [FRITM]: 1974–86)

Washington Area Military and Draft Law Panel Newsletter (location unknown [DRAFRES]: 1970–73)

We Are Everywhere (USS *Coral Sea* [USAF/USN]: 1972)

We Are Somebody Too (Karlsruhe, West Germany [service branch unknown]: 1971)[18]. No copies of this paper exist in public collections.

We Got the Brass [Vietnam ed.] (Tokyo, Japan [USA/MC]: 1970)

Why (Naha, Okinawa [service branch unknown]: 1971)

Wildcat (Chicago, Illinois [USA/MC—Military Action Committee]: 1973–75)

The Wiley Word (Neu Ulm, Germany [USA/MC]: 1972). This paper was renamed *The Word* with the publication of vol. 2, no. 1.

Wish (Cherry Point Marine Corps Air Station [USA/MC]: 1969). Merged with *Head-On!* to form paper *Head-On Wish!*

The Witness (Schwäbisch Gmünd, West Germany [USA/MC]: 1970)

Women Hold Up Half the Sky (Yokosuka, Japan [VET]: 1974)[19]. This was one of three GI papers specifically dedicated to the problems of women in the military. The others were *Whack*, which is included in Harry Haines' list, and *Women's Voices*.

Women's Voices (Koza, Okinawa [service branch unknown]: 1974). No copies of this paper exist in public collections.

The Word (Neu Ulm, Germany [USA/MC]: 1973)

Worms Eye View (of Nixon's War) (Thailand [USA/MC]: 1972). This paper was produced by Army Intelligence personnel stationed in Thailand.

Write On (Bitburg, West Germany [USA/MC]: 1973)

Write On (Norton AFB, California [USAF/USN]: 1971)

Xpress (Staten Island, New York [USA/MC]: 1970–71). Affiliated with Fort Hamilton GIs United

Yah-Hoh (Fort Lewis, Washington [USA/MC]: 1970). This paper is the only GI underground known to have been produced by and for Native Americans. No copies of this paper exist in public collections.

Yand (Fukoka, Japan [service branch unknown]: 1970)

Your Military Left (Newsletters) (San Antonio, Texas [USA/MC]: 1970)

Your Military Left (series 2) (San Antonio, Texas [USA/MC]: 1971–73)

Zero (Paris, France [AMEX]: 1973)

Pamphlets and Project Reports

4th Of July Project
1972 GI Movement Calendar
1973 GI Movement Calendar
American Deserters

American Servicemen Have Rights—Do You Know Yours?
Amnesty: Why? For Whom?
Antiwar GIs Speak Out: Interviews with Ft. Jackson GIs United Against the War
Billy Dean Smith (Billy D. Smith Defense Committee)
Billy Dean Smith (Vietnam Veterans Against the War)
Black Marines Against the Brass
Brothers And Sisters (Fort Hood United Front)
Brothers And Sisters (FTA Project)
Brothers And Sisters (Green Machine Collective)
Brothers And Sisters (UFO Coffeehouse)
Call for Support (Fort Dix)
The Calm Before the Storm (The Center for Servicemen's Rights)
Camp Mccoy 3
Camp Pendelton Brig Riot
Camp Pendelton, California (Green Machine Collective)
Carolyn Kiiskila and the First Amendment Beat the Brass 5–0! You Can Do It Too!
The Case of Gary Lawton and Zurebu Gardner
Class Chauvinism a Problem in Creating the GI Movement (Code 7 Collective)
Comrades (Fort McClellan)
Comrades (The Oleo Strut Coffeehouse)
Court Martial Turned Around (American Servicemen's Union)
Dear Comrades (United States Servicemen's Fund)
Dear Folks (United States Servicemen's Fund)
Dear Friend (GI-Civilian Alliance for Peace)
Dear Friend (Vietnam Veterans Against the War)
Dear People (Potemkin Bookshop)
Decent Jobs (American Servicemen's Union)
Discharge in Store for Pvt. Glover (GI Civil Liberties Defense Council)
Do GIs Have Rights? The Case of Lt. Howe
Establishing National GI-Civilian Solidarity
February 16 March (I) (GI-Civilian Alliance for Peace)
February 16 March (II) (GI-Civilian Alliance for Peace)
Fight Racism (Progressive Labor Party)
For Immediate Release—11–11–69 (GI Civil Liberties Defense Council)
For Immediate Release—Tom Doyle Acquitted (American Servicemen's Union)
Fort Bragg Report (Fort Bragg Collective)
Fort Dix Coffee House Bombing
The Fort Hood Three: The Case of the Three G.I.'s Who Said "No" to the War in Vietnam
Fort Hood 38 Appeal (The Bond)
The Frame-Up of the Gainesville Eight: A Case of Political Repression
Free Billy Smith
Free Billy Smith: Black G.I. Framed on Frag Rap
Free Speech for GIs: The Case of Pfc. Howard Petrick, a Soldier Opposed to the Vietnam War
Friends (The Shelter Half Coffeehouse)

From the Shelter Half (The Shelter Half Coffeehouse)

From the UFO (UFO Coffeehouse)

Fundraising Appeal (The Bond)

GI Community

G.I. Joe's a Red!

GI Legal Self-Defense

The GI Movement and May 16

GIs Handbook on Military Injustice (American Servicemen's Union)

GIs Hit Back (4-page supplement published by *The Old Mole*, 1969)

GIs Organize (GI Airmen and Sailors Coalition)

GIs Speak Out Against the War: The Case of the Ft. Jackson 8; Interviews of Participants

GIs Struggle Against Army (Progressive Labor Party)

Guide for the AWOL GI

Hard Times

Harass the Brass: Mutiny, Fragging and Desertions in the U.S. Military

Hell No Don't Go! (American Servicemen's Union)

Here's Your Ammunition

History of the Fort Knox GI Movement (Fort Knox Coffee House)

Information Sheet (GI-Civilian Alliance for Peace)

Kangaroo Court-Martial: George Daniels and William Harvey, Two Black Marines Who Got 6 and 10 Years for Opposing the Vietnam War

Letter from Joe Goodman (United States Servicemen's Fund)

Liberate Okinawa

The Man Can't Win if Ya Grin

March with the New Antiwar Army

The Military Messes with Mobile Men

Mutiny Trial Defendants the Presidio 27' Profiles by Donna Mickelson; drawings by Louise James

"My Fight Is in the Ghettos of Philadelphia—Not in Vietnam!" by Pvt. Ronald Lockman

The New Exiles: American War Resisters in Canada

The Nine for Peace

No More Shit (USS *Coral Sea*)

On GI Civilian Solidarity

People's Armed Forces Day, May 20: Great Lakes Naval Training Center

People's Peace Treaty: to End the War in Indochina

People's Peace Treaty and Women

PL Press a Revolutionary Viewpoint (Progressive Labor Party)

Plan of the Day (USS *Coral Sea*)

Playboy Ad (Vietnam Veterans Against the War)

Post-Vietnam War Syndrome Library

Press Release—10-6-69 (GI Civil Liberties Defense Council)

Press Release—Ed Jurenas (GI Civil Liberties Defense Council)

Report 1974 (Pacific Counseling Service)

Report from the Great Lakes MDM (Great Lakes Movement for a Democratic Military)

Repression and the GI Movement

Riot Control, Hell No (The Oleo Strut Coffeehouse)

Sanctuary of Servicemen

Seize the Time (Black Disciple Party)

Smash the Bosses' Armed Forces (Progressive Labor Party)

Soldiers Against the War: The Story of Pvt. Andrew Stapp and the Fort Sill GI's

Soldiers Sue the Army: War Protest Issue (Special Issue of the *San Francisco Chronicle*)

Some Notes on the GI Movement and Great Lakes Movement for a Democratic Military

Statement of Aims (GI Civil Liberties Defense Council)

Stop Our Ship (USS *Coral Sea*)

Stop the Wars (American Servicemen's Union)

Strategy and Tactics for GI Organizing (GI Alliance)

Suggestions (GI-Civilian Alliance for Peace)

Support Our Soldiers

Support Our Soldiers, Bring Them Home (The Oleo Strut Coffeehouse)

Supporting the GI Movement (People's Coalition for Peace and Justice)

Terrorism and Harassment of the GI Movement

The Trial of Juan Farinas

The Truth about Deserters

They Love It but Leave It: American Deserters

Turn the Guns Around (Progressive Labor)

Untitled Report (The Home Front Coffee House)

Universal Unconditional Amnesty

Up Against the War: A Personal Introduction to U.S. Soldiers & Civilians Fighting Against the War in Vietnam

A Warship Can Be Stopped

We Resist Because: Statements of Conscientious Non-Compliers with Military Conscription

We the Undersigned (USS *Coral Sea*)

We Won't Go: Personal Accounts of War Objectors

What's Happening in the Navy

NOTES

1. It is unclear how many issues of the latter paper were published; the Deering Library has a single issue in their collection. Given the date provided by the Deering Library for the publication of *The Road*, the date provided by Swarthmore College for the single issue of *Dig It!* (June 1971) is incorrect.

2. David Cortright, *Soldiers in Revolt* (New York: Anchor Press: 1975), 291.

3. In an editorial, published on the front page of the first issue of *Hair (Revived)*, the staff explained why they had decided to begin publishing the paper: "A year ago last July the newspaper *HAIR*

was first published by G.I.s here at Misawa. After the third issue had been printed, the paper was stopped by the brass 'for the use of base facilities' and its editors were shipped out PCS. We are reviving *HAIR* because we feel this is one means of promoting peace and unity among ourselves and with our brothers and sisters here in Japan" ("Why Hair?" in *Hair (Revived)* 3+1 [December 1, 1970]: 1).

4. *The Knot* is listed in the October 1971 issue of the *GI Press Service*. *My Knot* was included in a listing of GI newspapers "currently being published" prepared by the staff of the House Committee on Internal Security for publication in May 1972. The only known copy of *My Knot* preserved in a public collection was dated by the Historical Society of Wisconsin as January 197?.

5. The editions of *The Second Front* preserved at the Tamiment are listed as being published by the American Deserters Committee. In the GI press, the publisher of the 2^(nd) *Front International* is listed as the International Union of American Deserters and Draft Resisters (*Veterans Stars and Stripes for Peace*, vol. 1, no. 7).

6. Swarthmore College Library website, 2010.

7. This acronym is an adaption of the term FRITA—Friends of Resistors In The Army—that was coined by Max Watts to describe organizations supporting GI Resistors. I have changed it to Friends of Resistors In The Military, because by 1969 the centers of GI resistance had spread to every branch and subset of the armed services. FRITA itself was an adaption of the term RITA—Resistors In The Army—first used by Dick Perrin in January 1968.

8. This first iteration of *a'Bout Face* was published from July 4, 1970 through August 27, 1971. The last issue of this paper was vol. 2, no. 7. The Deering Library catalog, which has detailed notes on the GI papers in its collection, makes no mention of a relationship or affiliation between the two papers sharing this title.

9. While sharing name and place of publication, this version of *a'Bout Face* was limited to three issues with the first, vol. 1, no. 1, being published on September 27, 1971.

10. *Battle Front* and *Eyes Right* are the only conservative GI newspapers I have been able to identify. Because the GI Press Project has one mission to preserve all newspapers, newsletters, pamphlets, project reports, and posters without regard to size of organization or ideology, it is important to include conservative and anti-communist materials.

11. See note 2 above.

12. Listed in *GI Press Service*, vol. 2, no. 8.

13. This was an issue of the Progressive Labor Party newspaper *Challenge* that was produced and distributed by GIs at Fort Lewis. I am not aware of it being distributed to bases outside of the Seattle/Tacoma area.

14. Published by Soldiers' Free, Democratic, Guerilla, Anti-Fascist, Revolutionary, Peace and Freedom Loving Liberation Press.

15. Published as a supplement to *All Hands Abandon Ship*.

16. Listed in the August 1969 issue of *Bragg Briefs*.

17. Listed by David Cortright.

18. Listed by David Cortright.

19. *Women Hold Up Half the Sky* was published by the women's collective of Yokosuka Chapter of VVAW/WSO; "it covers the problems of women in the military, and women's efforts to change the conditions which oppress them and limit their growth" ("What is VVAW/WSO," special issue of *Fall in At Ease*).

Fast Times in the Motor City: The First Ten Years of the Fifth Estate, 1965–1975

BOB HIPPLER

Harvey's Trip

In 1965, Norma Ovshinsky Marks decided to move to Los Angeles and take her seventeen-year-old son, Harvey, a senior at Detroit's Mumford High School, with her. Ovshinsky wasn't too happy about going. "To begin with," he recalls, "I had to speed up my Mumford graduation by going to summer school and missing most senior class ceremonies. I was well known at school and would have been a class officer. When I got to Los Angeles, I was desperately homesick for Detroit and my high school friends."

Wandering around Los Angeles in a funk about his predicament, Ovshinsky happened upon the Sunset Strip. There he saw a couple of sights that piqued his interest: a gathering place called the Fifth Estate Coffeehouse, and nearby a functioning underground newspaper, Art Kunkin's *Los Angeles Free Press.*

Ovshinsky began hanging out with the denizens of the coffeehouse and soon began helping out any way he could on the *Los Angeles Free Press.* He was captivated by its antiwar politics, its concern for developing a radical Los Angeles community, and its coverage of the local music scene, which in coming years was to produce legendary groups like Arthur Lee's Love, Jim Morrison's Doors, and Roger McGuinn's Byrds. "Soon I became obsessed with coming back to Detroit and publishing an underground paper which would bring people together there, like the process I saw happening in Los Angeles," Ovshinsky recalls. He wasn't even sure who his target audience would be, except that it would include freeks (with two e's, the original Detroit term for hippies) and politicos of various kinds, including civil rights activists, whose Selma, Alabama, confrontation during that spring got the sixties rolling in earnest. Somehow he would, as a journalist, help unify the disparate counterculture developing on the streets of Detroit.

Acting on his obsession, Ovshinsky abruptly ran away from his new home in Los Angeles and returned to his father's house in suburban Detroit. His father, Stan Ovshinsky, a noted inventor and electronics whiz, loaned him $300 for the new paper, which Harvey named the *Fifth Estate*, after the coffeehouse. The first *Fifth Estate* office was in Stan's basement.

Why the name "Fifth Estate?" An issue of the paper from 1975 provides an explanation:

"The term 'estate' harkens back to the era of the French Revolution when society was declared as being divided into the three estates of the royalty, the clergy, and the common people. By the 1920s, the power of the U.S. press was so formidable that it could make and break politicians, foster wars, create drug hysteria, etc. and so it was dubbed the 'Fourth Estate' by some wag. So, the fifth is one up on the fourth. Dumb, huh?"

Actually, the name has at times not been well understood in brass-tacks, blue-collar Detroit. Jim Kennedy helped distribute the paper as head of Keep on Trucking, a group that emerged from the *Fifth Estate* itself after a brief 1970 power struggle between Kennedy and Peter Werbe. He said that a frequent reaction he got from people in his travels was "Fifth what?"

Ovshinsky and several high school friends put out the first issue on November 19, 1965. "I decided on a tabloid form," he says. "The problem was, I didn't know a tabloid had to have at least eight pages, so I submitted only six pages to the printer. Nobody at the printer told me anything; they just ran the paper as it was submitted." So the first *Fifth Estate* had two blank pages. Good for taking notes!

"For the first issue, we stole ads from other publications and printed them, just to make it look like we had some support," he continues. "Also, we put a date on the issue, but forgot to put the year." The *Fifth Estate* announced itself as "Detroit's new progressive biweekly." Its first headline was "Bob Dylan: In Memoriam," for an article that bemoaned Dylan's switch from acoustic to electric guitar. The issue was dedicated to Norman Morrison, the American antiwar crusader who had burned himself to death right outside the office of Secretary of Defense Robert McNamara. The new paper was well received by young people in the downtown Wayne State University area, who were starved for any alternative to the dull *Detroit Free Press* and the reactionary *Detroit News*.

Detroit—1965

Detroit in 1965 was both better and worse than it is in the first decade of the new millennium. It was a bustling, prosperous factory town of 1.5 million people, not the depressed, aging city of under 900,000 that it is today, albeit with more power for blacks. But politically it was more conservative than today, more dominated by the auto companies, with the Detroit Police Officers Association (DPOA) and to some extent the United Auto Workers (UAW) as Blacks were a large and growing minority in the city, gradually taking over the manufacturing and service jobs, and gaining political power as their numbers grew. They were about five years away from gaining a majority on the city council, and eight years away from electing Detroit's first black mayor, Coleman Young, who served from 1973 to 1993.

As blacks gained in numbers, the white-dominated DPOA was beginning to get increasingly politicized. By 1969, off-duty police officers would spend long hours registering voters, and the DPOA would financially back a "white hope" mayoral candidate in a successful bid to prevent Richard Austin from becoming the city's first black mayor. The DPOA would also endorse eight city-council candidates in that election—all white.

According to social critic Ralph W. Conant, author of *Prospects for Revolution*, as the sixties wore on, "the sharp rise in crime rates, urban rioting, student unrest, and war demonstrations . . . precipitated the latent political activities of the police unions." Carl

Parsell, president of the DPOA, said, "We have found that our negotiating power is tied to getting greater political power."

While the police were getting more political, the blacks were getting less and less satisfied with police job performance. As early as 1957, almost half of Detroit blacks surveyed said that police service was "not good" or "definitely bad," says Conant. Two-thirds of the blacks referred to anti-black discrimination and mistreatment by police officers. A Detroit poll taken in 1965, notes Conant, revealed that 58 percent of the black community stated that law enforcement was not fair and equitable.

There were other problems. The book *American Odyssey*, by Robert Conot, says that "in the third generation of the auto industry, blacks continued to be stuck in the lowest-grade jobs and excluded from professional, supervisory, white-collar, and skilled positions. Twenty-three percent of General Motors employees in the Detroit area were black, but of 11,125 skilled workers, only 67 were black. . . . Twenty-six percent of Chrysler employees were black, but of 7,425 in skilled jobs, 24 were black. . . . Forty percent of Ford employees at River Rouge were black, but of 7,000 in skilled categories, fewer than 250 were black."

Finally, housing was a chronic Detroit crisis. The city hoped to demolish 20 percent of its houses within ten years, they were so rundown. But though Detroit had 380,000 households with low-enough incomes, only 12,000 public housing units were available.

As far back as the 1943 riot, scarce housing had been a factor, with blacks being over-charged for slum dwellings, competing with the whites who did the rioting.

In 1925, Detroit had a small-scale riot when a crowd of five hundred whites tried to force a black doctor, Ossian Sweet, out of his new house. Sweet and several friends fired a shotgun, killing one. At a sensational trial, they were defended by Clarence Darrow and acquitted.

In 1965 these problems were getting worse, but to most outward appearances Detroit was still a huge one-horse factory town, the animal in question being the horseless carriage. Detroit's cultural narrowness was already then legendary, and the sense of airlessness was palpable. For baby boomers flooding downtown to escape an even more miserable existence in suburbia, the *Fifth Estate* filled a great void.

Buoyed by good street sales at 15 cents a copy, and a few head-shop ads, Ovshinsky and friends produced a second issue. But they ran into the first of the *Fifth Estate*'s many hassles over the years with the commercial printers hired to run off the paper. Besides being the year of Selma, 1965 was also the year of the massive U.S. escalation in Vietnam, with hundreds of thousands of troops being deployed. "I can't print a picture of an American flag with the stripes as bayonets," declared the printer when he saw the *Fifth Estate* cover, which protested the U.S. invasion.

Finally, black activist Rev. Albert Cleage, of the Shrine of the Black Madonna, agreed to print the issue. He was the first printer who stuck with the *Fifth Estate* for any period of time, and thus deserves credit for helping get it off the ground.

Creating and selling the second issue gradually broadened Ovshinsky's circle of acquaintances, and several of them commented that if he was starting a Detroit underground paper he definitely should talk to John Sinclair.

John Sinclair was a local Detroit artist, musician, and reefer-head who had started a project called the Artists' Workshop. "I remember my first visit to John Sinclair's place as wonderful," Ovshinsky says. "It was a homey yet intellectual atmosphere. John's wife Leni was cooking some exotic dish, John Coltrane was on the stereo, and we were surrounded by books. John was twenty-four, which seemed ancient to me at the time. He was also the first adult, besides my parents, who encouraged my idea for a new paper."

Sinclair, however, had one big problem. He was targeted by the authorities because he openly promoted drug use. The *Fifth Estate* began to report on his busts and helped fight police entrapment practices in the community. This was the beginning of an adversarial relationship that the paper would have with the Detroit cops for years. Crusading against police abuse was to become a big priority, especially after the Detroit rebellion of 1967.

Sinclair agreed to write a column for the *Fifth Estate*, which was originally called "Coat Puller," but was later renamed "Rock and Roll Dope." The name pretty much summarized Sinclair's political program. The role of drugs in the revolution was to be a recurring controversy on the *Fifth Estate*, with drugs definitely falling from favor by the early 1970s. Then, too, the drugs on the street in the early years—weed, mescaline, and LSD—were much more attractive than the Quaaludes, angel dust, and amphetamines of later years. Who changed the supply? A good subject for another brief history.

In 1967, Sinclair founded the White Panther Party, which was to become the single most popular youth political grouping in late-1960s Detroit. The White Panther philosophy was an amalgam of Eastern religious insights, drug-oriented rites patterned after Native Americans, a love for music—including black jazz and blues, psychedelic rock, and heavy-metal riffs—and a long-haired hippie political militancy modeled on the namesake Black Panther Party.

In 1967 the White Panther Party was probably the political group that most influenced the editorial policy and general style of the *Fifth Estate*. However, after the 1967 Detroit rebellion, the Motor City political scene got too heavy for the White Panthers, and they moved to more sedate Ann Arbor, occupying a large house right across from fraternity row. The geographical distance, plus an increasing disdain for drug use on the left, reduced their influence on the paper.

John Sinclair's book *Guitar Army*, which became popular after he began a ten-year sentence for marijuana possession in 1969, helped to continue the White Panthers' popularity. As late as 1973, Jim Kennedy said that in his travels out of state distributing the *Fifth Estate*, the strongest youth political force he saw was the White Panther Party.

Despite the encouragement from Sinclair and many new friends, after two issues, the *Fifth Estate* had a bank account of close to zero. "I didn't think we were going to make it," Ovshinsky recalls. "I went around to all the political people I knew, from civil rights groups like the Student Nonviolent Coordinating Committee to antiwar groups like the Detroit Committee to End the War in Vietnam (DCEWV). Finally I announced at a meeting at the DCEWV Building that we were closing up shop. Up stepped a guy in a T-shirt and a Beatle haircut who said he'd like to help, we should keep this thing going. It was Peter Werbe."

Enter Peter Werbe

Werbe, twenty-five, had been an instant convert to the *Fifth Estate* from the time he saw the first issue. "I was at a University of Detroit blues concert," he recalls. "Harvey came down the aisle selling the paper. I was flabbergasted! I'd always thought that the print media and the people in power were inaccessible, and here was a paper that said things could change. It knocked my socks off."

With new support from Werbe and other volunteers, the *Fifth Estate* moved out of Stan's basement and into an office next to the DCEWV at John C. Lodge Freeway and West Warren. The paper worked closely with the committee, and for a period devoted the middle four pages of each issue to the committee's newsletter. John and Leni Sinclair soon moved into an office upstairs and encouraged the talented psychedelic artist Gary Grimshaw to contribute to the paper.

The *Fifth Estate* used the offset production process—in fact, the massive introduction of cheap offset technology was a major factor in making possible all the alternative presses of the Vietnam era.

The layout person worked with a row of backlit pages at light tables, applied the actual headlines, photos, and type, and had a clear view of what the final product would look like. The best layout person who ever worked at the *Fifth Estate* was Cathy West, a young woman from a working-class background in the downriver suburb of Wyandotte. As of the third issue, she was officially on the staff and spent more time there than any woman except Marilyn Werbe, Peter's wife. Cathy was a good friend of the paper in the years after she left the staff. Sadly, she died in Detroit in 1984.

Reminiscing about the earliest days of the paper, Ovshinsky says, "It was a thrill to be involved in it. Most of the people I was working with were older, but nobody ever treated me like a kid. Also, the essence of the sixties was a belief that things might change, as indeed they did, though not as much as we hoped for. The movements for women's rights and student rights were just taking off. It was a very optimistic time.

"Peter Werbe was radical from the start. I wanted to bring people together—he wanted them together if they agreed on a political program. He wanted to provoke people into action, which he really valued more than words. He was an angry guy at times, and I always said, 'I'm glad you're on *our* side.'"

During these years, the youth scene began to explode. According to Werbe, "People were just streaming into the downtown area, many wanting to get involved in the paper." Amid the increasingly hectic activity, the *Fifth Estate* did not even have regularly scheduled staff meetings. "We were eventually overwhelmed with material for the paper. Everyone wanted to do something. It was almost a process of automatic writing."

A Political Heritage

While the political establishment in Detroit was stodgy, in a longer historical perspective, and on a grassroots level, the city provided a fertile environment for a radical newspaper. Detroit was a strong union town and had a tradition of radical activity in those unions. The Communist Party (CP) had controlled the Rouge Plant local until about 1950. Sol Wellman, who went to prison as state CP chair in the 1950s, used to come by the office and discuss the issues of the day. (He was also a Spanish Civil War veteran.)

The Trotskyist Socialist Workers Party operated a popular meeting place on Woodward called Debs Hall, named after Eugene V. Debs, the single most dominant figure in American socialist history, who was active from the 1880s to the 1920s. Several Trotskyists were on the *Fifth Estate* staff over the years.

And there were other resources. The Catholic Worker movement had strong roots in Detroit, with activists who followed the teachings of Dorothy Day and Thomas Merton. Activist Sheila Murphy Cockrel came out of this milieu. In addition, the Protestant community in Detroit still felt the influence of Reinhold Niebuhr, who was pastor of Bethel church on West Grand Boulevard from 1915 to 1928. In the book *Detroit Lives* (Robert Mast, editor), Episcopalian activist Hugh White recalls that "I did a fair amount of work under Reinhold Niebuhr at Union Seminary." (Niebuhr taught there after his Detroit days.)

Around that same time, in 1930, Detroit blacks founded the Black Muslims, or Nation of Islam, who later produced Malcolm X (known in his younger days as "Detroit Red"). Also, the city had one of the nation's largest liberal Jewish communities, which produced a half-dozen *Fifth Estate* staffers. In 1963, the year of John F. Kennedy's assassination and Martin Luther King's March on Washington, Detroit saw a massive civil rights march of over 100,000 people, led by the late Rev. C. L. Franklin, the father of Aretha Franklin. Students for a Democratic Society (SDS) was started in nearby Ann Arbor and Port Huron, with the help of the United Auto Workers, who gave SDS the use of a large meeting hall in Port Huron, which no longer exists (SDS began its history with the 1962 Port Huron Statement).

On a more immediate level, political opposition to the hideous day-to-day reality of the Vietnam War steadily grew, especially since the war was visible daily on television. However, young people did not need a TV to know the war was affecting them—all they had to do was read their draft notices that came in the mail. In working-class Detroit, many young people knew friends who, without student deferments, were sent to Vietnam. As the war dragged on, many were killed or injured.

The result of this social pressure was to breed strident revolt among many young people. "The paper was dominated by a spirit of generalized rebellion," Werbe recalls. "If you could break one rule, why not break all the rules? And if you do that, why just put a new set of rules in their place?" Even the rock-music scene got increasingly political as drug busts and draft convictions produced the same repeated image: a young person led off to jail for simply trying to live freely.

With time, the *Fifth Estate* began to prosper on a modest scale. Record-company media buyers began to notice the underground press and run ads there, convinced that such papers were reaching the nonconformist kids who were listening to new groups like the Grateful Dead, the Jefferson Airplane, Mitch Ryder and the Detroit Wheels, and (lest we forget) John Sinclair's high-intensity rock group, the Motor City Five, whose favorite haunt for performing was Detroit's fabled Grande Ballroom.

A typical record ad from the period read: "Country Joe and the Fish Are You—The things that you are: questioning, idealistic, involved, concerned with the love, the confusion and the excitement of the life you live today." As a result of steadier ad income, the paper even began to pay a subsistence wage of $25 a week to full-time staffers.

Plum Street

Then a break came that put the enterprise on even more solid footing. In 1966, the city of Detroit decided to designate a block of Plum Street as "Detroit's Art Community," where offbeat music, studios, bookstores, and head shops would be featured. Mayor Jerome Cavanagh even spoke at the kickoff ceremony.

After a staff debate, the *Fifth Estate* decided to move its office to Plum Street and also open a small bookstore there. "Peter was ambivalent about moving," Ovshinsky recalls. "He didn't want to lose our base near campus. But I liked the sense of community that was developing there. And also I was worried about paying our bills."

Also about this time, Werbe's wife Marilyn joined the staff and began to take an active role in writing, editing, and layout. She is still active on the *Fifth Estate* and falls about one year short of tying Peter as the staffer with the most seniority. In both cases, it's about forty years.

Sales at the *Fifth Estate* bookstore were 90 percent periodicals, with the rest being items like T-shirts, bumper stickers, and buttons. "The bookstore saved the paper and helped us get established," says Werbe. It also marked the high point of the *Fifth Estate*'s hippie-psychedelic era, before the politics got tougher and harder in 1967 and 1968.

After about a year, commercialism began to take its toll on Plum Street, and the flower era lost its luster as the bad chemicals drove out the good (at least they seemed good at the time). Plum Street began to seem less and less the place for a political newspaper, and the area around the West Warren office continued to take off as a center of progressive activity. The staff decided to move back to the West Warren location. "By the time we left, we were glad to get out," Werbe recalls.

Within another two years, the Plum Street scene collapsed completely, and the block became deserted as businesses moved out. Semi-trucks roared by the forlorn storefronts, and it was hard to imagine how anybody could have thought Plum Street would last.

Love for Sale

Downtown Detroit continued to fill up with young people escaping bleak suburbs like Livonia, Warren, and Southfield. In the case of the *Fifth Estate*, many also came from college campuses and from out of state. People wanted to change their lives, and in many cases that meant forgetting hometown sweethearts and seeking out somebody new. To put it briefly, hormones raged.

Norman Mailer stated, "The middle class is preoccupied with sex; the working class is drenched in it." Nevertheless, Detroit was still an old-fashioned town, and seeking out a satisfactory love life could be a sometime thing. Amid political struggle and a subsistence living standard, sexual relationships could be intense, but not necessarily stable. Low-rent, one-night stands were not unknown. Amid a city approaching a black majority, interracial affairs were not the rule, but certainly were not rare.

Many *Fifth Estate* staffers and friends began living collectively in a big house in the Cass Corridor called Boone's Farm Commune. Shared rent and food expenses alleviated some of the financial pressures, while occasional parties and long evenings listening to rock music under the influence of mind-altering substances made it a darn sight easier to socialize. "Revolution as ecstasy" became a byword.

Despite all the factors militating against it, several relationships among the *Fifth Estate* staff and friends lasted for years and years.

In an era of sexual liberation, John Sinclair eventually concluded that the increasingly serious, Marxist-oriented *Fifth Estate* was a little staid for his tastes. In 1968, while still writing a column for the *Fifth Estate*, he started his own underground paper, the *Warren-Forest Sun*, and gave it the motto "Sex, Drugs, and Rock and Roll." The late Barry Kramer also found the *Fifth Estate* rather reserved and lacking in music coverage, and so started *Creem* rock magazine as Detroit's sensual answer to *Rolling Stone*.

Society's attitude toward sexual matters was slowly changing. Not until 1970 did the first girlie magazine dare to show pubic hair. In nearby Ann Arbor, police were busting movies and plays that would not raise an eyebrow today, and the *Fifth Estate* covered the stories. In 1967 the chief of police tried to confiscate a film by Jack Smith called *Flaming Creatures*. Students blocked the door to the projection booth and later staged a sit-in at the station house. The film was not shown, and an obscenity trial followed.

(Director John Waters has referred to Jack Smith as the greatest of the underground film makers. *Flaming Creatures* has been described as a homosexual drag film, with many of the scenes done for humorous effect. There was much soft-core nudity on screen and a spirit of satire.)

Two years later, a play called *Dionysius in '69*, which featured scantily clad actors but no nudity, also caused controversy.

Sexual variety and experimentation also became the order of the day. Detroit's gay and lesbian community, which had existed in the shadows for decades, began to come out of the closet. A gay commune was established in the Cass Corridor. A group of activists put out the first issue of the *Gay Liberator* in 1970. It published regularly until 1977.

Sometimes, in the search for sexual fulfillment, things got a little kinky. The following letter and reply were published in 1969 in the *Fifth Estate*'s "Dr. HIP-pocrates" column, by Dr. Eugene Schoenfeld:

Dear Dr. Schoenfeld:

A couple of weeks ago my girlfriend and I got loaded and were making love. She told me that she wanted to show me something new that would be a real thrill to me. She said that one of her old boyfriends liked to have her do it to him often, so without knowing what it was, I agreed to let her try it.

What she did was to stretch my scrotum out tightly, then she took a pair of finger nail clippers and cut a small hole in the sac. I began to get scared then but she said not to worry, it was fun and didn't hurt much. Next she stuck a small plastic straw into the hole in my sac and started blowing air into it.

My sac got bigger than a baseball, but surprisingly it didn't hurt much and felt kind of good. I began to worry that it might burst so she stopped blowing and removed the straw. Then she quickly put a piece of adhesive tape over the hole to keep the air in. Then we continued with intercourse and I had a climax that was out of this world.

Afterwards she removed the tape from my scrotum and squeezed the air out with her hand. Then she dabbed my scrotum with rubbing alcohol (to prevent infection she said) and retaped the hole. When she put the alcohol on it, it burned like hell. The next day my penis was swollen to about double its normal size and it itched like hell, but two days later it was OK again. What I want to know is, could this practice cause me any harm? And what caused my penis to swell the next day?

REPLY: I should point out firstly that more bacteria exist in the mouth than in any other body orifice. Our skin is a natural barrier to bacteria and other microorganisms which are not normally found in the bladder or scrotum. Infections of the bladder may continue up the urethra to the kidneys. Infections of the scrotum? Not a pleasant prospect. Even more dangerous is the possibility of an air embolism. Air forced into a closed tissue space may enter the bloodstream, go to the heart, lungs, or brain and cause sudden death or stroke.

Holy Toledo! How did any urban youths survive those years?

Summer of Love?

In the spring of 1967, Detroiters decided to organize their own "Be-In," in tribute to the famous San Francisco "Be-In," which had starred Allen Ginsberg and Timothy Leary. According to Werbe, "Several thousand people showed up on Belle Isle and people were generally having a great time." Bands entertained the crowd, and balloons and Frisbees floated around. "It was a fusion of politics and counterculture, world revolution and the Age of Aquarius. It was all the same to us."

However, the Detroit Police Department provided a harbinger of things to come. As the crowd streamed home across the Belle Isle Bridge, mounted officers began harassing the revelers, in particular focusing on a biker element. By the time the crowd was on Jefferson Avenue, the cops were riding up and down the street, picking out individuals to sandwich against buildings, knocking people down, and even breaking windows.

The daily Detroit papers blamed the mess largely on the bikers. "They said that the Be-In crowd attacked the police, which was preposterous," says Werbe. The bias of the mainstream media, and their cover-up of the police misconduct, illustrated clearly what the role of an alternative paper could be. The *Fifth Estate* provided eyewitness accounts of police beatings, and showed how the cops ruined the Be-In.

The Belle Isle Be-In was Detroit's attempt to participate in the 1967 Summer of Love. However, it was not the defining event of the summer that it was intended to be. Instead, a few weeks later in July, another event occurred that would define 1967 in Detroit history: a massive racial rebellion, worse by far than the riot of 1943. As large areas of the city burned, several square miles of the downtown were cordoned off for three days. The National Guard killed over forty people, by official count, and finally the 82nd Airborne and the 101st Airborne were called in. The 1967 cataclysm was vividly described by Detroit blues artist John Lee Hooker in his song "The Motor City's Burnin'." During the rebellion, the Detroit police attacked the *Fifth Estate* office with tear-gas grenades, another dose of Detroit reality during the flower power era.

The upheaval of 1967 turned the *Fifth Estate* staff into what Werbe calls "participant journalists." As Ovshinsky recalls, "We really began to go out and dig up stories about the events. There was more to the situation than met the eye."

In tone, the paper became more sober. The following editorial appeared immediately after the rebellion:

> If there was any *one* thing which caused the Detroit Rebellion, it was police brutality. . . . Most white people do not believe there is any such thing as police brutality. They have never seen it, nor have they experienced it. And as Robert Tindal of the NAACP said at a meeting recently, "Some people have got to get beat over the head themselves before they can believe anyone else was beat."
>
> he Detroit Police Department is the epitome of systematic institutionalized racism. Twenty-four years after the race riot of 1943 when the department had 143 Negro policemen, it has today only 200 Negro officers in a force which is over 4,300, and in a city where 33 percent of the citizens are Black. It is the unbiased, the unprejudiced, and the non-sadist who is the exception in the Detroit Police Department.
>
> The police mentality is police brutality. It goes with the badge and the gun. Especially the gun. A gun is particularly good to have and a shotgun is even better if you are sexually insecure about your virility as compared to the "natives" you are supposed to be guarding.
>
> The "New Detroit" needs a new police department. It should be mostly Black and it should be controlled by the people it is supposed to protect. They should decide who is hired and who is fired. . . .
>
> It was police brutality when the police murdered three men in the Algiers Motel [during the rebellion].
>
> It was police brutality when the police ordered William Dalton to run and then shot him in the back.
>
> It was police brutality when Negro Recorders Court Judge Elvin Davenport was arrested two years ago and taken to the police station because he was in Lafayette Park at 2 A.M. and a rookie cop didn't know he was a judge and mistook him for a nigger in a white neighborhood late at night.

The 1967 Detroit rebellion happened in part because the nonviolent civil rights movement had failed to achieve significant change in the North, and because the society seemed to condone violence, as in Vietnam, as a means to achieve ends. Once the upheavals in Detroit and other cities happened, many nonviolent leaders "recognized the riots as a phase of the movement that . . . prepared the way for change in governmental action and policies," says Ralph Conant. The 1967 rebellion was a forceful assertion, however chaotic, of the black presence in the city.

The Black Struggle

Especially in the wake of the rebellion, the *Fifth Estate* reported on the upsurge of black activism in Detroit. The League of Revolutionary Black Workers was organized at Dodge Main, the second largest Detroit-area auto plant after Ford's River Rouge complex. (It has since been closed.) The Black Panther Party was also active in the city, aiming to organize the "lumpenproletariat." (The lumpenproletariat is defined as individuals who are dispossessed and uprooted from the economic and social class with which they might normally be identified—the working class. Permanently laid-off auto workers and people of color who have suffered lifelong discrimination are examples.)

One leader of the League was John Watson, who also became editor of the Wayne State University newspaper, the *South End*, in 1968. Under Watson, the paper's masthead carried such slogans as "One class conscious worker is worth 1,000 students," and "1968—year of the urban guerrilla." Watson also increased press runs to 50,000 at times and distributed copies to Detroit-area auto plants. After leaving the *South End*, he edited an important black paper, the *Inner City Voice*.

For a time, the League had sizable support among black workers, who were an increasing percentage of the workforce. The United Auto Workers, then still headed by Walter Reuther, got worried. Peter Werbe recalls one night when some *Fifth Estate* staffers accompanied League members to a Dodge Main union meeting. The hall was guarded by a phalanx of UAW "flying squads," tough union members, some of them veterans of the battles of the 1930s.

One flying-squad member came up to Werbe and said, "If you don't want to get hurt, why don't you hippies get your ass back to Wayne State University?" Werbe began to take his advice and head in the opposite direction, when he ran into an adventurist *Fifth Estate* supporter who said, "Don't worry," and showed him a weapon under his overcoat. However, cooler heads prevailed and the meeting was conducted peacefully.

The League and the *Fifth Estate* also helped to publicize the case of James Johnson, a black auto worker who, after being fired, returned to his auto plant with a rifle and killed three supervisors. Johnson's Detroit trial jury was given a tour of the plant and, after viewing the wretched working conditions, returned a verdict of not guilty by reason of insanity. The League composed a song about the incident called "James Johnson Needed a Thompson."

Another leading League activist was the late Ken Cockrel, a brilliant young black lawyer who was undefeated in jury trials for many years in the 1960s and early 1970s. He won legal rulings that ended the practice of blacks being tried by all-white juries, something that still happens in states like Louisiana and Florida. From now on, a person would indeed be tried by a jury of his or her peers. In subsequent years, Cockrel was elected to the Detroit City Council.

The Black Panther Party was involved in providing free breakfasts for schoolchildren and calling for community control of the police. One time the Panthers organized thirty people to picket a local police precinct. Hard as it may be to believe, the police had sharpshooters stationed on the roof. Late one night, the Panthers called the *Fifth Estate* office and asked for armed support in an expected confrontation with police. Werbe replied that they must be out of their minds. However, there was no organized chain of command at the paper, and indeed later that night two staffers were standing in the middle of 14th Street with rifles in their hands. Luckily for their health, the police had withdrawn from the area.

At times the League and the Black Panthers had almost a rivalry. "The Panthers were more mass based, while the League was more vanguardist," recalls Werbe. "We did more stories on the Panthers partly because they were more accessible, while the League cadre was impenetrable. I remember meeting with Watson and Cockrel. They complained about lack of coverage, but it was hard to get stories out of them."

The League did get some media exposure through a media project called "Newsreel," which was located in the same building as the *Fifth Estate*. In a film called "Finally Got the News," Watson explained the League's ideology and activities.

League activists affected a macho style. Watson went around with an attack-trained, muzzled German shepherd for a period in the late 1960s. The adventurist *Fifth Estate* supporter mentioned earlier had a muscular, aggressive Bouvier dog. Werbe recalls his own usual garb of a black leather jacket and Levis. A shotgun in a rack next to Werbe's desk was a permanent feature of the *Fifth Estate* office. The entire atmosphere was definitely pre-feminist. For both the black activists and the *Fifth Estate*, this melodramatic style led to a political approach that was confrontational and could involve a lot of posturing.

While the *Fifth Estate* and the black groups were on the same side of the barricades ideologically, they did not have a close relationship. For the *Fifth Estate*, the groups were an entrée into the world of revolutionary action among oppressed people. For the black activists, the *Fifth Estate* was a way to publicize their program and give them credibility outside the black community.

There were also differences in lifestyle that caused friction. Dave Riddle recalls one argument he had with John Watson, in which Watson criticized the "poor boy act" of *Fifth Estate* staffers who lived on subsistence salaries. He tended to view some staffers as ex-suburbanites who were slumming in the inner city. "The hell with that," said Watson. "The more money I make, the happier I am."

To be fair, both sides were plowing new ground in a city that had seen two major racial upheavals within twenty-five years. In a catch phrase of the day, "Nobody ever said it was going to be easy." Over the years, with the decline of the auto industry into a state of permanent crisis, auto-worker militancy declined, and the League folded. However, today's workers look back to its heritage of fighting discrimination before the days of affirmative action and standing UAW committees on the subject. As for the Panthers, soon after they started providing breakfasts, the Nixon administration decided it might be a good idea and started the program that survives to this day. And Fred Hampton, the martyred leader of the Chicago Panthers, originated the concept of the "rainbow coalition," which has been used by Jesse Jackson.

Detroit Police Abuse

The *Fifth Estate* also worked with black activists in the years after 1967 to expose the chronic abuses of the Detroit Police Department. The paper covered the 1968 police attack on anti–George Wallace protestors, which sent people to the hospital, and the harassment of the Poor People's March the same year. With both articles, dramatic photos showed the police abusing their powers.

In 1969, a black political group called the Republic of New Africa was holding a meeting in a black church when a police officer was killed nearby. The police arrested the whole churchful of people—men, women, and children. The next morning, black judge George Crockett released all but three on their own recognizance, and came under attack from the white-controlled press for doing so. The *Fifth Estate* defended Crockett.

The 1969 incident galvanized the community and almost resulted in the election of Richard Austin as Detroit's first black mayor. A nonentity named Roman Gribbs squeaked by him, and as a result the Detroit police were allowed to run rampant for four more years. In 1972 and 1973, the *Fifth Estate* helped document the activities of Detroit's worst-ever police misconduct—the STRESS decoy unit. STRESS stood for "Stop the Robberies, Enjoy Safe Streets." One policeman would pose as a staggering drunk, and when a mugger attacked, six or so of his colleagues would leap out of the bushes and arrest the mugger or, more often, shoot him. The decoy unit killed fourteen people, almost all of them black, within one year.

Outrage over the STRESS unit and several other major police incidents finally resulted in Coleman Young's election as Detroit's first black mayor in 1973. Under his administrations the police department gradually improved, with affirmative-action programs dramatically increasing the number of women and blacks on the force. Murderous stunts like the STRESS unit were largely eliminated.

It is worth noting that for all its support of black causes, and all the articles it printed from black contributors, the *Fifth Estate* never had a full-time black staffer in the period covered by this history, 1965–1975. Recalls Werbe, "Black journalists didn't want to work with us when the *Inner City Voice* or the *South End* existed, and that sort of separation of radicals by race on the publications of the era was overwhelmingly the rule. If there were more than a handful of black writers on any of the 500 underground papers, I'd be surprised."

South End Story

John Watson's term as editor was only part of the picture at the *South End*. Wayne State University's student paper went through a series of dramatic changes starting in 1967. It was then that editor Art Johnston changed the paper's name—until that point it was called the *Wayne State Daily Collegian*. The new name expressed an empathy with the less prosperous south end of the campus, which bordered on the Cass Corridor. The north end of the campus abutted on the Detroit Civic Center.

Werbe remembers Johnston as a "hippie cum hillbilly biker" and "a rough-hewn writer-poet" and says that "starting with Johnston, the *South End* became an underground paper." Johnston was followed by Watson, whose term as editor shook Wayne State up completely. (Campus conservatives tried but failed to remove him from his post.) Cheryl McCall continued the new activist tradition as summer editor in 1969 (in later years she made an acclaimed documentary on runaway kids in Seattle). John Grant was the next editor—he eventually wound up on the post-1975, anarchist-libertarian *Fifth Estate*.

A cross-pollination between the two papers went on for years. Jim Kennedy, certainly another rough-hewn working-class poet, started out at the *South End*, became a staffer at the *Fifth Estate*, and then left to form Keep on Trucking, which for years distributed the *Fifth Estate* and many other alternative publications to stores and head shops. Alan Franklin, a clever writer with a gift for political criticism and satire, started at the *South End* and eventually joined the post-1975 *Fifth Estate* staff. Bob Moore left the *South End* to become a *Fifth Estate* staffer and media columnist.

Ken Fireman, a Trotskyist who was on the *Fifth Estate* staff in 1972 and 1973, left and shortly after became editor of the *South End*. During his campaign for editor, he described his politics as "left of center," which indeed they were. Fireman later worked for the *Detroit Free Press* for years, and later worked in Russia.

Werbe recalls participating in a virtual *Fifth Estate* "takeover" of the *South End* in the wake of murders of students at Kent State and Jackson State in May 1970. The paper had retreated politically since John Watson. It took a long afternoon of heated political argument to persuade the *South End* staff to issue extra editions about the student strikes protesting the Nixon invasion of Cambodia and the killings that followed.

Fifth Estate also had connections with another college paper, the *Michigan Daily* of the University of Michigan. The late Jeff Goodman and I were both senior editors in 1965, later becoming socialist activists and joining the *Fifth Estate.* Goodman was on the staff in 1973 and 1974. Bob Moore was a *Michigan Daily* senior editor in 1966, and also a *Fifth Estate* staffer in 1973 and 1974.

Confront the Warmakers

Several months after the 1967 rebellion, several *Fifth Estate* staffers went to the first really massive Washington antiwar demonstration, the "Confront the Warmakers" action described in Norman Mailer's *Armies of the Night.* Atop the building housing the *Fifth Estate* was a large billboard featuring a skull crowned by a U.S. Capitol dome. As of fall 1967, tie-dyed hippies were still putting flowers in GI gun barrels and attempting to levitate the Pentagon, but a more militant faction got into battles with the police. Most of all, the sheer size of the demonstration, over 100,000 people, showed that "things were getting heavier," in the phrase of the day.

Nobody knew how heavy things were getting, however, until the fall of 1968 at the Democratic Convention in Richard Daley's Chicago. "The Movement," as it now was called, had talked for months about how over 100,000 demonstrators would show up to demand that the war end. The unstated premise was that at least some Democrats would be willing to listen (no similar crowds went to the Republican Convention). Instead, the nation was treated to a gruesome display of Democratic police brutality against the fewer than 10,000 protestors who did show up. Added to the 1968 assassinations of Martin Luther King Jr. and Robert Kennedy, Chicago gave the nation a definite air of political instability. The ensuing election of Richard Nixon raised justified fears that the veteran McCarthyite anti-Communist would really go after the progressive movement.

According to Werbe, "The years 1967 and 1968 were a watershed for the *Fifth Estate*, transforming us from dewy-eyed hippies to hardcore opponents to the system. Things took on more of a military aspect. The city had burned and cold-blooded murder had taken place in the streets. Sometimes we felt on the defense. The forces against us were enormous, and there had been casualties. How would we keep up the pace? Somewhere in the process, we lost our sense of humor. We began to identify with the enemies of the U.S., like the Black Panther Party and the Viet Cong—and correctly, too. We were looking for allies to take part in a social revolution. When you look back, it might seem ridiculous considering the true balance of forces at the time."

It was hard to get a perspective in those days.

Many people recall 1967 to 1969 as a period in which events began to develop in a furiously rapid manner. Demonstrations grew from 100,000 one year to one million two years later. Students went from peaceful petitioning to seizing university buildings, all in the same period. Black nationalists overtook the civil rights movement, and strident radical declarations were met with systematic police violence. In Vietnam, the United States went from rosy predictions of "the light at the end of the tunnel" to the devastating Tet Offensive that forced Lyndon Johnson from office. Time and events seemed crazily telescoped, and to many young people revolution indeed seemed possible, especially after the student-inspired general strike in France. Of course, many young people had little knowledge of American history (the schools saw to that) or of radical history (the 1950s McCarthyite repression saw to that). These factors impeded their judgment, but not their enthusiasm!

During this period, the *Fifth Estate* explored topics not covered by the establishment press until many years later. One half-page article discussed anti-Semitism among blacks. Professor Leonard Fein of Harvard was quoted as saying that if every black person in the U.S. was an anti-Semite, there still would be more white anti-Semites in the country. Another article described Catholic priests in Latin America who had turned to guerrilla warfare to fight social injustice. Another reported how male and female college students had protested the arrival of a *Playboy* photographer on their campus by disrobing in front of him (pictures were included).

The *Fifth Estate* was also an early supporter of Palestinian self-determination. Nick Medvecky, as managing editor of the *South End* under Watson, had written articles supporting the Palestinians. As a supporter of the paper, he made several trips to the Middle East, and was there to see the PLO's ascendance to control of the refugee camps. He provided eyewitness coverage to the paper. In September 1970, staffer Dave Riddle did an article examining the oil companies and the Israeli-U.S. alliance. The headline said, "The Middle East Will Be the Next Viet Nam." An accurate prediction.

The Political Landscape

During these years, the *Fifth Estate* changed as quickly as the times did. Tommye Wiese, who had played an important role on the paper for two years, left the staff. As well as participating in writing and editing, Wiese had typeset the entire paper every two weeks. Werbe recalls that, as a woman playing such an important role, Wiese had "democratized and collectivized" the paper, making it no longer the domain of several male political heavies. Her departure was related to the fact that, as a Trotskyist, she was becoming more and more active in the Socialist Workers Party.

Some background might be helpful here. The New Left, as the Movement had come to be called, was instinctually anarchist, anti-hierarchical, and believed in a concept called "participatory democracy," which had been popularized by the early SDS. It was radically democratic, in the sense that everybody counted and everybody was expected to take an active role in raising his or her own consciousness and participating in his or her own political destiny.

The Socialist Workers Party, on the other hand, was out of the Old Left socialist tradition and was by definition hierarchical, since it was a type of Leninist group. Trotskyist groups such as the SWP called for defense of the Russian revolution against its enemies, but also called for a political upheaval within the Soviet Union to overthrow the government created by Stalin after the death of Lenin and the expulsion of Trotsky. The SWP very carefully planned and built coalitions around single-issue demands like "Bring the Troops Home Now." In times of mass upheaval like the 1960s, it was the most effective group around at bringing people together.

However, the SWP was notorious for not doing any education within the coalitions, which were often composed of people who mistrusted each other and had no clear reason as to why they were together in the first place, despite the fact that the SWP had ample knowledge and resources for education. Sometimes they wouldn't even admit they were socialists (of course, many socialists besides the SWP have shared this trait). The result was that their coalitions tended to fall apart after the single issue had been achieved, or even after a strong demand had been made. The potential for manipulation was strong in such a situation.

Also on the political scene were the "Stalinists" (Communist Party-oriented) and the "Maoists." They had their own reasons for disliking the Trotskyists, since the "Trots" were very critical of the governments in Moscow and Beijing. Also, there was a Movement hangover from decades of Moscow-Beijing propaganda that had accused Trotskyists of everything from being agents of Hitler to having contempt for peasants. The Stalinists and Maoists had a convergence with the New Left in that at least they said who they were and did believe in education for socialism. (Their commitment to democracy was a lot less clear.)

There were further complications. The fact that Mao Zedong's ideology was actually a variety of Stalinism tended to be lost because many young activists took a positive view of the Chinese Cultural Revolution. And Ho Chi Minh's Vietnamese Communists, themselves a local variety of Stalinism, had tremendous prestige because of their heroic fight against U.S. troops. Many New Leftists and even many Trotskyists, as well as the traditional Stalinists and Maoists, thought well of the Chinese and Vietnamese. In addition, there was widespread support for Fidel Castro's Cuban revolution, which was Moscow-oriented. All this militated against the Trotskyists, who actually had better-developed political ideas and better organizational skills, though the SWP made poor use of both.

On top of all this, the *Fifth Estate* had an informal policy during its 1965–1975 period that staffers could not be "card-carrying" members of outside political groups. The only possible exception to this had been John Sinclair and his White Panther Party, but most of the time Sinclair was only a columnist.

The net result was that Tommye Wiese had to choose between the *Fifth Estate* and the SWP. She left the staff and went on to be a dedicated SWP activist for many years. All the above did not prevent another Trotskyist, Ken Fireman (not an official SWP member), from moving into an important role on the paper, really steering political policy under different conditions in 1972.

There were further *Fifth Estate* changes around 1969. John Sinclair and his White Panther Party had moved to Ann Arbor after the 1967 rebellion, and he stopped writing his column after people became more critical of the drug-oriented lifestyle. The late Sol Plafkin was a people's lawyer who had helped staffers out of many scrapes. But he was basically a reform Democrat, and stopped writing his column as the paper moved further left. Alan Gotkin, an editor, writer, and crack photographer, left to begin a career as a union printer. Political heavy Frank Joyce left the staff to help start the group "People Against Racism."

Eventually the *Fifth Estate* became too radical for its founder. "I began to withdraw around 1967 or 1968, to get a bit bored," says Ovshinsky. "I think some people on the staff also began to view me as an impediment." Finally, an issue in early 1969 featured pictures of several handguns along the bottom of the cover, with the remaining space containing the word "NOW" in six-inch high letters. "I was outraged. That was it for me. I don't think I was missed after I left." About the same time, Harvey got his draft notice, applied for and got C.O. (conscientious objector) status, and did his alternative service at Lafayette Clinic. Then, with the help of some clinic staff, he founded the youth service group Open City. He remained there only a short time before leaving to begin his new career as an independent filmmaker.

Other staff changes included two socialist activists joining the paper in 1970. Dave Riddle arrived after a stint with Ann Arbor's Radical Education Project, and I arrived after trying to make a go of an Ann Arbor music magazine called *Big Fat.*

The political tenor of the time was getting more serious, and the paper got more serious, too. Staff meetings became regularly scheduled, and decisions were now often made by votes, not just consensus. Political discussions got more urgent and sophisticated, reflecting the experience of the staff. The *Fifth Estate* was coming of age, as can be seen from a staff editorial that appeared in early 1969 (see sidebar 1).

────────────────── SIDEBAR 1 ──────────────────

FIFTH ESTATE STAFF EDITORIAL FROM FEBRUARY 1, 1969

We believe that people who are serious in their criticism of this society and their desire to change it must involve themselves in serious revolutionary struggle.

We do not believe that music is revolution. We do not believe that dope is revolution. We do not believe that poetry is revolution. We see these as part of a burgeoning revolutionary culture. They cannot replace political struggle as the main means by which the capitalist system will be destroyed.

The Man will not allow his social and economic order to be taken from him by Marshall amps and clashing cymbals. Ask the Cubans, the Vietnamese or urban American Blacks what lengths the system is willing to go to, to preserve itself.

We see the working class of this country and the world as a requisite part of the revolutionary process. Students can play an important role, but without the economic power the working class commands by virtue of its productive capacity, no real change will be possible.

We define the working class very simply. It consists of those individuals who are forced to sell their labor for subsistence and who have no control over, and are alienated from, the means of production.

We think that calls for people to drop out or not "join the machine" make sense to only a few privileged children of the affluent. Most people just have to work those awful straight jobs and feel intimidated when a long-haired parent-financed dropout points an accusing finger at them.

We oppose people who consider themselves serious revolutionaries dropping out. A revolutionary does what is necessary, not what provides him with the most personal comfort.

That means you stay in ugly poisonous cities because you know that is where the real action will be.

That means you stay in college. Not to study the irrelevant and boring course work, but to organize among students because you realize the role students will play in a revolutionary movement.

That means you stay in the army and organize other GIs against the war.

That means going into a factory to work and organize among workers before the Wallace people do.

It means dropping into American society and breaking out of your hip, chic, mod intellectual circles, where everyone knows the latest rock group and dope from San Francisco and has the proper revolutionary hero on his wall. It means that instead of putting up posters of Che, we try to be like him. That means us too.

The Youth Revolt

In the fall of 1969, *Fifth Estate* staffers traveled to Washington, DC, to attend and report on the massive Moratorium demonstration against the war, an action involving over one million people. Daniel Ellsberg later claimed that the Moratorium caused Nixon to cancel a scheduled massive military attack on North Vietnam. The 1969–1970 school year also saw an unprecedented number of college demonstrations against the war, culminating in May 1970, when four students were shot to death at Kent State and two at Jackson State for protesting the invasion of Cambodia. Medvecky remembered a Wayne State protest meeting where "enough militant resolutions were passed to start a revolution."

During this period, *Fifth Estate* staffers took a long second look at student activism and concluded that students might be a more vital "agent of change" (in the phrase of the day) than previously thought. They were influenced by writers such as Jerry Farber, whose *Student as Nigger* described the real lack of student rights, and the actual treatment students got from the authorities.

The student ferment was so intense that it began to reach into the Detroit high schools also. The *Fifth Estate* responded by running articles that criticized high school dress codes, drug busts, and the general notion that the Bill of Rights stopped at the high school door. Other articles showed how the social-studies and history textbooks often ignored the lives of working people, and the cultures of blacks, Mexicans, and Native Americans.

"This demographic bubble had arrived which faced the draft and many other problems," says Dave Riddle. Facing censorship, many of the high-schoolers wanted to start their own unauthorized student papers, and the *Fifth Estate* helped by letting hundreds of students use the office mimeograph machine to run off their proud creations. The *Fifth Estate* also set up a speakers bureau, through which staffers went out to address youth audiences.

Millard Berry, who joined the staff in 1970, was important in this period of youth organizing. He also helped edit a column in the paper called "Dope-O-Scope," which ran down what kinds of marijuana, LSD, and other drugs were available on the street, and at what prices. By 1971, the title of the column was changed to "Detroit Roulette," and it soon disappeared from the paper.

"We weren't just reporting, we were going out and stirring up trouble and agitating," says Riddle. The summer of 1970 saw virtual high-school-youth uprisings at Detroit's Balduck Park and Memorial Park. The Detroit police, as usual, were willing to go more than halfway to quell any disturbances. Riddle himself was arrested at one of them. Though the high school activism, along with other student protests, trailed off after 1970, many young Detroiters got their first introduction to political activism through the *Fifth Estate* that year. And after the decline of student activity on both the high school and college levels (including the fall of Students for a Democratic Society), the *Fifth Estate* grew even more as a key focus for Detroit radical organizing in the 1970–1975 era.

Enter Feminism

The 1969–1970 period also saw both the women's movement and the gay movement reach a critical mass in terms of their impact on the Movement. The SDS convention of June 1969, which resulted in the group splitting into "Weatherman" and Marxist factions, devoted one full day of its three days to women's issues, with women chairing the sessions. June 1969 also saw the famous Stonewall rebellion in New York City, a three-day uprising in which gays and lesbians fought back against the cops and inaugurated the modern gay liberation movement.

By 1969, the *Fifth Estate* was publishing articles with a militant feminist tone. The following is from a review by Nancy Holm of the *S.C.U.M. Manifesto*, by Valerie Solanas (Solanas, who seriously wounded artist Andy Warhol by gunfire in 1968, founded the Society for Cutting Up Men the same year): "She describes some elemental truths of our society: 'The male is . . . obsessed with screwing; he'll swim a river of snot, wade nostril-deep through a mile of vomit, if he thinks there'll be a friendly pussy awaiting him. He'll screw a woman he despises, any snaggle-toothed hag, and further pay for the opportunity.'"

Concludes Holm: "Paul Krassner, who comments on the manifesto, has some things to say about violence—but doesn't know much about Solanas. Both (Krassner and publisher Maurice Girodias) try to make her a fool, both laugh, but I'm really astounded that a woman hasn't killed 23 people from a tower in Houston, Texas, like [Charles] Whitman did a few years ago."

It was from such primal bursts of energy that the early feminist movement arose.

By 1970, two women who advocated strong feminist positions had joined the full-time staff—Cindy Felong and Barbara Carson. Traditionally, women on the paper's staff had done much of the necessary day-to-day work and received little credit. But now Felong, Carson, and the other women began to question this division of labor.

The nature of staff meetings began to change. "Until 1970 most meetings were basically dialogues between the men," says Riddle. Now the women began to speak up, proposing articles on feminism, and taking more of a role in writing, editing, and news decisions.

Especially in the area of feminist politics, progress often comes step by step, and seemingly small incidents have meaning. In 1970, I was doing a brief obituary for Jimi Hendrix when Felong remarked that I should comment on the occasionally sexist content of Hendrix's lyrics. Upon reflection, I recognized that she had a point, and inserted such a sentence. At that time, neither I nor any other male staffer would have come up with the idea independently.

Carson was the first staffer to argue forcefully for the inclusion of gay and lesbian news in the paper as a priority. (There had been some coverage in the past.) At first, she got some support, some opposition, and a good amount of indifference. Some of the opposition was from gays who were themselves only halfway out of the closet. These people were not really antagonistic; their consciousness had simply not reached the necessary point. Raising it could at times seem like a thankless task.

People began to grow politically as they realized what a complex struggle feminism entails, especially in a racist society. Felong at one point described the shock she and others experienced at a feminist meeting, held in one of the women's houses, when a black maid walked into the room. On another occasion, the *Fifth Estate* ran a graphic description of a local woman's experience of being raped in broad daylight. The article identified the rapist as black, and several auto workers the staff knew complained that it only added to anti-black stereotypes.

Change brought some conflict, as it often does. At one point Carson interrupted Peter Werbe when he was criticizing a fellow male staffer. She basically told him to give it a rest, as the current saying goes. The implication was that he was overdoing his role as the dominant staff male. Another time, Werbe suggested that a certain male staffer take on the task of answering the phone whenever it happened to ring during a staff meeting, and Felong pointedly stated that it might be better to rotate the duty or leave the phone off the hook. Werbe recalls that "I tried to be true to the idea of equality of everyone no matter what their 'status' and to encourage and accept collective decision making."

Actually, Werbe tended to be a bit of a lightning rod—he was a dominant influence due to his political experience, argumentative ability, and organizational skill. The fact that his actions were more open to sharp criticism made the staff more democratic, and made everybody more willing to question and be questioned when necessary.

Riddle remembers Werbe as the staffer most vocal in support of the largest feminist project ever undertaken at the *Fifth Estate*—the Women's Issue of March 8, 1971, the sixty-first anniversary of International Women's Day. Written entirely by *Fifth Estate* women and their feminist associates, the issue had a cover featuring female cartoon characters such as Lucy, Blondie, Little Lulu, and Olive Oyl, all with their fists in the air.

The lead article, called "The Rising of the Women," said in part:

We are fighting for an end to unequal wages, unequal job opportunities and dehumanizing welfare. We want an end to the "tracking" system in schools based on race, sex, or class. We want an end to the oppression of women within the family by establishing laundry and food co-ops and day care centers. We don't want our bodies used for testing untried drugs, nor do we want them used to sell the products of Madison Avenue.

We want the freedom to control our bodies: to decide whether we want a child or an abortion. We want the freedom to develop our creativity and to have relationships with whomever we choose—male or female.

We want to know our history. . . .

We live in a society that is historically rooted in racism and sexism. This country maintains itself by controlling and destroying the lives and resources of people in other countries. . . .

We feel that liberation for all people can only be found in a classless society where the social system is designed to meet human needs, not profit, and where people have control over all the forces that affect their lives.

We want to come together with sisters and brothers to build a revolutionary movement for a new society. And we must create a strong women's movement to insure that our liberation will be a conscious part of the change that's coming.

The Women's Issue called for free, legal abortion on demand, with no forced sterilization—a set of slogans that would fill the banners of the abortion rights movement for the next two decades. The Women's Issue was published almost two years before the historic *Roe v. Wade* decision that legalized abortion across the country. At the time, abortion was legal only in California and New York.

The Women's Issue publicized a demonstration that was to occur five days later in Lansing, the capital of Michigan. "If abortion becomes legal, fewer women will have to submit to the humiliation and danger of illegal operations," said the article on the Lansing action. "Organized crime in Michigan will take a substantial cut in its third most lucrative enterprise."

The issue also featured articles on Angela Davis, who was in jail at the time on a murder charge, and Elizabeth Gurley Flynn, the longtime Communist Party labor activist. Another essay examined day-to-day sexism at the youth service organization Open City. (Ovshinsky had by this time left Open City, and the organization was dominated by an activist named John Martin, whose leadership was criticized by many.) A "Letter from Prison" came from Jane Kennedy, a Catholic peace activist.

The Women's Issue was the only issue of the *Fifth Estate* that ever sold out down to the last copy. The standard press run was 15,000; the sellout necessitated an additional press run of 5,000.

However, the Women's Issue almost didn't get distributed at all. One article, called "Love All Ways," was written by a lesbian who lived at Boone's Farm Commune, where many members of Keep on Trucking also lived. It said in part:

> We have gotten a lot of pressure about being dykes, primarily from men in our commune. Men who are insensitive to their own feelings and are not used to the idea of love not based on sex roles. At times they have succeeded in bringing me down. I've almost believed their insecure lies and ceased to trust my own feelings. But fuck that shit! I know lesbianism is not a sickness. Lesbianism is a healthy growth of sister love. DYKE POWER!

In terms of male domination, Keep on Trucking made the macho *Fifth Estate* staff look like a feminist bastion. They were infuriated by the article, and sat on their hands for a couple of days, refusing to touch the issue. They only relented after they saw street sellers drawing crowds of young women anxious to read about feminism in Detroit.

Cindy Felong and Barbara Carson remained on the *Fifth Estate* staff until the end of 1971, when both left to embark on other projects. Following Felong and Carson, other women were full-time staffers, but none were in the same league, as far as pushing feminism.

However, the general awareness of the staff had risen to the point where the paper covered feminist issues pretty steadily over the next few years. A sample of articles includes a report of a "wet in" by Wayne State University women demanding child care, and an article supporting women who protested the cancellation of a feminist radio show. Books reviewed include *Small Changes*, by Detroit's Marge Piercy, and *Complaints and Disorders: The Sexual Politics of Sickness*, by Deirdre English and Barbara Ehrenreich. A feature called "The Speculum Underground" explains the women's self-help movement, and Beth Cady of the International Socialists examines "Women's Liberation—1974." Gay and lesbian coverage also continues, but tends to be reprints from the *Gay Liberator*. The *Fifth Estate* had no openly gay staffer until I rejoined it in January of 1973, having "come out" as a gay person in 1972.

Despite the continuing articles, the paper in fact reached a plateau in terms of feminism and gay liberation, and then began to backslide, especially in the quality of internal staff relations. Riddle recalls that many forces were competing for attention—antiwar activity, labor news, police abuse, you name it. It is interesting to compare the *Fifth Estate* to the *Great Speckled Bird* in Atlanta. For years the *Bird* had a women's caucus that pushed feminism within the staff and in the paper. In its last two years it also had a gay caucus. For whatever reason, the *Fifth Estate* never advanced that far.

Blue Collar Blues

As the various waves of activism swept the Movement, the *Fifth Estate* both participated in and reported on them. But what probably made the paper unique among its contemporary alternative publications was its labor coverage.

Detroit was first of all a blue-collar union town, and many staffers came from union families. In addition, the Marxist ideology that influenced the paper over the years put a strong emphasis on the working class. The result was a wide variety of worker-related coverage, some of which, of course, overlapped with the continuing struggle of blacks, women, and students. In fact, *Fifth Estate* staffers saw the labor movement as the background, and potentially the support, for all other attempts to change society.

To begin with, the paper did historical articles on labor. In 1970, Bryce Crawford did one on the 1932 Ford hunger march, which led to five workers' deaths at the hands of Detroit police. By 1932, the Great Depression had become so severe that one Detroiter died of starvation every seven hours, according to a local doctor at the time. Workers marched on the Ford Motor Company plant in Dearborn demanding the right to unionize, jobs for laid-off workers, and the abolition of spies and goons. They were met with great violence, red-baited in the *Detroit Free Press*, and blamed by authorities for the debacle. (Ford was unionized in 1941.)

In 1970, I did a piece on a big 1945 UAW strike. The demand of the strike—"Open the Books"—was actually revolutionary in nature, and has not been raised in the years since.

The extent of labor coverage in the *Fifth Estate* can be further documented by perusal of three issues from the early 1970s.

In the May 13, 1971, issue, a female Teamster member interviewed by Cindy Felong described female workers as being relegated to the lowest-rung jobs, and then facing further discrimination when the union did not support their grievances. The women strongly supported male truckers then on strike, were not yet interested in feminism, and had no separate caucus. "A lot of them, when you really do get to talk to them, do resent their husbands controlling their paychecks and men controlling what they do. When you get into a one-on-one situation, then a lot of these feelings come out."

In the same issue, an article entitled "Union Democracy" examined United Auto Workers elections: "Democracy in the UAW breaks down in at least three areas. (1) Auto workers do not participate in local meetings. (2) Election procedures are biased in favor of the present entrenched UAW machine, the 'Green Slate.' (3) The union local operates as a pork barrel in many cases, with special privileges going to members who toe the Green Slate line."

The piece concluded with one worker's comments criticizing the UAW leadership: "The UAW is getting too big, self-centered and corrupt . . . the UAW tries to appease workers rather than represent them in dealing with the auto companies."

In the April 22, 1972, issue, an article on the UAW Convention in Atlantic City began on a historical note:

> There was one Atlantic City convention of particular significance. Young rebellious members of the stodgy American Federation of Labor turned their 1935 convention into a forum of political conflict, resulting in a fistfight between the tough leader of the United Mine Workers, John L. Lewis, and Big Bill Hutchinson, who represented the pinnacle of AFL provincialism. . . .
>
> Out of the convention was born the Congress of Industrial Organizations (CIO) which went on to change the face of the American labor movement, leading to the growth of the UAW, and its historic Flint sit-down strikes of 1937. The CIO was led by John L. Lewis, built on the commitment of many socialists and communists, and driven by the fury and militancy of hundreds of thousands of rank and file workers.

The piece detailed the struggle of UAW opposition caucuses to democratize their union, while the leadership used the convention to indulge in nostalgia, memorializing Walter Reuther.

Another article in that issue described a boycott of food-service operations by workers at the Warren Dodge Truck Plant. "While management personnel have a full-service hot food cafeteria, the production workers must put up with machine food and a sandwich line." The boycott had spread to the Chrysler Jefferson Assembly Plant (now closed), where the vending company "raised prices from 25 percent to 50 percent." The piece concluded: "The food issue may seem small, but it's a very clear-cut example of who causes inflation."

A third article described the firing of Audrey White, a black female worker at a small auto-supply plant in Hamtramck. She had told the foreman where to get off when he had made a racist remark. The article goes on to criticize the shop steward, who the article charges with being an example of the poor protection Local 155 UAW gives to its members. The piece described how, earlier in 1972, two hundred Local 155 members had actually been mad enough to picket Solidarity House, the UAW headquarters, and indicated that further action was planned as a result of this latest incident.

In the August 12, 1972, issue, the paper reported on the aftermath of the July heat strikes, in which fifty-one paint-shop workers walked off the job, causing the entire Chrysler Jefferson Assembly Plant to shut down. "At a press conference called after the walkouts, United Justice

Caucus spokesman Bob Carter asserted the right of workers to leave the plant when the heat became unbearable. . . . Jordan Sims, co-chairman of the United National Caucus, also spoke in support of these demands: 'Working people are the greatest natural resource this country has. Their lives and health must be protected above all.'"

A second piece in that issue was called "Kaymac Strike Ends . . . So Does Kaymac." A supposedly hip head-shop supply operation in the Detroit suburb of Royal Oak, Kaymac hired very young women at very low wages. When they organized a union and went on strike, the company hired scabs from a temporary agency. That tactic was defeated when the foremen walked off the job. The strikers began to get support from other unions. Finally the company went bankrupt rather than recognize a union.

A third article reported on the Norwood, Ohio, anti-speedup strikes against the new General Motors Assembly Division, a bitter struggle that got nationwide publicity in 1972.

The *Fifth Estate* reported on and supported many other union developments, such as the spectacular rise of the public employees' unions (including teachers) in the 1960s and 1970s, the rise of Cesar Chavez and the United Farmworkers, and even attempts to unionize the prisoners at Jackson State Prison.

To sum up, the *Fifth Estate* was an alternative paper of the 1960s and 1970s, but its staff did not forget the 1930s, when industrial unionism was won, with Michigan as a main battleground. The great gains of that early period in turn made possible the progress of the later decades. The paper supported unions but, as the above articles make clear, always criticized sellout union bureaucrats, those folks known to workers as "pork choppers" or "pie cards."

In Detroit, with its boom-and-bust economy, unemployment was always just around the corner. It was vital to defend your basic rights as a worker—the right to have a job with decent pay, benefits, and working conditions; to join a union and strike if necessary; to participate in the union democratically; to speak up at the workplace. If you didn't have these basics, all your other rights were moot, because you were caught up in a day-to-day struggle for survival.

When Reaganism arrived in the 1980s, its first attack was on unionized workers—the PATCO strikers. The hallmark of the era was forced union givebacks and union-busting. Only after that pattern was set did the right wing proceed to further attacks on civil rights, abortion rights, AIDS funding, student loans, and more. The anti-union era was started by Reagan and continued by the two Bushes. The waning of that era is shown by the tremendous growth of the Service Employees International Union, the organizing successes of the Teamsters, the persistence of the United Farmworkers Union, and the militancy of the California nurses.

The Tank Plant March

While the labor movement is the background for other social changes, it is undeniable that the main background for the *Fifth Estate*'s entire existence was the Vietnam War. The first issue of the paper came out within months of the massive 1965 U.S. invasion, and the last issue (before the paper became a monthly) came out within months of the final fall of Saigon to North Vietnamese troops. Youth resistance to the continuing war was the single biggest factor that kept the paper going.

In retrospect, it is still amazing that U.S. imperialism staged such a protracted effort and met with such complete defeat. People who were ten years old when the U.S. invaded were in some cases parents with children when Saigon fell.

At the outset of 1971, the *Fifth Estate* staff began to plan the biggest mass action ever instigated by the paper—the march on Chrysler's Warren Tank Plant. Conveniently, the paper had moved to larger offices, at Second and Canfield, which were more suitable for large meetings. (Longtime *Fifth Estate* bookkeeper Bill Rowe quipped that the rundown West Warren building should be officially preserved as a Detroit historical site. It was torn down a few years later.)

One idea of the march was to achieve some organizational independence from the DCEWV, which had led several marches down Woodward Avenue, with speeches at Kennedy Square—a pattern that had become limiting and boring to many activists. The paper wanted instead to have a demonstration in a (then) white working-class suburb that was, in effect, a main supply area for the war, sending both tanks and troops.

A series of organizational meetings with regional antiwar activists took place. Dave Riddle and I wrote a 40-page illustrated pamphlet that showed how the war had disrupted the economy, with especially negative effects on blacks, women, youth, and older people. And, in the end, all our efforts paid off as between 2,500 and 4,000 people participated in the march, which was held on April 30 (see sidebar 2).

SIDEBAR 2

EXCERPTS FROM *FIFTH ESTATE* REPORT OF APRIL 30, 1971 MARCH, FROM MAY 13, 1971 ISSUE

The Warren tank plant march was the first such event of that size in the all white, conservative city of Warren. Many people predicted that it would end in a police riot and/or a right wing attack on the march.

As it turned out, although the march organizers had previously estimated that perhaps as many as 1,500 people would show up, the march drew anywhere from 2,500 to 4,000 people, kept itself together and repulsed the small number of right wingers who showed up to harass the march.

Along the route of the march . . . the marchers met with general acceptance, if not always enthusiasm, from onlookers. A few people stood outside of their homes waving American flags. But this wasn't always taken as hostility by the marchers, especially since there were about as many American flags as NLF flags on the march. A surprising number of people who drove past the march in their cars gave marchers the peace sign or the fist.

As the march went past Warren Woods High School, students crowded to the windows and shouted their support. The march stopped and many ran up to the windows chanting, "Join us, join us!" One student leaped out a window and joined the march. He was followed by 20 or 30 more coming out the windows.

When the marchers finally ran into right wing resistance, even that was colored by a general acceptance of anti-war sentiment. Donald Lobsinger's Breakthrough was at the tank plant to meet us with his two dozen anemic punks and their banner, "America Forever,

Communism Never!" But among the patriotic hecklers there was another large banner which read: "Peace? *Yes.* Communism, Never!"

The organizing for the march included a lot of speaking engagements in high schools and among liberal groups in Macomb County. Workers at the tank plant were leafleted several times concerning the fact that we were not there to threaten their jobs. . . .

An older woman I spoke to during the march down 12 Mile Road was wearing a nurse's uniform. I asked her why she was there, marching next to younger protestors who kept running through the "We don't want your fucking war" chant.

She said that she was marching for her son, who couldn't be there. I asked her why, half fearing that she would say her son had been killed in Vietnam. As it turned out, he couldn't be there because he would have lost his job if he missed work. "I'll probably lose mine for doing this, but it's worth it," she said. Her son was draft age and didn't intend to go. She was supporting him.

That's basically why we didn't get trashed in Warren.

Another major 1971 event in Detroit was the Winter Soldier Investigation, a series of public hearings organized by the Vietnam Veterans Against the War and lawyer Mark Lane. More than one hundred Vietnam veterans testified about war crimes they had participated in or witnessed. One was a young John Kerry, who later told the U.S. Senate Foreign Relations Committee, "How do you ask a man to be the last man to die for a mistake?" *Fifth Estate* staffers attended and reported on Winter Soldier.

On a national level, spring 1971 also saw the May Day demonstration, which attempted to shut down Washington through nonviolent resistance and used a poster of Gandhi with his fist in the air. There was also a bigger demonstration in the nation's capital, almost as big as the original Moratorium. These marked the high tide of national opposition to the war, which was being dragged out to the nth degree by Nixon, with over a million useless casualties, as he gradually withdrew U.S. troops. Also in 1971, Daniel Ellsberg leaked "The Pentagon Papers," which documented decades of U.S. government perfidy regarding Vietnam. The uproar caused by the papers led to a Nixonian obsession with secrecy and leaks, which ultimately led to the administration's downfall.

Dee-troit City

Many exciting political events happened in Detroit during the period of this history, but what was life like on the street for the activists involved (and for everybody else, for that matter)? An essay by Jim Kennedy from the December 8, 1973, issue captures some of the ambience:

The southwest side of Detroit is a half unnoticed slice of the Motor City that lies between downtown and the downriver suburbs. . . . Unlike much of Detroit, people still are out on the streets shopping and looking around at 8:00 on an autumn night. . . .

Down around Clark Park is Detroit's Chicano [barrio]. . . . Large, sprawling and mostly poor, the area has, between the cultural centers, the small businesses and the Catholic Church, held a tight sense of community. To the west, past Patton Park, is Salina, the largest Arab ghetto in the country.

Scattered throughout . . . are small pockets or neighborhoods left over from years before. Retirees, skilled workers, Detroit cops and city workers who live isolated from the ethnic communities, grumbling and paranoid about the whole area going to hell.

For sure, southwest Detroit is unique and a little strange, but if you want to spend some time and know what you're looking for, anyone can find a groove to float in. . . .

For myself I'll spend a lot of snowy nights this winter at the Bittersweet Bar on Vernor.

It's mostly a young crowd—kids who work for Ford, Great Lakes Steel, move slag for Levy, or work at the railroad. That is, when they're not pissed off, laid off, or unemployed.

I mean we sit around and get drunk on a drizzling Friday night, rapping and listening to a killer juke box until Marge throws us all out. Or in the summer stand around outside the Chat n' Shoot Pool Hall next door and smoke weed till the cops cruise by and we've got to move.

The Bittersweet—really gets off on the name—is the place to be in this community if you're young and crazy. Chicanos, bikers, greasers and street freeks generally get along despite the air of impending violence. . . .

It's strictly a West Side Doper scene—Super Fly trying to get older. Doing the West Side shuffle—all night long. Drunken haze. Marge unplugs the pinball. Snow on Vernor. Fourth Precinct rollers. 3 A.M.

> *"Ooh la la*
> *I wish that I knew then*
> *what I know now*
> *when I was younger"*

Frank Joyce once joked that Detroit activists should form a group called "radical alcoholics." Other favorite hangouts were the Jay-Cee Bar (near Wayne State University) and the Bronx Bar (across from the *Fifth Estate* office).

Detroit also had a street-level blues music scene that was less famous than Motown. The book *Detroit: I Do Mind Dying*, by Dan Georgakis and Marvin Surkin, describes it: "The singers often had colorful names and played unusual instruments. The [most well-known] was John Lee Hooker, but there were many others, including Washboard Willie, One-String Sam, Dr. Ross . . . and Bobo Jenkins." (Dr. Ross was a one-man band who I saw at the 1970 Ann Arbor Blues Festival.) Roselyn, a folk singer, told *Fifth Estate* reporter Pat Halley in 1973, "Anybody who plays music in Detroit plays blues sometimes."

1972's Key Phrase

The Warren Tank Plant march and the Women's Issue had been the highlights of 1971. In the months following them, many *Fifth Estate* staffers realized that the high-stress job was burning them out, the low pay (now up to $50 a week) was slowly bankrupting them, and they might want to embark on other projects (perhaps even find a real job), at least for a while. (It was the rare *Fifth Estate* staffer who lasted more than two years at a stretch.)

By mid-1972, a whole group of staffers had left, not out of various political disagreements, like much of the 1969 exodus, but out of general exhaustion. Those leaving, besides me, included Cindy Felong, Barbara Carson, Dave Riddle, Millard Berry, and—after seven and six years respectively—Peter and Marilyn Werbe.

Len Schafer, who had been on the staff since 1970, began to take on a more important role. He was skilled at investigative reporting (including an exposé of mishandled funds at Open City), editing, selling, advertising, layout, rewiring the office, and just about every other skill necessary to keep the paper coming out. Mike Neiswonger joined the staff in 1972, his main strength being graphics and layout. Ken Fireman took Peter Werbe's place as resident political heavy.

The year 1972 was slow politically, at least relative to the first two years of the decade. One cartoonist said that two words on everybody's lips then were "Fuck it." Just before the year began, John Sinclair finally got out of prison after spending two years at Marquette on the "10 years for two joints" conviction. Three days ahead of his release, 15,000 supporters came to a benefit concert featuring Allen Ginsberg, Abbie Hoffman, John Lennon and Yoko Ono, Phil Ochs, Bobby Seale, and Stevie Wonder. The biggest local issue in Detroit was the continuing abusive activity by the STRESS decoy unit. One cover of the *Fifth Estate* read, "$500 Reward for Information Leading to the Conviction of Any STRESS Cop for Murder." The paper also listed the "top ten" STRESS officers in number of people killed.

At one point in 1972, a crowd of 2,000 blacks shouted down police chief John Nichols at the City Hall Auditorium after the police ransacked the black community, hunting for three young men involved in a shootout following a police raid on a dope house. All three died, either in 1972 or following years, either at the hands of police or in unsolved murders.

On the national level, the Chinese Communist Party virtually assured Nixon's reelection by inviting him to Beijing. A couple of months later, the North Vietnamese destroyed his military war strategy with a big spring offensive that sent tanks right across the demilitarized zone between North and South Vietnam. Nixon responded with saturation B-52 bombing of the North and the mining of Haiphong's harbor, exhausting all ideas the Pentagon had ever suggested, as if to show he'd tried everything. Even after this, the Soviets allowed him to come to the Moscow summit. Nixon's domestic political war strategy was more successful than his military efforts: he thought that as the draft faded away so would student protests, and he was right.

The McGovern campaign drained off a lot of national political energy during the year, only to end in Nixon's landslide reelection. In June, in the middle of the campaign, several mysterious burglars were caught breaking into the Democratic National Headquarters in the Watergate Hotel.

In Detroit, some of the baby boomers started to desert the economically declining downtown area in search of brighter economic horizons. Today's pattern of a poorer, black-governed inner city, and prosperous, mostly white suburbs was beginning to take shape. This factor along with the decline in political activity and the departure of key staff began to give the *Fifth Estate* a case of the financial woozies. As recently as 1971, the paper had been printing

32-page issues. Now it was down to 20 or 24 pages. It published an emergency financial appeal and initiated a monthly "sustainer" program. Mike Neiswonger later recalled that some issues did not have enough ads to pay for the front cover, let alone all 20 to 24 pages.

Lyndon LaRouche Debunked

The beginning of 1973 saw an upswing of political activity from the nadir of 1972. The Detroit black community, fed up with police abuse, mobilized to elect veteran progressive politician Coleman Young as the city's first black mayor. (Among his other accomplishments, Young had appeared as a "hostile witness" before the House Un-American Activities Committee (HUAC) in the 1950s, telling off the McCarthyites. HUAC was not abolished until the early 1970s.)

The *Fifth Estate* endorsed no one in the mayoral race and supported no candidates for office during its 1965–1975 history. The staff took the position that elections changed little, if anything, and only diverted attention from the source of the problems, the capitalist system. The paper preferred direct-action methods instead. Whether this was the correct policy is open to question. In the 1960s, blacks and their allies fought and sometimes died in the South for the right to vote. And the fact that blacks can now vote in most of the South has certainly brought on significant changes.

Nationally, in January 100,000 antiwar activists went to Washington for the last major Vietnam demonstration. Peace accords were about to be signed, but activists did not trust the U.S. to abide by them. Also nationally, the Watergate scandal began to unfold in earnest, promising to render Richard Nixon more and more ineffective as president. Spiro Agnew, his vice president, resigned in a separate scandal, when it was revealed he had accepted stuffed envelopes of cash in the White House. Another major national development was the dramatic 71-day occupation of Wounded Knee by the American Indian Movement.

Dave Riddle and I decided to rejoin the *Fifth Estate*. Riddle was sick of assembling pickup trucks for a living, and I was sick of delivering pizzas. Within several months, several talented new staffers also joined, including Jeff Goodman and Bob Moore. Ken Fireman left the staff and, shortly after, badly broke his leg in the first inning of a *Fifth Estate* softball game (it was cancelled). After recovering, he went on to become editor of the *South End*.

The reconstituted staff held an emergency strategy meeting, fully cognizant that the paper had damn near folded in 1972. The staff decided that distribution was the biggest problem financially, and that if circulation went up, advertising revenue might follow. This decision led to the conclusion that depending almost solely on Keep on Trucking for distribution was a mistake, and that instead the paper should start installing coin-operated (25 cents) newsracks across the city. The paper ordered them in lots of ten from a small business in Georgia. By the end of the year, the eighty newsracks had more than doubled distribution income.

In this context, it is appropriate to mention the role played by unpaid volunteers in ensuring the *Fifth Estate*'s survival over the years. One such volunteer, the late Pete Kwant, donated his labor and his pickup truck to installing the first twenty newsracks across the city. The day he took out the first ten newsracks, as he rounded the first corner, two newsracks fairly leaped off the truck and crashed to the unforgiving pavement. Kwant and the staffers with him picked them up and banged them back into shape, and all ten newsracks went into operation that day.

(As an additional note, four full-time staffers who played significant roles on the paper have yet to be mentioned: Mark Mayer and Doug Larkin from 1970–1972, and Teresa Garland and Dennis Witkowski from 1973–1974.)

Several of the new 1973 staffers, along with Len Schafer, also plunged into a renewed campaign to secure paid advertising. The ad workers created an advertising brochure, which featured on its cover a picture of Canadian youths in an antiwar march at the Blue Water Bridge. The ads began to roll in.

Politically, the staff decided to concentrate on local investigative news reporting and political analysis, something readers hardly ever found in the daily papers. Issues of the paper began to appear with as many as twenty local news stories.

Soon the paper became personally involved in two controversial Detroit news stories. The first was the political exposure and debunking of Lyndon LaRouche.

The U.S. public is now familiar with Lyndon LaRouche as a right-wing extremist with neo-Nazi politics who has run for president several times. In 1973, he and his group, called the National Caucus of Labor Committees (NCLC), which had originated during the 1968 Columbia University crisis, were still posing as Trotskyists. (LaRouche got his start in the 1950s in the SWP.) Several local activists known to the *Fifth Estate* had joined the Detroit chapter, which eventually quit the national organization en masse in 1981.

The LaRouchians' strategy up to 1973 had been to subtly draw off energy and members from other progressive causes in various ways. When the National Welfare Rights Organization (NWRO) became prominent, the NCLC founded the National Unemployed and Welfare Rights Organization (NUWRO) as an ersatz clone. When Detroit garbagemen went on strike, the LaRouchians formed a Strike Support Coalition, which was used for NCLC speechifying and recruiting, rather than to aid the strikers in any material way. The NCLC joined student groups to gain use of university buildings, which were used for "classes"—mostly propaganda, finding new members, and loudly denouncing any political enemies who happened to show up. (All these tactics are similar to today's New Alliance Party, which is headed by former LaRouchian Fred Newman. For example, they formed the Rainbow Lobby, which has no relation to the Rainbow Coalition.)

In mid-1973, the LaRouchians underwent a change that strained their credibility in the eyes of many observers. Their behavior became erratic and confrontational. Instead of quietly leeching off other leftist groups, they suddenly launched "Operation Mop Up," a self-described attempt to destroy the Communist Party, which by its alleged dominance was hindering the Left. NCLC goons nationwide began to break up any meeting involving CP sponsorship or participation.

While seemingly "Trotskyist" in its opposition to the Communist Party, Operation Mop Up actually more closely resembled 1930s campaigns by the CP itself to break up fledgling Trotskyist gatherings. Operation Mop Up was anti-democratic and a threat to the entire progressive movement. Activists across the country united to defend their meetings from LaRouchian goon attacks. In Detroit, people arrived at one major socialist meeting with boxes of literature under which lay billy clubs for everybody. When the NCLC attacked the meeting, the crowd grabbed the weapons and chased the goons downstairs and out of the building.

The *Fifth Estate* saw the seriousness of the crisis and responded by issuing a special four-page supplement, with a long staff editorial denouncing the LaRouchians, including much of the analysis just laid out. The article pointed out that, with their violent tactics, the LaRouchians were acting more like fascists than socialists. The supplement also contained an article by Keep on Trucking. While the text indicated they were partially taken in by the NCLC propaganda, the piece ended by saying that Keep on Trucking would physically retaliate for any attack on the *Fifth Estate* office. (Threats had been received.)

The four-page supplement and staff editorial put the *Fifth Estate* at the center of the controversy and made it, as Dave Riddle says, "one of the first to blow the whistle on LaRouche." The cover of the supplement had two big words in block letters—THE LEFT—with the blocks breaking up. This picture illustrated what was happening in Detroit and nationwide. The *Fifth Estate* met the crisis head-on, but the nature of it did not bode well for any progressive projects.

The Guru Gets Pied

The second controversial story involved the rise of religious cults. With the dropoff of political activity, a lot of young people were apparently still searching for something—anything—to believe in. Religious cults moved in to fill the psychological need and soak up the energy, often giving back little in return.

People in many cases gave all their worldly possessions to these groups; took part in long sessions called "love bombing," where attention was showered on them (actually a form of indoctrination); and submitted to control over the most minute aspects of their daily lives. They also worked at fundraising for next to nothing.

Some examples of these cults included "Moses David" and the early Jesus freak movement, and Sun Myung Moon, whose church was already well enough developed in 1974 to lead demonstrations against impeachment. The black community was also affected. Jim Jones's congregation was growing in San Francisco, and Jonestown—the nation's wake-up call about the danger of cults—lay four years in the future.

In 1973, still another cult was growing in power and influence: the Divine Light Mission of the fifteen-year-old Guru Maharaj Ji, who claimed to be God himself. The Divine Light Mission had attracted followers in chapters across the country, including Detroit, and the guru himself embarked on a national tour.

Total amazement gripped the *Fifth Estate* office when staffers first heard that Rennie Davis, an antiwar organizer par excellence since 1965 and an architect of the 1971 May Day demonstration, had announced in California that he was now a supporter of the young guru. Quite simply, credibility again was strained, and staffers even made several long-distance calls to the West Coast to confirm the news.

Soon the guru visited Detroit on his national tour, and the Detroit City Council, not having enough to do, with a major national recession and automotive slump approaching, decided to give the guru the key to the city. What he had done for Detroit in his fifteen years was unclear.

Pat Halley was another new *Fifth Estate* staffer, and the only one ever to advocate pandemonium as a political solution (see figure 1). He went to the city council chamber posing as an admirer of the guru, carrying a bouquet of flowers. However, under the flowers was concealed a shaving-cream pie, which Halley threw in the face of the Guru Maharaj Ji at a strategic moment (see figure 2). [Ed.: Halley tells his own story for the first time in "Looking for Utopia" at the end of this article.]

FIGURE 1: Pat Halley is up against the car being rousted by Wayne State University cops while Peter Werbe holds out a press pass insisting on his right to be present to observe what's happening. Photographed on Lodge Service Drive around the corner from the Lodge and the *Fifth Estate* office on Warren. Date unknown but likely early seventies. Photographer unknown. From *Fifth Estate* archives.

With city council president Mel Ravitz suddenly sounding very unliberal, in fact yelling for Halley's head, the master of pandemonium dashed down multiple flights of stairs and out of the City-County Building without being caught.

A Ken Kelley article describes what followed:

"I don't want the man hurt or arrested," explained the embarrassed child-god to his followers and the press as he wiped the soap from his face.

However, one week later the pie-thrower was brutally beaten from behind by two of the guru's top devotees. The two men, one an older Indian and the other a young American, had tried to reach Halley for several days after he threw the pie. They told him they wanted to "expose" the Guru Maharaj Ji as a fraud.

The older man claimed he had traveled all the way from India for that purpose. To track down the story, and aware of warnings from other *Fifth Estate* staff members not to accompany the men alone, Halley led them to his apartment.

"For forty-five minutes or so they told me what a great thing I had done, that the

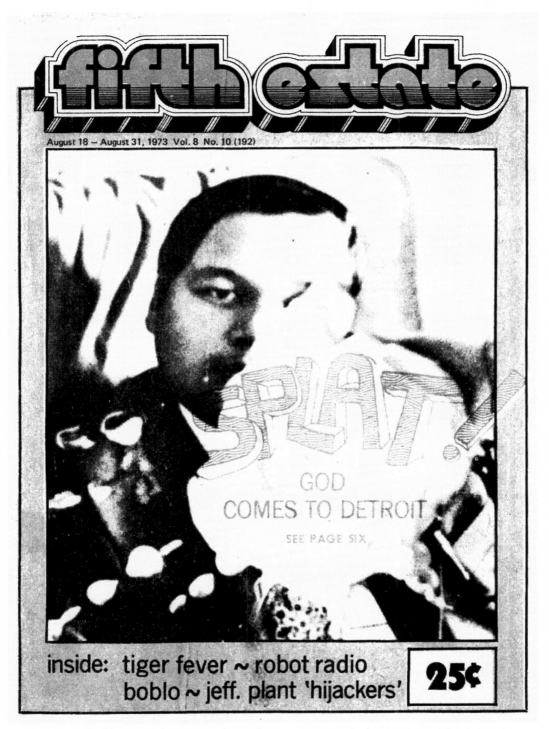

fifth estate

August 18 — August 31, 1973 Vol. 8 No. 10 (192)

SPLAT!

GOD
COMES TO DETROIT

SEE PAGE SIX

inside: tiger fever ~ robot radio
boblo ~ jeff. plant 'hijackers'

25¢

FIGURE 2: Cover of *Fifth Estate* volume 8, number 10 (August 18–31, 1973), showing Guru Maharaj Ji getting splattered with pie thrown by staffer Pat Halley. Photo by John Collier.

guru was evil, and that they would show me hypnotic techniques he employs so that I could tell the world," he recalls. "The older man told me to close my eyes, which I did, while he walked behind me. I heard the sound of metal scraping metal, and I thought it must be some kind of flashlight they used to produce their divine light or something. Then I saw the light all right—and lots of stars. I didn't realize what was going on till I heard my blood splatter on the wall."

He screamed; the men fled. Luckily friends were next door and managed to get him to a hospital. He had received six skull lacerations and contusions; for the rest of his life Halley will have a plastic plate over his cerebrum where the skull bone was shattered. . . .

The men were identified as 25-year-old Richard Fletcher and 55-year-old Jupteswar Misra. . . . When I talked to Rennie Davis, he admitted to me that the two are still very much a part of the DLM. In fact, the Indian turns out to be Mahatma Fakiranand, one of the first two mahatmas to give knowledge in America. . . . "Was he stripped of his mahatmadom," I asked. "No he wasn't—he was just shipped off to Europe and he's there now giving knowledge."

Rennie Davis added, "I really feel Maharaj Ji is doing everything—he had the pie thrown in his face, and he had Fakiranand do that. The whole thing is one gigantic *lila* (i.e., game) that operates on many levels." Including, apparently, felonious assault and its cover-up.

Though felony warrants were issued for their arrest, Halley's assailants were never caught or prosecuted. Following the Halley incident, the *Fifth Estate* ran a series of articles investigating the nature of religious cults. If all was peace and love, why did the bloody fangs come out so quickly when a hippie pantheist pulled a harmless prank? What else lay hidden behind the clouds of incense, the hypnotic chanting, and the beautiful altars (which in the Detroit guru house had stacks of money on them)?

The *Fifth Estate* again deserves credit for some early whistle-blowing. But again, the crisis was essentially a negative phenomenon. Young Americans were blindly following a half-baked punk from India rather than thinking for themselves how to live.

As in the case of LaRouche, people were turning to the irrational rather than to the rational, to mysticism and mindless violence rather than to struggle and analysis. The fact that Rennie Davis was now leading them down the primrose path was doubly shocking.

"Roots of the Underground"

The third major *Fifth Estate* event of 1973 was a fifteen-part series called "Roots of the Underground," an in-depth look at the rise of an "adversary culture" in the United States, starting with the immediate post–World War II period, continuing through the "Beat" period of the 1950s, and on into the 1960s and 1970s.

The series was retrospective in nature, raising questions such as: Where did we come from? How did we get this way? Who were the forebears of the present era of antiwar activism, sexual liberation, experimentation with drugs, and talk of revolution? The various articles examined both the political and cultural aspects. After the furor of the late 1960s and the early 1970s, it seemed a good time to reflect.

Featured were samples and analyses of works by some of the writers and thinkers whose writing has changed American life; these included the following:

- Lawrence Ferlinghetti, the owner of City Lights bookstore in San Francisco and author of *A Coney Island of the Mind* and *Unfair Arguments with Existence.*
- James Baldwin, black activist and author of *Another Country* and *Go Tell It on the Mountain.*
- Beat poet and later culture hero Allen Ginsberg, author of the famous poems "Howl" and "Kaddish."
- Jack Kerouac, author of the classic beat novels *On the Road* and *Dharma Bums.*
- Paul Goodman, the anarchist educational theorist and godfather of the New Left, author of *Growing Up Absurd*, *People or Personnel*, and the classic novel *The Empire City.*
- LeRoi Jones (later known as Amari Baraka), early black nationalist figure, poet, and author of *Preface to a 20-Volume Suicide Note.*
- William Burroughs, author of *Naked Lunch.*
- Paul Krassner, comedian and editor of *The Realist.*
- Diane DiPrima, author of *Revolutionary Letters.*

"Roots of the Underground" was an interesting series, but it's worth noting that, in total, it featured fourteen males and only one female, a lopsided score in anybody's playbook. Early feminists such as Gloria Steinem and Ti-Grace Atkinson could have been included, as well as black female writers such as Angela Davis and Lorraine Hansberry.

Trouble in Lotusland

Toward the end of 1973, something began to go wrong on the *Fifth Estate* staff, though it was hard to tell just what. Traditionally the staff operated in a somewhat relaxed manner, alternating their paid vacations as convenient.

Len Schafer took his vacation, and in his absence the staff voted 7–4 to begin running personal ads again, including sex ads. The *Fifth Estate* had banned these ads in 1969, not wanting to become a "meat market." Local gay activists had asked the paper to reinstate the personals, on the grounds that gays had fewer ways to meet than other people, but the ban had stood.

When Schafer returned, he thought something had been done behind his back. As the only openly gay staffer, I had pushed for repeal of the ban, but not because Schafer was on vacation. The issue just came up while he was gone. Both Schafer and Mike Neiswonger were incensed and threatened to quit. The personal ad ban was reinstated without a formal vote to do so.

Then I took my vacation. When I got back, Pat Halley had already thrown his pie, gotten beat up, and landed in the hospital. I probably would have voted against the pie-throwing had I been present, because that "Yippie" type of activism was not my style. When I saw that Halley had almost been killed, I quickly concluded that he had underestimated the guru and his group.

During the same week as the pie-throwing incident, the staff also voted to make Cathy Kauflin a full-time member. Even though Kauflin was an excellent graphic artist, the move was a departure from common practice in that up to that time, all full-time staffers had participated in the writing and editing processes.

As the months went on, Kauflin came under increasing criticism from several staffers (including me) for not taking part in the preparation and editing of articles. Instead, she continued to do what she had always done, mainly artwork, typesetting, and putting together the *Fifth Estate* calendar, which had become one of the big attractions of the paper. Eventually she left the staff under a dark cloud, never having been accepted as a full-time staffer. Kauflin went on to do important editorial and graphic work on pamphlets for Fredy Perlman's Black and Red Press (see final section for more on Black and Red).

The fact that staffers criticized Kauflin, or just sat and watched rather than supporting her once she was on the staff, showed that sexism was still a problem on the *Fifth Estate.* The fact that the staff was making policy in such an erratic manner—and with so little real agreement on what should be done, and so much mistrust of each other's judgment—indicated that more trouble was on the way.

As 1974 dawned, another political event took place that, like the LaRouche and guru affairs, caused staffers to question what was going on, and to examine their political beliefs. Several of the socialists on the staff decided to initiate a protest march against high energy prices and mounting unemployment. Progressive and leftist groups around the city were called, and an initial meeting or two were held. To put it mildly, things went sour. The *Fifth Estate* "Detroit Seen" column of March 2, 1974, described the situation well:

> The proposed "Energy Crisis" march that we announced last issue has run into deep trouble. . . . From an initial brainstorming group of enthusiastic independents, the planning meetings have been transformed into dialectical shootouts between small left sects, each one trying to put its pet line over. . . . The tone of the last meeting was set by a debate over whether or not to exclude the Trotskyists from the planning sessions. . . . The motion was defeated, but most of the original people involved in the action, including most of the *Fifth Estate* staff, have already walked out of the meetings, disgusted by this dinosaur mentality. . . . For those who wish to try and salvage a march from this zoo of narcissistic heavies, the meetings are Tuesday nights. . . . Earth Center spokesman Marvin Surowitz reports that the karma was so bad, the center had to be exorcised for a couple of days after each meeting.

The flop of the 1974 march, coming after the two weird episodes of 1973, had an effect on everybody on the staff. The socialists stayed firm in their beliefs, at least judged by their activities in following years. But they began to lose faith in the paper as an instrument of change.

To begin with, everybody knew that the publication's current prosperity was due to the coin newsracks, hard work hustling ads, and continuing public outrage over Watergate. It was not due to any grassroots political groundswell in Detroit—the leftist groups who were flipping out trying to organize the march were evidence of that. The largest-selling *Fifth Estate* issue of 1974 had none other than a bug-eyed Nixon on the cover, with the words "Jesus F-cking Christ" underneath. (Yes, there was no letter *u.* In effect, we censored ourselves there.) And Watergate was slowly coming to a close, with Nixon's resignation approaching.

Also, all American troops had been out of Vietnam for a year now, drastically reducing public concern over the war. And discontent over Vietnam had been the single biggest factor in the paper's survival.

Everybody also knew that a major recession was coming, and that downturns affected Detroit especially heavily, cutting into the incomes of all businesses, including marginal small ones like the paper. It seemed doubtful the publication would survive it.

Dave Riddle, a socialist, and Bob Moore, whose politics were radical-liberal, had worked together on the paper for a year and a half. They both quit within two weeks of each other, without informing each other they were going to do so. Jeff Goodman, another socialist, took on a more passive staff role, working on the office books and not always even attending staff meetings. A third socialist, myself, retreated to a part-time staff role, working mainly with the newsracks, which had been one of my pet projects from the start.

Looking back, the attitude of the socialists at the time is deserving of criticism. Socialism is a collectivist concept, with people working together in a cooperative way. Yet when confronted with adversity, the socialists acted very individualistically. Socialism also advocates progressives seizing power to effect change, outflanking the right wing. Yet the socialists passively gave away the power on the *Fifth Estate.*

Len Schafer and Mike Neiswonger reacted differently to events. They began to shed their progressive beliefs, and became more interested in the paper solely as a business proposition. Schafer was coordinating advertising, and Neiswonger directed layout, so they already had a firm grip on the financial/production process of the paper.

Both Schafer and Neiswonger began specifically to reject socialist ideas. This first came out in staff discussions, and only later in the paper itself. Two incidents were typical. A staffer did an article on the meaning of the May Day tradition, and wanted to use a drawing of a Maypole with it. Neiswonger suggested using tanks rolling through Red Square. On another occasion, a Marxist study group called, wanting to run a small ad for a meeting. Such ads were often done for a minimal rate or for free; Schafer insisted on charging full commercial rates.

When local feminists held a women-only conference, both Schafer and Neiswonger were offended and said it was sexist of the women not to admit men.

Staff meetings began to take on a backbiting tone. One disgruntled staffer described them as "litanies of bureaucratic procedure, accompanied by the hounding of singled out individuals." The quality of writing in the paper began to drop as socialist staffers and contributors stopped producing. For example, Marxist analyst Jim Jacobs would soon quit writing for the paper.

Schafer and Neiswonger were reacting not only to the immediate political situation, but also to very real events in their lives stretching over several years. Schafer openly admitted that he had become a bit cynical after working hard on the *Fifth Estate* staff for four years, and watching the Movement decline for most of that time. Neiswonger was the victim of a bad experience before he ever joined the paper. He had arrived as a virtual refugee from the Detroit Organizing Committee, a group whose members studied stacks of Stalinist texts and held ten- to twelve-hour meetings three times a week.

Both expressed some interest in anarchist ideas, as opposed to socialist ones, but neither ever wrote a major article for the paper in that vein. In reality, both were on the fast track out of politics altogether. Schafer became a well-paid advertising executive in San Francisco, cutting a dashing figure in a three-piece suit; Neiswonger was spotted in the mid-1980s as a public spokesman for the Michigan Consolidated Gas Company, justifying rate increases.

In describing the process that went on at the *Fifth Estate*, Dave Riddle recalls Isaac Deutscher's analysis of what went on in the Soviet Union from 1920 to 1940, albeit on an immeasurably larger scale. "The class struggle receded, and bureaucracy moved in and took over. Stalin himself was a symbol of the steep decline of the class struggle." (Isaac Deutscher was the biographer of Leon Trotsky.) Schafer and Neiswonger probably would not want to be compared to Stalin, but the analogy tells as much about his politics as about theirs.

My parting of ways with the *Fifth Estate* came over the subject of whether to put the word "gay" on the cover. Since I had rejoined the staff in January 1973 as an openly gay person, the *Fifth Estate* had increased its gay coverage markedly. The gay and lesbian movement was growing stronger locally; the new Gay Community Center was only a few blocks from the *Fifth Estate* office. I urged greater coverage and wrote some of the articles myself. Gay Pride Week in 1973 was the subject of an entire centerfold.

Finally, there seemed to be enough going on in the city to merit a cover story. Tentatively called "Gay Life in Detroit," it featured a cover illustration of a cop punching a gay on the chin and saying "Fag!" in a word balloon.

On layout night, Schafer, Neiswonger, and others began raising objections to putting the word "gay" on the cover (the word "fag" was, as noted, already there). As the staff debate went on, my position suffered from the fact that *Fifth Estate* had no women's caucus—or, for that matter, any feminist women on the staff at the time—and no gay caucus. In addition, Schafer and Neiswonger got some support from the part-timers and volunteers, who each had a vote, for the unstated reason that at least the two financial/production people were sticking with the paper, while the socialists like me seemed to be fading away. Full-time male staffers like Halley and Moore were no help.

Schafer said that "special interests" were getting too much space in the paper (a distant early warning of Reaganism). Neiswonger said that "gays have their own paper in this city" and "people might think we're a gay paper." By a narrow vote, the staff decided to strike the word "gay" from the cover. (The alternative was not designated. Cheery Life in Detroit? Deviant Life in Detroit?)

Now it was my turn to threaten to quit—leaving off the word "gay" negated the whole point of the cover story, which was that gays and lesbians were at last coming out of the closet in old-fashioned Detroit. Two hours later, the vote was reversed and the G-word went back on the cover. But the fight took so much out of me that I quit two weeks later anyway, in spring 1974.

In retrospect, it might seem hard to believe that an allegedly radical paper was afraid to put the word "gay" on the cover. To me it was a lesson that while change comes, it can be at an agonizingly slow pace, and at times at a very high price. To be fair, gay and lesbian coverage continued in the paper after the controversy, including another centerfold for 1974 Gay Pride Week and various other articles.

About a month after I left the staff, the *Fifth Estate* suffered its third incident of 1974 involving sexism. The following exchange of letters to the editor in June 1974 outlines the problem. The first letter was from a feminist collective that included Miriam Frank, a prominent activist in the women's health movement.

To The Editor:

"Notes from the Speculum Underground" was a regular column contributed to the *Fifth Estate* by the Detroit Women's Health Project from August of 1973 to very recently. This column was about the sexual politics of the American Health System and . . . reported research and technology on women's health as developed by local activists in the women's health movement.

One of the main provisions of our agreement to contribute to the *Fifth Estate* was that there be No Political Editing (censorship) of our copy . . . our experience has been that male-dominated left groups traditionally censor, ignore, misinterpret or crudely co-opt the unique voices of women . . . and we had no reason to believe the *Fifth Estate* would be an exception to that situation.

We have learned that the *Fifth Estate* no longer wants to keep to that original agreement of No Political Editing and would prefer not to carry Notes from the Speculum Underground without their ultimate control of our copy's political content. This is of course not acceptable to us.

The *Fifth Estate* staff made the following reply:

The last article of the column mentioned above . . . was not left out of the *Fifth Estate* *primarily* for political reasons [italics mine—BH]. . . . It was much longer than the average length which was previously agreed on . . . it also repeated material already covered in the first installment and it had many grammatical errors. . . . We do not share the mystifying notion that certain social, sexual or political groups have a monopoly on insights into the inner workings of human oppression—including the particular oppression of women perpetuated by the male-dominated profit-corrupted health care system. It is the editorial intent of the *Fifth Estate* to expose this system . . . and not to promote one group or clique's "unique voice" on the matter.

In the following issue, Jeff Goodman, the last socialist on the staff, wrote the following individual letter in answer to the staff reply:

There definitely was political editing of the last column . . . the changes made were not merely mechanical, shortening or grammatical in nature. They included deletion of the whole first page of the column, which basically constituted the introductory political rap and projected anger at the "male-dominated, profit-corrupted health care system" which the *Fifth Estate* deplores. . . . The basic problem seems to have been that the *Fifth Estate*, in fact, demanded changes in the political content of the column, and the people of the Women's Health Project were unwilling to enter a lengthy struggle over these changes.

The *Fifth Estate* maintains that a newspaper must have the right to edit copy for political content; this is true but it is at best a completely ambiguous principle, which, having no political content of its own, can be used to justify anything. The real question is why did the *Fifth Estate* demand these changes in the first place? Why does the *Fifth Estate* now have only one woman on its full-time staff and not even a regular column by any of the women's groups in Detroit? Surely you can participate in the general oppression without being capable of knowing as much about the unique aspects of women's oppression as women themselves. Perhaps it is the lack of ability of some *Fifth Estate* staffers to comprehend even the general oppression of other people . . . which makes them so uptight that THEY take on the role of God, declaring that no other particular group of people could possibly know enough to speak for themselves.

"Notes from the Speculum Underground" did not run again, and Goodman quit the staff soon afterwards.

Some of the events described so far in this section were not pretty, but they did happen, and can be learned from. The saving grace is that the paper somehow came back from all these hair-raising difficulties. Even while the old *Fifth Estate* was sinking into bureaucracy and feminist-baiting, a new one—the post-1975 *Fifth Estate*—was being born within its husk.

Wildcat at Dodge Truck

The first sign of the new *Fifth Estate*, one with serious anarchist-libertarian politics, was a series of articles by Millard Berry and Alan Franklin starting on August 8, 1974. The articles analyzed the June 1974 four-day wildcat strike by auto workers at Warren's Dodge Truck plant. (A "wildcat" is a strike not authorized by the main union, in this case the UAW.)

Dodge Truck had many young white workers influenced by "countercultural" values, and many young black workers as well. They went out on strike spontaneously when five metal-shop workers, including a union steward, were fired after they complained jointly about bad working conditions. The UAW did not support the walkout by its rank and file, said the wildcat was caused by "communists" and "outsiders," and actually called the local police to evict 150 striking workers from their own union hall (a total of about 6,000 were on strike).

On the fourth day of the walkout, the UAW assembled huge flying squads numbering hundreds of workers to cross the picket lines, break the wildcat, and keep the plant open. The local police arrested about thirty workers, and the company pitched in by firing another fifty to one hundred who refused to return to work.

The *Fifth Estate* articles outlined the skullduggery by the UAW, and also criticized the activities of Marxist organizers who had been agitating in the plant for years, among them the original steward who was fired. The articles said that the Marxists' local plant newsletter was not critical of the union leadership, did not fight for democracy in the union, and did not win the support of the workers. They added that the Marxists themselves were taken by surprise by the wildcat, but once it started, tried to co-opt its energies by appointing a steering committee and excluding all other literature besides their own from meetings.

The articles then described the fourth day of the strike—it was losing steam (partly due to the leftists' tactics) and the UAW-Chrysler-local police forces were getting ready to shut it down. The authors said that the Marxists, along with leftist allies who did not work in the plant, pushed for an ultra-left attempt to prolong the walkout, resulting in the mass arrests and firings, and turning a wildcat that might have made a serious point to both management and union into a rout.

Here is how Alan Franklin described the UAW:

Any UAW member in the plant has painfully concluded that the union long ago gave up representing his interests and became instead a simple adjunct of the company, enforcing work discipline that foremen and supervisors by themselves could never hope to impose.

This is the logical and inevitable result of the contradictions inherent in any organization which claims to "represent" the interests of others. Unions are not now essentially "healthy" organizations which require only a cleaning up of leadership to "begin once again serving the workers' interests." They have not been "betrayed" by the corrupt fat cats, they are the betrayal themselves.

Millard Berry criticized the Marxists as follows:

These organizers share the basic view that the working class . . . is the only segment of capitalist society capable of overthrowing capitalism itself and constructing a socialist society in its place. They also believe, however, that the workers cannot properly evolve their own critical analysis of capitalism, nor any tactics or strategy to radically transform it, but must have them *injected* from outside the class.

The Marxist organizers use an authoritarian, hierarchical party. This party would take on the task of administering the new society, after the overthrow of capitalism, *in the name of the workers.*

Ex-staffer Dave Riddle replied to the Dodge Truck articles in a letter to the editor. (Both Riddle and Berry had worked at Dodge Truck in the early 1970s.)

Anarchism is the position espoused by both the authors . . . and by the *Fifth Estate* newspaper. This position, which idealizes the day-to-day resistance of workers to capitalism, unfortunately provides no alternative to capitalism and no means to assure that any alternative can be reached. Not one constructive word on what to do to move beyond capitalism appears either in the pages of the *Fifth Estate* or in the writing of the people who produced the articles. Instead, anarchism condemns every initiative for change short of an unspecified scenario for spontaneous revolutionary upsurge.

So the articles condemn unions as a whole, holding that the CIO originated in a ruling class ploy to buy off an angry work force in the '30s. The authors . . . presumably feel that today's migrant farm laborers are fools to try to organize their own union and that mine workers would give up their union and place themselves once again in the tender care of the coal operators.

The terms of the anarchist-Marxist debate in Detroit were now defined, and the future course of the *Fifth Estate* was clearly indicated.

Long Live the *F.E.*

After the old model *Fifth Estate* heaved a great sigh and died in July 1975, the anarchist-libertarian activists regrouped. Leading the new effort were Peter and Marilyn Werbe. Franklin and Berry made great contributions, and also joining were John Grant, formerly of the *South End*, and Dave Watson, a longtime friend of the paper.

A particular inspiration for the renewed project were the late Fredy Perlman and his wife Lorraine, whose Black and Red Press published a steady stream of literature, pamphlets, and books in the 1970s, and which in fact was the fountainhead of anarchist-libertarian thought in Detroit during that decade. Black and Red Press and the Werbes helped to inform and critique the 1974 Dodge Truck articles.

The new staff tackled the problem of bureaucracy frontally by abolishing all paid positions ("We no longer will relate to people in this way") and abolishing all paid advertising. They established a bookstore with a much more complete selection than its distant Plum Street ancestor. Its purpose was to help support the publication, and to serve as a focal point for its ideas and political organizing.

The new crew brought a burst of creativity into the office at Second and Canfield, the scene of so many *Fifth Estate* achievements, and the occasional mind-boggling interstaff argument, in the previous five years. The *Fifth Estate* continued to publish, for the first five years as a monthly and after that as a quarterly with a worldwide circulation of 5,000. Its politics could best be described as anarchist, although it has extended classic anti-capitalist, anti-statist libertarian politics to include opposition to the industrial system itself and the civilization it has spawned.

In recent times, the *Fifth Estate* has been particularly strong in supporting, and constructively criticizing, the radical environmental movement. In an issue called "How Deep Is Deep Ecology?" the *Fifth Estate* endorsed Earth First!'s militant, direct-action tactics, but added that environmentalism should go beyond "saving wilderness" as a final objective, and should also become a revolutionary movement for social change, or there will be no wilderness left to save.

The paper criticized Edward Abbey, in many ways the inspirational godfather of Earth First!, but whose views were considered by many to be racist and anti-immigrant. Similarly, it criticized an Earth First! founder: "Unfortunately, Dave Foreman and others writing in his private business, the *Earth First Journal*, continue to issue forth racist refugee baiting . . . and other patriotic ravings that make us barely want to be in the same room with them."

Despite these criticisms, the *Fifth Estate* recognized Earth First! as an important grassroots organization capable of growing away from the backward views of some of its founders. "No compromise in defense of Mother Earth" is a fine starting point, and Earth Firsters have repeatedly demonstrated a willingness to do more than talk, to put their bodies or even lives on the line. The summer 1990 issue of the *Fifth Estate* had a photograph of redwoods on the cover, with the headline "Bombing Won't Stop Redwood Summer." It stressed the importance of defending Earth First! from police attack, whatever the ideological differences.

In the winter 1990 issue, the *Fifth Estate* editorialized:

We endorse the idea of radicalizing the 20th anniversary of Earth Week. . . . The attempt to fashion it as a domesticated spectacle has already begun with every hack politician, mainstream institution, and even notorious polluters declaring allegiance to the 1990s as the "Environmental Decade," all the while planning business as usual. These fakes are preparing to make it a week of festivities celebrating "concern" for the earth and the system's ability to fix its problems.

We at the *Fifth Estate* intend to be active in Detroit asserting the opposite contention: that the wreckage of the biosphere comes directly from the operation of the capitalist system and not from "ill advised policies," "lack of information about sound alternatives to pollution," and the like. Industrial petro-chemical production—the cornerstone of world capitalism (even when labeled "socialism")—is incompatible with an ecologically viable world.

The 1965–1975 *Fifth Estate* did not emphasize environmentalism as the current *Fifth Estate* does. In those days, the environment was not widely recognized as the overriding issue it is today, and did not have as important a nook in the radical kitchen. On the other hand, echoing the editorial just quoted, it is arguable that moderate-to-liberal environmentalism—as opposed to the brand advocated by the *Fifth Estate*, Earth First!, or even Greenpeace—is the Mom's apple pie of American "armchair radicals" today. It is a lot safer to join the Sierra Club than to picket with union strikers, defend an abortion clinic, or stop the Ku Klux Klan from marching in the nation's capital.

The current incarnation of the *Fifth Estate* is also a strong supporter of women's prerogative to control their bodies and their reproductive lives without government intervention or legal restraint. Soon after George H. W. Bush was elected, *Fifth Estate* staffers went to a massive pro-choice rally in Washington, DC (300,000 strong), as part of a seventy-person "anti-authoritarian contingent."

While supporting women's struggles, the paper was critical of the National Organization for Women's leadership: "NOW and its liberal allies decided to forego a march, such as the one last April which brought 600,000 people to the capital in support of abortion rights, and instead have the only event of the day be a rally where those attending would be held captive to speeches by an endless parade of mainstream feminists and Democratic Party politicians. It is usually the case that after experiencing the exuberance of a mass march, participants tend to drift away as rally speakers begin to drone on. This time, NOW assured that to attend was to sit and passively listen."

The anti-authoritarian contingent's leaflet explained the group's position: "In order to create a lasting community of resistance, we must establish systems for health support (midwives, health collectives, etc.) so that we are no longer vulnerable to the patriarchal medical establishment or an oppressive government. Why grovel before the courts and legislatures again to ask for that which is *already ours*? Let's take control of our bodies and our lives!"

The winter 1990 issue is dedicated

to the memory of the 14 women slaughtered in Montreal December 6 at the hand of a patriarchal maniac. As he lined up his victims and methodically shot them, he expressed a hatred for all women and said he wanted "to kill feminists."

In the memory of these dead sisters, we pledge, "We're all feminists here!"

In more recent years (since 2000), the *Fifth Estate* has ceased being a 100 percent Detroit project. Much work is done at a rural Tennessee collective, and some is done by a group of activists in New York City. Motor City staffers also contribute.

Titles of recent issues include "Revolution: Spain–1936, Venezuela–2006?" and "I.W.W. and the Revolt against Work," plus a literature issue featuring Ursula K. LeGuin, Diane DiPrima, Gary Snyder, and Allen Ginsberg. Most importantly, in 2005 the *Fifth Estate* published a 100-page fortieth anniversary issue: "Supporting Revolution Everywhere" since 1965. (The first three words are a direct quote from an FBI report on the paper.)

This last, brief section has been a glimpse into the post-1975 *Fifth Estate*; its more detailed history must be written by somebody who knows better the events and issues of these years in Detroit.

As a veteran of the early *Fifth Estate* days, I look forward to another season of social change in the United States. Karl Marx's "old mole of revolution" has been burrowing for quite a while now, and she may pop her head up at any moment. Now that the snake oil of Reagan and the two Bushes has bankrupted the country and led it into economic decline, there are great opportunities for progressive organizing. The true agendas of the 1930s and 1960s have yet to be fulfilled: most workers do not have a union, countries still suffer under the yoke of neocolonialism, and politicians still win elections by appealing to racism.

Many activists are working to accomplish the needed changes—feminists defending abortion clinics and causing "pro-life" political hacks to run for cover, workers and their allies opposing "free trade" agreements and globalization, blacks protesting continual racist incidents, immigrant labor organizers winning the basic rights of workers (again) in the fields, factories, and offices of this vast country. Most importantly, the public has rejected George W. Bush's bogus "war on terror" and illegal occupation of Iraq, in the process giving control of Congress back to the Democrats.

It is for my *Fifth Estate* comrades, and all today's progressive activists ("those infinitely different from us, and infinitely like us," in the words of novelist Victor Serge) that I have written this history.

ACKNOWLEDGMENTS

I would like to thank Harvey Ovshinsky, Peter Werbe, and Dave Riddle, whose comments represent a major portion of this article. Ovshinsky, who founded the *Fifth Estate* at age seventeen, was on its staff from 1965 to 1969, and is now an independent filmmaker in Ann Arbor. Werbe has been on the paper's staff for its entire forty-plus year existence, with the exception of two or three years in the early 1970s. He is now a radio talk-show host in Detroit, expounding his revolutionary anarchist philosophy over the airwaves. Riddle was on the staff during most of the 1970–1974 period, and since then has been a Teamsters Union activist and a historian of the Detroit Left.

▬▬▬▬▬▬▬▬▬▬▬▬▬▬▬▬▬ APPENDIX ▬▬▬▬▬▬▬▬▬▬▬▬▬▬▬▬▬

LOOKING FOR UTOPIA (by Patrick Halley)

In 1973 I decided that I *had* to start writing for the *Fifth Estate*, Detroit's revolutionary "underground" paper, or become a werewolf and fade into some wilderness unknown.

The times were ablaze with change, and the world was but a tinderbox only waiting for the right match.

I had been on the road, à la Jack Kerouac, for six months, hitchhiking up and down the West Coast, singing for quarters on street corners from Vancouver, British Columbia, down to L.A., and in major cities between Detroit and the Coast. My little theater troupe, "The Shadow People," also took me around the Midwest, where we performed wild skits and bizarre "assaults on Western Culture" on the streets, in coffeehouses, bars, and outdoor concerts—wherever and whenever we had the slightest opportunity to vent creative spleen. In a word, I was afire.

But working for a biweekly underground paper was a more disciplined pursuit, with deadlines, heavy scheduling, and editorial responsibilities that forced me to hone my writing skills and adapt to compromising with a collective of equally imaginative and fermentative individuals. I couldn't be as crazy, yet I could be more effective because we had a wider audience with the *Fifth Estate*, and other members of the collective were very talented people with experiences in teaching and writing. One fellow, Michael Neiswonger, was a former head of the English department at Cass Technical High School in Detroit; another, Bob Hippler, was the former editor of the University of Michigan's college paper; another guy had a PhD in economics; and so on—and all of us had a slightly different view of Utopia, though we were certain that it was "just around the corner."

I was certain that "Utopia is already here, but people just don't know it yet."

Via the *Fifth Estate* we not only worked frantically to end the war in Vietnam, we also wanted civil rights, economic justice, women's equality, gay liberation, ecological awareness, free speech, legal drugs, and all manner of New Left issues. We were on a tidal wave of change and were more than willing to sacrifice not only our careers but our lives to make the world a place where we could live for love and creativity and not merely for economic prosperity—with all of the social evils that unrestrained capitalism necessitates.

Working on the *Fifth Estate* was rewarding and stimulating, but it wasn't so very easy, largely because the paper was (and is) collectively run. Every rule, every single article that we printed, was debated and voted upon, because the operation of our paper was itself a socialist experiment. Begun in 1965, the *F.E.* by 1973 was staffed by anarchists, socialists, liberals, and even apolitical activists oriented by single issues. Arguments often raged into the night. Sometimes fisticuffs would come into play, only to be broken up quickly and settled eventually with marijuana or a trip to the bar. Despite our different backgrounds and political orientations, however, our first principle insisted that we operate with no boss or editor in chief to make anyone toe the line. It worked. We fought, but we wanted history to show that a socialist experiment could work, and that's why we made it work!

The Guru Cometh

I made myself and the *Fifth Estate* world-famous in 1973, in one of the many bizarre instances of Detroit politics, when I threw a pie in the face of a renowned guru. The year before, the Supreme Court had broadened the scope of U.S. tax-exempt laws to enable obscure religious groups to receive tax-deductible donations that previously only traditional major Judeo-Christian religions had been entitled to. One immediate result was the rise of the "Moonies," the "Krishnas," and various fundamentalist Christian groups that seemingly surged from nowhere.

In August of 1973, guru Maharaj Ji, the fifteen-year-old "perfect master," arrived in Detroit to inaugurate his "Divine Light Mission"—a religious cult started in India—and he was to receive the key to the city. The *Fifth Estate* was alerted about his coming by the Yippies in New York, who indicated that this guru was a hustler and a fraud, and I volunteered to investigate him and his sect. Having been involved with Buddhist and other Eastern religions, I felt that I could at least feel out this sect and determine if it was a genuine movement for peace or another capitalist scam.

I went to a meeting of the Divine Light Mission, previous to the guru's coming, and found that the Yippies were correct. The guru's technique was to attract affluent suburbanites into the cult, indoctrinate them, and then get them to donate all of their money to him, even to work in businesses that he started. It worked. Even George Harrison, the erstwhile Beatle, gave a Rolls-Royce to the corpulent mogul of spirituality. But I could see at their meeting that the deceptive methods of recruiting were more like a pyramid scheme than a truly religious function. My friend and I were ejected from the meeting for heckling the guru's head Detroit disciple.

When the guru came to town a few days later, on August 7, 1973, the local press hailed him as a messenger of peace and brotherhood. His disciples (advance men) hailed him as a combination of Jesus, Buddha, and Krishna—the new "God." The Detroit City Council had plans to give him a testimonial resolution and the key to the city, but my radical friends and I were ready to give him hell. At the foot of the City-County Building in Detroit, we passed out leaflets to satirize the occasion. Since this guru was "God," our leaflet had a list of demands that "God must meet, or leave the Universe in shame." It was signed, "No-Name, Ambassador of the Animal Kingdom."

In compiling this list, knowing that the major press would most likely pick it up, I decided not only to satirize the guru and religion in general, but also to throw in some anarchist concepts to prick society as a whole. The demands were:

> End to all suffering, pain, and hostility immediately. . . . Money should grow on trees. . . . God must clean house—no more pollution. . . . No more work—let the angels do it. . . . Extend the life span of people, with perpetual youth. . . . Large mountains in Michigan. . . . No more gravity—let people fly. . . . No more winter. . . . Free the Devil and all political prisoners. . . . Abolition of all private property, bosses, and government. . . . More money for teeth from the Good Fairy. . . . No more premature orgasms. . . . Communications with all civilizations in the Universe. . . . PEACE, PEACE, PEACE, PEACE, PEACE, PEACE, PEACE, PEACE.

This was participatory journalism, radical in itself at the time. Not only did the New Left writers write news, we also tried to make news. After our brief demonstration, we alerted the media that an event was to occur with the guru that shouldn't be missed. In the council chambers, surrounded by gushing worshippers of the guru, I sat with a corsage of flowers that concealed a cream pie. When the guru entered the dais, surrounded by aides, I came forward with the corsage. He glared disdainfully down at me, in his expensive suit, as I approached him, so without hesitation I launched a perfect throw from fifteen feet that hit him square in the face.

Pandemonium ensued as I flew out of the council chambers. My friends in the balcony laughed uproariously; furious disciples clutched at my arms as I raced down the aisle with a mob of screaming "gurunoids" and policemen following in hot pursuit. I raced down thirteen flights of stairs and out the door, and lost myself in the swirling crowds of downtown Detroit citizenry. I did it; I didn't even wind up in jail!

Serious Repercussions

My friends and I had a great time watching the videotaped event on the evening news. I was particularly satisfied when Bill Bonds reported the list of demands on the channel 7 news at 11:00 o'clock. My momentary utopia was sobered out of me the next day when I read the newspapers. I had carefully prepared a statement to the commercial press: "This pie should be seen not only as a protest against the guru, who I consider a fraud, but also against what I consider to be thousands of years of illegitimate religious authority." The *Detroit Free Press* quoted me as saying, "I hate authority. God is an authority. Therefore, I hate God."

What I thought was a perfectly quotable anarchist statement for all time was instead twisted into a grotesque statement of someone who is insane, or worse. The *Free Press* used this misquote to attack me in the editorial page the next day as a racist and religious bigot. They said that the "guru only came to town preaching brotherhood and peace, which Detroit needs so badly, only to be insulted by a misguided and confused zealot."

Of course the *Free Press* had no way of knowing that people would pay good money a few years later to kidnap their own children from the guru and other cults and have them "deprogrammed," because they didn't investigate him. But they did investigate me, and I still don't know if it was merely sloppy reporting on their part, or an attempt to get back at the alternative press for our constant harping about them and the commercial press at large. A revolution is never without enemies.

A week later, however, I was vindicated, because the press had to report that I was beaten and almost killed by two of the guru's disciples, who attacked me with crowbars and crushed my skull. This was the first battle in the war against cults and represents a real "scoop" by the alternative press. Because the New Left and the alternative press were really at the forefront of peace and equality in the early seventies, we had to constantly be on guard against opportunists attempting to co-opt these trends for personal, political, and corporate gain.

Back to the Presses

The notoriety of this pie-throwing incident helped expand interest in the alternative press, and that is one of the reasons we did it. *We* did it, as I've always insisted, because, like everything associated with the *Fifth Estate*, the pie-throwing was a collective effort. I depended on others to help defend me physically, and also the paper retained a lawyer and guaranteed me money for bail, fines, and other related expenses. In fact, while I was being besieged by howling gurunoids in the council chambers, one of my comrades knocked down two assailants who would have hemmed me in. I would have been torn up badly if that mob had caught me in the aisle.

But everything the *Fifth Estate* did was a result of collective effort. As I said, we wanted to prove that we could manage a business without a boss, demonstrating in practice one of the concepts we professed: workers' control, or self-management. We *had* to prove that anarchy was not chaos, not pie-in-the-sky (or in the face) idealism, but a form of organization that is viable, practical, and desirable.

Working on the *Fifth Estate* showed that I could be imaginative and daring as an individual while still functioning within a socialist group. We were then at the crossroads of many political movements and groups, and for the sake of internal harmony maintained an "independent socialist" philosophy. All of us were convinced that some sort of socialist form of organization must replace the capitalist structure on a national and local level. Some staff persons were hardcore anarchists, but some were active in Communist or Socialist parties. A few of us were even liberals, working for a more benign capitalist government. The *F.E* was so fluid, it was constantly reflecting the personal evolution and transformations of about thirty or more part-time and full-time writers.

But we did function as a classic anarchist group, in the sense that we didn't, in principle, affiliate with any outside group or party, and we did not have any chairman or editor in chief. Instead, we voted on every decision, and even edited each article collectively. This did indeed make for lively arguments, and, I think, contributed to a creative atmosphere, providing one had a thick skin and could defend one's own perspective.

The topics we wrote about reflected this diversity and combativeness. We would publicize such events as gay rallies, drug busts, feminist activities, antiwar efforts, union strikes, government corruption, new publications, films, and art gallery openings. At the same time, we never hesitated to cross horns with other groups in the New Left movement and, in fact, considered it necessary, in our role as newspaper people, to help foster internal criticism and debate, as well as to confront frauds and opportunists on the left.

For instance, during the Patty Hearst debacle, when she declared her mission to join the SLA (Symbionese Liberation Army) and then joined them in bank robberies and social-ist communiqués, I contrived, and we printed, a "Patty Hearst Look-Alike Contest" that savagely ridiculed her and the SLA, and which was reprinted in other alternative papers. Another staffer, Bob Moore, maintained a media column that constantly rated and berated commercial and socialist radio, television, and print media.

The *Fifth Estate* was only one of many alternative papers, and I was only one pie-thrower. Aron Kay, a Yippie from New York, pied George Bush in 1974 while Bush was CIA director. Numerous mayors and small-town politicians around the country have been pied since, and I hope the tradition continues. I won't pick up the pie again, because its singular use was appropriate for the time and I find its echo in numerous performance art pieces that have merged theater with life—but that's another topic. Besides, becoming a cult hero goes against the grain of an anarchist-communal viewpoint and would have vulgarized and trivialized the purity of that particular moment.

Thus, when that very *Free Press* reporter who had misquoted me called to tell me he had been commissioned by *Rolling Stone* magazine to do a cover story on me, I refused to cooperate. It reflects the mercenary nature of the commercial press, and a lack of integrity, that a reporter can switch sides on an issue abruptly and without consequence to himself while his subject's very life may be radically influenced by his coverage of events.

The major function of the underground press was to scoop up the life that falls between the cracks of our dehumanizing, corporate mass media and to publish information in defiance of that press and the large corporate advertisers who influence its tone and content. The shareholder-owned Detroit commercial press has Chrysler Corporation and Ford, for instance, who profited handsomely in the manufacture of tanks and army trucks during the Vietnam days. So the *Fifth Estate* people were not surprised when certain antiwar demonstrations were never reported by the *News* and *Free Press*. We could also write virulently against the oil companies and the food processors, or against union-busting firms that the *News* and *Free Press* conveniently overlooked. We would even reject lucrative advertising money from companies we thought to be sexist or racist or big war supporters. Needless to say, we never made any money, and that no doubt contributed to our attrition.

Some of the issues we confronted and prompted seemed too fringe or extreme for the commercial papers at the time, but we can see now that we were merely ahead of our time. We remember when nuclear power seemed inevitable and how we were labeled kooks for opposing it. We were advocacy journalists, a new concept at the time, and promoted feminism, gay liberation, nuclear disarmament, and other facets of the waves of change. We didn't start these movements, but we actively publicized groups and events that worked toward progressive change when the commercial media ignored or ridiculed them. Much of what we helped accomplish is taken for granted now, and our ideas have influenced the mass editorialists who are still trying to catch up with the waves of change that occurred in the sixties and seventies.

One of the best examples of the damage caused by the negligence of the commercial press is the present ecological crisis. It was the alternative press that warned, even screamed, of the dangers of a mass-consumption society—of off-shore drilling, factory pollution, and uncontrolled growth. As the greenhouse effect starts exacting its toll on the world, I get no personal satisfaction knowing that my own small efforts for ecology were ignored or scorned, but I sometimes wish I had been wrong.

If the efforts of the men and women of the underground press haven't succeeded in overthrowing capitalism or disarming the militaries of the world, they may have at least spared Nicaragua and other small countries from invasion by Old Glory. We helped stall the nuclear industry. We helped the women's movement get respect and helped swell its ranks by covering feminist events in the early days when no one else would. The list of victories goes on, but the struggle for ideas is a continuous process and *our* best hope is that our contributions may have influenced other people to continue the struggle in whatever societal roles they play today.

America is still dominated by the interests of enormous corporations, and by a vast bureaucratic government that is actually remote from the average working person. The newspapers in this country, already huge corporations, are themselves merely links on a chain pulled by overlapping mega-corporations that may own several factories, oil companies, and international investment firms as well.

Today the media is still the "watchdog" in America—but for big business, not the common people. The *Fifth Estate* and a few other small presses still exist, but in emaciated form, a victim of the times. I do hope, and dare predict, that the underground press will rise again, to greater heights and influence in the future. The ecological and political awareness fostered by the alternative media has affected society and we can see its influence. But a few generations down the road? New wars and new issues, plus the inevitable destruction of a capitalist system that *requires* continual growth, will necessitate another popular uprising.

I know that someone will be there to challenge unbridled power and to fight against the enemies of freedom and natural integrity. I know because it has always been such fun all along.

Fag Rag: The Most Loathsome Publication in the English Language

CHARLEY SHIVELY

It's been over four decades since that Friday evening, June 27, 1969, when New York City police raided the Stonewall Bar on Sheridan Square; instead of going quietly into the waiting vans, the motley crowd of queers and queens attacked the police. Stonewall was closed, but sporadic street rioting continued in Greenwich Village for the next few days. The event quickly became the Bastille Day of an emergent, nationwide gay and lesbian liberation movement.

In Boston, the Gay Liberation Front (GLF), through a publications collective, would soon be putting out *Lavender Vision*, *Fag Rag*, Good Gay Poets books, *Boston Gay Review*, Fag Rag Books, *Street Sheet*, and numerous broadsides, posters, and flyers. Boston's GLF participated in its first demonstration March 15, 1970 (against paying taxes to support the Vietnam War), organized a community center, maintained a hot line, and carried on wildly. As a formal organization, Boston's GLF had ceased to exist by 1973; however, despite the obstacles of gentrification, police repression, plagues, and paradigm shifts, *Fag Rag* continued into the nineties. What will happen in the 2000s we can't predict.

Like the New Left, the Gay Liberation Front both benefited from and repudiated groups that had struggled through the dark ages of the fifties and before. During the 1920s, gay papers in Paris and Chicago were seized by the police. Catholic deputies of the Third French Republic succeeded in destroying *Inversions* (1924–1925). Of the two issues of Chicago's *Friendship and Freedom*, every single copy has been lost or incinerated; those working on the paper were arrested. After the 1873 Comstock Law, printing presses and post offices in the United States were closed to any publication that did not denounce homosexuality. The district attorney in Boston prevented publication of an 1882 edition of Walt Whitman's *Leaves of Grass*. In 1928, Radclyffe Hall's *Well of Loneliness* was declared "obscene" and banned in both London and Boston; Hall and her lover fled England. Even such relatively uncloseted figures as John Addington Symonds, André Gide, and Jean Cocteau first published their defenses of homosexuality (*A Problem in Greek Ethics*, 1883; *Corydon*, 1911; *The White Paper*, 1928) anonymously and/or privately.

As late as 1958, the U.S. Post Office excluded any publication that favored homosexuality.

In 1954, they busted *One Magazine* (1953–1968), a journal allied with the homosexual liberation Mattachine Society. The lower court judged *One* "obscene, lewd, lascivious and filthy"; the appeal judge called it "cheap pornography." In 1958 the Supreme Court overturned the lower courts without comment. Even so, in 1960 postal inspectors reported several Smith College professors for receiving homosexual publications. The most famous (Whitman biographer Newton Arvin) was allowed to retire quietly; he died while the cases were still in the news.

What a contrast with the sexual liberation of the sixties. When district attorneys went after magazines and newspapers, prosecution increased circulation. Boston's *Avatar*, for instance, was busted for using the word "fuck," and in 1964 the *Evergreen Review* ran afoul of a Long Island DA who got excited over a picture. They published my own thoughts on the DA's "Browning Evergreen 32." The poem called for closing "the (too oppressive) printing press / . . . Let's worship together / (without sex) and / play the electric (forgetting / the human) organ."

In his 1964 defense of the *Evergreen Review*, Edward Steichen didn't mention browning (anilingus) or playing with one's organ: "If human beings in the act of making love are indecent then the entire human race stands indicted. As long as the act of lovemaking is in itself not declared illegal and the extermination of the human race presented as a goal of civilization, lovers will continue to make love and babies will be born and it will be interpreted by the artist." Of course, "homosexual acts" were then illegal in every state except Illinois, which decriminalized such acts in 1961. In the same issue in which my poem was published, there was an advertisement from *One Magazine* for "The Homosexual Viewpoint." I'm not sure why I didn't send my dollar along for a sample copy. I had few reservations about my sexuality and certainly had no plans of making babies. I was reading Allen Ginsberg, John Wieners, Jean Genet, William Burroughs, and Simone de Beauvoir's *Must We Burn Sade?*

What I needed to pull me into gay consciousness came only with the Stonewall Rebellion. On the night of the uprising of gays against the police in New York's Sheridan Square, I wrote "Exiles' Kingdom":

1.

flower exile
filament
broken stalks
washing memories
together bracken
water lilies
disengaged
sport spurt spear
spree spent heads
wiggling for
more time

2.

Soon flowers
soon cut sleeves
open bouquets waiting

waiting awhile longer
everywhere flourishing
flooding child
finding foot
flowing mountain
milk final finial
flood food floor
homecoming earth
suncaked
sunflower
shelter seed
room soon will
soon will bloom
another lagoon
other kinds of
kingdoms come

(June 27–28, 1969)

I first learned about Stonewall in *WIN*, the counterculture War Resisters League magazine. I began attending Boston's Student Homophile League, whose Wednesday-night political group quickly evolved into Boston's Gay Liberation Front; the GLF group participated in the Black Panthers' Revolutionary People's Constitutional Convention and organized both a publication and a community-center collective. The principles put forward at the RPC conventions in Philadelphia in September and in Washington, DC, two months later drew on gay experiences and in turn provided direction for GLFs around the country.

In November 1970, Boston's GLF published the first issue of *Lavender Vision*, with a staff that was half lesbian/half gay male. Soon after it appeared, most of the male staff members moved to San Francisco; the lesbians wanted to use the name *Lavender Vision* for an all-lesbian publication (issue number 2 came out in April 1971); the remaining male publication collective then adopted the name *Fag Rag*. Our first issue appeared in June 1971 in time for the New York Gay Pride March to commemorate the Stonewall Rebellion.

Fag Rag was one among a whole network of GLF papers that included New York's *Come Out*; Detroit's *Gay Liberator*; Toronto's *Body Politic*; Berkeley/San Francisco's *Gay Sunshine*; Washington, DC's *The Furies*; Oakland, California's *Amazon Quarterly*; and many more. All these publications offered a brisk brew of sexual liberation, anarchism, hippie love, drugs, peace, Maoism, Marxism, rock-and-roll, folk song, cultural separatism, feminism, effeminism, tofu/brown rice, communal living, urban junkie, rural purism, nudism, leather, high camp drag, gender fuck drag, poetry, essays, pictures, and much more.

Publication could be an act of liberation, an act of publicity for those outside the centers of power. Passive consumers of the various media came suddenly both to record and to create another reality. Even now, the original 1969 lesbian/gay liberation viewpoint is largely excluded from popular consciousness. Jill Johnston of *Lesbian Nation* wrote that the existing media provides "more an obstruction than a channel . . . somehow the incoming information is blocked or distorted instead of passed through intact or at all. the media is its own agency. or else it's a strict customs agency and very little cargo is permitted to pass." Even counterculture rags would at best allow an issue or a column for what they saw as a marginal viewpoint; they themselves struggled under the conservative putdown that the counterculture men were all pansies and the women all lezzies ("freaking fag revolution").

Divisions and Unities

Often painful conflicts arose from the individual desires of women, African Americans, gay males, lesbians, and other groups to separate into their own collectives. Such separation was needed because of the long history of oppression, silence, and suppressed consciousness. Separation came both from hostility found in self-styled comrades, and from frustration in developing a self-consciousness. Profound contradictions around race, gender, and class could not just be glossed over with well-meaning but otherwise meaningless professions of a common struggle. A *Fag Rag* number 8 (Summer 1973) editorial declared, "We have to create our own existences; we have to create our own media; we have to create our own community." A first step was to find out who "we" were; what "we" wanted; who our enemies were, who our friends were; what our history was; what our future was.

Fag Rag's first great separation was to accept a division between gay men and lesbians. *Fag Rag* never pretended to speak for more than a small group of gay men; the intellectual and political imperialists, on the other hand, want to speak for vast bodies of people, who are actually de-voiced by being conglomerated into a whole of which they are not an active, participating part. *Fag Rag* did not create the separation between men and women, and *Fag Rag* never pretended that this separation was meaningless. Where sexuality is not an issue, coed groups make sense, but the sexuality of gay men and lesbians cannot be homogenized easily.

Although a seemingly trivial issue, the different positions of men and women in body exposure cannot be covered over. For instance, at dances, some women do not feel comfortable exposing their breasts in front of other men—particularly bisexual men. And some are not happy to see men nude; the cock could represent both patriarchy and rape. Since some women don't want to expose themselves in front of any man, some demanded rules against men going topless (if not bottomless). Part of this attitude comes from a long heritage not of our making: straight men love to watch lesbians, but they freak out when they see two men making out. Women, on the other hand, have less often enjoyed watching men make out (although there is a report of one group of university wives who meet together to watch gay male porno movies). In the heterosexual society, women who expose themselves are likely to be raped; men who expose themselves are likely to be arrested for indecency.

Among lesbians, some women feel uncomfortable with men around; other women seek their companionship. Likewise, among gay men, some are more companionate than others with lesbians. In addition, both lesbians and gay men relate to straight men and women in diverse ways. Homogenization tries to paper over these differences and say we are all one big group; such homogenization would wipe out differences. These differences are like dialects, which television attempts to eliminate in order to develop a single market for advertisers and manufacturers. The more separate groups there are, the better chance we have of surviving. While separate groups are needed in order to develop freedom on both sides, combinations can be made. Thus *Fag Rag* participated with a group of women who began a lesbian journal, *Bad Attitude*, the first issue of which appeared with *Fag Rag* number 41 in 1984.

A group from *Fag Rag* participated in the 1971 protest at Atlantic City against the Miss America contest. Among the groups protesting was the Vietnam Veterans Against the War. Their flyer framed the position of women, men, and Vietnamese: "How to Dehumanize: a woman . . . enter her into a beauty contest where she is an object to be admired for her ability not to say or do anything significant; a man. . . . enter him in the military where his individuality is crushed and where he learns to respond to the order of KILL!!!" And how to dehumanize "Vietnamese women or children . . . emphasize their slant eyes or their 'funny' way of life. Equate their poverty or hunger with laziness, call them GOOKS. Depersonalize their humanity to the point that they are no longer human and they become the casualties, killed by American MEN."

Feminism provided a perspective for *Fag Rag* no less than the Vietnam veterans. Allen Young, an early member of the *Fag Rag* collective, wrote that "Gay liberation without feminism . . . cannot really deal with the source of homosexual oppression. For that source is the system of sex roles propagated by a male supremacist society." GLF groups met in consciousness-raising and study groups that were based on the model of women's groups, which themselves were based on models from the Chinese Revolution of speaking bitter tears. The links between racism, sexism, class oppression, and homophobia were studied in our groups, in our own lives, and in the society around us. One day, while we were riding in a '69 Volkswagen Bug, one of the early Mattachine Society leaders from Washington told me quite firmly that consciousness-raising groups were a waste of time. First we must become liberated, he insisted. Then we would have time for the luxuries of self-examination. I said that without changing our consciousness, we would only recapitulate existing oppressions.

Style has remained an enduring division, even though fashion changes every day. Men wearing "women's clothing" have petrified many faggots and not a few women; that the lines can be crossed so simply confuses philosophers who want clarity and stability in their systems. In *Fag Rag* number 3, we ran an interview with Boston's most famous drag queen, Sylvia Sydney; and several *Fag Rag*'ers—such as Clover, Maya Silverthorne, Mijo, myself, Teddy Mathews, Bunny LaRue, and John Wieners—participated in cross-dressing on stage. Here is another division not of our making and perhaps more rigid in the first decade of the 2000s than in 1970. For instance, in businesses, the military, and universities, women can wear suits or ties, but few men can survive unless they approximate the looks of straight men.

Another division (likewise not of *Fag Rag*'s making) was that between the bar gays and movement gays. Some distinction was made by many Gay Liberationists between "gay" and "homosexual" in the early seventies. Being gay was being liberated; being homosexual was being retrograde. *Fag Rag* from the beginning tried to avoid alienating or attacking vulnerable parts of the gay community: hustlers, drag queens, boy lovers, bath orgiasts, bar queens, leather, rest area/tea room, and bush players were often condemned by Gay Liberation Fronts. In the first editorial (see sidebar 1), *Fag Rag* called for the creation of a new gay community: "We realize that it is very easy for any group of people to become elitist and cut off from the very people they claim to speak for and about. . . . The fact that we are in Gay Liberation does not mean we are liberated, it means instead, that we are working towards liberation."

SIDEBAR 1

AN OPEN LETTER TO GAY BROTHERS

It's taken a few months to get this newspaper together. We've worked hard writing articles—informational and opinionated, taking photographs, laying out the paper. It's been especially difficult deciding what format, information, and opinion is most relevant to the Gay Community. We realize that it is very easy for any group of people to become elitist and cut off from the very people who they claim to speak for and about. We feel that the future of this paper will depend very much on your feelings and interest.

It may be naive of us to expect that people will take the time to verbalize their criticisms, but the movement for the liberation of Gay People should not belong to a small group of people with exclusive ideas. It is up to you to broaden the scope of a newspaper and the range of activities of Gay Male Liberation with your criticisms and ideas. It's not easy to accept criticism, but this is the only way we can grow, and relate to a wider range of people.

We spend lots of time in Gay Male Liberation talking about the separation we feel from the larger Gay Community. This separation seems to come in part from a whole set of political beliefs (and rhetoric we use to express those beliefs) which aren't shared by many Gay People. But there seems to be a more fundamental reason for this separation—there seems to be an unspoken sentiment among Gay People not in Gay Liberation, that coming to Gay Male Liberation means making a commitment to a certain set of political beliefs, to a certain kind of life style, most particularly a commitment to being open about Gayness all the time. This is not true—all of us live with pressure all the time, though most of us believe in theory that we should be open at all times, we often aren't—for fear of losing a job, a home, a straight friend, just for plain fear. The fact that we are in Gay Liberation does not mean we are liberated, it means instead, that we are working towards liberation.

It has been a lot of fun doing the newspaper together, sharing ideas, gaining insight into each other's experience in "coming out" and discovering the perspective of the American academic and public attitude toward Gays. We are coming closer together, overcoming fears about being Gay and attempting to create more of a communal feeling among people.

On the following page is an address and some telephone numbers which can be used to direct any comment or criticisms about the newspaper and Gay Liberation activities. Of course, this does not preclude personal contact with members of Gay Male Liberation as a means for criticism.

GAY LOVE TO ALL

Reprinted from *Fag Rag* 1 (June 1971), by Mark Heumann and Kevin McGirr.

Those who have worked on *Fag Rag* over the years have come from diverse political directions. All have shared in some ways in the African American liberation; in the antiwar movement; in the student revolts. And all took up a call for revolution rather than simple reform. The "front" in Gay Liberation Front came from the Algerian and Vietnamese Liberation Fronts. One of our marching slogans was "Ho Ho Homosexual, the ruling class is ineffectual; Ho Ho Ho

Chi Minh, the NLF is going to win." Protesting U.S. bombing in Laos and in North Vietnam, the collective participated in the seizing of the local NBC station during the evening news. Inside the station, a statement was read (but not broadcast because they went off the air for half the program). My task in this action was to call other stations, tell them what was happening, and then hang up. As instructed, after I had finished my calls, I ate the phone numbers.

Fag Rag, of course, never endorsed any political candidate and never believed in begging the ruling class to grant us concessions. The closest we came to ever adopting any specific program was our "ten-point demands" (see sidebar 2), which were derived from the September 1970 "Statement of Demands from the Male Representatives of National Gay Liberation" at the Revolutionary People's Constitutional Convention in Philadelphia. Wearing a leopard-skin robe (handmade by Larry Anderson), I read *Fag Rag*'s 1972 version to the Democratic Platform Committee, and the demands were widely distributed in the demonstrations at the Miami conventions in 1972. Point 8 called "for the return of all United States troops to within the United States borders as the most effective way to end American imperialism." Number 10 concluded globally: "We call for the self-government and self-determination of all peoples irrespective of national, sexual, party, race, age or other artificially imposed categories. . . . All coercion and dominance must end, equality must be established and we must search together for new forms of cooperation."

SIDEBAR 2

BOSTON GLF'S 10-POINT DEMANDS PRESENTED TO THE DEMOCRATIC CONVENTION IN MIAMI BEACH, JULY 1972

Boston GLF urges that the following principles be incorporated in the 1972 Democratic Party Platform:

1. We demand an end to any discrimination based on biology. Neither skin color, age nor gender should be recorded by any government agency. Biology should never be the basis for any special legal handicap or privilege.

2. We demand an end to any discrimination based on sexual preference. Everyone should be free to pursue sexual gratification without fear of rape. Governments should neither legalize nor illegalize these forms of gratification. And no one should be restrained in movement (either immigration or emigration), in employment, in housing or in any other way for being a faggot or lesbian.

3. The United States government should not only end discrimination based on dressing habits but should positively encourage more imaginative clothing. No member of the armed forces or other government agency should be forced to wear a "uniform" to conform to either biological gender or hierarchical position. For instance, if they prefer, women should be allowed to wear short hair and pants; males, to wear long hair and dresses.

4. All economic discrimination against faggots and lesbians should be ended. We should not be denied either employment nor promotion because of our sexual preference

or dress habits. We should have the same tax advantages as heterosexuals living in nuclear families. And like all people, we should have free access to sufficient food, housing, medical service and transportation in order to lead a full and rewarding life. We specifically support a guaranteed annual income of $5,500 for every individual, and we call for a redistribution of the national wealth. Resources and power must be taken from straight, white heterosexual men and redistributed among all the people.

5. We call for an end to all government (or other) research on "homosexuality." Our preference is no disease; all chemical, electric or hypnotic "treatments" to "cure" us should be outlawed. Government funds now being used for "mental health" should be given to groups of lesbians, faggots and other "mental patients" so that they may organize themselves in counseling and community centers to administer to their own needs.

6. Rearing children should be the common responsibility of the whole community. Any legal rights parents have over "their" children should be dissolved and each child should be free to choose its own destiny. Free twenty-four hour child care centers should be established where faggots and lesbians can share the responsibility of child rearing.

7. All lesbians or faggots now imprisoned for any "sex crime" (except rape) should be released immediately from brigs, mental hospitals or prisons. They should be compensated at $2.50 an hour for each hour of their confinement and all records of their incarceration should be destroyed. Lesbians and faggots imprisoned on other charges should be protected from beatings and rape at the hands of their jailors or inmates, and no one should be denied quick release or parole for engaging in "homosexual acts" while confined.

8. We call for an end to all aggressive armed forces. We support the Vietnamese people's Seven Point Peace Program and call for the *total* withdrawal of all United States and United States-supported air, land or naval forces from Vietnam. Moreover, we call for the return of *all* United States troops to within the United States borders as the most effective way to end American imperialism.

9. Within the United States, we call for a disbanding of all armed forces, secret police (FBI, CIA, IRS, Narcotics squads, etc.) and uniformed police. Arms should be used only to protect the people and to prevent rape. For this purpose, we call for the formation of a people's police to be organized by those now most subject to police brutality: third world groups, women, lesbians, faggots and poor people generally.

10. We call for the self-government and self-determination of all peoples irrespective of national, sexual, party, race, age or other artificially imposed categories. Our liberation cannot be complete as long as any person is the property or the slave of another in any way. All coercion and dominance must end, equality must be established and we must search together for new forms of cooperation.

A division between anarchists, Marxist-Leninists, Maoists, and others aroused great excitement in *Fag Rag*'s early years. The *Lavender Vision* came out just after the GML

(Gay Male Liberation) collective returned from the Revolutionary People's Constitutional Convention (November 1970) in Washington, DC. The first two issues of *Fag Rag* carried all the news of the 1971 May Day demonstrations in Washington. Various strains appeared over political differences. Thus the issue of Cuba bothered some of the returned veterans of the Venceremos Brigades. All the copies of *Out Out Damn Faggot* written by members of the 4th Brigade and highly critical of gay oppression in Cuba were "lost" by members of earlier brigades working on *Fag Rag*, but a copy of the play was recovered and published in *Fag Rag* number 3. The gay male liberation group met in the Red Book Store (named, of course, after Chairman Mao's pocket guide to revolution). When their Cuban posters were stickered with "This oppresses faggots," staff members of *Fag Rag* were blamed. We were also blamed when the shawls woven to raise money for the Palestine Liberation Organization disappeared. Some of the divisions from various leftist ideologies disappeared as the leftist groups disbanded or lost interest in homosexuals. In 1972, for instance, the Socialist Workers Party sent organizers into the gay community, but meeting resistance, they departed to organize the handicapped.

A division between cultural revolution and political revolution could be resolved by anarchism, which allows more room for differences. Such a position often developed more by default than from consensus. In *Fag Rag* number 7/8 (Winter–Spring 1974; see figure 1), Larry Anderson summarized the dilemma *Fag Rag* faced with the passing of an active gay male liberation group. On the one hand, he asks: "Is *Fag Rag* a homosexual literary magazine which will publish anything of quality referring to writing style, regardless of content—written by homosexuals?" Or should *Fag Rag* carry on the GML struggle through the publication. "Is *Fag Rag* an anti-racist, anti-masculinist publication from some gay community of thought saying there's exploitation, needless and meaningless insults and belittling rampant in this world and it's reflected everywhere else: we don't need it here; LET'S TRY SOMETHING ELSE!?" *Fag Rag* from the beginning tried to bridge this gap. Poetry and art provided a way of being both political and cultural emancipation, of fighting the revolution, and of realizing self-expression.

Praxis

The difference between publishing regularly and coming out when ready expressed different lifestyles and expectations that cut across political lines. Some hoped to find emancipation from the "straight" press: murders, advertisements, puffs for the government, puffs for the middle class, all delivered on a predictable—daily, weekly, monthly, quarterly, yearly, millennial—schedule. A friend once called up and said, "Oh, I've just been talking with Susan Sontag and she says you're very interesting, but you must come out more often; you must reach a larger audience." While some wanted *Fag Rag* to become famous, others argued on the same point that we had an obligation to the movement both in Boston and elsewhere to provide regular news and comment for "all the shit coming down."

In *Fag Rag* number 1, we never promised a second issue, and throughout our history no one was ever able to bet safely that another issue would be out. Called quarterly from time to time, *Fag Rag* came out four times only in 1974. For a while, a weekly *Street Sheet* was published with regular announcements and news; it was mimeographed, given away free, and widely circulated in Boston. But despite the urging of greater regularity, *Fag Rag* never

FIGURE 1: Cover of *Fag Rag* number 7/8 (Winter–Spring 1974), in which Larry Anderson discussed *Fag Rag*'s attempt to deal with the division between cultural revolution and political revolution. From *Fag Rag* archives.

became a laxative/enema regular; we were loose from the beginning. Anyone want to bet on when the next issue will be out?

In June 1973, the Boston *Gay Community News* was founded. They relieved *Fag Rag*'s *Street Sheet* of having to come out every week, and the two projects came to complement each other. I myself participated in *GCN* from the beginning until its last issue in 1992; I helped edit some articles and wrote for the paper as early as their second issue. In 1974, we rented offices together with some other gay groups (an archives, distribution agency, and campaign offices for Elaine Noble), but while the other groups soon separated, *Fag Rag* and *GCN* continued to share offices. The two groups did not always see eye to eye, however; a paroled prisoner had, in fact, built a wall between the two. In one squabble over religion and heterosexuals, *GCN* objected to our slogans on the wall—"God Is Dead Now Let's Kill the Church" (written by a graduate of Harvard Divinity School) and "Two, Four, Six, Eight: Kill a Straight and Masturbate"—by scribbling words like "infantile" across our part of the office. The *GCN* collective met and voted whether to demand an apology or to expel *Fag Rag* at once. The vote ended in a tie; we didn't apologize, but we did cover our own and their graffiti with copies of *Fag Rag*. *GCN* responded by putting copies of their own paper on the wall.

FIGURE 2: Cover of *Fag Rag* number 2 (Fall 1971): Flaming Faggot issue. A charred copy of this issue hung over the altar at a fundraising and information meeting at Arlington Community Church after the 1982 fire destroyed the office. From *Fag Rag* archives.

Time and common oppression brought *GCN* and *Fag Rag* closer together. During the June 1982 Gay Pride activities, for instance, *Fag Rag* under Tom Reeves's leadership led a march on Boston police headquarters calling for the immediate abolition of the vice squad. The next month, on July 7, our offices were torched by, we believe, a combined SWAT team of off-duty Boston firemen and policemen. Coincidentally, the owner of the building was visiting China with the mayor. (We had found the mayor lingering suspiciously outside our office on the night of June 27, 1979.) Federal investigators took part of the floor to Washington for study, but could only conclude there was no evidence.

The 1982 fire certainly brought us all closer together; the Glad Day Bookstore, *GCN*, and *Fag Rag* received an outpouring of goodwill and community support. With the money raised, new office space was found and new equipment was acquired. At a fundraising and information meeting at the Arlington Community Church, the charred issue of *Fag Rag* number no. 2 with a flaming faggot on the cover (see figure 2) was hung over the altar.

Fag Rag separated itself from both the rest of society and the mainstream of the gay community in at least two ways—in a commitment to poetry, and in the celebration of man-boy love. The GLF began a Good Gay Poets group who first published Aaron Shurin's "Exorcism

FIGURE 3: Cover of *Fag Rag* number 4 (January 1973), one of two issues that included poetry pages laid out by the Gay Liberation Front's Good Gay Poets group. From *Fag Rag* archives.

of the Straight Man Demon." The original Good Gay Poets group included Aaron Shurin, Ron Schreiber, myself, David Eberly, Charles River, and John LaPorta. Collectively, the Good Gay Poets laid out poetry pages in *Fag Rag* number 3 and number 4 (see figure 3). Salvatore Farinella, David Emerson Smith, and Freddie Greenfield helped extend gay male poetry far beyond the ordinary.

From the beginning, *Fag Rag* supported sexual freedom for people of all ages. In 1977, Anita Bryant led a campaign against the sexuality of children and was the force behind the defeat of a Dade County ordinance that would have granted human rights to homosexuals of any age (see sidebar 3). Heterosexuals and many straight-identified homosexuals suddenly turned to identify an age of consent for sexual freedom that would exclude people younger than themselves. Tom Reeves, whose "Red and Gay" was published in *Fag Rag* number 6 (see figure 4), led the battle in Boston against a local Anita Bryant DA, whose witch hunt was stopped by the Boston Boise Committee. Out of that committee, GLAD (Gay Lesbian Advocates and Defenders) and NAMBLA (National Man Boy Love Association) were founded. Tom Reeves's vigorous leadership and forceful articles stunned and startled the emotionally dead, and enlivened and inspired the oppressed.

CHARLEY SHIVELY'S KEYNOTE ADDRESS AT THE BOSTON LESBIAN AND GAY PRIDE MARCH ON JUNE 18, 1977, PROVIDED A FIERY DEMONSTRATION OF *FAG RAG*'S DISLIKE OF HOMOPHOBIC INSTITUTIONS

Boston Bible Burning

Everything that we are
we owe to each other.
What we are
we owe in no way
to the straight society around us.
(Cheers)

I have a Harvard Ph.D., and I teach at Boston State College: they say I'm not fit to teach gay history:

I have here the committee report calling me unqualified.

I have here my Harvard diploma.

They are worth only burning.

(Cheers for the burning papers)

In today's march, we passed by the John Hancock Insurance and the Prudential Insurance buildings: these companies have one hundred, two hundred, a thousand times more space than all the gay bars and all the gay organizations in Boston.

I have here an insurance policy and a dollar bill.

This is what they're worth: Burning.

(Cheers at the flames!)

I have here the text of the crimes against chastity, Chapter 272, Verse 32 of the Massachusetts Criminal Code:

"Whoever commits the abominable and detestable crime against nature, either with mankind or with a beast, shall be punished by imprisonment in the state prison for not more than twenty years."

The laws of the state against us are only worth burning.

(Cheers and shouts of Burn it! burn it!)

I have here the Bible. Leviticus, Chapter 20 says: "If a man also lie with mankind, as he lieth with a woman, both of them have committed an abomination: they shall surely be put to death; their blood shall be upon them."

And "A man also or woman that hath a familiar spirit, or that is a wizard, shall surely be put to death: they shall stone them with stones: their blood shall be upon them."

(Cheers and shouts of Burn it! Burn it! combine with, No, no, Not the Bible: you can't burn the bible.) After the Bible drops into the flames and ignites, an excited demonstrator grabs and stamps on it with his feet.)

Nine million witches have been burnt to death under that verse. And how many gay people we will never know, but the word "faggot" comes from tying us to the feet of the nine million witches as they burned to death, which is what it means to say "burn a faggot."

So, when Anita Bryant quotes those verses, she's talking about our MURDER!

WE CANNOT COMPROMISE; WE CANNOT SINK INTO RESPECTABILITY. Some among us may think you don't have to worry.

those who are Christian can blame our troubles on the atheists and Jews

those who are rich can blame our problems on the poor

those who are white can blame the Black and Third World peoples who are in struggle

those who are conservatives can blame the radicals

those who are well-dressed can blame the sloppy dressers

those who are educated can blame the uneducated

those who are alcoholics can blame the sober

those in their closets can blame the out-front for our troubles

those who have sex in private can blame those in public places

those who are monogamous can blame the promiscuous

those who are celibate can blame the sexual

those who are bisexual can say they only did it for a lark.

We cannot remain alone and terrorized and divided. Because we face a test: a test to see who among us is the weakest, who among us will go first, who among us will be destroyed first.

Some say let the weirdos go, and we will be safe. Perhaps let the radicals go, others say. Send Susan Saxe to jail. *(Shouts of "Free Susan Saxe!")* Some say send the pedophiliacs to jail. Some say send the pornographers to jail.

But when the time comes, we are not going to be asked what degrees we have, how rich we are, who we know or what we have accomplished. They will only ask, "Are you queer?" And when they come for the queers, they are going to come for us all. So. WE MUST COME TOGETHER OR WE WILL SURELY BE DESTROYED.

Reprinted from *Fag Rag* no. 20 (Winter 1977): 31.

Loose Practices

Within the staff of *Fag Rag*, an anarchist commitment to having everyone participate in every part of the paper led to many battles between the more "professional" and the more "amateur" members. This process among ourselves was as critical to us as our public presentations, our poetry, or our struggles against a repressed and repressive society. The "pro" side wanted *Fag Rag* to be better organized, to publish more regularly, to have an office, and to perform the other functions expected of a journal. "Professionalism" also involved what kind of writing got published; the search was for "high-quality" writing, not half-digested, sloppy, lackadaisical work that would be rejected if we did not know the author. The professional also sought "brand names" like Gore Vidal or W. H. Auden. These names inevitably sell papers because they are known and people want to know more about celebrities.

50¢

Boston, Mass.   Fall-Winter   1973

FIGURE 4: Cover of *Fag Rag* number 6 (Fall–Winter 1973), which included "Red and Gay" by Tom Reeves, who led the battle in Boston for sexual freedom for people of all ages against a local Anita Bryant–type district attorney. From *Fag Rag* archives.

The amateur side argued that the people writing the paper were more important than any consumers or audience. They wanted to destroy the dividing lines between author, publisher, and reader. The amateur thought only intermittently about continuity; today I'm working on the paper, but if Alaska or Bolivia strikes my fancy tomorrow, I'll be off. Freedom means not only getting away from established society but also not reduplicating that society's values within the counterculture. In writing, the amateur tended to believe not only "first thought best thought" but also that every piece submitted must be printed—word for word.

When the paper started, most of us had had little experience with publications—except as passive readers. One exception, Allen Young, who worked on several issues after number 2, brought and shared a wealth of experience from the Liberation News Service and his training at the Columbia School of Journalism. Some others had training here and there—mimeography, photography, typing—which we also shared. But for all of us on the paper, *Fag Rag* was a virtual school of gay male journalism. We emphatically tried to have everyone learn to share and do all tasks. Of course, in the rush of typing, layout, and printing, someone with accumulated skills might have to do more.

We never solved the problem of unequal experience. The untrained, on the one hand, often didn't want to acquire any of the accumulated wisdom about layout, writing, typing, and other skills needed to produce a newspaper. Everyone seemed eager to be an "editor" (more often "the" editor) — that is, make decisions about what should be printed and how the paper should be run. But when it came to shit work, some people would be off dancing. On the other hand, the trained often hoarded their skills and enjoyed the leverage they gained over the unskilled.

In writing, for instance, verbal ability is a tremendous asset in getting along. Every middle-class child learns verbiage early and relatively easily; other children acquire literacy only through a struggle. Being inarticulate is a social condition in the United States. I know this firsthand, since my father did not read or write and my mother only finished grammar school. But I have also learned that writing is no magic gift of the gods, given usually to the rich and well-born; it is a learned, communicable technique. (What a paradox: They tell us that the art of communication is incommunicable!)

Editing then raised problems. Some articles need rewriting, need cutting, need criticism, need help. How can that be done without the sheer exercise of power? A poem comes in from a pubescent boy, touching and beautiful, but ends disastrously with his defining his gayness by exclaiming, "at least I'm not a cunt." In a "professional" journal, a secretary (an office here called "corresponding person") just mails out a preprinted rejection slip and that's it. But literary rejection is just as painful and horrifying as sexual rejection. And some of the same games are played in literature as in cruising places. Somebody personally explained to the youth why being a faggot did not necessarily mean hating cunts, but our cutting his poem couldn't help but increase his castration anxieties.

What we have yet to create is a "gay" or "faggot" style of writing. We might be able to finger some writing as alienating, academic, straight, impersonal, and boring — but we still lack a common style, medium, vocabulary, or even literature. There is the Queen's Vernacular, but much of that is more an affectation of a saloon or salon society than a literature. Is it a first step in a new direction? Or is it only false consciousness? Perhaps the postmodern condition allows no common language to anyone? But that condition rapidly eradicates any and all vernacular (except perhaps that of the academics).

Editorial decisions were never easy; we always tried for the anarchist ideal of universal consensus. One trial came around the issue of whether or not we should print an interview with Gore Vidal. Those favoring publication of Vidal found defenders in the *Boston Globe* (January 19, 1974): "Any periodical that won't publish it, no matter what the reason, doesn't deserve to stay in business." In a heated meeting over the article, someone got so overworked that he vomited. The interview ran with a summary statement of misgivings about some of its contents. Less easily resolved was an issue around some of the arguments derived from Michel Foucault that "homosexuals" and "homosexuality" were only recently invented. Although I wanted to print an article by a *Fag Rag*'er who had attended the master's lectures in Paris, the group rejected it and the author left. Eventually, in *Fag Rag* number 29 (see figure 5), Mike Riegle and Giles Barbedette translated from *Le Gai Pied* number 1 (April 1979) Foucault's "The Simplest of Pleasures [Suicide]." The French celebrity's article sparkles with a wonderful irony and wit — quite alien to his many Anglophone imitators.

Typesetting underwent a revolution parallel to gay liberation; the easy access to mass-production printing and the sixties' movements are intimately interconnected. Without mimeograph, xerox, and photographic negatives for printing plates, the underground press

FIGURE 5: Cover of *Fag Rag* number 29, which included a translation by Mike Riegle and Giles Barbedette of Michel Foucault's "The Simplest of Pleasures [Suicide]." From *Fag Rag* archives.

would have been very different. Changes in production between 1970 and 1990 were awesome. Continuing changes into the new millennium have transformed publication and perhaps will eliminate print publication with the various Internet possibilities. Beginning in 1453 when moveable type was invented, type was set by hand; in 1886, newspapers began using Linotype machines. But suddenly, as microchips and other technologies began to flourish, the number of people who could put out a paper vastly multiplied. In 1970, *Fag Rag* had access to the *Old Mole* offices, which included a rented IBM Composer, a machine that had a changeable typeset ball (like the later Selectric) but that could also justify columns (right and left sides flush); to justify, the typist had to type each line twice (once ragged right edge; second time even right edge). We never justified. Everyone struggled through learning the machine; those who knew how to use it passed what they had learned on to others.

When we lost the office and the Composer, we had to fend for ourselves. By a clever improvisation, Mitzel rented an IBM executive office typewriter that used a carbon ribbon and had limited proportional spacing. We then laid out the typewritten pages and had them reduced about 10 percent in size. For *Fag Rag* number 12 (see figure 6), we returned to an IBM Composer. David Stryker had worked many years as a typesetter at the reactionary *Boston*

FIGURE 6: Cover of *Fag Rag* number 12 (Spring 1975). With this issue, *Fag Rag* went back to using an IBM Composer to lay out pages after a brief experiment with an IBM executive office typewriter. From *Fag Rag* archives.

American Herald, but in the mid-seventies, seeing the need for typesetting in the gay community, he started a part-time business. Ken Sanchez, who worked for Stryker, was able to type out *Fag Rag* text (with some volunteer help) after hours; we paid a dollar an hour for using the machine. Stryker's business expanded and he bought a Compugraphic, a machine that used a computer linked to a camera, which produced typeset galleys. Stryker charged basically at cost per issue; still our typesetting costs quadrupled. He saw it as a sacrifice for the movement; others saw it as an inroad of capitalism. The Compugraphic was more expensive and more complicated; only a few *Fag Rag*'ers learned to use it. In one case, when we had typeset John Wieners's *Behind the State Capitol* (1975) on a movement Compugraphic, the entire text faded and had to be reset (because the developer had not been properly changed).

After the 1982 fire, most of the relief money raised was used to buy a used Compugraphic machine, which was used until 1990, when *GCN* bought a new desktop publishing assembly and dumped the Compugraphic in the famous dustbin of history. I learned to use the Compugraphic twice, but never quite mastered it. Desktop publishing almost instantly wiped away all the skills learned on the Compugraphic, and a great gap always existed between the computer-literate and those who lacked access to the machines and the communication they allowed. Even those skilled in one program or machine found their learning constantly obsolete with so-called upgrades, and seldom found training transferable to other machines and programs.

Page-layout skills were easier to learn and easier to share. Each page had to be assembled from galley text, photographs, headlines, page numbers, graphics, and other material. From the beginning, everyone working on the paper took pages for layout—sometimes in teams, sometimes alone. *Fag Rag* layouts were always in the best tradition of the underground, and each person in the collective developed his own style of layout. The unmistakable handwritings—wild, teasing, timid, mean, giggling, quick, slow, sad, lingering, longing, panting, loving, humping, pumping, each quite distinctive—always worked together.

Still, there were some bitter divisions over layout. In *Fag Rag* number 2, some members of the collective felt the cover was too Anglo; others thought it was an exciting long-haired ideal. We finally agreed to run the cover, but we also struggled to include more non-Anglo images in the paper. Visual artists were often uncomfortable with these discussions; they also resented the lack of respect shown for the integrity of their work. Too often, artists felt that others saw their work as only illustrative. For one issue, a particularly verbal person suggested that the editorial for the issue appear on the cover without any graphic. Covers always were agreed on by the whole staff through consensus.

Printers posed many dilemmas for *Fag Rag*. Once we had decided to print in thousands of copies, we could neither do the printing ourselves nor use movement printers. Thus anti-capitalists faced off with the capitalists. A collective had to mesh with authoritarian bosses. They distrusted us (even though we paid in up-front cash) because *Fag Rag* carried no advertisements. One of the printers almost pleaded with us to take ads, do more issues, make more money. They also found it difficult to work with a whole group of people who had to make final decisions about color plates, corrections on the negatives, number of copies to be printed, and other issues. In fact, we all had to quickly learn the mechanism of presenting "camera-ready copy," "screening," "half-toning," "windows," "double-burning," "color plate," "negatives," and other mysteries of the web press. Mitzel even signed up for an adult education class on printing, and we all learned to share our knowledge.

Printers exercise a great power of censorship. Supposedly they are only in business to make money, but about a dozen printers who refused to print us themselves went bankrupt. A half dozen who printed us also went bankrupt. Before *Fag Rag* began publishing, movement papers in Boston had used a sympathetic printer, but by the time of our first issue it had gone out of business (sabotaged by the FBI, according to some reports). One printer refused to print *Fag Rag* because we carried a picture of a nude black man. Another printer submitted our copy to their most conservative daily communicant bookkeeper and asked her opinion. As luck would have it, her son had been a sexual partner of mine and we were good friends. She knew he was gay, and she was grateful for support and legal help the son had received in a rest-area arrest. She reported back that *Fag Rag* did not represent her way of life, but that she believed it should not be censored. We had less luck with a Brooklyn printer, where there was a pressman who was a Jehovah's Witness (with a *Playboy* pinup on his desk) who threatened to shut the plant down if they printed such filth. Another printer claimed that "high school girls" had to handle the material; another said "Bibles run through those presses," without asking our opinion of bibles. In fact, one large midwestern plant told us that "Christians regularly pass through their plant" and they could not risk exposing them to *Fag Rag*.

The contradictions between a revolutionary rag and the market economy appeared even more markedly once the paper had been printed and we faced distribution. For the first issue, we debated whether to give it away free or to charge. By compromise we settled on ten cents as a fair price for those who could afford to pay. The most we ever charged was $3.99. Like Boston's other underground papers, we sold papers on the streets and at gay events. In June 1971, following the New York Gay Pride March, we took home two hundred dollars in dimes. We offered subscriptions for anyone who wanted to send a contribution or a request. Later we offered lifetime subscriptions for five dollars. In *Fag Rag*'s first twenty years, about half our income came from subscriptions, and half from sales either on the streets or in bookstores.

In 1970, few bookstores would carry *Fag Rag*. Outlets run by straights were never very favorable. One corner store in Harvard Square took a stack of *Fag Rags*, but when we came to collect on the bill, they physically threatened us. Another porno store on New York's 42nd Street took the papers, but on the four or so times we came to collect, we were told that only the manager could pay us but that he was not there. Another bookstore in Atlanta (now out of business) said they couldn't sell the paper because it contained pictures of black men. Consequently, we were overjoyed as the example of the Oscar Wilde Memorial Bookstore in New York began to spread, and more and more lesbian and gay liberation bookstores opened their doors. Gay publications helped the gay bookstores, and gay bookstores helped gay publications.

Continuing Struggles

Fag Rag may have entered the market economy and discovered a niche in that market: sex, radical, national (if not international), male, revolutionary, literary, and irregular. *Fag Rag* never faltered in trying to find a voice for faggots and their culture. A new Berkeley, California, magazine (*OUTLOOK*) by contrast promised in its prospectus "something attractive and engaging enough that I could even hand it to a politician—or my mother—and say, 'Here, this is what gay people are thinking about these days.'" Thus the family and state become hidden censors; only god (the third part of the fascist trinity) is not mentioned. Among gay publications, respectability means money and acceptance; but most faggots bypass such sanitized writings as they look for "something a little more meaty." An issue of *Fag Rag* number 9 was placed in the Grolier Bookstore (a store devoted entirely to poetry); a priest picked it up and dropped it in shock when he opened it to Roger Stearns's drawing of a bathhouse orgy.

Fag Rag never tried to placate our enemies or soft-pedal our sexuality. In 1973, I drove some cast members to the University of New Hampshire, where Jonathan Ned Katz's play *Come Out!* was being presented. In return for the favor, I had been told I could sell copies of *Fag Rag*. When an official of the university intervened, I said I'd just give copies away; when he denied that proposal, I said, "Let's just pass them out as program notes" (since the issue contained a review of the play). Police spies at the performance rushed copies of the paper to Governor Meldrin Thompson, the *Manchester Union Leader*, and Warren Rudman, then the state's attorney general. Mitzel's witty article "How to Proselytize" caught their attention. The governor demanded an immediate probe of *Fag Rag*, which he called "one of the most loathsome publications in the English language." (Presumably he considered all publications not in English as loathsome.) The *Union Leader* called for the immediate expulsion of all homosexuals at the university, and in an editorial, publisher William Loeb suggested that god might destroy Durham, New Hampshire, as he had Sodom and Gomorrah. *Fag Rag* was labeled "unspeakably filthy," and the "most rotten, filthiest, degrading piece of literature" they'd ever seen.

The literary/movement dialectic in *Fag Rag* played itself out most pointedly in grant applications. In the first decade of the 2000s, after the barbarian invasion of the eighties, and despite some softening of attitudes in the nineties, few remember the days of the early seventies when the NEA (National Endowment for the Arts) began dribbling funds into African American, women's, and gay publishing. To apply for a grant from the federal government violates fundamental anarchist principles. Lawrence Ferlinghetti of City Lights Books denounced the NEA money as contaminated and contaminating. The money, he said, could be seen as a bribe to buy out militancy and divert revolutionary energies into safer "literary" projects. The arts could be kept on a leash. Publications once dependent on the fed's trough could be brought to heel by leash tightening when the rebels began to get out of control.

Those opting for grants argued that the excluded should demand what was rightfully their own, and that while the government money was contaminated, so were all money transactions. Thus City Lights Books might not take grants, but they did charge for the books and magazines that they published. In their dealings with *Fag Rag*, the bookstore acted like most other straight bookstores: suspicious of gay publications, slow to pay, and reluctant to display.

Those seeking grant support found no easy welcome in the NEA. First *Fag Rag* approached the money trough through NEA's subsidiary CCLM (Coordinating Council of Literary Magazines), which itself was a somewhat defanged organization, less radical than COSMEP (Committee of Small Magazine Editors and Publishers), and thus funded by the NEA. In a 1974 letter to COSMEP, William Phillips, founder of the anti-Communist *Partisan Review* and then chair of CCLM, claimed that CCLM's "aim is to respect and reward quality." "Quality" was then and has remained a term to describe straight, white, middle-class literature, whose "quality" excludes the African, Asian, Native American, women's, or gay voices. CCLM nonetheless played a mediating role between the NEA and foundations that, in Phillips's words, "are afraid of the radical, experimental nature of magazines and 'dirty' things in them."

In 1972, *Fag Rag* applied to the CCLM and they threw our application away (or claimed never to have received it). In 1973, we tried again and were turned down. We then offered (threatened) to appear in person to appeal our gay rage case; consequently, *Fag Rag* received grants in the fall of '74, '75, '76, and '77 and in the spring of '80. But the winds of reaction were gathering. In 1976, a new CCLM director had to fight the NEA for funding of little mags. "One of the reasons we were given for the attempt to cut off CCLM's grant," he wrote, "was that its participatory program created too much trouble and turmoil among the membership."

Fag Rag questioned some of the literary standards of the small presses no less than the grand presses. They lived by a system of mutual back-scratching: you support our grant, publication, whatever; we'll support you. In order to counter some of those politics, *Fag Rag* adopted a rule of not printing reviews or interviews, since they were too often disguised advertisements, or at best, celebrity self-promotion. That rigorously pure stand soon gave way to our sponsoring an affiliate organization, the *Boston Gay Review*, which first came out in the mid-seventies. Although the two rags were independent, they overlapped, and the initial issues of *BGR* were funded entirely by *Fag Rag*. On its own, the *BGR* sold slowly. I asked the manager at the East Side Bookstore (which was then selling about a hundred *Fag Rag*s per issue) why they hadn't sold a single issue of *BGR*. "The word 'gay?'" I asked. "No," he answered, "the 'Boston' kills it."

Boston Gay Review published many reviews of lesbian and gay books. The review set a high standard in reviews of poetry, which were not equaled until the *James White Review* from

Minnesota began publication in the early nineties. And while the CCLM shut off *Fag Rag* for causing too much "trouble and turmoil," they funded *BGR.* The secret guideline for publications then included tranquillity (synonymous with "quality" in their rhyme schemes), but some misread poetry, thinking it incompatible with agitation.

Not only did the group who put out *BGR* overlap with *Fag Rag*, but the two groups also overlapped with the Good Gay Poets. In the early seventies, William Burroughs and John Giorno did a benefit reading in Boston for *Fag Rag*, which led to the publication of a volume of my own and of Sal Farinella's *San Francisco Experience*; that book then led to John Wieners's *Behind the State Capitol* in 1975. In 1976, the Good Gay Poets received a grant directly from the NEA to publish six books of poetry. That was followed in 1978 with another NEA grant to *Fag Rag* for the publication of Arthur Evans's *Witchcraft and the Gay Counterculture*, which had appeared serially in *Fag Rag*.

One of the problems of government grants and of government surveillance has been the tracking. Even CCLM had to report in 1974: "We've been audited four times, and we are an open book to the [National] Endowment [for the Arts], the New York State Council on the Arts, the Internal Revenue Service, the General Accounting Office, the New York State Department of Social Services and the New York State Attorney General's Office." Files! Files! These not only generate information for government agencies but they also train the people to think in terms of double-entry bookkeeping. Andy Warhol's clever exploitation of the government demand for monitoring his life resulted in his delightfully name-filled and profit-making diaries. But the vitiated qualities of our lives and our literatures are revealed in his telling pages; they would have us all become accountants for the Office of Management and Budget.

Whatever the merits of grants, government funds for *Fag Rag* ceased quite abruptly with the election of Ronald Reagan. Reagan simplified the NEA so that artists could clearly identify it and the government as their out-and-out enemy. All magazines and artists should be self-supporting. To become too dependent (whether on government or foundation or spouse or patron) weakens efforts to become self-supporting. *Fag Rag* for better or worse depended on the voluntary labor of its members and on its readers. Publication for the fun of it. The editorial in *Fag Rag* number 27–28 (see figure 7) defended "self-indulgence, living our lives for ourselves, following our own desires, passions, feelings. The opposite to self-indulgence is denial, the theme of all gay oppression."

Fag Rag's relationship to prisons in many ways defined the publication: We did not say no to grant support; we did not say no to individuals who donated money to keep us afloat. But we appealed beyond them to a wider audience, which too many other publications avoided. In every issue we published writings from prisoners, and the paper was sent free to those incarcerated in prison, mental hospitals, or the armed forces. In 1972, among our demands at the Miami conventions was that "All lesbians or faggots now imprisoned for any 'sex crime' (except rape) should be released immediately from brigs, mental hospitals or prisons. They should be compensated at $2.50 an hour for each hour of confinement and all records of their incarcerations should be destroyed." The group took up the cases of many prisoners, such as Eddie Rastillini, who was arrested in 1970 on trumped-up boy-love charges and then killed in prison under so-called "suspicious conditions." The Massachusetts Civil Liberties Union refused even to consider his case, and another, more conservative gay group maintained that he was where he belonged.

FIGURE 7: Cover of *Fag Rag* number 27/28. In this issue, the staff editorial defended "self-indulgence, living our lives for ourselves, following our own desires, passions, feelings," as the opposite of "denial, the theme of all gay oppression." From *Fag Rag* archives.

The link between the sex radicals of *Fag Rag*, the movement of Chairman Mao, and the more acceptable gay movement was, in the nineties, epitomized in Mike Riegle, who held together the Red Book Prison Project, the *GCN* Lesbian/Gay Prisoner Project, and the *Fag Rag*. He was also office manager for *GCN*. (Amy Hoffman's incisive 2007 memoir, *An Army of Ex-Lovers: My Life at the Gay Community News*, discusses the relationship between *Fag Rag* and *GCN*, in particular the important role of Mike Riegle, who was an important figure in both publications; after his death, both publications more or less stopped.) Prisoners are not likely soon to take a cruise to the Caribbean, take in a play in New York, or buy a new waterfront condominium on the Pacific coast. You don't need a market researcher to tell you that they won't buy many cases of Chilean wines or new cars. *Fag Rag* didn't pretend to "help" prisoners, but it did provide a place where this gay voice could speak and be heard by other prisoners. Freddie Greenfield jumped from parole into the collective and was the poetry editor for the next decade, until his death in 1989. His own book, *Were You Always a Criminal?*, was published by *Fag Rag* just before he died. At one COSMEP meeting in Philadelphia at a workshop on prisoner writings, one editor complained of the "poor quality" of writings from prisoners, and said if they just sent in something good, it could be published. Half facetiously, I answered, "If you want to raise the quality of prison writing then you should do some time."

The vision of the sixties was that the old world had died, that the divisions between good (quality, rich) and bad (poor, oppressed) could no longer hold. Some said the first shall be last and the last first; the more secular saw every threat not from the wretched of the earth, but from the established powers who controlled the press and used it to crush life, creation, and beauty. Fewer people have given up than they would like us to believe; and those who say the sixties are dead are only saying their prayers. To understand why we have struggled, you need to feel that continuing hope for a new world, which denied will only rise again. In May 1960, I went on my first march against Woolworth's segregated lunch counters; that November, I wrote the following prison/out-of-prison poem.

MILLENNIUM

tongue clog
drain fountain
bow broken
bed shaken
strictly still
stiff legs running
one day
love lick
lasts only
until passed
sun shadows spin
pieces disintegrate
gold leaves fallen
worm chocked apple
sudden sparrow dead
prison lock melting

The Kudzu: Birth and Death in Underground Mississippi

DAVID DOGGETT

Yes, there was an underground press in Mississippi in the sixties. How could there not be writers in the land of Faulkner, Tennessee Williams, Richard Wright, and Eudora Welty? We called our paper *The Kudzu* after the notorious vine that grows over old sheds, trees, and telephone poles throughout the South. How did it come about that a bunch of Mississippi white kids, descended from rednecks, slave owners, and Bible-thumpers, published for four years in the state's capital a running diatribe of social, economic, and political revolution, a proclamation of sexual liberation, illegal drugs, and heretical mysticism? How does anyone, anywhere rise above the overpowering flow of one's native culture, the suffocating, vise-like grip of the familial and communal, birth-to-death universe view? Why and how is the swim upstream begun, and if it is abandoned, why? Such faltering steps make up the progression of human history.

Since it is the beginnings and the ending of this phenomenon that hold the most fascination, I have chosen to go into some background history leading up to the founding of *The Kudzu*, most of it from a personal perspective. I have also included some discussion of national events, such as the disintegration of the Southern Student Organizing Committee and Students for a Democratic Society, because I believe that ultimately these events were involved in the demise of not only *The Kudzu* but the entire underground press.

From today's perspective, the fifties and early sixties were sealed in an unbelievably complete and rigid conformity, a straitjacket of convention in every area of life, which had been reinforced and tightened on our parents by the desperation of the Depression, the horrors of World War II, the harsh threat of totalitarian communism, and the doomsday fear of thermonuclear destruction. Our generation knew none of this. Even The Bomb had been around since we were born; it was just part of the backdrop of life. The straitjacket didn't fit us, and we slipped out of it. It was simply inevitable that such a smothering blanket of convention would be rebelled against by such a different generation as ours, even in Mississippi.

Sweet Home Mississippi

All the horror stories about Mississippi are true, and more; yet while the reactionary face of Mississippi has appeared monolithic at times, there have always been some few, white and black, who have struggled with progressive ideas. And in spite of its notoriety, in many ways Mississippi is like other places in this country, more so now than before. Mississippi gained some ground in the Kennedy and Johnson years, and the rest of the nation has stagnated or lost some ground in the years from Reagan to Bush II. But before the sixties, there were things about Mississippi that were truly different. Mississippi was extreme. Segregation was state law. Most whites openly professed white supremacy, right-wing militaristic "patriotism," and fundamentalist Christianity. They also had repressive, Victorian sexual attitudes and were oppressively anti-intellectual. Intellectual activity threatened the simple-minded prejudices of the lower class, and for the middle and upper classes, thinking out loud was simply considered impolite. These attitudes were enforced by beatings, jail, lynchings, shootings, and bombings.

I grew up in several small towns in North Mississippi. My father was a Methodist minister; my mother was an elementary school teacher. My first memories are of several small towns in the Yazoo-Mississippi Delta. The Delta is a flood plain that covers the northwest part of Mississippi between Memphis and Vicksburg. At that time it was dominated by cotton and soybean plantations, and over half the population was black. I went to grammar school in Indianola, home of bluesman B. B. King. I went to junior high school in the hill country east of the Delta, in Oxford, home of William Faulkner and the University of Mississippi, "Ole Miss." We moved from Oxford a few months before James Meredith entered Ole Miss and became the first black person to attend a white school in Mississippi. To accomplish that breakthrough, Bobby Kennedy had to call in the National Guard, and there was a pitched battle with young toughs from Oxford and neighboring towns, in which a reporter was killed by gunfire. Guys I played football with were in the mob. In 1964 I graduated from Elvis Presley's old high school in Tupelo, in northeast Mississippi.

As a small boy, growing up in small-town Mississippi had been a Mark Twain–Norman Rockwell heaven, with long summers spent with buddies romping through the bayous catching frogs and turtles, and roaming the forests and fields with 0.22 rifles, taking potshots at small game. But as I entered the world of ideas in high school and college, Mississippi became a hated prison of provincialism from which to escape. I loved classical music, jazz, and folk music, but on the radio was only country music and rockabilly. I read Bertrand Russell and Jean Paul Sartre, but my father was the only adult I ever met outside of a college campus who knew who they were.

In some other decade, like so many other Southerners, I would have simply left the South as soon as possible and headed for one of the nation's urban, intellectual centers. But in the sixties something different happened. People from the urban, intellectual centers came to Mississippi with the civil rights movement. So I stayed for a while and struggled with Mississippi's extremism. While in college in the mid-sixties, I joined up with the black civil rights struggle, "the movement."

My family went back to before the Civil War in the South; some owned slaves, most were too poor for that. Half of my male ancestors at the time of the Civil War died defending the Confederacy, although there was apparently reluctance on the part of some. But by my grandparents' generation, much of the old failed heritage had given way to strong belief in religion and education. My parents were college-educated liberals, dedicated to community service in the church and schools. For them, racism was unchristian. The religion didn't stick with me, but the fervor for good works did.

So if by college I was a thoroughgoing atheist, nevertheless I was passionately concerned with the secular struggle for moral progress, for freedom, equality, justice, and an end to economic disparity. Atheists are the most moral people I know. They act to create human progress, not because they are trying to get into heaven. So, God may have been dead—but without moral struggle, history would be meaningless, just the daily rat race ending in a grave full of dirt. Racism was the product of a history that was not meaningless to me. Slavery and the fight to maintain it was a catastrophe for the humanity of the South, white as well as black, and had taken lives and fortunes from my family. Racism was the vestige of this curse, the old evil still alive—just as Faulkner, Mississippi's historian, whom I met while living in Oxford, told of it. For Faulkner's writing to Mississippians is barely fiction, but rather a more-or-less straightforward telling of our antecedents.

Antecedents I

In 1964 I entered Millsaps College in Jackson, Mississippi's capital. Millsaps is a small Methodist-affiliated liberal arts college. It has a good academic standing regionally and was a tradition in my family. All of my father's five brothers and sisters went there. One of my uncles had been editor of the school paper in the thirties and had done some journalistic sparring with the reactionary Jackson daily papers. My father was on the board of trustees while I was there. During my first year, I joined a fraternity, dated a cheerleader, and hung out at jazz clubs. But it was an act I was not cut out for. During my sophomore year I resigned from the fraternity and moved into a dorm room with Lee Makamson, the only other overtly liberal and political student on campus. Lee was a political-science major from a working-class Jackson family. He said that if he had been alive during the early days of the labor movement, he would have wanted to be involved in that great moment of history. So now, in his own time, he wanted to be involved in the civil rights movement. Together we made contacts From the beginning of my politically active years, I believed that most white people in Mississippi, like most Americans, were good people in their hearts. But they were kept isolated and ignorant by the circumstances of history and the conservative leadership of society. The only solution to the problem was massive doses of new information. Writing and publishing were the keys. Together Lee and I published a few issues of a mimeographed newsletter we called the *Free Southern Student*, which we mailed out to a handful of students around the state, white and black. It consisted mostly of civil rights news. But this really didn't catch on, and we were pretty much ostracized at Millsaps, which like most schools in the South was still languishing in the apolitical, silent fifties.

That same year, I became associated with the Southern Student Organizing Committee (SSOC, pronounced "sock"). SSOC was to the Deep South what Students for a Democratic Society (SDS) was to the rest of the country. In fact, SSOC and SDS became formally affiliated as "fraternal organizations," whereby members of each organization sat as token members on the other's governing council. SSOC had been founded a couple of years earlier by white

Southern students who were originally in the Student Nonviolent Coordinating Committee, SNCC, which was at the militant forefront of the civil rights movement. With SNCC oriented toward the black community, it became clear that there needed to be a special organization oriented toward young Southern whites.

SSOC was headquartered in Nashville, and also had strong groups in Atlanta, North Carolina, and Virginia. Like SDS, SSOC was not a political party with a set ideology, but rather a catalyst for direct action for various left-liberal and progressive causes, and a facilitator for public education about these ideas. SSOC's main activities were publishing literature and holding conferences that brought together people from all over the South. The original focus, mostly civil rights, gradually gave way to discussions of the war in Vietnam and U.S. imperialism, women's liberation, labor issues, and all the other progressive issues of the day. Stokely Carmichael, a major SNCC leader, would show up at SSOC conferences to goad us fledgling white radicals into the forefront of movement issues.

My first big action in the civil rights movement was the James Meredith march from Memphis, Tennessee, to Jackson, Mississippi, in the spring of 1966. Meredith was a maverick and loner, not closely tied to the mainstream movement. He started his march out of Memphis, to urge black voter registration, virtually alone except for the press. As soon as he crossed the Mississippi state line, he was shot in broad daylight, non-fatally. Suddenly the movement leadership flocked to the site and quickly started a real march. Now led by Stokely and others, a rag-tag group of whites and blacks marched through the Mississippi Delta of my childhood, headed for Jackson. They maintained Meredith's purpose of encouraging voter registration among local blacks.

I had been at a SSOC conference in the Smoky Mountains when the march started, and a few of us decided to join in. The cry of "Black Power" made its debut on this march. As Stokeley and the black marchers started this shocking new chant, the minority of white marchers looked around at each other and tentatively raised our fists in solidarity. The climax of the march came just above Jackson in Canton, where we were tear-gassed by the Mississippi Highway Patrol, and many people were beaten with billy clubs and rifle butts. I was quick enough to escape unscathed; but those who were slow to move, including women and a white guy on crutches, were knocked to the ground and severely beaten. I will never forget the sickening sight of those goons in gas masks beating helpless people lying on the ground.

After the march, I passed that summer in Jackson working with Jan Hillegas, a Northern transplant who ran the Freedom Information Service, providing the movement leadership and civil rights attorneys with political research and paralegal work, and who served as a sort of documentarian for the movement.

Trouble in SDS: Part I

At the end of the summer, I went to Clear Lake, Iowa, for the national convention of SDS. While the usual topics of civil rights, the Vietnam War, and U.S. imperialism were discussed there, the most heated debate centered around an issue that had great foreboding. Membership in SDS was going ballistic at that time, and it was clearly becoming the biggest and most active student organization on the American Left. Old Left, doctrinaire organizations such as the Communist Party (CP) and the Progressive Labor Party (PL) cast jaundiced eyes on SDS and saw a grand opportunity for recruitment and manipulation. Without declaring their affiliations, these people were attempting to take over SDS at the local and national levels, and were trying to enter their party lines into the SDS agenda. There was a motion to require SDS members to reveal their affiliations. The people with such affiliations claimed this would be dangerous, given the anticommunist environment in the country. SDS leaders pointed out that the FBI and the government certainly knew these affiliations, so only the SDS membership was in the dark. CP and PL cried "red-baiting." "How can that be?" responded the SDS leadership. "We are the ones in most danger of persecution here; we are the real The danger was not merely that some of the conservative Old Left agenda would be foisted onto SDS at the national level, but that miring meetings in tedious parliamentary battles over the old failed dogmatisms would turn away the thousands of middle-class American college students who were attracted to SDS because they wanted more "participatory democracy." But CP and PL practiced dogmatic centralism. It was a case of fundamentally opposing world views. Nevertheless, SDS was an insecure "New Left" organization and was cowed by the "red-baiting" epithet. The move to require disclosure of outside affiliations failed to carry, and the issue went unresolved. It was a mere opening skirmish in a protracted struggle that would end in disaster for everyone involved.

Antecedents II

In the fall, I was back at Millsaps College in Jackson studying sociology and cultural anthropology. That year, Millsaps became the first school in the state to voluntarily integrate. In a very low-key manner, four black students entered Millsaps. Some minor harassment surrounded this courageous act; most memorable was an incident in which one of the black students' tires was slashed, and my buddy Lee Makamson helped change the tire in front of a jeering crowd of fraternity boys. But Lee had grown disinterested in publishing, so alone I published a single issue of a newsletter called *The Mockingbird*, a play on the name of the official Mississippi state bird. The newsletter generated little interest, and I didn't feel like carrying on completely alone.

Shortly, however, a new dynamic arose: the hippie movement. While the civil rights movement and the New Left had been my only means of escape from the straitjacket of Mississippi, increasingly those few young people in Jackson who might have joined me grew long hair and played rock music instead. Not that they felt no kinship with the movement, but integration was moving along without their help, was actually moving faster than anyone had expected, and black separatism and the violence of ghetto riots estranged sympathetic whites. Also, the New Left leaned more and more toward a theoretical and rhetorical approach that intimidated all but the most intellectually oriented young people. Besides, the new hippie movement was far more glamorous. So, during my last two years at Millsaps, sex, drugs, and rock 'n' roll took precedence over political activism among those few young people in Jackson inclined toward rebellion. The straitjacket fifties were finally giving way to the Beatles and the Stones, the Byrds and Hendrix, grass and acid, miniskirts and the Pill, even in Mississippi.

One incident alone during this period brought the emotional impact of the civil rights struggle temporarily back to the forefront. In the spring of 1967, a sequence of loosely organized events surrounding student protest about traffic passing through the center of the predominantly black Jackson State College campus culminated in the police shooting a local black civil rights worker, Benjamin Brown. A number of facts tended to discredit the official story that Ben was part of a street crowd attacking the police. In fact, he was shot in the back. At best, he appeared to be a victim of typical police overreaction; at worst, he had simply been recognized as someone associated with the movement, and was murdered by a cop.

The following morning, several of us at Millsaps made up some quick placards and organized a march to city hall. We were prepared to march with as few as five students, and were amazed to find twenty people lining up to march. Now this may not seem like many people, but only two of us had ever been in a political demonstration before. And this was Mississippi. Everyone on the march was calling forth completely unknown consequences at the hands of school, family, friends, future employers, and the Ku Klux Klan, not to mention the police, who the night before had gunned down a man in public.

It was the first demonstration of this type in memory, maybe ever, carried out solely by Mississippi whites, and it was a little different from your usual movement march. The president of the junior class, who was also a first-string lineman on the football team, took my placard away from me and led the march, a gesture that I suppose was meant to show it was not just the usual hippie-politicos who were outraged about the killing. I guess I should have been insulted, but of course I wasn't. And the campus karate champ strolled along beside the line to protect us from any threatening bystanders we might encounter. The march went without incident. The police escorted us in a routine manner, almost politely. The public reacted with confusion and shock more than hostility.

When we arrived back at Millsaps, practically the entire student body turned out in front of the student union. Many of them were concerned that we might have been taken to represent the entire school. We replied that we never intended to give that impression, but did anyone really want to defend the killing? There were a few apologists for the police actions, but most people knew in their hearts what had really happened. There was a lot of heated debate, and the scene became intense as white Mississippi confronted itself. That evening, all of our families were dragged into the turmoil when the march made NBC's evening news. The publicity also threw a kink in the school's big drive to raise funds from conservative alumni to match some promised Ford Foundation money.

That march was a powerful experience for all of us. Then something with implications for the future happened. Nothing. As organizers, we blew it. We were unable to follow through with any permanent organization to capitalize on this catalyzing event. Virtually none of the new people on the march wanted to become part of the movement, or SSOC, or the New Left. They wanted no part of our theorizing and rhetoric, our conferences and our fervent writings. The excitement settled back into the previous apolitical stupor.

Trouble in SDS: Part 2

That summer, while working again for Freedom Information Service, I went to an SDS workshop on power-structure research at the University of Chicago, and to an SDS leadership retreat in rural Michigan. The retreat was scheduled immediately before the SDS national convention in Ann Arbor and was supposed to be a strategy-planning session for dealing with the Progressive Labor problem. But Abbie Hoffman showed up along with the Diggers, a sort of hippie community-service group from California, and SDS was harangued for being too stodgy and political while masses of young people were becoming hippies and Yippies, Hoffman's term for political hippies. SDS was catching it from two sides: from the Old Left–style dogmatists, and from the anarchistic Yippies, who wanted to revolutionize even the way political organizing was done.

Back down south, SSOC had a meeting to elect a new chairperson. The founding members of SSOC had by this time moved on to other activities and had left a leadership vacuum. One of the two candidates was Tom Gardner, a sincere but straight left-liberal. The other was Ed Clark, a PL hack from New Orleans. A third group led by Mike Welch of Memphis had recently moved into the Nashville office as staff members. They asked me to consider running. I was flattered but disbelieving. I had one more year of school, I told them—the chair had always been a full-time position. That would be no problem, they responded; it would be good for SSOC's image to have a student chair. What would my platform be? they wanted to know. I was clear on that. I would be Yippie-like; I would bring SSOC out of its straight political past into the wave of the future, the Youth Culture—sex, drugs, rock 'n' roll, and New Left politics. They weren't very happy about that, but they had to defeat Ed Clark of PL, and they had some problem with Tom Gardner that was never clear to me. However, it was all to naught, because the majority stayed true to SSOC's roots and voted in Tom Gardner. It was an odd meeting, and I came away perplexed.

The Quickening

That fall at Millsaps, the political atmosphere finally began to heat up. We decided to start a "Free University" off campus. Bill Peltz, a cultural-anthropology instructor who had the year before come from Columbia University, joined the effort. We would have "courses" that would be self-taught discussion groups on everything from revolution to poetry. Someone stole the fraternities' freshman mailing list, and we sent out a mailing about the Free University to the entire incoming freshman class. The Millsaps administration ended up with copies of the letter and "freaked out," as the vernacular of the time so aptly put it.

A new president, business professor Benjamin Graves, had recently been brought in to kick off the big Ford Foundation matching-grant fund drive. He summoned three of us Free University ringleaders to an intimidating meeting of the entire administration and the faculty department heads. There, he began to lecture us at great length about being irresponsible and jeopardizing the fund drive. He had no grounds for any action against us; he just wanted to browbeat us into submission. As he droned on and on, our liberal friends on the faculty shuffled their feet in embarrassment but failed to come to our defense. We could see he did not expect and did not intend to allow a response from us; I realized I had to call his bluff. When he failed to recognize my attempts to respond to his harangue, I interrupted him in mid-sentence and gave an impassioned speech, the gist of which was that fundraising to pay for an education that discouraged free inquiry was a moral travesty against the spirit of the institution and the founding principles of the nation. It was clear we would not be so easily intimidated. The meeting came to a strained conclusion.

We were a new breed of students. The administration had never seen such brash independence. The academic dean called up my parents and told them he thought I had mental problems and that they should take me out of school and seek psychiatric help. He even suggested a Jackson psychiatrist. My parents, bless their hearts, didn't go for it. They were having their own problems with my rebelliousness, but they knew I was not insane. We talked it over and decided to again call the administration's bluff. I would be examined by an out-of-town psychiatrist of our own choosing to settle the matter. I visited a psychiatrist in Memphis, where I went through a few standard tests and explained the situation in Jackson. He reassured my parents I was fine, and he wrote a letter to the Millsaps administration giving me a clean bill of health.

Thus the Free University got off to a fiery start. Unfortunately it was overly ambitious and fizzled out before the semester was over. Nevertheless, the New Left had finally arrived in white Mississippi. In addition to this new political development, there was by now a very visible contingent of hippies on campus. In the spring, the administration announced their intention not to renew Bill Peltz's contract. The alumni had gotten upset about his research into social change in Mississippi, and the administration was uptight about his fraternization with the most rebellious elements of the student body. In response to this and other issues, a number of us began publishing a little mimeographed publication of satire and comment called *The Unicorn.* Unlike my previous publishing attempts, this one was immensely successful. I'll never forget the experience of walking into the school cafeteria right after the first issue had been circulated and seeing a huge room full of people actively reading our writings.

The trick that made it all so different from our previous attempts at publishing, the trick it took the hippies to teach us, was to break the mold of the political tract, to make the publication more general in appeal and content. We had access to an electronic stencil maker that could copy illustrations, so we had artwork and cartoons. We also included poetry and music commentary. Writers from the censored school paper wrote for us. Everyone on campus read *The Unicorn.* We could have made money if we had sold it instead of giving it away for free. Unfortunately, we couldn't save Bill Peltz's job. He left Millsaps, but stayed in Jackson to set up Southern Media, for the purposes of documenting social change in Mississippi and training local people in documentary techniques. That spring we had an antiwar demonstration involving dozens of students. We called it a Peace Parade, decorated cars with colorful crepe paper, and rode through downtown Jackson like a football homecoming parade.

The Birth

Upon graduation in 1968, I became a full-time organizer for SSOC and was paid a subsistence salary of $15 a week. Underground papers were springing up all across the country, including the South. Atlanta's *Great Speckled Bird* had just started, and many of the staff members were old SSOC friends of mine. I decided that my primary mission as an organizer would be to start an underground paper in Jackson. I felt that there were many young people ready to move in Mississippi, but that they were too cut off from what was happening around the country and around the world. It all came back to my belief that information provides the fuel for progress. I went to Atlanta and lived in the basement of the *Bird* office on 14th Street for a month or two while I learned how to lay out a paper for photo-offset printing. It was a very hot time in "Hotlanta." The yet-unrecorded Allman Brothers played practically every night at a club down the street, and hippies gathered in nearby Piedmont Park.

When I got back to Jackson, I tried to line up a printer. Unfortunately, they were all too expensive, and they looked at me funny. I was the first hippie they had ever seen. Finally my movement contacts put me in touch with a black printer in New Orleans who published the *Louisiana Weekly*, a regional black newspaper. The *Weekly* people were friendly; they let us print on credit; and, most important of all, they couldn't be touched by political pressure from Jackson. The four-hour drive to New Orleans was inconvenient, but it was workable.

When school started up in the fall of 1968, I gathered together about a dozen interested Millsaps students and we started *The Kudzu*. The name came out of a brainstorming session. I forget who suggested it, but once it came up it was favored virtually unanimously. Under the masthead, we would run a trailer: "subterranean news from the heart of old Dixie."

At first I was the only full-time staff member; the rest were students (see figure 1). A mainstay of the staff was Cassell Carpenter, a woman whose family owned Dunleith, one of the premier antebellum mansions of Natchez. My love interest at the time was Peggy Stone, a sophomore also from Natchez. She had long, red hair, and a rebellious spirit to match my own. We had met the previous year when she entered Millsaps. This year her parents sent her to school in Louisiana to get her away from me. But she came to town on weekends and eventually dropped out of school, and we moved in together. Everett Long had transferred over to Millsaps from Mississippi College, a conservative Southern Baptist school. He had just returned from being arrested during the demonstrations at the 1968 Democratic National Convention in Chicago. He was a well-read intellectual, as well as a major source of capricious humor in the early *Kudzu*. Mike Kennedy, another source of humor, was a local high-school dropout who drove around in an old black Cadillac hearse. Our recreational-refreshments connoisseur was Mike Cassell from Canton. He had recently left New College in Sarasota, Florida, under a political cloud. He worked part time for the Illinois Central Railroad, and two years before had unloaded the tear gas that had been used on us at Canton in the Meredith March. Alan Bennett and Jeff Livesay were budding underclass intellectuals who hung around a lot. Doug and Lynn Rogers dropped out of Millsaps and got married. They had a Volkswagen bus and a capuchin monkey. Lynn was an artist and poet, and Doug was an all-around man. Several other Millsaps students, local high-school students, and recent college or high-school dropouts hung around and contributed intermittently.

We took out a post office box as our official address, but we had no real office at first. The first issue of *The Kudzu* was laid out on the kitchen table of Cassell Carpenter's off-campus apartment. It was eight pages, tabloid size. Our goal was to publish once or twice a month. Organizationally, the staff was small enough that a maximum of democracy could be practiced. We decided on the content of each issue more or less by consensus. There wasn't much ideological bickering, simply because we tried to let everyone involved have some space to write whatever he or she wanted. We ran a fairly typical sixties smorgasbord of spacy hippie ramblings, rock-music reviews, cartoons and comics, and straight political coverage of the war in Vietnam, the civil rights movement, labor struggles, and the New Left. Being in Mississippi, we were naturally a little tamer than the *Berkeley Barb* or the *Rat* in New York.

There was no specialization on the staff, and no titles were ever listed with our names. People outside the staff invariably assumed I was the editor, but in fact we never had an official editor. Some people used pen names, some of us used both our real names and pen names, and we sometimes included in the staff box the names of our cats and dogs and completely

FIGURE 1: *Kudzu* staff 1968–69. Standing (*from left*): Everett Long, Cassell Carpenter (Nigel the cat), Mike Cassell, Mike Kennedy. Kneeling: David Doggett (Ivanhoe Ecclesiastes the Mississippi hound dog). According to author David Doggett, "Nigel and Ivanhoe Ecclesiastes regularly made it into the staff box to give the FBI fictitious people to puzzle over. For all I know they both have FBI files." *Kudzu* staff photo by Nancy Davis.

fictitious people, just to keep the police and FBI guessing. We more or less worked on all phases together throughout the publishing cycle. We would write for a few days and have a meeting or two on what was going in the issue. Unsigned articles were approved by consensus, since responsibility for them fell upon the whole paper. Signed articles were considered to be the sole opinion and responsibility of the signer. Individuals frequently took responsibility for whole pages or double pages of layout. We ran whatever state and local material we could come up with and filled remaining space with national articles from Liberation News Service. We freely ran articles, artwork, and cartoons from other underground papers, which was encouraged by the Underground Press Syndicate. Our production facility consisted of a single IBM Selectric typewriter, the kind with the little rotating ball. We started with one ball, and eventually got another one that printed a sort of script italic. The machine had no margin justification or proportional spacing. It was simply an electric typewriter. We took turns typing, everyone considering it one of the more onerous chores. We pasted up the layout with household glue. Typically we finished the layout at five o'clock in the morning, then piled in some claptrap car or VW bus and rushed down to New Orleans to make the printer's nine o'clock deadline.

During the press run, we would visit with Bob Head and Darlene Fife, the editors of the *NOLA Express*, and partake of the pleasures of the French Quarter and hippie New Orleans. At Buster Holmes' Restaurant you could get a big plate of red beans 'n' rice, which always included a chunk of smoked pork or sausage with a two-fisted size piece of cornbread, all for a quarter. Or we would pick up mufalleta sandwiches and some wine and have a picnic in some park. After a siesta, we would pick up our load of *Kudzu*s and haul it back up to Jackson.

When we got back to Jackson with the new edition, we all hand-addressed the subscriptions and then went out to the campuses and the streets to sell papers. Our initial price was 15 cents a copy, of which the seller got to keep half. Everybody on the staff gave all the proceeds back to the paper, but there were a few people at the local high schools and at the bigger college campuses around the state who made a little pocket change in the bargain. We started with no advertising at all, and never got very many ads. Most issues didn't make enough to pay for the press run, much less any staff salaries. If it hadn't been for the SSOC money and periodic donations from my parents, I would have starved.

The Arrests Begin

Our first issue made a big splash at Millsaps, and a few copies found their way to most college campuses around the state. With our second issue, we really took off. Over a dozen arrests of *Kudzu* vendors, including virtually everyone on the staff, were made at a local high school by deputy sheriffs. Actually, the staff never made a conscious decision to sell the paper at high schools, and if the issue had been formally raised, we might have decided not to make direct sales there at all. But before the issue was considered, high school students and recent graduates or dropouts started the ball rolling themselves.

Chuck Fitzhugh, the son of a local Episcopal rector, and Jimmy "Cap" Capriotti were selling *The Kudzu* at Callaway High School in a suburb where they lived just north of Jackson. The principal came out and started jerking the papers out of the hands of students. He then sent for a deputy sheriff who was directing traffic and had the two arrested (see figure 2). They were charged with obstructing traffic, a complete fabrication because they weren't even in the street. Chuck and Cap were released on bail, and the next day the whole staff went back with them to the same high school and attempted to sell papers at the close of the school day. Deputies arrived in force and all eleven of us were arrested. Chuck and Cap were singled out and beaten, although neither was seriously hurt.

Bill Peltz, the former anthropology instructor, was there to document the events for Southern Media. While taking photos of the beatings, he was arrested, his camera was taken,

FIGURE 2: "The shock troops" (*from left*): Jimmy "Cap" Capriotti, Mike Cassell, Chuck Fitzhugh. According to author David Doggett, "We called those three the shock troops because they were at the head of our first wave of arrests for selling the paper. Mike was a *Kudzu* founder and writer. Cap and Chuck were high school students at the time, and were arrested for selling the paper at a high school. It is an interesting comment on how young some of the people were." *Kudzu* staff photo by Nancy Davis.

and the film was destroyed. No charges were given for any of us, which is improper arrest procedure. When I requested that they state what the charges were, I was picked up and thrown bodily into the back of a sheriff's car. They took us to jail and thought up all the charges later.

Eventually all of us were charged with vagrancy and/or blocking traffic. The vagrancy charge was particularly disingenuous, since we were in the act of selling papers for our livelihood. And in further double-think fashion, those who were beaten were charged with assault. Resisting arrest and assaulting an officer were added to my charges, presumably because of my query. My old civil rights attorney friends, with the help of a local liberal attorney, Sebastian Moore, got us out on bail right away. I asked Sebastian how he got involved with the movement. He told the story of how, after some local civil rights altercation, he had walked in the courthouse and found the cops on one side of the hall handling their billy clubs and looking mean, and the young people of the civil rights movement on the other side of the hall, holding hands and singing. Right then he knew which side he was on.

On the third day following the original arrests, we all went back to Calloway, accompanied by over twenty additional people, mostly Millsaps students. We sold every paper we had, and no arrests were made. We had won, and the publicity was priceless. When the cases went to court, the charges were dropped for all but five of us. The officers told a bunch of obvious lies that had no consistency. For one, they all denied having arrested me. The judge gave them a recess to get their stories straight. We put ten witnesses on the stand who all denied the deputies' stories. The judge—who was the state attorney general's brother—upheld the charges. In his concluding speech, he claimed *The Kudzu* was a "propaganda sheet" rather than a "real newspaper," and he lamented the lack of respect for law-enforcement officers. It was clear we were on trial for the content of the paper, not any illegal actions. The cases were appealed and eventually all the charges were dropped, except the two original obstructing-traffic charges. The bond on these, though, was lowered to $25 each, so we forfeited bond rather than waste any further resources on the case. It was really sort of a pathetic Keystone Kops episode.

The second round of arrests came within a month, when four of us were arrested and charged with "pandering to minors." The Jackson city police came at us with crib sheets telling them how to make the arrests. The city felt our use of four-letter words and selling papers to city high school students were grounds for charges. That case eventually made it into federal court before it was dropped.

An accurate account of arrests and major incidents of harassment would take a whole book. We averaged several arrests a month somewhere in the state throughout the first year of publication. Occasionally beatings were involved. There was a lot of petty harassment with traffic tickets. We had good lawyers who always got us out of jail promptly and never expected a fee. A handful of local liberals put up their suburban homes for property bonds when the bail was set high. The charges were invariably dropped. After all, we weren't doing anything illegal. We were just trying to publish a newspaper. After initial minor confrontations over free speech, the major college campuses in the state became open to us; however, a number of the smaller campuses banned us, and we didn't have the resources to open them up.

Equally as troubling as the arrests were the more personal incidents of harassment. A number of college students associated with the paper were financially cut off by their parents. Some high school kids were expelled from school and sent to military academies. The police visited Cassell Carpenter's landlady, and she was promptly evicted. We found other quarters and kept going. Our office was nothing but the front room of a small apartment, and several of us slept in two bedrooms in back. We were afraid to sleep in the front room because of bomb threats.

We lived a stressful lifestyle that was only overcome by youthful exuberance and comradery. We were charged with "vagrancy" and called "lazy hippies," but we worked sixteen hours a day while welcoming a constant stream of out-of-town movement and New Left visitors. There were also a lot of high school runaways, sometimes followed by their parents and cops. We got threatening phone calls all day and night. Once somebody put some shots through our front window. We found the lug nuts loosened on the front wheels of the old VW bus we had bought with SSOC money. On the trips to New Orleans, we had lots of breakdowns and a couple of minor wrecks. When *Rolling Stone*, the rock music magazine, did an article on the underground press, they called us the most courageous underground paper in the country, and said *The Kudzu* had the look of a paper actually printed on the run. Truth to tell, we did not have a slick publication, but we were alive and kicking.

We really didn't think that much about the danger of it all. In those days in Mississippi, just having long hair and doing psychedelic drugs was dangerous. The political danger didn't seem like so much on top of that. We worked hard and played hard. Every Sunday afternoon, we joined an informal gathering at Riverside Park in North Jackson for free rock music and revelry. Sometimes at night we would go out with a dozen or more people to hidden clearings along the banks of the Pearl River Reservoir. There we all stripped off our clothes and went swimming and sat nude around a campfire. Once we had a late-night nude party in a law office in a downtown high-rise. One nude couple rode up and down the elevator, opening the door at every floor just to see if there was anyone there to flash. Fortunately, no one else was in the building.

In the Halls of the SSS

The draft was at its height in those days. Every young male who wasn't in good standing in school was called up. Many tricks were tried to flunk the physical, but few worked. Some people moved to Canada. Liberation News Service (LNS) reported that a memo had been sent around by the Selective Service System telling local draft boards not to draft writers from underground newspapers. Underground papers were springing up inside the armed forces, and apparently the government was trying to minimize that problem. The LNS report sounded too good to be true, and we didn't put much stock in it. I had applied for conscientious-objector status, but I had not stated that I was an absolute pacifist, and I had not heard from the draft board. Then I was called in to take the dreaded physical. I loaded up a satchel full of *Kudzus* and headed to the Jackson draft site on the appointed morning.

When I got there, I began giving out *Kudzus* to all the guys sitting around waiting for the procedures to start. When the officer in charge came in, he was startled to see a room full of inductees with *Kudzus* up in front of their faces. He came over to me and told me to stop passing out the papers, and he ended with, "That's an order."

I looked him in the eye and returned, "We have freedom of the press in this country, and I am not in the army yet, and I don't take orders from anyone." The room went silent as we stared at each other. The guy clearly was accustomed to unquestioning obedience. He had no reply. He finally told me to wait there, and he left the room. He came back shortly and asked me to accompany him to see the head of the center. The top dog explained that if I continued to distribute papers, they would charge me with disrupting the draft procedures, which carried the standard penalty of five years in prison and a $5,000 fine. He handed me a phone and said I could consult with my lawyers. I called one of our lawyers. He said we could fight it in court but we might lose, so I decided to go along with them. They took my satchel of papers and locked them up until I was ready to leave. Then they assigned a soldier to accompany me through the entire proceedings to hold the stack of registration forms they gave me, and to make sure I didn't pass out any more literature. So throughout the physical, I stood there in line in my underpants like everyone else, except there was this guy in uniform standing beside me holding my forms.

I was in good health and couldn't fake any physical problems. And I gave the IQ test my best shot. I didn't want them to think I was a dummy. But in the appropriate boxes, I checked off that I was a bed wetter and a homosexual, and I checked off that I used several illegal drugs, none of which were addictive. They called me into the doctor's office. When I told him I quit wetting the bed as a kid, he marked through that question. Then he asked me if I loved men. I knew they could easily discover I lived with my girlfriend, so I said, "Well, I love men and women." He asked me when the last time was I had slept with a man. In the back of the *Kudzu* office I slept in a room with several men and women, so I said, "Last night." He asked me how often I did drugs. I think I said, "Often." He marked "homosexual drug addict" across the bottom of the form in big red letters, and said he was sending me in to see the psychologist. I went in to see the psych. He said, "We're giving you a temporary deferment." And that was the last I ever heard from the Selective Service System. But none of these kinds of ploys had worked for others. Several *Kudzu* males went in for physicals within the next year, and none were drafted. Maybe there really was something to the LNS report of the memo against drafting underground press people; too bad more guys didn't take advantage of this de facto deferment.

The Beginning of the End

In those first several months of *The Kudzu*, activity rolled along at high speed. The future seemed to be opening up to us. Then, just as we were hitting our stride, politics dealt us a low blow. A call came from SSOC headquarters in Nashville. An SDS national convention was coming up in Austin, Texas, in less than a week, and Progressive Labor was campaigning to have SDS break ties with SSOC and denounce SSOC for being liberal and counterrevolutionary. There had been a lot of discussion recently within SSOC about Southern consciousness, along the lines of black consciousness and women's consciousness, which had both recently become powerful organizing approaches. PL embraced a doctrine opposed to the separate organization of separate constituencies; consequently, PL opposed black separatist organizations such as the Black Panthers, and even opposed national liberation movements such as Vietnam's National Liberation Front. For PL, everyone was either a worker or a capitalist; nothing else mattered. Centralism ruled.

The old reactionary Southern nationalism born with the Civil War was very much alive throughout the South. Anyone organizing in the South came up against it constantly. Few Southern whites still felt slavery had been a worthwhile cause; but most Southern whites had strong feelings about losing the heroic struggle of the Civil War, and about the subsequent economic, political, and cultural subjugation of the region. Outside the South, a southern accent generally invoked patronizing responses. Southerners were assumed to be poorly educated and ignorant, folksy and unhip. White criminals in movies and TV all too frequently had southern accents and were depraved and dumb. There was discussion in SSOC about trying to turn these pervasive feelings of inferiority and persecution into a progressive force.

Nationalism had been a potent force for revolution, from the Bolsheviks to the Viet Cong. In many respects, the South could be considered the first colony of Yankee imperialism. The compelling moral cause of abolition had inspired the Northern states into the Civil War; but the outcome of the war was not only freedom for the slaves but also the economic subjugation of the agrarian South to the industrial North. Far from being truly free, blacks emerged as the poorest inhabitants of an economically devastated region.

In one of the civil rights law offices I had worked in, there hung a color-coded map of the United States, which indicated per capita income on a county-by-county basis. The thirteen states of the old Confederacy stood out clearly from the rest of the nation, and the areas of the South with the highest proportions of blacks were the poorest areas of all. The exceptional poverty of the South, white and black, was so striking that I literally stared at the map with my mouth open the first time I saw it. At the time, I had never heard about Southern consciousness. I learned an entire history lesson in a visual instant. The overt chains of slavery had been loosened, but the boot heel of poverty remained firmly on the black man's neck. The sincerity of the nation in this matter is open to question to this day, as seen in the widespread white hostility toward affirmative-action policies and any discussion of reparations, or even official apologies.

This pattern of sending the troops in for a great moral cause and emerging with a colony primed for corporate exploitation and cultural domination is all too familiar in American history. In such respects, Southerners should feel some empathy with Third World countries, especially, in those days, Vietnam. Was there much difference between General Westmoreland's defoliation of the Vietnamese jungle with Agent Orange and General Sherman's famous burnt-earth swath from Atlanta to the sea?

This powerful line of thought had tremendous appeal to many of us. A favorite SSOC button was a pair of black and white hands clasped in a handshake across the center of the Confederate battle flag. That design was a spinoff of an old SNCC button that had the Confederate flag behind a lantern, which symbolized the light of freedom. Yet that flag and those powerful emotions of Southern pride had for so long been so thoroughly submerged in the whole sordid quagmire of Southern right-wing fanaticism, that the prospect of raising the specter of Southern patriotism made us all a little queasy. We looked on the idea with awe — what an organizing tool! But if the beast of Southern nationalism was called up again, would it not lurch uncontrolled to the right as always before? No one knew the depth of right-wing instincts in the Southern mind better than people in SSOC. We had all been in mortal combat with the monster all our lives.

Thus, although the concept had been discussed at the past couple of SSOC conferences, no one in SSOC had fully embraced Southern consciousness. At one closed staff meeting, an organizer in South Carolina was criticized for participating in the burning of a Confederate flag. Two of the main critics of that action were Lynn Wells, program secretary, and David Simpson, Georgia organizer. Both had taken the discussions about Southern consciousness very seriously. But as I remember, no action was taken against the organizer who burned the Confederate flag. There was no official SSOC policy in place regarding Southern consciousness.

Mike Klonsky, SDS national secretary, had made a hasty junket to Nashville five days before the spring 1969 Austin national SDS conference to check out SSOC. Mostly he had talked with Lynn and David. He was tentatively supporting SSOC. Considering the problems facing SDS, I couldn't believe anyone in SDS cared about this issue. I could understand that leftists outside the South might be uncomfortable about Southern consciousness, so I would have understood if SDS wanted to issue a policy statement against the idea. But to try to destroy SSOC over an issue that was not official SSOC policy was a gross overreaction. About a third of SSOC's forty staff members held a harried meeting in Austin the evening before the anti-SSOC resolution was to be introduced. Lynn and David were panicked. They convinced the rest of us that the only response we had was to thoroughly renounce Southern consciousness and to put on a big show of being contrite over this grave political error. Wow, had they changed their tune. No one was happy about this response, but nobody felt like jumping up on such short notice and trying to explain the whole history and program of SSOC to a hostile SDS convention either.

When we went into the convention the next day, PL hacks from New York and Boston were everywhere putting out a line that made SSOC out to be on the verge of becoming the next Ku Klux Klan. SDSers from California and Minnesota who had never heard of SSOC before were sucking it right in. I suddenly realized we were in deep trouble. Ed Clark and Fred Lacy of New Orleans PL introduced the anti-SSOC motion. PL presented Southern consciousness as a major policy of SSOC. They said it was offensive to blacks and was a transparent sham revealing the true, unreformed, right-wing character of the white Southerners in SSOC. They took a bunch of out-of-context liberal statements on various subjects from SSOC literature of years past and said that this is the way these people talk, they are not revolutionaries. Hell, that was the way everybody in the movement had talked a few years back. But now liberalism was the kiss of death; we were all supposed to be radical revolutionaries now. Politics had become fashion; nothing was as hated as last year's ideology. PL charged that SSOC got money from liberal foundations, some of which received money from the CIA. Again, this was a problem every organization in the civil rights movement had been wrestling with in recent years. It was a twisted attack on SSOC, but it was devastatingly effective.

SDS conventions had become rigorously parliamentarian. Four speakers were allowed to speak for or against the motion, and each was strictly timed for something like three minutes. Mike Klonsky had flipped his position; he got up and complained that SSOC was not sufficiently contrite about its Southern-consciousness error and was liberal beyond redemption. David and Lynn both gave wimpy, apologetic speeches and requested that the motion be tabled until the next SDS convention. I thought we were supposed to have two more speakers, but somehow two slugs from the New York Communist Party that none of us had ever seen before were given the mike. They gave horribly inane speeches to the effect that SSOC was a wonderful liberal organization with a lot of potential if given some help, and thus the CP supported SSOC. SSOC died right there. By this time everyone in SDS hated the CP. The New Left considered them a sick joke. The CP was scorned both for its slavish kowtowing to Moscow all the way back to Stalin, and for its Three Stooges attempts to enter the mainstream of American politics. Nobody else in that room had given a thought to the cesspool of mainstream American politics since kindergarten. The debate was over. The motion passed. SSOC was denounced and excommunicated, and further, SDS vowed to go into the South and organize in competition with SSOC.

This was the beginning of the end—for SSOC, for *The Kudzu*, and for my involvement in the movement and the New Left. I'm not sure when SDS's end had begun, but its final act was well underway, and this was just a small scene from it. There was a final meeting of SSOC in the summer of 1969. About half of the people there were from SDS, including Klonsky and Mark Rudd, fresh from the Columbia University takeover. Their dogmatism and rhetoric overpowered the fledgling Southern New Left. In one memorable moment between sessions, a SSOC woman went up to Mark Rudd and took off her blouse and challenged him, "All right, Rudd, pull off your clothes and show me that you're human, too, that everything you do doesn't have to contribute to the revolution." Rudd responded, "No, everything I do does have to contribute to the revolution, and besides, I like being repressed." Seriousness and guilt won the day. At the end of the conference, SSOC dissolved itself. Within months, SDS itself splintered at the infamous Chicago conference. *The Kudzu*, like the rest of the New Left, struggled on for a few more years. But the vine had been severed at the roots; it was merely a matter of time before the fruit withered.

How could this have happened? One year SSOC and SDS were raking in new members so fast they couldn't keep up with it; a year later they had both self-destructed. There are many layers to this complex tragedy. A major problem, which was obvious to all of us even at the time, was simply the superficiality and youthfulness of the participants. It was a student movement, and as long as it remained that, there was action and growth. Although older people left school and left SSOC and SDS, many of them continued their activism in more permanent activities—community organizing, social work, electoral politics, journalism, civil rights, poverty law, community medicine, teaching. In fact, contrary to the popular media image of sixties activists becoming self-absorbed yuppies, most of the activists I knew in the sixties are today left-liberals involved in low-paying, altruistic professions.

But in the late sixties, when the prospect suddenly loomed of transforming the New Left student organizations into a national mass movement, trouble arose in SDS and SSOC. The Old Left–style organizations, which earlier had been grateful simply to purvey their wares openly in the marketplace of ideas for the first time since McCarthyism, suddenly saw a historic moment approaching, and began maneuvering to make a grab for the reins of control. Students, dividing their energies between school, politics, and just being young, couldn't hold off the onslaught of these professional political hacks. The students' instinctive aversion to hierarchical authoritarian organization left a wide opening for the traditional Old Left–style disciplined infiltration that occurred.

Stabbed through the Back Door

Not long after SSOC's demise, it became clear that, unbeknownst to the local membership and much of the staff outside of Nashville, the Communist Party had taken over the Nashville office and many key staff positions. I knew there were people on the SSOC staff who were members of the CP, but I had no idea how many until it was all over. It had seemed so harmless. As one of them put it, it was more like SSOC had organizers in the CP than the CP had organizers in SSOC. Progressive Labor and the Communist Party were sworn enemies, so once the extent of CP infiltration became clear, PL's obsession with destroying SSOC also became clear. PL had tried to take over SSOC by having Ed Clark elected chair, and had failed. The CP had crept in the back door and had succeeded. The whole new cohort of SSOC staffers who talked me into running for chair all turned out to be CP members. Evidently they had run me for chair so they could have an absentee chair off in Mississippi, giving them free rein at SSOC headquarters in Nashville. Tom Gardner's election was an inconvenience for them, but nevertheless the stage was set for a power struggle in SDS between PL and the CP, with SSOC as a political football. When PL saw SSOC was lost to the CP, PL decided to use its dominance in SDS to destroy SSOC. With typical clumsiness, the CP stuck those two speakers in front of the mike in Austin to defend SSOC. Due to the CP's low status in SDS, that strategy backfired and SSOC became history. The whole Southern-consciousness flap was a red herring thrown out by PL for gullible SDSers.

As the extent of PL's power in SDS became clear, SDSers chose one of two options. Many of the national leaders of SDS, such as Klonsky, Mark Rudd, and Bernadine Dohrn, took a "we're more revolutionary than thou" tack. They appeased PL on issues they considered of less consequence, like the SSOC question, and on other issues they sought to outflank PL with more aggressively revolutionary rhetoric and actions. This strategy eventually culminated in the Weathermen's "days of rage" in Chicago, and forced many key people into the ineffectual role of underground fugitives from the FBI. They were forced into overextending their positions beyond anything a mass movement was prepared to support. What was to have been the vanguard of a popular uprising ended up as a small, isolated bunch of ineffectual extremists.

Much of SDS's local membership took another approach. In disgust, they abandoned the national level of the organization to the sectarian hacks and the extremists. The national leadership splintered into several factions, none of which had any popular support. PL and the CP were left in control of only their own members. And the goose that laid the golden egg was dead. The Old Left had reached up out of the grave and engineered one last grand failure to cap half a century of impotence in the United States.

Six years after all of this, in 1975, I wrote an article about *The Kudzu*, SSOC, and SDS for *Southern Exposure*, a quarterly published by the Institute for Southern Studies of Atlanta and Chapel Hill. The entire section describing the shenanigans of PL and the CP and the deaths of SSOC and SDS was cut out by the editors. I have no idea what their motives were. Even then, after the SDS/SSOC debacle, many independent leftists and liberals looked the other way rather than stir up any controversy that might be misconstrued as anti-communism or red-baiting. Until 1992, when the original version of this article appeared, to my knowledge the full story of how SSOC ended had never been told. The story has since been told in more detail in Gregg Michel's *Struggle for a Better South: The Southern Student Organizing Committee, 1964–1969*, which was published by Palgrave in 2004.

I wrote a number of editorials in *The Kudzu* decrying the mindless red-baiting by right-wingers. But apparently many more people in the civil rights movement and the New Left than I cared to admit at the time were unrecognized members of doctrinaire leftist parties. They didn't state their affiliations, and good leftists and liberals were not supposed to ask. Maybe now, long after the Cold War, and after the economic, political, and moral bankruptcy of all the Old Left regimes around the world is so widely recognized and admitted, some sunlight can be shed on what happened in this country at the close of the sixties.

I am not regressing to anti-communism here. On the contrary, it appears that members of Old Left organizations may have to be given credit for major contributions to the birth and growth of the New Left, in the South as well as the rest of the country. Would that they had better understood the limitations of their ideology and their machinations. The sixties were not the forties or fifties. There came a time when the Old Left should have shown its hand to the New Left, when the old ideologies should have been put forth openly to stand or fall on their own merits. They would have fallen, of course—not because of anticommunist prejudice, but because they were out-of-date, inappropriate, and ineffectual ideologies for this country. Knowing this, perhaps, the old secrecy was cravenly maintained in an unforgivable scam perpetrated on the only people in this country who had the slightest understanding and sympathy for the Old Left.

In 1994, there was a thirty-year reunion of SSOC veterans at the University of Virginia. A young history graduate student there, Gregg Michel, was writing a dissertation and planning a book on the history of SSOC. Looking over a draft he handed out, I was deeply troubled by the superficiality of it. On a panel discussion reacting to his draft, I pointed out the ludicrousness of his mentioning that early SSOC chairperson Ed Hamlet was a Baptist, while there was a complete lack of mention that the entire final Nashville staff had become Communist Party members. Even at that late date, there were those who didn't want to open that can of worms, and who argued that, in the day, we strove to ignore such political affiliations and to unite all progressives into the struggle.

At that point I had been involved in hard science, as a research biologist, for twenty years. I said that, look, regardless of our instincts in the sixties to protect all liberals and leftists from the harsh persecutions of the day, in the interest of academic objectivity, if this was to be a legitimate historical work, the whole story had to be told. From the start of his project, I believe Gregg had been intrigued about the origins and activities of SSOC—about the seeming contradiction and drama of white Southerners becoming involved in the civil rights movement. When he stumbled across the twisted sectarian story of SSOC's last days, I think he was surprised and at a loss as to how to handle it. But with my appeal (and that of others) to the objectivity principles of history as an academic discipline, it became clear he would have to greatly expand his project to include the whole story. Therefore, when his book, *Struggle for a Better South: The Southern Student Organizing Committee, 1964–1969*, came out in 2004, it included substantial coverage of the sectarian squabbles of SSOC's last days. Gregg attempted to interview most of the principals, although for their own reasons some were uncooperative.

But, back to my *Kudzu* story, the SSOC/SDS end game is still not the whole story of the death of the sixties. There was one sinister strand of this web that had not unraveled and revealed itself yet. That comes later in *The Kudzu*'s history.

The Ink Keeps on Flowing

After the traumatic ends of SSOC and SDS in 1969, at the end of *The Kudzu*'s first year, we kept going in Mississippi. There was no more SSOC money, but that had never been an essential part of our financial base. We picked up a few paying ads and received a steady trickle of donations—most local, but some from out of state. Some staff members had outside jobs, and activity had to be scaled back somewhat. Sixteen issues appeared during *The Kudzu*'s first year; it took us another three years to put out another sixteen issues. Our writing became a little less awkward and shrill, and our layouts got a little neater and more professional looking. We continued to try for a balanced mix of culture and politics. Ironically, the real groundswell of youthful rebellion was just barely getting started in 1969 as SDS and SSOC self-destructed. In the next few years it seemed like virtually every family had at least one son or daughter who "went hippie." Radical politics was only one parental worry out of many. My own parents had more sympathy for my political activities than for the rest of the trappings of the new subculture, the wild hair and clothes, the drugs and sex.

Several *Kudzu* staffers had gone to one of the first big pop festivals, near Miami, at the end of 1968. This was after Monterey and before Woodstock. We had press passes to Woodstock, but passed it up because of the distance. Because of its proximity to New York, Woodstock had the biggest attendance and got all the media attention, but festivals before and after Woodstock had the same musicians and the same impact on the attendees. There were two monstrous Fourth of July festivals near Atlanta. At the second one, several hundred people tore down the fence of a swimming lake next door to the festival, stripped naked, and went for a communal skinny dip. Couples took turns assuming various positions from the Kama Sutra and going down the tall sliding board together to the applause of the nude crowd. At the climax of the festival, Jimi Hendrix played his famous version of the national anthem. But it wasn't all so beautiful; crowd facilities at all of the festivals were atrocious. We tried to come down from the clouds somewhat by pointing out the exploitive nature of the music industry as a lesson in the problems of corporate capitalism.

We put on two festivals of our own in Mississippi that we called Mississippi Youth Jubilees. We obtained use of the grounds of a former college that had been used for years as a civil rights conference site, Mt. Beulah, near Edwards, Mississippi, and brought in a bunch of local musicians. We also had political speakers and discussion groups about civil rights, the peace movement, women's liberation, and other current issues.

At the first festival, a big fat Mississippi highway patrolman named Loyd Jones showed up, taking license numbers and giving people tickets for missing taillights and other minor infractions of the law. Jones was notorious among blacks all over the state for his alleged harassment and brutality. Many blacks called him Goon Jones. At one point he cruised onto the festival grounds in his patrol car. He refused to pay admission, but produced no search warrant. We surrounded his car and confronted him. Some people started breaking bottles in front and back of his car so he couldn't leave. A big confrontation followed between the people who broke the bottles and some pacifists. Finally the pacifists picked up the broken bottles, and Jones left. We parked cars across the entrance to prevent his return. There were intense discussions about violence and pacifism all over the festival for the rest of the weekend. Jones had been a priceless catalyst.

During the next year, Nixon invaded Cambodia, and National Guardsmen shot down unarmed students at Kent State University in Ohio. In Mississippi, Goon Jones and a group of fellow patrolmen marched onto the campus of predominantly black Jackson State College and shot into a crowd of unarmed students, killing two. *The Kudzu* was the only paper in Jackson that presented the students' accounts of the killings. The bullet-splattered women's dorm was my most famous photo and *The Kudzu*'s most dramatic cover (see figure 3). Among the many demonstrations following these killings was a march around the governor's mansion by Millsaps students and faculty. Three years before, when Ben Brown had been killed at almost the same spot at Jackson State, twenty Millsaps students had marched. This time it was almost two hundred. We considered that progress. Still, two people had to die to get people moving. And it was still Mississippi—the patrolmen were exonerated.

Narc Wars

While arrests of *Kudzu* staffers had tapered off after the first year of publication, the increasing numbers of counterculture participants and the increasing presence of recreational drugs in

FIGURE 3: Cover of *Kudzu* volume 2, number 6 (May 1970), showing a bullet-splattered women's dorm at Jackson State College in Mississippi following the murder of two unarmed students. *Kudzu* staff photo by David Doggett.

Jackson gave the police both the incentive and the excuse to constantly harass *The Kudzu*, which they perceived as an instigator of the drug culture. We became more or less personally acquainted with the entire vice squad as they subjected us to constant surveillance. At one point, the vice squad rented an abandoned apartment on the grounds of our office-residence. They parked in our driveway and arrested and beat staff members who also tried to park there. Many people we knew spent time in jail or prison for possession or sale of small quantities of marijuana. We were very careful ourselves and had no drug arrests of staff members during our first two years.

Nevertheless, harassment by narcotics agents resulted in my worst jail experience, but it was not in Mississippi. In May 1970, several of us covered a small pop festival and environmental rally at Denham Springs, Louisiana, near Baton Rouge. The local sheriff had deputized a bunch of his redneck cronies in this rural area, and undercover narcs disguised as hippies had been brought in from New Orleans. A hidden police compound was set up behind a fence next to the festival site. Over the course of the weekend, between one and two hundred people were seized, dragged into the secret compound, booked, and sent out to local jails and prisons. The pretext for the arrests was usually drugs, but most of them were bogus. Very few of those arrested were selling or even in possession of drugs. Many people were beaten on the festival site as they were arrested. Once inside the compound, almost everyone was beaten during the "booking procedures." Some were gassed with mace and sadistically tortured. It was a true nightmare. No announcement was made from the stage concerning this continuing assault on the peaceful festival goers.

I started taking pictures of what I thought was a brawl between festival goers. It turned out to be one of the "arrests." Narcs dressed as hippies were beating several people as they dragged them to a police car. When the narcs saw me taking pictures, I was seized, my camera was confiscated, and I was thrown in the car and driven through a fence gate into the adjacent police compound. I was beaten during the strip search and not allowed to make a phone call for a day and a half. Over the course of three days, I was transferred to several jails. At one point I was in a Baton Rouge cell block, wearing a prison uniform, along with a *Newsweek* reporter and almost thirty other festival goers. After three days, an American Civil Liberties Union attorney finally located me and got me released on bail. After a great deal of difficulty I got my camera back, but the film was gone and the camera had been maliciously damaged on the inside.

When people were finally brought up for hearings, local court-appointed lawyers tried to force innocent people to plead guilty against their wills. Charges against me were dropped. Unfortunately there was only one ACLU attorney in that rural area, and it proved too difficult to bring any charges against the law officers responsible for this atrocity. This was one of the worst examples of the American police state gone amok I knew of since the old days in the civil rights movement, when demonstrators likewise were arrested in large groups and beaten and tortured.

From today's perspective, it is difficult to understand the symbolic importance of illegal drug use for both the counterculture and its persecutors. Today we look askance at the sordid abuse of addictive drugs by movie stars and rock stars, and drug use has gained an unfashionable association with inner-city addicts and their petty crime, and with money-crazed dealers and their violent crime. But in the sixties and early seventies, the use of illegal psychedelic drugs was an act not only of social rebellion but of political rebellion, since the state forbade it. It was a line drawn in the dirt by parents and police that millions of young people stepped across in defiance of frequently severe consequences.

The drug-induced psychedelic initiation rite was like a religious awakening. But it was not really a new religion that one awoke to; rather, it was chemically induced culture shock. The psychedelic experience was an instant way to step outside one's native culture and look on society from an estranged perspective. The hysterical response of the authorities served to heighten the alienating effect. While the drug tripper was trying to manipulate his or her own mind into a different perspective, the state was desperately trying to keep the minds of its youth in the old straitjacket. Thus drugs became a radicalizing political experience for millions of young people, who otherwise might never have so forcefully experienced the shocking hand of thought control in their society.

The drugs, being physical things that influenced thought, forced the thought police to step out from behind the curtain of psychological manipulation and attempt to physically control the drugs and those who used them. People who might never have made the intellectual effort to understand U.S. imperialism, or the moral effort to empathize with oppressed blacks, suddenly found themselves persecuted as outlaws because they simply wanted to alter their own mental perceptions. The drug war was a major political battleground of the sixties and seventies.

Year Three

By our third year of publication, we had survived forty-two *Kudzu*-related arrests and were undaunted. But the financial situation was discouraging. It was clear that *The Kudzu* would not pay for itself anytime in the foreseeable future. We were taking turns holding outside jobs to support the paper. At various times I did paralegal work full-time for the American Civil Liberties Union and other civil rights lawyers in Jackson. Except for myself, the original staff had turned over completely. Bill Rusk, on probation for draft violation in California, had become a mainstay on the staff while also working long hours as a cab driver.

We made plans to start a community center called Edge City, named after the destination of Ken Kesey's bus, Further, in Tom Wolfe's book *The Electric Kool-Aid Acid Test*. The hope was that the center could make money by having rock bands play on weekends, and by housing some small businesses such as a craft shop and a used book and record shop. *Kudzu* staffers would try to earn a living working at the center. We sold $5 memberships, the members elected a board of directors, and the board formed a nonprofit corporation. We brought legendary bluesman Mississippi Fred McDowell down from the Delta for a fundraising concert. Jack Cohn, a young local businessman in the wholesale clothing trade, gave us several thousand dollars, which was to be paid back only if the venture was successful. We rented and renovated an old parking garage in downtown Jackson and opened for business. Edge City met with moderate success at first.

In other events that year, *Kudzu* staffer Mike McNamara decided to go to Cuba with the Venceremos Brigade. Mike was a big red-headed guy, a former high school football guard from Vicksburg. He had been a writer and distributor of *The Kudzu* up at Ole Miss, and had moved to Jackson and joined our staff. He raised some money and went with Venceremos to Cuba to spend a summer cutting sugar cane. He cut so much sugar cane, he got elected a brigade leader.

J. Edgar's Spooks

In *The Kudzu*'s third year, we began to get heat from the FBI. We had always felt that the FBI had us under close surveillance. During our first year, several *Kudzu* staffers and associates were questioned by FBI agents. Some people were asked to become paid informants. One of the main women on our staff came to an early staff meeting and told of being offered money to meet with FBI agents clandestinely on a regular basis to keep them informed of our activities. She would be paid $50 for each meeting. We were intrigued. We decided that she should become a double agent. She was to go along with the FBI's scheme, take the money, and try to find out as much as possible about the FBI's knowledge and operations. We weren't breaking any federal laws and had no plans to, so it was all just a game with us. Also the money wasn't bad. At the time we each lived on about $20 a month and were struggling to pay the printer's bill with each issue. Why not play a little game with them, feed them either trivial information or misleading stuff, and take some of their money to use for our own purposes?

Our staff member had one or two meetings with the FBI. They had her lie on the floor of the back seat of their car while they talked. Then she had to sign a receipt for the money. After each meeting she came back and reported at a staff meeting. After one or two meetings, the FBI must have realized they had been had, because they stopped setting up meetings. The main benefit we got out of the game was that we learned to recognize several agents. And from that knowledge, I discovered FBI agents could be identified at demonstrations because of the brand of camera they used. Reporters and the state and local police always used Nikon cameras, the standard professional workhorse. Federal people used Beseler Topcon cameras. Topcon even advertised in photo magazines that they had a federal contract.

After those early contacts in our first year, the FBI dropped into the background until our third year. Unbeknownst to us at the time, the FBI in 1970 was carrying on a national campaign called COINTELPRO. As part of that program, informer-provocateurs all over the country were paid both to spy on activist groups and to disrupt and discredit them. In early October of 1970 we ran a statement by three Alabama attorneys that revealed that Charles R. Grimm Jr., a Tuscaloosa Police Department undercover narcotics agent who had a close relationship with the FBI, had thrown objects at police and set fire to buildings during student disturbances at the University of Alabama the previous May. The statement noted, in fact, that Grimm had been virtually the only violent participant in some of these instances, that he had urged students to use guns and dynamite, and that he had offered to help them obtain such items. He became a member of the University Committee on Unrest and Reconciliation, where his militant approach appeared intended to divide the university community.

Our article also enumerated several similar instances where apparent police and FBI agents provocateurs were involved around the country. We followed the article with an editorial criticizing the FBI for vigorously pursuing the Black Panthers and white radicals alleged to be involved in violent or criminal activities, while in the South, churches were bombed and burned and blacks were murdered while the FBI looked the other way and failed to successfully investigate.

Soon after that article was published, there came a knock at the *Kudzu* door. It was the first of several occasions in which FBI agents rushed into our office-residence with guns drawn, claiming they didn't need search warrants because they were "in hot pursuit of fugitives." The "fugitives" were national figures such as the SDS Weathermen or various Black Panthers. FBI agents actually looked under our beds once for Columbia University SDS leader Mark Rudd. We had no connection with any of these "fugitives" and the FBI well knew that, since they had us under constant surveillance. They were very hostile and spewed a lot of verbal abuse, such as "Punks like you don't have any rights." They threatened to shoot us down on the street if we had our hands in our pockets, since we might be going for a weapon. Around us they dropped the FBI's famous professional image. They were garden-variety right-wing thugs to the core.

Finally, on October 26, the Jackson police marched into our house with a search warrant. Then, while holding eight of us at gun point in the front room, they ransacked the office and house, intentionally breaking several personal items and stealing address books as they worked (see figure 4). They "found" a small bag of marijuana none of us had ever seen before, and off we went to spend a night in jail. They threw a few punches during the booking procedures. The local papers had a field day. However, it was one of the few times we ever got a reasonable judge, J. L. Spencer. In a surprise move, he released us on our own recognizance and merely bound the case over to a grand jury for investigation. He correctly noted that there was no chance for a conviction, since the marijuana was not found on anyone's person and in fact none of us was even in the room when it was found. The charges were eventually dropped.

On the surface it was just one more case of harassment among many. But as time went by and we pieced together additional information, the incident took on a deeply sinister meaning with far-reaching implications. Word came back through the legal community that the FBI had set up the raid. The search warrant had been obtained on the grounds that an informant had witnessed the use and sale of marijuana in our house the night before the raid. At first we assumed that was a complete fabrication. But on thinking back, we realized that there had been some grass smoked in the house that night, although none was left on the premises. Further, one person present at the time had not smoked any: Don Cole. He was a long-time acquaintance of all of us, and we suddenly suspected that he was almost certainly an informer-provocateur.

Don Cole was one of the first leftists I ever met. Way back in 1965, when Lee Makamson and I published our first mimeographed newsletter, Don Cole appeared on the Millsaps campus out of nowhere. He was not a student. He was a short, nerdy guy with glasses and short hair who worked in a hardware store in the small town of Raymond, north of Jackson. He claimed he was a Communist, and his first advice to Lee and me was for us to go to Vietnam and join up with the Viet Cong. We never took him seriously after that, but just considered him a harmless wing nut. He later claimed to be a member of the Progressive Labor Party; yet in spite of that organization's militant Maoist image, he was never close to anyone in the Jackson activist community, and he maintained his job in the hardware store in Raymond, where he lived. He sort of "checked in" on a regular basis, but never really participated in any organizations, although he was frequently at meetings, hanging around the fringes. He showed up at demonstrations unannounced and handed out tracts containing the most embarrassing, stereotypical, and irrelevant Communist rantings imaginable. He was always jolly and friendly to all of us, and we just sort of ignored him.

FIGURE 4: Author David Doggett's office after police raid, October 26, 1970. *Kudzu* staff photo by Bill Peltz.

Suddenly it all made sense. In fact, Jan Hillegas, of Freedom Information Service in Jackson, not long before the FBI-instigated raid, had said that she suspected Don Cole of being an informer. Some photos had disappeared from her office under circumstances that convinced her Don had taken them. Don had been such a seemingly harmless fixture around town for so long that I hadn't really taken Jan seriously. But we finally became convinced that if there was any real testimony for the search warrant that led to the *Kudzu* raid, it had to have come from Don Cole. That little snake—all those years of embarrassing us at demonstrations with his ridiculous Communist literature, and now he had gotten our house wrecked and caused us a night in jail. I was annoyed, and we passed the word around, but at that point I still didn't get the really big picture.

The Headless Horseman

The Kudzu struggled on. We hosted a conference for the underground press of the Southeast at Mt. Beulah. Tom Forcade of the Underground Press Syndicate came down, and people from all over the South showed up. There was some speculation that the raid on our office had been an FBI attempt to disrupt our organizing of this conference. And the timing of the raid right before the conference was certainly suspicious.

A major topic of discussion at the conference was the vacuum left at the national level by SDS and SSOC. We were all concerned that without a strong national organization to connect with, those of us in provincial areas might sink back into isolation, and we were uncertain how long we could hold out that way. The underground press was increasingly writing about a revolution that was not happening. There were huge liberal initiatives for civil rights and peace; there were lots of hippies and Yippies pretending or naively believing that music and love and outrageous humor would cause permanent change; and there were black and white militants strutting around with guns and getting thrown in prison or forced underground. In the name of revolution, banks were being robbed and cops were being shot. But it wasn't going anywhere.

I was not a pure pacifist, and I had written in *The Kudzu* in support of violence in self-defense. We kept a loaded 12-gauge shotgun in our house. But the "vanguard" was getting way ahead of its troops. A few years back, I read that a former SDS Weatherman confessed they had committed "the militarist error." It figures they would have a doctrinaire term for it. Too bad there's no orthodox doctrine that instills common sense. They were leading a suicidal charge that few people were foolish enough to follow. It was all beginning to look too crazy.

There was no preeminent organizational vehicle with real popular support, no aggressive but sane democratic leftist organization to fill the void left by SDS and SSOC. The New American Movement and a few other groups tried to pick up the ball where SDS had fumbled it, but somehow nothing ever took off again like SDS.

Year Four

In 1972, *The Kudzu*'s fourth and final year, the Republic of New Africa (RNA) set up house in Jackson. RNA wanted to press the United Nations for a chunk of the southeastern United States as reparations for slavery and its aftermath. Their goal was to set up a black homeland. In spite of its seeming impracticality, let's be honest, there was justice in that demand. Without much enthusiasm, we dutifully wrote about their views. But most of white Mississippi took great offense at these notions, especially the law 'n' order gang. Within months, the FBI and Jackson Police Department staged a raid on RNA's headquarters. Both sides were heavily armed. When the police fired tear gas into the building, RNA members claimed they thought it was gunshots and fired back in self-defense. A Jackson vice-squad officer was shot in the head and killed. By this time we knew all of the vice squad all too intimately. As luck would have it, the officer killed, Louis Skinner, was the only member of the vice squad who treated us fairly and professionally in all of our encounters. He was a genuinely nice guy who was simply in with the wrong crowd. Now he had been at the wrong place at the wrong time. His death was totally unnecessary. The raid was purely a trumped-up act of political repression. And so it goes. Every time someone is killed, even if it is the "enemy," humanity loses.

After that incident, the Republic of New Africa leaders, like many other black militants, were mired in courts and prison. Activity was winding down, not only for the militant black movement and the New Left, but for the underground press and *The Kudzu* as well. Sometimes the *Kudzu* staff only consisted of Bill Rusk and me, and we both were doing outside work. New issues came out less than once a month. We had little advertising; almost no newsstands would carry *The Kudzu*; and street sales were too poor to provide incentive to street hawkers. Jackson was simply not a large enough city to support an alternative press. We could have probably gotten more ads and sales at the major college towns around the state, but we didn't have the resources and time to do the constant traveling required for that. In the beginning we had been perceived as pioneers and martyrs, and people rose up to help us. But by the fourth year, we were taken for granted as more of a business, which of course we never were. We had seen all of this by the end of the second year, which is when we started working on Edge City.

But Edge City had never really gotten off the ground. Soon after it opened, a gang of bikers started hanging out at a bar around the corner and harassing people. At one point I had to pull out a shotgun and hold off several bikers at gunpoint for almost half an hour while the police took their time in answering our phone call for help. The bikers weren't happy with the standoff and immediately went over to our house, beat up Bill Rusk, and stole a bunch of stuff. They swore to see me dead. I moved out of the house and slept with a .38 revolver under my pillow for the next month. Eventually we made a strained peace with the bikers. But the whole affair did little to enhance Edge City's public image as a fun place to be.

But the biggest problem for Edge City was that the police refused to issue us a dance permit. They tried to extort us into hiring city police as security guards, but we felt that their presence would scare people away, and that having police around would simply make it easier for them to spy on people and to harass people with petty drug arrests and traffic tickets. Maybe we could have taken them to court and eventually gotten a dance permit, but in the meantime, without dancing we couldn't keep up the rent and staff salaries. We had a rock or rhythm-and-blues band play most weekends, but most of the bands we could afford were okay as dance bands but weren't good enough to pull off an all-night concert with no dancing. Also, we didn't serve alcohol, because we didn't want to exclude high school kids. Without dancing for the high school kids or drinks for older people, the entertainment just never took off. Edge City didn't last long.

Death with a Whimper

Edge City's closing was pretty much the last straw for me. We could have kept *The Kudzu* going for a while longer with the trickle of donations we got, but when we realized that none of us would be able to quit our outside jobs to work full-time on *The Kudzu*, I decided it was time to move on to other things. In the beginning of *The Kudzu*, I really had thought I was starting on a lifetime career. When I finally admitted that dream was over, I was devastated. My whole identity was tied up in *The Kudzu*. I wandered around the South for two depressing years before I got seriously involved in another career. How much revolution would occur, I had never really known. But I never envisioned that it would all just dissipate into nothing. As with the end of SDS and SSOC, again I had to ask, what had happened?

Postmortem

To be sure, we had changed history. Blacks were voting and electing people to office in the South. President Johnson left office. The troops came home from Vietnam. Never again in our lifetime, we believed, would this country enter into war as blindly as before. Nixon was eventually to be run out of office. Women were moving out of the kitchen and into the workplace. Gay culture was increasingly open. Everyone knew what the word "ecology" meant. The harsh conformity of the fifties had been broken. Breathtaking changes had taken place in every area of culture. Thus, much of what we perceived as a winding down was not so much a dissipation as an integration of our goals into mainstream society. But there was no national structure, no comprehensive national organization or publication to carry on the original vision of the New Left and the counterculture. How could that be, when there were once so many of us with such a similar vision?

Indeed, the vision was never lost for the individuals. To this day, if you talk to anyone who was active in the sixties, you will discover that he or she still has that vision of racial harmony, of an economic system that nurtures those at the bottom rather than adds to their numbers, of a political system with participatory democracy rather than sham representative democracy, of a culture in which work and play are fun and creative rather than desperate and destructive, and in which there is international appreciation and cooperation in maintaining the environment. But we have been reduced to individuals, when we once were a mass movement.

Several years ago, I acquired my FBI file through the Freedom of Information Act. The documents in my file were not merely about surveillance. The FBI was far more sophisticated and creative than we ever imagined them to be. We knew that they watched us. But we had no idea how much they tried to manipulate us. When *The Kudzu* started, the FBI reasoned that since we were all students with conservative parents living in small towns throughout Mississippi, it would be a simple matter to put fear into our parents and thus enormous pressure on us. Agents visited not only our parents, but also the friends, neighbors, and employers of our parents around Mississippi. These people were questioned about us and our families in an intentionally intimidating manner. Many of my friends were estranged from their families for years after those days. People were financially cut off, transferred to other schools, forced into psychiatric treatment, and subjected to other experiences—and all of this permanently changed many people's lives. Who knows how much of the trauma we all went through in those days was intensified by this cynical meddling by the FBI?

Being young, there was a lot of amorous coupling among us in those days. The FBI sent fake letters about false infidelities in attempts to break up couples. There were FBI memos discussing who were effective leaders among us and who were ineffective, and memos about what types of rumors might turn people against the strong leaders. There was communication between the FBI, the Mississippi State Sovereignty Commission (a notorious right-wing McCarthyesque group), and state and local law-enforcement organizations. There were also communications between the local FBI agents and agents further up the chain of command outside the state.

At some point, after I had absorbed what a sophisticated campaign the FBI carried out against us in Jackson, I began to wonder what schemes they had hatched against national organizations like SDS and SSOC. SDS may have been the greatest threat to the corporate ruling class in this country in the twentieth century—not simply because the ideology of SDS, economic as well as real political democracy, was so threatening, but because so many middle- and upper-class young people were flocking to SDS and the ideas SDS promulgated. At its height, there were rapidly growing SDS chapters on virtually every college campus in the country. On many campuses, SDS was the biggest and most powerful student organization, rivaling conventional student government. But although the top universities in the country had been intermittently shut down, SDS was not immediately threatening to shut down any factories or mines. Far worse—these middle- and upper-class young people were setting out to carry these ideas into the mainstream media, into electoral politics, and into all of the professions and all of the positions of influence and power that they would inevitably inherit from the older generation. J. Edgar Hoover's FBI would not stand idly by for that.

Don Cole was a member of the Progressive Labor Party. Don Cole was at the 1967 SSOC conference with Ed Clark when PL tried unsuccessfully to take over SSOC. Ed Clark and Fred Lacy of PL engineered the rejection and destruction of SSOC by SDS. The in-fighting between PL and SDS ended in the disintegration of SDS. The premier organization of the New Left, the political manifestation of the counterculture, did not make it into the seventies.

I have talked to people from coast to coast who recall that in their city there were members of PL who were known or suspected of being informer-provocateurs. PL was universally disruptive. Possibly there were many people in PL who knew nothing about the FBI. Surely some well-intentioned people were sincerely idiotic enough to screw things up as badly as PL managed to do. Surely SDS's youthful ineptness contributed to its fatal inability to deal with that threat. But I would like some day to know what role the FBI had in all of this. Was PL an FBI creation from the beginning, or did the FBI merely use PL so cleverly for its own purposes? Everyone knows the FBI was in the Communist Party USA. How much of the CP's actions came from the FBI? Certainly the death of the New Left cannot be blamed solely on FBI skullduggery; there was self-inflicted damage aplenty. But how different would things have been without such disruptions? Would there have been a PL threat to SDS? Would SDS have surmounted the threat instead of splintering? Would Liberation News Service have thrived intact? Would the Black Panthers have gone further politically? Would the underground press have become a permanent part of the nation's mass media?

And what of the conclusion of *The Kudzu*'s small part in it all? Well, finally, after *The Kudzu*'s tale is told and the years have intervened, it becomes clear that Mississippi was and is not so different. It wasn't the Ku Klux Klan that stopped *The Kudzu* in the end; it was economics, the legal system, the FBI, our own youthfully superficial political polemics, the loss of an effective national connection, and changing times—the same forces that dealt killing blows in the rest of the country to the sixties' counterculture, its New Left political organizations, and its voice, the underground press.

Since I left Mississippi, I have lived in Atlanta, Washington, DC, New Orleans, Nashville, Knoxville, Los Angeles, Boston, and Philadelphia. In 1991, when I wrote the first version of this history, a greater proportion of U.S. citizens were in prison than in any other major nation. A greater proportion of black males were in prison in the United States of America than in the Union of South Africa under apartheid. Now, in 2008, the number of people in prison surpasses every other nation. In no major nation are citizens more fearful of their own city streets than in the United States. Our cities have higher infant-mortality rates than many Third World countries. In these cities today, the segregation of the white suburbs and the black inner cities is in many ways as complete as Mississippi's old segregation. We have de facto apartheid. The first slaves did not come into Mississippi; they were brought into Boston harbor. The curse of the abomination of slavery and its aftermath in America was not erased by the Civil War, and it does not fall on the South alone. The curse is alive in every major city in this country.

And there are new problems as well. The environment is more threatened than ever. We have gone from the savings-and-loan scandal of the nineties to the current housing credit crisis, with other political/economic scandals and crises in between. Together these constitute the biggest public theft in the nation's history. The big banks and Wall Street have massive bad debts. The public has become addicted to huge personal debt at devastating interest rates. The government itself has an unthinkably huge debt. With these financial manipulations and the increasingly regressive tax structure, in the past decades there has been a tremendous transfer of wealth from the poor and the middle class, both inside and outside the United States, to the international corporate upper class. Well-paying jobs and benefits dwindle. Healthcare is increasingly unaffordable and unattainable, and is manipulated by the insurance industry so that risks and costs are increasingly unequally shared, which defeats the whole purpose of insurance. Even as the Old Left regimes of the Cold War have crumbled in Eastern Europe, American capitalism can scarcely relish the victory as it wrestles with these problems and plunges into yet another recession. Catastrophe continues in the Middle East because of our blind addiction to the oil of kings and dictators, and our longstanding arrogance and ignorance toward the millions of poor people in that region. Malignant, medieval, theocratic fascism, rather than being effectively defused by modernism, is exacerbated by arrogant and incompetent militarism. And to deal with all of these problems, we have a perennially paralyzed government of destructive, divisive, right-wing administrations and feeble Congresses.

Would history have gone in all of these directions if the counterculture, the New Left, and the underground press had continued? We will never know. We can pick over the bones and try to understand the causes of the patient's death. Many's the night some of us have lain in bed and done that. But we can scarcely imagine what the patient would have done had it lived on, what its influence would have been. We can only wonder now, as the reverberations of our voices, created then, now fade in the halls of time.

The Wong Truth Conspiracy: A History of Madison Alternative Journalism

TIM WONG

he 8½ years I spent working on alternative newspapers in Madison chronicled very clearly the transition from the sixties to the eighties. In 1971, when I first worked on *Kaleidoscope*, the hippie era ("sex, dope, *Kaleidoscope*") was still in full swing. A large alternative community existed in Madison. It was clearly an alternative to the dominant community, but that alternative was not clearly defined, nor were its recognized differences destined to remain as differences. Smoking marijuana, for instance, was enough to make one "alternative," but by the end of the decade such nonpolitical "alternative" behavior had become institutionalized. The nonpolitical drug user was no longer implicitly attracted to the alternative political media or community.

In response to this transition, the alternative press made a similar transition. Dope columns, both glorifying drug use and evaluating goods for sale—often including those sold by staff members—were as prevalent in papers of the early seventies as they were absent by the end of the decade.

In addition, the rise of feminist and gay consciousness was challenging the heterosexual male domination of the political movement and alternative newspapers. This meant that alternative newspapers contained both more articles on feminism and the women's, gay, and lesbian movements, and fewer articles glorifying "free love" and other forms of primarily male sex. Exclusively women's and gay newspapers developed as well.

Political content changed greatly throughout the decade. The existence of the Vietnam War, the draft, Richard Nixon, and "life drugs" (marijuana and psychedelics) as liberators made being antiwar and anti-establishment easy, almost natural, in the early seventies. By the middle of the 1970s, the end of the draft and the war resulted in relative demilitarization. The exposure and prosecution of the main Watergate figures led to post-Watergate reforms, and the opening of the Democratic Party in 1972 and other electoral reforms led to the ventilation of the "smoke-filled rooms." All of these events led many people to make their peace with the establishment. By the end of the decade, radical politics were no longer "in," even in relatively radical Madison.

The Origins of the "Revolution"

I got my start in journalism during my college years at Carleton College in Northfield, Minnesota. The four years I was there—from 1965 to 1969—probably ushered in more changes to the college than any four years in the college's 145 years. Required chapel attendance had been abolished in 1965; men were still required to wear ties to Sunday lunch in school year 1965–1966; "open houses," where members of the opposite sex could visit dorm rooms (virtually all students lived in dorms), were limited to four hours a week, a shoe needed to be placed between the door and the jamb, and three feet needed to be on the floor. By 1969 virtually nobody wore ties or went to chapel, and unlimited open houses had been instituted (dorms were integrated the following year).

These "student power" reforms coincided with a dramatic shift to the left in the predominant campus political attitudes. During my freshman year, as an early opponent to the Vietnam War, I was regularly pelted with water balloons as I walked back to my dorm. On one occasion, several people came into my room and overturned my bed while I was sleeping. On another, my mattress was thrown out of my fourth-story window (fortunately I was not in bed that time). Yet three years later, many of my early tormentors, whether genuinely or conveniently (due to the draft), were actively antiwar.

Carleton's student newspaper, the *Carletonian*, reflected this shift. My first story for the paper concerned the disciplining of a student for bringing a couch into his dorm room (at Carleton, there was no off-campus housing). By the time I was editor in 1969, we subscribed to Liberation News Service to give our national and international news coverage a radical slant, and to College Press Service for its student power coverage.

Madison underwent a similar political conversion during the late 1960s. Mario Savio, a leader of the free speech movement in Berkeley, had identified Carleton in 1965 as the Midwestern campus most likely to erupt into revolt—most people at Carleton were bemused at the prospect. In reality, of course, change happened much faster in Madison. In October 1967, police violently attacked demonstrators sitting-in to protest recruitment by the Dow Chemical Company, makers of napalm, at the University of Wisconsin (UW) Business School. This police attack on nonviolent protesters merely served to swell the number of willing participants. Over the next three years, as many as 30,000 people took part in marches against the war, the number varying in inverse proportion to the likelihood of widespread trashing taking place.

The demonstrators felt the UW administration showed clear complicity in the Vietnam War effort by refusing to shut down the Army Math Research Center (AMRC), a campus organization that did war-related mathematical research, and the various ROTC branches. Demonstrations invariably started on the Library Mall, an open area between two libraries, with one or more incendiary speeches, followed by a march or a war-whooping run to the target building—frequently Army Math, as it was called, or one of the UW administrative buildings. ROTC buildings were less often the targets, primarily because they were over a mile from the Library Mall.

A black student strike in February 1969 attracted widespread white radical student support. As time went on, though, radical activity was no longer limited strictly to the campus. Many student radicals had moved several blocks southeast of campus into what was known as the Mifflin-Bassett neighborhood. When that area "declared independence" from Madison and the United States, it was renamed Miffland. In 1968 the White Front Grocery on the corner of Mifflin and Bassett closed, and a number of people organized to rent the building and establish a food cooperative, which opened on January 13, 1969. The existence of the co-op gave people the sense of controlling their own destiny; the co-op became the symbol of Miffland. The alternative community was becoming a reality.

In May 1969, Mifflin Street residents decided to have a block party to celebrate the coming of spring. While most residents were indifferent to what city reaction would be, more "responsible" types such as alderperson (and later mayor) Paul Soglin investigated getting a permit. City officials said no permit would be necessary because the 500-block of West Mifflin had very low daily traffic counts, particularly on Saturdays. Nonetheless the police department determined to keep the street open, and a three-day riot ensued, spreading to other student neighborhoods besides Miffland. Political feeling continued to become more militant. Many people began arming themselves in anticipation of the "revolution." A loose coalition of demonstrators calling themselves the Bobby Seale Brigade, after Black Panther cofounder Bobby Seale, loaded their backpacks with rocks and trashed business storefronts during each Madison demo between 1969 and 1971 or 1972. Madison sent a contingent of protesters to the Days of Rage protest in Chicago in the fall of 1969.

In February 1970, university teaching assistants went on strike and won a favorable settlement. Three months later, Nixon invaded Cambodia, and Madison, like most university communities, exploded, particularly as word of the Kent State and Jackson State murders spread. Numerous buildings were firebombed in various sections of town. A Kroger's supermarket, which had long drawn resentment from the student community for its perceived higher prices and lower quality than other Krogers in Madison, was burned to the ground. A week of rioting ensued, featuring barricades, pitched battles with police, and helicopters with spotlights flying overhead. The police responded with a blanket of tear gas throughout the Mifflin-Bassett neighborhood, firing tear-gas canisters through windows in the Mifflin St. Co-op and most houses on the 500-block of West Mifflin and some on surrounding streets.

On August 24, 1970, the Army Math Research Center on campus was bombed by the so-called New Year's Gang, resulting in relatively little damage to Army Math, but causing substantial damage to the physics department, housed in the same building, and killing a researcher who was working at 5 A.M. when the bomb went off.

The straight media usually portray the Army Math bombing as the beginning of the end of the antiwar movement. In reality, the Kent State and Jackson State killings—which showed people both how vulnerable and how powerless they were against an armed state—were probably more responsible for the reduced participation in antiwar protests. The leveling off and reduction in the number of U.S. troops in Vietnam and the subsequent ending of the draft succeeded in ending protest by all but the politically committed.

In Madison, though, energy flowed into creating a wide variety of alternative economic institutions. In addition to the Green Lantern Eating Co-op, which had existed for several decades, and the Mifflin St. Co-op, Whole Earth Learning Community (a food co-op) on the east side and Eagle Heights Food Co-op on the west side emerged, as did Common Market, a food "buying club," and ICC, a cooperative trucking group. There was also a book co-op, a musicians' co-op, a printing collective, an alternative publications distributor, two clothing cooperatives, a bicycle co-op, a photography co-op, and at least twenty-one housing co-ops.

Alternative newspapers flourished as well. Madison's first, *Connections*, published its initial issue on March 1, 1967. It was the most campus-oriented of all of Madison's undergrounds, and reflected the increasing militancy of the campus—focusing on the increasingly violent confrontations with the police during demonstrations. *Connections*'s last issue appeared in May 1969. Roughly concurrent with *Connections* was *The Call*, the newsletter of the UW chapter of Students for a Democratic Society (SDS), the largest radical political group in the United States during the second half of the 1960s. *The Call*'s avowed purpose was to "help clarify radical thought and action on the New Left here, by providing a place for the exchange of opinions, analysis, and information." *The Call* reprinted articles by national SDS writers such as Carl Oglesby and Tom Hayden, and featured local articles on organizing, including one whose title indicates humor wasn't totally lacking: "Elephants in the Ivory Tower: The Tusk That Lies Before Us."

Other more obscure titles published in the late sixties were *Links*, the "Voice of the Wisconsin High School Underground," *Underground Underdog*, *Psst!*, *Oscar's Underground Ghetto Press*, *Madison Free Press*, the first community-oriented paper, . . . *And Beautiful*, and *Bad Moon Rising*.

Madison's second significant alternative paper, *(Madison) Kaleidoscope*, first appeared on June 23, 1969, less than two months after the demise of *Connections*. Some staff members worked on both papers. Underground comics were a regular feature of *Kaleidoscope*. The quality of layout improved over *Connections*, and the writing reflected the increasing self-confidence of the growing counterculture. The Madison paper took its name from the *(Milwaukee) Kaleidoscope*, which first appeared in 1967. *(Milwaukee) Kaleidoscope* published a "second section" devoted exclusively to features on music, arts, and literature, which was widely distributed, including in its Madison namesake.

Shortly after the Army Math bombing in August 1970, *Kaleidoscope* received and printed a statement on the bombing by the New Year's Gang, the group that had claimed responsibility. When editor Mark Knops refused to reveal the source of the document, he was sentenced to, and served, six months in jail for contempt of court. (It is certainly questionable whether Knops even knew the source; so great was our contempt for mainstream society, though, that Knops refused to cooperate on principle.)

While Knops's courageous and defiant action increased the alternative community's respect for the paper, it also hastened its demise. By late 1970, the majority of the staff was questioning the paper's hierarchical structure and some of the paper's politics that they felt exploited women. Knops's absence gave this portion of the staff the opportunity to think about (and to some extent work on) a paper without an editor and without sexism. When Knops returned from jail and tried to reimpose the *status quo ante*, a split was inevitable.

Student Dropout Gets Involved

Following my graduation from Carleton in June 1969, I moved to New York City and worked enough odd jobs to afford food and my half of the $40 rent of a dump on the Lower East Side. In September I moved to Madison to attend graduate school at the University of Wisconsin in Ottoman and Middle Eastern history (I had lived in Turkey and Iran for 6½ years during my childhood). I soon discovered that I was much more interested in the antiwar movement, the counterculture, and Madison in general than the stifling atmosphere at the UW history department. I dropped out for the second semester, but discovered that employers in Madison were very conservative. I was offered two different jobs on the condition that I cut my hair—I refused, after ascertaining that women workers were not required to have short hair. My faith in the judicial system was not bolstered when my discrimination suits were dismissed.

I was seriously contemplating buying a short-haired wig when I was offered a job from a woman for whom I had worked at Columbia University the previous summer. As quickly as it took to buy my way out of my lease, I moved to New York. I got there on Sunday, May 3—the day before the Kent State murders. By Tuesday, I had persuaded my boss to let us go out on strike with full pay for a week—thank you, Stephanie, wherever you are! I also discovered I had elevated status among the Columbia students because I was a "worker." The excitement soon died down, though, and I went back to work. In September, two weeks after the Army Math bombing, I moved back to Madison to pursue my "exciting" life as a graduate student. Once again Madison proved more exciting than graduate school, and I dropped out for good at the end of the semester.

I first came into contact with Madison alternative journalism in the fall of 1970 by "hawking" *(Madison) Kaleidoscope.* At that time, people took bundles of a hundred *Kaleidoscope*s on consignment and sold them on the street. There would be hawkers on every corner of State Street and on a few other university streets; good hawkers could sell a hundred papers in an hour on the first day back from the printer, either by getting the "good corners" or by being obnoxious, intimidating, or persuasive. Anyone willing to invest several hours could sell a couple of hundred papers every two weeks: hawkers kept a dime of the 25-cent sales price.

During the time I hawked papers, I imagined the *Kaleidoscope* staff to be very cohesive and cliquey, and hopelessly closed to outsiders. There were probably two explanations for my feeling this way. Having come from a school of 1,300 in a town of 8,000, I was intimidated (even after a year of living in Madison and New York City) by the size of the university and the radical community. My shyness was compounded by my happening to interact with the staff at its least gregarious moment—the day staff members brought the laid-out pages to the printer and returned a couple of hours later with the completed bundles of papers. I realized later, once I became a veteran of newspaper publishing, that the core staff get less than adequate sleep the night or two before publication and feel a close affinity with their compatriots; in their burned-out condition, they might not have felt like interacting with strangers. I didn't realize this at the time, though, and thought that *Kaleidoscope* didn't need new staff. I never showed up during layout time, when I might have felt more welcome.

In the summer of 1971, I became involved in People's Office, a switchboard that provided services ranging from arranging overnight housing for visiting out-of-towners, to reciting that night's campus movies, to "acid rescue." That fall, as a result of a volunteer shortage, personnel from People's Office, which was housed in the same building as *Kaleidoscope*, were asked to help arrange *Kaleidoscope*'s calendar of events. I took the opportunity to work on the paper in other capacities as well.

In the four or so issues of *Kaleidoscope* I worked on, I recorded my experiences working as a corn detassler that summer along with a contingent of mostly fourteen- and fifteen-year-old boys, wrote a fantasy history of the revolution (bylined the Purple Sunlight Brigade), and compiled news shorts about government atrocities here and abroad for a feature called "In the Belly of the Monster." I was fascinated by the collection of underground papers *Kaleidoscope* had lying around, and loved the stimulation.

The *Kaleidoscope* Split

It was an interesting period. I happened upon *Kaleidoscope* shortly before it split into two papers. On one side was the group around editor Mark Knops, recently returned from his stint in jail for contempt. Knops was a perfectionist who felt the need to apply the editor's prerogative to have the final say over the paper's appearance. Much of the staff, having become accustomed to functioning as a collective during Knops's absence, objected to the hierarchy. While Knops's product was more graphically pleasing and coherent, the other side's was more spontaneous, and their instincts definitely more democratic.

The split, which occurred in November 1971, resulted in two biweekly papers, *Take Over* and the *King Street Trolley*. The two papers shared the *Kaleidoscope* office space and went to press on alternate weeks.

The faction led by Mark Knops, which became *Take Over*, was essentially unwilling to adapt to the changes brought into the movement by increased feminist consciousness. Members were predominantly male, and the ideological split brought out the worst sorts of machismo. During negotiations over the split, some of their followers showed up in motorcycle jackets and strutted around as if intent on bloodying some heads. Early *Take Over* articles glorifying prostitution probably reflected a reaction to the *Trolley* politics as much as Knops's bizarre notion that prostitution was a "revolutionary" alternative to the nuclear family. *Take Over*, during its eight years of publication, was "left-liberal" and anti-establishment in its politics, but it never really embraced current leftist thinking, although it was clearly sympathetic. This gave staffers independence and the license to be more creative and irreverent, but it also isolated them politically from the radical community.

The majority faction of *Kaleidoscope*, which became the *Trolley*, felt that the hierarchy, with Mark Knops as editor, was antithetical to the sorts of revolutionary changes they were pursuing for society. They started the trend, followed by both *Free For All* and *No Limits*, of having no editorial staff positions on the paper. While certain people clearly fulfilled those functions, no one was credited as such. They also felt the need to reach out to people who were not white males, through the newspaper if not in person. This evolving ideology was somewhat confining, and made them easy targets for the arrogant *Take Over* antagonists. Nevertheless, the general ideology portrayed in the *Trolley* set the tone for all subsequent Madison alternative papers through the nineties. The *Take Over* faction dismissed them as "Stalinoid creeps." Yet the Trolleyites were neither Stalinoid nor creepy. Instead they were dedicated leftists reflecting the evolving ideology of their time.

Overall, as individuals, people on both staffs shared many common political views, including opposition to the war, support for the "revolution," and hatred of police and mainstream capitalists. Yet, the papers they produced were vastly different. The *King Street Trolley* resembled *Kaleidoscope* in its political content and its not particularly pleasing graphic appearance. This was not surprising, as the vast majority of the *Kaleidoscope* staff had migrated to the *Trolley*.

In stark contrast, *Take Over* was sensationalist. Stark headlines and *National Enquirer*–type features were the rule. A feature story about how a worker at the Madison Oscar Mayer plant had allegedly fallen into the butchery and had been ground into and mixed with the sausage product (and how Oscar Mayer officials were covering up the story) was typical. Another cover story featured an "interview" with an IRA terrorist, which I only discovered years later was completely fictitious. *Take Over* was humorous and entertaining, interested in selling newspapers, and only coincidentally interested in converting people to leftist politics. One could say that *Take Over* strove to be the Madison political establishment's underground newspaper. Relatively unconstrained with news about the alternative community, *Take Over* was perfectly suited for that role. The *Trolley* and later *Free For All* and *No Limits*, on the contrary, geared themselves to the alternative community.

After a few months, when it became clear that *Take Over* would not become a financial success and press runs dwindled from the hoped-for 10,000 to 2,000 or so, Mark Knops ceased his active participation. Knops was a sort of enigma. He had basic leftist tendencies, but he felt strongly that the "masses" were uninterested in leftist politics or ideology, and that these had little or no place in an underground paper. While he was probably right that most people weren't interested in our dreams about the new society, I questioned the purpose of publishing a paper if propagandizing for the Left was not a part of it. The paper soon slimmed down to a core of five people, and actually became slightly more political in content.

Having been so new to *Kaleidoscope* at the time of its demise, I was ambivalent about where to put my energy—except that I knew I was interested in working on some underground newspaper. As a result, I was the only person who actually worked on the first several issues of both *Take Over* and the *Trolley*. Because the *Trolley* had a large staff and essentially ignored me, while, on the contrary, *Take Over* had promised me several pages of copy per issue, I began working exclusively for *Take Over*. Soon, I stopped working at People's Office and even quit my typist job at the University of Wisconsin.

At *Take Over*, I saw my role—in addition to the shit-work functions of circulation manager, exchange manager, main typist, and other unnamed, unglorified, but essential activities—as inserting enough leftist political news into the paper to make it palatable to the sizable leftist political community, in effect neutralizing the often sexist, usually politically irrelevant stuff in the rest of the paper. It was a tentative alliance at best. We did feel a certain kinship, as we were aware that, in these pre-Soglin days, we were under constant police surveillance, although none of us was ever personally confronted. When the *Trolley* folded in the late summer of 1972, I took it upon myself to argue for an increasing amount of leftist news. This put me in conflict with the rest of the staff, who felt such material was boring. I began to realize that I had made a mistake in ultimately siding with *Take Over*, despite the opportunity it had afforded me of filling several pages of each issue with material as I saw fit. Staff members did approve of my continuation and expansion of *Kaleidoscope*'s "Belly of the Monster," news shorts excerpted from other underground papers and, increasingly, humorous or bizarre filler stories rewritten from the straight press. I renamed the column the "World Truth Conspiracy," and changed it to the "Wong Truth Conspiracy" several issues later.

They were less taken, however, with my other contributions. As I pushed more and more strongly for additional national and international news in the paper (I wasn't yet focusing on local news), I ran into increasing resistance from Michael Fellner, the de facto editor who also solicited all the advertising. He didn't want to hustle more ads just to accommodate my pedestrian leftist news-service stories. I began feeling resentful that my editorial (not to mention administrative) work was not being appreciated. While on vacation at the end of 1972, I realized my further participation with *Take Over* was impossible.

Take Over continued publishing on a fairly regular basis until May 1979. It maintained its humor, irreverence, and good layout until the end. *Take Over* devoted a lot of space to local politics and had a special relationship with left-liberal Mayor Paul Soglin, who was in office initially from 1973 to 1979. They criticized him and his administration from the left. Yet, in 1977, when conservative challenger Nino Amato came in first in the mayoral primary (with Soglin placing second) and the pundits gave him a chance of beating Soglin in the general election, *Take Over* ran a feature story linking Amato to the Mob. I don't know whether the article was true, or more likely a typical *Take Over* mesh of fact and fiction, nor whether the story had a decisive impact on the outcome of the election. Amato filed suit, but Soglin won the election.

Probably the high point of *Take Over*'s existence was in about 1976 when they printed parodies of Madison's two daily newspapers. The *Capital Times* cover headline read "Nixon Suicide Attempt Fails," while the flip-side *State Journal* was headlined "Nixon Recovering from Ordeal." They placed these papers inside *Cap Times* and *State Journal* vending machines, and managed to sell 10,000 copies of that well-done issue. Jim Danky summed up *Take Over* aptly in an article he wrote for the *Harvest Quarterly* in 1977: "Needless to say, the paper has never failed to successfully call attention to itself."[1]

For instance, following the election of Paul Soglin as mayor in 1973 and his appointment of a liberal police chief, the Mifflin Street block parties became legal and institutionalized. Thousands of people descended upon Mifflin Street each May. Little known by the average partygoer was that all the profits from the party went to *Take Over*. After *Take Over*'s demise, the Mifflin St. Co-op took charge of any profits made, distributing them to groups requesting donations to further their underfinanced causes until the Co-op's own demise in 2006.

In 1989, Michael Fellner organized a reunion for veterans of Madison's underground papers. It was billed as a celebration of the twentieth anniversary of Miffland's declaration of independence. Fellner graciously invited former *Trolley* people, and others, including me, with whom *Take Over* had had difficulties. As the idea evolved, radicals from the late sixties and early seventies were invited, regardless of their involvement in alternative journalism. The event occurred around the July 4th weekend, from Friday through Tuesday the 4th, and included workshops, picnics, and parties. It concluded with a pro-choice rally and march to the Capitol. While *Kaleidoscope* and *Take Over* were adequately mentioned throughout the weekend, there was no mention of the *King Street Trolley*, *Free For All*, or *No Limits*. Those who had left Madison before 1972 and attended the get-together never learned of any other publications besides *Take Over*.

Free For All Founded

Following my split with *Take Over*, I started volunteering full-time at the Mifflin St. Co-op, which was located across the street from my house. A couple of weeks later, I learned that a group of people from People's Office were seeking to start up a new alternative newspaper—one that was in fact alternative to *Take Over*. Interestingly, while People's Office still found out-of-towners places to "crash" and housed the Acid Rescue office, callers were no longer told what movies were being shown on campus. Differentiation between campus and commercial movie-showing was no longer significant—both were considered mainstream and irrelevant to a leftist switchboard.

I was exhilarated at the prospect of working on a new paper. I was thrust into the odd position of being considered a veteran all-around journalist by the others, odd because my all-around experience stretched back less than a year and a half. At the *Carletonian*, I had been involved in all aspects of writing for a newspaper, but layout and other technical chores were done by the printer, the publisher of the town's weekly newspaper. Since coming to Madison, I had become knowledgeable about many aspects of newspaper production also, but other jobs—such as shooting a process camera—I had never done. Because I at least knew where the alternative community's process camera was, and because I knew how to load it, I was a relative expert.

The first issue of *Free For All* appeared on March 1, 1973—about six weeks after the first serious organizational meetings occurred, and six years to the day after Madison's first underground, *Connections*, had appeared. It was produced at night in the basement of a UW campus church basement (campus church basements have played a role in Madison leftist politics for several decades). One of the founders, a dope dealer, happened to be a very persuasive ad salesperson (he later made a fortune selling T-shirts), while the rest of us tried to pull in a few ads beyond the semi-obligatory ones from the alternative and cooperative communities. Our financial security dipped considerably after the second or third issue, when he faded from the scene.

Free For All differed from its recent predecessors in that it was circulated free and was dependent for its livelihood, after that initial two-month period, solely on advertising, plus a minimal amount from donations and subscriptions. By this time, there were enough co-ops and marginal alternative businesses in Madison to keep the paper afloat. Record companies—once the lifeblood of most underground newspapers—had by this time abandoned the political, self-avowed "revolutionary" newspapers and thrown their money instead into the less threatening and more apolitical, or at best quasi-political, music-oriented rags such as *Rolling Stone*.

Free For All carried on the role *Kaleidoscope* and the *Trolley* had previously borne—being the newspaper for the alternative community. *Take Over*, on the other hand, with its sensationalism and its general orientation, was the "alternative" newspaper for the straight community. This explains why alternative papers with three to four times the circulation were much less well known at the time than *Take Over*.

Although I didn't recognize it at the time, the transition to *Free For All* symbolized the end of the sixties. Staff members on Madison's earlier "underground" newspapers had been an integral part of the alternative community. While that community didn't encompass all young people, we went on the assumption that we spoke for all youth who weren't still brainwashed by their upbringing and past. Many of the people making up the *Free For All* core, however, had no ties to the alternative community. Although they had leftist politics, they decidedly were not part of the "cultural revolution"; some were even openly contemptuous of those for whom drug use was a way of life. They understood, less naively than we, that the majority of youth were not going to rally to our cause, and certainly that drug use by itself was not revolutionary.

It was the end of a euphoric era, when we had assumed that only a few more excesses by the government were needed to generate a mass uprising against the state. Instead, movement was in the other direction. The Chicago police violence in 1968, the open declaration of war against the state by the Weather Underground and other revolutionary groups in 1969, the Kent State murders in May 1970, and the August 1970 Army Math bombing caused many people to wonder how committed to the struggle they really wanted to be.

By 1972 and 1973, Nixon started withdrawing U.S. troops from Vietnam, while radicals and left liberals (including Madison's Paul Soglin) found out they could get elected to public office if they really tried. Government in many places—certainly in Madison—did become more open. Radical people were appointed to city committees. In Madison, the police chief, who many in the progressive community considered to be a fascist, was replaced by a liberal one who allowed demonstrators to do virtually everything except break windows. Those who remained in the leftist community were consciously separate from mainstream society—they were convinced that "working within the system" didn't work.

Free For All put out several issues in succession. While not exceedingly well written, and falling considerably short of professional graphic standards, it had a warm feeling. Its purpose was to support and be a part of the "alternative community," which was defined as both the people who subscribed to a notion of a political lifestyle different from that they had grown up in, and also the economic and political institutions—mostly cooperatives—that had sprung up to consolidate their alternative visions. At least thirty untrained but eager people worked on the first issue. It soon became apparent, though, that only a small minority of those thirty people were willing or able to commit the time needed to make a newspaper an ongoing reality.

The initial momentum of better-than-monthly publication was halted temporarily when four underground-paper people from Lansing, Michigan (including Ken Wachsberger, the editor of this book) pulled up in our driveway and asked my girlfriend and fellow *Free For All* staffer Marie and me if we wanted to go to Boulder, Colorado, for a conference of the Underground Press Syndicate (see figure 1). A few minutes later, we were on the road to Colorado nonstop in the back of a "driveaway"[2] pickup truck to attend a loosely structured affair and shoot the shit with people with whom we exchanged papers.

Our return home was delayed for a series of reasons. First, we had to go to Murray, Utah, and then Denver, Colorado, to deliver the pickup truck and then a ChemLawn truck. In both towns, we were investigated by suspicious local gendarmes, and en route to Denver the chemical fumes challenged my liver. In Denver, we had to wait for the police to release our eastbound driveaway car. That car turned out to be owned by Herb Score, the one-time phenom pitcher for the Cleveland Indians, whose career was ruined when his forehead caught a Gil McDougald line drive. Score was then working as a play-by-play announcer for the Indians in Cleveland, which was, conveniently, Ken's hometown. The previous driveawayers had been stopped somewhere in Kansas and found to have a trunk full of marijuana. The car must have been held for evidence, or maybe the company couldn't find anyone who wanted to go from Denver to Cleveland. On the way back to the Midwest, I had the Michigan people drop Marie and me off in Lincoln, Nebraska. There we stayed with staffers from the *(Lincoln) Gazette*, including Milton Yuan, the only Asian-American I met in my years in underground journalism. He was disappointed to find out that I was not actually of Asian descent: he had hoped to find "another Chinese American who had gone wrong." The *Gazette* later split into two, the older staff keeping the name *Gazette*, and Milton and the others forming the *People's Dispatch*. The two papers shared the *Gazette*'s typesetting machine, until the *People's Dispatch* refused to give it back one time and moved to Detroit to be good Stalinists.

By the time we got back to Madison, *Free For All* had come out again. It was a graphic disaster, even by *Free For All* standards. Most of the graphics were too small and too dark; the staff hadn't rented a proportionally spaced typewriter and didn't reduce the size of the type when making negatives. The paper didn't come out again for almost three months.

FIGURE 1: Participants at Alternative Press Conference in Boulder. Front row (*from left*): Steve Vernon (*with cigarette*) and Jim "Red Bear" Rieben (*with toothpick*), both from Lansing, Michigan's *Joint Issue*, and Sandy Shea from Liberation News Service (*slouching on the right*);. Second row: Ken Wachsberger (*black beard*), *Joint Issue* staffer and future editor of Voices from the Underground Series. C.Berlet/PublicEye.org.

We did manage to come out in September 1973, helped in large part by generous fall advertising budgets eager to greet returning students. Ads appealed directly to our perceived readership. One, from a liquor store, said, "Everybody Must Get Stoned." The graphic showed an underground comic character passed out on the street, bottle in hand, with the caption "Falling Down Drunk Stoned." A new hole-in-the-wall business that has since become one of Madison's largest camping/scuba/clothing stores ran an ad exclaiming, "Good Shit!! At Great Prices," with a picture of Spiderman saying, "Drop In! Or Else!"

The September issue reminded Madison that *Free For All* was back, and that we desperately needed staff. One person who answered the call, in late 1973, was Michael Kaufman. Michael was unemployed, looking for work, and had lots of energy to work on the paper, even when he finally got a job. I was paying rent with money saved from my earlier typist job, volunteering at Mifflin St. Co-op in exchange for "wages" that could be applied toward food and other co-op products, and was, therefore, able to live job-free. Together we did the bulk of the work for several issues.

Free For All varied from issue to issue, with few stable features. Two of them that did appear regularly were written by me: the "modestly" titled "Wong Truth Conspiracy," a two-page spread of news shorts I had also written for *Take Over*, and "On the Road to Fascism," a surprisingly good (as I reread it thirty-five years later) summary of domestic political news, focusing, until his resignation, on Nixon, who was known in the column as Nixswine. I always considered "Wong Truth Conspiracy" a sort of loss leader for the alternative papers I worked on, humorous yet political writing that (I hoped) drew the reader into the more substantive, serious, and political stuff comprised by the rest of the paper. Anonymous observation of people on the days the new issues came out confirmed that Wong Truth was invariably the first section people turned to. (We always referred to the column as Wong Truth as the two-page spread's heading was vertical, with "Wong Truth" on one page and "Conspiracy" on the other.) I watched to see how long they read the paper after finishing the column. Michael later also contributed a regular feature, "Revolution Abroad," a synopsis of what was going on in the Third World, particularly in countries where Marxist-Leninist regimes had taken over, or where Marxist guerrilla groups were active.

In the spring of 1974, another Miffland resident and Mifflin Co-op volunteer, Rick Caprow, joined the staff, and Michael brought in some people from the housing co-op where he lived. The staff was beginning to grow, and we knew the paper was going to survive its infancy. As long as a staff is extremely small, the urge to keep that paper alive predominates, and factional disputes are kept to a minimum. Once the staff grows and stabilizes, there is time to analyze the different political viewpoints represented. Michael was talented and basically easy to work with. He also was a convinced Maoist/Communist who thought anarchism was nonrevolutionary and "petit bourgeois." Phil Davis, on the other hand, the major person Michael had brought in, was of anarchist persuasion and certainly anti-Soviet and anti-China. I had libertarian instincts but was not an overt anarchist. Rick was outspokenly anarchist and showed me that my libertarian instincts were in line with present-day anarchist thinking.

FFA Leans towards Anarchism

Rob Lerman and Nomi Schwartz, paper people from the beginning, basically were dubious about the ruling "Communist" regimes, but didn't think (Rob especially) that it was our job to attack the "Left." Despite their presence and Michael's, the paper took a decidedly anarchist drift. Typical of this period was an article Rick wrote about a speech he and I had attended, given by Bob Avakian, the head honcho of the Revolutionary Union (RU), a Maoist sect that had received the "China franchise" (the right to speak for China in the United States) from the Maoist regime. Because Avakian considered himself a dangerous revolutionary and therefore a ripe target for assassination, we were frisked before being allowed into the room. Chairman Bob rambled on for several hours about the need for "Communist revolution." We wrote it up under the headline "Stalinism: RU Serious?"

The article itself was a report on Avakian's speech, with frequent digressions into repudiations of the RU perspective. Along with the article was a "discussion piece" entitled "Which Way Goes the Movement?," an attack on the theory that the vanguard party should lead the "masses" to revolution, balanced with a reminder that the revolution meant destruction, not seizure, of power, and that it involved much more than just the economic question of who controlled the means of production.

Quoting from literature of another vanguard group, Detroit's Motor City Labor League, Rick expressed genuine indignation that an allegedly leftist group could talk about "lines [being] drawn so that we can precisely chart the path to revolution . . . [and] achieve the necessary unity of will so that the Party can impose iron discipline in order to lead the proletariat to deal the necessary death blows to decadent capitalism" (this wasn't Rick's and my idea of smashing the state). Rick added, "To get a historical perspective on the mentality I am talking about, remember that one hero of these 'vanguard parties' is none other than modern history's number two mass murderer Joseph Stalin. I am serious, they praise him and quote him in their literature. One has to struggle to keep from going blind with rage at the thought of it." To add insult to injury, one of our graphics on the pages was a profile of Stalin, designed as a mug shot, with the serial number added 5369417PIG.

The article provoked reactions. Externally, several RU adherents and/or their student affiliates, the Revolutionary Student (we always said "Stalinist") Brigade, set the papers sitting inside the doorway to our building afire. Internally, our own skepticism that China provided the guiding light for the movement, as reflected in our discussions inside the office and by our snide remarks in the paper wherever we could sneak them in (the "Wong Truth Conspiracy" was a natural), was distressing to Michael. He managed to convince Lucy Mathiak, his woman friend who was herself a marginal contributor, and Rob and Nomi to request a meeting to discuss their futures on the paper, in light of *Free For All*'s obvious drift toward an anarchist philosophy.

At the meeting, held around November 1974, we decided that the paper should include all factions of the Left, including Michael's brand of quasi-independent Maoism. In retrospect, we probably should have told the non-anarchists to fuck off and start their own paper if they needed an outlet.

The anarchists were in a position of strength in late 1974, but chose not to capitalize on it. We felt that *Free For All* would be a better paper for Michael's and Rob's contributions. In fact, the *Free For All* of 1975 was a fairly good newspaper. Following a month-long trip to the East and South around the end of the year, I helped start the Madison branch of the People's Bicentennial Commission (PBC). The idea, primarily the brainchild of Jeremy Rifkin, was to re-create scenes of the rebellion that had taken place two hundred years before, use selective quotes that made the Founders sound radical, and reenact historical events on their 200th anniversary—in general, to counteract the celebration of capitalism that the corporate mainstream was planning to commemorate. I spent six months working with PBC. During that time, my involvement at *Free For All* was limited to doing the Wong Truth and inserting articles about the PBC.

When I rejoined the staff full-time in about the middle of 1975, there was a different feel to the paper. It seemed to crave more structure. We had experimented during the first half of 1975 with the idea of a paid staff by paying Rick $100 a month to coordinate all publication tasks, but he had burned out and moved to Sturgeon Bay, Wisconsin, to become a ship welder. Phil seemed to have become less of an anarchist.

At about this time, *Free For All* moved from its first long-term home to an office in the university YMCA. Although the space was much bigger and the atmosphere in the Y much more leftist, the move was somehow symbolic of a change. We had been in a large room above a store on State Street, the street that bridged the eight blocks between the state capitol and the university. One neighbor was a strange character who would come next door to our office and ask, "Does anyone want to come next door and smoke a j[oint]?" Those who did—he always had good dope—were frequently subjected to a lengthy monologue on the subject of cancer.

FIGURE 2: Cover cartoon for *Free For All* volume 3, number 13 (September 18–October 7, 1975). Courtesy DreamWorldDragon Press.

The memories of that office are countless. The stimulating conversations we had with staffers and visitors, from both Madison and out of town, the arguments, the frequent all-night sessions—in short, everything that characterized the early years of *Free For All*—took place in that dingy room. One lasting, annoying memory is the green flying bugs that infested our office in the summer and kamikazeed on our layout pages, the price we paid for renting a hole-in-the-wall office that had no screens on the windows. I never felt comfortable in the new office. Michael's presence was felt heavily. Yet that fall something happened that gave anarchism its last hurrah on *Free For All*. A talented artist had shown up, and we had recruited him to draw some front covers for the paper. His first was a three-part graphic depicting "the Capitalist Way," "the Communist Way," and "Another Way" (see figure 2). The first two drawings were similar: in both pictures, workers at the bottom were trudging along, chained together. The air was full of pollution from numerous smokestacks. Above the trudging workers was an animal with a whip: in the "Capitalist Way," a massive pig was portrayed as the owner of Swine Works; in the "Communist Way," a similar-sized rat was in charge of the People's Foundry and the People's Steel Works. Below those two drawings was "Another Way," an idyllic (definitely naive) portrayal of an apple-picking collective—the sun shining, everyone happy.

Most of our readers who contacted us loved it and supported the cover's thesis that we needed a revolutionary alternative to the twin oppressive systems of capitalism and communism. But Michael was furious. Even though he understood (I think . . . I hope!) that the state-capitalist bosses were no better than the capitalist bosses from the workers' point of view, he didn't feel the Left should be the ones to point that out. We thought it was exactly the Left that should point it out. In reacting to reader responses, Michael redoubled his efforts to purge the paper of the anarchist ideology. Although Rick, the energetic anarchist, had moved away, several people with decidedly anarchist leanings had joined the paper. Unfortunately they played mostly minor roles and were unreliable. Many others, primarily of a leftist but nevertheless "don't rock the boat" mentality (their "boat" was the cooperative movement and the Left in general), joined the staff on Michael's side.

I began to wonder whether I should spend time and effort resisting the takeover of *Free For All* by a bunch of humorless leftists. One major difference between my way of thinking and theirs was in determining when the paper should publish: my idea was that we were an "alternative" paper and therefore not a "news" paper. I felt we shouldn't publish on a specific date if we didn't have enough good material to make it worthwhile; they felt that we should publish on a regular schedule, to make our calendar of events useful and "because we promised our advertisers we'd publish." Were we a totally "alternative" newspaper or an alternative version of a regular newspaper? The development of *Isthmus* in Madison and other liberal but definitely calendar-oriented weeklies around the country took over that role for the "alternative" newspapers, and made "revolutionary" biweeklies that revolved around a calendar of events obsolete—most advertisers preferred a professional-looking paper with no threatening politics to a graphic disaster with emphatically leftist politics.

Origins of the Split

Between January and the late summer of 1975, a new need for order and structure descended upon the paper. We had always printed publishing schedules, but we had always been flexible as to whether we adhered to that schedule (and, in fact, we rarely did). Now, it had become an obsession to publish on the date forecast in the previous issue. More than merely irritating to someone with social plans on the night before publication (always a late night, sometimes all night), this made volunteers think being on the paper was work rather than fun. Naturally, when there was "work" to do, we needed to pay someone to do it. Looking back to Rick's monthly paycheck earlier in the year as precedent, staffers talked increasingly of the need to hire people to produce the paper.

The amount we could afford to pay, however, was totally inadequate for even subsistence living. Furthermore, with a paid staff, unpaid people volunteered less often—particularly for the shit jobs such as soliciting advertising. This added pressure on the paid staff assured rapid turnover. Nevertheless, the paper's reliance on whoever was paid staff made them "more equal" than the volunteer staff. Given the various political factions within the newspaper, the then-dominant faction would make sure a person of their political persuasion became the paid staff member. For these reasons, the paid-staff concept at this juncture of *Free For All*'s existence really couldn't work.

In late 1975, an incident occurred that further delineated the split in thinking on the paper. An article in the December issue of *Take Over* revealed that two people involved in the movement in the early seventies had actually been police agents. One of these people, Steve Featherston, had been one of the founders of *Free For All* and had worked at People's Office before that. According to Steve, he had been recruited in Missouri by George Croal, a notorious Madison policeman who was particularly identified with spying on and harassing the Left. Steve came to Madison and dutifully reported on his comrades in People's Office and *Free For All*. He stopped his work for the police some time in 1973. While he was never a major contributor to the paper, he was a frequent visitor, co-authored baseball columns with me, wrote fitness columns, and generally contributed good humor to his environment. He was genuinely working-class, unlike most of the staff, and I remained a good friend of his.

In response to the *Take Over* article, Steve wrote another article, entitled "Free For All's Informer Tells His Story," for the January 1976 *Free For All*. In that article, which he signed "MPD706," Steve referred to the *Take Over* article, confessed to everything, and asked people's forgiveness for something he had done without thinking about the consequences. (The longer he hung around his informees, the more guilty he felt about his job. A few months after he quit working for the pigs, he tried unsuccessfully to hang himself.) Since Steve still hung around the paper, Michael demanded a "trial" for him, an inquisition at which this self-righteous, holier-than-thou leftist could set down the conditions for Steve's continued participation on the paper. After enduring more abuse than I would have tolerated, Steve adjourned with me and a few others to our favorite bar. This unnecessary humiliation of an obviously repentant ex-informer left a very bad taste in my mouth.

Around this time, nationwide, a movement was being organized by Marxist-Leninist types to take advantage of the hard times people were experiencing. The Weather Underground had also distributed its book *Prairie Fire* around this time, an exciting event for many of us. The idea was to sponsor "Hard Times" conferences around the country. One was held in Chicago in January 1976, and about ten people from *Free For All* attended. Simultaneously, there was a drive in Madison to establish a "Community Union" to direct political activity on the left. The anarchist community immediately dubbed it a "community onion." The CU's intent was to have a board of directors to decide what political activity was appropriate for the "community" to participate in.

The idea was not totally without merit. Politically these *were* "hard times" for the Left. Several years had now passed since the Left in Madison could muster more than a couple of hundred people at political demonstrations. It was becoming apparent that the mass movement of the late sixties and early seventies had been the exception to the norm, rather than the beginning of a general uprising against the establishment. A central organization in town that was in contact with movements in Madison and other cities and that had a few paid full-time staff members was no doubt helpful in publicizing activities.

But more dominant was another group of people more interested in controlling the movement and establishing themselves as the vanguard of the movement, the enlightened few who could guide the wavering movement onto the correct path. To them, these hard times called for more leadership and more unity. Usually unspoken (although not always) was the fact that it would be their leadership and that they would impose the unity.

On *Free For All*, Michael viewed the Hard Times movement nationally and the Community Union locally as a godsend. A majority of the staff appeared to agree with him that the CU was a good thing. Members of *FFA*'s anarchist minority, who shared the suspicions of Madison's nonauthoritarian Left, argued that staff members as individuals could participate in the CU as they saw fit, but that the paper itself should not take a stand pro or con, given the differences of opinion about it among the staff. Our point of view was rejected, and *Free For All* became the major advocate and cheering section for the Community Union.

While the core staff during that time remained very small, there were twenty or thirty people who came to meetings or milled around the office during layout sessions. Structurally, members didn't hold formal titles; officially, at least, we were all equal. Yet a subtle change took place during 1975: the staff had evolved into a "collective." This change involved more than semantics. While a staff was a group of individuals who gathered to produce the paper, a collective was a politically cohesive collection of individuals who met to produce the paper. The paper tried to reach agreement by consensus. Those who disagreed with the majority opinion and therefore stood in the way of consensus (as defined by the majority) were branded "consensus-blockers" and people who couldn't "work collectively."

One "collective" decision had been to keep to a regular publication schedule. To back up that schedule, they set rigid deadlines, particularly for submission of copy. Traditionally I had spent the first several days of layout hanging around the office, trying to keep volunteers busy, editing people's articles, typing them, and laying out other people's pages. About 36 hours before publication, I would go to work on my articles—the two-page "Wong Truth Conspiracy" and the one to four other pages I had agreed to write and lay out. My routine never caused us to miss a publication date. But this schedule was unacceptable to the "collective" under the new regime. (I would be disingenuous if I didn't admit that writing my articles late in the process irritated others I worked with over the years, and I have always been very good at procrastination.)

Consistently not meeting these newly imposed deadlines cast me as an "individualist" resisting the collective will. Conveniently forgotten was the fact that I single-handedly did more to get the paper under way during the first few days of the issue's layout than most of the people who showed up at collective meetings to forge the "collective will."

Although I am usually not given to conspiracy theories, in retrospect I think a conspiracy was working against me during the early part of 1976. Every staff sets copy deadlines for articles. The deadlines exist for people whose writing ability or reliability are in question, and/or for people who submit their articles and let others process them further. But for those who write their articles, type them, find graphics, lay them out, and don't delay publication in so doing, a deadline seemed less necessary. It had been an unspoken agreement on *Free For All* that, unless the author asked others for feedback, articles written by members of the core staff were not edited by others. For instance, Michael's "Revolution Abroad" column found no fault with any two-bit dictator as long as the dictator proclaimed himself a Marxist-Leninist. I was a little repulsed by Michael's glorification of petty dictators, albeit proclaimed leftists, but felt he had the right to write what he believed in, especially if he awarded me that same right. Since I did all the work on my articles, solicited input from others on graphics, honored self-imposed deadlines (even if it meant staying up the last 48 hours straight), and still had time to do the camera work on the paper, I felt that the newfound insistence on deadlines for all had been specifically designed for me.

In March of 1976, a dispute during layout saw me accused of being "anti-woman" as well as an anti-collective "rugged individualist." While the story list for any given issue, although fluid, was established early on, one of the last decisions usually was about the front cover, mostly due to lack of any ideas rather than a surplus. Often we solved the dilemma somewhat unsatisfactorily by printing one or more stories on the front page. For an issue in late February 1976, though, we had come up with two ideas and had agreed to do a split cover. "My" cover was a graphic accompanying an article urging people to withhold part of their utility bills to protest an illegal rate increase the local utility, Madison Gas & Electric, was collecting in defiance of a court order. The organization behind the protest, People United for Responsible Energy (PURE), had asked us to help publicize the effort, and we had responded by saying we would devote part of the front page to their story. The other plan for the front cover was a graphic to introduce the centerfold, which listed the schedule of events for International Women's Day. The dispute arose when Nomi finally found a graphic she liked for the cover—because it was vertical, it could only take the whole cover or a fourth of it. Since we had promised PURE that we would publicize the bill protest on our cover, and because I thought standing up to a monopoly was as important as publicizing the upcoming celebration and series of workshops, I held out for half of the front cover.

This was the way most disputes during layout were resolved: the majority present at the time of the dispute prevailed. Because of who was in the office that night, the other side prevailed: the PURE story was relegated to page 5, and the Women's Day graphic took up the whole front page. I felt not giving PURE front-page publicity at a time when they were trying to build momentum for the payment-withholding and for their organization was wrong. My advocacy on PURE's behalf, though, was not taken by the other staffers as advocacy on behalf of a community group who had asked us for much-needed support. Instead, my advocacy for PURE was proof positive that I was anti-woman, anti-feminist.

Another mindset gaining currency at that time—perhaps it was a new variant of white middle-class guilt about "skin privilege" that developed during the Black Power movement of the late 1960s—was an attitude that favored certain groups over others. For instance, women had higher status than men; gays and lesbians higher status than straights; "workers" (presumably blue-collar) higher status than non-"workers" and students; non-whites higher status than whites. The origin of these attitudes made sense—it was a rebellion against the white male (heterosexual) power structure, the system we were trying to replace with one that was more humane. Yet these attitudes, when carried to their extreme, caused friction. The quarrel cited above was one example. The paper's willingness to redo a page or two the night before we were going to press in order to accommodate the request for space of a women's or gay group (a request we denied to other groups) was another. Those of us who thought such favoritism was inappropriate were branded "anti-women," "anti-gay," or anti-whatever.

Another point of difference on the paper concerned the Wobblies. In 1974 the paper had become an Industrial Workers of the World (IWW or Wobbly) union shop. For a period, more than twenty of us carried Wobbly "red cards." As time went on, however, most staffers let their memberships lapse, but several of us stayed on. The local Wobblies were a source of fresh talent on the paper. They came as ardent proponents of anarcho-syndicalism—a point of view that rubbed the paper's Marxist-Leninists the wrong way because of the Wobbly belief that labor unions should be revolutionary rather than business unions.

Our criticism of the Eastern European and other "Communist" regimes for their basic authoritarianism and elitism, including the fact that labor unions in "Communist" countries were docile adherents to the party line and totally subservient to the state, reignited long-expressed concerns by some that we shouldn't be criticizing the "Left." We countered by saying that any government that could only stay in power through creating a police state was definitely not leftist. This tension lay mostly under the surface, but it was there nonetheless.

Although we all shared the one incentive to get the paper published, these combined tensions created a rather unpleasant atmosphere around the paper through 1975. By the beginning of 1976, we probably all realized in our subconscious at least that a split was inevitable.

The paper still consisted of about four or five people who did at least 80 percent of the work, plus a much larger group of people who came to meetings and/or hung around during layout sessions. This latter group probably considered themselves staff people even though they didn't do much. These hangers-on tended to have the politics of those who had brought them into the paper. By this time our faction had about ten adherents, the other side not quite twice as many. We thought them grim and humorless; they thought us nuisances who, through our constant questions about the paper's direction, kept the paper from realizing its true potential.

The unpleasantness led me to withdraw somewhat. On a few issues in the spring of 1976, other people on the staff wrote and laid out the Wong Truth. The first incident that led directly to the paper's eventual split occurred when I asked that the paper not use the name Wong Truth Conspiracy on those issues that I didn't work on. Rather than simply change the name, the other faction of the staff inserted a contest box saying in part, "RENAME WONG TRUTH! *Free For All* believes in change. After three years of the old one, we finally revised our masthead last January. But we've used the 'Wong Truth' name since Volume 1, Number 1, 47 action-packed issues, and *frankly, we're bored*" (my emphasis). This was inserted without my knowledge, and since the column contained my name, I thought it appropriate that I see what they were running before it went to press.

I wrote a letter in response for the following issue, stating that "I was appalled to see the distortion of facts contained in the contest box in last issue's Wong Truth," and going on to delineate some of the problems I saw occurring on the paper. My letter was printed, along with seven responses (on a page entitled "Stimulus-Response") attacking me and my letter and essentially boiling the whole controversy down to a personality conflict centering on my inability to get along with the "collective" or to work "collectively." Needless to say, no one sharing my feelings about the paper was invited to write a response.

The "Stimulus-Response" page threw me for a loop and further decreased my interest in working on the paper. Ironically, at the same time that I was withdrawing voluntarily from the paper, the other side was plotting my expulsion. The "collective" (i.e., Michael, Rob, and Phil) called for a meeting to expel me. A recent Wobbly recruit, Frank Callahan, incensed at the majority's treatment of me, had vowed to increase his involvement on the paper, specifically to be confrontational and irritating to them. For his efforts over the course of just two issues, Frank was elevated to the status of codefendant in the "purge trial."

The only mention in writing of this meeting was in a letter written by seven staff members who were critical of the "Stimulus-Response" page. The letter said in part, "The nature and layout of the page leads one to believe that Tim, in his rugged individualism, singlehandedly is obstructing the decisions of the otherwise unified 'collective.' This is hardly the case. In reality, over the last six months, many of us at *FFA* have been frustrated by the grim and humorless ordeal that producing *FFA* has become. We have come to question this mythical monster called the 'collective.' Is the collective the three individuals who, without informing anyone else (not even their friends, let alone Tim) went and took Tim's name off the *FFA* [bank] account claiming that at a 'collective' meeting new officers had been elected?" It then described the upcoming meeting, and continued, "Do purges constitute collective process? How many of us will have to be removed before the paper 'functions' collectively? We urgently await the day when *FFA* will once again become the open community newspaper it once was."

The Split

The stage was set for a split, and it occurred. The expulsion meeting actually discussed four options: (1) to continue as usual, (2) to expel Frank and me, (3) to split the paper in two but continue to share the same facilities on a rotating basis, and (4) to split the assets. Although the major elements of the "collective" faction favored the expulsion option, they could not muster the two-thirds vote needed to bring that about. Since they had a paranoid distrust of our honest intentions (witness the bank-account shenanigan), they rejected the office-sharing option.

Being in the minority, we favored the "continue as usual" choice, but this choice was unacceptable to the other side. That left only the option of splitting the assets. It passed on a 20–9 vote. The only real difference between the expulsion and assets-splitting was that the latter guaranteed our side some stake in the paper. Otherwise, the effect was the same: the seven members of our group not up for expulsion would not have stayed on the paper had the two of us been expelled.

The "collective" then set a meeting to discuss how the assets would be split—they picked a day on which they knew we couldn't attend. Only one person from our side showed up, and he left before the vote. The outcome would not have been different had we been there. Considering that we were not, we were lucky to receive half the cash in the bank (our share was $750) and half of the layout supplies. They got to keep the office, the name of the paper, and, most importantly to me, the post office box. The P.O. box was critical, because that was where our incoming mail came, including all the other underground papers from around the country that I had worked with almost exclusively from the beginning to get exchange subscriptions. They kept the two functioning typewriters and gave us one whose worth did not much exceed its value at a recycling center.

Their bitterness against us and their paranoid assumptions that we would try to destroy their paper pervaded their writings about the split. They framed the issue as a few dissidents against the otherwise unified "collective." In a guest editorial in the UW student newspaper, *The Daily Cardinal*, they wrote: "The basic division began over the role of collective action and the individual's responsibility in a collective. . . . Some individuals have interpreted [*FFA*'s billing itself as an 'open community newspaper'] to mean 'for anyone to do whatever she/he wants.' . . . Unfortunately, there were a few staff members who valued their individual right to dissent to the exclusion of the rights of either other individuals or the collective as a whole." Blithely ignored was the fact that over a third of the staff at the "purge trial" refused to expel these "few staff members" for their crimes against the "collective." In other words, a significant minority of the paper's staff refused to accede to the dominant faction's desire to rid itself of the nuisance minority, pious and self-righteous pronouncements about the "collective" notwithstanding.

Their editorial continued with a rewriting of history, designed to suit their political goals rather than the actual facts. They had proposed the meeting to divide the assets to occur two days hence. I and several others said we could not attend that night because of an IWW meeting. They decided to schedule the meeting for that night regardless, and their version read: "The rugged individualists once again demonstrated their contempt for the *Free For All* collective by failing to attend the meeting."

I'm not sure what Rob, Michael, Phil, and others thought we were going to do to them immediately after the split. Their *Cardinal* editorial continued: "Given these individuals' low regard for group process, however, we doubt that the last word's been spoken. [We wondered: were we to submit to their collective will even after we weren't part of the collective?] *Free For All* will likely come under heavy attack soon. It's up to readers who have enjoyed and supported what *Free For All* has been trying to do recently to demonstrate that support now. . . . *Free For All* is still YOUR community newspaper. Accept no substitutes!"

In their next issue, late August 1976, their back page consisted of an expanded rewrite of their version of the *Free For All* split, newly entitled "How We Spent Our Summer Vacation," and what became a standard feature of the post-split *Free For All*, a whining plea for money. Their new last paragraph on the split contained this gratuitous sentence: "The rugged individualists now have the where-with-all [*sic*] to put out their own paper, or play the stock market if they want to, free from domination by their imagined oppressors."

Rather than feeling a need to attack their paper (physically or in writing), we felt that their humorlessness and constant whining about lack of money were their own worst enemy. We felt that unless they brought in some new staff not afflicted with the grim Hard Times/Community Union attitude, they would fall under their own dead weight.

While I was much too emotionally involved in the paper to be objective about the split, Jim Danky's article on the Madison underground press[3] seemed to affirm our point of view: "The anarchistic spirit that produced *Free For All* was only one source for its staff and readership.

Other persons were interested in more controlled progress towards goals and this led to a staff division which produced [No Limits]."

Before delving into *No Limits*, a few footnotes about *Free For All* are in order. Within a year of the split, most of the people from the majority faction had stopped working on the paper. The paper underwent a steady decline in appearance, due in no small part to their essential purge of the most experienced and creative layout people. *Free For All* limped along until 1981, a slave to its calendar of events, with rarely a story worth glancing at after about 1977 or so. The begging for donations became the dominant feature of the paper along with the calendar of events, which drove the requirement to produce the paper on a regular basis. Most of the work was now done by the overworked, underpaid paid staff member. The result was a monotonous, boring paper—truly the end result of what I had predicted if *Free For All* tried to seriously pay staff in its then-underfinanced position.

A typical issue appeared in April 1977, eight months after the "purge trial." It contained two quarter-page requests for money. The one on the back page, the usual location of their pleas for money, was headlined: "Did you know that we need your help!" and continued, "Hmm, you say. Two pleas for money in one issue! Things at *Free For All* must be pretty desperate. Well, they are and they aren't. *FFA* can go on the way it's been going for quite some time yet, struggling to pay for each issue and leaving a trail of burnt out staffers in its wake. But it takes a lot of money and energy to put out the paper, and right now, both are in short supply." Then they begged for $1,000 to pay two people $60 a week for two months, "by which time they will have (in theory) improved the quality of the paper, sold a bunch of new ads, and found other ways of funding *Free For All* to keep it going from there." Judging from their continuing pleas for more money, no one bit in a significant way at their request.

A few months later, they offered to cease publication unless the community bailed them out, and held a "community meeting" to discuss their problems. The response was apparently sufficient to persuade them to limp along, which they did for another four years.

One of the more amusing (or is "pathetic" more apropos?) incidents in the history of the post-split *FFA* was when a *No Limits* staffer (a person not known to them) answered a job notice *Free For All* had posted with the Job Service, the state employment agency with which many unemployment compensation applicants feigned compliance in order to get their unemployment checks. The *Free For All* interviewer informed the applicant that the earring he was wearing in his left ear needed to be removed. Political buttons were also taboo, and a haircut was suggested. Quoting from the December 1978 *No Limits*, the story continues, "The interviewer asked the applicant if he owned a sport coat and tie. Assuming that *FFA* was somewhat left in its politics, the applicant laughed and replied, 'Good god. Of course not.' *FFA* made it quite clear that they were not joking and that the sport coat and tie were prerequisites for employment. We deal with businesses that respect a 'clean attire,' spoke the interviewer."

The final footnote on *Free For All* is what happened to Steve and Michael. Steve, the erstwhile informer, returned to St. Louis and got a job at the General Motors plant there. He was later transferred to a new GM plant in Oklahoma and became a vice president of his local, and later became an organizer for the United Auto Workers itself. In the tradition of radical unionists and contrary to customary business union practice, while Steve was the local VP, he insisted on working half time in the plant. Michael, on the other hand, the ardent "communist" who harangued Steve so about his youthful indiscretion, moved to New York and volunteered at the *Guardian*, an orthodox leftist weekly. When the staff unionized and went out on strike, Michael, I was told, crossed the picket lines and helped the "communist" managers produce scab issues until the strike was settled.

The Origins of *No Limits*

No Limits was virtually the antithesis of *Free For All.* Having received our share of the money and supplies, we saw no urgent need to produce an issue immediately. We had lost our office, our name, and our incoming mail to the other faction of the paper, which continued to produce issues under the influence of the temporary high stemming from their victory over us. Only gradually did it sink in that getting the paper out required the same amount of energy as before, that all their loyal voters during the purge trial weren't willing to contribute energy during layout sessions, and that they needed to put out the paper without the services of several people (us) who had previously contributed essential time, energy, and talent.

A little less than three months after the purge trial, in late October 1976, *No Limits* produced its first issue. We arrived at the name *No Limits* by getting together and, quoting from the first issue, "playing the game of free association in various states of altered consciousness." Many of the 199 names were awful. Following the first list, we voted on the ones we liked best. The semifinalists were Black Swan, Black Tornado, Black Hole, Eclipse, Constant Comment, Off My Toes, Permanent Vacation, Dispossessed, Wildcat, Subversive Times, Phlebitis Times, Total Eclipse, Under Toe, Dream World Dragon, Morning Glory, Synapse, and No Limits. Synapse and Permanent Vacation ended up being the most serious challengers to *No Limits.* Other suggestions included Madison Mosquito, Purple Sunlight, Free For All, Long Live Death, Black Carp, Sour Grapes, Enemy of the People, The Tyrant's Foe, Zero for Forty, Madison Hot Shot, Sugar in the Gas Tank, Black Pajamas, Rugged Individualist, Frankly We're Bored (these two were references to the *Free For All* split), Black Blood, Wicked Messenger, No Compromise, Nixon's Bloodclot, Spherical Orange, Black Orange, Swamp Gas, Bela Kun's Necktie, Methane Messenger, and Unlimited Pleasure. (Twenty-six of the names contained the word "black," reflecting the fact that anarchists rallied behind the color "black," much as communists identify with the color red.)

What we discovered when we got together to produce the first issue was that, while we were all anarchists, anarchism encompassed several very different points of view. The primary distinction was between anarcho-syndicalists and other types of anarchists. Anarcho-syndicalists are anarchists who believe that the working class will rise up against the employing class and overthrow the government they dominate. Other types of anarchists oppose all types of hierarchy, including government, but do not see workers, through their control of the means of production, as the critical force in revolution. All but two of the *FFA* rejectees were in the Wobblies, and therefore sympathetic to anarcho-syndicalism. The two who weren't, Bob Brubaker and Scott McPherson, were strong advocates of their position, assuring that the paper would reflect both of these currents of anarchist thought.

Our first issue had two front covers, one of *No Limits* and one of *Free For All.* The *No Limits* cover was an election cover, encouraging a "Vote for Nobody." It exhorted: "If you think nobody should run your life, vote for nobody. Nobody keeps campaign promises. Nobody deserves to live off your taxes. Nobody can legislate your freedom. Nobody is the perfect candidate. If you *think*, vote for Nobody for President." The graphic was a picture of Gerald Ford sitting at his presidential desk, with his head whited out. The amazing feature about the cover to me was that it was graphically sophisticated—a "duotone," red on brown. *Free For All* had never had the graphic capability to produce such a cover. Scott, who had basically been scorned during the eight months or so he had hung around *Free For All* and only had one "article" printed (a graphic of a phony UW survey of student apathy he had distributed during one student registration week), produced the cover, with the various colors in perfect registration, no less. The rest of us were impressed.

The second page consisted of the list of names we had considered, several ads (including one for me, running for Dane County Registrar of Deeds on the "Abolish Private Property" ticket), and a statement of "Who We Are" (see sidebar 1). The issue was laid out in the basement of our five-bedroom cooperative house, giving us the license to say in our staff box: "Working out of a near east side basement, we are Madison's only true underground newspaper."

SIDEBAR 1

WHO WE ARE

We are a group of people who associate ourselves with the emerging movement for a free society. As part of an anti-authoritarian tradition of social revolution, we fight for an end to the tyranny of capitalism and the state over our lives, and against all forms of authority, hierarchy, and bureaucracy.

We see *No Limits* as a contribution to this movement—providing a forum for libertarian ideas and analysis of local, national, and international events from an anti-authoritarian perspective. *No Limits* will also provide news and general information which is of interest to the Madison community.

Some of us are members of the Industrial Workers of the World (IWW); others of us are members of a Madison libertarian communist group called Aurora; many of us are associated with the Social Revolutionary Anarchist Federation (SRAF).

The decision-making process at *No Limits* reflects our convictions about the structure of a free society; all decisions are made democratically and by consensus. Our view of consensus includes respect for the rights of the minority. By allowing for differences of thought and opinion within the paper, we find it possible to work together cooperatively and with a sense of unity.

No Limits will be published on a monthly basis. We will print 10,000 copies each issue, which will be distributed free at various locations in the Madison area. Unfortunately, until we become independently wealthy from your subscriptions, we will be forced to finance *No Limits* from advertisements.

If you feel any affinity for what we are doing, we encourage you to join us in working on *No Limits*!

From *No Limits* 1, no. 1 (October 1976): 2.

Page 3 featured a debate on voting. My article, entitled "Why You Should Vote," said that, although 95 percent of electoral candidates had essentially identical positions, some candidates, particularly in small districts such as city council or county board, were radical enough to vote for and did make a difference compared to their opposition. I contended that the mainstream media concentrate vast amounts of attention on electoral races, and that even radicals on the ballot were allowed to state their positions, an opportunity they would never have were they not candidates. I further argued that people who took not voting seriously by urging people to not vote "tend to convince those to their side who would vote most radically, leaving unaffected the traditional voters to whom the two-party system provides a choice." I made a pitch for writing in for almost all offices, suggesting that "the time spent writing-in in the booth is more annoying to the octogenarian election officials and more discouraging to voters waiting in line than simply sitting at home. Almost everyone wastes 15 minutes a day doing nothing, and voting is just another way of doing the same. The main point is: don't take voting seriously. Even more importantly, don't take *not* voting seriously."

The other point of view—entitled "Don't Vote, Revolt!"—began: "Another election, another chance to choose a leader. A chance to delegate your responsibility to one more master masquerading as the solution to the desolation and decomposition of this society." The article admonished readers to "decide if you like the flavor of not controlling the most basic aspects of your life. . . . Choose the taste of shit or the taste of vomit; that's what capitalist elections are all about. . . . This year less than 50 percent of the eligible voters will obediently march to the polls to give their support to class society." It continued, "As for referenda, they rarely if ever pass, and the effort spent voting could (in the instance of the marijuana referendum [to decriminalize pot, which did pass]) probably be better spent getting high illegally!" As to leftist candidates: "Naturally, there are the so-called socialist and communist candidates, the left wing of capital. These charlatans are really part of the same rotten stew as the republicans and democrats. They want to 'lead us,' they 'know what's best for us.' By reinforcing the myth of elections, these 'socialist' and 'communist' cretins are in reality the best friends of the system because they suppress the idea that people can and have run their own lives directly; without parties or bureaucrats."

This debate epitomized our positions—I at the far left of mainstream society; the writers of "Don't Vote, Revolt!" simply outside of it. I frequently felt that their position was mostly an intellectual one, one that did little to relieve the oppression felt by most people more directly affected by capitalist society. The proponents of each position were no doubt embarrassed by the other position. This dichotomy existed as long as Bob and Scott worked on the paper.

Our "back cover" was mostly a reprint of the controversial *Free For All* three-way cover, with the last panel originally entitled "Another Way" changed to read "The 'Free' for All Way" (see figure 3). The oppressor in our panel was a longish-haired person in the likeness of *FFA*'s Michael holding a whip and a *Quotations from Chairman Mao*. The factory was named "The 'Collective' Works," and had three puffs of smoke emerging from the stack labeled "repression," "guilt," and "'revolutionary' self-sacrifice." The panel also contained a "'consensus' slaughterhouse," with a door marked "Anarchists enter here." Also on the page was a box entitled "Voices of the Revolution"—graphics of Lenin, Stalin, and Mao—and a quote from Mao outlining the "discipline" of the party (i.e., the subordination of everything to the Central Committee). In addition, we ran a takeoff of an inane column by the then-editor of the *Capital*

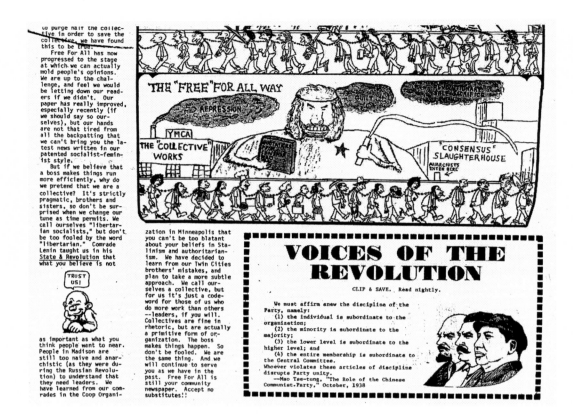

FIGURE 3: Bottom third of back cover cartoon for *No Limits* volume 1, number 1 (October 26–November 8, 1976). Courtesy DreamWorldDragon Press.

Times, Madison's afternoon daily newspaper, whose title, "Hello Wisconsin," we changed to "Hello Collective." The takeoff article rambled on about people's need for a boss, and *FFA*'s willingness to be that boss. We changed *FFA*'s masthead from "the Tyrant's Foe, the People's Friend" to "the People's Foe, the Tyrant's Friend," and we changed their whining slogan "20 cents would help a lot!" to "$20 would help a lot!" The "Inside" box noted: "*FFA* Exclusive: UW Gets New Computer. . . . [page] 3."

The centerfold was our response to the *FFA* split. In our response, we explained why we believed the formation of the Community Union and their purge of us were related (see sidebar 2). The article was entitled "Thus Spoke the 'Collective.'" It included graphics of Lenin and Stalin saying, "I'm a Libertarian Socialist"; a picture of Lenin saying (quoting *FFA*'s Phil in the *Daily Cardinal* article), "Tim's group call themselves anarchists—it's because people like him call themselves anarchists I won't call myself an anarchist anymore"; and a photo of Lenin and Stalin, with Lenin saying, "*Free For All* is still your community newspaper," and Stalin responding, "Mao, more than ever."

EXCERPTS FROM "THUS SPOKE THE 'COLLECTIVE'"

Near the end of 1975, however, *Free For All* became infected with a malaise that has threatened to relegate the Madison "movement" to the dustbin of history. Lacking an obvious focal point such as the Vietnam war or even "Free Karl [Armstrong]," the movement was floundering. The answer appeared to some to lie in increased unity among the Left—sacrificing diversity in hopes of somehow becoming more effective in organizing "the people" or "the workers." A prime focus for these frustrated intellectuals was the Community Union, an organization they hoped would "finally unify the Left." Rather than simply seeing the CU as an informal umbrella organization that could help coordinate the diverse activities of the "Left"—which might have been useful—they preferred to saddle the organization with a ready-made bureaucracy and non-debatable "principles of unity." Showing the limitations of their trust in the people, these bureaucrats ensured the CU's demise, which occurred almost immediately, despite *FFA*'s valiant attempts to portray it as something much more benign than it was.

Whether through conspiracy or not, a clique developed on *Free For All*. They maintained that *FFA* was not run efficiently and was consequently no fun to work on. Instead of quietly fading away and leaving the paper to those who still knew how to have fun and produce a good newspaper at the same time, these jerks took measures to guarantee that the paper was no fun for anybody. They insisted that all staff people conform to their methods of working at *FFA*, and laid endless guilt trips on people not "collective" enough to fall in line. . . . Worse, they increasingly got on the cases of those who disagreed with them. Yet, consistent with their strong orientation towards leaders and refusal to believe in individualism, they tended to see most of the staff dissidents as "Tim's lackeys." . . .

The possibility of an open libertarian socialist community paper was denied by the advent of a bureaucracy which maintained that readers were too stupid to think for themselves. This position paraded itself as "collectivism" and "consensus" decision making. In reality it meant that the "leaders" wanted nothing they didn't like in the paper and demanded an absolute veto power. The majority faction's use of the term consensus, even on their own terms, was a joke. Their consensus could more correctly be called democratic centralism. The majority got its way and the minority was supposed to shut up to avoid problems. The junta's conception of the paper was that of a Monolith. If everything wasn't equally boring and non-controversial, the readers might get confused and the "correct line" might be lost in the richness of different ideas and perspectives. If people began to think for themselves, then what would be the point of *FFA* "leaders"? . . .

As for us, we refused to be sacrificed for "the cause," as though our common revolutionary project were not based upon our need for a qualitatively richer life. We will not burn ourselves out for "the revolution." . . . A newspaper is not an end in itself, a god to be bowed down to. . . . "Revolution ceases to be as soon as it is necessary to be sacrificed to it" (wall painting, France, 1968). We found *FFA*'s "serve the people" mentality and its corresponding humorless guilt-tripping an altar of alienation; and we have had enough of alienation and religion. . . .

Free For All doesn't want to print anything too radical or it might scare advertisers and distributors, decreasing the budget for the paid bureaucrats. They don't want to print anything too critical of the "Left" because they are afraid of criticism from a handful of co-op Leninists. *Free For All* is to be totally "positive," pumping pages of boring uncritical monologue into the "fray" of the latest camp "struggle" of the "representatives" of "the workers." . . .

The majority faction's accusation that some of us are anti-feminist, anti-gay, and out to "destroy" the co-op movement is totally unfounded. It stems from their desire to smear us, thereby supposedly increasing their credibility to the aforementioned movements. As the "true" community organ of the co-op movement they have trouble understanding that there could exist more than one tendency in the wide network of alternative economic collectives and cooperatives. As guilt-ridden "leaders," any criticism of certain authoritarian tendencies within the women's movement by us is "sexist" and "anti-feminist." Where they dug up the anti-gay bit one never knows, and one wonders why they haven't accused us of being racist and anti-Martian in addition.

From *No Limits* 1, no. 1 (October 1976): 8–9.

Reaction to the first issue was positive. We received numerous letters. A few, from doctrinaire anarchists, charged that we weren't anarchist enough, but the bulk were complimentary: "I was most pleased to find another left paper with an understanding that the revolution (and its publications) is not supposed to be boring; it's supposed to be *fun*"; "*Free For All* is clearly deteriorating (deteriorated) to unreadable crap. *No Limits* is great"; "*Free For All* seems to have lost some of its guts in the last four months. Now I know where it went—to *No Limits.* Keep up the fine work"; "I have been missing *Free For All* for many months now. It's been delivered all right, but the fun had seemed to be going out of it. . . . We'll both keep ignoring those who think revolution only happens with clenched fists and gritted teeth"; and "Saw the new paper and I'm very impressed and I'm also looking forward to seeing *FFA* sink into a sea of mindless layout and boring articles; from the look of things, they're well under way."

The early issues (we put out two in 1976 and six in 1977) were a combination of the staff's two strains of anarchism. Bob and Scott, also known as Panda Bear and Polar Bear (we called them the Bear Brothers), produced their stuff both in *No Limits* and independently (primarily before the paper started) under the name Aurora. Polar Bear's work was graphically oriented and given to pessimistic, macabre descriptions of society. His specialty was using other people's letterheads (e.g., Madison Mayor Paul Soglin and various UW departments and administrative offices) to have them making absurd statements. The two also did good satires of the more doctrinaire Left—one poster (reprinted with different names in a later issue of *No Limits*) talked about the 57 varieties of Leninism ("all of them unfit for human consumption") and was distributed widely throughout the Midwest. Panda Bear's stuff was intellectual. As time progressed, their contributions shifted gradually from political anarchism (criticism of more authoritarian strains of the Left) to situationism and nihilism, particularly the French and Italian strains. For instance, the August-September 1977 cover proclaimed: "The society that has abolished every adventure makes the only adventure the abolition of that society!" The back cover glorified the looting that took place during the 1977 blackout in New York City. Frequent features were collages of graphics and magazine and newspaper headlines that presaged the collapse of society.

The balance of the paper contained stories on the labor movement (such as Ed Sadlowski's race for president of the United Steelworkers Union), anarchist politics (articles on Spanish anarchism and anarchist political prisoners around the world), the environment (focusing on efforts in Wisconsin to defeat plans to build a fourth major nuclear-power plant at several different locations and to build a copper mine in northern Wisconsin), local election coverage (noting the candidacies of avowedly leftist candidates for political office), and, of course, the ever-popular collection of short articles still modestly entitled the "Wong Truth Conspiracy."

We occasionally gave certain people the liberty to lay out two or more pages without any editorial interference on our parts. For instance, Ben (Zippie) Masel wrote a two-page defense of his spitting on then–presidential candidate Scoop Jackson in late March 1976 coincident with his trial a year later for that heinous "crime." We allowed a member of the American Indian Movement (AIM) to lay out an eight-page spread entitled "Native Struggles Spring '77."

Because of Scott's graphic talents, the anarcho-syndicalists produced only two of the first nine covers. One was a photo of three scientists walking briskly away from a nuclear power plant with a mushroom cloud superimposed on the top and a quote from nuclear power critic David Brower: "Let's put it this way: if we're wrong, we can do something else. If they're wrong, we're dead." The centerfold consisted of a collection of short news articles on nuclear power in Wisconsin, as well as a review of McKinley Olson's *Unacceptable Risk*, a book hostile to the "peaceful atom."

The other cover was a photo of early twentieth-century electrical engineer Nikola Tesla sitting nonchalantly underneath a "Tesla coil," an oscillator that produced flame-like electrical discharges up to 125 feet long. The headline exclaimed: "How the Russians Put Us in the Deep Freeze," with the kicker, a "No Limits exclusive interview." In addition to a sidebar describing Tesla and his contributions to science, we ran an "interview" with an alleged Soviet scientist visiting the University of Wisconsin who claimed that Soviet use of Tesla's theory succeeded in shifting the jet stream north in the Soviet Union (and therefore south in the United States), which was responsible for the bitter-cold winter of 1976–77 in Wisconsin we were then experiencing.

The last issue of the first half of *No Limits*'s existence appeared in April 1978. The cover was vintage Bear Brothers: a picture of a "comic book" cover entitled "In the Presence of Wage Slavery." Scott had changed the captions of a militaristic comic. One terrorist thug was telling the victim, "You will get a job or you will die!!! What is your choice?" The victim says, "Here it is!" and on a piece of paper is written "Death!" Four of the background figures have their faces replaced with those of Jimmy Carter, Leonid Brezhnev, Imelda Marcos, and Idi Amin.

The issue was a nice blend of the two general schools of thought on the paper. The centerfold was a graphic argument against advertising, directed primarily against TV advertising, but basically rubbing in the fact that the Bear Brothers were not very comfortable with our reliance on advertising for the revenue needed to print the paper.

The back page was a review I did—entitled "Reader's Digest" and using *RD*'s logo—of three diverse publications: the Lyndon Larouche–led National Caucus of Labor Committees (NCLC) publication *New Solidarity*, the official North Korean newspaper *Pyongyang Times*, and a *Time* magazine "exposé" of socialism.

New Solidarity had recently determined that the villain behind everything they didn't like was now Great Britain, rather than the Rockefeller family. In just a few pages, they managed to blame Britain six different times, including for the interesting "fact" that "the Panama Canal treaty debates are little beyond a British plot to overthrow Carter and install British agent Walter Mondale in the White House." Several British agents, including Americans in high government positions, were "identified."

The second publication, the *Pyongyang Times*, devoted its space to accounts of the week's activities of the "Great Leader" Comrade KIM IL SUNG (caps in original), including receiving the Austrian ambassador and receiving a message from the dictator of Madagascar. In addition, the "Great Leader" sent telegrams to various fellow dictators around the world, including the emir of Kuwait, the shah of Iran, and Emperor Bokassa of the Central African Empire. The space devoted to something other than praise for the "Great Leader" went to attacks on South Korea, flatteringly described as "flunkeyist traitors," "the traitor for all ages," "flunkeyist splittists," "fascist hangmen," et cetera ad nauseam.

The *Time* eleven-page article on socialism divided the world into five economic systems: Marxist-Leninist, social democratic, Third World socialist, mixed economy, and capitalist. The highlight, in *No Limits*'s opinion, was a "Communist" joke: "Brezhnev invites his mom to his plush villa in the Crimea. He shows her the yachts, art treasures, and his fleet of foreign cars. After a table-groaning banquet, he asks, 'Well, Mama, what do you think? Not bad for your little boy?' To which Mom replies, 'My son, it's very impressive. But what if the Communists come to power?'"

One article got us into trouble with Madison's leftist political establishment. We wrote an article entitled "Rotten Eggs in Willy-Op?" decrying the firing of Willy St. (Grocery) Co-op staffer and former IWW member Bob Steffes for political reasons. The mentality of the majority was strikingly similar to that of the gang at *Free For All* that had forced us out. The terminology was slightly different: Steffes was offensive to the "socialist feminist" rest of the staff.

We wrote: "The major point is that being a woman or a feminist is not radical per se. . . . A woman is not inferior or superior to a man. . . . Should a white man be miserable, ashamed, and guilt-ridden for life because he can't be a lesbian or a black militant? Obviously not, but socialist feminism is melting into liberal feminism with a double side order of guilt. . . . Almost two years ago, the (white male) power-grabbers forced a split in the staff of *Free For All*, culminating in the founding of *No Limits*, because they could not tolerate political differences. One can choose to ignore a newspaper, but near east-siders need to shop at their co-op. . . . Remember, it is usually those who call for political unity who make it impossible for it to exist, except under their firm tutelage."

We added parenthetically at the end of the article: "No doubt we will be accused of being 'sexist' or 'anti-feminist,' because we have refused to censor our opinions about this and other subjects—we have and are being punished financially by co-ops and other leftist businesses for our allegedly 'anti-leftist/co-op' attitudes. We deny these accusations, and reaffirm our opinion that revolutionary feminism is an essential part of any strategy for radical social change."

Of course, this attack on the co-op did piss them off; later that year when I wrote an article for the co-op newsletter, which at that time was still in the hands of the Steffes faction of the membership, the co-op staff published their own newsletter, calling our newsletter the voice of *No Limits*, a "racist, sexist, and unconstructive local newspaper." At the time of the split, *Free*

For All staffers had gone to many of *FFA*'s advertisers, begging them not to advertise in *No Limits*. Many leftist businesses never advertised in *No Limits*, which was otherwise a natural market for them.

The Second Phase of *No Limits*

We didn't realize it at the time, no doubt, but that issue marked the end of an era for *No Limits*, as well as the beginning of another. That was the last issue either of the Bear Brothers worked on. Panda Bear, in an undated letter printed in our next issue, which appeared eight months later, in December 1978, wrote that because of *No Limits*'s acceptance of advertising, he "no longer desire[d] to participate in the *No Limits* project." Bob stayed in town for a while longer, but Scott left town to hitchhike around the country. He was known to have ended up in Austin, Texas, where he personally struggled with the hopelessness of life he so frequently and eloquently expressed in *No Limits* and his other writings. In the late 1990s I got an unexpected e-mail from him stating that he was now planting trees in the countryside. I responded, but never heard back.

Despite the political acrimony, particularly over the issue of advertising, and the frequent disdain in which we held some of each other's writings, the personal relations were completely harmonious—there was absolutely no sign of the personality conflicts the *Free For All* clique used as an excuse to purge those of us with whom they disagreed politically. (I subsequently heard from a mutual friend who had seen or heard from Bob that he had moved to Japan to teach English as a second language. She also mentioned that he claimed he had never been political, but had gone along with Scott, who was sincerely political, as a means to attract women [!!!]. I later learned he had died, a victim of respiratory problems.)

Several other changes occurred with this issue. In the spring of 1977, I had quit my "job" as a newspaper carrier for Madison's afternoon daily newspaper to take a job as a "limited term" typist with the state of Wisconsin. That job ended when state employees went on strike, and I, too, went on strike—in my case, as a worker without benefits—essentially quitting. Several months later I landed a job as a typesetter with a fledgling publisher of academic journals. The April–May 1978 issue exhibited some of the fringe benefits of that job—typeset ads, subheads, and even a typeset Wong Truth. The sharpness of the typeset copy helped the paper shed some of its ragtag appearance.

The other major change with this issue was the emergence of a new person, Steve Spoerl, as a major contributor to the paper. He had been recruited by Panda Bear when both of them worked at one of the university libraries, and had written an article for the previous issue. Steve's bizarre interests helped him fit right in, and he wrote articles on mostly obscure subjects.

One of his stories, obscure at the time, printed in the first issue he wrote for (December 1977), was perhaps the first American mention of the Pol Pot–guided mass murder in Cambodia. The article, drawn from British sources and entitled "Cambodia Goes to Pot," ended with a quote from Khieu Samphan, one of the country's leaders: "In five years of war, more than a million Cambodians died. The present population of the country is five million. Before the war it was seven million." When asked what happened to the other million, Samphan was annoyed: "It's incredible the way you Westerners worry about war criminals." Other articles on that two-page spread entitled "Class War in Revolt," taken mostly from other anarchist publications, were critical of Chinese repression of its critics from the left, Rumania's bloody crushing of a coal strike, and the "monolithic state-capitalist regime" in Mozambique. That latter article, entitled "Mozambique: 'Marxist' Mess," succeeded in alienating us from the Marxist People's Bookstore, another logical advertising source.

In part because I was working full-time, and partly because the Bear Brothers and their graphic skills had abandoned the paper, *No Limits* did not appear again until the end of the year. A major impetus of the issue was the effort of Patrick Murfin. Murfin had been a former general secretary-treasurer (GST, the top executive post) of the IWW and a longtime Chicago (where IWW headquarters was then located) Wobbly. He was one of the more intelligent people I have ever met. He was also a heavy drinker who had been kicked out of Chicago by a few macho Chicago Wobblies who accused him of drinking away much of the union's income during his tenure as GST. He had been "ordered" to go to New Orleans to live with a Wobbly he couldn't stand. Instead of going, however, he hitchhiked to Madison, an "overnight" stop on his way to the Pacific Northwest. His "overnight stay" lasted four months.

Although he paid only one month's rent and didn't contribute his share toward his consumption of food and beer, he was a pleasant addition to our cooperative house. On the occasional times he found work, he typically spent his entire paycheck in various skid-row taverns following payday. But he revitalized the Madison Wobblies and was a major force behind our December 1978 issue. He organized a Wobbly lecture and film series at the State Historical Society that combined history and present-day imperatives for radical workers. He contributed two articles to *No Limits*, both incisive analyses of local politics—one about proposed bus fare increases, the other on the "ruling class blueprint for Madison." Murfin, through his incessant reading as well as conversations with townspeople, had developed an understanding of local politics far better than that of most Madisonians. We looked forward to more of Murfin's contributions in future issues, but he disappeared one day as quickly as he showed up; going down to Chicago "for a few days" over Christmas, he never reappeared in Madison.

Another newcomer to this issue was the Revolutionary Anarchist Alliance, the creation of Greg Jamrock, whom I considered to be a very neurotic individual. Greg was almost constantly accompanied by his girlfriend Mary, who nevertheless didn't seem to be part of the RAA effort. The RAA, which later changed its name to Count Down, subscribed to the same brand of anarchism as the Bear Brothers, but did so with considerably less graphic and semantic talent. Their departure after the February 1979 issue marked the end of any non-syndicalist anarchism on *No Limits*, and the paper developed a coherence it had never had before.

The paper's politics never really changed, though: it maintained an anti-authoritarian brand of leftism to the end, but gone (with the Bear Brothers and the cheap imitation RAA) were the anarchist polemics. What remained were articles written predominantly by Steve and me that focused on specific subjects, sprinkled with a liberal dose of "gentle asides to the reader" that revealed our political point of view. In some ways, the anarchist politics of *No Limits* of 1979 resembled the *Free For All* of 1974.

The first cover of 1979 was a photo by Diane Arbus of a white guy wearing an Indian headdress and holding an American flag—we ran it because the photo bore a striking resemblance to our then-governor Lee Dreyfus. Page 2 of that issue featured a story on the strike against Checker Cab, while page 3 evaluated the various candidates for mayor three weeks before the primary. At the bottom of page 3 was a subscription ad, typical of the sub ads we had run throughout *No Limits*'s existence, that featured a picture of the recently deceased Nelson Rockefeller and a caption from beyond the ad that asked, "Rocky, are you sure you renewed your subscription to *No Limits?*" Rocky answers, "I think so. I'd die before I'd let my subscription run out!" The headline on the right says, "Subscribe Now! Before You Die Too," along with the subscription rates.

The fourth page was an article by an outside contributor describing the situation in Iran between the fleeing by the shah to take a "vacation" in the United States, and the takeover by the fundamentalist Ayatollah Khomeini. Page 5 featured my analysis of Carter's 1980 federal budget and my article entitled "Con-Con Is a No-No," which warned against the then-popular thrust to call a federal constitutional convention to require a balanced federal budget. None of us imagined that the Great Prevaricator Ronald Reagan, an advocate of "Con-Con," would take Jimmy Carter's relatively small $60 billion budget deficit and, through voodoo supply-side economic theory, take it to four and five times that.

The next two pages were Steve's analysis of current events in China, a strong attack on the thirty years of Maoism, and a prophetic prediction that the authoritarianism would not cease there even if China decided to play ball with capitalism and become one of the countries that runaway corporations in the United States moved to in order to produce their goods at slave wages to maximize profits at the expense of laid-off American workers.

The centerfold consisted of a story on Kerr-McGee and the death of Karen Silkwood, and other shorter articles on nuclear power (mostly about setbacks to the nuclear industry) and how the labor establishment was doing big business's dirty work by opposing environmental goals.

The back half of the paper consisted of the Wong Truth, a story on prison revolts, and the first of a series of articles on jazz figures (in this case, Dexter Gordon) based on interviews conducted by Steve's high school friend Chuck France, who also did much of the work (but received little of the credit) on the film on Madison's antiwar movement, *The War at Home*. This was one of the few issues that did not have a baseball column and/or quiz, one of the more frequent features of *No Limits*, reflecting my obsession (and Steve's) with major league baseball.

The last two inside pages were an anarchist tract entitled "Ten Theses on the Proliferation of Egocrats," an intellectual, almost incomprehensible attack on authoritarianism, lifted from (and credited to) a brochure we had received—this was one of Greg's last contributions.

The back cover, a "genealogy" of the various authoritarian leftist splinter groups, listed thirty-eight different "Marxist" groups and the parent groups from which they had split, presented on a time continuum. Originally printed in some sectarian leftist paper as an attack on a different strain of Leninism (Trotskyist versus Maoist or some such), we credited it to the U.S. Association for the Study of Scientific Marxism-Leninism (Enver Hoxhaist) under the headline "Tired of Your Present Job?"

USASSML(EH) has recently split into three separate factions, with several careerist positions open for you, the Scientific American. All you have to do is reiterate our party line and you can become a central committee member, cadre, or rank-and-file member. We have openings for people who wish to join our central committee and make policies for our comrades around the world without regard to local conditions, and for those fluent in Albanian who could translate the latest mumblings from the great comrade leader Enver Hoxha. To show how scientific our organization is, refer to our family tree below. It took many splits to achieve our all-correct political line.

The next issue appeared in July. It featured a cover picturing traffic jams, an aerial photo showing how freeways had severed a city, an auto junkyard, and a German billboard urging everyone to wear gas masks "before we are all poisoned." It was entitled "$5.00 a Gallon and . . ." (on top) and "Sugar in Every Gas Tank" (on the bottom). The centerfold was a polemic on car usage and the hidden subsidies paid to the automobile industry and its infrastructure, along with a shorter article on the future of Amtrak. Every prediction about how catering to automotive interests would deteriorate the quality of life in cities has come true in Madison. Even today, a nominally environmentalist mayor has committed to spending millions of tax dollars to build or expand highways and roads on the periphery of town serving mostly sub- and ex-urbanites, while forcing a 50-cent fare hike on Madison's bus system.

Several articles in the paper were written by nonstaff members—an indication that the paper was beginning to be taken seriously by the leftist community—one on the Black Hills and mining, one on Nicaragua, in addition to Chuck's jazz interview. Steve contributed his articles—one on the budding conflict in Yemen and another on the militarization of space. Probably the most important article in this issue, from the standpoint of an anarchist paper taking a position on current anarchist events, was about the trashing of an anarchist bookstore in Philadelphia by a group of ultra-leftist anarchists who ruined the store (by stopping up the sink and turning on the water) because they felt "a store is a store is a store." The article quoted extensively from the trashers' pamphlets and the bookstore's response and concluded that the trashers had no right to vandalize an anarchist bookstore for any reason—especially this store, which was totally staffed by volunteers. When one of the trashers came through Madison on her way to the West Coast, several of us went to a fish fry with her. Panda Bear felt favorably disposed to the vandalism, in much the same way he felt our taking advertising in *No Limits* had totally compromised everything we had to say in the paper. The rest of us were rather appalled at the self-righteousness of her attitude.

The last four issues of *No Limits* came out, amazingly enough, in regular two-month intervals. We were attracting outside articles; I was able to contribute a lot of typesetting to improve the graphic appearance. Articles in these issues dealt extensively with local issues, such as urban planning, local electoral politics, and bike trips.

But the staff responsible for producing the paper had melted to three—Steve and I, who still did the bulk of the writing, and Vicki Drenning, my "significant other," later wife, and now ex, who performed much of the unheralded administrative work around the paper. When Vicki decided she was no longer interested in working on the paper, we reevaluated our purpose and decided to fold. Unlike many papers that folded, we had an adequate treasury and were in the process of producing another issue when we called it quits.

The *No Limits* of 1979 and 1980 had changed a lot from its 1976 origins. It placed a stronger emphasis on radical environmentalism; doctrinaire political preaching was less apparent. In part, I think, this resulted from our understanding that classical anarchist thinking had to be updated to deal with the present reality of the state (and we were not about to undertake this project). The state was now far more than the apparatus by which the ruling capitalist class maintained its minority stranglehold over the rest of society. Rather, the state was a major provider of social benefits to the needy elements of society. One could certainly argue about the efficiency of governmental programs and complain about the status quo nature of the two dominant political parties, but to regurgitate anarchist philosophy of the late 1800s and early 1900s in the pre–New Deal period when the state provided little other than the military for foreign excursions and wars, and a police force to side with the employer against employees seemed to us a little naive.

No Limits produced fifteen issues in a little over three years. The last issue was printed on January 31, 1980. *Free For All* limped along a little longer, meeting its long- and well-deserved death on December 3, 1981.

Subsequent Madison Journalism

Madison had no alternative newspaper for several years. In 1984, the other faction of *Free For All* held a reunion to which I was invited. It was fairly pleasant; the hatchets seemed to have been buried. (Michael did not show up from New York.) Rob tried to use the get-together as an excuse to put out one more issue, but he found no takers. Later that year he did put out an issue.

Rob kept working on the idea of putting out a paper on a regular basis. He eventually formed a staff that produced a newspaper called the *Phoenix*, which first appeared in March 1985. The paper lasted through the fall, publishing less than ten issues. Steve from *No Limits* got involved in this paper and, after Rob got a job in New York City, almost single-handedly put out several of the later issues. I wrote an article for the first issue on my concept of a light or heavy rail transit system for Madison and surrounding suburbs, but didn't participate beyond that. The paper was, despite Steve's valiant efforts, essentially a continuation of *Free For All*, in its gloomy politics and tone and the constant whining about the need for money. The lack of appreciation for Steve's efforts by the neo–*Free For All* clones dimmed his enthusiasm, and the paper died with the next issue.

In 1987, a two-sided, one-sheet calendar of events (along with historical remembrances of those dates) appeared under the name the *Insurgent*. After about a year, the broadside evolved into a newspaper, and continued biweekly publication for several years. The paper suffered from a doom-and-gloom outlook, with the humor prevalent in its broadside days largely gone. Also gone was one of the most useful features of its broadside days, evaluations prior to each semester of various UW professors and selected courses. Instead, with a staff dominated by white males, it reflected their all-too-familiar guilt over being white and male. Another paper or two appeared into the early- to mid-90s, always short-lived.

Now that the eight long years of the Bush administration are finally over, it will be interesting to see if history does repeat itself. President Obama's campaign for president, although heavily bankrolled by Wall Street and other corporate interests, also drew millions of young and idealistic supporters and campaigners. Millions of people really seemed to believe Obama's campaign slogan of "change." Would Obama actually be different? Could Obama bring about change, even if he wanted to? Because Obama was an opponent of the Iraq war from the beginning, many Americans seemed to have great expectations both that he would end the war and that he would bring forward many long-postponed policy initiatives. His backtracking from his previous positions during the election campaign was excused as campaign expediency. But what excuses his post-election actions: hiring a right-wing Democrat as his chief of staff, bringing in a financial team that had ushered in and championed the deregulation during the Clinton years that brought about the depression of 2008, drastically expanding the unwinnable war against Afghanistan and spreading it to Pakistan, maintaining the secrecy and pro-torture policies of the Bush administration, and pursuing health care reform, but saying from the start that single-payer, the only plan that can increase coverage and control costs, is off the table? Granted, Obama looks good when compared to the Democratic congressional leadership, which seems to be a totally owned subsidiary of America's vilest corporate interests. But that only reminds us what we knew back in the 1970s, that Democrats really aren't much better than Republicans.

As it becomes apparent to many of his idealistic campaigners that Obama is just another corporate-owned politician who primarily serves the interests of big business—even if he has a black face and offers a sprinkling of good policies here and there to differentiate himself from the Republicans—how will they respond? It is even more frustrating that Obama is clearly very smart and we keep thinking he should know better than to pursue the policies that his administration is pushing.

Is history cyclical? Can we expect a period of political turbulence every twenty to thirty years, followed by reaction, which in turn spawns a new round of change? Or have the changes in society, in culture, the vastly expanded entertainment and diversion options, turned most people, even young ones, into apolitical adapters? As millions of people lose their jobs while Congress bails out the millionaires who caused the economic downturn, will people be able to radicalize and demand change to our political institutions?

Will the young people of today clamor for the change the politicians weren't able to bring about? Will the 2010–2020 version of newspapers help mobilize people? Or are the entrenched interests even more dominant than they were forty years ago? Will we, the rank-and-file citizens, denounce Congress as the tools of the power brokers who finance their campaigns, and demand the change Obama wasn't able to deliver? Let's hope that eventually we can answer, "Yes, we can."

NOTES

1. James Danky, "Still Alive and Well: The Alternative Press in 1977. Part II," *Harvest Quarterly* no. 6 (Summer 1977): 17–22.
2. "Driveaways" were a common method of long-distance transportation in those days: car dealers or other people needed their vehicles transported from one location to another—we provided the driving; they provided the gasoline credit cards (we filled quite a few other tanks during the Boulder conference); and everyone ended up happy.
3. Danky, "Still Alive and Well," 17–22.

New Age: Worker Organizing from the Bottom Up

PAUL KREHBIEL

When I started work at Standard Mirror Company in South Buffalo in the spring of 1968, I had no idea how profoundly that experience would change my life.

My first day on the job is still emblazoned in my mind. When I walked into the factory, I was assaulted by loud crashing and banging sounds. Black and green pipes and hoses crisscrossed everywhere, hissing like coiled cobras. The once-white walls looked like old teeth, coated in a yellowish-brown film after years of smoking. My nostrils sucked in the stink of sickening smells.

A gray mist hung in the air, like fog in a Hollywood movie. But it wasn't romantic or intriguing. The mist was deadly. It had ground-up glass in it. After four hours in the foggy room, I felt like someone had rubbed sandpaper over my throat.

This was not a torture chamber. It was one room in the auto-parts factory where I worked, eight hours a day, five days a week. I spent almost half of my waking hours in that factory. I was twenty years old and a fine-grinder operator in the finishing department, which was next to the foggy room. We made rearview mirrors for cars and trucks. Standard Mirror had all of the contracts for Ford and Chrysler nationally.

Fortunately I didn't spend a lot of time in the foggy room unless someone was out sick. On most days, I just passed through it. A wall divided most of my department from the foggy room so we didn't breathe in too much ground-up glass where I worked. But we got soaked laboring in water and polish, and the heavy forms we lifted all day let our arms and back know they had had a good workout well before the end of our shift.

The foggy room was the glass-cutting and beveling department; the ground-up glass in the air came from the beveling machines. Lubricant poured onto the rearview mirrors so the hard cutting tool wouldn't chip the glass while grinding off the sharp edges. The resulting ground-up glass and mist floated up and out of the beveling machine and eventually covered the room.

Both sweat and blood went into making those mirrors. The glass cutters were constantly cutting their fingers on the sharp glass because their high production quotas forced them to work too fast.

Production Quotas

The company established production quotas for every department, and each quota was set so every worker moved quickly. Management tried to convince us that production quotas were based on "scientific" principles, and not just the bosses' arbitrary whim to get us to work faster. A management representative, with a stopwatch and a clipboard, would observe and time workers as they performed the various tasks that made up their jobs. These time studies were conducted under optimal conditions (material being right next to our machine), which were not the same as normal factory production conditions (we had to walk across the department to find our material), so inevitably the company's time study revealed that the worker could work faster and produce more. Since we all were working hard and steady, we saw these time studies as simply a way to sugarcoat a job speedup so the company could increase its profits. Every time a time-study man came around, we cringed because we knew the result was going to be more work.

The outside world had no idea about any of this. The newspapers and TV stations never reported on our unsafe, hard, and hectic factory jobs. Most news coverage about factories involved the types and amounts of products produced, business expansions and contractions, changes in business ownership, and management complaints about taxes or other "unfavorable" business conditions. On the few occasions when the media talked about workers, we were usually cast negatively, such as when there was a strike. At that point the media would portray workers as greedy, unreasonable, irresponsible, or lazy, and quote management sources to this effect. Rarely were the voices of workers heard. There were a few exceptions to this scenario, but not many. And Buffalo was a heavily working-class, blue-collar union town, with hundreds of thousands of union workers employed in huge steel mills and auto factories and other workplaces.

An article about Standard Mirror, which was a typical business article, appeared in our city newspaper, the *Buffalo Evening News*, in early 1968, not too long before I began working there. The local owners of Standard Mirror had just sold the company to a larger firm in Ohio, so the article quoted top executives about how the sale improved the company's chances for growth and increased profitability. The article was illustrated with a photograph of two young female workers. The caption underneath explained that they were removing side mirror assemblies from racks after they had been run through the electrostatic spray booths and baking ovens. Not a word was said about the chemicals, or fumes, or ground-up glass, or other unsafe working conditions, or a company management that drove us to work harder and faster.

At the time, I didn't think much about it—that's the way the world was.

Then came the summer of 1968. It was one year after the "Summer of Love" in San Francisco, but that historic summer didn't have much to do with us or most blue-collar workers. In the summer of 1967, I was slopping around in mosquito-infested swamps doing manual labor on a surveying crew helping to lay out roads and sewer lines. But in the summer of 1968, I was involved in a union campaign to stop the auto-parts company from increasing the work quota in my department. I worked in a department that ground out imperfections on the surface of rearview mirrors and then polished them; but more importantly, this slow-down campaign ground out the myth that we were helpless in the face of unreasonable management edicts.

I had started to take an interest in the union before this campaign after I saw our union steward verbally rip into the personnel manager for trying to force the workers in the beveling department to produce more than their quota. I was impressed that this union steward stood up to the company on behalf of fellow workers; his courage helped give me and other workers confidence that we could stand up for ourselves. When the company tried to raise our production quota, we organized an intense campaign to stop it. We began by following all the safety rules, purposely working more slowly than normal, and having more problems and accidents than expected. After three weeks of chaos, we failed to make the higher quota, so management had to abandon the speedup. We won! I was ecstatic. I learned that workers didn't have to simply take whatever management dished out to us. That was an important lesson.

Workers and Vietnam

This was also the time when the war in Vietnam was really heating up, and the military draft was targeting blue-collar workers as prime candidates for foot-soldiering on the front lines. Young workers did the bulk of the fighting and dying in Vietnam, as they do in all wars, and young black workers were doing more than their fair share. A number of young workers from Standard Mirror, including some guys from my department, were drafted and sent to Vietnam. One came home and returned to his job at Standard Mirror with a serious leg injury from the war. His leg could not bend at the knee. He limped, and he had to stand on that bad leg eight hours a day as he worked at his machine.

I didn't know much about the war in mid-1968, but the endless killing and maiming of people appeared senseless and shocking to me. I talked to soldiers who returned from the war and saw they had been deeply affected by it. Politically, I could understand World War II, despite its horrors. Monsters like Hitler had to be stopped from goose-stepping across the world, taking over one country after another, and starving, gassing, and slaughtering millions of people. My dad had served in World War II and I was proud of him. But Vietnam seemed different. I didn't see how a small, poor country of peasant farmers on the other side of the globe was a threat to the USA or anyone else. Something wasn't right about the war in Vietnam, and even though my high school guidance counselor suggested that I sign up for the army because I wasn't "cut out for college," I wasn't so sure that was the best course for me.

The war, along with my experiences working at the factory, and witnessing the abuses of racism and poverty in the community drove me to learn about these social problems.

I heard that students at the University at Buffalo (UB) were involved in a powerful antiwar movement and other social-justice movements on campus. I left Standard Mirror later in 1968, and while I felt out of place on any university campus, I started going to UB to see if I could find answers to my questions. I worked at temporary factory jobs or other part-time blue-collar jobs, and started sitting in on classes and attending antiwar meetings. I read a powerful antiwar book, *Vietnam! Vietnam!*, by Felix Greene, and I began to understand the real history of the war and why the U.S. really got involved in Vietnam. I enrolled in night school at the university for the spring semester of 1969.

There, I met other young workers who were taking classes and who were active in the antiwar movement and other progressive political movements, and in their unions. Some were members of the Buffalo Draft Resistance Union (BDRU), and others were members of Students for a Democratic Society (SDS), or other progressive organizations. I learned more about all of those organizations, attended their events, and took courses taught by progressive teachers who were opposed to the war, racism, poverty, and the exploitation of workers. It was exhilarating!

I learned that the government and the mass media lied to the American people about the war. Americans had been told that our military was in Vietnam to help protect the right of the Vietnamese people to choose their own form of government, when in fact our government had canceled elections scheduled for 1956 because the guy it wanted to win had no chance of winning. Then, our government sent in troops to force the Vietnamese at gunpoint to give U.S. big businesses raw materials, exploit extremely low-paid almost slave labor in Vietnam, and gain new markets. The Vietnamese resisted this raping of their country, and the war that ensued led to the deaths of tens of thousands of my peers, and to the slaughter, ultimately, of millions of Vietnamese. I was outraged! I also learned about how capitalism's drive for profits exploited workers and society and led to wars, theories about socialism, and why our society suffered from so many social problems. I was learning about strategies to correct them, and was becoming a good student in the process. I learned these lessons in classes, from books I was reading, and from the progressive student organizations in which I participated.

Radicals and Organizers

Eventually I joined both the BDRU and SDS, and I became friends with the workers who were in those organizations. Several of the top leaders and many activists in the Buffalo chapter of SDS had worked in steel mills and other factories in Buffalo, so our SDS had a distinct pro-worker and working-class outlook. I even met two progressive, left-wing, working-class students who had worked at Standard Mirror.

By the latter part of 1969, I had become one of the leaders of the BDRU. Throughout the time I was a student at UB, I spent many mornings each week at the draft induction center passing out antiwar leaflets and talking to young workers who were being drafted. One of my main arguments was that I didn't think that young workers should fight in Vietnam to enrich big corporations, many of the same corporations that exploit us as workers right here in the U.S. Many of these guys had the same blue-collar backgrounds as the guys I worked with at Standard Mirror, so I felt at home with them.

I was also active in antiwar activities on campus, including the national SDS-led campaign to eliminate the ROTC (Reserve Officer Training Corps) programs and war-related research from our campus and others across the country. The war in Vietnam, as many of us saw it, was the mutual slaughter of workers from both countries for someone else's benefit.

I was involved in other campaigns at UB, too. One was to have the university hire black union construction workers to help build the new UB campus in Amherst, since most of the construction unions were made up overwhelmingly or almost totally of white workers. Another campaign was to build the grape boycott in western New York to help the United Farm Workers union in California in its battles with growers to win union recognition and a union contract.

UB administrators repeatedly refused our demands to stop their support for the war, and failed to seriously address many other issues that students brought before them. Eventually this led to confrontations with the police, and this precipitated a semester-long strike at UB in the spring of 1970. Our demands included ending all war-related activities on campus, hiring the black construction workers, and opening a workers' college on campus for workers, with courses on labor history, collective bargaining, building stronger unions, and establishing a social-justice labor movement. I worked on the committee to set up the workers' college. All of this was going on during our strike, which many of our unionized teachers and professors supported.

Our nation's campuses were in turmoil in the late 1960s and early 1970s, and this rebellious spirit spread to other sectors of society. Growing numbers of soldiers were refusing to fight in Vietnam—some were throwing hand grenades at especially abusive officers. Blacks and other people of color and women were fighting for equality, and increasing numbers of workers were backing up their demands for respect and improvements on the job with wildcat strikes and other job actions. When four students were killed at Kent State during antiwar protests in May 1970, following Nixon's invasion of Cambodia, we were still on strike at UB. These killings enraged us and led to a new round of mass demonstrations and riots on our campus and in the university district. Other campuses around the country went out on strike following these killings. Our strike ended at UB only after the Buffalo police and right-wing vigilantes shot and wounded twelve students.

Throughout this time, I saw the insidious role that the mass media played. It never reported on the true history of U.S. involvement in Vietnam, or the truth about the antiwar movement, or about our strike at the university, or the truth about the struggles of workers and their unions.

While the radical and left-wing students discussed how to expand these progressive movements into the community among the large majority working-class population and create an alternative newspaper, we were winning important victories at UB from our student strike. We got ROTC removed from campus. We won a number of educational reforms, including the establishment of a black studies program, Puerto Rican studies, a women's college, and an environmental college. While we didn't win the establishment of a workers' college, many of the courses we were developing were adopted by another very progressive college called Social Sciences College.

The student strike was over in June of 1970, and I was one of a number of student activists who talked about starting an alternative or "underground" newspaper in Buffalo. There had been other earlier attempts, but the results had been low-distribution newsletters with limited life spans.

Forming Our Own Newspapers

The initial underground newspaper in Buffalo was *Cold Steel*. It was started by a mixture of student activists, antiwar organizers, socialists, progressive workers, hippies and youth-culture advocates, and several sympathizers of the violent group the Weathermen, who had what I saw as a counterproductive philosophy of criticizing everyone who didn't agree with them, and engaging police in street battles. There were about twelve people on the staff. The front and back pages and the centerspread were in two colors, and the rest of the 16-page tabloid paper was in black and white.

I wasn't happy with this conglomeration of forces and wondered how they would survive working with each other. They didn't. The first issue of *Cold Steel* came out in the summer of 1970. The paper was to be a monthly, and was financed by collecting donations from readers. There was no hierarchy, so therefore there were no editors. The staff made decisions collectively. Since we thought some retribution was likely for publishing this newspaper, none of the articles were signed. Few of us had any faith in the authorities, and some of the writers and activists saw themselves as being part of an underground movement. The major article in the first issue was on the student strike at the university. Other articles represented all of the political tendencies of its staff, including the views of the Weathermen, which I knew would turn off the vast majority of people. When some of them drifted away, I saw their departure as an opportunity to bring more sanity to this project. So, I got heavily involved in the second issue, writing the feature article on the history of U.S. involvement in Vietnam from a worker's perspective. The article appeared on the inner four pages, like a center supplement.

We published 10,000 copies of that second issue of *Cold Steel*, and then another 40,000 copies of my Vietnam history as a stand-alone piece, and distributed them at schools, workplaces, and in neighborhoods all across Buffalo over several months. Both publications were paid for through donations. Fifty thousand copies of the truth about Vietnam made important inroads into the thinking of whoever got our newspaper, and I felt good about that. But I was also aware that we were competing with huge corporate-controlled TV and print media that filled the heads of 1.5 million Buffalo-area residents with misrepresentations and lies every day, so we needed to keep publishing our views regularly.

Unfortunately, after the second issue of *Cold Steel*, there remained on staff a number of irresponsible and counterproductive people—some called them the "lunatic fringe"—and I felt I couldn't work there any longer. Others felt the same. *Cold Steel* lasted one or two more issues and then folded. I knew that other movement leaders, including many of the workers I met at the university, were talking about starting another alternative newspaper aimed at working families. I contacted them, and we held several meetings in the summer of 1970 to discuss this new project. About fifteen people were involved.

We decided to start an independent workers' newspaper and return to organizing workers. We selected this focus for several reasons. First, many of us were workers and we felt most comfortable among this group. We also knew that workers had a specific set of serious problems that needed special attention. We believed that workers, especially those in manufacturing industries, occupied a unique place in society where they could put tremendous pressure on the economic and political system if they were well informed and organized. If workers developed progressive ideas, they could influence people in power to adopt or accept more progressive policies and programs. Many of us had read *Labor's Untold Story*, a labor history book by Herbert J. Morais and Richard O. Boyer, published by the very progressive United Electrical Workers Union (UE). That book was popular among leftists and radicals because it highlighted the work of progressives, leftists, and rank-and-file workers in the labor movement since the Civil War who led massive campaigns for the betterment of all workers and society as a whole. We were fascinated by the accounts of the great movements for the eight-hour work day; improvements in wages, hours, working conditions, and workers' rights; the winning of legal rights for trade unions; the establishment of health insurance, pensions, social security, unemployment insurance, and Medicare; and gains in fighting racism and other forms of discrimination.

Many of us had also read Marx and Engels, and we saw daily at work the exploitation and oppression of workers that they attributed to capitalism. Many of us were critical of capitalism, and we believed some form of socialism would create a fairer and more humane society—just like many of the union leaders of the 1930s and 1940s believed. Many big gains were made during those earlier decades, and some smaller ones were made in the fifties and sixties. We wanted to build the type of mass movements, especially among workers and their unions, which achieved so much in the 1930s and 1940s, again in the United States in the 1970s. Some in our group wanted to see a national revolutionary movement develop that could ultimately overthrow capitalism and replace it with socialism—what we saw as the democratic rule of workers and other sectors of the population, in place of the current rule of big business. That was a pretty ambitious undertaking for a group of young workers, most of whom were in their early and mid-twenties.

Empowering Workers

Finally, we decided that we would focus most of our attention on workers in Buffalo and western New York. We would distribute most copies of our paper to them at their workplaces, where they could talk about the articles with their coworkers. We believed this strategy would help them develop faster politically and increase their power sooner through collective on-the-job education and action. Also, distributing the paper regularly at their workplaces ensured that we would have regular contact with our readers. We also made plans to get the paper distributed where we worked, and saw it as an organizing tool everywhere.

The organizational structure of the paper was simple. We were all leery of hierarchies, so we had no editors for *New Age.* Instead, we all met to discuss what should go into each issue, and everyone had an equal say and vote. We strove for a consensus, but a majority vote was enough to include an article for publication. We had no set policy for bringing new people into the work of the paper other than agreement with our general principles and goals. Overall, that system worked well, though at times we had political differences among the staff. Everyone was a volunteer; we had no paid staff. We all wrote articles and laid out the paper on someone's kitchen table, and since none of us had training in journalism, the paper had a unique look to it, with some pretty creative layouts. Some articles weren't laid out in neat boxes, so we put lines around them to keep them separate. Lots of photographs and graphics helped liven up the pages.

We decided to distribute the paper for free, but ask for donations to pay for the printing costs, which were our only expense. We published 10,000 copies of each issue, in black and white. We found that it was cheapest to print on the front and back of one large sheet, 34" × 22", which we folded into sections, so we used that format. We folded the paper over three times so we had the equivalent of a 16-page paper with each page being 8.5" × 11". We found an offset printer to run 10,000 copies for about $110. We always raised enough money through donations from the workers who received it to pay the printer and have a little money left over to buy more supplies.

We set five major goals for our project:

1. to help workers organize and empower themselves on the job to better fight against the abuses they faced, win immediate improvements, and strengthen their unions;
2. to build solidarity among workers in other unions and other industries;
3. to build the antiwar movement among workers and their unions, and alliances between workers and the antiwar movement;
4. to fight against racism, sexism, and other forms of discrimination and build alliances between civil rights groups and workers; and
5. to build international labor solidarity.

We decided to do this in a two-part plan. First, we believed the best way to build workers' power was from the bottom up, so we would use our newspaper to report on the campaigns of workers on the job in Buffalo and western New York to improve conditions, primarily at work, but also in their communities. We would inform them of their rights and workers' efforts to expand those rights, and provide information about issues related to our five goals. Second, we would build on this increased worker consciousness and solidarity to create a worker-controlled organization that could work both inside and outside their unions to influence political, economic, and social institutions to advance the interests of working people, their families, and the broader society.

I went back to work at Standard Mirror in September of 1970 and worked with our group to produce the first issue of our newspaper. We named it *New Age*, after a progressive workers' newspaper by that name that had been produced in Buffalo in the early 1900s. Little did we know that later that year another "New Age" movement would come to Buffalo and that it would become much more widely known nationally. We were two different worlds with the same name. The other New Age opened a restaurant with a big sign with that name across the top of the building. Inside the building, hippie-like folks ate tofu and bean sprouts, read tarot cards, and gazed at crystals. Our *New Age*, on the other hand, was a movement of beer-drinking, hammer-wielding, radical factory and service workers who were trying to build a stronger, more progressive labor movement. Amazingly, we got along fine with the other New Age group; we even advertised their restaurant in our paper, and they put a stack of our papers in their restaurant for their patrons. I'm sure the FBI was confused and asked themselves, "What the hell kind of political group is this New Age movement?" There was a little overlap since some hippie-like factory workers and a few of our members ate at their restaurant. We took the concept of being nonsectarian to a new level.

We knew our society did everything possible to make the voices of workers nonexistent, so we pledged to open the pages of *New Age* to workers to write their own articles and letters, and we would help them if they asked. We gave priority coverage to workers who were engaged in struggles with their employers to improve their wages and working conditions — and especially to those who were on strike, and to those who were fighting for progressive social gains for society as a whole.

The first page of our first issue, which came out in September 1970, had a drawing of a hand holding a wrench with the name "New Age" written on the wrench. In the background was a wheel, with four screws and three smokestacks. In large letters we wrote: "This paper is to help build a new age in America. The age where workers and their families control their own lives." That was probably the best and most succinct summary of what we stood for.

I lived in an old apartment building at 1528 Main Street at West Ferry. My roommate, Steve, was a year or two younger than me and worked at Republic Steel. Across the hall were two friends of ours who were several years older than me. Wayne worked at Bethlehem Steel and Carl worked at Allied Chemical. Since I worked in a section of the auto industry, between the four of us, we worked in the largest industries in Buffalo and western New York, employing over a hundred thousand workers.

Carl told me one day in the early summer of 1970 that he thought his union might go on strike at the end of June. I mentioned this to our *New Age* group and said I wanted to interview Carl for an article if they went on strike. Everyone agreed.

Oranges and Poisons

One day soon after that, I was coming home from work and I saw a tall, lanky man in work clothes not too far ahead of me. He was almost to the door of our apartment building.

"Hey, Carl," I called. He turned around. I was startled by the bright orange glow on his face. I had seen that look before, but it looked brighter that day, as if someone had painted his face. His skin looked normal only from about two inches above his eyes up to his scalp. A thick clump of light red hair was sticking up.

"What happened to you?" I asked when I caught up with him.

"We were making orange dye today," he said. He unlocked the weather-beaten plywood door to the old condemned brick building where we lived.

"What's that for?" I asked.

"Oranges," he responded as we climbed the creaky wooden stairs.

"You mean the ones we eat?"

"Yup. All those nice orange oranges you see in the store . . ." He turned and looked at me. "They're painted orange so they sell better at the market. So any time you see me come home like this, you know we made orange dye for oranges that day."

"Why do you have that stripe across your forehead with no orange?" I asked.

"That's from my hardhat. It covers my forehead and hair."

I asked how safe the orange dye was.

"You ever peel an orange with your teeth?" he asked.

"Yeah. All the time. Why?"

"You ever feel anything on your lips?"

"Yeah. A little stinging sensation. I figure it's from the orange peel."

"Nope. It's from this fuckin' orange dye. There's all kinds of shit in the chemicals we use, not just the orange dye. Some guys feel a stinging on their skin; some feel nausea." He turned to unlock his apartment door.

I reminded him about the rank-and-file workers' newspaper that a group of us were starting and told him we were writing articles for the first issue. "We want to write about the kinds of problems people are having on their job," I explained, "like your problems with the chemicals." I invited him to join us at our next meeting at John's apartment. John was a bartender at a working-class bar in south Buffalo.

"Well, I'm pretty busy with the union and strike preparation," Carl said, "so I don't have much time."

It was the summer of 1970. A rash of strikes had been going on all over the country for over a year, more strikes than in many years past. In March, for example, over 200,000 postal workers had gone out on strike, surprising everyone. It began in New York City, but spread to over 650 other locations in cities across the country in two weeks. That set the tone for the rest of the year and beyond. Workers were in the mood to fight the crappy conditions they had put up with for so long. I believe it was a sign of the times. The campuses were literally on fire, soldiers and veterans were protesting against the war, and this fighting and protesting sentiment had spread to workers.

Several weeks later, I learned that Carl's union did go on strike, and I asked again if I could interview him.

He agreed, so I got my notebook and pen and joined him in his apartment.

"So, what's going on?" I asked him.

"A lot," he began. "We went on strike June 29th and we've had some battles. Maybe you've read about 'em in the papers?"

"Yeah, something. But I couldn't get a very good picture of exactly what has happened. There were some arrests?"

Carl explained, with anger in his voice, that there had been fifteen arrests so far. "The papers made it sound like it was our fault when, in reality, the company and the police provoked our people and set them up to be arrested to try to intimidate us."

According to Carl, the company had hired a large number of salaried workers to do production work, and they were being escorted in and out with police protection. "Some people say this is legal, but they're still playing the part of scabs. When they come in and go out, a contingent of police breaks our picket lines to let them in. These strikebreakers are doing somebody else's work while he's on strike; they're trying to prevent us from getting a living wage. Guys get angry when this happens, and when we try to maintain our picket lines, the cops rough us up and then arrest us. Most of the arrests have taken place due to confrontations with the scabs and scab trucks."

Carl had told me earlier that summer that the working conditions were bad. I asked him for more details.

"Essentially, the buildings are old," he began. "Many of the buildings were built around 1916 and 1920. Many machines are old and obsolete. The plant is poorly lit, and in some places you can't see. It's extremely dusty and dirty. The men work with such gases as phosgene, such chemicals as caustic, and a thing called H acid—which will eat through your clothes. There are also aniline, nitric acid, hydrochloric acid, and others—many of which eat away at your skin; plus you inhale the fumes of ammonia. There are guys who have worked there for years who can walk through dense concentrations of ammonia and not feel it. You wonder what has happened to the nerves in your eyes, nose, and mouth."

Industrial Murders

In addition, Carl explained, safety devices in the factory were practically nonexistent. "The machines are unsafe and the company doesn't care. If you die, you're just another number. Guys that have been here twenty and twenty-five years can tell you of between six and ten deaths, like guys going into vats of acid and what's left of them you can literally pick up with a spoon and put into a matchbox. One guy told me of an accident where a guy was painting a tower, and some fumes came along—the guy passed out and started falling. He hit the side of the tower, and it split his head open—he was probably dead before he hit the ground. There's another case where two guys went into a vat to repair it. The poisonous fumes were still there and they passed out—for good."

I asked him if any of those deaths had happened recently. "We rarely see anything in the papers about them," I said.

"Let's not call them deaths; they're industrial murders," he corrected me. "I don't know how long ago they happened, but some of the older guys were here then. But in the last six months, two guys died of heart attacks. One guy was scheduled to retire in about three weeks; you can't tell me that working at Allied didn't contribute to their dying prematurely."

Carl told me that a majority of the workers at the plant were white. In his department, about one-third were black or Spanish-speaking. The blacks and Latinos were the ones, he said, who seemed to hold the dirtier jobs, like cleaning presses for longer periods of time. Few people of color were pipefitters, carpenters, or lab personnel. He also said that well over 40 percent of the plant workers were under thirty years of age.

"The general feeling is that we can't go back, not for what they offer us," Carl continued. "Fifty-four cents over three years is an insult. We've had little support from District 50 of the union, there's no strike fund, and that hurts. The company's now protesting our right to get unemployment checks. Nobody's really starving—we have about 400 guys on welfare—so we'll hold out. We want $1.10 increase over the next two years and improvements in other benefits. The only demand we got is a union shop."

I asked about the morale of the workers.

"It's rough going," Carl admitted. "But when somebody has his back pushed up against the wall, he realizes he can't back down."

He said that two guys on the bargaining committee got busted by the cops, and one got beaten up pretty badly. "One of the things the strike has shown is the relationship between the company, the cops, and the courts," he concluded.

On the positive side, however, the people were beginning to see how issues at work and in society were linked, he explained. "During a strike, people get a chance to do some reading and thinking. You look at certain issues like the war, taxes, Tricky Dicky Nixon, and a number of workers are beginning to see the connections. They pay for the war, not only with their taxes, but with the blood of their sons—some are Vietnam vets—and none seem too happy about the war. If they can now see that the repression at home, the repression of unionists, the repression of minorities, and the repression of students are all tied together with the war and the bosses' need for greater profits, that big businesses have to expand or die, it will be a big victory."

FIGURE 1: One man in a group of Allied Chemical workers who picketed at the New York State Employment Center in Buffalo to protest the company's efforts to delay the unemployment checks they were entitled to while on strike. From "Allied Chemical: On Strike!" in *New Age* volume 1, number 1 (September 1970). From *New Age* archives. Courtesy Paul Krehbiel.

Carl said just what we were looking for. I wrote up the story in interview form, but we used the name "Tom" instead of Carl to protect him from retaliation by the company.

I did some research on Allied Chemical to supplement the interview and found that many members of the company's board of directors also sat on the boards of other major companies and news media, and had held top government positions. Here are three examples: John T. Connor, chairman of the board, was also on the board at General Motors and had been the secretary of commerce under President Johnson; Alexander Trowbridge had also been a secretary of commerce and worked for Standard Oil in Latin America; Arthur Bebee was on the boards of the *Washington Post* and *Newsweek* magazine. Allied Chemical workers didn't get good coverage from those media. I wrote this up in a box that was laid out with the article.

I also checked on the coverage from our local newspapers. On June 30, 1970, the *Courier-Express* ran an article headlined "Three Pickets Arrested at Buffalo Dye Works." The article named the three workers, gave their home addresses—which was completely unnecessary—said the three were members of the Allied and Technical Workers union, and noted that they were arrested for picket-line altercations including "illegal possession of a dangerous instrument [a club]," "obstructing governmental administration," and "disorderly conduct." There was nothing in the article about the police breaking the picket lines by beating the workers so they could usher strikebreakers into the plant. The article referred to the police "subduing" one picketer, but didn't say he was doing anything, and to two other picketers who "interfered and were also taken into custody," but again didn't spell out what this alleged "interference" was.

I asked Carl what had happened. He said that when the police were breaking the picket lines and the workers were trying to maintain their line, some pushing took place and the police beat the strikers and arrested them. When two workers came to the aid of a beaten coworker, they were arrested for "interfering." There was no mention of this information in the article, or in two other articles about the strike that appeared in the local corporate-owned newspapers, nor was anything said about the unsafe working conditions or other grievances of the workers, except that they wanted more money. The June 30 article quoted the plant manager as saying the company's offer of a 54-cent-an-hour increase over two years was "a good, solid offer." The article quoted the local union president asking for a $1.10 pay increase over two years.

I took my article to the next staff meeting and read it to the group. People liked it, and it became the lead article in our first issue. When we laid it out, we put in a photograph of Allied Chemical workers picketing at the New York State Employment building, demanding their unemployment checks (see figure 1). The workers won that fight and received their checks. We also ran a photo of the closed company gate with the workers' "On Strike" signs attached to it.

Auto Workers and Farm Workers

In this same issue, we ran an article about the half-million members of the United Auto Workers who were about to go on strike at General Motors and Chrysler. We had two big General Motors plants in Buffalo; one wasn't that far from where I grew up. That article was interesting to me for personal reasons. My company, Standard Mirror, produced all the rearview mirrors for Chrysler nationwide. I wondered if a strike at Chrysler would result in a production slowdown at Standard Mirror. Some people wondered if any of us at Standard Mirror would be laid off. But I saw the strike of the UAW workers as a strike for us, too, because they were sending a message to all employers that workers deserved better wages, benefits, and working conditions. If the auto workers at General Motors and Chrysler made important gains, that would encourage workers at Standard Mirror to demand bigger improvements, too. Or, some workers at Standard Mirror might apply for jobs with the major auto companies; an exodus from our company might put pressure on Standard Mirror to improve our wages, benefits, and working conditions to keep enough workers on the job. I wondered if our union could do anything to support the UAW in their struggle.

Other articles included "Nixon's Attack on the Unions," a short article on a strike of taxicab drivers at Madison Cab Company in Buffalo, an article attacking Nixon for widening the war in Vietnam into Cambodia, one by a nurse and doctor at Buffalo General Hospital exposing the shortcomings in our health care system, and an interview with a migrant farm worker working the fields south of Buffalo.

I remember meeting and being part of the interview with the migrant farm worker. We all thought it was important because we wanted to build support between rural agricultural workers and urban industrial and service workers. We met her at the apartment of two *New Age* staffers, Tom and Lynn.

Lares was a tiny lady, looked to be in her forties, and was very thin, with long jet-black hair pulled back and tied behind her neck. Some stray ringlets swirled around her deep-brown suntanned face. She wore jangly earrings and a brightly colored fluffy blouse with a red sash around her waist, and a sky-blue cap tilted sideways on her head. She looked like a gypsy, and her mere presence in the room commanded attention. We had been told that she was working and organizing in the tomato and beet fields south of Buffalo, near Dunkirk, and that she wanted to tell her story.

We sat in a circle and introduced ourselves. Lynn asked Lares to begin by telling us about herself and her work.

"I was born in Puerto Rico and came to the United States as a young girl," she began. "I've been doing farm work off and on since 1943. I live in the Dunkirk area and work with approximately 3,000 migrant workers in the fields there."

We learned that about one-third were Puerto Ricans, one-third were blacks, and one-third were whites.

"It is my belief that the people who work in the field are the cultivated crop," she explained. "Before you begin to talk about beets or tomatoes or string beans, you have to talk about this special crop that is the people who have been cultivated with such care and attention and a sort of devilish amount of planning. It is one of the means of cultivating a special species of skilled farm workers that you free them of having to read or write. This is taken care of in Puerto Rico and the South."

"Have the migrant workers organized themselves into unions of any kind?" Tom asked. Most of the people in the room were union members. Buffalo had one of the highest rates of union membership in the nation.

"There have been attempts," said Lares. "We've touched all types of possibilities, but haven't lifted any off the ground." I knew of Cesar Chavez and the United Farm Workers in California, but I didn't know of any established unions in western New York that organized farm workers—so I guessed the farm workers in the eastern United States had to figure it out on their own. That might be hard without some help, I thought.

Jim, a worker in a unionized paint factory, anticipated my thought. "What are the main obstacles?" he asked.

"One of them is welfare," said Lares. "We earn so little, we can get welfare. You become halfway skilled at living on welfare and not dying, which by itself is quite an accomplishment. Then, the work in the fields begins and you consider that work extra. You report less than what you earn so you don't get taken off welfare. What you make in the fields you don't inspect too carefully, and you don't give too much of a damn what your wages and hours are. You don't want to report an employer who may be breaking the law and cheating you for fear of losing your welfare."

"What about health and safety?" Lynn asked. "What happens if there is an accident?"

"If the accident is a good enough one, usually the worker perishes. Agriculture is the third most hazardous industry in the United States, but farm workers don't have the protection that other workers do."

We all were impressed with Lares's understanding of the sophistication of a system designed to keep poor people down. We wrote up the interview and gladly included it in our first issue. We printed 10,000 copies of that September 1970 issue and gave Lares a bundle to take back to the fields. The rest we distributed at the two big General Motors plants in Buffalo, to the Madison cab strikers, at Standard Mirror, and at other workplaces. After Carl read the Allied Chemical interview, he asked if we could bring 400 to 500 copies to their picket line. I agreed, and we set a time and day when I would meet him there. When I approached Allied Chemical carrying a bundle of papers, I saw about fifteen guys picketing and immediately recognized Carl. As I neared him, he stepped out of the line and walked toward me. We greeted each other, talked for a minute, and then he asked for a paper. As he was reading the Allied Chemical article, a couple of guys nearby saw him and came over.

"Look at this," Carl said. "Finally, someone is telling the truth about our strike." He read aloud a couple of sentences, and the first guy reached up to hold one side of the paper. Carl gave the paper to him and asked for another copy. He read two more sentences out loud so other workers would hear him.

"Remember how the *Courier Express* lied about the confrontation on our picket line?" Carl asked his coworker. "Well, here is what really happened, right here in this article."

His friend looked at it more closely. "Yeah. That's exactly how it happened," he said.

Carl motioned for me to come closer, and I did. He introduced me to both workers as a member of the group who published the paper, and said I worked at Standard Mirror.

One of the guys, Jack, said his mother-in-law used to work there, and he asked if I knew her. I said I didn't. It turned out that she worked there before I did.

"She told *some* stories about that place," Jack said. "People getting soaked working in one department and breathing ground-up glass."

"Those conditions still exist," I said. "That's one of the reasons we started this newspaper. The public doesn't know about the conditions any of us work under. We have people working on the paper who work in different industries—steel, auto, flour milling, and others—and no one knew what it was like working in another industry until we got together to put out this paper."

"That's for sure," Jack said. "Boy, have we been screwed by the newspapers since we went on strike. They ignored our issues and just focused on the violence. Then they claimed that we started it. And that's a lie!" I could hear the emotion rising in his voice.

He called several other picketers over. We exchanged greetings, and Jack showed them the article. "Here's a paper that's tellin' the truth," he said.

I asked if they wanted more, and they said they did. I gave them a bundle. They asked if we were charging for the papers, and I told them we didn't have a set price but were asking for donations to cover the printing costs. A bunch of the guys handed me coins and some dollar bills, totaling about $12. Our printing costs were a little over $100, so that was a good start.

Later that day, back at our apartment building, Carl told me that everybody read the article and people talked about it. They liked it and felt good that someone finally had paid attention to their issues.

"Did they read any of the other articles?" I asked.

"Well, I noticed a couple of guys reading some of the other articles, but they didn't say anything about them. I'm sure they'll like the articles about General Motors and the UAW, and the other articles about workers, but I'm not sure how they'll respond to the one about Cambodia. You've got to remember, this is probably the first time they've seen something so critical of the U.S. government, and it might make them feel uncomfortable. They all consider themselves strong, patriotic Americans. But they're not happy with the way the government is treating them in this strike, so maybe they'll think about the Cambodia article. But I wouldn't expect too much of a change in their thinking very soon. It will probably take some time."

"I understand," I said. "Just the fact that some of them are reading the Cambodia article is important. That's a good first step.

DuPont Workers on Strike

While the Allied Chemical workers were out, we heard that workers at DuPont in Niagara Falls had gone on strike, too. I volunteered to go up there to talk to them.

Niagara Falls is spectacular. Millions of tourists from around the world go there to see this incredible natural wonder. Honeymooners and lovers are seen walking by the falls hand in hand; some put out blankets on nearby fields to enjoy this romantic setting.

Yet, only several miles from this heaven on earth was a living hell. Most people never saw it or knew it existed. It was a row of putrid chemical factories, hidden from public view by big concrete walls and thick rows of trees and bushes. The city of Niagara Falls was smart enough to know that the sight and smell of these monsters so nearby would kill the lucrative tourist trade. Several years after the DuPont workers' strike, one of these polluters, Hooker Chemical Company, made the news when its chemical waste leached into people's yards and homes, causing a rash of birth defects and illnesses.

I drove up to talk with the DuPont strikers in September of 1970. I parked near the plant and saw a group of men holding signs and picketing outside. I grabbed several copies of our first issue of *New Age*, walked over to them, and introduced myself. I told them I was with an independent workers' newspaper and showed them the front cover. They looked, but with expressions on their faces that said, "Who is this guy?"

I turned the paper to the article on the Allied Chemical strike in Buffalo and told them we were a group of rank-and-file workers who were supporting the workers there. That got their attention, and one asked to see the article. I handed him the paper, and several others gathered around to read it (see figure 2). When they saw I was telling the truth, they warmed up to me.

I told them I wanted to talk to them about their strike so I could write an article about it. The taller man directed me to a beat-up trailer that was across the street on Buffalo Avenue. "That's our strike headquarters," he said. "Go over there and ask for Al."

I thanked him and crossed the street. I knocked on the door of the trailer, and a husky middle-aged man opened it. I introduced myself and told him why I was there, and he invited me in. Another man, Sam, was sitting at a table reading some papers. I talked to them briefly about our group and the Allied Chemical strike and showed them the article about it.

"This is good," Al said after reading part of it. "It's nice to see some honest reporting about workers for a change. We've been following the Allied strike the best we can, because what happens there will have a bearing on us. These chemical companies stick together."

I agreed. "We're hoping it'll be okay to write an article about your strike," I said. "The guys at Allied will definitely be interested." The Buffalo papers weren't covering either strike fairly.

Al was happy to comply. "It's pretty unique," he began. "First, this is the longest strike against DuPont in Niagara Falls ever—one week! There are several reasons for this. First of all,

FIGURE 2: Striking worker at DuPont in Niagara Falls reads *New Age* while on picket duty. From *New Age* volume 1, number 3 (November 2–18, 1970). From *New Age* archives. Courtesy Paul Krehbiel.

DuPont is incredibly centralized and brutal. Their idea of collective bargaining makes General Electric look like a labor organization!" I had remembered reading somewhere that DuPont was a major supplier of war material to Nazi Germany. That could explain a lot. Several years later, I saw the book *DuPont: Behind the Nylon Curtain*, by Gerard Colby Zilg, that confirmed the DuPont business connection to the Nazis.

"The basic issue is this," Al continued. "The men have had it up to here just running around like little dogs with their tails between their legs. They want to be able to leave the plant in the evening saying, 'I feel tired as hell, but, damn it, I still have my dignity!'"

He explained that all orders for running the company came direct from Wilmington,

Delaware, the headquarters. "They've sent in supervisory personnel from out of state to run our machines, to try to keep production going and break our strike."

"Just like at Allied Chemical," I added.

"That's what it looks like," Al continued. "We heard that some picketers were arrested there, but we didn't know the details. Your article helps explain that much better."

Through the article, he could see they had a lot in common with the Allied Chemical workers. "We've got what you call an independent union, too. We're in a federation with some other DuPont plant unions, but this is informal. They can't go on strike with us, legally. If DuPont in Tonawanda went on strike, the courts could call it a secondary strike and order the men back to work down there." The DuPont plant in Tonawanda wasn't far from where I lived. I drove by it often. It was a modern building and looked nice from the outside. Just like Standard Mirror. The public had no idea what hellish places these were on the inside, I thought.

"Our union has no strike fund," Al continued, "and we can't file for unemployment insurance for forty-nine days. And, of course, we remembered what happened to the Allied Chemical workers with their checks in Buffalo." I could see he knew that these big corporations and the courts were powerful forces working together against them. Yet they went on strike anyway. I wanted to find out what drove these men to take such action. I remembered the bad conditions at Allied Chemical, and wondered if working conditions were a factor at DuPont.

"Working conditions are lousy," Al said. "You can never prove to the compensation board that you feel sick because you've spent twenty years with strong chemicals, but what do you think? The average guy lives two and a half years after retirement, and we have a lot of heart attacks. We make mostly polyacetate for dry-cleaning solutions, and a compound that goes into leaded gasoline. This has a lot of the guys thinking, because they know leaded gasoline might be outlawed in an anti-pollution bill soon. DuPont tells us they've got their chemists working on new products for this, but we're trying to make sure."

"At the present time," Al continued, "the strike is going terribly. Truck traffic is almost normal through almost all the gates. We see guys in white shirts and ties driving trucks to the North Tonawanda chemical truck terminal. You should see these guys. Driving over curbs, scraping poles. I'd be worried if I were a citizen anywhere along Buffalo Avenue in LaSalle or North Tonawanda and knew that an untrained guy was driving a huge rig filled with poisons. I guess the cops don't find it in the public's interest to see if these guys are qualified drivers."

Racism in Industry

The similarities with Allied Chemical were striking, I thought. I asked what it was like for black and Puerto Rican workers.

"DuPont will do the minimum for minority workers," Sam said. "They don't want them working here. We have no black foremen, and well under 20 percent of the workers at DuPont/Niagara Falls are minority." Both Al and Sam were white. I was impressed at their understanding of the plight of minority workers and the implication that if people of color made up 20 percent of the population of the area, which they did, they should make up 20 percent of the population in the plant. Popular culture, especially the mass media, routinely portrayed American workers as a whole as being backward and white workers as being racists. That certainly wasn't true with these guys, nor with the Allied Chemical workers I had interviewed a month earlier. I thought about how this media propaganda was a conscious attempt to divide workers and weaken them so they couldn't stand up to their employers.

"It's ridiculous," Sam continued. "Two kids, black and white, grow up together, go to school together, go to Vietnam together, and then all of a sudden the white guy is up here at work and the black is down there on the street." Even though the conditions at DuPont sounded terrible, Sam and Al knew it was better to be employed at DuPont with all the problems, abuse, and hazards, than being unemployed.

"It's almost a strike out of desperation," Al exclaimed. "Look at our demands: a general wage increase of just 20 cents an hour for everyone, and a 4-cent increase for working evenings or nights. And look at what DuPont is offering. No wage increase and a 2-cent increase in the wage differential. Those guys in Wilmington think we're a bunch of fools up here in New York, and they think they can break us."

"Why do you think DuPont is fighting you guys so hard?" I asked.

"If we won," Al explained, "it would be a sign to the workers at the other eighty-seven DuPont plants that DuPont could be taken on locally. It would encourage a lot of other so-called 'weak unions'—weak in form, but strong in the spirit of the men."

I knew Al was exactly right. I marveled at their political astuteness. They knew their strike was much bigger than just the workers at DuPont Niagara Falls—it could set an example for every worker at DuPont wherever they worked. And they knew that what happened to the Allied Chemical workers was important to them.

"If we lose," Sam added, "lots of men are beginning to think twice about this whole management-labor thing . . ."

"The name of the game is definitely power," Al said. He paraphrased several statements published recently in a small local independent newspaper: "Let's not forget that never has industry with all its billions done anything to diminish the profit-increase graph unless they were forced into it. If it wasn't for unions, weak as many are, industrial workers would still be working sixty hours a week for 25 cents an hour."

I agreed.

These guys knew that bosses acted as a group to increase corporate profits at the expense of all the workers, and workers were in an opposing group to resist increasing exploitation. Whether they would have called themselves the working class and the bosses part of the capitalist class, I don't know. But they definitely understood the relationship between the two groups and had some idea of class consciousness. I thanked them for the interview and told them I would bring back copies of the next issue with their story in it. They thanked me, we shook hands, and I left.

The DuPont strike story appeared in the October 1970 issue of *New Age*, illustrated with a woodcut graphic of a wealthy-looking boss in front of a smoke stack. The caption simply said: "The Class Enemy." I took copies to the DuPont workers and they were very appreciative of our support.

Labor Solidarity: United States and Vietnam

While we were preparing the October issue, I was reading a book written by a Vietnamese Buddhist monk, Thich Nhat Hanh, titled *Vietnam: Lotus in a Sea of Fire*. I learned about the terrible poverty and high unemployment in Vietnam, and the poor wages and working conditions of those workers lucky enough to have jobs in South Vietnam, under the sponsorship of the U.S. government. I thought about the similarity of terrible conditions for the workers at DuPont, and about how the unemployed in both countries were even worse off. I had heard that DuPont had overseas operations, and I tried to learn where they were and what the wages and working conditions of overseas DuPont workers were like. I wondered if DuPont or Allied Chemical operated in Vietnam.

I didn't find them there, but I did find a number of U.S. construction companies working in Vietnam and decided to write an article about the similarities between workers in the U.S. and workers in Vietnam. I figured if these American chemical-company workers already saw that they had common interests with other workers in the United States, they could see that they had common interests with the workers in Vietnam and other foreign countries. This was the first step in building international labor solidarity, another of our goals.

I began the article by pointing out that U.S. construction companies went to South Vietnam mostly to build military bases to help the U.S. war effort "against the Vietnamese people, [while] making big money for themselves."

I named four U.S. companies, including Brown & Root, which helped finance Lyndon Johnson's presidential election campaign. (Years later, Brown & Root became a part of Halliburton, which became a major supporter of President Bush the Second and Dick Cheney, who left his positions as chairman and chief executive officer of Halliburton to become vice president. When Bush and Cheney invaded Iraq in 2003, Halliburton received multimillion dollar contracts from them to build military installations in Iraq.)

I wrote that the U.S. construction companies employed 4,200 Americans, 41,800 Vietnamese, and a small number of Filipinos and Koreans. I explained that the Americans mostly served as managers and bosses and received "pay beginning at $1,000 per month . . . plus an exemption from paying U.S. income taxes." That was very good money back then. And it was much higher than American workers earned in the United States and many, many times more than the Vietnamese earned. From Hanh's book, I learned that Vietnamese workers "are getting an average of $35 a month, or 14 cents an hour," and they were forced to work sixty-hour weeks! I put that in the article.

I continued, "It is no wonder that Thich Nhat Hanh . . . stated: 'Each morning sees swarms of [Vietnamese] people on the dumps and trash heaps of the city [Saigon then, Ho Chi Minh City now] and especially on those adjoining American installations. An ordinary worker cannot earn enough to support himself.'"

I then wrote that the American bosses operating in Vietnam "get rich and the Vietnamese starve." I knew that some American workers in the United States were so low paid that they did go hungry; in fact, I knew some workers at Standard Mirror made so little that they qualified for food stamps. I ended the article by writing: "We should see more clearly now that when we fight against the company and the bosses, we are not fighting alone. . . . The South Vietnamese workers have been fighting U.S. bosses for years. The people that are taking

FIGURE 3: "Worker Solidarity" poster, which illustrated the article "U.S. Firms Profit in Vietnam," from *New Age* volume 1, number 2 (October 1970). The article explained that the reason for the war in Vietnam was the desire of U.S. multinational corporations to acquire cheap raw materials, cheap labor, and new markets in Vietnam and Southeast Asia. It argued that workers in Vietnam and workers in the United States had much in common and should support each other in their struggles with their employers. Graphically the poster showed the unity of workers of different countries, unity of men and women workers, and the unity between industrial workers and agricultural workers. Courtesy the artist, Paul Krehbiel, who acknowledges the influence of Cuban artist, René Mederos.

advantage of the Vietnamese are the same people who are taking advantage of us. Know your friends, know your enemies."

When the article was laid out, I put under it a drawing I had done of a Vietnamese farmer and American worker together with large letters that said: "Worker Solidarity." The article was headlined "U.S. Firms Profit in Vietnam." I later made a poster for *New Age* using that graphic (see figure 3).

Right below that article was an article written by a construction worker, warning fellow construction workers not to get manipulated by misdirected patriotism and flag waving by their employers or government and construction union leaders into supporting the war in Vietnam and attacking antiwar demonstrators. This was right after New York City construction workers were incited to beat antiwar protestors, and practically every mass-media outlet gave top-priority coverage to this inflammatory action. Our *New Age* article ended: "Workers do love this country and respect the flag. But nobody ever said that workers had to love, honor and trust this country's ruling class, the rich, the big corporations. Vietnam is their war, not ours. Stand up for the flag but don't support a war in Asia that profits the rich and robs the working people of this country and Vietnam."

One of our goals was to make *New Age* a school for workers. We regularly ran articles about important struggles in labor history, especially when there were lessons that could help workers today in their current battles. In the October 1970 issue, we ran an article on the front page about a militant national railroad workers' strike in 1877. We knew that contract negotiations among American railroad workers' unions and their employers were going poorly in the fall of 1970, and that the workers might go on a national rail strike in December 1970. We wanted to give them an example of what other railroad workers did during another national rail strike.

We also wanted to expose the mistreatment and sometimes brutality of the authorities toward *all* workers, both in the United States and in other countries. This would help in building support for the railroad workers in the United States, and international labor solidarity. We wrote that in Pittsburgh during the 1877 railroad strike, authorities shot and killed some workers, and the strikers responded by burning down the roundhouse. We weren't advocating violence, but we wanted workers to know that if the police were violent toward them, there was a history of American workers fighting back. It was also the height of hypocrisy for the U.S. government to draft and then order American workers to kill workers in other countries so U.S. corporate owners could get richer, but then arrest, maim, or kill those same American workers when they tried to defend themselves against U.S. or National Guard attacks here at home.

Other articles in the October issue were about:

- the great union-student-community coalition that formed to support striking taxi drivers, members of Teamsters Local 558, who were working for Van Dyke Cab company in Buffalo;
- facts for auto workers who were on strike at General Motors about GM's huge profits, and how they could easily afford to meet the auto workers' contract proposals;
- women workers who met at the Buffalo YWCA to talk about fighting for better wages

and working conditions for women workers, and closing the wage gap between men and women;

- a strike of auto mechanics in Buffalo who were in their eighteenth week; and
- the League of Revolutionary Black Workers in Detroit and how they were fighting inside the United Auto Workers union to make the union more responsive to fighting the racial discrimination against black workers in the auto plants, along with an announcement of a meeting in Buffalo with members of the League who traveled to Buffalo from Detroit.

Chilean Workers and Socialism

Finally, we had an article in that same October 1970 issue on the monumental struggle of workers in Chile to throw off generations of exploitation by foreign multinational corporations by electing a strong, pro-worker government. This pro-worker government, called the Popular Unity coalition, had been elected on September 5, 1970, and the corporate mass media in Buffalo and across the United States were in a frenzy to denounce it. We received reports from a number of independent sources and wrote our own article supporting the new labor government and challenging the denunciations. What got U.S. corporations and their media most lathered up was that this new labor government would likely make it much harder for foreign corporations to exploit the Chilean people as ruthlessly as before. The way they presented it to the American people, however, was that the new government was headed by a leader of the Socialist Party, Salvador Allende, with strong backing by the Communist Party of Chile. Decades of smearing socialism in the United States laid the foundation to scare the American people into supporting possible action by the U.S. government against this new government, even though it was elected in a democratic election—exactly what the U.S. government says it wants for all countries of the world. Our headline was "Socialist Victory, Imperialist Defeat in Chile."

We began the article by explaining the poor conditions that most Chileans and Latin Americans lived under. We explained that "poverty [and] starvation" plagued millions of people, where the "per-person average income in Latin America is around $250 a year (it is over $2,000 in the U.S.)." That meant the average resident in the United States made eight times more than the average Latin American. We wrote that "world health groups have calculated that four Latin Americans die EVERY MINUTE of preventable disease or starvation, and that US companies extract $40,000 in profit EVERY MINUTE from Latin America." This was in 1970. It's much more as I write this in 2010.

We noted that half the children never saw the inside of a school. Based on the program of the Popular Unity coalition government, we reported that it pledged to develop a jobs-creation program to drastically reduce the 18 percent unemployment rate, and to spend money on schools, affordable housing and health care, and programs to eradicate malnutrition. The government was going to raise the money for these programs by nationalizing many of the foreign-owned industries, such as the huge copper industry that provided 81 percent of the world's copper.

We warned about U.S. corporations initiating opposition or even retaliation against the Popular Unity government, including the possibility of "CIA-financed invasions" in league with "disgruntled rich Chileans." At the same time we believed that support for the Popular Unity government was widespread in Chile and would grow stronger as the success of these programs was felt by the people, and that the government could protect itself against an attempt to overthrow it.

We were right about the first prediction. Six months later, in the May 1971 issue of *New Age*, we reported that most private banks had been nationalized, workers' salaries increased substantially—some by as much as 60 percent—pensions and other benefits were improved, jobs were created and unemployment went down, a new ministry was preparing to build and open thousands of child-care centers, and the vote for Popular Unity candidates went higher in the next round of elections. But we were wrong about our second prediction. On September 11, 1973, conservative and right-wing generals in the Chilean military led by General Pinochet, and supported and guided by the Nixon administration, the CIA, and wealthy corporate Chileans and Americans, led a coup against the Allende government and overthrew it. Thousands of Chileans were killed; many were imprisoned, tortured, and disappeared; and a right-wing dictatorship descended on Chile that returned control of Chile's natural resources to U.S. multinational corporations. This ruthless military dictatorship remained in power in Chile with U.S. government and business support for seventeen years, and Chilean workers' wages, living conditions, and unemployment severely worsened.

I knew that a lot of workers in the Buffalo area wouldn't necessarily agree with everything we wrote about the workers in Chile, largely because of the incessant antisocialism and anticommunism that we were bombarded with daily by the government, corporations, and the mass media. But I and the other workers on the staff thought it was important to publish these articles for several reasons. First, this was a big story, covering the front pages of the mass-circulation, corporate-owned daily newspapers and getting top billing on TV stations. Second, it was a story about workers in Chile organizing to improve their hard lives, a theme totally ignored in these same stories. Also, our government consistently railed against socialists and communists as being undemocratic. Yet, here was a case of socialists and communists being elected to power through democratic elections, and now they were being attacked verbally and threatened militarily. The hypocrisy was glaring, and we wanted to build support in the United States for the people of Chile in the hope that it would make it harder for the U.S. government to violently overthrow this elected government.

My own support for the Chileans was because I believed strongly in workers acting in their own interests *and* for the general welfare of the whole society. That is what I saw the Popular Unity government attempting to do. That government said it wanted to establish socialism—a system where workers have more control over their lives, and where goods and services are produced to meet the needs of all the people, not just to enrich the wealthy, which is a major feature of capitalism.

Socialism has done much good in the world by bringing jobs, education, health care, and a better life to millions of people. We don't learn about that in our corporate-owned mass media. Conversely, problems that crop up in the course of creating socialism, and the wrong-doings of some who profess to be socialist and communist leaders get full coverage, and give a slanted, untruthful picture of socialism.

Socialism is so young in its ideas and practices in all of human history that it needs time to experiment. Unfortunately, every time the advocates of socialism try to implement

FIGURE 4: Cover of *New Age* volume 1, number 3 (November 2–18, 1970). The issue included feature articles about, and that urged support for, U.S. unions that opposed the war in Vietnam, chemical workers on strike at DuPont and two smaller chemical companies in nearby Niagara Falls, and the wildcat strike movement among auto workers at Fiat in Italy. The graphic, by German artist Kathe Kollowitz, shows worker solidarity. From *New Age* archives. Courtesy Paul Krehbiel.

their vision and programs, capitalism and its armed might moves to crush them. Those of us working on *New Age* believed that the Chilean people had a right to experiment with their version of socialism, free from outside interference.

Patriotism in Black and White

In November 1970, we covered more militant strikes at chemical companies in Niagara Falls at Varcum, and a wildcat strike at Airco-Speer. Workers at both companies were represented by the Oil, Chemical, and Atomic Workers Union. In both strikes, the companies had the cops break the workers' picket lines to usher strikebreakers into the plants—just like at Allied Chemical; and in both strikes, workers resisted. Confrontations broke out, and property damage occurred at the plants.

In the November 1970 issue of *New Age* (see figure 4), I wrote a labor history article about Eugene Debs, the leader of the American Railway Union and a leader of the national rail strike in 1894. We headlined the story "Eugene V. Debs: A True Patriot." I wrote that Debs stood up not only for the rights of railroad workers, but for all working people everywhere, and that made him a great patriot. He also was a socialist, and in 1917 he publicly opposed U.S. plans to go to war in Europe in World War I, saying the war would be a mutual slaughter of workers from many countries to enrich the rich, the big corporations, and the banks. He was jailed for his opposition to that war, and for his union leadership and socialist political beliefs; yet he was so popular that he polled a million votes for president of the United States while sitting in jail. I wanted readers to know that socialism wasn't a "foreign" ideology, but had strong roots in the history of our country, and that it was common for far-sighted union leaders and union members, other workers, and people from many walks of life to see that socialism offered a solution to the incessant exploitation, oppression, and wars of capitalism.

In that same issue, we ran an article on the strikes of workers at huge Fiat auto plants in Italy to stop job speedup, initiated by rank-and-file workers and supported by progressive students.

And I wrote a history of the Vietnam War, including how U.S. policy supported the wealthy and corrupt in Vietnam and kept Vietnamese workers weak and poor, and how the growing number of unions in the United States were calling for an end to the war.

In the December 1970 issue, we had two feature articles on the national United Auto Workers strike at General Motors. One article was an interview that we did with a striking worker at the Tonawanda GM plant in the Buffalo area. The other article was about workers—especially black workers organized in a Black Panther caucus, who were on strike at a big GM plant in Fremont, California. These workers talked about GM's divide-and-conquer tactics to keep the workers disunited, the dehumanizing pace of the assembly line, how black workers were assigned the hardest and most unsafe jobs. They also talked about the contract fight for the "30-and-out" proposal to give full retirement benefits to an auto worker after thirty years on the job, how the workers had to reform the union to make it more responsive to the members, and how young workers were leading the way.

Other articles were about

- the efforts of Buffalo's city garbage workers to make improvements on the job and in their union—including their fight to establish a grievance procedure;
- how to apply for food stamps (I knew workers at Standard Mirror who used that information to get food stamps as copies of *New Age* circulated around the plant), Medicaid, and welfare;
- the settlement of the Allied Chemical strike and contract, and ideas on how the workers could prepare to get a better contract next time (and their thanks for the support of *New Age*); and
- a strike of tens of thousands of workers in Spain, precipitated by the repressive policies of its fascist dictator Franco, that was organized secretly by underground workers councils. Interestingly, Franco was the hero of General Pinochet, who overthrew Salvador Allende in Chile two years later.

And we had a major feature article titled "To My White Working-class Sisters." The author began: "We are the invisible women, the faceless women, the nameless women. . . . No one says we are beautiful, no one says we are important." She wrote that, while working as a switchboard operator, someone asked: "'Are you the switchboard?' Naturally—since we are looked on as extensions of the machines we operate—not as human beings." She ended her article by writing: "As white working-class and poor people we must begin to be proud of ourselves, our histories and each other; we must unite and support ourselves. . . . Once we respect ourselves, we will find it necessary to struggle with a society and with jobs which tell us we are worthless. In that struggle we will learn that the anger of black and brown people which we have feared for so long has the same direction as our anger, that their enemies are our enemies, and their fight our fight."

I and others were emotionally moved by this extraordinary talk from the heart. I believed it was exactly what we needed in our paper. Not only did it make important connections, but it was spoken in a voice that would resonate with whoever read it. While we were a predominately white group, we recognized the special oppression of people of color and women and wanted to give special attention to their stories. We believed that the white working class as a whole were treated as invisible, faceless, nameless, and worthless. We knew these included Italians, Irish, Poles, and other white ethnic groups from eastern Europe, because many members of *New Age* were from these groups. So, in this issue we ran articles about other white, working-class ethnic groups as well.

In our January 1971 issue, we published a labor-history article titled "The Fighting Irish," about the Molly Maguires, militant Irish-American union organizers in the Appalachian coal fields in the late 1800s. When Bernadette Devlin, the fiery Irish civil rights organizer who got elected to the British Parliament from Northern Ireland, came to Buffalo to speak in early 1971, we ran an article about her talk titled "Irish Revolutionary in Buffalo" (see figure 5). We quoted her first words: "There are only two breeds of humans—those who work and those who live off the fruits of other people's labor." She called for the unity of Catholic and Protestant workers, and between workers in Ireland and Great Britain and everywhere. We ran the article with a picture of her speaking and a photo of Irish workers with their distinct Irish caps. After her talk, a group of about ten of us—many from *New Age* and including a number

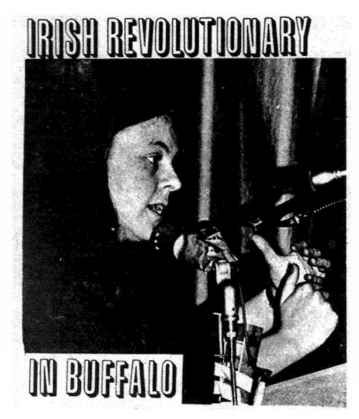

FIGURE 5: Bernadette Devlin—Irish revolutionary, socialist, and the youngest member of the British Parliament from Northern Ireland—spoke in Buffalo in February 1971 to a large crowd at Buffalo State College. Notes author Paul Krehbiel, "After her speech, we took her out to McGinty's and other Irish working-class bars in South Buffalo where we all sang Irish revolutionary songs over pitchers of beer." From *New Age* volume 1, number 7 (March 1971). From *New Age* archives. Courtesy Paul Krehbiel.

of Irish American workers from Buffalo—took her to McGinty's and other Irish bars in South Buffalo, where we sang Irish revolutionary songs late into the night over pitchers of beer.

In the April 1971 issue of *New Age*, we ran another labor-history article, titled "Sacco and Vanzetti: Italian-American Labor Heroes." Our goals were to inform Buffalo workers of all ethnic backgrounds about these two great working-class organizers who were framed and executed on trumped-up charges in the early 1920s, and to reach out to the large Italian-American working class in Buffalo to help instill pride in their history and culture. I did a pen-and-ink drawing of these two labor leaders to illustrate the article. We also wanted to show all workers that their hopes and dreams were similar. Like most white, ethnic, working-class groups, Italian Americans were largely ignored by the corporate media, except when members of the Mafia were arrested. Then the mass media would routinely note their Italian backgrounds. Our goal was to show that the overwhelming majority of Italian Americans—like most groups—were honest, hard-working members of society, making their contribution to the betterment of our communities. Irish, Italians, and Polish—all predominately working class—made up the majority of Buffalo's population. German Americans were another large group, and African Americans made up about one-third of the city's population, so all of these groups were important to reach.

We had articles in every issue exposing racism in the workplace, and what black workers and their allies among whites and others were doing to combat it. In the June and July issues,

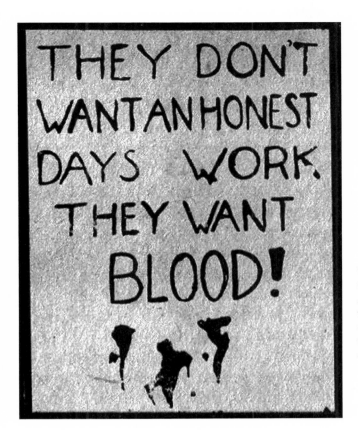

FIGURE 6: Striking Acme steelworkers union members, practically all African Americans, wrote this hand-made sign to express their feelings about their employer. From *New Age* volume 1, number 10 (June 1971). From *New Age* archives. Courtesy Paul Krehbiel.

we had articles about the strike of steelworkers at Acme Steel. Over 90 percent of the workers were black (most of the rest were Puerto Ricans) and they labored under conditions right out of Dante's *Inferno*. I visited the plant with several other staff members to talk to the workers, who were members of the United Steelworkers union. The plant was built in the 1890s and it looked like little had changed since then. The men labored on dirt floors, in a dark and dingy mill, with no ventilation, and had to push carts loaded with steel by hand. They showed us scars and burn marks on their hands, arms, and faces that they had received from the foundry. These men made as little as $2.05 an hour—well below steelworkers at the larger mills—and told us they were getting little help from their international union. Many had silicosis, tuberculosis (which had been largely wiped out in the rest of the country), and lung cancer. Many were in such poor health that they couldn't pass a medical exam anywhere else, and were condemned to stay at Acme. The owner was a local right-winger who was a leader in the American Legion. These workers had pulled wildcat strikes over these barbaric conditions since 1957, and had a reputation for militancy. The picketers carried hand-made signs, including one that read, "They don't want an honest day's work. They want blood" (see figure 6). Red paint was splattered across the bottom of the sign. We took a photo of that sign and some of the strikers and ran them with our articles. The commercial dailies ignored the plight of these men, or condemned them when they had wildcat strikes, as if they were un-American. We saw them as patriots, fighting for justice, not only for themselves but for all workers.

Steelworkers Take on a Giant

Because of steel's role as the most important industry in Buffalo, we published regular articles about steel and steelworkers. In January 1971, we had two features about Bethlehem Steel, the largest mill in the area and the fourth largest steel mill in the United States, employing 18,000 workers. In a front-page article headlined "Bethlehem Steals," we wrote that the company, which was located on Buffalo's southern border in Lackawanna, was trying to steal from the Buffalo area by scaring elected officials with threats of big layoffs, and maybe even closing the plant. According to the company, the Buffalo area wasn't a good place to do business: taxes were too high, pollution laws were too stringent, workers' wages and benefits were too high, the steelworkers and their union were too demanding, and equipment was too old and inefficient. Every couple of weeks, for months, Bethlehem laid off workers, until the total on layoff reached over three thousand by the end of 1970. The message was clear: Bethlehem Steel was a major financial power in western New York, and if the community didn't buckle under to the company's demands, it would cripple Buffalo.

We said this was blackmail, a company scare tactic to get more tax breaks from state, federal, and local elected officials (the company already had had its taxes reduced from $188 million in 1960 to $80 million in 1969), as well as breaks on complying with pollution laws—which would allow the company to continue operating old, high-polluting machines and furnaces that poisoned the air and water, while scaring steelworkers into not going on strike on August 1, 1969, for fear of losing their jobs. But we also noted that the company had just installed over 90 new coke ovens (this mill had 1,000 coke ovens), three new basic oxygen furnaces, and new equipment in the 10- to 12-inch bar mill, all signs that the company wasn't planning on leaving anytime soon. Our goal was to inform the steelworkers about the company to give them the strength to go on strike if they felt they weren't getting a fair contract during negotiations, and to get all levels of government not to buckle under to Bethlehem's unreasonable demands.

The issues for steelworkers were improvements in wages, benefits, and working conditions, and especially in stopping company efforts to eliminate jobs and negatively change job descriptions, and to speed up jobs at will. We interviewed one of our *New Age* staff members who worked at Bethlehem Steel to get a better idea of exactly what steelworkers were thinking. We titled the article "From the Coke Ovens." Mike (we didn't use his name in the article) had just been transferred to the coke ovens from another department, and here is what he said about his new job:

It's one of the worst jobs in the mill. I work on top of the coke ovens as a lid man. When you open a lid, thick black smoke pours out, along with intense heat and gasses. I wear a respirator—which keeps out some dust but not the smoke, a heat shield which is cumbersome, special gloves and shoes because I'm walking right on top of a blazing furnace. In the winter, with the cold wind blowing off the lake, you can be freezing from the waist up and boiling from your waist down. I feel dizzy in the intense heat and I'm exhausted. One day flames 10' thick shot up out of the furnace along with thick smoke, and I backed up to get away from the flames and almost backed into another open coke oven hole. When I told my foreman that I felt I hadn't had enough training yet to work

FIGURE 7: Cover of *New Age* volume 1, number 10 (June 1971), with the lead story supporting workers at Bethlehem Steel in South Buffalo. The article urged the workers, the government, and the Buffalo community to rally together to oppose the company's blackmail threats to close the mill unless their demands were met. Company demands included another series of lower taxes, waivers in complying with pollution laws, and givebacks by the United Steelworkers union in upcoming contract negotiations. From *New Age* archives. Courtesy Paul Krehbiel.

alone on the coke ovens, he sent me to the company doctor. The company doctor said that I just needed to get used to it and be more careful. He then added that he thought guys hired off Jefferson Avenue coped better on the coke ovens than guys who were transferred there from somewhere else in the mill. Jefferson Avenue is a major street in Buffalo's Black community; normally 90% of the workers assigned to the coke ovens are Blacks. Since the company can transfer anyone there, some people are afraid to challenge the company too much for fear of being sent to the coke ovens.

We published all this in *New Age* and didn't let up in following issues:

- February 1971: We did another feature article on the Lackawanna plant titled "Interview with a Steward at Bethlehem Steel." His name was Ken (we didn't use his name in the article, though he may not have cared), and he worked closely with us. He was the chief steward for his department and he was a militant union leader. He talked about the many confrontations he and other workers had with management to stop management abuse and protect the rights of workers.
- May 1971: We ran an article headlined "Steelworkers Unite." We published a list of demands that we got from rank-and-file steelworkers, including a call to set up strong strike committees.
- June 1971: We blasted Bethlehem Steel again with a front-page article headlined "Bethlehem

Steals from the Niagara Frontier" (see figure 7). We hammered the steel giant for being a tax evader, a major polluter, and an abuser of workers and the community.

- July 1971: We announced the formation of a community-based Steelworkers Strike Support Committee, which we and other groups initiated.

Bethlehem continued to threaten the Buffalo area, especially about closing the plant. The company used similar tactics all over the country and averted a national steel strike in August of 1971. But that didn't mean steelworkers or their communities were happy. There were many smaller strikes, work slowdowns, and job actions, and the steelworkers at the Bethlehem plant in Lackawanna were leaders in these rebellions. Several decades later, in 2006, Diana Dillaway wrote in her book *Power Failure* about the corporate crippling of Buffalo; that top-level management at Bethlehem Steel headquarters in Bethlehem, Pennsylvania,

remained oblivious to the needs of local managers and labor at the Lackawanna plants in the Buffalo area. During the 1970's at any one time, six thousand to seven thousand union grievances were pending in Buffalo, and the Lackawanna plants were ranked high in terms of lost time because of strikes. . . . This out-of-touch style of management lit the fires of labor militancy, leading to a combative atmosphere reinforced by the sheer numbers of workers at the Lackawanna plants.

As our friend and militant chief steward Ken said in his February 1971 interview, "When I leave Bethlehem Steel, I intend to leave with the same dignity as when I started." I was proud of our role in supporting the steelworkers and the Buffalo community.

My Struggle in Auto Parts

While all this was going on in steel and other industries, events were heating up in the auto industry. I was active in the United Glass and Ceramic Workers at the auto-parts plant where I worked. We were preparing for negotiations, since our contract was going to expire in September 1971. I was friends with a couple of other young progressive workers, and we had a lot of ideas about what we should be asking for. Many other workers also had good ideas, and they were brought up at union meetings. Proposals for modest wage increases and improvements in shift differentials and pensions garnered strong support. Large wage increases, like the $1.00 an hour some of us advocated, were seen as unrealistic, as were ideas to get union control over hiring and firing, and seeing the company's financial records. But a small group of us younger workers felt those issues were important.

Our group then decided to compile all the good ideas and get them out to the entire membership and let everyone decide what they wanted. We talked to workers in different departments to learn about their problems and concerns. While many agreed with our more radical proposals, they thought it would be nearly impossible to achieve them. Our small group started going over our contract, and writing language that would make improvements. We formed the Progressive Action Caucus inside our union, and we put out a leaflet with the caucus name on it and the list of ideas. We didn't criticize the current union leadership, but instead focused on the improvements that we thought workers wanted.

I was the primary author of our leaflet. I began by listing many of the problems in the plant. "There is the increasing job speed-up in almost every department. In the last 2–3 years, the quota on the 48 lines has gone from 288 chucks up to 448 per shift." A chuck is a round form that holds the rearview mirrors so the surface of the glass can be ground perfectly smooth and polished. I continued: "In department 3 the block-splitting quota has gone up on almost every job. . . . In the press-room, one job quota went from 700 pieces to 1,000 pieces . . . and the list could go on and on. And there is no end in sight. Each time they give one of their phony 'scientific' time-studies, we know that they're going to raise the quota again."

We described the terrible working conditions in most of the departments: "Certain bosses treat us like slaves. And we are afraid to say anything for fear of being fired. . . . How much more of this are we expected to take? We are human beings, not machines or slaves. We are tired of being used and abused by a small group of people who never have to cope with these conditions." This part expressed the long-pent-up anger, humiliation, and fear that many workers felt, and now we finally said out loud on a written leaflet what everyone thought.

We then quoted net earnings figures from the company's annual report to stockholders, proving that Standard Mirror could easily pay us decent wage increases and fix the other problems.

Next we listed eleven ideas for contract proposals and urged all the members to give their thoughts for contract negotiations. We suggested a significant wage increase with a cost-of-living allowance, deleting the no-strike provision in the contract as well as the entire management-rights section. We urged setting up one board with workers on it to gain some control over hiring and firing, and another board to determine production schedules. We wanted union access to the company's financial records, improvements in safety and health in the plant—especially by putting filters on the machines that made the ground-up glass— freedom for any union member to post notices on the bulletin board, and better pensions.

We knew some of these ideas were unrealistic, but we thought it was important to list them to get workers to think about them. In essence, these proposals called for the workers to have greater control over their work lives in our factory. I saw these proposals as important building blocks in moving us toward a fairer, more just and democratic society.

Once the leaflet was completed, we had it distributed at the front gate in February 1971. The workers loved it! They took stacks to pass to coworkers and taped them up on the walls and told any supervisor or boss who walked by, "This is what we want!" I wrote an article about this campaign in the March 1971 issue of *New Age* (see appendix), which we distributed at the plant.

I began the article by describing the problems in the plant, and then quoted the company's report to stockholders: "Standard Mirror continues effective efforts to streamline production methods and lower costs . . . [and introduce] automation." Then I wrote: "No new automation had been introduced; they have just constantly cut the workforce . . . and forced the remaining workers to work twice as fast! . . . On the 48 line . . . one guy . . . had a heart attack and had to quit."

Unfortunately, I had been laid off around Christmas along with some other workers, but I was hoping to be called back. Then another worker who was a friend of mine told me that a top boss told him one day: "We think Paul had something to do with that leaflet. He's smart, but he should use his intelligence to try to help the company, not fight us." I filed a charge at the National Labor Relations Board and gave the board agent that piece of information since it looked like company retaliation for union activities. But when the board agent wanted to talk to this worker about testifying in my case, the worker got scared. He had a child with a lot of medical problems and was afraid that he would get fired and lose his medical insurance.

One response to my article was a letter from a Standard Mirror worker, which we published in the April 1971 issue. The worker thanked us for a great article and criticized the international union officials for not doing enough to help us.

I tried to keep up with the struggles at Standard Mirror and contract negotiations, and I wrote another article about the factory and the workers that was published in July 1971. During this period, *New Age* was working to set up a Steelworkers Strike Support Committee in anticipation of a big strike in the steel industry that fall, and I didn't have time to keep up with the contract negotiations at Standard Mirror.

But bigger problems were looming in front of us. Some internal problems that had existed at *New Age* for a number of months got worse in July 1971.

Women in Revolt

The women in the group felt that *New Age* wasn't giving enough attention or coverage to the problems that women workers faced, and especially on jobs that primarily employed women, like waitresses, nurses, telephone operators, hotel maids, and other jobs primarily in the service sector. While we had some coverage of these female-dominated jobs, it was true that we hadn't given nearly as much attention to them as we had to the male-dominated jobs in manufacturing. The group that started *New Age* was comprised largely of men, and our thinking had been to concentrate on basic manufacturing industries because we believed that economic pressure applied there would have a much bigger impact on the economy and political system than pressure applied to the service sector. But when the women in the group confronted the men with their criticisms, I and many of the other men on staff recognized that we had made a big mistake. More and more women were entering the job market and becoming important members of the working world. Growing numbers were getting more active in their unions.

Women also made up about half of the staff of *New Age*, which now totaled twenty people. Many of the female members of the group were our wives and girlfriends. They had made these complaints earlier and now felt that the men on staff hadn't taken them seriously enough. The women presented an ultimatum to the men: allow the women to produce the August issue by themselves as a special all-women's issue, and agree that half of all future articles be about women—because, they argued, women make up half the population.

The men agreed to the all-women's issue and to giving more attention to women's issues and jobs, but were divided about having half of all future issues be exclusively about women. What about articles on companies or unions that involved both men and women? It seemed to me that most issues—wages, benefits, and working conditions—affected both men and women, and that our main focus should be on the big issues that affected most everyone. If there was an important strike that involved both men and women, but writing an article about it would push the percentage of all-women's articles to less than half, would we have to scrap it, at least for that issue?

FIGURE 8: Cover of *New Age* volume 1, number 12 (August 1971), the special all-women's issue. The women wrote articles on female telephone operators, waitresses, housewives, women and the war in Vietnam, and "invisible" women. The entire issue was a moving tribute to women's struggles for recognition, equality, dignity, and respect. From *New Age* archives. Courtesy Paul Krehbiel.

As we debated this demand, the women worked on the August issue. It was tagged on the front cover "Women's Issue" (see figure 8). Inside it contained excellent articles on the working lives of telephone operators and waitresses, women and the war, housewives and the family, rape and self-defense, birth control, and more, including a reprint of the great article on "Invisible Women" that we had run earlier.

On the front page, they began by explaining who they were and why they put out this issue:

We are a varied group from 18 to over 40 years old; married, divorced, and single; with children and without them. A few of us work, a few of us are on welfare, a few are dependent on their husbands for support. But despite all these differences, what unites us is the belief that *because we are women* we share a special set of problems.

For almost a year now some of us have worked with men to put out *New Age*, a newspaper addressed to the working people of Buffalo, both men and women. We have done this because we believe the real conditions of our lives—the way we must struggle just to survive—are not reflected in the daily press. It ignores the fact that, as an economic class, working people in this society are oppressed. That is, because we do not own the places where we (or our husbands) work, we have no say in the decisions that are made about what will be produced, what our working conditions will be, and how the profits will be used. As long as we, as a class, have no control over these decisions, then we will have no security from economic hardship, no power to determine the kind of society we live in, and no real control over our lives.

But although the major conflict in this society is between we who work for a living and those who live off the profits of our labor, still women *as women* suffer a special kind of oppression. As workers we are in the same situation as men except worse; our unemployment is higher, our pay scales lower, our job insecurity greater. But there is more.

Because it is generally women who handle most of the day-to-day details of survival, it is we who are most aware of the lousy quality of life in this society and especially of public services. . . .

It is we who feel the economic squeeze worst as we run from store to store, hunting for bargains. . . .

It is we who tremble to be out alone at night. . . .

It is we who suffer from lack of free public birth control and abortion services. . . .

And because we bear almost all the responsibility of caring for children, it is we who are most aware of the lack of free public day-care facilities . . . we are the most aware of the impersonal, over-crowded and authoritarian schools our children must attend. . . .

[It is] we who worry about the chemicals that they put into their bodies with every bite of food and the filth they consume with every drink of water and every breath of air. . . .

So we have put out this special issue of *New Age* in the hope that some of the articles will be of help to women in solving the problems they face every day and that other articles will raise the questions of *why* we face these problems. If you would be interested in getting together with some of us please contact us.

They then listed the *New Age* post office box and a telephone number.

The special women's issue was powerful. In "Politics of Housework," they wrote: "We women have been brainwashed more than we can imagine. Probably too many years of seeing television women in ecstasy over their shiny waxed floors. . . . Men have no such conditioning. They recognize the essential fact of housework right from the very beginning. Which is that it stinks."

The author explained that both she and her husband had jobs, and that they agreed to share the housework since that seemed fair. "Then an interesting thing happened," she wrote, and she shared the dialogue that had been going on between them: "'I don't mind sharing the housework,' he said, 'but I don't do it very well.' Meaning: 'Unfortunately, I'm not good at things like washing dishes and cooking. What I do best is a little light carpentry, changing light bulbs, moving furniture.' (How often do you move furniture?) Or, 'I'm so lousy at it that it would be easier for you to do it.'"

Another article explained what it was like to work at an all-female job as a telephone operator at a switchboard. "The operator must enter her chair from the left and leave from the right. She must face the switchboard at all times, never turning her eyes to the side or looking behind her. She may not swing her arm across the back of her chair. She may not cross her legs. She may not chew gum. . . . If the operator wants to go to the toilet, she puts on her overhead light to signal the supervisor. . . . If permission is granted, the operator signs out and must be back in three minutes. . . . This is rude and dehumanizing." The author concluded the article by writing: "Many women who work go home at night to another full day's work of child-care and housework. Burdened by two jobs at the price of half of one, they have little spare time. Kept out of the world in an isolated marginal existence, [women's] . . . egos were long ago smashed by despair. Women have a tough job ahead. But the rage is there, and some day it will explode." That's what was happening inside *New Age*.

In "Women and the War," they wrote of a poll that showed that 74 percent of women would have refused orders by the military to kill innocent women and children at the My Lai massacre in Vietnam, while only 21 percent of men said they would refuse such orders. They continued: "Women living in ⅔ of S. Vietnam have a 60 percent chance of giving birth to a deformed child because of our government's chemical warfare. . . . Thousands of Vietnamese women await the births of their children with terror instead of joy. . . . 400,000 Vietnamese women have been forced into prostitution (one per GI) in order to feed their families." The article also explained that the U.S. government and military had dehumanized the Vietnamese by calling them racist names, making it easier for U.S. troops to rape Vietnamese women and girls and slaughter innocent people. "What kinds of attitudes can we expect returning veterans to have toward women they live with here at home?" the author asked.

Both the women and the men distributed this issue.

But we weren't able to come to an agreement on the number of articles that should be devoted exclusively to women for future issues of the paper. This dispute, and there may have been others, cast a pall over the project, and the women's issue was the twelfth and last issue of the paper. *New Age* died in September 1971, one year after it started. The group broke up, and several of the personal relationships ended; it was a painful demise to a promising project.

Globalism versus Labor Solidarity

Despite its short life, *New Age* helped many workers in the Buffalo area see that they weren't alone with their problems, and that working with their coworkers would help them resolve issues and make improvements in their lives. I knew about similar rank-and-file workers' newspapers that were being published in Chicago, Detroit, Philadelphia, and other industrial cities in the early 1970s. We often exchanged our papers with each other, and reprinted or wrote summaries of each other's articles. Of course, it is hard to measure our success in Buffalo; most of my evidence is from workers who told me the paper helped them at work, in their community—and sometimes even at home. While I had disagreements with some of the articles and actions we took, overall I think it was a terrific project. Differences of opinion on issues were good, in my opinion, as long as we all agreed with our basic principles and goals. These differences helped to better define those issues in all their complexity, and they reflected the real world—people do have different opinions and it is important to discuss them, and not try to impose one view on everyone.

New Age also helped teach us a great deal about working people in Buffalo, especially at a unique time of great change in the economy, jobs, and politics. We learned about workers with diverse backgrounds of race and ethnicity, but also recognized so many common problems and dreams that united them. We gave a voice to the nameless and faceless people, as one writer so eloquently put it—that great majority of people whom the commercial daily media ignores or slanders, and showed that all of these workers are absolutely essential to the life of any community and our country.

We worked to combat racism and sexism—with varying degrees of success and failure. We worked to raise awareness of the importance of supporting our fellow workers in other countries, and to exposing wars that were little more than the mutual slaughter of working people for the advancement of wealthy corporations and banks.

We tried to alert the community to the dangers of the coming global economy. I'm not sure we could have stopped the massive plant closings that threw millions of workers out of their jobs and crippled Buffalo and most other industrial cities across the United States in the late 1970s and early 1980s, unless the unions and powerful allies had taken up that fight right then—or preferably many years earlier. Of course, for most of the black community, and low-income people of all groups, life was always hard. But the die had already been cast decades earlier. Bethlehem Steel and other corporate and banking giants had been using their tremendous economic clout to dictate to steel towns and influence all levels of government for many decades.

This clout gave them the power to get our government and military to install puppet dictators in power in more vulnerable foreign countries, like South Vietnam, and then get those dictators to repress their own people and any signs of labor unrest. Under these terrible conditions, the corporations could get away with paying foreign workers a fraction of what they paid U.S. workers.

The last piece of the puzzle was put into place when these corporate titans built the infrastructure in these foreign countries—the roads and power stations and transportation facilities that enabled them to set up shop there. All of that infrastructure was ready by the 1970s and 1980s. Then, Bethlehem and other corporations didn't have to deal with their

U.S.-based workers. They simply closed up shop here, laid off millions of workers and crippled countless communities, and built their manufacturing facilities overseas in low-wage havens. They called it "globalization." Standard Mirror closed in 1977. Bethlehem Steel in Lackawanna was effectively closed in the early 1980s, and some 18,000 steelworkers lost their jobs. Many other manufacturing companies closed in Buffalo and nationwide over a ten- to fifteen-year period beginning in the mid-1970s, destroying communities and radically changing the economy of our country. Years later, I spoke with an Italian who worked at Fiat and who was visiting the U.S. She said that the unions and rank-and-file workers—the ones we wrote about at Fiat in 1970 when they were staging wildcat strikes—and left-wing political and workers party legislators who were mostly socialists and communists were so strong in Italy that they stopped many plant closings. They made it so costly for a company to close a plant in Italy and move overseas that many simply remained in Italy.

Unfortunately, the U.S. union movement didn't do nearly enough for many years prior to the plant-closing disaster to save their factories. Nor was enough done to support those low-paid workers in foreign countries, to help them raise their wages so they could live decently and not undercut our wages. This really was an example of the old labor adage—which was forgotten by too many unions: "An injury to one is an injury to all." And that means *all* workers, everywhere—even in other countries. That was why we at *New Age* published regular articles forty years ago on the importance of building international labor solidarity.

Some people have asked why the unions in the U.S. were so conservative and failed to prepare for plant closings and other big problems. There is no one answer. But one critically important factor was the terribly destructive role that the McCarthy red-baiting period of the late 1940s and 1950s played in removing so many of the good, progressive, and smart labor leaders with solid union principles from their positions in many unions. Many were said to have been socialists or communists—and a significant number were. Together, the good solid trade-unionists of any political persuasion and the good leftist trade-unionists were among the best labor leaders our country has ever had. Those workers who opposed them were often politically conservative, and not a small number were mediocre unionists; with the help of their employers, the government, and much of the mass media, they drove the leftists and progressives out of union office. Then, many of the vacant union leadership positions were filled by these conservatives. Those were the union leaders whom many from my generation met when we first went into the work force, and why we started organizations like *New Age*. Over the past four decades, significant progress has been made in many unions. But we still have more to do.

Labor solidarity among workers all over the world is needed more than ever today, as I write this in 2010. But it must be genuine labor solidarity, based on mutual respect. It can't be a large union trying to bully or coerce workers in other countries into supporting a weak form of unionism that won't adequately address workers' problems and issues. Unfortunately, as a former staff member at Service Employees International Union, I've seen SEIU's "labor-management cooperation" carried to such an extreme that SEIU members' interests were short-changed. Seeing that made me believe the numerous reports I've heard about how SEIU, under the direction of union president Andy Stern, is trying to impose its weak model of unionism on workers in other countries. That is not the way to build genuine international labor solidarity. It must be built on mutual respect, and on solid union principles of fighting for the best possible improvements for union members, and all workers, and society as a whole.

New Age was important for me personally because it started me on a life-long career of labor activism and labor journalism. I worked in the trucking industry for years, and got involved in union rank-and-file activities in the Teamsters union, including the successful national Coors boycott. I've worked in other industries, was always an active union member and was an elected steward and officer, and participated in countless labor-supported campaigns. I've written hundreds of labor articles and leaflets for a variety of labor organizations and newspapers over the past forty years. In the mid-1980s, I was the managing editor of the *Furniture Workers Press*, the national newspaper of the United Furniture Workers of America, AFL-CIO. In the late 1980s, I was an organizer for the United Electrical workers (UE), the most politically progressive union in our country. UE had been promoting, since its founding in Buffalo in 1936, many of the goals we adopted at *New Age* in 1970. I also joined US Labor Against the War shortly after the United States waged war on Iraq in 2003.

In all of this work, I have tried to advance the goals we set for ourselves in *New Age*: to empower workers on the job to win greater improvements; to build interunion, national, and international labor solidarity; to give special attention to the issues of people of color and women and fight all forms of discrimination; to educate workers on how the corporate world exploits workers to maximize profits and how to effectively fight for economic, political, and social justice; to create labor-community coalitions to maximize our strength and win improvements for all; and to organize labor support to stop U.S. government military intervention in other countries with the goal of enriching corporations at the expense of working people.

There have been starts and stops in this work, but I have seen progress on every front. For one, union leaders elected Richard Trumka, the progressive president of the United Mineworkers Union, as the president of the AFL-CIO in 2009. *New Age* was instrumental in setting me and many other workers on this path to strengthen and revitalize our labor movement.

APPENDIX

STANDARD MIRROR: SWEATSHOP IN SOUTH BUFFALO
(by Paul Krehbiel, originally written anonymously)

Progressive Action Caucus Forms Inside Plant

Standard-Mirror Company is a small manufacturing plant located on Buffalo's southside. Auto rear-view mirrors are produced here, and Standard Mirror has most of the nation-wide contracts for both Ford and Chrysler motor companies. In 1968 their net sales were over $85 million, and are growing each year.

But while the owners get richer, the workers work harder and get poorer. Standard Mirror is located in a primarily poor white neighborhood, made up largely of Polish people. It is from this Polish community that Standard Mirror draws its labor force. Most of this surrounding community has had a lack of educational opportunities and lack of job opportunities. For these reasons many have no choice but to work at Standard Mirror. The bosses there know this, and take advantage of it by paying low wages (around $2.70–$2.80 per hour for production work), by speeding up job quotas, by neglecting safety conditions, and by generally looking down on the workers as slaves or inferiors.

Standard Mirror sold out to Lamsons and Sessions in Ohio in 1968. Since then things have gotten worse, for the workers that is; things have gone well for the owners. The bosses at Lamsons and Sessions probably don't even know who the workers are at Standard Mirror. But these parasites make a lot of money off the workers at Standard Mirror and they never lift a finger. In their 1968 stockholders annual report they said, "Standard Mirror continues effective efforts to streamline production methods and lower costs. All manufacturing operations are being analyzed intensively to find new areas in which automation can be applied. Increased productivity and better profitability are resulting from these programs."

No new automation has been introduced; they have just constantly cut the work force down, and forced the remaining workers to work twice as fast! In some departments, job quotas have doubled in the last 2 or 3 years. On the 48 line, rear-view mirrors are put into round forms called chucks. These weigh 30–40 pounds, and they are put through different grinding and polishing processes. Three years ago the quota was 288 chucks per shift. A year and a half later, the quota went up to 360, and in 1970 the quota was up to 448! One guy who was there about 15 years had a heart attack recently and had to quit. Other middle-aged workers on the second shift quit because they couldn't take the inhuman job speed-up.

Standard Mirror also cuts costs by getting rid of workers. Three years ago, there were 210 workers; by December of 1970 there were 118, and more have been laid off since. People have been putting up with these worsening conditions for years, and have always felt that there was little they could do about it. But people can be pushed just so far; due to these conditions, a caucus was formed inside the plant this winter.

Progressive Action Caucus

A leaflet written by the Progressive Action Caucus of the United Glass and Ceramic Workers of North America AFL-CIO, CLC, was distributed at the plant in the middle of February. Following are excerpts:

> Working conditions are terrible. People working on the suntools get soaking wet every day and everyone in the glass-cutting room is constantly breathing air that has powdered glass in it. In the molding room people are getting hand burns, cut hands, and people are forced to work on the machines when they can't keep up.
>
> Glass-cutters get cut fingers while trying to keep up with quotas. People on the 48 line get sore arms and backs from carrying around the chucks all day, and get soaked from the polishing due to leaky aprons and boots, or sometimes lack of boots. There is poor or no safety guards in the press room and nothing to muffle the loud pounding noises. The shipping and assembling plant is crowded; there are not enough trucks available in Plant 1, and it's already too crowded. The machines keep breaking down

in every department, and certain bosses and supervisors treat us like slaves. And we're afraid to say anything for fear of being fired. And now a lot of people are being laid off.

How much more of this are we expected to take? We are human beings, not machines or slaves. We are tired of being used and abused by a small group of people who never have to cope with these conditions.

One of the things that we can do is to work at a regular speed, even if they raise the quotas again—let's face it, there's got to be a limit. Many jobs are now set at higher than what a normal human speed should be. If everyone does this, the company can't fire everybody. And if they do fire someone, remember that we have the power to stop production throughout the entire plant.

The leaflet went on to suggest demands that should be brought up to the union bargaining committee, which would in turn be submitted at the September contract negotiations. Basically the points were:

1. $1.00 wage increase; 2-year contract; and the cost-of-living allowance. No one gets less than $3.00 per hour.
2. Omit the No Strike Provision so that the workers can strike over neglected grievances.
3. Get union control over hiring and firing so as to insure job security.
4. The right to see the company's financial records.
5. Union control over production schedules so as to stop the terrific job speed-up.
6. Get higher shift differentials—possibly 14¢ and 20¢.
7. Force the company to institute health and safety measures—safety guards on all presses, and filters on all glass-grinding machines.
8. The right to post notices on the bulletin board without the supervisor's approval.
9. Omit paragraphs in the present contract that outline the company's rights.
10. Not make group leaders responsible for meeting production standards until he and every worker has a say in setting those standards.
11. Extend the pension benefits.

Then the leaflet said:

We must begin to take up these issues—in our union meetings, in the plant, and outside. And we must unite and begin to organize around these and other demands in order to win them from the company. The company is already organizing to take things away from us.

Management isn't going to give us these rights; we are going to have to fight for them.

PROGRESSIVE ACTION CAUCUS
United Glass and Ceramic Workers
of North America AFL-CIO, CLC

Pass this on to others. If anyone is harassed, punished or fired for reading or possessing this leaflet, we will respond with legal and affirmative action against the company.

The response was tremendous. Workers came out to get more leaflets to take in to pass around. People taped copies to the walls for others to see. One woman said, "I've been working here for more than 20 years and this is the best thing that has happened here—it's about time somebody did something." Others said that when negotiations come around, they are going to slap this leaflet down on the table, and tell the company, "This is what we want."

This article originally appeared in *New Age* 1, no. 7 (March 1971).

Ain't No Party Like the One We Got: The Young Lords Party and *Palante*

PABLO "YORÚBA" GUZMÁN

Who Am I?

The group of college-age Latino males who would later join with two other similar group-ings to become the New York chapter of the Young Lords Organization (YLO) was called the Sociedad de Albizu Campos (SAC) when I joined in May 1969. Six or seven of us met Saturdays in Spanish Harlem—El Barrio. I was eighteen at the time and had just come back from a semester of study in Mexico, part of my first year's work at the State University of New York at Old Westbury. Before leaving for Mexico, I had already been politically active for two years, organizing at my high school for citywide rallies against the Vietnam War, against outdated bureaucratic codes for students, fighting racism, participating in mobiliza-tions in Washington, DC, organizing among both African American students and the radical hippies. I am a Puerto Rican and Cuban in whom the African genes are obvious, and in those pre–Young Lord days, Puerto Ricans in New York often tended to identify either with blacks or whites. From an early age, my father and maternal grandfather had instilled in me a sense of healthy skepticism toward the basic BS that defines this country's fundamental hypocrisy, racism, and the legacies of slavery.

For instance, my folks told me how the Japanese were rounded up during World War II, but not the Germans; how the land was stolen from the Native Americans; how Africans were brought here in chains. How separate and equal was really separate and unequal; how the color of our skin meant we would have to work two or four times as hard as whites alongside us just to keep up. My folks spoke English at home because, they said, "We don't want you to have a Spanish accent; on top of your dark skin, that would be two strikes against you in this country."

My father often told the story of how, a naive product of El Barrio at nineteen, he had gone into the navy after seeing *Anchors Aweigh* and gotten assigned to the carrier *Midway* shortly after the war ended. A movie was being shown on the flight deck, and he told a black friend from the South, "Let's go up front. There's some good seats there."

Johnson pulled my father back and said, "Whoa, Guhz-man, that's for the white boys."

"What are you talkin' about, Johnson? We just fought a war against Hitler, that stuff is dead, we're all Americans in this together—"

"You been watchin' too many movies, Guhz-man."

"I'm gonna sit up front."

Sure enough, my old man got his ass kicked and tossed in the back row of seats where the colored sailors were supposed to sit. Johnson helped my father up to his feet and said, "Ah *tol'* you they was only for the white boys, Guhz-man."

"But I'm Puerto Rican."

"They don't care what kind a nigger you is."

My parents were almost prevented from taking their room at a hotel in Atlantic City for their honeymoon because it was not for "colored." My mother started crying, but my father, now a military-trained veteran of Racism USA, began talking to her in Spanish, essentially telling her to follow his lead. The clerk bit: "Oh, pardon me," he gushed, "I didn't *know* you folks were Mexican." My folks look about as Mexican as the Huxtables. All the kids, my cousins and I, were told these stories so we could be prepared for what life unfortunately had in store. We'd be told about how my grandmother lost her thumb during an industrial accident at the garment factory where she worked in New York while the ambulance attendants argued about taking her; or how my mother was denied giving the valedictory address for her high school class, even though she had won a scholarship to the Fashion Institute of Technology (she was told she had "too much" of an accent, even though she was born and raised in East Harlem and my grandparents were bilingual).

So, early in my life I learned about this country's true history. I was further influenced by reading the stories of Nat Turner, Harriet Tubman, and Frederick Douglass; by learning of W.E.B. Du Bois and Marcus Garvey; by studying the life and words of Malcolm X and the Southern civil rights movement, of Stokely Carmichael, H. Rap Brown, and the Black Panther Party.

This all fit in with where I was coming from culturally as well; the soul music of the era was my music, for example, in a way that the rock that I loved could never be. Not until the Lords and the expanding of my Latino consciousness could I appreciate salsa as an integral, *necessary* part of my heritage, and not "just" the dance music of my folks. My parents had been born in Spanish Harlem, and I was raised in the South Bronx, so our outlook was decidedly (North) American, as opposed to being heavily Puerto Rican. In my ghetto, (North) American meant black, baby, 'cause we certainly weren't livin' on the flip side. To be "Puerto Rican" or "Latino" before 1969 in New York, for those of us raised there and not recent immigrants from the islands, was not clearly understood. Or appreciated yet.

My entire life experience, then, pointed toward me joining the Black Panther Party. During my first semester in college, a friend and I had even worked up the nerve to go to the Panthers' Harlem branch, with the intention of inquiring about signing up. But we were totally intimidated, both by our own sense of awe and by the militant stance that often crossed over into arrogance of the members we talked to. It was something, that arrogance toward newcomers; I never forgot.

We came away with issues of the Panther paper, and my God, look at these pictures! The cartoons! The articles! References to an international struggle, Panther chapters all over the country, Panthers being attacked all over the country, Panthers in black leather picking up the gun. The rhetoric! Back at school, we slapped five over the *boldness* of these . . . *Niggers*, is what we said, not knowing any better. But with the kind of respect Richard Pryor used when he said (before he finally dropped the term) God, who works in mysterious ways, brought some good out of slavery, because he took the *best* out of Africa, the strongest, who survived the terrible journey, and took all the "tribes" that had been warring in Africa, the Ibos and Zulus and Masais, and in the Americas he forged one tough new tribe—*Niggas.* Now, this is a passé, even reactionary term, but back in 1968 that was the kind of audacious, charismatic, Afro-American figure we thought the Panthers were—and we wanted some of that. I had seen some other "underground" and "movement" newspapers before then, but nothing like *The Black Panther*—especially when compared to the leading black paper in the community, the *Amsterdam News*, whose coverage, to us, defined Uncle Tom.

I had gone to Mexico with this mindset, as Paul Guzman (Anglo pronunciation all the way), aspiring black militant; but after three and a half months in a country where everyone was a Latino and quite conscious and proud of that heritage, I came back to the States as Pablo "Yorúba" Guzmán, ready to listen a little more to the rap fellow student Mickey Melendez had been laying down since I had gotten out to the Long Island campus in late August of '68. Inspired by Ray "Masai" Hewitt of the Black Panther Party, I took the middle name "Yorúba," from an African "tribe" whose influence was prominent in the creation of Latino culture in the Caribbean and elsewhere the slave trade functioned. For instance, the religion called Santeria in Cuba and Puerto Rico (vodún in Haiti, macumba in Brazil) has its roots in the Ife tradition of the Yorubas of Nigeria. However, my ignorance of matters was such in 1969 that for a long time I mispronounced the name, giving it a Spanish "yuh-ROO-bah" (with a light twirl of the "r") inflection—until once in late '69 or early '70, I believe, when Peter Jennings profiled us for ABC. Having spent a lot of time on assignment in the Mother Continent, it was Jennings who told me that the correct pronunciation was "yuh-roo-BAH," but that latter never really caught on among most Latinos.

Mickey Melendez had been reaching out to me; and to Felipe Luciano, another "Afro-Latino," if you will, and classmate of Mickey's at Queens Community College; and to Juan Gonzalez, a light-skinned Puerto Rican who was active at Columbia University's SDS (Students for a Democratic Society) chapter. His message to us all was that those days of identifying with either black or white North Americans, even if on a radical trip, were over; it was time to look within and without and begin organizing in our own barrios. Creating a *Puerto Rican* movement. Maybe even building into a pan-*Latino* movement.

Puerto Rican?

Mickey was the first guy to go into some detail with me about the militant history Puerto Ricans had, something to be every bit as proud of as African (North) Americans are of their rich militant past (all this "ethnic" specification that becomes so necessary at times in this land of deliberate misinformation, this nationhood identification in this instance, in this land where language is purposefully used to obfuscate rather than enlighten, can at times become a bit unwieldy, *¿como no?* "African (North) American," oy . . . but, so long as you get the idea . . . and understand what kind of centuries-laden propaganda we're up against . . .). Mickey told us about Don Pedro Albizu Campos, president of the Nationalist Party of Puerto Rico, who fought against U.S. colonization of the island from the twenties until his death in 1965, a death very likely hastened by his exposure to x-rays while in an American prison. Mickey told us also of how Albizu Campos was Harvard-trained, and yet could not proceed as a lawyer beyond certain well-defined, racist limits; of Campos's skills as an orator; of the blood Nationalists shed in 1937, while preparing for a peaceful march on Easter Sunday in Puerto Rico's second-largest city, Ponce, when they were fired upon by U.S. imperialists. And why Oscar Collazo and other Nationalists attempted to assassinate Truman in 1950 (an erroneous news report had circulated on the island that Albizu Campos had died during one of his several incarcerations, and so it seemed logical to the *Nacionalistas* that "Well, if they killed *our* President . . ."). In 1953, Lolita Lebron and her two Nationalist companions fired upon the U.S. Congress from the visitors' gallery while the Congress was debating Puerto Rico's status. Mickey explained to us that the Nationalists wanted to highlight Puerto Rico's colonial status, in particular that every important decision about the island was made not in San Juan, but in Washington, DC; that the U.S. grip on the island's affairs was such that it had no vote in Congress; and that the highest court of appeals for a case that began on the island was in Boston, not San Juan, prior to the steps that would take an ultimate appeal to the Supreme Court.

Mickey had us look into a Puerto Rican history we never knew, of a resistance first to Spanish imperialism—known as *"El Grito de Lares"* ("The Shout of Lares")—led by Ramon Emeterio Betances and the other original patriots in 1868, and even of fights against the *conquistadores* by the indigenous Taino people in the 1500s, most of whom were massacred by the Spanish (see figure 1). We found out how Puerto Rico fell into U.S. hands, a prize won in the Spanish-American War along with Cuba, Guam, and the Philippines, even as those early nationalists of 1898 were celebrating their first month of hard-won autonomy from Spain (see figure 2). The U.S. Marines just dismissed what parliament Puerto Ricans had assembled. All this was contrary to what little some of us had "learned" of Puerto Rican history, that 'Ricans were practically running up to the Americans on the beach wailing, "Save us!" from the nasty Spanish. What hogwash.

What our research showed us was that, by the Spirits, we *did* have a fighting history to be proud of! We *had* resisted, and fought back, against the Spanish, forging a unique Puerto Rican identity in the process that was equal parts African, Taino, and Spanish, along with some other European and Asian strains. A *Latino* identity that was new and bold to the world, as much a claimant to the mantle of the *Americas* as our large, unruly, and ever-voracious neighbor to the north. And we *continued* to fight against the *Yanquis*, from day one to the present. Our whole history was one continual line of struggle for self-determination. We found out that Puerto Ricans had been in New York since the end of the nineteenth century, had always formed political and cultural organizations, and had always fought to be treated as equals "here." We even found out that, by the 1960 census (and who knows, perhaps earlier), there were *some* Puerto Ricans in every state—including a sizable population in Hawaii, where many had been brought in the late 1800s to work the sugar-cane plantations. It would not be long before we as the Young Lords Party would connect with Hawaiian activists and have an affinity group on our behalf in those islands, even as we labored to raise consciousness of the *real* story of Hawaii on our part of the mainland.

Our instrument for telling this story, as well as for passing along the Puerto Rican history we were uncovering, and the twin reasons at the root of why the Young Lords existed—liberation for Puerto Rico and equality for Puerto Ricans in a radically realigned United States—would be our newspaper, *Palante.*

FIGURE 1: Cover of *Palante* volume 2, number 12 (September 25, 1970). As staff members learned of the resistance struggles of Puerto Ricans, including those against Spanish imperialism—or "*El Grito de Lares*" ("The Shout of Lares")—they published articles in *Palante* informing the community. Courtesy Young Lords Party.

FIGURE 2: Cover of *Palante* volume 2, number 14 (October 30, 1970), featuring a story about Young Lords Party member Julio Roldan, who was murdered by police in Spanish Harlem, and the armed takeover of People's Church following the funeral procession. Courtesy Young Lords Party.

Pre-Young Lords

"Palante" loosely translates into "forward," or "ahead," or even "right on!" depending on the context. Bottom line, it's a progressive *motion* word familiar to the people. From the beginning, we took to heart the words of that noted Chinese philosopher: "Speak to the people in the language they know and love." In the early days of the Young Lords Party, we also waged a war against movement rhetoric. We *hated* rhetoric, movement jargon, and phraseology that could only be understood by "well-read" activists, and not the people we were trying to organize.

Time to back up a bit.

Excited as we all were by our research, we were also excited by current events. The year before, 1968, had been a hell of a year. The Democratic convention in Chicago, uprisings—so-called "riots"—in 150 cities following the murder of Martin Luther King, all against the backdrop of acid, acid-rock, 'Nam, the Pill, Black Power, you name it—it was all happening, and happening NOW. Almost on the same Saturday, as I recall, the second or third SAC meeting that I attended, we got hit with two news items: two other groups of young Latinos were just getting started in New York, as we were; and, in Chicago, what had been a gang had "gotten politicized" and—under the direction of the Chicago Panthers and together with a former white gang called the Young Patriots—had formed the Latino component of "the Rainbow Coalition." We read about this ex-gang in the June 7, 1969, issue of *The Black Panther.* One of our group, David Perez, whom Mickey had recruited to Old Westbury from Chicago, confirmed that these Young Lords (now the Young Lords Organization, or YLO) were indeed real, but he offered us words of caution because he knew, coming from Chicago, what we would find out later: that the YLO had not been able to shed its gang-like ways, that they were undisciplined and not committed to radical change. Unfortunately, we didn't pay attention to his warning. Hey, it was in *The Black Panther*! And Fred Hampton and the Chicago Panthers (as everyone knew, the second-baddest Panther chapter outside of the original Oakland bunch) were behind it! Come on, Dave!

David approved of our plan to send a mini-delegation to Chicago in June 1969 to seek the green light to organize as the New York chapter of the Lords, but he continued to voice his reservations to deaf ears. At the same time, we agreed to reach out to the group we heard was trying to organize on the Lower East Side, and to the other group organizing in Spanish Harlem.

The Lower East Side group, we found out, was led by a guy named José Martinez, who seemed to be a movement pro—a Cuban from Florida who joined SDS and made contacts in Chicago when Panthers, Lords, and Patriots came to the SDS convention there in 1968. But when we got to Chicago, YLO chairman José "Cha-Cha" Jiminez told us that, contrary to what Martinez might be saying, he had not authorized Martinez to begin organizing the Lords in New York.

I was part of the group that went to Chicago in June 1969 in Mickey's Volkswagen to meet these Young Lords in the People's Church we had read about. From the start, I was excited to see that they had a newspaper, *YLO*; but all I saw were hundreds of copies of the same issue. "Does this come out weekly or monthly?" I asked, but never quite got answered. Such petty questions of detail, and anything having to do with discipline, I later found out, quickly got lost in the Viking hall environment of hale and hearty warriors surrounded by banners acknowledging their past fights against Chicago police brutality and against Mayor Richard Daley's brand of politics. We walked into this with rose-colored glasses. We *wanted* some heroes, badly. We were excited when Cha-Cha took a liking to us and said we could organize as the New York chapter. Of course, we had to fly him and another guy back out to New York to make it official. Once in that city, however, in response to our questions about what we should do and how we should begin, I remember one piece of advice he gave us: "Our people in the community are going to join us only through *observation* and *participation.* We can preach till we're blue in the face. But at some point, they're only going to understand after they see us throw down and after we move them to throw down themselves." This advice fit in perfectly with our already blossoming anti-rhetoric stance.

It also was what the third grouping that would merge into the New York Young Lords was doing all along. While we in the SAC were meeting every Saturday like the college intellectuals most of us were, and while the José Martinez Lower East Side group was trying to get in good with the various "movement" factions that historically populated the Lower East Side, even though there was a sizable Latino population there, this third group was going out among the people of Spanish Harlem, picking a particular block, rapping with the people about the revolutionary changes going on in society at large, some of which they saw on TV or read about on the news, and then trying to connect those changes with the need to make revolutionary change in the immediate society around them. Right now. These guys pointed to the incredible garbage piling up in ghettos like East Harlem, garbage that went far beyond the bushwah that the propagandists in the society outside the ghetto tried to drill into the minds of those in and out of the ghetto, that the garbage was of "those" pigs' own making. True, barrio citizens had a certain responsibility for their/our own mess; but a greater fact of life was that garbage was only getting picked up once or twice a week—as opposed to the "high class" areas further south on Park Avenue, in the tony "Upper East Side"; or in all- or nearly all-white "middle class" enclave/neighborhoods like Howard Beach, Throggs Neck, and almost all of Staten Island, where garbage pickups were more frequent. A small point, perhaps, but it sure highlighted the difference between those with access to power—those who could make politicians jump through hoops and get things done for them, or those whom the politicians wanted to please with a few bones like frequent garbage pickup, more police protection, and better hospitals and schools, so they'd have something tangible to show for buying into the Great (White) American (Skin Privilege) Dream—and those who were being permanently shut out of the power game.

Garbage in the ghetto, by the way, ain't just about coffee grounds and discarded milk containers. "Garbage" is also abandoned automobiles, broken appliances like refrigerators, the squalor that surrounds burned-out buildings and rubblestone lots, which kids play in because the playgrounds have gone to seed, while rats dance and junkies shoot up. "Garbage" is refuse dumped into ghetto areas by unscrupulous, often mob-controlled private carting companies who sometimes drop hazardous medical and other industrial wastes while looking for a short end run.

So a lot of smaller issues were wrapped up in the seemingly "unglamorous" but larger issue of garbage in the ghetto. In their instinctive way, the third pre-Lord formation had hit upon the issue that would get us going, while the other two groups were still stumbling about. This third bunch was actually a photography workshop led by Hiram Maristany, a masterful photographer from El Barrio who became our first chronicler. And while all of us were certainly *young* Lords, Hiram's group was even younger, about fourteen to sixteen as compared to our nineteen to twenty-three (when we began, I was eighteen). Hiram's guys were also different from the other two groups in that they were *of* the barrio and destined to *remain* in the barrio, whereas guys like me had either punched a ticket to college or the service *out* of the barrio, or else weren't from the barrio at all. So from the beginning, we thrashed out a lot of class questions among ourselves, which helped us in a very real way to understand theories of class. Hiram's group had naturally proceeded from shooting pictures of their surroundings to asking questions, and Hiram encouraged them to hit the streets.

Another important person in those early days was an architect named Mauricio . . . Gomez, I think his last name was. He was Cuban, slightly older than most of us in the SAC. He came to us from the Real Great Society (RGS), an anti-poverty group formed by ex-gang members with branches in El Barrio and the Lower East Side. Mickey also had been in RGS. We used their barrio offices for our Saturday meetings. At one of those meetings, Mauricio showed us a copy of "the Master Plan" for New York that a friend on the City Planning Commission had slipped him; basically it showed that the very liberal administration of Mayor John Lindsay was still tied into the same old power elite, and was working on a plan that most New Yorkers wouldn't see manifest until a decade or two down the road, which called for "urban renewal" of ghetto areas that really amounted to "spic removal": a bulldozing of tenements, and their replacement with co-op- and condo-style housing that barrio residents could not afford. We saw draft studies that pointed out how a basic transportation infrastructure of buses and trains already existed in Harlem and East Harlem, and that as apartment space dwindled in Manhattan below 96th Street, and as costs for living in suburbia rose, perhaps efforts should be made to reclaim the untapped areas of the city—us—and make them safe for the baby-boom wave to come. They weren't called yuppies then.

Within the next couple of years, as the arson fires of the South Bronx in the early seventies so vividly illustrated, speculators also got their hands on the same draft reports we were studying . . . which we knew would have shocked certain power brokers, who (a) figured we couldn't read the tea leaves in such documents, and (b) were later astounded to learn we could gain access to such stuff. One of the reasons for the Young Lords' success was such class and race presumption: we were constantly underestimated, or else mistaken as some gang of semiliterate ghetto toughs. While some of us certainly *were* tough, many more of us *became* tough as a result of the Young Lords.

The Garbage Offensive

For instance, one present-day media figure with a Young Lords association—though he was never a member—was Geraldo Rivera. Gerry was one of our lawyers back then; indeed, his involvement with us had as much to do with his own emerging sense of identity as any of ours. Gerry was more than ready to put not only his services but his body on the line, participating in many of the early battles with police that grew out of what were initially peaceful demonstrations by us. In fact, Gerry applied for membership a couple of times, but we kept telling him he played a more important role as one of our lawyers; we were certain that the authorities would try to find a way to discredit or disqualify Gerry from representing us if they could spear his "officer of the court" position by tarring him with some lie about the Lords. Gerry was our lawyer from about October of 1969 right up to just before he began with (local) ABC in New York; in fact, his first major assignment with ABC was getting into the Tombs, the Manhattan prison, soon after the uprising due to overcrowded conditions and the specific unclear circumstances surrounding the questionable "suicide" of one of our members, Julio Roldan, on October 15, 1970, a day after he had been picked up by cops in Spanish Harlem for "disorderly conduct." That incident had prompted an armed takeover of the People's Church following a funeral procession of two thousand people for Julio; the resulting standoff with the city finally ended about a month later in the creation of the Board of Corrections, designed to monitor prison conditions (see figure 3). We were offered a choice to nominate someone for the panel; we chose Gerry, but the city said no, so closely associated was he with us already. So José "Chegui" Torres, former light-heavyweight champion, columnist, and city council ombudsman, who was the first prominent "establishment" Puerto Rican to support us, got the nod.

Mauricio was obviously experiencing some rapid changes in those early days. He was someone who could have easily bought into privilege, a light-skinned Cuban professional from a petty-bourgeois family; but the course he had been heading on through grad school was not personally satisfying, and he came to RGS to give something back to the barrio. At first, his RGS involvement included "liberal, reform, charitable" anti-poverty work in East Harlem; but his involvement changed when to his surprise RGS led to the SAC, which led to the YLO. It was Mauricio who told us about Hiram's group and, if I'm not mistaken, José Martinez's group. And it was Mauricio who became one of the important voices for unity instead of factionalism, for trying to bring the groups together and organize under the Chicago motion—rather than the minority view, which wanted to ego-trip on its own (obviously, you can tell where I was in the debate).

By June of 1969, the three groups had come together and had begun working as the Young Lords in New York. We had adopted the same purple berets that the Chicago Lords wore, which we later found out distinguished their "colors" from those of rival gangs. We had just thought it was to distinguish their berets from the Panthers' black ones. In the beginning, much about the YLO was based on the Panther Party, from organization ("democratic centralism") to ideology ("Marxism-Leninism–Mao Tse-tung Thought"), since we figured the Panthers were at the cutting edge of what was happening with revolution in this country, and if it was good enough for them, it was okay for us. Gradually, as we gained experience of our own, we became more critical and made our own refinements. But basically, our initial revolutionary thrust was pretty much as H. Rap Brown once put it: "If Amerikkka says wear a blue suit, wear a pink one; if Amerikkka says be quiet, talk loud; if Amerikkka says it's great, say AMERIKKKA AIN'T SHIT."

We had challenged the José Martinez group's desire to begin organizing in the Lower East Side by pointing out that, with so many groups bumping into each other down there, we would have difficulty maintaining our identity, and we would wind up wasting time getting sucked up into one or another factional debate. Better, we said, and they agreed, to invest our meager resources into a well-defined community like El Barrio, the spiritual home of all New York Puerto Ricans, and a place lacking radical activity. We picked up on Hiram's group's idea of making garbage the first issue to organize around; what we in SAC contributed was to give it a radical edge. We would not just clean the streets; we would also point out *why* this stuff wasn't being picked up and yet *other* people's garbage *was* getting picked up when we all paid

FIGURE 3: Cover of *Palante* volume 3, number 3 (February 19, 1971), with a photo of members of the Young Lords central committee. What originally was an all-male leadership came to include women, as Young Lords members confronted leaders about the Latin *machismo* in the organization. Courtesy Young Lords Party.

tax dollars. Sunday mornings, we picked a block and, wearing our purple berets, swept up, collected, and tried to get people to join in. We talked as we went, and at the end we summed up the experience by holding a rally. Unfortunately, our rallies were pitiful. People barely listened. And most of us were frightened to speak out loud.

Felipe Luciano, however, had no problem speaking to people. This guy had ego and personality to spare. Mickey and I desperately tried to get him to commit to us, but he had one foot in the black cultural nationalist movement in Harlem, and with the other he was testing the waters in a couple of other places. This boy got around. A former gang member with family roots in Spanish Harlem and Brooklyn, Felipe had done time for manslaughter for killing with his fists a guy who had messed with his brother. In prison he got his GED equivalency diploma, and he was paroled to a study program at Queens College where he met Mickey. His burning intellect and exhibitionism brought him to the world of radical black theater; he was a founding member of the Last Poets. In the black radical universe of the time, many cultural nationalists were polar opposites of the political nationalists such as the Panthers, and here Felipe and I differed; however, Felipe became tight with one of my idols, H. Rap Brown, who encouraged him to organize within his Latino community, as we were also telling him. Still, it was a long while before Felipe would commit to us on a full-time basis.

But when he did show on those early Sunday mornings when we were trying to organize through garbage collection, he energized the block. He certainly had the gift of gab. Another contribution was made by David Perez, in many ways the most inherently nationalistic Latino among us. David was born in Lares, Puerto Rico, from where Betances had launched the first fight for independence, and was brought to Chicago when he was ten. He was the most *jíbaro* of all of us, the most rooted in the peasant aspect, the rural campesino side of the Puerto Rican experience. By comparison, the rest of us were city slickers, heavily mainland-rooted. There was a class distinction among Puerto Ricans and other Latinos, a derision by mainlanders toward island arrivals, or even by San Juan metropolitan residents toward country cousins, who were regarded as *jíbaros* not with pride but as "hicks," as a putdown. Through David, we began to change how the word *jíbaro* was used, to find some pride in this part of us, even to gain some humility. David figured out that our early rallies had failed because we were still lacking that nationalist component that tied us like cement to people; when he brought out the Puerto Rican flag at the afternoon rallies that climaxed the Sunday cleanings, attendance doubled and tripled, because we had hit a nerve. Still, we couldn't get people to join up afterwards. They listened, they observed, they went home. Shit continued.

Until Felipe and Juan Gonzalez hit upon an idea. Juan Gonzalez was certainly the moral and organizational engine that bound and drove us in the beginning. Once Juan decided that Mickey's message was right, that he was needed more among Latinos than white radicals, he threw himself into this thing, whatever it was going to turn out to be, full time. With his example as an inspiration, I soon realized I wasn't going back to college. The idea he and Felipe hit upon was to take the people with us to the local sanitation facility so they could help us get more brooms and other supplies to clean up better.

For two or three weeks, people saw us get the runaround from a bureaucracy that was supposed to serve the community but could give a hang for it, and their frustration rose to a level that matched our own. We would go to one sanitation department office, and they would send us to another. That place would tell us that we weren't in their jurisdiction, or that they weren't authorized to give out brooms, or that we'd have to take it up at a higher level on the food chain . . . where we'd be told this was a local matter and get sent back to square one.

Finally, we took this frustration and, on Sunday, July 27, at the end of one rally, we took all the garbage—all the abandoned cars, all the refrigerators—and laid it all across Third Avenue at 110th Street, which was a major intersection. Then, with traffic blocked from all sides, we set the stuff on fire. When the police came, we took off our berets, so we could blend in. Sure enough, the cops reacted like an occupational army and began using their nightsticks on anyone hanging out on the corner. This action provoked a retaliation of bricks and bottles, which in turn prompted the cops to call for backups, who also got attacked; in minutes, the Young Lords of New York were in their first battle. Later, we signed up our first recruits.

Knowing the power of the mimeo machine from my high school and college days, I knew we had to follow up immediately so people would know that what had happened wasn't some drunken event, that it had been organized, and why; using the movement contacts of Gonzalez and Martinez, I mimeographed thousands of leaflets and spent the night with a few other guys blanketing East Harlem.

This became our modus operandi. The police response meant we could spend no time sweeping up a block now, since they'd bust us at once; so we went right to the barricades, blocking intersections, setting fires—and when the cops came, it was hit-and-run time, from rooftops, doorways, wherever.

The summer of '69 we called the Garbage Offensive, and it was some series of battles; our numbers grew as the cops brought in more troops to augment the two precincts that occupied El Barrio. Our battles grew from weekly to daily encounters; we called in false alarms to get cops to respond, and when they came back to their cars they'd find the cars trashed—literally, with some of the garbage we were talking about dumped in their vehicle, with broken windows and slashed tires. The police quickly became an issue as they moved through the neighborhood seeing nothing but "hostile spics," not a disciplined small group of Young Lords. They knocked over the domino games men had been playing on the sidewalk for generations, they broke heads, they made vulgar remarks to women passing on the street. They were our best organizing tool.

And after each day's confrontation, that night would be spent leafleting. All the while, I kept calling Chicago for more than that same issue of the newspaper. We *needed* a newspaper, not just for money—to spread the word. An organizing tool. Chicago promised, but delivered I think one more new issue in the next nine months. This was unacceptable.

Building an Organization

In our early division of labor, I was designated minister of information; actually, most of us wanted almost any job except that of chairman. Except for Diego Pabón, who came to us somehow from one of those "go slow"–type "left-wing" outfits, à la the Movimiento Pro Independencia, the "traditional," "respectable" CP (Communist Party) USA-Moscow–type revisionist party of Puerto Rico. Diego became chairman by default; the rest of us really wanted Felipe, but he would not yet commit. Juan was our minister of education, and, as our best strategist, he immediately began laying down plans for what to do *after* the Garbage Offensive, even as we were still in it. Juan would take us into organizing among health workers, and using the high tuberculosis and lead-poisoning rates among our young people as an issue around which to organize, to raise more consciousness about why such great differences existed in this otherwise rich society. But that would come later, toward the end of 1969. David was our first minister of defense.

The last person to be added to what was the original central committee was the youngest member of the organization. Juan "Fi" Ortiz, fifteen, was Hiram's best photography student. Even at his young age, Juan was in many ways the most profound and even-balanced of us all. Soon after we made him chief of staff, he and his cadres became the most indispensable part of our organization, which was probably a surprise to the various police agencies infiltrating and surveilling us. Fi's staff operation, our super-personnel department, oversaw organizational development, personal problems, and other internal issues. They were our monitoring backbone.

José Martinez's Lower East Side Group, we found out, was riddled with police agents. Martinez himself soon took a hike.

Certainly not in the same category, because his contributions to our early development were enormous, but Felipe Luciano, still our best-known member, left after about ten months. The split at the time was bitter; it began with Felipe being disciplined for sexism, and ended with the realization that we were on opposite sides of an ideological gulf. The rest of us went along a more "socialist" path, while Felipe continued as a more "militant reformist," if you will. After he left, the central committee never again had a chairman. Instead, we began to decide policies democratically as a collective.

We began with a hard core of thirteen, plus a sole woman whom Mauricio introduced into the group, a strong Cubana named Sonia Ivanny. From the beginning we were forced to confront machismo, bred into the Latin culture in its own special way. As more women came into the organization, they expanded into the leadership, including what would be the core central committee of five men (see figure 4). Diego—too much attached to his respectable and traditional Latino background, and unable to grasp the changes taking place in the ways men and women related to each other—didn't last as chairman for more than a month; Felipe finally agreed to stay with us full-time. Women like Sonia rising to positions of leadership were part of the battle against sexism that was waged constantly in the organization. In that sense, we saw ourselves as part of the overall movement of human liberation awakening across the country—beginning, in our time, with African Americans, and then spreading to other oppressed peoples of color, then to women, and then gays. Every step of the way, we were with it, recognizing women's and gay caucuses within the organization as legitimate forms that corresponded to various points of the organization's internal development. We made a point of building ties with women's and gay groups, just as we had with Panther chapters and I Wor Kuen, the radical Asian group in the Chinatowns of New York and San Francisco.

Interestingly, the most controversy our positions in *Palante* caused in the Latino community—as we spread in 1970 to the Bronx, Philadelphia, and Lower East Side, and in 1971 and subsequent years to Bridgeport, Connecticut; Santurce and Aguadilla, Puerto Rico; plus, through affinity groups, places like Boston and Detroit—was not over independence for Puerto Rico, opposition to the Vietnam War, or building socialism (or something *else*, at least) in America. No, the most hell we caught was in exposing the racism that affected too many Latinos and caused either some Caribbean Latinos to deny their African heritage, or some Latinos generally to despise African Americans. We also caught hell for promoting equality between men and

FIGURE 4: Cover of *Palante* volume 3, number 13 (July 24–August 7, 1971). The cover shows another informative historical feature piece, about Puerto Rican resistance struggle against U.S. imperialism, including how the U.S. took over the island as a prize after the Spanish-American War. Courtesy Young Lords Party.

women, for denouncing the mocking of gays—anything on the front against sexism. Sexism and racism, those were the most sensitive buttons we pushed among those we tried to organize. And we never shrunk back from the fight.

As with anything else, though, questions and attitudes of race and class affected us within the movement even as we were supposedly about trying to fight for change in the world outside. A flash point came around late 1969 when a radical women's manifesto was published in newspapers like the *Rat*, I believe, which caused a furor among the women in the organization. The manifesto touched upon some issues that needed to be criticized in certain posturing organizations. For instance, remnants of machismo still existed in YLO at the point where a militant defiance of reactionary authority crossed over into petty toy soldiering, becoming a caricature of true militancy. In addition, a double standard was practiced by some male members—leaders in particular, we were to find out—who were having affairs behind the backs of their significant others.

But when the manifesto asked sarcastically if the women in the Young Lords were Young Ladies, well, in trying to make a point they missed the mark badly. Granted, if we had had our druthers, we in New York would certainly have chosen another name; but there was a history to that gang's name, and there was something to be said about a gang that was trying to change its ways. It was not yet for us to change that name; it would have been presumptuous.

But what ticked off "the ladies" of our organization even more was that many of them had interacted with the mainly white radical women's movement and found too many of them to be essentially about bourgeois and petty-bourgeois complaints; they wanted *in* to a system the rest of us found basically corrupt. Or else their alternatives were sectarian, pitting women against men in a way that somehow still let the basic problem off the hook. The guys in the leadership barely prevailed, but we convinced the women not to go and kick ass, which they wanted to do. But their anger at being used by women who in the main were dabbling in radical change (like so many white men) but did not really want to see opportunity afforded equally to working-class women, particularly those of color, proved prophetic: I look around, for instance, at the newsrooms I have worked in (except for a period at a black-owned company) and see a great many white women, usually of petty-bourgeois background or attitude, in various positions, though it is still their male counterparts who dominate at the top; while I see more women of color than I did twenty years ago, they are still in the minority.

The Garbage Offensive established us in El Barrio, and word of our presence zipped along *radio bembe*, the grapevine, to barrios throughout the city. Oh, we scored a victory: the fighting had made its point. Sanitation promised at a public meeting, attended by Lindsay's representatives, to put more garbage cans on the corners, to work with residents looking to borrow brooms and other cleaning tools, and—most importantly—to add another day of collection. Sadly, as we were about to achieve our first victory, we lost Mauricio. His rise to commitment had come full circle: what was a Cuban with skills and a commitment to social change to do if not return to Cuba, Mauricio reasoned, and help build socialism? It would be many, many years before I saw Mauricio again.

Getting Past Square One

Using a leaflet as best I could as a poor substitute for a newspaper, my energies took in all forms of media. Truth be told, I was a media freak. Still am. I wanted us to use every form of media our people were exposed to: radio, TV, live concerts, speeches, seminars, rap sessions, graffiti, posters. I was concerned with the angle Lords wore their berets, how they spoke in public, who spoke, and where. I drafted the first thirteen-point program (see sidebar) and thirty rules of discipline. I coined phrases like "poverty pimps" to define anti-poverty fat cats, and tried to blend slang into our prose whenever I could.

SIDEBAR

YOUNG LORDS PARTY: 13 POINT PROGRAM AND PLATFORM

THE YOUNG LORDS PARTY IS A REVOLUTIONARY POLITICAL PARTY FIGHTING FOR THE LIBERATION OF ALL OPPRESSED PEOPLE

1. WE WANT SELF-DETERMINATION FOR PUERTO RICANS, LIBERATION ON THE ISLAND AND INSIDE THE UNITED STATES. For 500 years, first spain and then the united states have colonized our country. Billions of dollars in profits leave our country for the united states every year. In every way we are slaves of the gringo. We want liberation and the Power in the hands of the People, not Puerto Rican exploiters. QUE VIVA PUERTO RICO LIBRE!

2. WE WANT SELF-DETERMINATION FOR ALL LATINOS. Our Latin Brothers and Sisters, inside and outside the united states, are oppressed by amerikkkan business. The Chicano people built the Southwest, and we support their right to control their lives and their land. The people of Santo Domingo continue to fight against gringo domination and its puppet generals. The armed liberation struggles in Latin America are part of the war of latinos against imperialism. QUE VIVA LA RAZA!

3. WE WANT LIBERATION OF ALL THIRD WORLD PEOPLE. Just as Latins first slaved under spain and the yanquis, Black people, Indians, and Asians slaved to build the wealth of this country. For 400 years they have fought for freedom and dignity against racist Babylon. Third World people have led the fight for freedom. All the colored and oppressed peoples of the world are one nation under oppression. NO PUERTO RICAN IS FREE UNTIL ALL PEOPLE ARE FREE!

4. WE ARE REVOLUTIONARY NATIONALISTS AND OPPOSE RACISM. The Latin, Black, Indian and Asian people inside the u.s. are colonies fighting for liberation. We know that washington, wall street, and city hall will try to make our nationalism into racism; but Puerto Ricans are of all colors and we resist racism. Millions of poor white people are rising up to demand freedom and we support them. These are the ones in the u.s. that are stepped on by the rulers and the government. We each organize our people, but our fights are the same against oppression and we will defeat it together. POWER TO ALL OPPRESSED PEOPLE!

5. WE WANT EQUALITY FOR WOMEN. DOWN WITH MACHISMO AND MALE CHAUVINISM. Under capitalism, women have been oppressed by both society and our men. The doctrine of machismo has been used by men to take out their frustrations on wives, sisters, mothers, and children. Men must fight along with sisters in the struggle for economic and social equality and must recognize that sisters make up over half of the revolutionary army: sisters and brothers are equals fighting for our people. FORWARD SISTERS IN THE STRUGGLE!

6. WE WANT COMMUNITY CONTROL OF OUR INSTITUTIONS AND LAND. We want control of our communities by our people and programs to guarantee that all institutions serve the needs of our people. People's control of police, health services, churches, schools, housing, transportation and welfare are needed. We want an end to attacks on our land by urban renewal, highway destruction, and university corporations. LAND BELONGS TO ALL THE PEOPLE!

7. WE WANT A TRUE EDUCATION OF OUR AFRO-INDIO CULTURE AND SPANISH LANGUAGE. We must learn our long history of fighting against cultural, as well as economic genocide by the spaniards and now the yanquis. Revolutionary culture, culture of our people, is the only true teaching. JIBARO SI, YANQUI NO!

8. WE OPPOSE CAPITALISTS AND ALLIANCES WITH TRAITORS. Puerto Rican rulers, or puppets of the oppressor, do not help our people. They are paid by the system to lead our people down blind alleys, just like the thousands of poverty pimps who keep our communities peaceful for business, or the street workers who keep gangs divided and blowing each other away. We want a society where the people socialistically control their labor. VENCEREMOS!

9. WE OPPOSE THE AMERIKKKAN MILITARY. We demand immediate withdrawal of all u.s. military forces and bases from Puerto Rico, Viet Nam, and all oppressed communities inside and outside the u.s. No Puerto Rican should serve in the u.s. army against his Brothers and Sisters, for the only true army of oppressed people is the People's Liberation Army to fight all rulers. U.S. OUT OF VIETNAM, FREE PUERTO RICO NOW!

10. WE WANT FREEDOM FOR ALL POLITICAL PRISONERS AND PRISONERS OF WAR. No Puerto Rican should be in jail or prison, first because we are a nation, and amerikkka has no claims on us; second, because we have not been tried by our own people (peers). We also want all freedom fighters out of jail, since they are prisoners of the war for liberation. FREE ALL POLITICAL PRISONERS AND PRISONERS OF WAR!

11. WE ARE INTERNATIONALISTS. Our people are brainwashed by television, radio, newspapers, schools and books to oppose people in other countries fighting for their freedom. No longer will we believe these lies, because we have learned who the real enemy is and who our real friends are. We will defend our sisters and brothers around the world who fight for justice and are against the rulers of this country. QUE VIVA CHE GUEVARA!

12. WE BELIEVE ARMED SELF-DEFENSE AND ARMED STRUGGLE ARE THE ONLY MEANS TO LIBERATION. We are opposed to violence—the violence of hungry children, illiterate adults, diseased old people, and violence of poverty and profit. We have asked, petitioned, gone to courts, demonstrated peacefully, and voted for politicians full of empty promises. But we still ain't free. The time has come to defend the lives

of our people against repression and for revolutionary war against the businessmen, politicians, and police. When a government oppresses the people, we have the right to abolish it and create a new one. ARM OURSELVES TO DEFEND OURSELVES!

13. WE WANT A SOCIALIST SOCIETY. We want liberation, clothing, free food, education, health care, transportation, full employment and peace. We want a society where the needs of the people come first, and where we give solidarity and aid to the people of the world, not oppression and racism. HASTA LA VICTORIA SIEMPRE!

By September 1969, we had opened our first office, on Madison Avenue between 111th and 112th Streets, and I was determined to keep alive all of our earlier fire from our summer of fighting in the streets; everything that you have been reading until now, I tried to capture in every media release that went out. The following month we opened our second office, in Newark, New Jersey.

Our second great offensive would be in late December 1969, when we occupied a church for its space so we could have breakfast and educational programs. Earlier that month, on December 7, we had come to petition the church for permission to use a room there to run a breakfast program. We had been requesting permission from them for two months already with no luck. This time, they had responded by calling in the police to break our heads; thirteen arrests were made. The gauntlet had been thrown down. So, on December 28 we took over the church and held it for eleven days while we ran free breakfast programs, educational workshops, clothing drives, cultural events, daycare centers, and more. Three thousand people took part, and many became members. After the first day of the takeover, I looked at my performance on TV, and I didn't like it. I'd use it later as an example to our cadres of what *not* to do. I was covering up my nervousness with what had quickly become a tired image of black leather and shades (personally, I *liked* shades); much too Panther-like, and by then the Panthers were rapidly becoming a stereotype, what with their outrageous rhetoric and little actual organizing (in New York, anyway, where infiltration had sapped much of their strength). The Panthers, I noted, too often confronted the reporter, which became the dominant image on screen; instead, the camera should be used as an organizing tool, I thought, recalling that it is a *medium*, an avenue *to* the audience we really wanted to reach, not the reporter. For the next news conference, I adopted a more collegiate, open look, and became less confrontational with the reporters; humor, I found, went a long way.

In October 1969, we had begun publishing a mimeographed packet that we called *Palante*. Still, we looked to Chicago for leadership. They didn't produce. Their paper came out too irregularly. Finally, on May 8, 1970, a month after we opened our Bronx branch, we published *Palante* as a full-sized tabloid newspaper for the first time (see figure 5). We couldn't wait for Chicago anymore. Chicago threw a fit. Our printing the paper was one of the issues that led to the split with Chicago later that month. The making of the paper was in itself a liberating act for us colonized individuals. Layout, setting type, photo-ready copy, mechanicals . . . wow! My team was superb. Richie Perez, a young high school teacher, had left his career to join us, and he had become deputy minister of information, my right arm. I could never have gotten

FIGURE 5: Cover of *Palante* volume 2, number 2 (May 8, 1970), the first issue of *Palante* as a full-sized tabloid newspaper. Courtesy Young Lords Party.

that newspaper out without him . . . and Mecca, and Americo, and all the rest. All of us doing this work for the first time, using equipment loaned to us by supportive organizations (thank you, *Guardian*, thank you Workers World Party, thank you *Rat*, thank you Liberation News Service, thank you Joe Walker of *Muhammad Speaks*, thank all of you many others). Most of us in our teens, many of us told by the educational system to forget about it, yet here we were, following in John Peter Zenger's footsteps. To do that work, write the articles, shoot the pictures, and then see it come together as a newspaper . . . what a feeling.

We sold *Palante* for 25 cents an issue. It was distributed mainly by us selling it on the street; secondarily, we had about 1,000 subscribers. Before long we were getting orders for subscriptions from servicemen all over the world, from prisons, from all points. We tried to get distribution on the newsstands, but were told by sympathetic dealers, who *knew* we'd beat out tired *El Diario* among Latino readers, that what they sold was controlled by the Mafia, or Mafia-like outfits, along with cigarettes in vending machines and private garbage collection. While they peddled smut magazines, they blocked *Palante*.

During our peak period of 1970–71, we were selling most of the 10,000 (occasionally 20,000) copies of each issue we were printing up every other week. At one point, we hit a weekly stretch. But we could only do so much. Frankly, we were quite flexible. Who knew what our circulation was? But judging from our feedback, our circulation was great. Articles in English and Spanish dealt with local and national issues, as well as events happening in Puerto Rico. We made a point of having at least one article from every chapter—demanded it, really—so every local area would read something of interest to them while also getting a sense of how broad our struggle was. We took articles from all members—though to ensure a body of material, the ministry of information crew, as well as the central committee and chapter leaders, got regular assignments. We also took articles and letters from readers outside the organization, or from people in other organizations. Basically, I decided what got in after consulting with the information ministry team that produced the paper.

In October, I started hosting a weekly radio show, also called *Palante*, over WBAI-FM. 'BAI is a listener-sponsored Pacifica station. We mixed talk with music, mainly salsa. We rallied around salsa, not wanting to cause the kind of political/cultural nationalist split that had affected the black movement. I saw part of my information duties to be organizing the artists, and so we reached out, successfully, to Ray Barretto, Eddie Palmieri, Tito Puente, and others.

The toughest, and yet in some ways the most exciting, issue to print came after June of 1970, when we announced our split with the Chicago group, unveiled our new symbol on the front page, and declared that we were now the YLP—Young Lords *Party*. We had debated dropping the name altogether, but figured we were the ones who had carried the organization's reputation around the planet (no lie: by this time, we were the subject of documentaries from Tokyo to Copenhagen). The previous November, I had been sent to Chicago to try and help salvage our alliance and, in particular, to try and help get a newspaper out. The problem was that while there were a few good people in Chicago, most members of the organization there had never left the gang ways . . . they may not have been out committing crimes, but they knew nothing about discipline, nothing about how to organize. It was a mess. Now I remembered David's warning.

There is so much more to convey, to share . . . but it will have to wait. Quite simply, we tried to put all our experiences into every page of the paper and into the organization, as

I have tried to put some of that feeling, some of why, as well as who we were, and are, in these pages.

While a few of us had been gang members, gangs went out of existence in New York by the late fifties (due either to people growing up, dying, getting locked up, or becoming strung out on heroin); most of the New York Lords had never been in a gang. The organization was always about radical politics.

And, personal liberation. Growth. Change without and change within. It was an exhilarating adventure. It had its downs—oh yeah—but overall, the period I spent as a Lord from mid-1969 to the end of 1974 was five of the best years of my life, and I know just about all the rest of us (at our peak, in New York City, we had close to 2,000 members in 1970–71) felt the same way. That period includes the nine-month stretch I would do in federal prison for resisting the draft because of Puerto Ricans' second-class citizenship status and Vietnam, while other similar offenders were getting six months' probation or community service in a V.A. hospital (I started my sentence May 30, 1973). I got tougher time precisely because of my Young Lords connection. And all the lessons I learned then have become an integral part of every aspect of my life, from what I do as a journalist to what I hope to pass on to the next generation.

Let a Hundred Flowers Blossom, Let a Hundred Schools of Thought Contend: The Story of *Hundred Flowers*

ED FELIEN

It began for me in the summer of 1967 at the New Left Convention in Chicago. I had been hired to teach Modern European Drama at Smith College in Massachusetts in the fall, my first full-time academic appointment. On the drive there from Minneapolis, I thought I'd stop in Chicago for a few weeks and check out the state of the Left.

The New Left Convention was sponsored by a broad coalition of peace and civil rights leaders, including Julian Bond, Ivanhoe Donaldson of Student Nonviolent Coordinating Committee (SNCC), Andrew Young of Southern Christian Leadership Conference (SCLC), Richard Hatcher, and Robert Scheer. I had heard about it through my local Du Bois Club. (Remember the Du Bois Clubs? They were an alternative to Students for a Democratic Society [SDS]. At this time, SDS said it didn't want any Marxists—of which I was one, though I was too much of an anarchist to join the party—in its organization, so anyone with a developed analysis, and particularly red diaper babies of Communist Party parents, joined the Du Bois Clubs. The organization existed until Richard Nixon personally, in classic Nixon anticommunist style, said something like, "It's typical of the Communists to try to confuse American youth with an organization that sounds like the Boys' Club." After that negative endorsement by Nixon, SDS became less exclusive, welcomed radicals of any stripe, and the Du Bois Club that I was staff advisor to at Hallie Q. Brown Community House disbanded.)

I went down early and met some people around Old Town. In the psychedelic spirit of love we set up a Free Bakery and gave away chocolate-chip cookies. The convention itself was much more uptight. The blacks did not want to have anything to do with the whites. The Westside organization, with black Chicago gangster machismo, wouldn't even allow the black delegations to meet with white delegations.

Martin Luther King gave the keynote address, and it was typically thrilling, and only slightly enhanced by hometown clown Eddie Fassbinder's dancing up and down the aisles in time to King's cadences.

A wealthy benefactor backed the convention with enough money to provide meeting rooms in the Palmer House Hotel and free meals. Along with the local chapter of the Brotherhood of Sleeping Car Porters, I was organizing lunches and dinners. At one point the owner of the storefront we were renting on Michigan Avenue said he couldn't rent to us; he hadn't realized we were radicals, and now he wanted to back out of his agreement. I told him he was going to make a lot of people unhappy, and I couldn't be responsible for what they might do to his building once they learned they weren't going to get fed. Upon reflection he graciously relented. We cooked wonderful meals, and it all worked smoothly once it got started.

Dr. Spock was at the convention. A popular idea of the time was to run King and Spock for president and vice president as an alternative to the Democratic and Republican parties. But the final consensus of the convention, one that I still agree with, was to not get caught up in a national organization at all, and instead to organize locally. The big banner in the open hall read, "Don't Mourn, Organize." I left Chicago with my batteries fully charged.

Continuing on the way, a friend and I stopped off at Detroit to see the wreckage wrought by the Detroit riots.

By the time I got to Northampton, I wanted action. I wanted to do something about the war, about racism, about the roar of genocide committed in my name. I knew my politics would screw up the one chance I'd have at tenure and a good gig. After all, Julie Nixon was a student at Smith at the time, and the price of job security was political compliance and a respectful silence. One of the ways I would later measure my political effectiveness (aside from not being reappointed) was that my class was visited by strange men in blue suits and white socks. These obvious Secret Service types stood out as the only men in a class of 140 women. They sat at the back and took notes.

At the time, the only political action in town was a weekly vigil sponsored by the Quakers. I went. I was able to convince myself that going was at least better than doing nothing, but I wanted to do more. I remember one time, for instance, when some local rednecks drove by and shouted at us. I shouted back, and this quiet, meek woman next to me elbowed me in the ribs and hissed, "You're supposed to be nonviolent." After one of the vigils, I talked with some of the other people and asked, "Couldn't we do something a little more intense?" Jimmy Cooney said he thought we should picket the draft board.

Jimmy turned out to be probably the most important person in my life. An Irish renegade, he left the Communist Party in the thirties because they weren't radical enough, left New York City and bought a tobacco farm in Massachusetts, and began *The Phoenix*, a literary and pacifist quarterly that was the first to publish Anaïs Nin, Henry Miller, and others. From the first moment, we were soul mates for life.

We organized a series of meetings and had over 150 people show up for a Monday-night demonstration in front of the draft board. About fifty counterdemonstrators (many of them Vietnam vets) from the Commercial College also showed up. We wanted the draft board to stop drafting young men for an undeclared war. At the very least, we wanted the board to begin issuing deferments based on an unwillingness to fight. The board refused to meet with us. I suggested that it would be a shame to waste the momentum, so after a quick meeting, we decided we'd try to meet with the head of the draft board (who was also the chief Democratic Party political hack and town clerk) at City Hall the next day at noon. He wouldn't meet with us then, either.

That next day, a hundred of us were met by sixty counterdemonstrators. Wednesday there were sixty of us and seventy of them. Thursday there were thirty of us and seventy of them. Friday there were Jimmy, his son Gabe, a vegetarian pacifist, ten young Smith women, and me—and seventy-five angry counterdemonstrators. They started pushing us around until they had us with our backs up against the wall. The Smith women started singing "God Bless America," and I thought I was hearing angels. Then, just when I thought it all might pass, the vegetarian started singing, "Gonna Lay Down My Sword and Shield. . . ." The vets knew that was a Commie song and they attacked. When Gabe and I got our heads split open, I said, "Okay, you win. But we'll be back tomorrow."

Inspired by a series of meetings over the weekend, over a thousand people showed up at City Hall on Monday to march in protest against the war in Vietnam. Later, some of the Smith women went on to work for Eugene McCarthy in New Hampshire. Some formed a strong chapter of SDS. And some of the rest of us started an underground newspaper, *The Mother of Voices*, that ran for a few issues in 1968 out of Amherst, Massachusetts. The paper had gonzo antiwar politics, and it was run by a crazed collective of graduate students. I wrote a few articles: "Rabbits Underground," a parable about getting your political act together before you take it on the road, and "Summary Report from Sgt. Pepper of Colonel Cooney's Looney Army," a summary of the demonstrations. Needless to say, these were not the kind of publications that would ensure my tenure.

The Mother was wonderful and exuberant and filled with infectious fun. It achieved a certain notoriety when the local chief of police sent his adolescent daughter into a local leather-goods shop to purchase a copy so he could bust the proprietor for obscenity and contributing to the delinquency of a minor. The lawyer defending the paper and the leather craftsman cited constitutional guarantees of freedom of the press, but the judge said he wouldn't recognize any foreign jurisdictions. That decision better than anything demonstrated the state of the union when the U.S. Constitution was declared a foreign jurisdiction in Massachusetts.

By the spring of 1969, school was finally out for me for a while. I was leaving the tenure track, getting off the fast track, and traveling down dusty country roads. I left Northampton on a truck with a troupe of traveling actors from hometown Minneapolis. When we arrived home, we lived together in the Eater Family Commune and did some antiwar guerrilla theater. Most of them went out to San Francisco at the end of that summer. I joined some other dropped-out antiwar activists in a small rural-town commune a hundred miles west of Minneapolis. After six months, I was anxious once again for urban action, so I visited San Francisco in the spring of 1970.

There, I got caught up in a street theater group I had known from New York City. One play we performed around The Day After demonstrations (the day after the Chicago 7 got sentenced) was a fairy tale about how it was in the interest of the ruling class in this allegorical country to keep people ignorant and fighting with each other so they wouldn't see how they were all being exploited. The demonstrators moved from downtown San Francisco to Berkeley and ended up trashing banks on Shattuck Avenue. The procedure was demonstrated for me by a Weatherman in a motorcycle helmet holding a 16-foot-long two-by-four. He simply poked it through the front windows of some of the more visible banks. This was a couple of days before the Bank of America was burned to the ground.

While out in San Francisco, I ran across *The Dock of the Bay*, a very left-leaning agitational paper that had full-page centerfold posters of revolutionary heroes like Ho Chi Minh. I also saw *Good Times* for the first time and was impressed with its straight-ahead politics and its community base. I thought that with those two ingredients and the psychedelic colors and

FIGURE 1: Cover of *Hundred Flowers* volume 1, number 2 (April 24, 1970), hyping the upcoming Honeywell demonstration. Courtesy Ed Felien, publisher, *Hundred Flowers*.

FIGURE 2: Cover of *Hundred Flowers* volume 1, number 3 (May Day 1970), celebrating the May Day celebration. Courtesy Ed Felien, publisher, *Hundred Flowers*.

burns of the *San Francisco Oracle* and the *(Chicago) Seed*, there should be enough style to sustain an underground newspaper in Minneapolis.

When I got back to Minneapolis, I began asking around and found two young guys freshly dropped out of college who were game to try a 16-page underground tabloid. Warren was valuable to the paper's early success because he could draw, and Dickie was essential because he was the only person who had had any real production experience doing a newspaper. We agreed it should be a weekly, and I contacted another dozen or so writers. We held our first collective meeting at my old rural commune, and we decided to call the paper *Hundred Flowers*. It was to pay for itself, and sustain the working collective, by ad sales and by selling for 25 cents.

Our first issue came out April 17, 1970. In it were articles about strikes, upcoming demonstrations, and ongoing community struggles against developers and rapacious landlords. On the back was a picture of Mao Zedong drinking a glass of something, and under it a quote by him: "A revolution is not a dinner party." We also quoted Mao's statement on "A Hundred Flowers," part of which predicted with tragic irony the massacre of students that took place during demonstrations nineteen years later in Tiananmen Square: "In socialist society, conditions for the growth of new things are radically different from and far superior to those in the old society. Nevertheless, it still often happens that new, rising forces are held back and reasonable suggestions smothered."

Our next issue was given over to hyping the upcoming Honeywell Demonstration (see figure 1). One ultra-leftist, who twenty years later would be a very centrist member of the Minneapolis City Council, wrote, "More and more of us are beginning to realize that we are part of a new generation, nurtured in the glutted womb of Pig Amerika's Empire and born into revolution," and he borrowed for his title the phrase "I'm going to smash down all your plate glass windows," from the Rolling Stones' "Midnight Rambler." We had music reviews of rock concerts and comics. The centerfold was a cartoon of two Viet Cong looking into the ears of a large tiger and saying, "Hey, it's not paper, it's plastic."

The cover of the third issue was a drawing celebrating May Day that was reprinted by Liberation News Service throughout the country (see figure 2).

The fourth issue celebrated the student strike at the university in protest of the invasion of Cambodia and the murders of four students at Kent State University. We also ran articles on the university community's resistance to the McDonald's–Burger King fast-food invasion. The centerfold was a wonderful photo of a car that had been driven through the front plate-glass windows of a Red Barn hamburger stand that we felt was trying to expand by buying and destroying part of an older neighborhood.

Our sixth issue upped the ante. Beyond just dropping out of society, we now wanted to secede from the Union because, we proclaimed, we could no longer be part of a tyrannical, imperialist government. A map on the cover suggested that we secede from the Union and join part of Canada to form North Country.

We rewrote the Declaration of Independence, leaving the first part, the boilerplate, and adding our own contemporary grievances (see sidebar 1). We also published the first analysis and description of the local capitalist cabal. Up to now we had been opposed to "capitalists." But it was time to get specific. Stephen Keating, president of Honeywell, the chief weapons manufacturer in Minnesota and the producer of the anti-personnel bomb, was a director of the First Bank Systems and a director of Dayton's Department Store. James Binger, chair of the board of Honeywell, was a director of Northwest Bancorp. One Dayton brother sat on the Northwest Bancorp board, and the other was with both the First Bank Systems and Honeywell. We named a few other names and showed how these interlocking directorships maintained economic control over Minneapolis and St. Paul.

SIDEBAR 1

HUNDRED FLOWERS' "DECLARATION OF INDEPENDENCE: UPDATE"

The People of the United States of America have a long list of unresolved grievances against the Federal Government: First, the President of the United States, without the consent of the people or an act of Congress, has involved the Government in foreign and imperialistic wars. The Constitution clearly states that it shall be the responsibility of Congress to "declare war, grant letters of marque and reprisal, and make rules concerning captures on land and water. To raise and support armies, but no appropriation of money to that use shall be for a longer term than two years."

The President has under his special jurisdiction a private Army (the Central Intelligence Agency), not accountable to Congress, which has repeatedly violated international law by engineering direct attacks on the Governments of Guatemala, Cuba, Lebanon, Indonesia, Cambodia, and Greece, to name just a few.

Article I of the Bill of Rights states that Congress shall make no law abridging "the right of the peoples peaceably to assemble and to petition the Government for the redress of grievances," and yet the President has on numerous occasions prohibited public gatherings and otherwise intimidated legitimate assemblies. The murder of four Kent State students is the latest example of this kind of violent suppression of public indignation.

It is our right, it is our duty to establish a new government to serve the interests of all the people. Communities must be allowed to control their own destinies. When giant Corporations have entered our communities they have subverted democratic decision-making and reduced the populace to meek submission to their will. The domination of Northern Minnesota by U.S. Steel is a case in point. These companies must now be turned over to the people who work in them. Workers must elect their bosses. Workers must determine, in cooperation with the community in which they live, the ends to which the products of their labor shall be used.

We, therefore, Joyously publish and declare all ties, treaties and taxes between us and the Government of the United States totally dissolved. And for the support of this Declaration, with a firm reliance on the Protection of Divine Providence, we mutually pledge to each other our Lives, our Fortunes, and our sacred Honor.

Our next issue was devoted to women's liberation. Then we did an in-depth analysis of redevelopment on the West Bank—of Minneapolis (where most of the hippies lived).

Next, we did a financial issue in which we laid bare the economic realities of running a newspaper and other small businesses. *Hundred Flowers* had to gross between $400 and $500 dollars a week to break even. About $250 went to publish a 16-page tabloid with photos and two colors. Most of the rest, about $200 a week, went to keep our urban commune in shelter, utilities, food, and so on. Our income came from two sources. We sold the paper for 25 cents. We had street vendors who got 10 cents of the quarter (if they were reliable, we got the other 15 cents). After a few weeks we had three head shops that acted as drop-off points. These major distributors got a nickel per paper for their trouble, so the dealers still got a dime and we got a dime. This arrangement could bring in around $200 a week, maybe a little more. We also sold ads (to be more precise, I also sold ads) that could bring in another $150 to $250 dollars a week. If it was a good week, we had ice cream and could go to a movie. If it was a bad week, we had brown rice and veggies into infinity.

In that issue, I wrote "A Serious Proposal for the Abolition of Money," in which I argued:

If we truly wish to disassociate ourselves from the Federal Government then we must treat its institutions like foreigners in our land. The Federal Government has legitimacy over our lives because we give it legitimacy over our lives. It continues because we continue to support it.

Jesus stepped on the coin — "Render unto Caesar the things that are Caesar's and to God the things that are God's." We can stop the Federal Government if we understand the meaning of this simple act. If we refused to recognize the power of money, then money would cease to have power. If we developed a system of distributing goods and services that was free, then the Government would no longer have the excuse to regulate and control our lives.

The article went on to outline what specific segments of society I believed should be free; I named some of them: food, land, public and commercial buildings, universities, medical care, police, and the courts.

The centerfold of that issue was a reprint of the Black Panther Manifesto, which announced, "The fascists have already decided in advance to murder chairman Bobby Seale in the electric chair." Alongside it, we ran two panels from a current issue of the comic book *Captain America*. In those panels, Captain America was saying, "Right! This is no time to quarrel amongst ourselves! Together we may hope to stand! But divided we must certainly fall! You'll notice that one of us is missing this fine morning, Thor! That one is our African Avenger . . . T'challa, the Black Panther." We concluded it with our own histrionics: "Bobby Seale is THE prisoner of war. He is the symbol of People's War. If White and Black America don't set Bobby free the blacks will go it alone. RACE WAR. Bobby Seale is our future on trial against America."

Two strains always coexisted in the pages and on the staff of *Hundred Flowers*: the political and the cultural. They didn't always rest easy, and eventually they were the reason we fell apart. I was one who wanted to publish stories about resistance struggles, and some of the others wanted to publish photos of themselves with LOVE written on their foreheads. We did both. The result was a bit schizophrenic, but in the early days, our differences were our twin pillars of strength.

Our eleventh issue was a religious one with a laughing Jesus on the cover and Meher Baba saying, "Don't worry be happy" in the centerfold. A hippie priest declared Jesus to be a "cosmic revolutionary," and I wrote about cultural terrorists like the Marquis de Sade, Rasputin, Oscar Wilde, Jesus, and Charlie Manson in an article entitled "Revolutionary Cultural Terrorists" (see sidebar 2).

SIDEBAR 2

REVOLUTIONARY CULTURAL TERRORISTS

Rasputin jolted the Victorian morality of his day. To many he seemed totally debauched—to others, of course, he seemed a saint. He would conduct drunken orgies all night, minister to the needs of the poor during the morning and cure the Czar's son with miracles in the afternoon. He embodied all the contradictions of Russia: debauched but devout, dogmatic yet mystical, a natural communist and a loyal monarchist. He was a supreme actor. He acted out all the major fantasies of his day. He blew everybody's mind by pushing every trip to its logical conclusion. He expanded the dimensions of the possible. Before Rasputin assumed absolute power, Lenin thought he would never live to see the revolution in Russia. After Rasputin gained power over the royal family, Lenin could accurately predict the revolution in six months. What was the change? Rasputin had elevated the level of social consciousness. He had made people aware of what was going on. As Peasant-King he was the ultimate wish-fulfillment of Russian culture.

One of the best treatments on this theme is Charlie Chaplin's "Monsieur Verdoux," the story of a man who murders his wives for their insurance and has no qualms about it. When the man is finally apprehended, he demands of the courtroom, "How can you dare to prosecute me? My crimes are on such a small scale. Why, your wars kill thousands of people—most of them young and full of life. I have but taken a few old ladies out of their misery and made their final moments beautiful."

It is a kind of cheap publicity trick for the Government to exploit the sensationalism of the Manson murders and to quickly dismiss their My Lai Massacre, their Kent State and Augusta murders, their brutal executions of Fred Hampton and Mark Clark, and many more. When viewed in the context of these acts, Charlie Manson's crimes do not seem so grotesquely extraordinary. The only difference between him and the Federal Government is size; they both claim God as their final authority.

From *Hundred Flowers*, no. 11 (July 1970).

Ronald Reagan introduced issue number 14, our Health issue, when we reprinted on our cover a Chesterfield cigarette ad he made in the forties. Under his photo we listed our four steps to stop smoking: first, you must want to stop; second, drink lots of herbal teas; third, try chewing a sassafras root; fourth, smoke herbs like marijuana, comfrey, rosemary, thyme, and eyebright or corn silks.

As the summer wore on, we became less political and a lot more cultural, part of the ebb and flow of the times. We were best when the two merged. When a young artist was murdered in a random act of senseless violence, we wrote an obituary and served as the vehicle of grief for the community. We had a respected role in the articulation of values for the alternative culture. At least we could all agree on sex, drugs, and rock-and-roll. As I was laying out the paper one afternoon, I heard a local rock station DJ say, in reference to someone else, "He'd swear on a stack of *Hundred Flowers.*"

We were intensely democratic in our decision making at the paper. No article could get in unless it was approved by three members of the collective. Most of the people who worked on the paper also lived in the house where it was produced. There were about twelve of us usually, but after members of the Hog Farm and another busload of migrating hippies pulled up outside one day, we had about fifty people in and out of the house for the next week. We tried to share responsibilities for housekeeping and cooking. Occasionally our domestic decisions became public policy. After a house meeting, we decided to print a poster in the paper entitled "WASH YOUR DISH" so we could cut it out and put it over the sink.

By our nineteenth issue we were finding it difficult to get a printer. We had gone through about thirty printers, which included every web-fed press capable of printing a 16-page newspaper within 150 miles. At first, small-town printers would print us, but then they'd tell us they were getting pressure from their advertisers, and they'd refuse. Once, after we had put together our Women's Liberation issue, we showed up at our printer and were met by the right-wing congressman from the district, Ancher Nelson, who personally looked over our camera-ready copy. A number of articles were critical of sexism in popular music. Another article reported on an action by some sisters who had protested sexist posters at a popular record store, The Electric Fetus. The article was entitled "Power Failure at the Electric Cock." When the congressman saw that title, he closed the folder and looked toward heaven. The printer would not print us. As we left, we turned back and I said, "Remember what John F. Kennedy said: 'If you make peaceful revolution impossible, you make violent revolution inevitable.'" We ended up being printed by the same printer in Milwaukee, Wisconsin, who printed the *(Chicago) Seed.*

The police took papers away from our dealers at the state fair. We seemed to have a legitimate basis for our paranoia, our persecution mania, our delusions of grandeur. Perhaps we were being persecuted. Maybe the revolution was just around the corner. Maybe it was just what we were smoking.

In early September, we learned that Che Guevara had been killed. The Bolivian military, three years earlier and acting on orders and advice from the CIA, had assassinated him by firing a revolver bullet straight through his heart while he was in captivity, but had managed to keep it a secret until now. I cried as I typed out his final farewell letter:

One day they asked who should be notified in case of death, and the real possibility of the fact affected us all. Later we knew it was true, that IN REVOLUTION ONE WINS OR DIES (IF IT IS A REAL ONE). Many comrades fell along the way to victory. . . . I CARRY TO NEW BATTLE FRONTS THE FAITH THAT YOU HAVE TAUGHT ME, THE REVOLUTIONARY SPIRIT OF MY PEOPLE, THE FEELING OF FULFILLING THE MOST SACRED OF DUTIES: TO FIGHT AGAINST IMPERIALISM WHEREVER I MAY BE.

In response to this murder, the New Year's Gang of Madison blew up the Army Math Research Center on the University of Wisconsin campus. The Army Math Research Center was the training center for the CIA group that engineered the capture and assassination of Che Guevara. Members of the Gang had given sufficient warning to allow people to clear the building, but a janitor disregarded their warning and, as a result, a researcher was killed in the explosion. Our work took on more serious implications after this.

In the same issue, Huey Newton urged everyone to choose between revolutionary suicide and reactionary suicide:

> If the penalty for the quest for freedom is death, then by death we escape to freedom. We are not alone. We have allies everywhere. We find our comrades wherever in the world we hear the oppressor's whip. People all over the world are rising up. The high tide of revolution is about to sweep the shores of America—sweeping away the evil gentry and corrupt officials.

Huey Newton was the centerfold in our next issue. On the cover was a drawing of the original seal of the United States proposed by Benjamin Franklin, John Adams, and Thomas Jefferson. It read, "Rebellion to Tyrants Is Obedience to God."

At the end of September, the death of Jimi Hendrix was the cover story for our twenty-first issue. By this time, some of our regular features were becoming standard: lead news on page 3; "People Rising Up All Over," a review of international news the other papers didn't print, on pages 5 and 6; a "Bulletin Board"; a calendar; and classified ads on the back page.

Two weeks later, a couple of us were promoting a "Gathering of the Tribes," an attempt at a conference of alternative energies. We wanted to translate the newspaper into a political action, a ratification of aspirations, our agreed-upon hopes. More than a hundred people showed up, at the church that was soon after permanently renamed the People's Center, for the three days of workshops and rap sessions. We had workshops on the Black Panther Party, free schools, gay liberation, women's liberation, ecology, organizing food co-ops, organic gardening, people's medical clinics, and more. We held general sessions where we talked about where we should be headed politically, and we heard reports from brothers and sisters who were facing jail and prison for anti-ROTC demonstrations and attempts to destroy draft files.

During the time we were putting together that issue (see figure 3), I got arrested for breach of the peace while covering a story about the demolition of single-family homes to make way for two-and-a-half-story walk-up apartment buildings. Some of the hippies who lived in the houses were protesting the demolition of the houses and the consequent increase in density in the neighborhood. The charges were eventually dismissed, but the police harassment was obvious: I was arrested for taking photos standing next to a television cameraman.

Finally, by the twenty-sixth issue, I snapped. I had been burning out. One or two all-nighters every week, typing copy, laying out, trying to manage circulation of 5,000 copies and sell ads: all this had taken its toll. For what seemed like the millionth time, I was the only one left at 3:00 A.M. to put the paper to bed. Was I the only one who took it seriously?

The differences between the others on the paper and me were becoming too great. I was ten years older than most of the others. I had finished my PhD. I had been marching against segregation and the war in Vietnam since 1963. They were bright and eager, but they had no

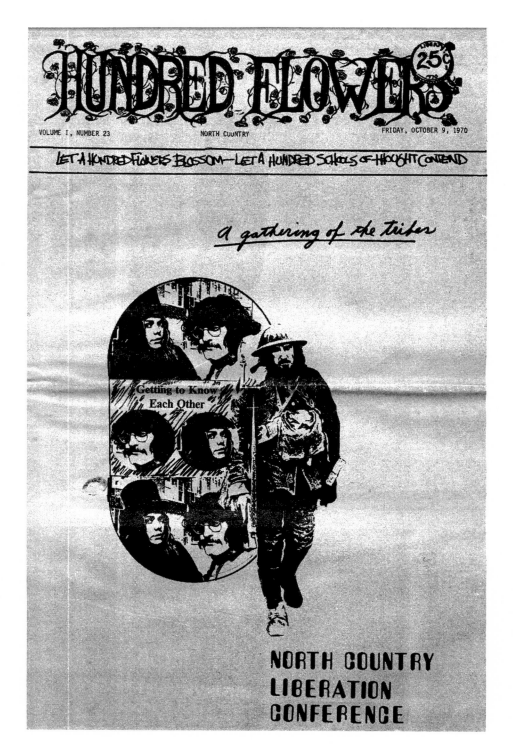

FIGURE 3: Cover of *Hundred Flowers* volume 1, number 23 (October 9, 1970), promoting Gathering of the Tribes conference. Courtesy Ed Felien, publisher, *Hundred Flowers*.

real idea of what they were in for. We didn't share the same frame of reference or the same political commitment. They liked the music, the drugs, the lifestyle, and they enjoyed being the center of the counterculture in Minneapolis. Compared to them, I must have seemed like a political fanatic.

I was typing and laying out the letters to the editor ("Readers Write On"). I had just typed a confused letter from a pacifist, a peace-and-love letter from a GI in 'Nam who was thankful he was in the artillery and not the infantry, and a letter from a hippie critical of the protest bombings of buildings by the Weather Underground. That was the last straw. I couldn't resist. I added a short response of my own to the first letter: "You are a chicken-shit bourgeois pacifist. Che said: 'Wherever death may surprise us let it be welcome as long as one more person comes forward to pick up the gun and intone our funeral dirge with the staccato of machine guns.' Yours, for a just peace, thorsten do-good."

This short statement provoked a major controversy. In the next issue, a colleague and I defended our positions in "Two Flowers on Violence: A Criticism of Bourgeois Pacifism." She was more eloquent than I:

> Do I dig violence? No. But tell me you don't believe in violence, and I say, "Bullshit." How much closer does Honeywell or the New Brighton Arsenal have to be before we believe in it.

I was more crude:

> We cannot any longer be pacifists: House Niggers with our heads in the sand hoping we won't get our asses shot off.

Members of the Black Panther Party were being assassinated by the Alcohol and Tax Division of the Treasury Department all over the country. Some of us were organizing a Black Panther Party chapter for Minneapolis. We had a storefront, the Kathleen Cleaver Community Information Center, and plans to start a breakfast program for children, and a transportation program to help loved ones visit their friends and relatives in prison.

Our Black Panther Party issue showed the schizophrenia manifest in the paper. I supervised pages of copy about the BPP that were almost rigidly orthodox, while the cultural hippies organized pages advertising a rally of support for the Minnesota 8 who were about to be sentenced to prison for attempting to destroy draft files. They entitled their section "Thanks for the Pie!" The centerfold was a blowup of a house fly that you were supposed to paste to a picket sign and bring to the demonstration.

The "Readers Write On" section of the paper brought the struggle out in the open. We reprinted the original pacifist letter, my response, a new response to me in which I was described as an "arrogant elitist in 'peoples' clothing," a new extended reply by me again attacking bourgeois pacifism, and a response by five members of the collective that agreed with the criticism of me as elitist and arrogant.

A few years later, the Weather Underground, in their self-criticism, said they were guilty of the Military Error. They were ultra-left when they thought that quick, violent acts would spark a mass uprising. Certainly, one judgment of history has to be that they were wrong.

I was wrong, too.

The way we criticize the present world is the way we build the new.

You don't fight fire with fire. You fight fire with water.

You catch more bees with honey than you do with vinegar.

All these platitudes are true. But, even though we were wrong to act angrily, violently, antagonistically, we were right to act. It was a much greater wrong to do nothing.

That was almost forty years ago, and I'm still not repentant.

But the split in *Hundred Flowers* was irrevocable. I was purged. Some readers wrote in, wanting to continue the debate, but the paper sputtered and finally folded after three more issues. The final issue came out December 11, 1970.

Those were heady days. The year 1970 was a turning point for America. Resistance to the war in Vietnam had matured into a permanent institution, a persistent and articulate counterculture. A new consciousness was being developed about capitalism, racism, and sexism. Being a part of those struggles was exciting.

It was good work. But I have no nostalgia for the genocide, the racism, the oppression of women that made that work so immediate and necessary. There is political work enough for today and even for tomorrow. It is no less important now, even though there's new music on the radio and the tempo has changed.

The Furies: Goddesses of Vengeance

GINNY Z. BERSON

n the winter and spring of 1972, while Richard Nixon and his minions were preparing to bug Democratic National Headquarters at the Watergate Building, twelve self-proclaimed revolutionary lesbian feminists—who were known collectively as the Furies—were putting out the first issues of what would almost instantly become the "legendary" *The Furies*. While Washington, DC, may seem an unlikely place for the birthing of such a major contributor to the exploding underground press in this country, in retrospect, and in light of what the Furies wrote about and stood for, it all makes perfect sense.

Washington, DC, was, after all, the belly of the beast, the very seat of power of the U.S. government. As such, Washington was also the focus and locus of hundreds of protest groups and demonstrations. Government offices were regularly occupied by groups as diverse as the National Welfare Rights Organization and the Committee of Returned [Peace Corps] Volunteers. The Black Panther Party was strong and active. Gay men and (fewer) women were coming out of the closet and talking about their civil rights. As the war in Vietnam raged, hundreds of thousands of people descended regularly on the Capitol grounds to march and rally, smash windows and fight with cops, circle the Pentagon and try to levitate it, block traffic and sit in the halls of Congress. Hippies and freaks dropped acid and contemplated their visions in the reflecting pool across from the Washington Monument.

D.C. Women's Liberation in the early 1970s was thriving. Consciousness-raising groups enabled hundreds of women to understand a critical lesson of this second wave of feminism: the personal is political. Women took the revelations that followed and established a host of services for themselves and other women, including rape counseling and child care. Women in the health fields began researching the Pill and testified in Congress to its dangerous side effects. Others began organizing and lobbying for changes in restrictive abortion laws—*Roe v. Wade* was not decided until January 1973, so for most American women abortion was still illegal. *off our backs*, a feminist monthly, was publishing news and opinion from around the

This article originally appeared in *The Furies*, no. 1 (January 1972). It was reprinted in *Lesbianism and the Women's Movement*, ed. Nancy Myron and Charlotte Bunch (San Francisco: Diana Press, 1975), 15–19. It is reprinted here with permission of Diana Press.

FIGURE 1: *The Furies* staff at layout (*from left*): Lee Schwing, Tasha Peterson, Ginny Berson, Jennifer Woodul. From staff archives.

country. Women Against Racism, Women Against Imperialism, and Women Against Population Control met regularly, marched together, wrote position papers, planned to change the world.

The particular confluence of forces that gave birth to *The Furies* was being duplicated all over the country. Straight women were tired of being the gofers and sperm receptacles for the white male Left. Lesbians were tired of being ignored by the gay liberation movement, and were being actively told to go back in the closet or get out by the women's liberation movement. It seemed that liberation went only so far. Women's liberation was considered bourgeois by the lefties—something to take care of "after the revolution." It was not even taken seriously enough to be considered a threat. Lesbianism was considered a bedroom issue by women's liberation—but leaders like Betty Friedan were very threatened because the mainstream media were already dismissing the emerging women's movement as a bunch of "bra-burning" lesbians. If that turned out to be true, women's liberation would have an even harder time gaining credibility and winning converts.

The twelve original Furies came from D.C., New York, and Chicago, having worked in all the movements, and having found no home in any of them. We were all white, rural and urban, working, middle, and upper-middle class. Our ages ranged from eighteen to twenty-eight. The primary organizer of the group was Rita Mae Brown. Rita had been a lesbian activist for years, being one of the authors of "The Woman-Identified Woman," the first authoritative definition of political lesbianism. She came to D.C. to organize, and she formed her first critical alliance with Charlotte Bunch, a straight (though not for long after meeting Rita) activist in the D.C. women's liberation movement. Rita had the fire and vision; Charlotte, one of the most visible founders of D.C. Women's Liberation, had the credibility and contacts; and they pulled together the rest of us: Tasha Peterson and Susan Hathaway, recently arrived from Chicago where they had worked on the Chicago 7 conspiracy trial; Nancy Myron, lesbian activist from New York; Joan Biren and Sharon Deevey, whose coming out into the D.C. women's liberation movement had caused a major split in that organization; teenagers Helaine Harris and Lee Schwing; Coletta Reid, married mother of two who lived down the street from the first all-women's house in D.C. and was one of the founders of *off our backs*, and one day asked her husband to leave; Jennifer Woodul, who came out while a student at Vassar College by the organizing work of New York Radical Lesbians, including Rita Mae Brown; and me, closeted my whole life, active in the Left and the women's movement (see figure 1).

Before the formation of the Furies, I had lived in D.C.'s first women's house, with Tasha, Susan, and Helaine, among others. We did massive quantities of grass, acid, mushrooms, and other drugs; went to meetings of Women Against (fill in the blank); and struggled endlessly about everything. I left that house after Joan and Sharon came out to me and I finally felt free to come out myself. The three of us moved in with a group of lesbians who had come from New York, one of whom was Nancy Myron. We thought that particular house would solve the problem of living among the straight "oppressor." But Joan, Sharon, and I were middle-class women with college degrees, who had no visible means of support but managed to live well. Our five housemates were working-class and all had straight, nine-to-five jobs. I began to develop an understanding of class in America. But the house lasted only one week. These two themes—lesbian and class consciousness—became the dominant themes of *The Furies*.

By July of 1971, the Furies had formed itself into a collective. Everyone had come out. Weekly meetings, which had begun in April as consciousness-raising sessions for the new lesbians, became more politically focused. We were going to define and build a lesbian-feminist ideology. We decided to publish a monthly newspaper—a way to reach other lesbians and would-be lesbians. In September or October of that year, we moved out of our houses in the northwest part of D.C. where most of the hippies and male lefties lived and into the (relatively) gay southeast section of the city.

By this time we had agreed to form a disciplined, revolutionary cadre. We developed an income-sharing plan, by which the more privileged among us got the best jobs we could find—in direct opposition to the value being promulgated by the political and hippie middle-class white male Left that only "oppressors" had well-paying jobs, and that we should all embrace downward mobility as a way to better relate to our working-class sisters and brothers. By doing this, we were able to supplement the incomes of the less privileged, and no one had to work full-time. We each put a percentage of our wages into the common pool (the greater the privilege, the higher the percentage). One of the working-class women was sent to printing school. The cars of those who had them became community property. We formed study groups that read and reported regularly on the functioning and malfunctioning of other revolutions. We stopped doing drugs.

Political Lesbianism

We struggled among ourselves to define our politics. Out of the morass of the white male Left, the hippie/freak/drug culture, the straight women's liberation movement, and the male-dominated gay liberation movement, we intended to develop a truly radical lesbian-feminist ideology. We rejected the glaring weaknesses we found in each movement—the male domination, the downward mobility, the glorification of feelings over thought, the priority given to personal relationships, the lack of strategic vision and practical organization.

We chose the name "The Furies," for our collective and our newspaper, after the three Greek goddesses—strong, powerful women, the "Angry Ones," the avengers of matricide, the protectors of women. They are part of the Orestes myth, and, according to our interpretation, their defeat marked a major victory for male supremacy; their ultimate betrayal came at the hands of Athena—"the creation of the male God, Zeus, sprung full-grown from his head, the first token woman." As I wrote in the lead article of the first issue (see appendix 1 and figure 2), published in January 1972:

> We call our paper *The Furies* because we are also angry. We are angry because we are oppressed by male supremacy. We have been fucked over all our lives by a system which is based on the domination of men over women, which defines male as good and female as only as good as the man you are with. It is a system in which heterosexuality is rigidly enforced and Lesbianism rigidly suppressed. It is a system which has further divided us by class, race, and nationality.

Although we called ourselves a "newspaper," our interest in news was relatively insignificant. While that first issue did contain a full page of "What's Going On?" that reported lesbian activities from around the country, future issues devoted less and less space to that information. In fact, we were quite sure that political activity was premature until a solid ideology had been developed. And that, we thought, was our primary task. In a nutshell, again from the lead article of issue 1:

> The base of our ideological thought is: Sexism is the root of all other oppressions, and Lesbian and woman oppression will not end by smashing capitalism, racism and imperialism. Lesbianism is not a matter of sexual preference, but rather one of political choice which every woman must make if she is to become woman-identified and thereby end male supremacy. Lesbians, as outcasts from every culture but their own, have the most to gain by ending race, class, and national supremacy within their own ranks. Lesbians must get out of the straight women's movement and form their own movement in order to be taken seriously, to stop straight women from oppressing us, and to force straight women to deal with their own Lesbianism. Lesbians cannot develop a common politics with women who do not accept Lesbianism as a political issue.

These themes were developed more fully in Charlotte Bunch's first article, "Lesbians in Revolt: Male Supremacy Quakes and Quivers" (see appendix 2):

the furies

lesbian/feminist monthly

January 1972   Volume 1

35¢

The story of the Furies is the story of strong, powerful women, the "Angry Ones", the avengers of matricide, the protectors of women. Three Greek Goddesses, they were described (by men) as having snakes for hair, blood-shot eyes, and bats' wings; like Lesbians today, they were cursed and feared. They were born when Heaven (the male symbol) was castrated by his son at the urging of Earth (the female symbol). The blood from the wound fell on Earth and fertilized her, and the Furies were born. Their names were Alecto (Never-ceasing), Tisiphone (Avenger of Blood), and Magaera (Grudger). Once extremely powerful, they represented the supremacy of women and the primacy of mother right.

Their most famous exploit (famous because in it they lost much of their power) involved Orestes in the last episode connected with the cycle of the Trojan War. Orestes, acting on the orders of the Sun God Apollo, killed his mother Clytemnestra, because she had killed his father. Clytemnestra had killed the father because he had sacrificed their daughter Iphigenia, in order to get favorable winds so his fleet could sail to Troy. The Furies tormented Orestes: they literally drove him crazy, putting him under a spell where for days he could not eat or wash his blood-stained hands. He bit off his finger to try to appease them, but to no avail. Finally, in desperation, Orestes went before the court of Athena to plead his case.

The point at issue was whether matricide was justifiable to avenge your father's murder, or in other words, whether men or women were to dominate. Apollo defended Orestes and totally denied the importance of motherhood, claiming that women were no more than passive sperm receptacles for men, and that the father was the only parent worthy of the name. One might have thought that Athena, Goddess of Wisdom, would have condemned Orestes, but Athena was the creation of the male God, Zeus, sprung full-grown from his head, the first token woman. Athena decided for Orestes. Some mythologists say that Zeus, Athena, and Apollo had conspired from the beginning, ordering Orestes to kill his mother in order to put an end, once and for all, to the religious belief that motherhood was more divine than fatherhood. In any case, that was the result.

The Furies were, of course, furious, and threatened to lay waste the city of Athens. But Athena had a direct line to Zeus, King of the Gods; she told the Furies to accept the new male supremacist order or lose everything. Some of the Furies and their followers relented, the rest pursued Orestes until his death.

ORESTES PURSUED BY FURIES

We call our paper The FURIES because we are also angry. We are angry because we are oppressed by male supremacy. We have been fucked over all our lives by a system which is based on the domination of men over women, which defines male as good and female as only as good as the man you are with. It is a system in which heterosexuality is rigidly enforced and Lesbianism rigidly suppressed. It is a system which has further divided us by class, race, and nationality.

We are working to change this system which has kept us separate and powerless for so long. We are a collective of twelve Lesbians living and working in Washington, D.C. We are rural and urban; from the Southwest, Midwest, South and Northeast. Our ages range from 18 to 28. We are high school dropouts and Ph.D. candidates. We are lower class, middle and upper-middle class. We are white. Some of us have been Lesbians for twelve years, others for ten months. We are committed to ending all oppressions by attacking their roots--male supremacy.

We believe The FURIES will make important contributions to the growing movement to destroy sexism. As a collective, in addition to outside projects, we are spending much time building an ideology which is the basis for action. For too long, women in the Movement have fallen prey to the very male propaganda they seek to refute. They have rejected thought, building an ideology, and all intellectual activity as the realm of men, and tried to build a politics based only on feelings--the area traditionally left to women. The philosophy has been, "if it feels good, it's O.K. If not, forget it." But that is like saying that strength, which is a "male" characteristic, should be left to men, and women should embrace weakness. Most straight women, to say nothing of men, feel afraid or contemptuous of Lesbians. That fear and contempt is similar to the feelings middle class whites have towards Blacks or lower class people. These feelings are the result of our socialization and are hardly worth glorifying. This

is not to say that feelings are irrelevant, only that they are derived from our experience which is limited by our class, race, etc. Furthermore, feelings are too often used to excuse inaction and inability to change.

A political movement cannot advance without systematic thought and practical organization. The haphazard, non-strategic, zig-zag tactics of the straight women's movement, the male left, and many other so-called revolutionary groups have led only to frustration and dissolution. We do not want to make those same mistakes; our ideology forms the basis for developing long-range strategies and short-term tactics, projects, and actions.

The base of our ideological thought is: Sexism is the root of all other oppressions, and Lesbian and woman oppression will not end by smashing capitalism, racism, and imperialism. Lesbianism is not a matter of sexual preference, but rather one of political choice which every woman must make if she is to become woman-identified and thereby end male supremacy. Lesbians, as outcasts from every culture but their own have the most to gain by ending race, class, and national supremacy within their own ranks. Lesbians must get out of the straight women's movement and form their own movement in order to be taken seriously, to stop straight women from oppressing us, and to force straight women to deal with their own Lesbianism. Lesbians cannot develop a common politics with women who do not accept Lesbianism as a political issue.

In this (see page 8) and following issues of The FURIES we will share our thoughts with you. We welcome your comments, letters, articles, fiction, poetry, news, graphics, and support. We want to build a movement in this country and in the world which can effectively stop the violent, sick, oppressive acts of male supremacy. We want to build a movement which makes all people free.

For the Chinese women whose feet were bound and crippled; for the Ibibos of Africa whose clitori were mutilated; for every woman who has ever been raped, physically, economically, psychologically, we take the name of the FURIES, Goddesses of Vengeance and protectors of women.

Ginny Berson

FIGURE 2: Front page of *The Furies* premier issue (January 1972). From staff archives.

In our society which defines all people and institutions for the benefit of the rich, white male, the Lesbian is in revolt. In revolt because she defines herself in terms of women and rejects the male definitions of how she should feel, act, look, and live. To be a Lesbian is to love oneself, woman, in a culture that denigrates and despises women. The Lesbian rejects male sexual/political domination; she defies his world, his social organization, his ideology, and his definition of her as inferior. Lesbianism puts women first while the society declares the male supreme. Lesbianism threatens male supremacy at its core. When politically conscious and organized, it is central to destroying our sexist, racist, capitalist, imperialist system.

Lesbianism, we said, is a political choice, not just a matter of sexual preference. To see lesbianism as exclusively a sexual act was to strengthen the dominant view of women as only sexual beings; furthermore, the popular conception of lesbians as not being "real women" reinforced that notion: a "real woman" is one who has sex with men. Lesbianism is political, Bunch went on, "because relationships between men and women are essentially political, they involve power and dominance."

In terms of actual "sexual preference," we believed that, in an ideal world, all human beings would be bisexual, capable of loving, intimate relationships with people of both genders. But we did not live in an ideal world, and that natural inclination had been suppressed in most people. Still, every woman (we didn't care about the men) had the ability—and the obligation—to reclaim that part of herself, and free herself from the personal and political bonds of male domination. While lesbian singer Alix Dobkin was singing, "Any woman can be a lesbian," we were saying, "Every woman should be a lesbian."

But lesbianism by itself is not enough. Even billions of women coming out would still not make a revolution. At worst, lesbians could be racist, classist, oppressive to other women and lesbians. They could opt for individual solutions to political problems. They could settle for political reforms that gave them certain civil rights but did nothing to change the power structure. "Lesbians must become feminists and fight against woman oppression, just as feminists must become Lesbians if they hope to end male supremacy. . . . The only way oppressed people end their oppression," wrote Bunch, "is by seizing power: People whose rule depends on the subordination of others do not voluntarily stop oppressing others. Our subordination is the basis of male power."

Our analysis of history concluded that sexism was the root of all oppression; the original imperialism was male over female: "the male claiming the female body and her service as his territory (or property)." Domination by men of other men based on race, class, and tribe ensued. At the bottom of every conquered group were the women. To this day, armies still regard women as spoils of war. Witness Bosnia or the Congo. Even among the more "liberated" socialist and nationalist fighters of the sixties, seventies, and eighties, women's place was always secondary, and women's "issues" had to wait until after the "revolution." For *The Furies*, there could be no revolution until male supremacy, the primary contradiction, was resolved. Today we would add religious fundamentalism of every brand to the list of rationales used to justify male supremacy.

While parts of the straight women's liberation movement agreed with our analysis of sexism, *The Furies* went a step further, to a place where straight women could not go and remain straight. We defined the institution of heterosexuality as the primary underpinning of male supremacy. Charlotte Bunch wrote:

> Heterosexuality separates women from each other; it makes women define themselves through men; it forces women to compete against each other for men and the privilege which comes through men and their social standing. Heterosexual society offers women a few privileges as compensations if they give up their freedom: for example, mothers are respected and "honored," wives or lovers are socially accepted and given some economic and emotional security, a woman gets physical protection on the street when she stays with her man, etc. The privileges give heterosexual women a personal and political stake in maintaining the status quo.

The very essence of heterosexuality in the twentieth century (not to mention the previous thirty centuries) was "men first." As lesbians, therefore, we believed that to continue working with straight women in women's liberation would mean our ultimate betrayal. "Lesbians cannot grow politically or personally in a situation which denies the basis of our politics: that Lesbianism is political, that heterosexuality is crucial to maintaining male supremacy."

We hammered home those points over and over, in the first issue and in every one that followed. Sharon Deevey's first article began with her personal story of struggling with her "sensitive" husband, her first lesbian relationship, and finally her realization that "Everything around me was . . . heterosexual—men and women together, and men most important. Books, movies, people in the streets, my family, my friends, and especially Women's Liberation: Birth control, bad fucks, and abortions!"

Rita Mae Brown added to the discussion with "How a Female Heterosexual Serves the Interests of Male Supremacy," taking on Roxanne Dunbar, in response to Dunbar's just published article "The Movement and the Working Class." Rita was reluctant to criticize another working-class woman, and acknowledged the importance of Dunbar's analysis of class in the United States and the failure of many political movements to effectively address class issues. But, "Roxanne attempts to smash Lesbianism by treating it as a personal luxury rather than dealing with it as a political ideology. This sweeping us under the rug as some great apolitical, individualistic freedom is classic heterosexual blindness." Rita made the point that has been echoed by feminists ever since—class struggle, race struggle, and national struggle are considered the "important" struggles because they include men. The struggle for the liberation of women in general, and lesbians in particular, is simply not taken seriously, because women in this world are not taken seriously.

We tried to make *The Furies* the newspaper for the complete lesbian—with regular features on developing physical strength and self-defense tactics; short stories, including one by me on a trip to the dentist (see appendix 3); poetry (by the likes of Judy Grahn, Pat Parker, Rita Mae, and others); discussions of the workings of capitalist economics in the United States and the world; the occasional movie review (when some political point could be made); photos (many by Joan Biren, who became JEB) and drawings of women; and history, always something about history.

We were a bit obsessed with history—we studied the Russian and Chinese revolutions and the structure of their parties, the Nazi rise to power, the Greek and Roman myths, the first wave of feminism in the United States, the beginnings of the lesbian and homophile movement in the 1940s and '50s. We looked for and found lesbians or remarkable straight women in history—women whose lives and/or loves had been kept secret from us—and we wrote about them: Queen Christina of Sweden, Emily Dickinson, Susan B. Anthony, Doña Catalina of Spain, pirates Anne Bonny and Mary Read. Part of our obsession with history was genuine curiosity about the women, especially the lesbians, who came before us. But part of it was a tribute to the serious role we believed we were taking on. We were going to create a revolution like nothing anyone had ever seen before. We had to know how other revolutionaries did it—to emulate what we could, and to avoid what we should.

Reading through *The Furies* in 1990, as I was writing the history of *The Furies* for the first time, I was astonished to realize that we never discussed the dynamics of personal relationships (issues such as monogamy or breaking up with integrity), except to bemoan the amount of time, energy, and attention relationships were getting from other lesbians and feminists. While we seemed to have changed partners regularly, we never allowed the comings and goings of various lovers to disrupt our political work.

Outside of the poetry and fiction, we never wrote about sex. Indeed, we made a conscious decision to specifically exclude any graphics that depicted female nudity. We were, in fact, determined to smash the popular conception of lesbianism as a purely sexual occupation; we had no intention of even acknowledging the frequently asked question, "But what do two women do in bed?"

Class

Class analysis and the development of class consciousness was the second dominant theme of *The Furies*. As a group, we struggled with the issues constantly, monitoring our own and each other's behavior. I cannot find a single article that did not mention class—even if class was not the point of the article. All of us were in different stages of class awareness, but we all understood that, to succeed, our revolution had to be for all women, not just the privileged.

Rita brought the clearest understanding of the workings of class to the collective, but Coletta, Tasha, and Nancy made their experiences as working-class women heard as well. As a middle-class woman, I was encouraged to understand my own position relative to both the working and lower classes and the upper-middle and upper classes, and to not allow myself the luxury of being frozen by guilt.

Nevertheless, in retrospect it seems that class guilt was a considerable force in our group dynamics. Being accused of classism by one of the working-class women in *The Furies* was tantamount to being accused of being male-identified. When in doubt about a particular issue, it was safer to shut up and follow the lead of the working-class women. Needless to say, this did not make for a healthy group process.

Issue number 3 (March–April 1972) was devoted largely to class. Nancy Myron described her own "Class Beginnings" as "the trash of the community" when she was growing up. Her sister, being not only poor but endowed with large breasts, was considered a whore and an easy lay, while young women with similar physiques but higher class standing were dated and considered respectable:

I'm not saying that the sweet magnolia blossoms of lawyers' daughters escaped objectification but that they had a less traumatic time of it. Someone has to be on the bottom to hold up the top. And in this case part of the female citizenry was projected into the shadows of alleys while the rest went steady with basketball stars.

Rita Mae Brown reviewed *The Last Picture Show* and slammed the movie as "being more dishonest than most in its packaged cinematic sensitivity":

First the technical dishonesty: Movies shot in black and white in the 1970s are artsy fartsy. Human beings see in color. . . . There's a class aspect to black and white movies in our times. Supposedly, the bleak screen will serve to heighten the viewer's sense of the drab, the working class, the impoverished. Those of us growing up impoverished were oppressed in living color and any deviation from that is a perversion of our lives justified in terms of "style." When our ceilings peeled they peeled from pea green to red to black to gray to blue and all together it was more hideous than anything shot in black and white.

My own contribution was "Slumming It in the Middle Class," in which I described the evolution of my class consciousness. It was important to us to describe our own processes because we desperately wanted other women to recognize themselves in us and make the changes we thought were necessary. If I had once been unaware but had learned to alter my behavior, so could others. So must others:

For many middle class women the women's movement has meant a reprieve from working for somebody else's revolution. Having gotten in touch with their own oppression, they are unwilling to see themselves as oppressors again, especially as the oppressors of other women. It is crucial that we stop this before our movement gets torn apart by middle class women's refusal to deal with their class privilege.

Class privilege included real material issues like the amount of money one makes and the degree of economic security one has; and behavioral issues like the romanticization of poverty and downward mobility, which ran rampant in the sixties and seventies. Class background often determined who dominated meetings, as well as who had time to attend meetings.

For the middle-class Furies, the sharing of material privilege with our working-class sisters came much more easily than changing the destructive attitudes—the ways of viewing the world, the standards of thought and action that we had learned to be the "right ways." Charlotte and Coletta wrote in "Revolution Begins at Home," in issue number 4 (May 1972):

Class supremacy is acted out in thinking that working class women are less together, personally and politically, because they do not act and talk the way we do. Their politics may not be expressed in the same manner, their vocabulary may not be as "developed," and so they are "less articulate" and treated as less important. Or they may be hostile and emotional so one can hardly trust their political judgment; after all, we've learned to keep ourselves in check, to be reasonable, to keep things in perspective. Looking down with scorn or pity at those whose emotions are not repressed or who can't rap out abstract theories in thirty seconds flat reeks of our class arrogance and self-righteousness.

It's hard to talk about how the contemporary women's movement addresses class issues because, while feminism continues to be a vital and motivating force (whatever it is called), it's harder now to identify and locate the "organized" movement. The large national organizations (such as Fund for a Feminist Majority and NOW) seem to do a better job of raising and supporting issues for working-class and poor women.

We almost always mentioned race and racism in our articles, but never thought or wrote extensively about the subject. We were aware that this was a failing; indeed, the fact that our group was all white was disturbing to us. However, we did nothing about it, believing that at some future point, having successfully dealt with the class issues among us, we would be able to focus more on race. It is clear that we focused so much on class because of our internal class differences; without the leadership of the working-class women in the collective, the middle-class women would have treated class issues the same way the all-white group treated race issues: important, something to be dealt with, but not urgent.

Power

We solicited, and occasionally printed, articles by other lesbians, particularly when they agreed with our positions. There was, however, one notable exception. In issue number 2 (February 1972), Rita wrote a perceptive article on "Leadership vs. Stardom"—a problem that was plaguing the entire women's movement, which had a tendency to trash anyone who was perceived as taking a vanguard role. Part of this tendency came from having the male, mainstream media declare our "leaders" for us. A leader was a woman like Betty Friedan or Gloria Steinem, who had "little or no political following. She has done something that the media finds noteworthy—written a book, founded a reformist organization, made a public fool of herself, etc. She serves male supremacy by being a token."

But a far more serious aspect of the problem was feminists' basic distrust of power, because of our horrendous experiences with male abuses. Many believed that power was inherently evil and corrupting. Our beliefs in egalitarianism translated into a kind of feminist lowest-common-denominator conformity. The most vivid example of this for me came while playing softball, one of my personal addictions. Every Sunday we organized softball games for women in one of D.C.'s parks. Some of us were really good. Others weren't. I was a very good shortstop, and a number of other players insisted that I play another position—that all the good players play someplace other than at their strength in order to equal things out. I offered another solution—I and some others would come early each Sunday and spend time working with and teaching less skilled players so we could all play better. For several Sundays in a row I arrived at the park, ready to coach. Nobody else showed up. We had yet to develop an understanding of the differences between "power to" versus "power over." This was an issue *The Furies* was ready to take on.

In a very casual manner in her "Leadership" article, Rita mentioned the need to form a national feminist political party to confront the power of the state. The principal opposition to the discipline and organization required to form a party, she asserted, came from anarchists, whom she accused of being middle class, cowardly, and anti-leadership. In issue number 4,

Katz (the only name she used), a white working-class anarchist from Boston, responded by calling instead for a "world of man-hating-dyke-gangs," "small groups based on friendship and common politics that you are so flipply disdainful of." Katz goes on:

> Are you ready to form a party in a movement where lesbians of color are not yet fully participant? Are you willing to form a party in a movement where most of its middle class members are classist? As a leader, are you ready to risk the codification of power? Let's see you kids get all of D.C. together so fine that you can justify such a call. And then I'll show you how well you did without any damn party.

I wrote our official response, "Beyond Male Power . . ." We acknowledged that the mention of party in Rita's article had been fairly offhand, without consideration given to the difficult questions that Katz raised. We also apologized for the misuses of the word "anarchy" and for its equation with emotionalism, cowardice, and individualism. But we stuck by our call for a party:

> Individual lesbians can and do carve out little niches for themselves in which they are as "free" as possible and in as little contact with their oppressor as possible. But, by themselves, they do nothing to change the balance of power. They do nothing to change the basic system which oppresses them and forces them into that solution. Small groups, acting on their own, with no national coordination or agreed upon action, do a little more. They expand the base of the niche and can improve the lot of large numbers of women. But their effectiveness is limited by their size and the degree to which they can coordinate their actions and their understandings with other groups. They still do not threaten the balance of power; they still don't bring about a major redistribution of power.

Needless to say, we never got very far with the creation of a party. In fact, some time between the fourth and fifth issues, the working collective dissolved. Many of us continued to live together, share income, work on common projects, and produce *The Furies*. By issue number 6 (August 1972), half the people working on the paper were new. We had seen *The Furies* as an organizing tool. We were now becoming unorganized ourselves. Our demise was caused by a combination of unresolved (in some cases unacknowledged) personal/political dynamics—which is a part of the story I will not attempt to deal with in this article—and a belief that we had said what we wanted to say in the paper and it was time to move on to other work. The dream of the tight-knit cadre, the vanguard of the revolution, was gone.

Response to *The Furies* was immediate and strong. The paper hit the lesbian communities around the country like a bombshell. Much of what we were saying about political lesbianism, and male supremacy, had been said before, in the "Woman-Identified Woman" paper *Lavender Menace* (out of New York City), and by Martha Shelley and Rita in *The Ladder*. But we were among the first to discuss heterosexuality as an institution, to devote so much thought to class analysis, and to go beyond the basic ideas of political lesbianism and male supremacy, expand them, and examine their ramifications for building a total politic. Lesbians throughout the country had experienced the same frustrations with the male Left, gay liberation, and women's liberation, and we were able to articulate an explanation, a direction, a cosmology, that many others were looking for. Women waited intently for each new issue to appear, and groups were formed to read and discuss the latest words from Washington, DC. For many straight

FIGURE 3: Subscription ad for *The Furies*. From staff archives.

women, *The Furies* was the impetus to come out. For many lesbians, *The Furies* gave political meaning and validation.

Exact circulation figures are lost, but Coletta remembers that we printed 3,000 copies of the first issue—we mailed out 1,200 free to the *off our backs* mailing list, sold quite a few through the women's and gay bookstores that were springing up around the country, and eventually sold the rest as copies of *The Furies* became collector's items.

We paid for the paper out of our own pockets—from the pool of money we collected each month from each woman's paycheck. We sold ads to women-owned businesses and services, but the cost for an ad was only $10, and we had very few of them. Most of our ads were, in fact, exchanges with other lesbian periodicals (see figure 3).

Needless to say, not all response was positive. We were accused of arrogance, elitism, communism, lesbian chauvinism, and general political incorrectness. Coletta told me a story about a trip she took to California during the summer of 1972. She was visiting a lesbian bar in San Francisco and had to get back to the East Bay, where she was spending the night. She asked a woman at the bar for a ride. When the woman found out that Coletta was a member of the Furies, she refused to give her a ride.

In all, nine issues were published over a period of fifteen months, with only Lee and Helaine left at the end from the original group. We had to change printers on a regular basis; there were no lesbian print shops then, that we could find, and male printers were too afraid of lawsuits, too afraid of being picketed, or just too afraid of lesbians to stay with us for very long. In the end, the only print shop that would handle *The Furies* was a pornographic press in Long Island.

Passionate politics leave their mark, whether positive or negative, or some of both. Out of the original Furies members came some of the women who founded and ran Diana Press, which published thirty-two books over a ten-year period; some of the women who founded Olivia Records, the national women's record company; some of the women who founded *Quest: A Feminist Quarterly*; some of the women who founded Women in Distribution. If we hadn't known before *The Furies*, we knew when we were done how to organize ourselves and others, and how to establish functioning, productive political projects—particularly those related to media. Some of us still hold a vision of a society that is free and just. Some of us still work diligently toward turning that vision into reality.

We're all quite a bit older now, and of the Furies with whom I still have contact I can say that we are not as angry, not as naive, not as self-righteous. For that reason, perhaps, I doubt that any of us now believe that we can create the movement that will change the world, but I would argue that our passion for justice has not diminished. As we outlined in the lead article of the very first issue:

> We want to build a movement in this country and in the world which can effectively stop the violent, sick, oppressive acts of male supremacy. We want to build a movement which makes all people free. For the Chinese women whose feet were bound and crippled; for the Ibibos of Africa whose clitori were mutilated; for every woman who has ever been raped, physically, economically, psychologically, we take the name of the FURIES, Goddesses of Vengeance and protectors of women.

NOTE

I want to thank Coletta Reid for helping to jog my memory about the details, and for helping me remember the context and the times in which we lived *The Furies*. The opinions herein are mine alone.

APPENDIX 1

THE FURIES (by Ginny Z. Berson)

The story of the Furies is the story of strong, powerful women, the "Angry Ones," the avengers of matricide, the protectors of women. Three Greek Goddesses, they were described (by men) as having snakes for hair, bloodshot eyes, and bats' wings; like Lesbians today, they were cursed and feared. They were born when Heaven (the male symbol) was castrated by his son at the urging of Earth (the female symbol). The blood from the wound fell on Earth and fertilized her, and the Furies were born. Their names were Alecto (Never-ceasing), Tisiphone (Avenger of Blood), and Magaera (Grudger). Once extremely powerful, they represented the supremacy of women and the primacy of mother right.

Their most famous exploit (famous because in it they lost much of their power) involved Orestes in the last episodes connected with the cycle of the Trojan War. Orestes, acting on the orders of the Sun God Apollo, killed his mother Clytemnestra, because she had killed his father. Clytemnestra had killed the father because he had sacrificed their daughter Iphigenia, in order to get favorable winds so his fleet could sail to Troy. The Furies tormented Orestes: they literally drove him crazy, putting him under a spell where for days he would not eat or wash his blood-stained hands. He bit off his finger to try to appease them, but to no avail. Finally, in desperation, Orestes went before the court of Athena to plead his case.

The point at issue was whether matricide was justifiable to avenge your father's murder, or, in other words, whether men or women were to dominate. Apollo defended Orestes and totally denied the importance of motherhood, claiming that women were no more than sperm receptacles for men, and that the father was the only parent worthy of the name. One might have thought that Athena, Goddess of Wisdom, would have condemned Orestes, but Athena was the creation of the male God, Zeus, sprung full-grown from his head, the first token woman. Athena decided for Orestes. Some mythologists say that Zeus, Athena, and Apollo had conspired from the beginning, ordering Orestes to kill his mother in order to put an end, once and for all, to the religious belief that motherhood was more divine than fatherhood. In any case, that was the result.

The Furies were, of course, furious, and threatened to lay waste the city of Athens. But Athena had a direct line to Zeus, King of the Gods; she told the Furies to accept the new male supremacist order or lose everything. Some of the Furies and their followers relented, the rest pursued Orestes until his death.

We call our paper *The Furies* because we are also angry. We are angry because we are oppressed by male supremacy. We have been fucked over all our lives by a system which is based on the domination of men over women, which defines male as good and female as only as good as the man you are with. It is a system in which heterosexuality is rigidly enforced and Lesbianism rigidly suppressed. It is a system which has further divided us by class, race, and nationality.

We are working to change this system which has kept us separate and powerless for so long. We are a collective of twelve lesbians living and working in Washington, D.C. We are rural and urban; from the Southwest, Midwest, South, and Northeast. Our ages range from 18 to 28. We are high school drop-outs and Ph.D. candidates. We are lower class, middle, and upper-middle class. We are white. Some of us have been Lesbians for twelve years, others for ten months. We are committed to ending all oppressions by attacking their roots—male supremacy.

We believe *The Furies* will make important contributions to the growing movement to destroy sexism. As a collective, in addition to outside projects, we are spending much time building an ideology which is the basis for action. For too long, women in the Movement have fallen prey to the very male propaganda they seek to refute. They have rejected thought, building an ideology, and all intellectual activity as the realm of men, and tried to build a politics based only on feelings—the area traditionally left to women. The philosophy has been, "If it feels good, it's O.K. If not, forget it." But that is like saying that strength, which is a "male" characteristic, should be left to men, and women should embrace weakness. Most straight women, to say nothing of men, feel afraid or contemptuous of Lesbians. That fear and contempt is similar to the feelings middle-class whites have towards Blacks or lower-class people. These feelings are the result of our socialization and are hardly worth glorifying. This is not to say that feelings are irrelevant, only that they are derived from our experience which is limited by our class, race, etc. Furthermore, feelings are too often used to excuse inaction and inability to change.

A political movement cannot advance without systematic thought and practical organization. The haphazard, nonstrategic, zig-zag tactics of the straight women's movement, the male left, and many other so-called revolutionary groups have led only to frustration and dissolution. We do not want to make those same mistakes; our ideology forms the basis for developing long-range strategies and short-term tactics, projects, and actions.

The base of our ideological thought is: Sexism is the root of all other oppressions, and Lesbian and woman oppression will not end by smashing capitalism, racism, and imperialism. Lesbianism is not a matter of sexual preference, but rather one of political choice which every woman must make if she is to become woman-identified and thereby end male supremacy. Lesbians, as outcasts from every culture but their own, have the most to gain by ending class, race, and national supremacy within their own ranks. Lesbians must get out of the straight women's movement and form their own movement in order to be taken seriously, to stop straight women from oppressing us, and to force straight women to deal with their own Lesbianism. Lesbians cannot develop a common politics with women who do not accept Lesbianism as a political issue.

In *The Furies* we will be dealing with these issues and sharing our thoughts with you. We want to build a movement in this country and in the world which can effectively stop the violent, sick, oppressive acts of male supremacy. We want to build a movement which makes all people free.

For the Chinese women whose feet were bound and crippled; for the Ibibos of Africa whose clitori were mutilated; for every woman who has ever been raped, physically, economically, psychologically, we take the name of *The Furies*, Goddesses of Vengeance and protectors of women.

========================== APPENDIX 2 ==========================

LESBIANS IN REVOLT (by Charlotte Bunch)

The development of Lesbian-Feminist politics as the basis for the liberation of women is our top priority; this article outlines our present ideas. In our society which defines all people and institutions for the benefit of the rich, white male, the Lesbian is in revolt. In revolt because she defines herself in terms of women and rejects the male definitions of how she should feel, act, look, and live. To be a Lesbian is to love oneself, woman, in a culture that denigrates and despises women. The Lesbian rejects male sexual/political domination; she defies his world, his social organization, his ideology, and his definition of her as inferior. Lesbianism puts women first while the society declares the male supreme. Lesbianism threatens male supremacy at its core. When politically conscious and organized, it is central to destroying our sexist, racist, capitalist, imperialist system.

Lesbianism Is a Political Choice

Male society defines Lesbianism as a sexual act, which reflects men's limited view of women: they think of us only in terms of sex. They also say Lesbians are not real women, so a real woman is one who gets fucked by men. We say that a Lesbian is a woman whose sense of self and energies, including sexual energies, center around women—she is woman-identified. The woman-identified woman commits herself to other women for political, emotional, physical, and economic support. Women are important to her. She is important to herself. Our society demands that commitment from women be reserved for men.

The Lesbian, woman-identified woman commits herself to women not only as an alternative to oppressive male/female relationships but primarily because she loves women. Whether consciously or not, by her actions, the Lesbian has recognized that giving support and love to men over women perpetuates the system that oppresses her. If women do not make a commitment to each other, which includes sexual love, we deny ourselves the love and value traditionally given to men. We accept our second-class status. When women do give primary energies to other women, then it is possible to concentrate fully on building a movement for our liberation.

Woman-identified Lesbianism is, then, more than a sexual preference; it is a political choice. It is political because relationships between men and women are essentially political; they involve power and dominance. Since the Lesbian actively rejects that relationship and chooses women, she defies the established political system.

Lesbianism, By Itself, Is Not Enough

Of course, not all Lesbians are consciously woman-identified, nor are all committed to finding common solutions to the oppression they suffer as women and Lesbians. Being a Lesbian is part of challenging male supremacy, but not the end. For the Lesbian or heterosexual woman, there is no individual solution to oppression.

The Lesbian may think that she is free since she escapes the personal oppression of the individual male/female relationship. But to the society she is still a woman, or worse, a visible Lesbian. On the street, at the job, in the schools, she is treated as an inferior and is at the mercy of men's power and whims. (I've never heard of a rapist who stopped because his victim was a Lesbian.) This society hates women who love women, and so the Lesbian who escapes male dominance in her private home receives it doubly at the hands of male society; she is harassed, outcast, and shuttled to the bottom. Lesbians must become feminists and fight against woman oppression, just as feminists must become Lesbians if they hope to end male supremacy.

U.S. society encourages individual solutions, apolitical attitudes, and reformism to keep us from political revolt and out of power. Men who rule, and male leftists who seek to rule, try to depoliticize sex and the relations between men and women in order to prevent us from acting to end our oppression and challenging their power. As the question of homosexuality has become public, reformists define it as a private question of who you sleep with in order to sidetrack our understanding of the politics of sex. For the Lesbian-Feminist, it is not private; it is a political matter of oppression, domination, and power. Reformists offer solutions which make no basic changes in the system that oppresses us, solutions which keep power in the hands of the oppressor. The only way oppressed people end their oppression is by seizing power: People whose rule depends on the subordination of others do not voluntarily stop oppressing others. Our subordination is the basis of male power.

Sexism Is the Root of All Oppression

The first division of labor, in pre-history, was based on sex: men hunted; women built the villages, took care of children, and farmed. Women collectively controlled the land, language, culture, and the communities. Men were able to conquer women with the weapons that they developed for hunting when it became clear that women were leading a more stable, peaceful, and desirable existence. We do not know exactly how this conquest took place, but it is clear that the original imperialism was male over female: the male claiming the female body and her service as his territory (or property).

Having secured the domination of women, men continued this pattern of suppressing people, now on the basis of tribe, race, and class. Although there have been numerous battles over class, race, and nation during the past 3,000 years, none has brought the liberation of women. While these other forms of oppression must be ended, there is no reason to believe that our liberation will come with the smashing of capitalism, racism, or imperialism today. Women will be free only when we concentrate on fighting male supremacy.

Our war against male supremacy does, however, involve attacking the latter-day dominations based on class, race, and nation. As Lesbians who are outcasts from every group, it would be suicidal to perpetuate these man-made divisions among ourselves. We have no heterosexual privileges, and when we publicly assert our Lesbianism, those of us who had them lose many of our class and race privileges. Most of our privileges as women are granted to us by our relationships to men (fathers, husbands, boyfriends) whom we now reject. This does not mean that there is no racism or class chauvinism within us, but we must destroy these divisive remnants of privileged behavior among ourselves as the first step toward their destruction in the society. Race, class, and national oppressions come from men, serve ruling-class white men's interests, and have no place in a woman-identified revolution.

Lesbianism Is the Basic Threat to Male Supremacy

Lesbianism is a threat to the ideological, political, personal, and economic basis of male supremacy. The Lesbian threatens the ideology of male supremacy by destroying the lie about female inferiority, weakness, passivity, and by denying women's "innate" need for men. Lesbians literally do not need men (even for procreation if the science of cloning is developed).

The Lesbians' independence and refusal to support one man undermines the personal power that men exercise over women. Our rejection of heterosexual sex challenges male domination in its most individual and common form. We offer all women something better than submission to personal oppression. We offer the beginning of the end of collective and individual male supremacy. Since men of all races and classes depend on female support and submission for practical tasks and feeling superior, our refusal to submit will force some to examine their sexist behavior, to break down their own destructive privileges over other humans, and to fight against those privileges in other men. They will have to build new selves that do not depend on oppressing women and learn to live in social structures that do not give them power over anyone.

Heterosexuality separates women from each other; it makes women define themselves through men; it forces women to compete against each other for men and the privilege which comes through men and their social standing. Heterosexual society offers women a few privileges as compensation if they give up their freedom: for example, mothers are respected and "honored," wives or lovers are socially accepted and given some economic and emotional security, a woman gets physical protection on the street when she stays with her man, etc. The privileges give heterosexual women a personal and political stake in maintaining the status quo.

The Lesbian receives none of these heterosexual privileges or compensations since she does not accept the male demands on her. She has little vested interest in maintaining the present political system since all of its institutions—church, state, media, health, schools—work to keep her down. If she understands her oppression, she has nothing to gain by supporting white rich male America and much to gain from fighting to change it. She is less prone to accept reformist solutions to women's oppression.

Economics is a crucial part of woman oppression, but our analysis of the relationship between capitalism and sexism is not complete. We know that Marxist economic theory does not sufficiently consider the role of women or Lesbians, and we are presently working on this area.

However, as a beginning, some of the ways that Lesbians threaten the economic system are clear: In this country, women work for men in order to survive, on the job and in the home. The Lesbian rejects this division of labor at its roots; she refuses to be a man's property, to submit to the unpaid labor system of housework and childcare. She rejects the nuclear family as the basic unit of production and consumption in capitalist society.

The Lesbian is also a threat on the job because she is not the passive/part-time woman worker that capitalism counts on to do boring work and be part of a surplus labor pool. Her identity and economic support do not come through men, so her job is crucial and she cares about job conditions, wages, promotion, and status. Capitalism cannot absorb large numbers of women demanding stable employment, decent salaries, and refusing to accept their traditional job exploitation. We do not understand yet the total effect that this increased job dissatisfaction will have. It is, however, clear that, as women become more intent upon taking control of their lives, they will seek more control over their jobs, thus increasing the strains on capitalism and enhancing the power of women to change the economic system.

Lesbians Must Form Our Own Movement To Fight Male Supremacy

Feminist-Lesbianism, as the most basic threat to male supremacy, picks up part of the Women's Liberation analysis of sexism and gives it force and direction. Women's Liberation lacks direction now because it has failed to understand the importance of heterosexuality in maintaining male supremacy and because it has failed to face class and race as real differences in women's behavior and political needs. As long as straight women see Lesbianism as a bedroom issue, they hold back the development of politics and strategies which would put an end to male supremacy and they give men an excuse for not dealing with their sexism.

Being a Lesbian means ending identification with, allegiance to, dependence on, and support of heterosexuality. It means ending your personal stake in the male world so that you join women, individually and collectively, in the struggle to end your oppression. Lesbianism is the key to liberation and only women who cut their ties to male privilege can be trusted to remain serious in the struggle against male dominance. Those who remain tied to men, individually or in political theory, cannot always put women first. It is not that heterosexual women are evil or do not care about women. It is because the very essence, definition, and nature of heterosexuality is men first. Every woman has experienced that desolation when her sister puts her man first in the final crunch: heterosexuality demands that she do so. As long as women still benefit from heterosexuality, receive its privileges and security, they will at some point have to betray their sisters, especially Lesbian sisters who do not receive those benefits.

Women in women's liberation have understood the importance of having meetings and other events for women only. It has been clear that dealing with men divides us and saps our energies and that it is not the job of the oppressed to explain our oppression to the oppressor. Women also have seen that, collectively, men will not deal with their sexism until they are forced to do so. Yet, many of these same women continue to have primary relationships with men individually and do not understand why Lesbians find this oppressive. Lesbians cannot grow politically or personally in a situation which denies the basis of our politics: that Lesbianism is political, that heterosexuality is crucial to maintaining male supremacy.

Lesbians must form our own political movement in order to grow. Changes which will have more than token effects on our lives will be led by woman-identified Lesbians who understand the nature of our oppression and are therefore in a position to end it.

This article originally appeared in *The Furies*, no.1 (January 1972). It was reprinted in *Lesbianism and the Women's Movement*, ed. Nancy Myron and Charlotte Bunch (San Francisco: Diana Press, 1975), 29–37. It is reprinted here with permission of Diana Press.

THE DENTIST (by Ginny Z. Berson)

All the way to the dentist she thought of Jennifer. Of how it got better all the time, every night. Of how incredible it felt to love someone like that. To want them so much that her body ached at knowing that it would be hours before they would be together again. Last night had been the best, and her insides stirred and trembled at the thought of their passion—hands lips legs tongue on ears neck breasts cunt—"I am loving you." Morning coming and not wanting to get out of bed ever—to hold each other, talk, make love. Thinking with sadness now, instead of her usual anger and scorn, that all women were not Lesbians, that all women did not know, would not let themselves know, feel, love again—Jennifer of "I am loving you," never said to her like that before.

The parking lot at the clinic was half empty. The day was gray and the ground was covered with puddles. The clinic was equally gray, the magazines in the waiting room at least six months old, one of the small prices one pays for not going to a private dentist. She sat with an old *Life* open on her lap, thinking of Jennifer. Her name was called and she moved quickly in the office, eager to get it over with. The dentist was surprised to see a white woman enter, and was ashamed for her. As he poked around her mouth he poked around her life: "Are you a student?" "Why aren't you married?" "Ah, but you do have a boyfriend?" A job? A family? A life? She answered in grunts, submerging her desire to tell him to shut up, can you just fix my teeth, can't you just be a dentist instead of a man? Of course not. She knew.

The nurse filled the needle. Her mouth wide open, his finger stretching it more, he poised over her and said, "If you come to my private office, I can give you much better treatment." "I can't afford it." "It could be free." The needle went into her gum but she did not feel it. Screaming, swearing, glass smashing, heavy feet stomping his face in, knees flying to his prick, kicking kicking over and over until there was nothing left but a useless sagging mass of flesh. A knife in his guts tearing them out while he retched on the floor in total agony and pain unimagined before. He pulled out the needle. "No thank you," she said.

He drilled and filled for the next twenty minutes, chatting all the while about his private practice, the great sacrifice he made by working at the clinic twice a week, how if any conflict arose of course his private patients came first—"A man has to make a living, doesn't he?" He only filled two—there were two more to do next week—she would have to come back. He handed her his card as she got up to leave. "Come see me some time." "Right, I will." He walked out of the office into the waiting room. "Next?"

All the way home she tried to think of Jennifer and couldn't.

From *The Furies*, no. 1 (January 1972): 4.

At This End of the Oregon Trail: The Eugene AUGUR, 1969-1974

PETER JENSEN

"Twenty years ago today," goes the Sgt. Pepper song and the memories of America's underground press. We thought we were Camus writing for *Le Combat* in Nazi-occupied France. An alien force had taken over our country: it talked peace and made vicious war; it owned both political parties. We were all that was left of the opposition, but we were everywhere in the streets in mass demonstrations and sinking new roots in old communities all over America. Above all, the media had caved in and was reporting inflated daily body counts for generals in Saigon and Washington. For all our "freedom of the press," the press was just another chain of corporations acting like a line of skimpily dressed cheerleaders for the boys in grunt green, who were fighting against the will of 80 percent of the people in a small but tough country 9,000 miles away across the world's widest ocean.

By 1969, it was obvious that the National Liberation Front (NLF) of South Vietnam was winning its war. This fact shook the established American Empire to its core. On April Fool's Day 1968, a Democratic president resigned. On Inhoguration Day 1969, a crooked Republican lawyer from Orange County was sworn in as president of some of the people some of the time. We knew we were in for a long air-war bombing campaign to punish the NLF for winning in the countryside, and megatons upon megatons of lies (see appendix).

Most of the people who started underground papers in their towns were in their twenties or thirties and were veterans (since 1960) of the peace and antiwar movements. Most were also far from home trying to live in college towns after they were done with school. The people who started the *AUGUR* in Eugene represented both fronts: antiwar and alternative community. Both groups of activists were action-oriented: they set out to make the news and then write about it. This style of journalism was not new in America. American revolutionary journalist Tom Paine wrote George Washington's newsletter, *Common Sense*, after each battle, explaining

---

Editor's note: Jensen is so, as he says, "suspicious and curious" about today's political climate that he requested, and received the editor's reluctant agreement, that his original piece from the first edition be reprinted rather than updated, "sealed up as a time capsule," he said. "My opinion has changed so radically from when I wrote the piece that it would require not just an update but a complete rewrite including in style and political beliefs. Maybe it's because I'm older and more cautious but I have no idea what's on the table now; this isn't the America we grew up in."

the strategic retreat to Valley Forge and the British warships' firebombing of Kingston, New York—a war crime to remember on the Hudson River. This kind of journalism demanded a very fierce, engaged objectivity. From the start in Eugene, antiwar demonstrations and new food co-ops, free clinics, and concerts got equal press.

What people called "the movement" of the sixties and seventies was an anti-fascist movement. Other wings of this movement were the liberation movements of Third World people and Native Americans; the women's liberation movement; a community-based war against narcs who were dealing drugs; the gay liberation movement; the radical environmental movement; the alternative small business movement; and what people called the hippie, alternative-culture movement. Most of us tried to embrace all of these wings: we wanted to forge a new majority. The *AUGUR* was started by a small crew of community activists around the Wootens' Odyssey Coffee House and the Oregon Country Fair (see figure 1); then it passed over to a group I belonged to—a collective of Students for a Democratic Society (SDSers) from the University of Oregon. But often, we could not serve all trends fully. At first, women on the *AUGUR* staff introduced our community to the basics of women's liberation. Later, around 1972, some lesbian and non-lesbian women broke off because they wanted to concentrate on women's issues and because they had become "separatists." They established *Women's Press*, a nationally important publication that still exists today as a regional publication. News of the women's movement, however, continued to receive major coverage in the pages of the *AUGUR*.

The streets of Eugene were filled with demonstrators—at least four major marches a year. The paper staff helped plan each march, called for it in the pages of our paper, went out and marched, spoke at rallies, took photographs, came back and wrote our stories and criticisms (see figure 2), sold ads, worked in the darkroom, did layout, took the paper to our printer, did distribution, and sold papers in the streets. Although some of us were experts, we held that everyone should learn to do everything. We tried to come out with a new edition every two weeks. We had a rotating editorship whose role was to coordinate the story list, and an ad sales coordinator for every issue. Most of us had other part-time jobs. Many of us counted on the income from each paper (a dime out of 25 cents) to help pay rents. We printed as many as 4,000 in each run, but we sent out almost 1,000 free subscriptions to prisoners, and we exchanged with many other collectives. Many of us got food stamps; for the first time, many of us lived below the poverty line while working hard and inventing new ways of cheaper and more natural collective living. I lived in an *AUGUR* collective house of two men and two women—a couple and two singles. I was too busy to worry.

At that time, Eugene had 54,000 inhabitants. Today, it has grown to 106,000, but it is still surrounded by a belt of farms and a further-out sea of cutover national and private forestlands. Organic agriculture and destructive forestry practices dominated our paper from the start. In 1970, women from the *AUGUR* collective attended a conference on women's health issues in British Columbia. There, they met a Cambodian woman doctor who had walked seven hundred miles in the jungles of Indochina and had flown to Canada from China. She told them of the massive numbers of cancers, birth defects, and miscarriages caused by spraying herbicides (among them, Agent Orange) to destroy the rain forests, which provided cover for the NLF. This was a war crime we called "ecocide." That same year, Air Force doctors halted the spraying, and an Oregon State forestry professor, "Spray for an A" Mike Newton, added water and sprayed Oregon forestlands with those same banned herbicides. Thus began a twenty-year battle to

the Augur

VOL. 1   October 14, 1969   Eugene, Oregon

Have you the courage
to start over?

FIGURE 1: Cover of AUGUR volume 1, number 1 (October 14, 1969), the first issue, put out by the small crew of community activists around the Wootens' Odyssey Coffee House and the Oregon Country Fair who founded the paper. Image from AUGUR archives. Courtesy Peter Jensen.

FIGURE 2: The AUGUR staff planned marches, participated in them, and then wrote about them. This photograph was from AUGUR volume 1, number 7 (January 20–February 2, 1970). The original caption read: "Marching through campus Thursday, radical students chanted, rapped with other students, swelled their numbers to over two hundred, and then diminished them in a two and a half hour exercise that marked the beginning of a winter offensive against ROTC, corporate recruiting, the buying of grapes, and for the establishing of a day care center for University staff and student's children. Activity ended for the day in Johnson Hall, the administration building, with a meeting in the hallway, a meeting that was joined unexpectedly by President Clark. He talked with the students twenty minutes or so. Meanwhile, twenty-five students joined the picket lines at the Huntington Shingle Strike across town." Photo by Rick Hillman. From AUGUR archives. Courtesy Peter Jensen.

stop the use of herbicides, which caused miscarriages, birth defects, and still-to-be-detected cancers in rural communities all around Eugene. The war had come home to America in an insidious way none of us had suspected; the fetuses of our people would suffer, while the so-called "right-to-lifers" were pro-industry and full of hypocrisy.

There were plans for a system of concentric freeways around Eugene, and more nuclear power plants in Oregon. The AUGUR staff helped lead the fight against those gross developments, and quality-of-life issues are still at the heart of Eugene community politics. In 1972, we campaigned for and won a citywide referendum requiring a vote on all new limited-access freeway proposals inside city limits. Some of us went into local politics: the Eugene City Council, the Lane County Commission, and the Oregon legislature. Many of us are still in activist organizations working for progressive social change, with this difference: we are now getting paid for our work.

It's interesting to note that all of the underground papers had so much in common. We had fun looking over other papers; we put them on our mailing list and exchanged with papers all over the country. We often took strength or articles or ideas from other papers. Some of our favorites were the *Great Speckled Bird*, the *Berkeley Tribe*, *Akwesasne Notes*, *off our backs*, *The Black Panther*, and the *Ann Arbor Sun*. Later, an underground press "syndicate" was born, and our very own news service, Liberation News Service (LNS), was sent every week from New York. LNS provided us with the best graphics, cartoons, stories, and short news flashes from many sources. Eugene is over six hundred miles from San Francisco or Seattle; we like it that way, but we needed big city information to turn out a good small-city newspaper.

There were many local roots here for radicals. Eugene was the hometown of Oregon senator Wayne Morse, one of two senators who voted against the war from the beginning. Ken Kesey, author of *One Flew over the Cuckoo's Nest* and *Sometimes a Great Notion*, lives up the hill in Pleasant Hill. In the early seventies, both were frequent speakers, and they represented well, for a while, two wings of Eugene's identity at that time: the serious political activist and the jesting cultural trickster. In addition, the Woodsmen of the World, some of them IWW (Industrial Workers of the World) Wobblies and wood products union activists, had built a dance hall here in 1932, and this WOW Hall was rebuilt and became a center for dances, concerts, poetry readings, theater, fundraisers, and community talent shows.

We found places in the local economy to sink our roots for money. One of the most important phases of forestry—tree planting: replacing the two hundred ancient forest species with ten-inch Douglas-fir seedling crop trees—was an unorganized and exploited part of the economy. The Hoedads were the first forestry workers' cooperative that did quality work at a living wage. This cooperative is just one of many that formed. Food production, farming, food distribution and sales, baking, restaurants, clothing, garages, music groups—people tried out all of the basic parts of the economy in cooperative form. In fact, we could not have published the *AUGUR* without these businesses. They were our advertisers; they provided our staff with jobs; their retail stores were some of our most important sales counters. And the more we developed, the more we found that we had been preceded by a wave of Eugene-area cooperatives in the thirties. The local milk distributor was started by dairy farmers as a cooperative in the Great Depression. One of the plywood mills was owned by four remaining members of a larger co-operative. We found that in many ways, the thirties had laid down a foundation for us in the sixties. We made it because they made it.

The *AUGUR* office was a confusing, exciting place to work. People with good ideas mixed with people with half-vast ideas. We were full of courage and paranoia, wisdom and foolishness. The FBI tried to shut us down. Agents approached our printer and tried to bully him, but he was an old union activist, and he smiled as he told us what he said to them: "I'm a small businessman and a capitalist. These people always pay their bills, and I need their money. Besides, I think their paper is a kick!" (Our printer had been a jazz musician in the 1930s.) He always helped us plan our color bleeds on the cover, our "tie-dyed art" covers. The IRS tried to shut us down. Agents came to our staff meeting and asked all the wrong questions, like "Who's in charge here?" A circle of rather hairy people just laughed at them. The agents had never before met a tightly knit group of anarchists, and we had a lot of fun with them.

Both narcs and local hard-drug dealers tried to shut us down. Agents threatened us from both sides of the "war on drugs." We were fond of publishing pictures of undercover narcs busting local pot growers and smokers, and we were fed these photos by a large shadowy collection of people who called themselves "People into Sabotaging Surveillance" (PISS). When we found that the owners at one drug paraphernalia store, who advertised with us, were dealing cocaine, we picketed them and published a story on their drug dealing. When we were visited by a local hood with polished black shoes, who offered us a drug profits deal, I ran for our camera, but he escaped while threatening us harm. Of course, once the Vietnam vets were back and organized into a four-hundred-member Lane County chapter of Vietnam Veterans Against the War (VVAW), we felt a lot safer. In fact, once they took over organizing the demonstrations, we often defeated or stalemated the sheriff's department in the streets. Soon, Vietnam vets and women were working as cops in the Eugene Police Department, and some of the police agents who attended our meetings were on our side!

One time, in 1971, we put out a paper for a demonstration that promised to be huge (four thousand) by Eugene standards, and pretending this would be the start of the "revolution," we called on all demonstrators to wear wool watch caps, heavy jackets, and bandanas for tear gas. We knew no one sane would wear all that stuff on a hot summer night in "mellow little Eugene," so we organized a seven-person camera team that consisted of one photographer with a flash and six defenders, and we took photos of all men in watch caps and heavy jackets; they all turned out to be cops, which made a nice two-page spread of undercover cop photos. And we sang: "All we are saying is pull down your pants." When things got really heavy in Cambodia in spring 1970, a couple of us were busted as part of the Eugene Thirteen, because we were on a list of folks who had held a bullhorn more than ten times each, and we were falsely charged with felony riot—"Must bust in early May / Orders from the D.A." (Bob Dylan)—under an unconstitutional law that had been passed to bust Chinese railroad workers. They had built Oregon's early rail lines in the late 1800s and then, once they were finished, were told they were not welcome to stay. We were part of this proud heritage. Charges were dropped three years later.

By 1973, with Watergate and all, the worm had turned on our enemies. I remember one peace demonstration a month after Nixon had bombed Hanoi and Haiphong on Christmas and lost one-third of his bomber force. We were getting ready to march, but the Eugene city council had issued us a march permit to start at 1:00 P.M., and our marchers were late in forming up. An older cop in a car told us we couldn't march, but a younger motorcycle cop with a beard drove up and asked me, "Where are we going, brother?" I nearly cried; it was such a change.

Often, we felt out of touch with modern Amerika, which we always spelled with a "k" the way Franz Kafka and my Danish grandparents had. We felt like immigrants from another time zone. The origin of the *AUGUR*'s name, meaning a bird priest from ancient Rome, was appropriate to Oregon, where there still is an environment with some birds to defend. Our paper's logo featured a bearded old guy in a toga reading meanings (auguries) from the patterns of flights of birds and writing down Nature's messages. The Lower Willamette Valley used to be home to hundreds of thousands of waterfowl, hundreds of bald eagles, and the Kalapooyan tribe. Now we have a few wintering eagles we share with Alaska, 60,000 ducks in a good year in local leftover wetlands, and nothing but stones, bones, and baskets left by the peaceful Kalapooyans.

Much has been written about the meaning of the culture of the sixties, and in Eugene, a city the *Wall Street Journal* called "a mecca for the terminally hip," that culture lives on as a mainstream for a quickly aging generation. The *AUGUR* was one of the mainstays of that

FIGURE 3: Cover of AUGUR volume 3, number 11 (March 24–April 7, 1972), publicizing an upcoming appearance by the San Francisco Mime Troupe, a favorite of the AUGUR staff as well as a supporter of the paper. Image from AUGUR archives. Courtesy Peter Jensen.

culture. We always had a poetry page, and I often edited it and printed the best local poetry I could find. Many of us did music and theater reviews; most of the music was political or rebellious. Remembering is as easy as putting on a tape. The San Francisco Mime Troupe was our favorite, and some of their local income went into printing our paper (see figure 3). The record stores were some of our truest advertisers. I always wondered why we were called the "alternative" culture. Sinatra was mainstream for his generation; why were the Beatles and the Grateful Dead not mainstream for ours? When I think of the passions and the big ideas of my own life, the culture of my generation is my blood's mainstream. What else was there: the death kulture of the Pentagon?

Much also has been written about sex, drugs, and nonviolence, and all that was a lot of fun for some of us. In Oregon, Nature gave us a somewhat gentler ride, as we tripped and skinny-dipped and tried to keep the faith. The movement here was quite artistic, and Nature inspired many of the graphics we printed in the *AUGUR*. There is something about a full moon rising out of a snow-covered volcano that neither a coyote nor a human being can resist. Nature makes us wail, and our photography, art works, and street guerrilla theater groups were full of the sexy juice of our mother Earth. Often, I felt we were overripe fruit dribbling down the chin of some giant faces, but when I compared that image with the body bags from 'Nam, I knew that our little messes were just humanity living it up somewhere in the surrounding galaxy. When our time is evaluated, I want to be there to make the case for our generation's culture starting the American Renaissance, no matter how long it lasts.

The underground press was full of this rebirth of science and spirit. The highs and the lows, the excitement and the bitter pain were all part of that coming out of the womb of our parents' world. They had endured the Great Depression and helped to win World War II; we inherited their survival instincts and their victories. Our paper helped to unify people and give them a shared vision of what was happening. Stories on organic gardening flowed into stories on ancient poets flowed into stories on Vietnamese villages being bombed with flaming napalm, but rebuilding into tunnels and caves flowed into feminist writings about women's orgasms and health clinics flowed into struggles of Native Americans to keep the culture of Raven and Eagle alive flowed into saving French Pete Creek with its streamside hiking trail flowed into nutritional information on organic foods flowed into medical and mental health care flowed into viewing an eclipse of the moon at 4:00 A.M. flowed into community housing and historic preservation flowed into the *AUGUR*'s cartoonists dueling the forces of darkness.

My main point is that cultural alienation ended; everything was connected to everything else, and our writing style was free to flow. Our paper layout reflected the electric rock-and-roll power of our culture. Sure it was new-lefty, trippy-hippy, but it moved us because it was our own, and if it failed us, we could always change. Anyway, you can't stick your foot in the same era twice. Here, by the Willamette and McKenzie rivers, it is obvious reality is always on the move. Often, we had to let those changes roll over the pages of our paper. Many layout nights, we were up until dawn making changes until the car left for the printer ninety miles away just up the Yaquina River from Newport on the Oregon coast.

The *AUGUR* went under in 1974. Sure, we were burned out, but it's still hard to say why. We learned that publications also have lives of their own. *Women's Press* continued for a few more years. Some of the *AUGUR* staff helped create the next community-based paper, the *Willamette Valley Observer*, which lasted from 1975 to 1984. Some of us started *10-point 5 arts magazine*, which lasted from 1974 to 1981. In 1984, a new community paper, *What's Happening*, took over the niche first occupied by the *AUGUR*, and it is doing well today. *What's Happening* is a free paper that survives and pays decent wages on advertising income only. What a far cry from earning 10 cents per copy of the *AUGUR* on the street corner to pay one's rent in the long-ago exciting times, when we thought we were making a revolution, and our excited readers thought so, too!

Now I'm forty-seven years old, teaching college, and working to raise money for conservation work in Oregon. I have an interesting box of all the old *AUGUR*s in my closet with a collection of photos with waxed backs. I tried to donate the papers to the periodical section of the University of Oregon's library, but a friend there told me they didn't have the money to microfilm them. "They'll get stolen issue by issue," he said. So they're still in my closet, and almost every time I clean, I get caught up and trapped in the past looking them over. Grassroots history is hiding in my closet. Actually, early in the history of the *AUGUR* (and I suspect this happened to most other "undergrounds" as well), Northwestern University in Evanston, Illinois, bought a library subscription and told us they had grant money (from Bell and Howell) to microfilm all the underground papers in America. So that's where our collective archives are for anyone interested in doing research on those times. We suspected that the CIA might have paid for all that microfilming, but who knows? Northwestern is one of the most heavily endowed universities. Anyway, leave it to the CIA to study the last domestic, democratic upsurge, while the next one builds behind their backs like a tsunami. It was CIA intellectuals who said that once 6 percent of the Vietnamese were willing to pick up a gun, the war was lost; but presidents don't listen to CIA "eggheads" either. By the time the White House and the Pentagon woke up, Vietnamese teenagers were armed to the teeth.

I don't know what can recreate those times for younger folks. Despite all the strange events between 1969 (and the end of the Vietnam War in 1975) and the present, I feel a connection to those times that will not die. The revolution never happened; our generation has not come to power in America with a transforming vision for democracy. Yuppies replaced Yippies in advertising. The Reagan years spread out against the sky like a war machine stalled within its own borders. The New Right enjoyed obscene amounts of media and money power—more than we even dreamed of—but what did it get them? Colonel Ollie North with chocolate cake on his face in Tehran? The idiot Contras? Reagan knighted by the English Queen? Tammy Bakker's eye makeup? Dan Quayle next to the White House? A Supreme Kourt that says you can burn the flag some of the time, but you can't control your body all the time? With these people, the right to life ends at birth! They still don't know what the hell they're doing. Remember Vietnam? Remember nuclear power? Remember Bhopal and Prince William Sound? They've been screwing up for decades and wasting the power of our country. Now, a trillion dollars deeper in debt, we still need a "rebirth of wonder."

But life, at the local level, goes on. The Vietnamese won their war for freedom and independence. The United States still needs a Solidarity movement and a radical, Gorbachev-type restructuring. Most of the liberation movements in the world have suffered and matured. Some have turned weird from too much pain. But the planet is in grave danger from the nonrenewable world economy. We knew it back then, and we were frightened in the sixties by our dark vision of the poisoning of the planet. That was like a bad acid trip back then. Now, we're twenty years further into the destruction, and the living Earth is in much more serious trouble, with continental-sized holes in the ozone over both poles and atmospheric warming. The destroyers of the planet can never say they weren't warned. Just as we chanted during the antiwar movement in the streets, they still need to respond when we say, "Join us!" Sometimes, twenty years ago today seems like yesterday. In the life of our species, twenty years is just one breath in and one breath out.

As the Voyager 2 space probe rounds Neptune and dives out of the solar system, it's painfully obvious that not all blue planets support life. Thanks to Carl Sagan and many others, the technology of the early seventies is still sending us family photos from the outer planets. Thomas Jefferson wrote that each generation needs to make its own revolution. I'm still waiting and writing. Goodbye, Voyager 2! Write if you find work.

APPENDIX

THE AIRWAR & THEN . . . MORE WAR! (by Peter Jensen)

While 40 thousand NVA trash Nixon's Vietnamization, & perhaps his President[i]al hopes, along with the NLF attacks out of Cambodia & the Central Highlands, here's a review of what has led up to this massive offensive. While we were at the Santa Barbara Conference on the San Diego demonstrations, we were told that all of the scattered attacks in Indochina were carried out by local militia, & that the NLF-NVA main forces were lying low. Now we know where they were & why. But the months & years preceding have been filled with deception & escalation by the most hated President of the United States. Using all the public relations power of his position, Nixon pretended to be winding down the war, but here are the terrible large numbers which describe an escalated war.

All the confusion about the war winding down was deliberate, guaranteed to give Nixon time to make the same devastating mistakes as LBJ. U.S. GI's killed in action did drop 90% in four years: 1968—15,000 killed, 1969—9,400 killed, & 1971—1,400 killed. & with the change to ARVN dead, the cost of the war was cut in half, from $90,000 for each American killed. Nixon, the supreme racist, had succeeded in changing the color of the corpses. Last year about 22,000 ARVN soldiers were killed, & according to Pentagon figures, total Asian military casualties per month have almost doubled: 4,300/month (LBJ) & 7,400/month (Nixon). The monthly civilian toll under Nixon is 130,000—compared to 95,000 under LBJ. The Liberal demand of 1968—that the South Vietnamese do their own fighting—has been turned into double genocide.

Nixon has also escalated the airwar & expanded heavy bombing to 4 countries. Since WW II, the U.S. Military has unsuccessfully attempted to bomb small Asian nations back into the stone age—the measure of U.S. barbarism can be summed up in this table of Pentagon figures:

```
KOREAN. . . . . . . . . . . . . . . . . . . . . . . . . . . . . . . . 1 million tons bombs dropped
ALL OF WW II . . . . . . . . . . . . . . . . . . . . . . . . . . . . . . . .2 million tons
VIETNAM (1965–68, LBJ's Operation Rolling Thunder. . . . . . . . . . . . 3,215,000 tons
VIETNAM & INDOCHINA (1969–March 72, Nixon's AIRWAR). . . . . . .3,776,000 tons
```

On top of that, Nixon's monthly average was way ahead of LBJ's: Monthly average, LBJ years—59,704 vs. monthly average, Nixon years—95,402 tons. If we add the projected tons that Nixon will drop until Nov. 1972, there will be a total of 4.5 million tons of bombs for Nixon's "wound down" war. Nixon has ordered the Air Force & Navy pilots to double LBJ's records of their bombing of Northern Laos—he has now dropped 6,000 lbs. of explosives for every person in N. Laos. Despite the fact that Nixon never announced that he reversed LBJ's 1968 decision to halt the bombing of North Vietnam, Nixon has ordered enough "protective reaction strikes" to be near LBJ's prehalt bombing levels. Now that the NVA offensive has ar[r]ogantly been labeled an "invasion," a 500 plane raid on N. Vietnam may be in the making, if U.S. planes can save ARVN first. Of course, the N. Vietnamese are the last to be deceived by talk of a bombing halt—in Santa Barbara we saw films of a recently bombed hospital near Hanoi. Nearby, protected by anti-aircraft batteries, people were draining & rebuilding a pond in a park to make it more beautiful.

Actually, these huge tonnage levels are deceptive, since the number of real heavy bombs dropped by Nixon has gone down in favor of more fragmentation & napalm bombs. The killing power & the numbers of these horrible anti-personnel weapons have increased under Nixon. The round metal bb pellets of older fragmentation bombs have been exchanged for impossible to x-ray, fiberglass, sharp-edged fragments. Often a surgeon can only slit the stomach from top to bottom, empty the contents, search for & remove the frags, replace the entrails & sew up the stomach like a football. One frag left in can be fatal. U.S. napalm has become more adhesive, & the super napalm with white phosphorus, "willy peter," now in wide use, burns right through flesh & bones, goes on burning inside until it is burnt out.

& the Electronic Battlefield, which has only lately come to the attention of the U.S. Senate, has actually been gaining in application since the days of Robert McNamara. There are already tens of thousands of sensors scattered all over Asia. Like the plastic plants on the L.A. Freeways, they are disguised as plants & designed to pick up footsteps & trucks. The sensors are supposed to radio data to a circling plane or drone, which relays the totals back to the Air Force's computer banks in Nakhon Phanom, Thailand. This center then orders air strikes. (Incidently, these computers are linked to the ones in the underground Pentagon & probably to the computer banks in San Diego, which select targets for bombing raids for all of Indochina.) In reality, these sensors can be triggered by a child running, a water buffalo, a tiger, or the wind; & the local communist forces have learned to move quietly, so that the Pentagon had to buy millions of "button bomblets," disguised as lumps of animal shit, that pop like firecrackers if they are stepped on.

It isn't difficult to see why the NVA & NLF have launched their offensives. Hundreds of thousands of troops are no longer necessary to carry out U.S. foreign policy. S.E. Asia is one big electronic battlefield, so what the armed forces need is not large quantities of oppressed, unskilled & undedicated soldiers, but qualified technicians & pilots. While we were down in San Diego looking over the convention & demonstration sites, we saw a fascist bumper sticker, which sums up Nixon's War: FIGHTER PILOTS DO IT BETTER. It doesn't seem to matter what more than 73% of the American people want—small nazi-type clubs of pilots (the all-white Black Widowers is infamous) simply love to kill & destroy in the name of America. But since the NVA troops brought SAM missiles & anti-aircraft guns with them, it's obvious they are prepared for the sharks of the air. & the Electronic Battlefield has vulnerable connections here in America. The credit for all the torture weapons & their new-fangled surveillance-intelligence systems counterparts goes to the Military Research Network (MRN). MRN is a network of university laboratories & research institutes without which the U.S. could not have attempted to suppress Asian national liberation struggles. Across America, in sabotage attacks not always covered in the straight press, military research centers have been located & bombed by the paramilitary wing of our movement. There have also been many acts of assembly-line sabotage, & these will increase. Overground propaganda attacks have been launched against war manufacturers: a boycott has been called on Wonder-(shit) bread, a subsidiary of ITT, because Wonderbread also makes electronic sensors, which organize the destruction of healthy, innocent bodies in 12 ways. The number of U.S. companies constructing Electronic Battlefield devices is huge. Only HONEYWELL & GENERAL TIRE & RUBBER COMPANY make complete weapons systems. Other companies make only one or several components. With your help, the AUGUR can do local research on industry & university projects—anyone with knowledge of local Dept. of Defense contracts should call or write us.

The result & stated goal of all this bombing has been (besides actual genocide) forced urbanization. One half of the population of South Vietnam is now homeless—there are 7 to 9 million displaced persons. In 1960 Vietnam was 90% rural—now it is 60% urban. The following figures for Saigon reflect the overcrowding in all South Vietnamese cities, however, many refugees are simply missing, with rumors of hundreds of My Lai's circulating among returning vets. Saigon, which was designed for 300,000, now contains 3 to 5 million people. It is the most densely populated city on earth, with twice the density of Tokyo. People live on rush mats in the streets as squatters, & all day & night the Saigon police are moving them out of the way of military vehicles. By the Saigon government's own figures, 60% of the people in the South Vietnamese capital have TB, & the Bubonic plague has reached epidemic proportions—10,000 cases a year reported. The streets are filled with mountains of garbage & huge rats. 50% of those who die in Saigon are under 5 years of age. There is virtually no medical treatment, since all the available doctors are in the ARVN. When there is amputation instead of death, there are no artificial limbs. Saigon is a city of orphans, amputees, & prostitutes, who, by the thousands, get their eyelids cut to have the "western look." In the cities, the destruction of Vietnamese civilization is completed by a combination of Amerikan & Japanese consumerism—Southern Comfort & Honda are making weird people out of the few urban Vietnamese who do have money. It is the progressive forces of Vietnam that are keeping the old ways alive—& this is in spite of forced urbanization & the destruction of the countryside. Since the war began, one quarter (3,000 out of 12,000) of the villages of South Vietnam have been totally destroyed. & there are 5 U.S. companies with bulldozers in the jungles, destroying 1,000 acres of forest a day. This kind of forced urbanization is a tactic that Samuel P. Huntington, chairman of the Dept. of Government at Harvard, & a long-time supporter of the war, openly advocated in *Foreign Affairs*, July, 1968. However, this attempt to dry up the human sea the guerrillas swim in has backfired, & the refugees may well be the quicksand that the U.S. & Saigon war efforts sink under.

Nixon still has a plan in his limp hands for neocolonialism which includes 25,000 U.S. advisors in Vietnam until 1975, $2 billion in economic aid to Saigon, & a projected strength of 1.1 million men in the Saigon army plus 147,000 men in the Saigon police force.

But even before this huge offensive, things were looking very grim for Nixon. Laos is 80% liberated—the Meo tribes have largely been turned into refugees. Thai troops are the only ones really fighting the Pathet Lao. Cambodia is 67% liberated—after 10–20,000 Lon Nol troops were killed in their first big offensive, the Cambodian dictator/general brought all of his troops home to defend the capital city. & Saigon has a $760 million deficit to the U.S., & the latest figures we've found show that in 1968, South Vietnam had to import 677,000 metric tons of rice as a result of isolation from the liberated zones & U.S. spraying & bombing.

And now the NVA & NLF main forces are smashing through the illusion of Vietnamization. Actually, Nixon had asked for this offensive by showing Hanoi & the NLF how weak the ARVN is in his foolish invasion of Laos. & Nixon has proved that he doesn't want peace. Since Jan. 25th, the day when Nixon announced his new 8 point peace proposal (with which he hopes to create the illusion that he is answering the 7 point proposal of the Provisional Revolutionary Government) the U.S. has conducted the heaviest bombing raids in 4 years in South Vietnam, launched a series of new air attacks against populated areas in the North, d[i]spatched a 4th aircraft carrier, the Kitty Hawk, to the Gulf of Tonkin where normally only 2 carriers have been deployed in recent years, sent 42 new B-52's to bolster the Indochina fleet, & announced the indefinite suspension of the Paris talks. In addition, he had started a relocation program, which, according to the PRG, will move one million people from their homes in the northern provinces in order to turn the area into a free fire zone for tactical nuclear weapons. Don't forget that Nixon advocated, when he was Vice-President, that the U.S. bomb the hills around Diem Bien Phu with nuclear weapons in order to save the trapped French forces.

These are some of the bitter reasons for the NLF-NVA offensive this Spring. Those of us, who long ago saw no hope in the American government for peace, wish the liberation forces victory! We believe that the Movement in the U.S. should join the offensive with all the levels of commitment & tactics open to us. Events that were coming up anyway include: a referendum against the airwar in California; the trials of Russo & Ellsberg in L.A. in May & June: & the huge, nation-wide actions planned for San Diego. Local meetings to discuss & plan for San Diego, on the Eugene & then on the Northwest levels, should be announced & take place soon. Just in case Nixon does something crazy, we should be ready to go out in the streets at short notice now. Next Wednesday, April 12th at 2:30 at the EMU there will be a rally to support the liberation forces of Indochina & at 3:30 in 150 Science let's make the UofO faculty finally vote to off ROTC NOW! JOIN THE OFFENSIVE!

From *AUGUR* 3, no. 12 (April 7–21, 1972): 3, 16.

Karl and Groucho's Marxist Dance: The *Columbus Free Press* and Its Predecessors in the Columbus Underground

STEVE ABBOTT

A metal canister imprinted with "No. 264 Multiple Baton Shell—For Use By Trained Police Personnel Only" stands on a bookcase in the house I now own in Olde North Columbus, a working-class neighborhood sandwiched between the ever-changing Ohio State University area and comfortably middle-class Clintonville. Loaded with short pieces of 1¼-inch dowel, these canisters were, along with tear gas and billy clubs, standard crowd dispersal materiel for urban police departments during the civil rights and Vietnam eras. This particular relic is part of a larger story, one perhaps partially explained by the books that surround it.

The writings of Malcolm X and Martin Luther King bump up against the poetry of Allen Ginsberg, Walt Whitman, Pablo Neruda, Kenneth Patchen, Marge Piercy, and Denise Levertov. Steinbeck's *The Grapes of Wrath* offers an echo to the turn-of-the-century urban deprivation chronicled by Jacob Riis's landmark *How the Other Half Lives*. Books on mysticism and religion blend with literature that has defined much of this century; the *I Ching* and *When God Was a Woman* share a shelf with Kafka's *The Trial* and Joseph Heller's *Catch-22*. Political extremes coexist comfortably here, where Tom Wolfe's *The Electric Kool-Aid Acid Test* and Abbie Hoffman's *Revolution for the Hell of It* rub covers with Marxist and anarchist treatises. Texts on drugs, meditation, and sensual massage provide a counterpoint to analyses of racism and community organizing; a book on natural foods relaxes next to transcripts of congressional proceedings of the House Internal Security Committee.

What may appear to be a library tour is, rather, evidence of a personal odyssey that represents the myriad influences and contending philosophies that typified the alternative/underground press during its heyday in the late 1960s and early 1970s. The *Columbus Free Press* (later the *Columbus Freepress*), in both its content and its internal struggles, reflected both its community and its time—a time filled with days of agony and days of wonder as the ideals of mystical transformation and principled political struggle contended for the lives of those involved.

The factors that gave rise to the underground press were many and varied—economic, social, political, philosophical, sexual. Two decades of changes in the wake of World War II had shredded traditions, social structures, and assumptions that had been integral parts of the fabric of life in the United States. A list is probably less helpful than explanation of what each item meant in terms of social change, but the attitudes, expectations, and dreams that drove the so-called counterculture emerged from a heady mix of factors that hardly begin to explain *how* they were so significant:

The post–World War II economic boom resulting from the destruction of most industrial nations' infrastructure and the consolidation of labor gains begun in the 1930s, giving rise to a more prosperous working class and a solid middle class. The ominous shadow of the mushroom cloud and the threat of nuclear war. McCarthyism and the Red Scare. The Beat manifestos: Jack Kerouac's *On the Road*, Allen Ginsberg's *Howl*. The second wave of the century's feminist movements. The constricting social templates projected by TV's *Father Knows Best* and *Leave It to Beaver*. The Ban the Bomb movement. The civil rights struggle and the televised brutality of institutionalized racism beamed into every home at dinnertime. Civil rights legislation and the decline of nonviolence and the rise of black militancy. Urban riots and cities in flames. Assassination of national dreamers. Introduction of the birth control pill. Development of the web offset press that made printing inexpensive. The emergence of rock 'n'roll as a cultural force, and the rise of influential black entertainers whose work influenced both black and white youth. The growing war in Southeast Asia and the Selective Service draft that fed the battlefield with young men who couldn't afford college or wrangle a slot in a National Guard unit. The rise of a separate "youth market" in clothing, entertainment, and recreation. The Peace Corps and belief/hope in the possibility of fundamental social change to improve the lives of others.

Columbus in the 1960s and '70s was a conservative place that reflected Ohio, which is sometimes referred to as the northernmost southern state or the easternmost western state. Except for Cleveland, Akron, and Youngstown in the state's industrial northeast, Ohio's cities then were largely overgrown small towns, with all the attendant parochialism the image implies. Yes, Ohio State had gone through some political dustups as part of the free speech movement that had swept the nation's colleges, and the city was annexing large parcels of Franklin County and growing at a rapid rate; but for the most part, the university had the reputation of being a football powerhouse, and the city's sense of itself, despite being the state capital, was tied to its college-sports identity and little else.

When the *Free Press* hit the streets of Columbus, Ohio, in October 1970, it was the most recent in a string of underground papers published in the city during the previous three years. Two issues of an underground first appeared early in 1968 as an extension of the Free University set up in the community adjoining the sprawling Ohio State campus. Put together by a mixture of counterculturalists and political activists, the first issue called itself the *Free University Cosmic Kosmic*; the second, like a new child in the family, had its own name: *Gregory*. A third issue never appeared.

Later that year, in November, a similar but decidedly more political group produced the first issue of *The People Yes*. The previous year had seen a takeover of the OSU administration building by black students demanding changes in university policies (and the subsequent indictment of thirty-four on charges of "kidnapping" a university vice president), and the firing of a popular professor for burning his draft card. OSU had a small but active Students for a Democratic Society (SDS) chapter, and the area abutting the campus had sprouted a large hippie community with numerous shops, many located on "Pearl Alley," a string of clothing stores, head shops, import stores, and a teahouse on nearby 13th Avenue. *The People Yes* reflected the sometimes uneasy alliance between radical politics and hippie counterculture in its first edition, which mixed license numbers of unmarked police cars and ads for roach clips with the SDS's nomination of a pig for president and an article on conscientious-objector counseling at a local church.

TPY covered the 1969 Counterinaugural following Richard Nixon's election, the ever-expanding war in Indochina, national and campus developments, and the ongoing police harassment of longhairs and political activists. A regular column, "Ask Doc Pettibone," responded to questions about basic countercultural concerns such as drugs and venereal disease, and much of its local news focused on links to national political issues—antiwar demonstrations and war research on campus. Its last issue appeared in May 1969. Later that year, Howard McHale and a few former *TPY* staff members published several issues of another paper, *Renaissance*, but it, too, soon went under.

By the summer of 1970, both the cultural and political landscape had changed dramatically. Woodstock had taken rock music and its countercultural trappings—if not its fading essence—to a mass level; the dark side of the same counterculture had been exposed by the Manson clan's murder spree and the debacle at the Rolling Stones concert at Altamont Speedway, where a young black man was knifed and stomped by Hell's Angels. In November 1969, the Vietnam Moratorium Committee had brought hundreds of thousands of demonstrators to Washington for the largest national antiwar demonstration in the nation's history. The Black Panthers were under increasing attack, as reflected most notably in the murder of Chicago Panther leader Fred Hampton.

Students had been shot by National Guardsmen at Kent State and by deputy sheriffs at Jackson State in May 1970. The mind-expanding possibilities of marijuana and LSD were being compromised by adulteration and by a heavy influx of amphetamines and the notorious sopors, "prescription hypnotic" depressants (also known as Quaaludes or methaqualone) that had begun to spread quickly throughout central Ohio. In the wake of these developments, *Purple Berries* (drawn from a line in the Crosby, Stills, and Nash post–nuclear holocaust song "Wooden Ships") appeared in June of 1970.

The tone of *Purple Berries* was the tone of a youth community that had seen the naked power of the nation's military, previously directed only at nonwhites, unleashed on Blanket Hill at Kent State one month before. Indiscriminate gassings and beatings by police, and the occupation of the OSU campus by National Guard troops during the student strike that coincided with the killings had pushed thousands of moderate students and community residents to question their cherished ideals of justice for all, honest government, and friendly policemen. *Purple Berries* was political, angry, and street tough—a reflection of the persona of its driving force, Yippie Steve Conliff, whose expansive, insightful article-tirades represented the action-faction approach to alternative media and the most in-your-face style yet in Columbus underground writing.

Purple Berries published eight issues between June and December, during that time being an uncompromising voice promoting the antiwar/anti-imperialist movement while championing the cause of "freaks" of the sociopolitical counterculture community who were the constant victims of police harassment. *Purple Berries* linked the actions of the U.S. government in Vietnam and in minority communities to the day-to-day intimidation and arrest of longhairs who smoked marijuana and listened to rock music—a less polemical, less sexist, and more humorous version of White Panther Party politics, minus the belief that rock 'n' roll was inherently revolutionary. (The paper, in fact, was printed on equipment operated by Mike Howard, a local White Panther whose Wildflower Collective became the Columbus alternative community's primary printer of leaflets and broadsides, as well as sponsor of free concerts and fundraisers for progressive community groups.) The paper's aggressiveness and total involvement with street life, however, typified the approach of the underground press: don't simply report news; *make* it and, like the corporate press, define what news is important to your community.

For example, in response to frequent police harassment and arrests of street people on petty pretexts—disorderly conduct, intoxication, possession of hallucinogens, vagrancy—in front of a popular local fast-food outlet, the BBF (shortened from its sixties appellation of Burger Boy Food-o-rama), *Purple Berries* challenged the power structure in a series of articles that advocated individual rights and community control. Minor skirmishes with BBF management and Columbus police grew into a sharp clash later that summer between the police D Platoon riot squad and hundreds of street people; in the fall of 1971, the same locale and the same issue would result in a riot that rivaled those of the spring of 1970.

Unfortunately, *Purple Berries* had ceased to exist by that time. Like so many other publications, *Purple Berries* struggled with money, apathy, and the factionalism of its community. Money problems eventually pulled the paper under following its December issue, its dire financial condition noted on its printed cover and mimeographed inner pages.

By that time, though, a new voice was already rising in its place. Even as *PB* had begun publishing the previous summer, another, decidedly less radical group of people, which included me, was already planning yet another paper. A journalism student and part-time employee of the OSU Libraries, I had been approached by another library employee, Bill Quimby, early in the summer of 1970. The student riots and the eighteen-day shutdown of the campus that spring had changed many people's views and opened large numbers to the possibility that the radical-liberal opposition might be onto something, and he wanted to start a publication to address that group. Initially, his idea was that of a digest of radical-liberal thought, drawing from other alternative and radical publications and creating our own commentary along the way. Another OSU student, Paul Ricciardo, was also interested.

Getting Started

We chose the safe, hopelessly bland name *Columbus Free Press* (in some ways reflecting our own politics at the time), rented a typewriter, and set to work. Bill and Paul hustled ads, Paul recruited a few other interested folks, I wrote a piece and, being the only person with any journalism background, directed layout. With the work of Sandi Quimby, Cheryl Betz, John Hunt, Roger Doyle, and assorted artists and hangers-on, we pulled together the first issue, an eight-pager, in a garage apartment on West 8th Avenue and hit the streets on October 21, 1970, with 2,000 copies that we sold for 15 cents apiece. Articles on Vietnam Veterans Against the War, Jimi Hendrix, and a mass demonstration against Nixon at an Ohio Statehouse speech; a reprint of a Julius Lester critique of white radicals; and reflections on the indictments of twenty-five Kent State students for activities the previous May 3-4—supported by six paid ads and free ads for the local tenants union and drug crisis center—made up the paper's initial content.

The second issue, which we sold for 20 cents, led with a cover story on the involvement of undercover Ohio highway-patrol officers in a student strike action that had precipitated a confrontation with police and led to the subsequent riots. (In a photo taken by a highway patrolman, Paul Ricciardo himself appeared standing between the two undercover agents.) Sporting a new masthead drawn by my high school friend and Cheryl Betz's roommate Jude Angelo, and featuring the words "An Alternative Newspaper Serving an Alternative Culture," the paper included reports on Vietnamese opposition groups and the Revolutionary People's Constitutional Convention, an Underground Press Syndicate reprint from San Francisco's *Good Times* (on rock music as a means of social control), an Allen Ginsberg article on the destructive impact of amphetamines, and a book review of Neil Postman's *Teaching as a Subversive Activity.* Like almost every other underground of the time, it included a plea for street sellers and interested participants. The layout had improved, and the *Free Press* looked something like a newspaper.

At the time, the *Free Press* had no coherent philosophy or clear political perspective. Bill Quimby's background was old-style loyal-opposition liberal; Paul Ricciardo's and my own were vaguely left-liberal pacifist, with active participation in the antiwar movement and the previous spring's student strike and a freak lifestyle being our points in common. My own politics came out of work with the War Resisters League, my cultural interests from the blues, rock music, and poetry. Our views would always be among the more moderate of the *Free Press*'s positions.

As political conditions in Columbus, and nationwide, became increasingly more repressive, those moderate views meshed uncomfortably with the demands by others on the staff for stronger response to these repressive conditions.

The fourth issue of the paper, appearing in January 1971, printed on the front page and inner pages the entire text of the Weather Underground's "New Morning, Changing Weather" communiqué; in it, they outlined the emerging types of political oppositions, many not linked to their own armed struggle except in a spirit of throwing off the control of white male domination.

The centerfold, black ink on yellow paper, was a poster of three GIs with peace symbols on their helmets walking through a rice paddy, framed by the slogan "Smoke Pot Where You Work—They Do." The ads had the unmistakable mark of Jude Angelo's light touch. And the general community response had been good.

The *Freep*'s situation, like its time, was full of contradictions, not the least of which was its printer. The paper was printed on the presses of *The Times*, a small weekly paper located in the rural community of Canal Winchester, southeast of Columbus. In Dick Eckleberry, its editor and publisher, the *Free Press* found a conservative who believed strongly in freedom of the press. In addition to publishing the weekly paper, he printed numerous circulars for local grocery chains; when lumber strikes in Canada threatened to reduce availability of newsprint in 1971, Eckleberry assured us that the *Free Press* would be printed even if it meant not having paper for his more lucrative commercial work. As he told us this, a framed picture of Barry Goldwater smiled at us from the wall behind his desk. Eckleberry kept his word, and he never raised any questions about the paper's content. Interesting times. . . .

Unlike the staffs of *The People Yes* and *Purple Berries*, people working on the *Free Press* were not at that point involved closely with political groups, and the tone of the paper reflected a more detached attitude even on local issues. Still, other influences were evident. By late January, participation from representatives of Ohio State University's Gay Liberation Front and a number of local feminists, including Mimi Morris (the pseudonymous Angela Motorman from *Purple Berries*) and OSU grad student Margaret Chisholm, was beginning to broaden the paper's perspective. New staff members Greg Frazier and Tom Moore showed up regularly to write and work on layout. Content ranged from analyses of events in Indochina to reprints of Furry Freak Brothers comix, from recipes for cooking with curry to reports of raids on local black activists.

Tradewinds, a local head shop/import store, served as the distribution point for street vendors. The store's merchandise and appearance had a definite *Free Press* feel: Glass cases displayed pipes, rolling papers, handmade jewelry, and natural soaps; racks of India-print bedspreads and Mexican peasant shirts were topped with shelves holding incense, candles, massage oils, and books of Eastern philosophy and radical politics. The walls were covered with rock-music silkscreens and political posters; and the bulletin board by the door was splashed with announcements of demonstrations, consciousness-raising groups, and concerts.

Tradewinds's owners had operated a shop on Pearl Alley during the days of *The People Yes*. In addition to the paper's own post office box, Tradewinds became a drop-off point for ideas, articles, and information for the *Free Press*, and a gathering place for hangers-on. Owners Judy Christopher, Alice Lehman, and Libby Gregory gave the *Free Press* a highly visible presence on High Street, the main drag through the campus area. Later, when Columbus police arrested numerous staff members, and its regular office seemed unsafe, the paper would be put together in Tradewinds's basement.

The Strains of Change

By early 1971, internal staff conflicts that had been only subtly bothersome the previous October, when the first issue hit the streets, began to emerge as major psychological strains. Changes sweeping the culture of the larger Movement that the paper sought to serve added to this internal pressure.

At the time, *Free Press* content had a strong cultural/entertainment base, an undefined counterculture air, buttressed by support for radical-liberal politics. Articles on growing marijuana faced reports on speeches by Angela Davis; record reviews and Sandi Quimby's wonderful (and inexpensive!) cooking recipes followed reports on demonstrations and trials. The paper was trying to maintain Bill Quimby's initial vision of being both a digest of the alternative press and a journal of its community's more immediate concerns. Its advertisers included concert promoters and "hip capitalists" of the local freak community, whose politics and attitudes were often highly suspect, but whose support helped pay our way.

In the May 17 issue, *Purple Berries* founder Steve Conliff brought his caustic, insightful style to the *Free Press* for the first time with a report on the recent May Day actions in the nation's capital. In the same issue, an article by Margaret Chisholm and Sandi Quimby entitled "Freep Feminism: A Declaration" enumerated a series of putdowns of women by local male politicos and business owners, most evident among them being the continuing assumptions that men were the only leaders in the hip/radical community (and in the *FP*), and that women were to play traditional roles even within the so-called alternative culture. The article concluded:

Take note, groovy-radical male chauvinist Columbus. Women of the *Columbus Free Press* hereby renounce pseudo-feminism and liberalism. No longer will we resign ourselves to piggish, put-down treatment from male movement lightweights or heavies "just for the sake of the paper." Peace and harmony, love and power, no longer take precedence over our self-respect.

In the past we have endured your insults in order to preserve solidarity in the Columbus radical community. We now perceive that community built upon the subservient chattel status of half its members is a sham. We are tired of being told we do not understand "The Revolution." A revolution that excludes half the population is hardly a revolution. It is not radical.

It is not even reform.

The article was accompanied by an Abbie Hoffman quote—"The only alliance I would make with the women's liberation movement is in bed"—and a passage from Mao Zedong's "Combat Liberalism." The times they were a-changin'.

And they were changing in ways none of us truly understood. How could we? All of us—female and male, gay and straight, black and white, anarchist and centralist, laid-back and revved-up, violent and pacifist, dopers and Democrats, rockers and Maoists, anti-authoritarians and anti-imperialists, a confusing convergence of the disaffected, disenfranchised, disillusioned, and disestablishmentarian—were vaguely united in the belief that the country operated in direct opposition to its espoused values, and that we as individuals and collectives had to do something about it, in our own interest and in the interest of the entire globe. The dream was a command.

We were feeling our way through emotions and perceptions about the need for immediate, apocalyptic change. The essential inequities of the political and social system had led some to a principled critique of, and opposition to, the existing order; others had become simply iconoclasts opposing the structures and strictures of the predominant (white male) culture.

We were experiencing personal and political changes that we could not fully grasp even as we advocated them—changes that put us at odds with our preexisting sense of who we were as individuals and as Americans. The future shock of history that had launched every post–World War II change—civil rights, rock 'n' roll, national liberation movements, rapidly evolving gender consciousness, protest actions, increased use of mind-altering drugs, growing tension between the individual and the mass society—had become a wave in the mid-1960s and, as the seventies began, had grown to a tide sweeping the world.

We believed that individually we could make a difference and collectively we could change the world. It was a rebirth of wonder.

The entire next issue of the *Free Press* was a women's issue; no male staff members worked on the 20-page paper (only the second to run 20 pages), which covered plays and music, radical motherhood, women's conferences, psychology, and struggles in the workplace, particularly offices. Its content, like other more generalized issues of the paper, combined post-hippie gentleness, anger-driven insight, and no-nonsense critique, and became the city's first public forum for a wide range of feminist concerns and an accurate reflection of the diversity of the women's movement.

Subsequent issues presented more local news and the initial appearance of Zorba the Freak, who would become one of the community's great mythic characters. Writing under the name Leon Karg, Steve Conliff created the persona of Zorba, "leader of the street people," whose utterances to "hippie fella" Karg revealed the political undertones of issues in an acerbic, wildly funny style that anyone could understand—and learn from. In his first appearance, Zorba took on the turf issue of street people versus the BBF; the Yippies had been active all summer around the issue, and a number of demonstrations, one including flyers for a "When Will It Burn?" sweepstakes, had led to confrontations and arrests. The "community control" aspects of the conflict had even drawn support from local Marxist and anti-imperialist groups. We wanted self-determination at all levels.

By the beginning of the second year of the paper, another trend had revealed itself: individuals representing various constituencies emphasized their particular issues during brief periods of activism on the paper. When several members of OSU's Gay Activist Alliance worked on the *Free Press*, for instance, more articles on gay issues appeared.

Internal Dissension

In volume 2, number 2, late in 1971, staff differences burst into the open with the front-page printing of an open letter from Steve Conliff under the heading "Up Against the Wall, *Free Press*" in white letters on a brick-wall background. In the previous issue, an article on the murder of revolutionary black leader George Jackson in Soledad Prison had run opposite an "Entertainment Guide"; in his letter, Conliff assailed the paper's focus on entertainment as disturbingly reflecting a "bread and circuses" approach to activism, protested the editing of references to revolutionary violence from his articles, and generally decried much of the paper's content as repetitive and liberal. His views, he said, were representative of those of many in the community "working toward a revolution in Amerika."

Although the *Free Press* had no named editor, I functioned as de facto editor and was largely responsible for the editing of articles. In fact, my own more liberal, culturally oriented politics had often been reflected in many articles. Coming out of a pacifist orientation that I was beginning to question seriously, I represented the less-militant wing of the paper's staff. The paper's printed response acknowledged some of Conliff's criticisms and generally said it was doing the best it could, but no one knew then how true one line from the Conliff letter was: "Things can't go on the way they have been going." The next few issues would make clear how rapidly "things," and the paper, were changing.

Everything was in flux. The paper was being produced in the large front room of an apartment rented by Bill and Sandi Quimby on High Street north of OSU. More people were swirling into the paper's charged, exhilarating operation and politics: photographer Evan Morris (brother of Mimi) and, occasionally, Chuck McCoy, both with experience on *The People Yes*; former marine and OSU Law School professor John Quigley; gay activist Jeff Arnold; Mike Jaschik and White Panther John Miernik; Tradewinds owners Alice Lehman and Libby Gregory; and Fred Andrle, a former college media instructor who, as advisor to the Ohio Wesleyan campus radio station, had allowed the studio's on-the-air destruction after the school administration condemned the shack that housed it.

Burned out from *Free Press* work, a part-time job, and class work for my final quarter at OSU, I temporarily withdrew from the paper early in October.

It seemed that every political and cultural activist in the country was a marked person. Official harassment, intimidation, and even outright assault by both street cops and right-wing groups were widespread, and to most of us, the nation and our own community seemed to be approaching fascism. Earlier in 1971, a local white supremacist group, the Minutemen, had distributed a list of "traitors" marked for death; everyone on the list was some combination of feminist, black, liberal, or radical. Articles appearing, often buried, even in mainstream publications revealed government contingency plans for suspending elections, declaring martial law, and interning political dissidents. Antiwar demonstrators were routinely attacked by police or hardhat labor unionists. Every day brought news of a new outrage in Indochina, in the courts, or on the street, and people's public and private worlds were routinely jolted to higher levels of intensity.

Nixon had called antiwar demonstrators "bums," and within weeks soldiers on a college campus had shot protesters; Vice President Spiro Agnew incited parents against their children, and a father in Michigan killed his daughter and her "hippie" friends. In a short time, the government's COINTELPRO (Counter-Intelligence Program) operation of spying, sabotage, and disinformation against domestic political activists would be exposed. A letter to the paper claimed, "Real genocide (final-solution type) is for real here."

The *Free Press* was not unaware that it had begun to rock the local political boat. Police harassment of street vendors and specific staff members was not uncommon. Although most of its outlets and audience were in the Ohio State area, the paper was expanding. John Miernik had begun selling ads, the advertising base was growing, and more stores around the city, even in shopping malls, were carrying the paper. We began doing outreach to local high schools and making contacts with antiwar and students' rights activists throughout the county.

Early in November, the old turf issue at the BBF exploded into a four-hour riot up and down High Street and onto the OSU campus. Hundreds of people were arrested, scores—including many uninvolved students attacked when county sheriff's deputies stormed into the Student Union building during the street battle—were beaten, and much of the area was gassed. The next issue of the *Free Press* covered both the riot and its aftermath in the courts; a separate article offered "legal self-defense" tips for use on the street or in street actions. Local labor strikes were given prominent play, and a front-page story by rock musician and music reviewer Cheryl Helm covered a different and chilling topic: a Los Angeles police informer's story of a plan by the FBI and Los Angeles police to use agents provocateurs to justify martial law in order to thwart the rising tide of opposition to the Nixon government.

The first *Free Press* split—more accurately a purge—happened in this apocalyptic atmosphere. Several staff members as a delegation visited me and asked if I would return to the paper to lend support to an effort to oust Bill Quimby; I agreed to at least attend the meeting where a new direction for the paper would be argued. The meeting took place at the *Free Press* "office" at the Quimbys' apartment, where it quickly rose to a shouting match as various Yippies and staff feminists, most notably Cheryl Betz, with whom I was living, argued with Bill Quimby and denounced him for sexist behavior. The meeting ended with Quimby quitting and ordering everyone out of his house.

The next day, in a scene played out in many versions in the alternative press, the *Free Press* files, layout materials, mailing lists, and various equipment were spirited away in the back of a station wagon. As the winter season began, the paper found itself in the basement of John Quigley's half-double on Indiana Avenue. There, with work tables squeezed between the furnace and a wall covered with revolutionary posters (as well as our own "Smoke Pot Where You Work" exhortation), the *Free Press* began to shape a new identity.

A strong viewpoint supporting the National Liberation Front in Vietnam appeared in succeeding issues of the paper as Colin Neiburger, late of Weatherman and active in the Gay Activist Alliance, joined a staff that was in various forms connected, either by membership or frequent participation, with most of the progressive organizations in the community, regardless of their political or countercultural slant.

The left-radical community in Columbus had never been large. Although it included thousands of freaks, most were involved more in the counterculture-dropout aspect of alternatives than in the political-organizing aspect. They listened to rock music, followed local bands, took drugs, worked marginal jobs, and hung out; they opposed the war because they or someone they knew might have to go, or because they didn't particularly like authority or government telling them what to do. This brand of self-determination differed significantly from the more "informed," even intellectual, approach of many "political" activists who were so serious they wouldn't dance. The social and political upheaval of the time generated a self-righteous sense of purity and certainty about how things should be, even as day-to-day events and changing personal and political relationships showed how uncertain the times really were. Our collective philosophy careened between two Marxisms, Karl's and Groucho's. It was a wild dance.

The "Crazy Horse Approach"

Strange coalitions were the order of the day. Members of the Progressive Labor Party would show up at Yippie actions against BBF; anarchists and street people would rally around Young Socialist Alliance banners at antiwar demonstrations. The Indochina Coalition, formed in the spring of 1972, was a virtual rainbow of political shadings that brought together the entire range of antiwar sentiment to organize mass actions. If any single group had organized a demonstration, ridiculous factionalism (aptly satirized later in Monty Python's movie *The Life of Brian*) might have prevented a large turnout; but when different groups worked together, the impact was multiplied. Coalition groups came to support each other on issues other than the war. One radical called it "the Crazy Horse approach: it's the same warriors showing up at different points on the ridge top."

With a regular office for the paper, the staff grew. Suzie Bird provided regular artwork; Margaret Sarber, a former SDS member and now a White Panther and Indochina Coalition leader, contributed occasional articles and did layout, as did Tradewinds owner Judy Christopher. Scott Williams, a Tenants Union organizer and independent activist, covered a variety of issues. Legal worker and former *TPY* staffer Sue Urbas shot photos. Many staff wrote under both their own names and a variety of pen names to protect their identities and to create shadow personae for police to wonder about, a strategy reflective of their strong anarchist and Yippie sentiment.

Free Press staff were in the center of much of what was happening. In February of 1972,

FIGURE 1: Cover of *Columbus Free Press* volume 2, number 10 (March 1–14, 1972). The *Free Press* takes aim at the Columbus police force. Courtesy the author.

Burton Cantrell, a minister, man of peace, and director of the Wesley Foundation, the Method-ist student center near the OSU campus, agreed to provide free office space to a number of community groups. The Columbus Community Food Co-op set up in the basement, and the Columbus Tenants Union and the *Free Press* moved into a shared office on the first floor. The Wesley Foundation became a center for community social and political activity where we planned, argued, celebrated, agitated, and danced.

In an effort to form its own "more perfect union," members of the Columbus Community Co-op, the Columbus Tenants Union, and the *Free Press*, along with members of the Open Door Clinic and Switchboard, the local crisis center, had formed the Community Union late in 1971. CU's goals were to provide a focal point for community alternatives—food, medical care, housing, media—and eventually to create a community center where these alternatives could be centralized and independently run. From the beginning, however, the Community Union suffered from its inability to work with large-scale democracy. The clinic and Switchboard were never very active in CU, but in the other three groups, factions formed quickly.

One of the Community Union's primary issues was community control of police; as the alternative community's mouthpiece, the *Free Press* was a militant representative of the com-munity distrust of, and animosity toward, police. The Columbus police were the enforcement arm of the dominant culture; their casual harassment of and violence toward blacks, gays and lesbians, freaks, and political activists were widely known in those communities and largely ignored in local media, particularly the *Columbus Dispatch*, which was owned by the powerful and conservative Wolfe family.

The *Free Press* covered CU's efforts to organize people around the need for a civilian review board to investigate police actions and expose undercover police infiltration of community meetings. Community organizations were my "beat" on the paper; clashes between tenants and landlords or police and citizens were regular copy. The *Free Press* took straight aim at the Columbus police department, both in news articles by me, and in more impassioned features by Steve Conliff. In a March 1972 issue covering a meeting demanding community control (see figure 1), I wrote that the police were "the best organized gang in town":

> The Police Department . . . runs itself. Tightly organized and ready to mobilize every civic group, news medium, and "patriotic" organization in the city against any threat to its presumptuous sovereignty posed by people it allegedly serves. The Columbus Police Department. Our very own military overseer.

In an article titled "Soporboppers: Serving the Pig," Steve Conliff drew the connection between the too-popular drug Quaalude and its impact on people's ability to resist police repression. Columbus was a popular test market for consumer products, and Conliff made an interesting case for government collusion in the "marketing" and distribution of depressants in the local freak community. Like heroin in minority communities, sopors reinforced a sense of listlessness and mindlessness, and police found users easy targets for arrest and good sources as informers. Conliff voiced the attitudes of many:

> Weed is a revolutionary drug because most people function at least as well on it as they do straight. . . . But I fear that catatonic sopor heads won't fare too well in the street

fighting. What saves us in the streets is our mobility and our brains, and fucked-up people exhibit little of either.

All this points up how the Vietnam era was not simply political upheaval in the traditional sense of demonstrations, collectives, position papers, and cadres; it was a dizzying mix of traditional political actions and eclectic social experimentation. While many activists remained true to the models provided by radicals historically, and in turn kept themselves separate, serious, and "politically correct," the social impact of music, drugs, and a variety of alternative lifestyles, living arrangements, and relationships created a curious and sometimes perplexing blend of militant purpose, self-deprecating humor, hippie self-indulgence, cosmic flair, and the contradictions embodied in meshing them. Bemused, we wondered aloud to what extent we were, in the words of an underground comix character, "bourgeois anarchists on an ego trip." Our *lives* were poems, political acts; how much of the re-creation we were going through was also recreation?

An "Open Letter to the Masses" in the March 15, 1972, *Free Press* noted conflicts within both the Community Union and the community at large:

> While "hippies" or "freaks" may in the early days have been predominantly middle class white kids, many of them merely out slumming prior to their eventual return to the corporate management power elite, today, through instantaneous communication and marijuana, a certain convergence of cultures has occurred. Woodstock Nation has absorbed a certain amount of input from the black experience, the Puerto Rican experience, the white greaser experience, the female experience, the military experience, the gay experience, the junkie experience, the prison experience, the daily unabating oppression of the poor experience; and the Counter-culture has increasingly come to resemble a class—a sort of cross between lumpen bourgeoisie and nouveau proletariat.
>
> But perhaps it would be more accurate to say that the Counter-culture has become a microcosm of the class system, for there exist classic Marxist class antagonisms between the penniless, vagrant, unemployed street person and the young, hip, suburban, dope-smoking liberal.
>
> Community-originating alternative institutions . . . have, more than anything else, fulfilled the communist slogan "Serve The People" on a practical, day-to-day basis, and have epitomized what we are supposed to be about.
>
> We are about people.
>
> But these alternative institutions are not ends unto themselves. Our food co-ops do not feed starving Latin American children—whom the US is starving; and our crashpads do not house Bengali refugees—who were driven from their homes by US-armed and -supported military; and our underground papers have not stopped the murderous bombing of Southeast Asia—by guess who. If freaks or youth or even Americans are the only people whose interests we serve, we are still imperialists, raping and pillaging the Third World for our own material comfort.

As a member of the Underground Press Syndicate, the *Freep* exchanged papers with dozens of other publications throughout the United States and Canada. We used them as sources for features, graphics, and posters, one of which encapsulated our approach to what we were doing. Reprinted from Washington, DC's *Quicksilver Times*, the poster proclaimed a determined, perhaps fatalistic, almost smug reminder: "There are two things you have to remember about making a revolution. One is that we're going to get our asses kicked. The other is that we're going to win."

As the antiwar movement grew locally and nationally, and our own community showed increasing diversity in its efforts at self-determination, the *Freep*'s staff spun through a bracing whirl of discussions, jobs, leaflets, meetings, concerts, trips, demonstrations, parties, and production work. We recognized the strength our work had generated.

When the Community Union leadership endorsed two liberal friends for local Democratic Party ward committee seats, disputes intensified. In an article titled "Unholy Alliance?" Conliff denounced the CU leadership and its exclusivity; many felt the CU was being too liberal, while others, basically in agreement with the dissidents, felt the level of conflict was unraveling what was a good-faith attempt at achieving necessary goals. Most *FP* staff thought we were being co-opted. How much the community would participate in existing political structures was an issue that cut deeply—and often.

We struggled with our contradictions. One article penned by Angela Motorman noted the recent prison releases of Angela Davis and Ted Berrigan as an introduction to an article on the imprisonment of Ralph Ginzburg, publisher of *Screw* magazine, after losing a ten-year-old appeal of an obscenity conviction. "As a feminist," she wrote, "I'm no fan of skin magazines, even self-proclaimed intellectual skin magazines, and personally I don't care much for Ginzburg's style, but as a civil libertarian I can't let this one pass unnoticed. . . . It's always easier to support the struggles of people whose politics and lifestyle you can identify with or at least admire. I still think Ralph Ginzburg is a slimy bastard, but I don't think he belongs in jail." The staff agreed to run the article with a headline chosen by the writer: "Creep Jailed."

The Indochina Coalition, many of whose members were *Free Press* staff, organized regular demonstrations against the war. The paper covered and supported efforts in state prisons to organize the Ohio Prisoners Labor Union (OPLU). In a front-page article, I wrote of the killing of an alleged drug dealer by Columbus police narcotics agents and called for a grand-jury indictment of the murderers. In releases from Liberation News Service (LNS), Underground Press Syndicate (UPS), and other undergrounds, we reported on FBI informants who helped plan a break-in at the Camden, New Jersey, draft office, and another agent who attempted to sell weapons to the Kent State Vietnam Veterans Against the War. We knew that police had the paper and members of its staff under surveillance; anxiety about infiltration by informants rose and fell.

This activism and militant anti-police stance led to the arrest, in May 1972, of several staff and numerous other local activists the day after a large demonstration protesting the mining of Haiphong Harbor in North Vietnam and the resumption of saturation bombing by U.S. warplanes in Indochina. Police attacked demonstrators blocking a main street near OSU, and the next day charged Margaret Sarber, John Miernik, Colin Neiburger, and former OSU student-body president Jerry Friedman with inciting to riot; I was charged with riot and malicious destruction of property. Two progressive lawyers who had been at the scene prior to the street battle were also arrested, one as he was trying to obtain the release of *Free Press* staff. Still, an eight-page *Free Press*, produced in the basement of Tradewinds, hit the street

FIGURE 2: Cover of *Columbus Free Press* volume 2, number 15 (May 17–31, 1972). Staff members are arrested protesting the mining of Haiphong Harbor in North Vietnam. Art by Susan Bird Conliff. Courtesy the author.

on schedule, with a Suzie Bird cover drawing of Margaret and John under the heading "Staff Jailed!" (see figure 2).

The next full issue of the paper followed the tradition of *The People Yes* and *Purple Berries* by running a list of license numbers of undercover police cars along with "Pig Pix," photos of undercover police. The license numbers had been obtained by a staff member during his lockup in the city prison, where one view overlooked a police parking lot.

That summer, many staff joined thousands of other activists at the Republican Convention in Miami Beach. There, *Freep* women were among the most combative with right-wing locals who prowled the demonstrators' campsite in Flamingo Park, harassing gays and females. We returned to Columbus with cracked heads, bail papers, large strips of decorative patriotic bunting, and renewed energy.

The paper had an intense local focus, covering tenants' strikes, the prosecution of a local black leader, and the efforts of Ohio Penitentiary inmates to get better treatment. In the issue following our return from Miami, Steve Conliff and I described the surreal events that had taken place. The cover of that issue included a box that brought the events together: "Pigs Harass / Tenants Win / CIA Plots / Prisons Boil."

My own views had swung around. Having decided early to resist the draft, I was now convinced that the moral-witness act of turning myself in on the steps of the federal courthouse would be, in the existing political climate, an empty gesture. Nevertheless, I decided that if I was drafted, I would not be pushed out of the country to Canada with other expatriates. The war was at home; I would go underground and continue to actively oppose the war from inside the United States. My draft lottery number was 116; the call-up for the year at my draft board reached 109.

Expanding and Raising Consciousness

The history of the underground press is incomplete without acknowledgment of the influence of drugs. Most *Free Press* staff used hallucinogens—marijuana and LSD. A few occasionally used speed, but all scorned the use of most other drugs, particularly sopors, which were prevalent on the street and regularly denounced in *Free Press* articles as counterrevolutionary because they dulled awareness rather than enhancing it. The same issue of a paper that featured gross caricatures of Nixon and Kissinger on the cover and an analysis of the politics of rape inside might have a cartoon on the back cover exhorting youth to "Build a better Amerika—Get stoned!"

We saw no contradiction; we embodied it. While more dogmatic activists shunned drugs as inherently counterrevolutionary, and while the mainstream press saw only "hippies" *or* "radicals," the *Free Press*, like its predecessors, encompassed both and included as staff members many who *were* both—not as separate viewpoints but as part of a larger liberation that included anti-imperialism, sexual freedom, and expanded consciousness, all operating to the sounds of mainstream and underground rock music and their exhortations to social and psychic change. Many a long night of layout (and countless other activities) included sessions to discuss issues and smoke a joint or two. It was a part of everyday life.

Articles on Indochina or the Black Panthers ran side by side with comix from Milwaukee's

Bugle-American; "The Continuing Story of God" comix, from Houston's *Hooka*, might appear on the page after an analysis of racism. Hippie culture mixed with political activism, spinning a synthesis that was alternately—and even at once—impassioned, communist, pagan, rational, flippant, mystical, hermaphroditic, anarchist, stoned, self-righteous, serious, whimsical, disciplined, and hedonistic.

We had grown up through one of the most dramatic economic expansions in history, following a war in which the economic strength of every other major country in the world had been literally or virtually destroyed. We had been brought up believing in liberty and justice for all, standing up for the oppressed, and making the world a better place. We had come to take ideals seriously and "reality" less so—or maybe more so; it was difficult to tell. We saw connections between the civil rights struggle and the gay rights struggle; we saw connections between ball-and-chain slavery and wage slavery. We saw connections between our own War of Independence and the desire of other peoples for the same opportunity our young country had: to form their own government—of the *people*, by the *people*, for the *people*—and make their own mistakes.

We learned how the U.S. government had picked up the remains of the British and French colonial systems in Southeast Asia and Africa, sheltered Nazis, undermined popular governments, blacklisted and even killed its own domestic opponents, and persecuted minorities at home while propping up dictators abroad. We had come to realize that our culture was, by inertia and/or design, a machine in which we would become small cogs, automatons programmed to consume prepackaged products, prepackaged ideas, and prepackaged futures. We had seen the birth of a sexual revolution that, unlike most other social movements in the world, was out of straight men's control because women and gays had begun to challenge the male definition of sexuality.

And we had grown up with the Beats, and with music: be-bop and doo-wop, and folk music, and the gospel and spirituals of the civil rights movement, and Bob Dylan, and rock 'n' roll. We had danced to Little Richard, Janis Joplin, the Beatles, and Aretha Franklin, and gotten stoned and tripped to Pink Floyd and Jefferson Airplane. The music was the soundtrack, and sometimes the statement, of our lives:

> Four dead in Ohio. . . . Goddamn the pusher man. . . . We can be together. . . . Some folks inherit star-spangled eyes / Oo, they'll send you down to war. . . . There's something happening here / What it is ain't exactly clear. . . . Bring the boys home. . . . And it's 1-2-3, what are we fightin' for? . . . War, children, is just a shot away. . . . We got to live together. . . . One toke over the line. . . . I'd love to turn you on. . . . How she walked like a woman and talked like a man. . . . We shall overcome. . . .

For a while, either Mimi Morris or I would call WCOL-FM, the underground radio station, and request Thunderclap Newman's "Something in the Air." As the staff labored through the night, the radio would announce a song "for the staff of the *Columbus Free Press*," and the office would fill with the song's chorus: "We got to get together sooner or later / Because the Revolution's here / And you know it's right."

And like the music itself, our lives and our beliefs were changing rapidly: how we saw ourselves as a nation in the world, as women and men, as human beings, as free individuals who were part of a larger striving for self-definition and community. For many of us, that search for self-definition included psychoactive drugs; we were both activists and psychoactivists.

A week before the 1972 election, many *Freep* staff and friends gathered for a Halloween exorcism of demons from the local headquarters of the Committee to Re-Elect the President. A massive police presence turned out to confront the Good Fairy, the Invisible Man, Aunt Jemima, several Vietnamese peasants, and a variety of wayward spirits seeking peace. Unamused police told us, "We're going to kick your asses." (*Mama said there'd be days like this . . .*) Yippie!

But always, the antiwar struggle and the resistance to repression unified us. Not planning to put out a paper at Christmas, we changed our minds and ran off a four-page mimeographed publication, "Cow Town Times—a holiday substitute for the *Columbus Free Press*," when we received word from a serviceman that large numbers of B-52 bombers and KC-135 refueling tankers were moving through Wright-Patterson Air Force Base near Dayton as part of a massive mobilization aimed at bombing Vietnam during the holidays. Other headlines included "Juries See Police Lies—Two Acquitted," "Madness at Statehouse: New Penal Code," and "Tight Assholes Ban Gay Newsletter." On the cover, Santa Claus raised a middle finger.

(Eventually, the "Cowtown" appellation became part of the entire community's vocabulary.)

Through early 1973, the paper continued to grow, adding as regular staffers Alison "Sunny" Graff, a martial-arts enthusiast and founder of Women Against Rape who often wrote as "Frieda P. Pole," and Eric Zeiters, a worker whose biker appearance, soft-spoken manner, and articulate insight brought a fresh element to the staff.

With its fiftieth issue, in March 1973, the *Free Press* changed its masthead and, at the same time, its name, to the *Columbus Freepress*. The paper began using color regularly. A new typewriter with slightly smaller type allowed us to fit in more copy; we worked harder at layout, and graphically the paper looked stronger. We ourselves felt stronger; most of the cases arising out of the previous spring's antiwar actions had resulted in dismissals or acquittals, although several Progressive Labor Party members and a few Yippies had been convicted and were spending time in jail. Roger Doyle went to Wounded Knee and sent back photos and stories on the American Indian Movement (AIM)'s showdown with federal and state police and local vigilantes; we ran a color poster commemorating Wounded Knee in the centerfold. The constitutional crisis of Watergate was exploding. Another civilian was shot by local police. The struggle continued.

Sexism in Theory and Practice

Part of that struggle was with male-female relationships. Within the *Freepress*, although it was in theory collective, a number of males who wrote a great deal played powerful roles. Steve Conliff, John Quigley, and I comprised different political viewpoints (Yippie, Marxist, and stoned social democrat, respectively) that were conveyed through our many articles, which we each wrote under a variety of names. The sheer number of words carried much influence simply because the paper depended on us for articles ranging from straight news, to satire, to analysis of community, or, in John's case, international issues. Too, certain staff concentrated on specific issues, thus becoming de facto "experts"—Colin Neiburger, for example, handled most writing on Vietnam. Since staff often disagreed on the specifics (though rarely the substance) of some political viewpoints, occasionally articles with conflicting analyses would appear in the same or subsequent issues.

On the other hand, the women of the *Freepress* staff—most notably Mimi Morris, Sunny Graff, Libby Gregory, Cheryl Betz, Kathy Wollard, Alice Lehman, and Judy Christopher—represented a varied cross-section of feminism. Their own articles and graphics in the paper, as well as their analyses of issues, covered a similarly wide range of viewpoints. Theirs was a continuing struggle to educate the men of the *Freepress* even as they struggled with sexism in its more general manifestations in society. Women's different sense of self, and the supportive connections they offered one another in a period of profound self-discovery, gave them a collective unity and power men did not share.

Like the use of drugs, the topic of personal relationships is often neglected in overviews of the period. For many progressives, sexuality and sexual behavior were not worthy subjects for introspection in the face of the war and racism, and discussion of complex sexual relationships and questions of identity may now seem relatively insignificant, perhaps even self-indulgent.

Today, many see the sexual revolution primarily in male terms. In some ways, the postwar sexual revolution, as typified by *Playboy*, simply reinforced the prevailing sexual double standard and served to legitimize the dominance of men in relationships. Men were allowed sexual freedom without commitment or responsibility—the requirements imposed by the economic relationship of marriage. Many "hip" and "progressive" men simply put a bell-bottomed blue-jeaned veneer on historic male behaviors, little understanding that the real sexual revolution was happening for *women*.

For women, their liberation from psychological stereotypes and economic dependence was, in fact, the acquisition of the power to choose their relationships rather than have them imposed by tradition and necessity. It was the changing attitudes of women that defined the sexual revolution and forced changes in the attitudes of men.

The sixties and seventies were a time of experimentation—politically, economically, socially, personally. The *Freepress* staff included several monogamous couples. Too, political comrades often became lovers, and a number of staff men and women were sequentially involved in sexual relationships with other staff members or other community activists, gay and straight. The hidden dynamics of these changing relationships, combined with our underlying imperative for CHANGE NOW!, often affected the issue-to-issue atmosphere on the staff. Often, both women and men found themselves trying to separate their intellectualized principles from their immediate and deeply felt emotions.

No issue better illustrated the complexities of our attempts to remake male-female relationships than the revelation in mid-1973 that I had been secretly involved for more than a year with another woman even as I lived with and received support from my partner of four years. The shock wave polarized the paper; *Freepress* women rallied around their wronged sister and isolated me; staff men, although rightly condemning my actions, recognized that sexism, male behaviors, and their own conduct were now subject to even more critical scrutiny. My own, and by extension all men's, hypocrisy was under fire. Numerous individual and group discussions followed, including one memorable four-hour meeting in which staff women ritually pilloried virtually every male staff member for various sexist behaviors. I was not purged from the staff, but my influence was irrevocably diminished.

With the loyalties of even progressive men now personally and intimately questionable, women received a powerful boost in confronting the inertia of male dominance on the *Freepress*. At the same time, they struggled with their own issues. Were women in heterosexual relationships literally sleeping with the enemy? As separatist views gained strength, could the feminism of a woman who had not explored a lesbian relationship be trusted? It was a confusing period of exploration and revelation, both of which generated ecstasy and conflict.

Women of varying politics continued to join the staff. Marianne Salcetti brought her feminism and formal journalism training to articles analyzing local labor actions and community-development issues; Pat Culp provided a satirical, warped sensibility to social commentary; Sandy Sterrett, writing as "Sandra Skinner," covered ecology stories and, later, community organizing. Their personalities and contacts, and the ongoing work of other staff women in women's organizations, strengthened the paper even as it continued its struggle with identity and finances.

The dichotomy between cultural and political "change" was always apparent but never clear. Articles on Israeli crimes against Palestinians faced record reviews; reports on the sterilization of poor women and the organizing efforts of tenants bumped columns with vegetarian recipes and advocacy of animal rights. Eric Zeiters's articles on police repression shared pages with Libby Gregory's cartoons of Polonius Potato, created after the FBI harassed local activists for "an attempt on the life of Vice President Agnew" in the form of a potato thrown at his limousine during a fundraising visit to Columbus in 1972. The revolution was broad-scale.

The paper's financial underpinnings, however, were not. It had numerous advertisers but no skilled business manager. Advertising revenues were supplemented by donations from working staff members, and occasionally by the then-honorable activity of dealing in marijuana and LSD. Two months after the paper's cover showed the backsides of four naked staff members over the plea "Help Save Our Asses!" a staff member worked a deal for 5,000 hits of purple microdot LSD. Many staff bought at discount, and the resulting sales allowed the paper to finish out the year more or less in the black, publishing every two weeks.

Then, in January of 1974, the *Freepress* confronted financial reality head-on by going free, dropping the 20-cent cost and expanding its press run from 2,000 to 10,000 (and ending the need to give a simple answer to "So why ain't it free?"). With a larger promised circulation, advertising increased even as the paper took a more militant stand on local and national labor conflicts and supported a strong community campaign for civilian review of police while exposing police informers. *Freepress* articles on a strike by Borden workers were the only media coverage in the city to support workers demanding compensation for a mysterious nerve ailment linked to chemicals at the Borden-owned Columbus Coated Fabrics plant.

Up Against the Police

The paper also exposed how Columbus police had attempted to use an informer to set up and arrest municipal judge Bill Boyland on drug charges. Boyland, a progressive lawyer for numerous community organizations as well as a number of *Freep* staff arrested for antiwar activities, had been elected in a popular campaign the previous fall, when his campaign headquarters had been kept under police surveillance; and the city's right wing, including many police, had circulated stories that the married Boyland was a secretly homosexual Communist who paid campaign workers in drugs. In the same story, I reported how the lawyer who had revealed the planned frame-up had himself been arrested when police raided his office and seized marijuana and pills being held as evidence in a client's file.

The militant antigovernment, antipolice rhetoric of the *Freepress* made it a natural target for reaction and repression. Harassment by police and direct attack by right-wing groups and white supremacists continued. Death threats came by telephone and by mail. A gunshot had been fired through the window of an apartment shared by feminist activists/staff members Mimi Morris and Sunny Graff, whose basement had housed the paper in the winter of 1971; windows in the paper's office at the Wesley Foundation were broken a number of times. The homes and vehicles of staff members and other political activists had been vandalized or burglarized, and intruders killed the pet of two activists during a break-in, leaving the message "Your [*sic*] next" on a mirror. Both Switchboard and the Third Avenue Food Co-op were damaged by arsonists. Police "field interviews"—ID checks—on the street were common.

Accordingly, many staff wrote articles, particularly highly charged ones, under a variety of names that revealed a taste for irony and bad puns. John Quigley covered international stories as Vanya, legal matters as Amy Cuscuria, and tenant-landlord stories as E. Victor. Colin Neiburger wrote Indochina analyses as Colinda Tomato or Jam-Cin; Mimi Morris appeared as Liz Estrada and Angela Motorman. Stephen Sterrett covered politics and the environment under the name Stephen Skinner. Libby Gregory wrote as Norma Jean Fish, Alice Lehman as Carolina Hunt. Steve Conliff wrote as Leon Yipsky or Leon Karg, the latter surname drawn from a fatigue jacket bought in a surplus store; when Karg had another article in the same issue, "Noel Grak" authored some articles. My own pen names included [Free] Lance Ryder, Dennis Menimen, and Houston Fearless, a brand name of earthmover. The bylines of "Neil Livingston," "Patterson Blake," and "Woodrow Thurman" combined various Columbus street names. Our own names graced many articles, but each byline was a choice trying to gauge the amount of risk or ego the writer might be investing.

(Ultimately, little of this mattered. In 1976, *Freep* staff gathered for a party at the house shared by Judy Christopher and me, and together we all filled out forms requesting our FBI files under the Freedom of Information Act. When we compared files many months later, we became convinced that John Miernik, who handled much of the paper's advertising and distribution, had been an informant for both the Columbus Police Intelligence Squad and the local FBI, reporting on even our birthday celebrations and relationships with lovers. Many, though not all, of the staff's pen names appeared in the FBI's files. The Revolution had clearly provided employment for thousands of file clerks, from the local to the federal level.)

Too often, though, our sense of theater led us mistakenly to measure our impact by the amount of repression we felt from police, in effect allowing them to define our influence in the community. Criticism of this tendency would later become part of the paper's internal political struggle.

In the face of intense organizing around both local and national issues, combined with the stunning revelations of the Watergate conspiracy and the Nixon administration's extensive list of dirty tricks, the staff tried to keep its sense of humor. One issue featured, in place of page numbers, the names of radical and progressive women; thus, stories were "continued on Elizabeth Gurley Flynn" or located on "Harriet Tubman." Cartoonist Paul Volker, following other local artists—Larry Hamill, Jude Angelo, and James Beoddy—began contributing humorous political comic strips and assorted artwork to the paper.

Many of us clearly were tired and overextended, but nonetheless determined to continue. Four years of intense activity; personal, political, and legal struggles; ongoing police and right-wing harassment; and the constant forming and collapsing of idealistic endeavors and personal relationships had taken a significant toll on many of us. On the one hand, we felt more certain of our direction; on the other, we were dazed and confused by the whirlwind of our lives. In a gigglingly funny article on the general state of the Movement, Steve Conliff reported the activities of the "Burn-Out Liberation Front"; in the next *Freepress*, in an occasional staff column titled "Goin' Through Them Changes," we wryly denied that the BOLF consisted entirely of *Freepress* staff members past and present. At the same time, no one contradicted me when I offered the mordant observation that our freewheeling, in-your-face attitudes would probably get us put up against a wall and shot if some of the political groups we claimed to support ever came to power.

In mid-1974, after several weeks of thought and discussion with staff and other friends, I took a job working as a bailiff in the municipal courtroom of Judge Bill Boyland. The contradictions were apparent from the outset, but the opportunities to cut some slack in the system for poor and working people—again, the question of reform versus revolution—prompted me to take the chance.

In addition to helping people get released from jail on low or recognizance bails and providing some empathetic understanding of the issues that brought them into the criminal "justice" system, I was able to work with and support a close friend whom the progressive community in the city had helped to elect. My appointment touched off a furor in the police department, whose representatives demanded my dismissal. I stayed for the next five years, and my contacts and access to information proved valuable to progressives on a number of occasions.

I was also weary of the *Freepress.* No less committed to the issues it addressed, I was exhausted (not unlike many other staff). Between the demands of the job and internal demands for a better understanding of what I myself believed independently of the group, I felt the need to leave the paper. I expanded my writing of poetry, and at a later date penned a celebratory "Poem for the Fifth Anniversary of the Columbus Tenants Union" for their annual community dinner.

Goin' Through Them Changes

The *Freepress* revamped its masthead and continued making connections between local, national, and international issues. Feminists like Sunny Graff increasingly linked their anti-rape work in the community with the rape of the Third World, particularly Vietnam. And there was still power in the dictum "The personal is political." In an article about police and media handling of several brutal assaults against women, Graff wrote:

> I am home alone and I am pissed off. I am sick and tired of being terrorized. I am tired of arming myself with mace and my whistle to take out the garbage at night. I am tired of being afraid to be alone.

I'm tired of being told I have no sense of humor when men casually laugh about rape and "scoring" women. I've heard degrading comments about women from every man I've ever known. I've seen women beaten, torn, ravaged and murdered. I've seen women who press charges against their attackers degraded and humiliated by male doctors, judges, attorneys, prosecutors, police officers and reporters. . . .

I am home by myself tonight—but I am not alone. I am with all the other women who feel my anger, who are tired of being victimized. . . . We are growing stronger every day.

In Vietnam, it was clearly only a question of time before the war would be over. Between February and May, three of the four front pages of the now-monthly *Freepress* focused on Indochina, including the printing of a communiqué from the Weather Underground following a bombing at the State Department, and articles on Cambodia and, in May, the fall of Saigon. Some of us went up to Larry's Bar to celebrate, and later walked down High Street to 15th Avenue, where we encountered other folks celebrating as well.

But the next day there it was, the question the staff had debated for several years but never really confronted: without the war, and without a broader critique of society, what would hold together the anger, disaffection, and flagging energies of the disparate groups that made up the so-called underground?

The paper was facing other realities as well. Two different entertainment publications, *Focus* and *Ragazine*, had begun publishing, and their rock 'n' roll and graphic-arts focuses were drawing advertisers away from the *Freepress*.

In another "Goin' Through Them Changes" column, the situation was laid out plainly but, as always, with some humor:

We have always maintained that we are a collective and that "everybody does everything." But this is not close to the truth. In fact, a few people have done the less exciting tasks of advertising and distribution. And a relative state of order has been maintained by personality politics. Power has been held by those able to stay up all night doing layout.

Last week the FREEP staff finally had the reorganizational meeting we've been dreading for years. First thing we realized is the changes we've gone through in our personal lifestyles. Two years ago we were hippies and politicos, students or part-time workers, with lotsa free time to put out a paper. Now we have all assumed straight identities and gone overground, stealthily infiltrating the work force at key points. . . .

We need distributors, advertising salespeople, and advertisers. If you've ever wanted to play underground paper, here's your chance.

The rest of the column explained the new process for handling the paper's content: articles would be submitted a week before publication, when there would be discussion and critique. Major tasks such as finances and advertising, office management, and distribution and correspondence would be handled by small staff collectives.

As 1975 began, the paper continued to be the voice of almost every revolutionary, reformist, or alternative viewpoint. An article on cultivating marijuana shared a page with a feminist critique of a proposed rape law; both faced a stern "Work towards Socialism" piece on the opposite page. Turning the page revealed health-food recipes. Other stories supported the development of community organizations—Datagang, a video collective; WFAC (Free Access Columbus), a nascent free-form radio station; the Moonshine Co-op Bar; the 16th Avenue Food Co-op, which was regularly distributing funds to other groups such as the Tenants Union, the Rape Crisis Center, and Switchboard.

Local issues—union strikes, tenant organizing, community control of police, development of alternative organizations, gay and lesbian rights—dominated *Freepress* pages, but international progressive politics remained a major element. Wedged somewhere between a political revolution and a cultural one, the paper and its content weaved wildly between seriousness and send-up.

Throughout 1975, community workers moved constantly in and out of the paper's production and writing staff. Tenant organizers Gayle Hoover and Steve Cohodas worked on several issues, and Scott Williams began writing and doing layout again; Skip Zitin contributed regular long hours. Jim Hiser played bass guitar, rhapsodized dizzily about John Lennon and Yoko Ono, helped with layout, and cranked out occasional articles. Marilyn Flower brought strong Marxist and feminist analysis. Gay activist Patrick Miller continued insightful, literate assessments of gay and lesbian issues, and Donna Smith (aka "Roxanne Role") covered rock concerts and wrote record reviews. The true responsibility for core work, however, still fell on a few.

A number of current and former staff became involved in the Prairie Fire Organizing Committee, the aboveground group supporting the Weather Underground, and local demonstrations supporting Puerto Rican independence attracted new police surveillance.

By the end of the year, however, disagreements within the paper were multiplying as the community itself saw its own struggles intensifying. Some staff, approaching issues and the paper itself from a Marxist-Leninist perspective, were increasingly impatient with the freewheeling content of the paper and its lack of coherent analysis of broader issues; debates over articles grew more pointed and prolonged.

As the *Freepress* continued into the nation's bicentennial year, some present and former staff felt the paper had lost its rebellious spirit; others countered that they sought revolution, not rebellion, and that reportage on the day-to-day economic struggles of the majority of working people was more important than radical-hippie self-indulgence.

In June of 1976, shortly before large numbers of present and former staff traveled to Philadelphia for the national demonstration coinciding with the national Bicentennial celebration, five staff—Mimi Morris, Kathy Wollard, Eric Zeiters, Evan Morris, and Marilyn Flower—formed a Marxist-Leninist study group and became a caucus within the paper. By then, the *Freepress* was broke and running on the energies of fewer than ten people and the financial support of John Quigley and several members of the caucus. Ad sales had been dropping off, and what ads Eric Zeiters was able to sell were insufficient to meet expenses.

The paper's focus soon reflected a Marxist-Leninist analysis and style. By the end of summer, rock 'n' roll coverage was gone, and articles contained a more obvious internationalist approach. More and more copy was reprinted from publications such as *Workers World* and the *Guardian*. The caucus insisted on principled struggle to resolve disagreements, and many of the more free-spirited staff felt it not worth the increased effort beyond the more casual style they were accustomed to. The caucus, in fact, regularly held a voting majority, depending on how many people showed up to work on an issue, but their power and influence came as much from their determined work as from their number.

In autumn of 1976, the *Freepress* moved from its 16th Avenue location to offices above the Moonshine Co-op Bar at 11th Avenue and North 4th Street. With the move came more space, worse conditions, and numerous additional and occasional helpers. Steve and Earlene Rothman (subsequently referred to as Earlene Dennison and Earlene Rackham), Patti McFarland, Jo Hoeper, and Darrell Browning, all active in Yippie, feminist, and tenant organizations, became regular workers on the paper.

The paper lurched toward the end of the year, mainly through the efforts of the caucus and four other regular staff members—Libby Gregory, John Quigley, Steve Rothman, and Earlene Dennison. Eight to ten others occasionally put in time on articles and production, but these people had no patience with the constant staff conflict over political positions. When Marilyn Flower departed at the end of 1976, disagreements within the paper stalemated.

The four non-caucus members saw the efforts of the four remaining caucus members as an attempt to convert the *Freepress* into a militant Communist Party organ. The caucus sought a more concrete analysis of issues that would make the paper an organizing tool for political struggle on a mass scale, and they approached the paper's work with disciplined seriousness. Such was the appearance and tone of the paper that a reader wrote a letter beginning, "Dear *Guardian*," and saying, "Why not reprint some articles from the *Columbus Freepress*?" As winter bore down on Columbus, the paper again uprooted itself to be produced from the apartment of a caucus member.

In the January 1977 issue, a full-page article written by the caucus said:

> Capitalism is the enemy. . . . We need decent housing and food, good healthcare and childcare, jobs, education, mass transit. Things we won't get from capitalism because there's no profit in serving the people. We need a new organization of society—socialism . . . and only through revolution will we get socialism. . . . In future issues the *Freepress* will develop and clarify the analysis and strategy necessary for socialist revolution. We welcome your comments and criticisms.

That statement defined the line between the caucus and the other four staff, a line with proponents of a political party on one side and a looser, less dogmatic group on the other. Thus, in early 1977, unable to reach unity on how to resolve their differences, and unable to produce a February issue for lack of money, the eight agreed, after long and rancorous debate, to disband the paper after one more edition, which would be put out when money could be raised to publish it and pay off debts.

Almost immediately, however, at least two of the non-caucus staff began recruiting former staff to work on a "reconstituted" *Freepress*, apparently planning to passively sandbag the paper's "final" issue. It was not a particularly glorious moment. When the caucus found out they had been betrayed, they seized the paper's equipment and files and produced a final special edition late in April, with the cover headline in bold red ink proclaiming "Celebrate Mayday!"

The 12-page paper ran a double-truck centerfold headed "The Future Belongs to Working People!" and a three-page article outlining the caucus view of the *Freepress*'s problems, their efforts to change them, and the betrayal of the staff's unanimous vote to disband the paper. They correctly analyzed the paper's historic character:

The prevailing mood on the *FP* was that the important thing was to be doing something, anything in a vaguely leftist direction; to look closely at what was being done, and why, spoiled the spirit and created bad feelings.

Near the end of the critique, the statement noted:

The members of the caucus believe the "new *Freepress*" will repeat many of the errors of the "old *Freepress*" as we found it ten months ago. The new staff contains various viewpoints and perspectives that can only find unity in the eclectic style of former times. We expect a resurgence of "youth and dope" culture, of a lack of seriousness in tone and style. OSU "community" news will again become the dominant theme of the "city-wide" *FP*. . . . But the weakness, the decisive error, will be a lack of any consideration of strategy, a return to wishful thinking and spontaneity as substitutes for organizing based on analysis.

For better or worse, it was a largely accurate prediction.

The "Reconstituted" *Free Press*

When the "new" *Free Press* (separate words again) came out in mid-May of 1977, both its content and the staff/contributors box looked much like the *Free Press* of several years earlier: an assortment of, in the words of a pointed article aimed at the caucus, "socialists, communists, anarchists, feminists, eclecticists, and various kinds of et ceteras," including several long-absent former staff. For a time, Conliff, Bird, Betz, Sarber, and I would contribute articles and production work. The article continued:

What the "reconstituted" *Free Press* is about is building the kind of movement that doesn't want to rule anybody, that aims to enable people to run their own lives. Everyone doesn't have to think exactly the same way, because revolution is an objective not subjective experience. There is no One Way. We look upon thinking anyone has all the "correct" answers as a mental disorder caused by reading too many books by dead men. The future belongs to the living.

The paper reflected its "et cetera" viewpoint, covering the Soweto uprising and demonstrations against the building of a gym on the site of the Kent State shootings, along with rallies to legalize marijuana and efforts to preserve urban green space. When the Ku Klux Klan held rallies at the Ohio Statehouse on July 4 and Labor Day of 1977, *Free Press* staff participated in large counterdemonstrations against them; photos taken by Sue Urbas and others at the Labor Day rally, at which members of the Committee Against Racism and the Progressive Labor Party were attacked by male bystanders who turned out to be plainclothes police, later helped acquit demonstrators charged with assault for defending themselves. (Several sympathetic court bailiffs and other employees helped identify undercover police in the photos.)

In August, Steve Conliff immortalized himself by pieing Governor James Rhodes, the "butcher of Kent State," at the opening-day ceremonies of the state fair (see figure 3). We never looked at pie-judging the same way again. Charged with assault (with a deadly banana cream

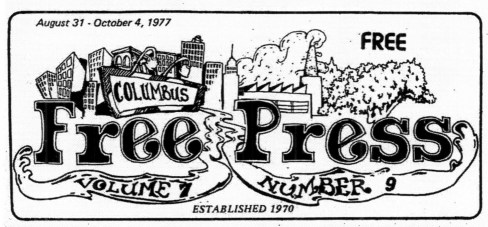

August 31 - October 4, 1977

FREE

COLUMBUS

Free Press

VOLUME 7   NUMBER. 9

ESTABLISHED 1970

Before

After

© PAUL VOLKER. 1977

★PIE JUDGING★
big hit with governor

PAGE 4

FIGURE 3: Cover of *Columbus Free Press* volume 7, number 9 (August 31—October 4, 1977). Staffer Steve Conliff immortalizes himself by pieing Governor James Rhodes, the "butcher of Kent State." Courtesy the author.

pie), Conliff was ultimately convicted of disorderly conduct in a jury trial and fined $100. Later, as always believing that pulling down the enemy's pants was almost as good as kicking him in them, Conliff ran as a write-in candidate against Rhodes in the Republican primary.

The paper moved into office space above Tradewinds, now two blocks north of its old location and directly across from the OSU Law School. The *Free Press* paid no rent; Tradewinds took in-kind ads in the paper.

Over the next three years, the *Free Press* gradually changed. Still progressive but decidedly less strident in tone, it spruced up its layout and gradually moved toward more generalized "alternative" and left-progressive news. A new typesetter sharpened the paper's appearance. Coverage focused heavily on neighborhood organizing around housing, zoning, and police brutality. Antinuclear articles and coverage of other environmental issues expanded. The paper ran a regular citywide calendar of political and cultural events in a format that has since been adopted by several other local entertainment papers.

No longer on the barricades but supportive of those who were, the *Free Press* was by this time one of the few remaining "alternative" papers that had begun the seventies. It was more and more the advocate, the commentator, representative of a broad community of opposition thought. The scene had changed, but the issues hadn't. Liberation News Service (LNS) stories and strong international coverage on the Sandinista, South African, and Palestinian revolutions were highlighted by an important 1979 story by John Quigley: his *Free Press* article was the first eyewitness account by a U.S. journalist of the Killing Fields horror of Kampuchea after the Pol Pot regime was driven out. It was disquieting and humbling to reflect on whether I had ever voiced support for the Khmer Rouge.

Libby Gregory served as managing editor, and in 1984, with environmental activist Steve Molk, John Quigley, and Yip-feminist/resident media critic Earlene Rackham as contributing editors, the paper again changed its masthead and began charging 50 cents for the 24-page monthly publication. The *Free Press* was an institution, a solid and dependable opposition voice that looked professional and more accessible to a wide audience. It began to bill itself—and does today—as "The Other Side of the News."

Some of its most unusual political education during this time was found in "Sexual Assault in Columbus," a regular column giving brief synopses, from police reports, of rapes reported in the previous month. Compiled by Libby Gregory, the column included reports in which women fought back or escaped, and information on whether a rapist had been charged in an attack. Sidebar articles debunked myths about rape.

It was painful, disconcerting reading. Some readers objected to the column, describing it as ghoulish and perversely pandering. Others saw it differently, believing that, by its dispassionate, relentless, page-long repetition of incidents of violence against women, it probably did more to educate its readership about the nature of rape and sexual oppression than many political analyses.

By 1987, though, core staff had dwindled to Libby Gregory, John Quigley, and Bob Roehm, who compiled the monthly calendar. All were working full-time jobs in addition to doing *FP* work. Hearing that Duane Jager, a former Tenants Union organizer, was interested in starting his own publication, they contacted him about taking over the paper.

Jager, who had more recently worked with the homeless, managed a soup kitchen and run for Congress, set up the not-for-profit Columbus Institute for Contemporary Journalism, and gradually assumed the role of publisher. In 1990, John Quigley was serving as senior editor, and former Liberation News Service collective member Harvey Wasserman, then relocated to Columbus, was writing a regular column on environmental issues.

Moving On

In a somewhat different form, and in a very different time, the *Columbus Free Press* (yes, the most recent shift in the linotype), and the spirit of the people who made it happen, lives on. No longer an "underground" publication, it provides a platform for progressive political news and views after weathering going dormant for several years in the early 1990s. After publishing its 25th anniversary edition in 1995, the paper suspended publication, reappearing the next year as a Web site sponsored by *Free Press* volunteer and community activist Tim Wagner. Two years later, the paper began publishing again as a quarterly journal, now under the leadership of Bob Fitrakis, a Detroit native, activist, and faculty member at Columbus State Community College. Fitrakis reintroduced a more in-your-face style to the publication. The paper later resumed monthly publication, which continues today.

Today the trappings of "the sixties" (and, more accurately, the early seventies) are window-dressing for everything from car ads to theme parties, and many of my own students rhapsodize about wishing they had been able to be part of what happened then. As much as I can appreciate the appeal of what in retrospect seems to have been a period of peace and love and a spirit of passionate engagement in political action, I explain that the time was also a period of intense cultural civil war that tore apart families, friendships, and lives in ways that make the so-called culture wars of the past fifteen years a relative frolic. In speaking to high school and college students about the alternative press and the antiwar movement, I get an opportunity to move their awareness beyond visual images and simple stereotypes into the complexities of the personal and political conflicts then that have molded our politics today. Similarly, my sister, a progressive spirit but never a political activist, asked me to take her and her two daughters to the Kent State twentieth anniversary memorial in 1990. "I want them to understand what happened, and what it was all about," she told me. And so it is important that we explain our own history.

Part of that history was made in the streets, where like colonial-era pamphleteers the members of the underground press spread the revolutionary word when even peaceful protest was often met with clubs, tear gas, and multiple-baton shells. The canister on the bookcase is, to me, a symbol of the importance of—and necessity for—dissent, and of what can happen when dissent becomes intolerable to those in power. Tiananmen Square has much in common with Kent State; in the run-up to the 2003 attack on Iraq, a calculated propaganda campaign by the Bush II administration—which relied heavily on right-wing radio talk-show hosts, newspaper columnists, and TV commentators—denounced and effectively silenced dissent in both Congress and the mainstream media. The consequences of the collective failure of political and journalistic nerve will have costly consequences for the country for decades to come.

Especially today, when cynical politicians and businesses blithely manipulate national ambivalence over the legacy of Vietnam by packaging aggression as patriotism and wrapping every imaginable consumer product in the flag, we must not simply tolerate dissent. We must encourage it. We must question, demand answers, root out the hidden agendas, and seek the other side of the story that independent media can provide. We must protect our victories and encourage further change. As citizens of a democracy on the brink of total subjugation to corporate control, we must demand that media provide both facts and informed analysis of what those facts mean in the context of past events and related conditions right now. The Internet and the proliferation of political blogs have opened up opportunities for disseminating information and commentary that were unimaginable in the early 1970s. Independent researchers and reporters have been able to prevent important stories from being ignored or buried by mainstream corporate media, and the increasing consolidation of major media systems spotlights how important the continued independence of Internet news has become. The efforts of phone and cable conglomerates, including Comcast, AT&T, and Verizon, to eliminate Internet neutrality, and thus control and dictate Web content, make clear that the struggle to provide alternative viewpoints via the latest technology is far from over.

Those of us who are interested in media must continually help others to understand that freedom of speech and freedom of the press are not about being able to say "fuck" on a TV show or in a magazine article; they're about being able to provide every citizen with information necessary to making informed decisions about self-government. In an age of bread-and-circuses distractions of every stripe—cell-phone ringtones/downloads, text messaging, endless Web surfing, 24/7 sports events on cable TV, "reality" shows, "wealth management" services, high-end fashion trends, Botox, Viagra, the latest health and exercise regimens, scandalous levels of conspicuous consumption—it's all the more important that each of us recognizes that our media's job is to *inform* us first and entertain us second. There's a good reason that the "press," as it used to be called, was referred to as the Fourth Estate (and a necessary bow here to Detroit's *Fifth Estate*, the longest-running underground paper from the period still in existence). Our news media are an additional component of maintaining freedom that is every bit as important as our executive, legislative, and judicial branches of government.

The life of the underground press was a life that acknowledged the possibility of change—fundamental change in attitudes and power relationships on a global, national, local, and, ultimately, personal level. Eventually, many of us realized that the heart of the struggle was not just learning to live with each other but learning to live with ourselves.

We were so much older then. . . .

It may seem that the story of the *Free Press* and its people was solely one of conflict. To think so, however, would miss the point of how our lives themselves—political, social, spiritual—are a process, a constant testing and reshaping of our personal realities. In those lives we have marched and danced, fought and celebrated, laughed and cried, been hurt and been healed. We have worked hard to find a way for all people to live in peace, in harmony with themselves and the earth, and to have their basic needs met. We have come to understand that as we work to create justice and peace, whether global or personal, we have to be in it for the long haul.

We sought to live our ideals and in the process discovered our fallible humanity. We made many mistakes, but we have learned and grown, and much of what we sought has come, in some form, to fruition. And we brought all of what we were to that struggle.

Many of us still do. We stood with our neighbors on street corners with protest signs in working- and middle-class neighborhoods, joined demonstrations, and contacted congressional representatives in the run-up to the attack on Iraq. Many of us continue work in thriving organizations once considered "alternative" but now woven into the fabric of everyday life, working to develop low-income housing and universal health care. Some work in social-justice groups within churches; others balance their political work with spiritual practices that include yoga and meditation.

In a participatory democracy, what the government does, or allows to happen, depends on *us*. Musician Steve Earle captured this reality in the song "The Revolution Starts Now" from the 2004 CD of the same name: "The revolution starts now / In your own back yard / In your own hometown. / So what you doing standing around?"

Take a look in the mirror. Every revolution begins as a spiritual or intellectual shift within and among individuals. In an economic system that offers freedom but encourages selfishness, the real revolution begins within us. The world continues to present opportunities for creating fundamental change, and the responsibility for creating that change is in our hands. Mahatma Gandhi said it simply: "Be the change you wish to see in the world."

And you know it's right.

"Raising the Consciousness of the People": The Black Panther Intercommunal News Service, 1967-1980

JONINA M. ABRON

The Death of Huey P. Newton

I was headed out the door to my job as managing editor of *Black Scholar* magazine in Oakland, California, when my phone rang the morning of Tuesday, August 22, 1989. The caller, a sister who had been a fellow Black Panther Party member in Oakland after first working in the party in Houston, Texas, rushed out the words:

"JoNina, have you heard? Huey's been shot. He's dead." She explained that a friend in Oakland had heard the news and called to tell her.

Shocked, I had barely hung up the phone when it rang again. On the other end was another comrade sister (in the party, women were "comrade sisters" and men "comrade brothers") calling to ask if I had heard that Huey had been killed. "I miss him already," she said.

Grief overcame me as I realized that Huey P. Newton, whose name thousands across the world once chanted in the cry "Free Huey!" and who had been an international symbol of black resistance to white oppression, was dead. Violence had consumed Huey's life almost daily in the twenty-three years since he cofounded the Black Panther Party, and violence finally took his life at age forty-seven.

The following Monday afternoon, August 28, at Huey's funeral, inside and outside east Oakland's Allen Temple Baptist Church, over 2,000 people—including ex-Panthers from Baltimore, Boston, Houston, Detroit, Los Angeles, Washington, DC, Philadelphia, and other places—mourned Huey's death and celebrated the enduring contributions that the Panther leader and the party made to the political empowerment of black and other disenfranchised people in the United States.

I was asked to speak at the funeral because I was an editor—the last editor—of *The Black Panther Intercommunal News Service*, the BPP's newspaper. As I stood crunched in line waiting to enter the sanctuary with Huey's family members and other speakers on the program—including ex–party leaders Bobby Seale, Elaine Brown, Ericka Huggins, David Hilliard, and Emory Douglas—I found myself looking into the faces of two Panther comrades whom I had not seen in fifteen years. We embraced—sad for the occasion that had reunited us, but happy to be reunited.

When I stood on the podium to speak, I nearly broke down and cried as I looked into the faces of my Panther comrades on the front pews. I thought about all the good and hard times we had gone through together "serving the people body and soul." I said that I had been privileged to serve in the Black Panther Party for nine years and that I would die a Panther. I know I said something else, but I don't remember what.

When Elaine Brown took the podium, it was the first time many ex-Panthers and party supporters had seen her since 1977, when she resigned from the party for personal reasons. Her capable leadership held the BPP together from 1974 to 1977, when Huey was in exile in Cuba after being charged with killing an Oakland prostitute. He had survived being shot by one policeman, and three years of prison for killing another policeman in the same incident; other confrontations with law enforcement; and numerous trials. In her comments, Elaine said she had thought Huey was invincible and that he would live forever.

Moving to the podium and putting a black beret on his head (in the party's early days, the Panther uniform consisted of a black beret, black leather jacket, and powder blue shirt), BPP cofounder and chair Bobby Seale brought the congregation to its feet in tribute when he raised his clenched fist and shouted the Panther rallying cry: "All power to the people!" Then he recalled how he and Huey met as students at Merritt College in the early 1960s, and how their mutual concerns about police brutality, poverty, and other problems in the black community led them to found the BPP in Oakland in October 1966.

Just as he had in the old days, in his familiar strident cadence, Bobby then recited from memory the entire BPP Ten Point Platform and Program. For a few minutes, it seemed as if the congregation at Allen Temple Church was at a Panther rally in 1968.

After the funeral, ex-Panthers, family members, and friends gathered for a reunion where we talked over old times and exchanged information about our lives since party days.

Later that afternoon, ex-BPP political prisoner Johnny Spain and I were among the guests on a program commemorating the legacy of the BPP on KPFA Radio in Berkeley. Johnny, who spent nearly twenty-two consecutive years behind bars, explained how in the late 1960s, while serving a prison sentence for murder in California, he joined the BPP because of his friendship with black prison leader George Jackson.

Murder Linked to Death of George Jackson

George was legendary in the California penal system for his effective organizing of black and poor inmates. He is generally credited with starting the Black Guerrilla Family. BGF was initiated as protection for black inmates against white racist inmates and subsequently became a focus of political education for black prisoners. During Huey's three-year imprisonment for killing an Oakland policeman, he learned of George's work and appointed him to the position of BPP "field marshal," responsible for organizing and leading blacks in prison. Many BGF members became Panthers.

On August 21, 1971, George, two other prisoners, and two guards were killed in San Quentin Prison's maximum-security section, the adjustment center, in what prison officials alleged was an escape attempt (see figure 1). Earlier in the day during a visit, the officials charged, a white attorney, Stephen Bingham, had smuggled in to George a gun, concealed in a portable tape recorder, and an Afro wig. During George's escape attempt, they maintained,

FIGURE 1: Cover of *The Black Panther* volume 7, no. 1 (August 28, 1971), commemorating George Jackson, who was killed in what prison officials questionably called an escape attempt. From It's About Time archives.

he concealed the gun under the wig. This theory was questionable, given that George was thoroughly searched before and after visits from his attorneys, family, and friends.

Johnny was incarcerated at the time with George in the adjustment center. He and five other black and Hispanic adjustment-center inmates—Willie Tate, Fleeta Drumgo, David Johnson, Luis Talamentez, and Hugo Pinell—were charged with assault, conspiracy, and murder in the August 21 killings. During the eighteen-month-long "San Quentin 6" trial, the prosecution conceded that Johnny did not kill anyone at the adjustment center, but maintained that he was trying to escape with George. He was, therefore, vicariously guilty under state law of killing the two guards. When the trial ended in August 1976, almost exactly five years after the incident, Johnny was the only one of the six convicted of murder. He was sentenced to two consecutive life prison terms. In August 1989, shortly before Huey's murder, Johnny's conviction was overturned.

What really happened at San Quentin that August day forty years ago may never be revealed. In an affidavit signed shortly after the incident, several adjustment-center prisoners declared that George risked his life to save theirs. At the time of his death, the twenty-nine-year-old prison leader was serving the eleventh year of a $70 robbery conviction and was about to go on trial with two other black inmates for the 1970 killing of a white guard at Soledad Prison. In his critically acclaimed 1970 book *Soledad Brother: The Prison Letters of George Jackson*—in part a forceful critique of racist violence and harassment of black prisoners—George said he did not expect to leave prison alive, because of his organizing of black inmates. Aware of this and determined to silence him, prison officials may have falsely led George and inmates close to him to believe that the BPP was going to break him out of prison. The party denied this rumor and charged that prison officials murdered George, a charge supported by testimony during the San Quentin 6 trial. Louis Tackwood, a black ex–police informant, testified that he was recruited to infiltrate the BPP as part of a plot by California law-enforcement officials to kill George.

In any case, when George was killed, many in the BGF blamed the party, Huey in particular, and relations between the groups soured. Exactly eighteen years and one day later, Huey was shot to death on a street in the same Oakland neighborhood where Huey and Bobby launched the party in 1966. Tyrone Robinson, who police said was a drug dealer, was convicted on October 9, 1991, for the first-degree murder of Huey. According to police, Robinson said he shot Huey in a dispute over drugs. Robinson was a low-level member of the Black Guerrilla Family, police said, and killed Huey in order to advance within BGF ranks. For whatever reason Robinson killed Huey, there is no question that at the time of his death, the BGF was not the same organization that George Jackson founded twenty-two years earlier (when Robinson was a toddler). And there is also no doubt that by 1968, three years before George was killed, then FBI director J. Edgar Hoover had already declared war on the BPP, charging that it was "the greatest threat to the internal security of the country."

Black Panther Party Founded to Oppose Police Brutality

Waiting to begin the KPFA program, and feeling more relaxed after the funeral celebration and more reflective from the emotions of the occasion, we laughed at the headlines as we passed around twenty-year-old issues of *The Black Panther*:

- "Nationwide Harassment of Panthers by Pig Power Structure"
- "Fascist Action Against the People of Sacramento"
- "White 'Mother Country' Radicals"

During the program, while discussing the history of the newspaper and the party, I said that I owed Huey and Bobby a great debt for starting the BPP and allowing me to participate in one of the most important black liberation movements in United States history. As we reminisced, I recalled the party's beginnings in 1966 and my own introduction to the party six years later.

Huey and Bobby founded the Black Panther Party for Self-Defense (Self-Defense was dropped from the name in 1968 to help give the party legitimacy as a political organization) because, as they later wrote in the party's initial Ten Point Platform and Program (see sidebar 1), "We want freedom. We want power to determine the destiny of our Black Community."

BLACK PANTHER PARTY PLATFORM AND PROGRAM

WHAT WE WANT, WHAT WE BELIEVE (OCTOBER 1966)

1. WE WANT FREEDOM. WE WANT POWER TO DETERMINE THE DESTINY OF OUR BLACK COMMUNITY. We believe that black people will not be free until we are able to determine our destiny.

2. WE WANT FULL EMPLOYMENT FOR OUR PEOPLE. We believe that the federal government is responsible and obligated to give every man employment or a guaranteed income. We believe that if the white American businessmen will not give full employment, then the means of production should be taken from the businessmen and placed in the community so that the people of the community can organize and employ all of its people and give a high standard of living.

3. WE WANT AN END TO THE ROBBERY BY THE CAPITALIST OF OUR BLACK COMMUNITY. We believe that this racist government has robbed us and now we are demanding the overdue debt of forty acres and two mules. Forty acres and two mules was promised 100 years ago as restitution for slave labor and mass murder of Black people. We will accept the payment in currency which will be distributed to our many communities. The Germans are now aiding the Jews in Israel for the genocide of the Jewish people. The Germans murdered six million Jews. The American racist has taken part in the slaughter of over fifty million black people; therefore, we feel that this is a modest demand that we make.

4. WE WANT DECENT HOUSING, FIT FOR SHELTER OF HUMAN BEINGS. We believe that if the white landlords will not give decent housing to our black community, then the housing and the land should be made into cooperatives so that our community, with government aid, can build and make decent housing for its people.

5. WE WANT EDUCATION FOR OUR PEOPLE THAT EXPOSES THE TRUE NATURE OF THIS DECADENT AMERICAN SOCIETY. WE WANT EDUCATION THAT TEACHES US OUR TRUE HISTORY AND OUR ROLE IN THE PRESENT-DAY SOCIETY. We believe in an educational system that will give to our people a knowledge of self. If a man does not have knowledge of himself and his position in society and the world, then he has little chance to relate to anything else.

6. WE WANT ALL BLACK MEN TO BE EXEMPT FROM MILITARY SERVICE. We believe the Black people should not be forced to fight in the military service to defend a racist government that does not protect us. We will not fight and kill other people of color in the world who, like black people, are being victimized by the white racist government of America. We will protect ourselves from the force and violence of the racist police and the racist military, by whatever means necessary.

7. WE WANT AN IMMEDIATE END TO POLICE BRUTALITY AND MURDER OF BLACK PEOPLE. We believe we can end police brutality in our black community by organizing black self-defense groups that are dedicated to defending our black community from racist police oppression and brutality. The Second Amendment to the Constitution of the United States gives a right to bear arms. We therefore believe that all black people should arm themselves for self defense.

8. WE WANT FREEDOM FOR ALL BLACK MEN HELD IN FEDERAL, STATE, COUNTY AND CITY PRISONS AND JAILS. We believe that all black people should be released from the many jails and prisons because they have not received a fair and impartial trial.

9. WE WANT ALL BLACK PEOPLE WHEN BROUGHT TO TRIAL TO BE TRIED IN A COURT BY A JURY OF THEIR PEER GROUP OR PEOPLE FROM THEIR BLACK COMMUNITIES, AS DEFINED BY THE CONSTITUTION OF THE UNITED STATES. We believe that the courts should follow the United States Constitution so that black people will receive fair trials. The 14th Amendment of the United States Constitution gives a man a right to be tried by his peer group. A peer is a person from a similar economic, social, religious, geographical, environmental, historical and racial background. To do this the court will be forced to select a jury from the black community from which the black defendant came. We have been, and are being tried by all-white juries that have no understanding of the "average reasoning man" of the black community.

10. WE WANT LAND, BREAD, HOUSING, EDUCATION, CLOTHING, JUSTICE AND PEACE. AND AS OUR MAJOR POLITICAL OBJECTIVE, A UNITED NATIONS–SUPERVISED PLEBISCITE TO BE HELD THROUGHOUT THE BLACK COLONY IN WHICH ONLY BLACK COLONIAL SUBJECTS WILL BE ALLOWED TO PARTICIPATE, FOR THE PURPOSE OF DETERMINING THE WILL OF BLACK PEOPLE AS TO THEIR NATIONAL DESTINY. When, in the course of human events, it becomes necessary for one people to dissolve the political bonds which have connected them with another, and to assume, among the powers of the earth, the separate and equal station to which the laws of nature and nature's God entitle them, a decent respect to the opinions of mankind requires that they should declare the causes which impel them to the separation.

We hold these truths to be self-evident, that all men are created equal; that they are endowed by their Creator with certain unalienable rights; that among these are life, liberty, and the pursuit of happiness. That, to secure these rights, governments are instituted among men, deriving their just powers from the consent of the governed; that, whenever any form of government becomes destructive of these ends, it is the right of the people to alter or to abolish it, and to institute a new government, laying its foundation on such principles, and organizing its powers in such form, as to them shall seem most likely to effect their safety and happiness. Prudence, indeed, will dictate that governments long established should not be changed for light and transient causes; and, accordingly, all experience hath shown, that mankind are more disposed to suffer, while evils are sufferable, than to right themselves by abolishing the forms to which they are accustomed. But when a long train of abuses and usurpations, pursuing invariably the same object, evinces a design to reduce them under absolute despotism, it is their right, it is their duty, to throw off such government, and to provide new guards for their future security.

The idea for the party's name came from a black self-defense group in Lowndes County, Alabama, which used a black panther as its symbol. The panther is known as an animal that only attacks in self-defense.

The two young men belonged to the community of Southern blacks whose families had migrated to Oakland during World War II and afterwards in search of jobs in the naval shipyards and other industries. Huey's family came from Louisiana and Bobby's from Texas during that period. Trying to escape the rigid segregation of the South, these blacks became victims nonetheless of California-style discrimination—on the job, in housing, and in education. In addition, by the mid-1960s, the Oakland Police Department had recruited several whites, also from the South, who brought their racist attitudes with them. Police brutality in Oakland's black communities was rampant.

Huey and Bobby formed the BPP partly as a response to this rise of white police brutality—which was occurring not only in Oakland, but in urban black communities across America—and partly because they believed, as did many black youth at the time, that the tactic of nonviolence successfully used by the civil rights movement in the South would not be effective in the large cities of the urban North.

At the time, it was legal for a person to carry an unconcealed gun in California. Point number 7 of the BPP platform called for "an immediate end to POLICE BRUTALITY and MURDER of black people" and advocated "organizing black self-defense groups that are dedicated to defending our black community from racist police oppression and brutality." It said further, "The Second Amendment to the Constitution of the United States gives a right to bear arms. We therefore believe that all black people should arm themselves for self-defense."

Huey, Bobby, and other Panthers conducted armed "community patrols of the police," during which they would observe police arrests and harassment of blacks and advise those arrested or harassed of their legal rights. Huey became famous (or infamous, depending on one's perspective) for standing on street corners, armed with his gun, quoting citizens' rights from a law book as outraged police looked on.

White Power Structure Responds

The black community had mixed reactions to gun-toting Panthers. Many—like me, initially—thought they were crazy and would get themselves and innocent bystanders killed. Others believed that blacks had no recourse other than to arm ourselves against mounting police brutality.

The white power structure was less divided. To them, the sight of armed black men was terrifying. Some whites may have been reminded of slave revolts, and slaves who joined the Union Army during the Civil War. The California power structure under the leadership of then-governor Ronald Reagan struck back. Legislation aimed at disarming the BPP, known as the Mulford bill, was authored and proposed by East Bay legislator Don Mulford. The bill sought to change existing law by making it illegal for an unlicensed person to carry a loaded gun, concealed or unconcealed, in a public place.

On May 2, 1967, an armed contingent of Panthers led by Bobby Seale marched into the California legislature in Sacramento to protest the Mulford bill. Later, on the steps of the state capitol building, Bobby read the party's statement protesting the bill, "Executive Mandate No. 1," later published in *The Black Panther* (see sidebar 2). The Mulford bill was later passed.

EXCERPT FROM "EXECUTIVE MANDATE #1," DELIVERED BY BOBBY SEALE ON MAY 2, 1967, ON THE STEPS OF THE STATE CAPITOL BUILDING, SACRAMENTO, CALIFORNIA, IN PROTEST OF THE MULFORD BILL TO RESTRICT THE RIGHT TO BEAR ARMS:

Black people have begged, prayed, petitioned, demonstrated and everything else to get the racist power structure of America to right the wrongs which have historically been perpetrated against Black people. All of these efforts have been answered by more repression, deceit, and hypocrisy. . . . The Black Panther Party for Self-Defense believes that the time has come for Black people to arm themselves against this terror before it is too late. The pending Mulford Act brings the hour of doom one step nearer. A people who have suffered so much for so long at the hands of a racist society must draw the line somewhere. We believe that the Black communities of America must rise up as one man to halt the progression of a trend that leads inevitably to their total destruction.

Nearing the end of my freshman year at Baker University in Baldwin, Kansas, I saw the televised footage of armed Panthers marching into the California legislature. The BPP, which had been a local group until then, gained national attention, and Panther chapters began to appear in major cities across the country.

Hoover Begins Infiltration Program

Unlike the Mulford bill, other attacks on the party were not so overt or legal. *War Against the Panthers: A Study of Repression in America*, Huey's 1980 doctoral dissertation at the University of California-Santa Cruz, is a detailed account of the government's harassment of the BPP—which was dominated by the FBI Counterintelligence Program (COINTELPRO). On August 25, 1967, FBI records show, the FBI launched a violent and illegal program to destroy the black liberation movement in America. In a memo, Hoover ordered forty-one FBI field offices to "expose, disrupt, misdirect, discredit, or otherwise neutralize the activities of black nationalist . . . hate-type organizations and groupings, their leadership, spokesmen, membership and supporters."

Initial groups targeted were the Student Nonviolent Coordinating Committee (SNCC), a civil rights group that played a key role in the Southern black voter registration drives of the early 1960s; Southern Christian Leadership Conference (SCLC), founded by Dr. Martin Luther King Jr.; Congress of Racial Equality (CORE); Nation of Islam; and the Revolutionary Action Movement. The BPP was added to the list in September 1968.

At Hoover's direction, FBI agents across the country planted spies and informants in the BPP and other black radical and civil rights groups in the sixties and seventies to destroy them from within. COINTELPRO was also used against white, Native American, Chicano, and Asian leftist groups during this period.

COINTELPRO operations against the BPP were numerous and vicious, and included:

- hundreds of false arrests. From January 1, 1968, to December 31, 1969, 739 BPP members were arrested, an average of more than one a day, with close to $5 million spent on bail;
- sending to churches whose facilities the party used for the Free Breakfast for School Children Program anonymous letters falsely accusing Panthers of teaching black children to hate whites; and
- securing respected establishment journalists to write negative articles about the BPP.

By July 1969, the BPP was the primary target of the "Black Nationalist" COINTELPRO. Ultimately, 233 of the total 295 authorized "Black Nationalist" actions had been carried out against the BPP. At least twenty-eight Panthers were killed as a result.

The worst of the COINTELPRO activities against the party was the planting of undercover informants, usually black, in party affiliates. A paid FBI informant in Chicago, William O'Neal, provided information that led to the murders by police of Illinois Panther leaders Fred Hampton and Mark Clark on December 4, 1969, in the westside Chicago apartment that was used as the local BPP headquarters. Fred, a brilliant, charismatic leader who built the Chicago BPP chapter into one of the largest and most successful in the country, was shot to death while asleep in bed, probably drugged by O'Neal. (After living under an assumed identity for twenty years, O'Neal committed suicide in January 1990.)

Details of COINTELPRO operations against the BPP were published in the April 1976 final report of the U.S. Senate committee investigating intelligence activities, known as the Church Committee for its chair, then-senator Frank Church of Idaho. The introduction to the 989-page report concluded:

Many of the techniques used would be intolerable in a democratic society even if all targets had been involved in violent activity, but COINTELPRO went far beyond that. The unexpressed major premise of the programs was that a law enforcement agency has the duty to do whatever is necessary to combat perceived threats to the existing social and political order.

Accusing the FBI of inciting violence between Panthers and other groups, the Church Committee declared:

It is deplorable that officials of the United States government should engage in the activities described below . . . equally disturbing is the pride which those officials took in claiming credit for the bloodshed that occurred.

First *Black Panther* Focuses on Denzil Dowell Killing

The first issue of *The Black Panther Black Community News Service*, a four-page mimeographed sheet published April 25, 1967, focused on the killing of Denzil Dowell, a twenty-two-year-old black man, by a white sheriff's deputy in Richmond, California. According to the official police report, Dowell was killed after he fled from the deputy, who had stopped Dowell and ordered him to show his identification. Dowell's family disputed the police account and charged that he was murdered. Residents of the area where Dowell was killed said they heard six to ten shots fired. The coroner's report said there were six to ten bullet wounds in Dowell's body, but the police said only three shots were fired. Police said Dowell jumped over a fence during their pursuit of him. Family members said a hip injury he received in a car accident some time earlier made it impossible for Dowell to jump over a fence. They also charged that the deputy who killed Dowell knew him and had previously threatened to kill him.

The family of Dowell asked the fledgling BPP to investigate the young black man's killing, which was ruled justifiable homicide. The combative editorial of the inaugural *Black Panther* set the paper's tone for the next four years. After listing "questionable facts" about the killing raised by Dowell's family, the newspaper said:

> The white cop is the instrument sent into our community by the Power structure to keep Black people quiet and under control . . . it is time that Black People start moving in a direction that will free our communities from this form of outright brutal oppression. The BLACK PANTHER PARTY FOR SELF DEFENSE has worked out a program that is carefully designed to cope with this situation.

Former BPP "revolutionary artist" and "minister of culture" Emory Douglas (see figure 2) coordinated layout and design of *The Black Panther* from the second issue of the paper until the last one in October 1980. In a March 1991 interview, he recalled the early days of *The Black Panther.* "Huey compared the party's need for a publication with the armed struggle of the Vietnamese people that was going on at that time," Emory said. "He said that the Vietnamese carried mimeograph machines wherever they went to produce flyers and other literature to spread the word about their fight to free their country. The party needed to have a newspaper so we could tell our own story."

Eldridge Cleaver Becomes First Editor

Eldridge Cleaver, one of the BPP's most controversial leaders, was the first editor of *The Black Panther.* In December 1966, only five months before the first issue came out, he had been paroled from prison after *Soul on Ice*, Eldridge's treatise on how being an oppressed black man in America led him to be a rapist, gained him national recognition. At Huey's invitation, he joined the party in 1967 after a BPP confrontation with police at the Berkeley office of *Ramparts* magazine, a white leftist publication. Eldridge was married to the former Kathleen Neal, who became BPP communications secretary and a well-known party spokesperson. Kathleen had been an activist in Nashville, Tennessee, in SNCC, and in June 1967, a short-lived merger of the BPP and SNCC began.

Huey believed that the party could become more adept at community organizing using the successful tactics SNCC had employed in the South. In "Executive Mandate No. 2" (see sidebar 3), published in the July 3, 1967, issue of *The Black Panther*, the BPP "drafted" SNCC leader Stokely Carmichael (now known as Kwame Tour) into the party with the rank of "field marshal." The alliance was formalized at a "Free Huey Rally" in Oakland on February 17, 1968, the twenty-sixth birthday of the incarcerated BPP cofounder.

FIGURE 2: Emory Douglas, Black Panther Party Minister of Culture and *The Black Panther* layout and design artist from issue two in May 1967 to the last one in October 1980, in 1969. From It's About Time archives.

SIDEBAR 3

EXCERPT FROM "EXECUTIVE MANDATE #2," IN WHICH THE BLACK PANTHER PARTY "DRAFTED" SNCC LEADER STOKELY CARMICHAEL (KWAME TOUR) INTO THE PARTY WITH THE RANK OF "FIELD MARSHAL." PUBLISHED IN THE JULY 3, 1967, ISSUE OF *THE BLACK PANTHER*:

So Let this Be heard . . .

Brother Stokely Carmichael:

Because you have distinguished yourself in the struggle for the total liberation of Black People from oppression in racist white America;

Because you have acted courageously and shown great fortitude under the most adverse circumstances;

Because you have proven yourself as a true revolutionary guided by a great feeling of love for our people;

Because you have set such a fine example, in the tradition of Brother Malcolm, of dedicating your entire life to the struggle of Black Liberation, inspiring our youth and providing a model for others to emulate;

Because you have refused to serve in the oppressor's racist mercenary aggressive war machine, showing that you know who your true friends and enemies are;

Because of your new endeavor to organize and liberate the Crown Colony of Washington, D.C., you will inevitably be forced to confront, deal with, and conquer the racist Washington Police Department which functions as the protector of the racist dog power structure occupying the Black Community in the same manner and for the same reasons that the racist U.S. Armed Forces occupy South Vietnam;

You are hereby drafted into the Black Panther Party for Self Defense invested with the rank of Field Marshall, delegated the following authority, power and responsibility:

To establish revolutionary law, order and justice in the territory lying between the Continental Divide East to the Atlantic Ocean; North of the Mason-Dixon Line to the Canadian Border; South of the Mason-Dixon Line to the Gulf of Mexico

. . . . So Let It Be Done:

Signed

Huey P. Newton

Minister of Defense

"Eldridge was a flamboyant person in those days, and his writing was provocative," Emory said in characterizing *The Black Panther*'s content under its first editor. Huey, Bobby, and other party members contributed ideas and articles to the paper. The newspaper also included articles from people in the community, a practice that continued throughout the paper's existence. Members of BPP chapters throughout the country wrote articles to report news and issues in their local areas.

When Eldridge first became editor, the paper was produced at the home of his attorney, Beverly Axelrod, Emory said. Later, production moved to the apartment where Eldridge and Kathleen lived in San Francisco. Production also took place at the homes of other party members who lived in the city.

The first two issues of *The Black Panther* were done on a mimeograph machine. Afterwards, the newspaper was typed, and graphics were done with instant type. Rubber cement was used to paste the galleys down. Kathleen and other BPP members typed and proofread articles.

Beginning with the third issue, Emory began to oversee the paper's format. "My job was to make the paper look appealing and to see that the art work was in line with the party's politics," he said. Under Emory's leadership, the newspaper's layout cadre used creative designs that most black newspapers had not widely used at the time. The front page of *The Black Panther* had a magazine flavor.

Emory Douglas: Revolutionary Artist

Emory would later outline his views as a revolutionary artist in a speech at Fisk University in Nashville, Tennessee, in October 1972. In the speech, which was printed in *The Black Panther*, the ex-BPP artist said:

> If we take this structure of commercial art and add a brand new content to it, then we will begin to analyze Black people and our situation for the purpose of raising our consciousness to the oppression that we are subjected to. We would use commercial art for the purpose of educating Black people. . . . No artist can sit in an ivory tower, discussing the problems of the day, and come up with a solution on a piece of paper. The artist has to be down on the ground; he has to hear the sounds of the people, the cries of the people, the suffering of the people, the laughter of the people—the dark side and the bright side of our lives. . . . We must understand that when there are over 20 million people in this country, hungry, then we, as artists, have something we must deal with.

When the party opened an office on Shattuck Avenue, a Justifax machine and later a Compugraphic machine were used for typesetting. Throughout the thirteen years of its production, *The Black Panther* was typeset at party offices by BPP members or others hired by the party.

Newspaper distribution was a party-wide activity. In 1967, Emory distributed *The Black Panther* in his hometown of San Francisco, where he sold papers in the then predominantly black communities of Fillmore and Hunter's Point. Huey, Bobby, Eldridge, and other BPP members would sell papers at their speaking engagements.

"Free Huey" Heard around the World

The BPP gained increased national attention and membership following the October 28, 1967, shooting incident involving Huey and two white Oakland police officers, Herbert Heanes and John Frey. The officers, who recognized the license plates of the car in which Huey was a passenger as that of a BPP vehicle, ordered the car to stop. In the bloody altercation that followed, Heanes was wounded and Frey was killed. Huey, himself seriously wounded, was arrested for Frey's killing.

A picture of Huey lying wounded and handcuffed to a hospital gurney appeared on national TV and in newspapers. The BPP, charging that Heanes and Frey had tried to murder Huey, launched an international campaign to get the BPP "minister of defense" out of jail. "Free Huey," a frequent headline in *The Black Panther* at that time, became the demand of black, white, and Third World progressive and radical groups around the world. As a result, hundreds of urban black youth across America joined the party.

On September 8, 1968, Huey was convicted of manslaughter in Frey's death. Three weeks later, he was sentenced to two to fifteen years in prison and was imprisoned until his release on August 5, 1970, after his conviction was overturned.

In 1968, Sam Napier joined the BPP in San Francisco; he was the party's dedicated circulation manager until his murder in New York City in April 1971 (see figure 3). "Sam had a great desire to distribute the paper. That's what he wanted to do," Emory said. Sam traveled all over the country securing distributors for *The Black Panther.* "He would call and tell us where he was and that he had gotten another route."

In the pages of *The Black Panther*, the BPP stated its views in speeches and writings by party leaders on "the correct handling of a revolution." In an article of that name published in the May 4, 1968, issue, Huey wrote:

> The Vanguard Party must provide leadership for the people. It must teach the correct strategic methods of prolonged resistance through literature and activities. . . . When the people learn that it is no longer advantageous for them to resist by going to the streets in large numbers and when they see the advantage in the activities of guerrilla warfare methods, they will quickly follow this example.

It was also common for the newspaper to print articles written by Cuban president Fidel Castro, Chinese leader Mao Zedong, and the late Mozambican president Samora Machel, as well as speeches and writings of party leaders.

"The paper gave black, poor, and dispossessed people a grassroots point of view on the news that they had never had before," Emory said in assessing the contribution of *The Black Panther.*

Thanks to Emory and other artists like Mark Teemer and Matilaba (Joan Lewis), *The Black Panther* published artwork that most people had never seen before. The BPP's contributions to popular culture of the era included the verbal and visual depiction of police as "pigs." The pig, because it is commonly thought of as a dirty animal, was chosen by the BPP as a symbol of police brutality in the black community. Many people bought the newspaper just to see Emory's latest cartoons of pigs dressed in police uniforms, which could be found in almost every issue from 1967 to about 1970. *Black Panther: The Revolutionary Art of Emory Douglas*, published in 2007, is a collection of some of Emory's finest work and includes essays by former Panther leaders Bobby Seale and Kathleen Cleaver and actor Danny Glover.

In its early years, the paper printed the names of BPP national and local leaders, as well as addresses of recognized chapters and branches. While this practice helped people who needed assistance to find Panthers in their local communities, it also, unfortunately, helped the FBI and police to infiltrate the party with agents provocateurs, the lifeblood of Hoover's COINTELPRO.

Eldridge Goes into Exile

Two days after the April 4, 1968, assassination of Dr. Martin Luther King Jr., Bobby Hutton, the first BPP member and the party's seventeen-year-old treasurer, was shot to death by Oakland police as he walked out of a house, hands above his head, to surrender. Eldridge and six other Panthers, including "chief of staff" David Hilliard, were arrested on conspiracy and murder charges in connection with Bobby's death. Fearing that he would return to prison, in late 1968 Eldridge fled with Kathleen, first going to Cuba and eventually settling in Algiers, Algeria, where he became "underground" editor of *The Black Panther* and head of the BPP's newly established international section.

By this time, the BPP-SNCC merger had begun to fall apart. In an article in the March 31, 1969, issue of *The Black Panther*, Bobby Seale and the late BPP "minister of education," Raymond

FIGURE 3: Cover of *The Black Panther* volume 6, number 13/14 (May 1, 1971), featuring Sam Napier, newspaper circulation manager from 1968 until his murder in New York City in April 1971. From It's About Time archives.

"Masai" Hewitt, criticized views expressed by Stokely during a visit to Scandinavian countries. Bobby charged that Stokely had "deviated from the Party's political line." An article in the August 16, 1969, *Black Panther* reported that David Hilliard had recently met with Stokely Carmichael in Algiers, and that it was unlikely that Stokely would continue as a party member. Writing from Algiers, in an "Open Letter to Stokely Carmichael" (*The Black Panther*, August 16, 1969), Eldridge attacked Stokely's "Black Power" philosophy:

> There is not going to be any revolution or black liberation in the United States as long as revolutionary blacks, whites, Mexicans, Puerto Ricans, Indians, Chinese and Eskimos are unwilling to unite in some functional machinery that can cope with this situation [capitalism, imperialism, and racism].

Back in America, changes were made in the editorial staff of *The Black Panther*. After Eldridge went into exile, Raymond Lewis became managing editor of *The Black Panther* and "deputy minister of information." By January 1969, Frank Jones had replaced Lewis. In March,

Elbert "Big Man" Howard and Bobby Herron became coeditors of the newspaper. By the end of March, "Big Man" replaced Frank Jones as managing editor.

During Eldridge's tenure as BPP "minister of information," which ended in February 1971, he encouraged a free speech movement in the party. Public statements by party leaders and the newspaper were filled with profanity. Although the profanity may have reflected the language of some activists of the period, it may also have offended some readers.

Newspaper sales declined, according to Emory. "We did a great disservice to the party and the people in the community," he said of the free speech movement. Huey, from prison, criticized it sharply, and it was eventually stopped. While Huey did not regularly oversee the format and contents of the newspaper, even when he was not imprisoned, if he wanted particular information included, his wishes were carried out, as they were in this case.

Even after his tenure as editor ended, Eldridge remained famous for his colorful speeches and writings, often filled with expletives castigating the U.S. power structure. In one article published in the November 22, 1969, issue of *The Black Panther*, he declared:

> A dead pig is desirable, but a paralyzed pig is preferable to a mobile pig. And a determined revolutionary doesn't require an authorization from a Central Committee [BPP leadership body] before offing a pig . . . when the need arises a true revolutionary will off the Central Committee. In order to stop the slaughter of the people we accelerate the slaughter of the pigs.

"One of the Most Effective Propaganda Operations"

The writings and speeches of Eldridge, Huey, Bobby Seale, and other BPP leaders that appeared in *The Black Panther* came under close government scrutiny at this time. On October 8, 1969, the Committee on Internal Security of the U.S. House of Representatives, chaired by then Missouri congressman Richard H. Ichord, authorized an investigation into "the origin, history, organization, character and objectives" of the BPP as reported in *The Black Panther*. A year later, on October 6, 1970, the committee issued a report of about 150 pages detailing the newspaper's contents from June 1967 to September 1970. The report included excerpts from *Black Panther* articles, cartoons, and photos of party leaders.

For the BPP, 1970 was a critical year. In a memo of May 15, Hoover described *The Black Panther* as "one of the most effective propaganda operations of the BPP. . . . It is the voice of the BPP and if it could be effectively hindered it would result in helping to cripple the BPP." Certainly, Hoover had cause for concern. *The Black Panther* had arguably become one of the most popular and colorful radical-left publications of the era. At 25 cents per copy, *The Black Panther*'s weekly circulation had surpassed 100,000. Subscriptions and contributors came from throughout the world, including France, Sweden, Denmark, England, Japan, China, North Korea, Mozambique, Guinea-Bissau, and Cuba. Of the "alternative" publications, only *Muhammad Speaks*, the newspaper of the Nation of Islam (NOI), was selling more copies.

Less than a week after Hoover's memo ordering FBI field offices to "cripple" the BPP, the San Diego FBI office proposed to spray a foul-smelling chemical called Skatol on copies of *The Black Panther*. In June, FBI headquarters concocted a plan to "ignite the fuel of conflict" between the BPP and the Nation of Islam by reducing sales of *Muhammad Speaks*. However, in July, the Chicago field office advised against pursuing this project, warning that, due to existing tensions between the two groups, "any revelation of a Bureau attempt to encourage conflict might serve to bring the BPP and NOI closer together."

In November 1970, FBI headquarters directed field offices to distribute copies of a column written by Victor Riesel, a white labor columnist, calling for a nationwide union boycott of handling *The Black Panther*, which was shipped around the country by air freight. The Church Committee could not determine the outcome of this plan.

FBI Plot Creates Rift between Huey and Eldridge

Earlier, in March 1970, the FBI had launched a COINTELPRO action to create a permanent rift between Huey and Eldridge. Each was isolated from the party—Eldridge in exile in Algeria and Huey in prison. Exploiting this situation, the bureau sent an anonymous letter to Eldridge saying that BPP leaders in California were trying to undermine his influence. As a result of this fake letter, Eldridge expelled three members of the BPP's international section.

Pleased with the apparent success of the first letter, the FBI followed it up with another one to David Hilliard, written to appear as if it had come from Connie Matthews, the party's representative in Scandinavia. The second letter claimed that Eldridge "has tripped out. Perhaps he has been working too hard." The letter suggested that David "take some immediate action before this becomes more serious." In May 1970, Eldridge called BPP national headquarters in Oakland and talked to David, Connie, and other BPP leaders. Suspicion was expressed that the letters had probably been sent by the FBI or CIA.

Nevertheless, the FBI continued with its campaign to cause dissension between Huey and Eldridge. About a week after Huey's release from prison on August 5, 1970, an FBI informant in Philadelphia distributed a fake "directive" to local Panthers questioning Huey's leadership ability. The fictitious COINTELPRO letters to Huey and Eldridge, alleging that each was critical of the other's leadership, continued throughout the rest of 1970 and into early 1971, and resulted in Huey's expulsion of several key members from the party, including Connie Matthews.

On February 26, 1971, during a TV interview, Eldridge criticized the expulsions and suggested that David Hilliard be removed as BPP chief of staff. As a result, Huey expelled Eldridge and the entire international section of the party. Their expulsions were reported in the March 6 edition of *The Black Panther*. The FBI program to create a permanent rift between Huey and Eldridge had succeeded.

In New York City, where animosities between the "pro-Huey" and "pro-Eldridge" groups were the greatest, several BPP members were expelled. In separate incidents there in March and April 1971, Panthers Sam Napier, *Black Panther* national circulation manager, and Harold Russell were shot to death.

In his critical essay published in the April 17, 1971, issue of *The Black Panther*, "On the Defection of Eldridge Cleaver from the Black Panther Party and the Defection of the Black Panther Party from the Black Community," Huey wrote:

We recognize that nothing in nature stands outside of dialectics, even the Black Panther Party. But we welcome these contradictions, because they clarify our struggle. We had a contradiction with our former Minister of Information, Eldridge Cleaver. But we understand this as necessary to our growth.

While praising Eldridge for his "great contributions to the Black Panther Party with his writing and speaking," Huey accused him of joining the BPP for the wrong reasons:

> Without my knowledge, he [Eldridge] took this [the *Ramparts* incident] as *the* Revolution and *the* Party . . . the police confrontation left him fixated with the "either-or" attitude. This was that either the community picked up the gun with the Party or else they were cowards and there was no place for them.

Criticizing the BPP for its free speech movement, which he said had isolated the party from the black community, Huey said, "The Black Panther Party defected from the community long before Eldridge defected from the Party."

Paper Embraces "Intercommunal" Struggle

Two months earlier, in February, Huey had changed the name of the newspaper from *The Black Panther Black Community News Service* to *The Black Panther Intercommunal News Service*. The change was made to reflect the party's shift from a largely black-nationalist perspective to one advocating an international or "intercommunal" struggle against racism and imperialism that cut across all color lines.

Regular features of the newspaper at that time, in addition to the party's Ten Point Platform and Program, included "People's Perspective," a column on national news events affecting black and Third World people; "Black and Community News," including articles about party leaders, programs, and events; "Intercommunal News," which featured news about freedom movements in southern Africa, Central America, and the Middle East; book excerpts and reviews and movie reviews; and a list of BPP "Survival Programs," such as the Free Breakfast for School Children Program (see figure 4), the People's Free Medical Clinic, and the Free Food and Free Legal Aid programs. *The Black Panther* was circulated internationally. African liberation movements and many foreign embassies subscribed to it. It was also popular on college and university campuses.

Elaine Brown and Ericka Huggins Become Succeeding Editors

Succeeding *Black Panther* editors included Elaine Brown and Ericka Huggins. The two women and Ericka's husband, John, were early party members in the Los Angeles BPP chapter founded by "deputy minister of defense" Alprentice "Bunchy" Carter, a former gang leader who had served time in prison. On January 17, 1969, Bunchy and John, the chapter's "minister of information," were shot to death during a meeting of black students at the University of California-Los Angeles. Five members of United Slaves (US), a black-nationalist organization founded by Maulana Karenga, were charged with killing the Southern California BPP leaders. Two of the five remained at large. The other three, brothers George and Larry Stiner and Claude Hubert, were convicted of murder. The Church Committee on Intelligence later revealed that

FIGURE 4: Participants of the Free Breakfast for School Children Program, one of many "Survival Programs" organized by the Black Panther Party and featured regularly in *The Black Panther*, in 1969. From It's About Time archives.

COINTELPRO instigated and then perpetuated rising violence between the BPP and US by sending inflammatory letters to the rival groups, claiming each was out to destroy the other. In a *Penthouse* interview published in April 1979, "Othello," an ex-agent provocateur in the Los Angeles BPP, charged that the Stiners and Hubert were police informants in US.

Following the deaths of Bunchy and John, Elaine, who had been communications secretary for the Los Angeles BPP chapter, became its deputy minister of information, the number two post in a chapter. She went to Oakland around 1970 and became editor of *The Black Panther*. Her writing and editing skills greatly improved the quality and professionalism of the newspaper. However, in late 1972, Elaine's tenure as editor ended when she ran for Oakland city council in a historic campaign with Bobby Seale, who ran for mayor. While the two BPP leaders lost the election in April 1973, they captured 40 percent of the vote, bolstering black political power in Oakland and paving the way for the election of the city's first black mayor, Lionel Wilson, in 1977. In 1975, Elaine was defeated in a close race in her second run for city council.

Ericka, while in New Haven, Connecticut, to bury her husband, was arrested and jailed for conspiracy and murder, along with seven other Panthers, in the May 1969 death of New York BPP member Alex Rackley. Ericka and Bobby Seale, who also was charged with Rackley's murder, stood trial together in a case that was regularly covered in *The Black Panther*. They were released from nearly two years of prison on May 24, 1971, when the jury deadlocked and a mistrial was declared (see figure 5). Moving to Oakland in 1971, Ericka followed Elaine as editor of *The Black Panther*, a position she held until about mid-1972. In 1973, Ericka became director of the Intercommunal Youth Institute (later renamed Oakland Community School), the BPP's community-based, award-winning elementary school.

David Du Bois Institutes Collective Decision Making

David G. Du Bois succeeded Ericka as editor of *The Black Panther*. During the summer of 1972, the stepson of W.E.B. Du Bois—the great African American historian and sociologist—returned to the United States following a thirteen-year absence. David had spent his time abroad working as a journalist and college professor in Egypt and Ghana and traveling in Africa, Europe, the Soviet Union, and the People's Republic of China, where he was a student for a time.

"When I came to the Black Panther Party, I was no spring chicken," David wrote in a 1990 unpublished article. "I was 47 years old and had cut my revolutionary teeth on street demonstrations with other [World War II] war-weary G.I.s in the Philippines demanding our right to go home and in the east coast student and veterans' movements of the mid and late 1940's." He became frustrated with the failure of these movements to "honestly and decisively" deal with issues impacting American blacks. Thus, in 1959 David began his exile from the United States.

Back in America in 1972, David began to research the achievements of the civil rights movement of the 1960s, which had taken place during his absence. At the top of his list was the BPP. Many party leaders, including David Hilliard and Eldridge Cleaver, traveled in Africa during the late 1960s, and David Du Bois met some of them in Cairo, Egypt, where he lived. "Through these contacts I learned firsthand much about the Party. . . . Most of what I learned increased an already intense admiration for these young ghetto blacks who had decided they had taken it long enough and were prepared to fight fire with fire," David wrote.

In November and December 1972, he visited the San Francisco Bay Area, where he finally

FIGURE 5: Cover of *The Black Panther*, volume 6, number 18 (May 29, 1971), with headline story celebrating the release of Ericka Huggins and Bobby Seale from prison after a deadlocked jury resulted in a mistrial. After the trial, Ericka succeeded Elaine Brown as editor of *The Black Panther*. From It's About Time archives.

met Huey and toured BPP programs in Oakland and Berkeley. Later, at a dinner with other party members, Huey shared with David his "fantasy" that David would become editor in chief of *The Black Panther*. David was a veteran journalist, and Huey was always concerned with improving the professionalism of the newspaper. Several days later, David began his three-year association with the BPP as editor of the party's newspaper. Huey insisted that David be a party employee, not a member, "making me, he hoped, less a target for the party's enemies," David recalled.

While assured by Huey that he would have complete freedom with content and format of *The Black Panther*, David nevertheless began his work cautiously. Reflecting on his early days as editor of *BPINS*, as the paper came to be known by party members, David wrote:

> The most serious initial challenge I faced was winning the confidence and the willing cooperation of the paper's staff. None had had formal journalistic training or newspaper experience, except that they had gained getting out the party paper. Their work methods had successfully produced the paper week after succeeding week. . . . "So who is this aging bourgeois outsider taking over and threatening changes," they [newspaper staff] said to me with their eyes and in their manner toward me.

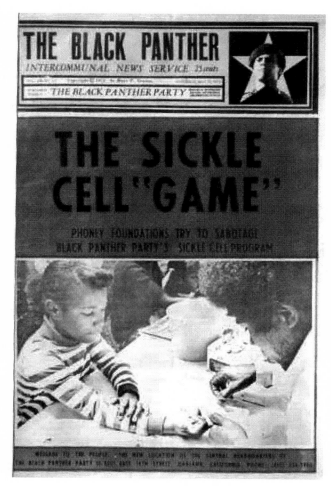

FIGURE 6: Cover of *The Black Panther* volume 8, number 10 (May 17, 1972), featuring one of a series of articles the paper ran to expose the medical establishment's apathy toward sickle cell anemia, a rare blood disease that afflicts primarily people of African descent, and to promote the Black Panther Party's free nationwide sickle cell anemia testing program. From It's About Time archives.

Being the stepson of W. E. B. Du Bois helped David's status with party members. Perhaps more important in helping him gradually win the staff's confidence, he insisted that the staff make collective decisions about the content and format of the paper. While weekly newspaper meetings were routine, David at first found it difficult to get staff members to express their opinions. With his encouragement, their reluctance abated in time, and they contributed ideas and opinions that continually improved *The Black Panther* and its status among BPP members.

In 1972 *The Black Panther* began a series of articles on sickle cell anemia, a rare blood disease that mostly afflicts people of African descent (see figure 6). For this reason, the party charged, medical science had made little effort to study the disease and develop a treatment for it. The party also launched a free, nationwide sickle-cell-anemia testing program.

Recruited to Detroit BPP Chapter

Meanwhile, the summer of 1972 was also eventful for me. My fiancé, Joe Abron, a Detroit native and Purdue University junior, joined the local chapter of the BPP. Having recently earned my master's degree in communication from Purdue, I worked in Chicago as public information officer at Malcolm X College and later as a reporter for the *Chicago Daily Defender*. Frequently, I went to Detroit for weekends to visit Joe and to do party work. We both firmly believed that black people who wanted to make social change needed to belong to an organization in order to have the greatest impact, so I soon followed him into the BPP.

By the time I joined the party, my views about the black struggle had been shaped by the Southern civil rights movement of the 1950s and early 1960s, which I observed at a distance during my childhood in Jefferson City, Missouri. I lived in the Missouri capital city with my parents and two younger sisters from 1953 to 1966. My father, J. Otis Erwin, a United Methodist minister (who died in 2003), established the Wesley Foundation at Lincoln University and taught philosophy and religion at the university, then a predominantly black school. From him and my mother, Adeline Comer Erwin, who had been a college music teacher before marrying my father, I learned that blacks with skills had a responsibility to use them to better the black race.

Watching television and reading news accounts, I was impressed by the courage of blacks and their white allies who often risked their lives to defy Jim Crow segregation laws in the South and demand the right of blacks to vote and to attend the schools of their choice. In the summer of 1964, when black and white students in SNCC and other civil rights groups launched a massive voter registration drive in Mississippi, I wanted to join them. My mother, however, told me it was much too dangerous for a sixteen-year-old girl like me to go to Mississippi.

At any rate, by the time I graduated from high school in May 1966, I had decided that whatever my career would be as an adult, I would use it to help black people. I spent the next four years in college at Baker University in Baldwin, Kansas, where I majored in journalism. When Dr. Martin Luther King Jr. was assassinated on April 4, 1968, I was near the end of my sophomore year. Dr. King's murder troubled me deeply and strengthened my resolve to get involved in the black movement.

That summer, I was one of six Baker students and a faculty member who spent eight weeks in the southern African country of Rhodesia, now Zimbabwe. Rhodesia was the first African country I had ever visited. My knowledge of Africa was so limited that I had assumed African blacks controlled their countries. In Rhodesia, I learned that the country had been under British rule since the late nineteenth century, and that blacks had launched an armed struggle to win their freedom. Living on a Methodist church mission, I worked for a black newspaper that was regularly censored by the government for printing news critical of the white regime, which the U.S. government supported. (Twenty-five years later, in 1983, I took another study trip to Zimbabwe, whose black-majority government had been in power for three years.) Returning to Baker with increased determination to work in the black movement after graduation, I became coeditor of the campus newspaper, the *Baker Orange*, during my junior and senior years. After graduating in May 1970, I went to Purdue to graduate school.

Party Work in the Motor City

By the time I joined the BPP in the summer of 1972, the COINTELPRO campaign against the party had taken its toll on Detroit Panthers. Many members had resigned and several were imprisoned, leaving less than a dozen members in the Motor City.

Afraid that a sheltered minister's daughter like me would not be accepted by streetwise party members, I began my apprenticeship as a would-be Panther selling *The Black Panther.* In platform shoes, I walked up and down endless drab hallways in Detroit housing projects, urging all who opened their doors to "Get your Black Panther news! Get your people's paper!" My Panther comrades and I had fun competing with Nation of Islam members for newspaper sales on Detroit street corners. For the most part, the competition was friendly and consisted of members of the two groups trying to out-talk each other for sales.

In August 1973, Joe and I were married. Four months later, in December 1973, he graduated from Purdue and we returned to Detroit to work full-time in the party. My main jobs were to work in the Free Breakfast for School Children Program; to drive for the Busing to Prisons Program, which provided transportation for relatives of prisoners to visit their loved ones at Michigan's Jackson State Prison; and to sell *The Black Panther Intercommunal News Service.* I worked hard and earned the respect of my comrades.

I became a writer for the *BPINS* in early 1974 after moving to Oakland with Joe and other members of the Detroit BPP chapter. At the time, there were thirteen comrades in the newspaper cadre, as we were called, consisting of writers, led by editor David Du Bois, and layout staff (paste-up and typesetting), led by artist Emory Douglas. In a given week, writers might be assigned to cover a city-council meeting, a community rally, or a speech by Bobby Seale and Elaine Brown. During my first few months there, I did a series on the party's alternative school, the Intercommunal Youth Institute.

In April 1974, shortly after my arrival in Oakland, local police raided a party facility on 29th Avenue in East Oakland where children from the Intercommunal Youth Institute often stayed. Several BPP members were arrested, and police seized party documents and files in the house. A few days later, while in a laundromat across the street from the apartment where I lived with Joe and other Panthers, I was approached by two white men who showed me badges identifying them as FBI agents.

"Hi, JoNina. We want to talk to you for a minute," one of the smiling agents said. "We know that you just came to Oakland to work with the Black Panthers. There's been trouble recently [referring to the 29th Avenue raid], and we don't think you want to be involved in that. Maybe we can help." His voice and manner were pleasant. Nevertheless, the familiar way he spoke, as if he knew all about me, terrified me. Panthers were trained never to talk to police without an attorney present. I told the FBI agents I had nothing to say to them and tore out of the laundromat back to my apartment, where I called party headquarters to tell them what had happened. I had experienced what I believe was a COINTELPRO action.

Crisis in 1974

Eight months after my arrival in Oakland, in August 1974, the party underwent another crisis. In separate incidents that month, police charged Huey with beating a black tailor, Preston Callins, and shooting a black prostitute, Kathleen Smith, to death. Afraid he might return to prison, Huey disappeared. A few weeks later, he surfaced in Havana, Cuba, where he lived in exile with his wife and Panther comrade, Gwen, for the next three years. The charges against Huey and his disappearance caused considerable confusion within party ranks and severely damaged our reputation in the community. Unsure of the party's future, and weary from years of courtroom trials and police harassment, party chair Bobby Seale and several other BPP Central

Committee members also disappeared. With Bobby gone, Huey, from Havana, gave leadership of the party to Elaine Brown and appointed her BPP chair.

As the party coped with the departure of its cofounders, *The Black Panther* continued its weekly publication schedule. Once again, "Free Huey" became a recurring theme in the paper. Other articles in the paper at that time reflected the expansion of the party's work and influence under Elaine's tenure as party chair. The BPP worked with such diverse groups as the United Farmworkers; the Zimbabwe African National Union, which was leading Rhodesia's armed black liberation struggle; and Oakland Concerned Citizens for Urban Renewal. She consulted frequently with David about the newspaper's coverage of the party's work with these groups.

The paper frequently reprinted articles from other leftist and progressive publications whose views reflected those of the BPP. Writers were given news clippings to edit. Such reprints were always attributed in an editor's note. Unlike most other leftist publications, however, there were no bylines on articles in *The Black Panther.*

Ideas and some copy for national and international news often came from establishment newspapers like the *New York Times, Los Angeles Times,* and *Washington Post.* However, our slant on the major news events of the day was almost always different than what appeared in the establishment papers. Under David's brilliant leadership, the quality, language, and appearance of *The Black Panther* substantially improved. The party purchased a good-quality offset typesetting machine and made greater use of party members with writing skills for proofreading and copyediting.

Membership Drops: *Black Panther* Becomes Biweekly

Police surveillance of the newspaper continued. According to a Los Angeles Police Department intelligence division memo of March 11, 1974, "The Black Panther has increased in journalistic quality, but decreased in circulation since the Panthers have concentrated in the Oakland area."

David's tenure as *BPINS* editor ended abruptly in early 1976 when his mother, Shirley Graham Du Bois, widow of Dr. W.E.B. Du Bois, became ill and David left Oakland to care for her in Beijing, China, where she died in 1977. Of his work with the BPP, David later said, "It irrevocably, mercifully changed my life." After his mother's death, David divided much of his time between living in Cairo, Egypt, and Amherst, Massachusetts, where for many years he was a visiting professor of Afro-American studies and journalism at the University of Massachusetts. When he was in the United States, David and I would often talk by phone about the pressing issues of the day. In September 1999, I invited him to attend a meeting of black activists that I helped to organize in Atlanta, Georgia. David's contributions to the meeting were invaluable and deeply appreciated by the mostly young people who attended. David died on January 28, 2005, in Amherst after a short illness. He was seventy-nine.

Following David as editor was Michael Fultz, the talented assistant editor, a Brooklyn, New York, native who joined the party in Boston while a college student. Michael became editor of *The Black Panther* when the BPP was mounting a citywide campaign to elect Lionel Wilson as Oakland's first black mayor (see figure 7). Elaine told party members that Wilson's election was an essential condition for creating a favorable climate for Huey's return from Cuba to stand trial on the assault and murder charges from August 1974. The newspaper was the party's official news organ and therefore a key component in the Wilson campaign and efforts

FIGURE 7: Author JoNina Abron (*center*) with *The Black Panther* staffers Micheal Ellis (*left*) and Micheal Fultz (*right*), at the time the newspaper's editor, in 1977. From It's About Time archives.

to bring Huey home. Elaine, therefore, often instructed Michael on the paper's contents. In addition to his responsibilities as editor, Michael often spoke for the party at meetings and other community events.

In April 1977, Wilson was elected mayor of Oakland, and in July, Huey returned to Oakland from Cuba. He was later acquitted of assaulting Preston Callins, but stood trial twice for the murder of Kathleen Smith. Both trials ended in mistrials, and charges were dropped in 1979. As a result of Huey's three costly trials and several unrelated arrests, party resources were nearly depleted and membership further declined. Soon after I became editor of the newspaper in March 1978, following Michael's resignation from the party, problems developed in my marriage to Joe Abron. He was among several Panthers who left the party in the late 1970s, and we later were divorced. BPP membership, variously estimated at highs of 2,000 to 4,000 nationwide, had dropped to a couple of dozen. Most members, although still dedicated to the party's principles, found it hard to stay in the organization as they got older and found themselves needing and wanting better living conditions for themselves and their families, which the party could not provide. The newspaper cadre had only six members, down from thirteen in 1974. With fewer people to produce the newspaper, *The Black Panther* became a biweekly.

Tragedy in Jonestown

The reduction in the newspaper's staff and frequency did not soften its stance on issues affecting black and poor people. One example was *The Black Panther*'s account of the November 1978 deaths of over nine hundred Americans, mostly black and many children, in Jonestown, a settlement in the Caribbean nation of Guyana.

The Jonestown dead were members of the San Francisco–based People's Temple, a church founded by the Reverend Jim Jones. The BPP had developed a close relationship with People's Temple, whose community programs for the poor in San Francisco and northern California were much like those of the party. I knew a few Temple members and considered them my comrades in the struggle. Charles Garry, longtime BPP attorney, was also attorney for People's Temple.

Stanley Nelson, director of the 2006 documentary film *Jonestown: The Life and Death of Peoples Temple*, said in a newspaper interview that his film attempted to portray the "thin lines between faith and zealotry." After I saw the film, I found myself wondering, where does religious faith end and zealotry begin? At any rate, in 1978, the BPP, based on our ties with the church, believed that Jones and several hundred church members had exiled themselves to Guyana and established Jonestown to protest racism and poverty in the United States. To Black Panthers, Jonestown was a serious indictment of life in America. The settlement could prove to be an embarrassment to the U.S. government if allowed to continue.

California congressman Leo Ryan, several Bay Area journalists, and attorney Charles Garry went to Jonestown in November 1978 to investigate complaints from relatives of Jonestown settlers. Authorities said that Temple members, afraid that they would be forced to disband Jonestown, committed suicide by drinking poisoned Kool-Aid at Jones's direction. Jones was found shot to death, apparently having committed suicide. Ryan and three journalists with him were killed while boarding their plane to fly back to the United States.

The BPP questioned whether the mass deaths were really suicide. In the beginning, we had no concrete evidence to support our suspicions. However, the strident media campaign to discredit Jones and People's Temple as a "crazy cult" in the weeks following the tragedy reminded many Panthers of the FBI COINTELPRO campaign against the party. Some party members, including me, were convinced that the deaths at Jonestown might also be the result of COINTELPRO actions.

To substantiate our beliefs, *Black Panther* writers interviewed members of People's Temple and their relatives; we read dozens of news articles about the church. I went several days without sleep to gather the story on Jonestown. For me, it became a personal crusade to tell the "real" truth about how the People's Temple members died.

Six weeks in the making, an entire issue of *The Black Panther* was devoted to what we called the Jonestown "massacre." I wrote the banner headline on the front page of the paper: "C.I.A. Linked to Deaths in Jonestown." I also wrote many of the articles in the issue. One of those, quoting other news sources, charged that a top aide to Jones had once been a CIA agent.

In the editorial, which I wrote, the Black Panther Party accused the CIA of destroying Jonestown with a neutron bomb, which is colorless and odorless and doesn't leave any evidence. This was a bold charge, even for the BPP, and I knew it had to be approved by Huey prior to publication.

In all my phone conversations with him, never had I been as nervous as I was that January day in 1979 when I read the editorial on Jonestown. Despite the public damage to Huey's image from the assault and murder trials he went through after his return from Cuba, he had resumed leadership of the party, and I respected him. After I finished reading him the editorial, he said to my great relief, "Good. Print it."

Many people thought the BPP's assessment of what happened at Jonestown was crazy. One woman said if she believed the BPP's account, she would have to start questioning everything the American government did. She said she was afraid to do that.

Among the Web sites dedicated to research and information about Jonestown is one created in 1999 by the Department of Religious Studies at San Diego State University. According to the Web site, documents about Jonestown that were eligible for mandatory declassification on December 31, 2006, were not declassified. Why?

It has been over thirty years since the horrific deaths at Jonestown, and I no longer believe that it was destroyed by a neutron bomb. However, until all the government documents about Jonestown are released, I believe the truth will never be known about the extent to which the U.S. government was involved in the destruction of Jonestown. Nevertheless, *The Black Panther*'s coverage of the event was but one example of the newspaper's boldness and in-depth reporting of news involving and impacting black and other disenfranchised people. Even though the programs of the Black Panther Party and its membership were all but decimated by the late seventies, and *The Black Panther* was forced to go monthly in 1980, the paper was still in demand by readers who wanted a non-mainstream analysis of the news.

The Last Black Panther, the First Commemorator

Thus, it was with great sorrow that, after thirteen years, the BPP was forced to discontinue the paper in October 1980. Much as I loved the paper, I was among those party members who persuaded Huey that we no longer had the human or financial resources to publish the "people's" paper.

Over a decade later, in November 1990, the Commemoration Committee for the Black Panther Party—composed of ex-Panthers and BPP supporters—began publication of *The Commemorator* in Oakland. The newspaper's statement of purpose reflects the original goals of the BPP and *Black Panther*:

> The newspaper encourages grassroots organizing and networking for people empowerment and community control of the institutions effecting change . . . the COMMEMORATOR IS A PROGRESSIVE COMMUNITY FORUM. It offers the community at large the opportunity to help solve some of the critical problems that affect us all. . . . the lack of decent shelter, medical care, education and employment for all people.

Beginning in the November 1990 issue and concluding in the March 1991 issue, the *Commemorator* reprinted an article written in May 1990 by ex-BPP chair Elaine Brown, "Responding to Radical Racism: David Horowitz Barely Remembered." Horowitz, former editor of *Ramparts* magazine, a leftist publication, was once a BPP ally. Elaine's article was written in response to a particularly bitter and racist article by Horowitz in the March–April 1990 issue of *Smart* magazine, in which the white ex-radical accused the BPP of being a "gang of hoodlums," and Huey of being a "thug who had terrorized the Oakland underworld in the seventies." In a stinging rebuke to Horowitz's reactionary charges, Elaine wrote:

> That Horowitz chooses to dismiss the holocaustal horror of the Black experience in America in his denunciation of Huey as a "crazy nigger" serves as clear and convincing evidence of his [Horowitz's] racism.

Calling Horowitz a "racist white rabbit who tries to confuse all who enter his wonderland," Elaine then accuses him of using Huey to discredit the progressive movement:

> Depicting the support of the campaign to "Free Huey!" by Whites and non-Panthers as the development of "a cult," Horowitz clucks a reprobate tongue at the serious work of literally millions of people. . . . There was no "cult," but a coalition by a mass of people consciously addressing yearnings and demands that came to focus on the freedom of one man, as he personified the capture of a collective freedom.

The April 1991 issue of the paper included an excerpt from Huey's doctoral dissertation, *War Against the Panthers*. In the December 1, 2005, issue of the *Commemorator*, which may be found on the Internet, ex–Black Panther and *Commemorator* editor Melvin Dickson wrote a tribute to the late Rosa Parks. (Anyone wishing to contact the *Commemorator* may write to the Commemoration Committee for the Black Panther Party, 4432 Telegraph Avenue, POB 62, Oakland, CA 94609, or call 510-652-7170.)

Memorial Issue of *The Black Panther*

Following on the heels of the *Commemorator*, in February 1991, in Berkeley, California, the Black Panther Newspaper Committee (BPNC), a nonprofit organization of former Panthers, published a Memorial Issue of *The Black Panther Black Community News Service*. The inaugural issue of the revived *Black Panther* looked like a *Black Panther* issue of the late 1960s. Using the newspaper's original masthead from the sixties, the front page of the paper featured the famous 1967 photo of Huey and Bobby dressed in the BPP uniform of black leather jackets and black berets, standing in front of party headquarters with guns, and the banner headline "The Struggle Continues." The editorial said in part:

> We were all members of the Black Panther Party who participated in the formation, organization, and day to day operations of Black Panther Party activities. . . . Because of our uncompromising work to build a strong Afrikan-Amerikkkan nation . . . many of us were forced into exile or underground, or were imprisoned by the U.S. government during its COINTELPRO war.

The editorial said that the BPNC came together out of a "compelling need" to address such critical issues in the African American community as drugs, unemployment, inadequate housing, "miseducation, legalized police terror and murder," and institutional racism—issues addressed in the BPP Ten Point Platform and Program. The editorial concluded:

> In the past *The Black Panther Black Community News Service* was an uncompromising voice for exposing these attacks . . . and for advocating an implacable stand to redress them. . . . We are proud to announce to you that uncompromising voice has returned!

The Memorial Issue was dedicated to the BPP's "Fallen Comrades," party members who were killed by police or other law enforcement agents, and political prisoners. The issue contained photos and biographies of some of the fallen comrades, and articles about the cases of several political prisoners. Other articles were written by some of those prisoners, several of whom were BPP members. Also included in the Memorial Issue were the BPP Ten Point Platform and Program, a chronology of party history from 1966–1971, a description and photos of party Survival Programs, articles on current national and international news, and a financial statement.

Renewed Interest in the BPP

Spurred by the autobiographies and memoirs of such former Panther leaders as Elaine Brown, Kathleen Cleaver, and David Hilliard, as well as the 1995 film *Panther*, there was a nationwide resurgence of interest in the Black Panther Party. This renewed interest by black youth, activists, and scholars contributed to the creation of "new" Black Panther groups around the country beginning in the early 1990s. Those groups included the Black Panther Militia, founded by former BPP member and former Milwaukee city-council member Michael McGee; the New Black Panther Party for Self-Defense, created in Dallas, Texas, by Aaron Michaels, which nationally grew under the leadership of the late Dr. Khallid Muhammad, previously the national spokesman for the Nation of Islam; and the New Panther Vanguard Movement in Los Angeles, established by Kwaku Duren, who in the late 1970s was appointed by Elaine Brown to coordinate the revived Southern California BPP chapter.

Unfortunately, some of these new Panther formations did not learn from the mistakes of the original Black Panther Party. Sectarianism, factional disputes, and personality cults that developed around various leaders prevented the new Panther groups from uniting under one umbrella. At the thirty-fifth reunion of the Black Panther Party held in 2002 in Washington, DC, Ron Scott, cofounder of the original Detroit chapter of the BPP, and I led a workshop on the new Panther movements. Some members of the New Black Panther Party for Self-Defense attended the workshop, and Ron and I criticized them for misrepresenting the history of the original BPP on the New Black Panther Party Web site by replacing Bobby Seale's picture with that of Khallid Muhammad in a famous photo of Huey and Bobby. The doctored photo was subsequently removed from the New BPP Web site.

The New BPP publishes *The Black Panther Black Community News Service*, which may be viewed on its Web site, www.newpanther.com. The New Panther Vanguard Movement (NPVM) revived *The Black Panther Intercommunal News Service*. Issues dated 1998 to 2001 may be viewed on the NPVM Web site, www.globalpanther.com. Several issues of the original Black Panther newspaper may be found on the Web site of It's About Time, www.itsabouttimebpp.com. A network of Panther alumni and supporters to which I belong, It's About Time organized thirtieth, thirty-fifth, and fortieth anniversary Panther reunions. (With former BPP members Madalynn C. Rucker and Ralph Moore, I organized the twentieth-anniversary reunion held in Oakland, California, in October 1986.) It's About Time is based in Sacramento, California, and coordinated by former BPP member William "Billy X" Jennings. To preserve Huey's legacy, Huey's widow, Frederika Newton, and David Hilliard, former BPP chief of staff, founded the Dr. Huey P. Newton Foundation in 1994. The foundation, which has a speakers bureau, has a Web site, www.blackpanther.org.

In 1998, *The Black Panther Party [Reconsidered]* was published by Black Classic Press, whose founder, W. Paul Coates, is a former BPP member. Edited by Dr. Charles E. Jones, founding chair of the Department of African-American Studies at Georgia State University, *The Black Panther Party [Reconsidered]* is perhaps the most comprehensive anthology of essays and memoirs written to date about the original BPP. (My essay "Serving the People: The Survival Programs of the Black Panther Party" is included.)

Enduring Contributions of the BPP

In October 2006, I joined many of my former Panther comrades and friends and supporters at the BPP's fortieth anniversary celebration in Oakland, California. As I rejoiced at seeing old friends, I was reminded that the struggle of African Americans for justice and equality, outlined in the party's Ten Point Platform and Program of October 15, 1966, continues. There is still no "land, bread, housing, education, clothing, justice and peace" for a vast majority of black people in America.

The Black Panther Party founded by Huey P. Newton and Bobby Seale arose from the unique economic, social, and political conditions that existed among black people in the United States in the late twentieth century. Those conditions cannot be recreated. Consequently, the Black Panther Party cannot be recreated. However, the various attempts to do so underscore the enduring contributions of the BPP to the empowerment of black and disenfranchised people throughout the world.

SELECTED BIBLIOGRAPHY

Alternative Considerations of Jonestown and Peoples Temple. Department of Religious Studies, San Diego State University: http://jonestown.sdsu.edu.

Brown, Elaine. *A Taste of Power: A Black Woman's Story.* New York: Pantheon Books, 1992.

Bush, Rod, ed. *The New Black Vote: Politics and Power in Four American Cities.* San Francisco: Synthesis Publications, 1984.

Carson, Clayborne. *In Struggle: SNCC and the Black Awakening of the 1960s.* Cambridge, MA: Harvard University Press, 1981.

Churchill, Ward, and Jim Vander Wall. *Agents of Repression: The FBI's Secret Wars against the Black Panther Party and American Indian Movement.* Boston: South End Press, 1988.

Clark, Ramsey, and Roy Wilkins, chairs. *Search and Destroy: A Report by the Commission of Inquiry into the Black Panthers and the Police.* New York: Metropolitan Applied Research Center, 1973.

Cleaver, Kathleen, and George Katsiaficas. *Liberation, Imagination, and the Black Panther Party: A New Look at the Panthers and Their Legacy.* New York: Routledge, 2000.

Committee on Internal Security, House of Representatives. *The Black Panther Party: Its Origin and Development as Reflected in Its Official Weekly Newspaper, the Black Panther Black Community News Service.* Washington, DC: U.S. Government Printing Office, 1970.

Donner, Frank J. *The Age of Surveillance: The Aims and Methods of America's Intelligence System.* New York: Vintage Books, 1981.

Durant, Sam, ed. *The Revolutionary Art of Emory Douglas.* New York: Rizzoli Publications, 2007.

Erikson, Erik H. *In Search of Common Ground: Conversations with Erik H. Erikson and Huey P. Newton.* New York: Norton, 1973.

Foner, Philip, ed. *The Black Panthers Speak.* Philadelphia: Lippincott, 1970.

Forman, James. "The Black Panther Party." In *The Making of Black Revolutionaries*, 522–43. New York: Macmillan, 1972.

Freed, Donald. *Agony in New Haven: The Trial of Bobby Seale, Ericka Huggins and the Black Panther Party.* New York: Simon and Schuster, 1973.

Hilliard, David, and Lewis Cole. *This Side of Glory: The Autobiography of David Hilliard and the Story of the Black Panther Party.* Boston: Little, Brown and Company, 1993.

Huey P. Newton Foundation: www.blackpanther.org.

Huggins, Ericka, and Huey P. Newton. *Insights and Poems.* San Francisco: City Lights Books, 1975.

It's About Time Committee: www.itsabouttimebpp.com.

Jackson, George. *Blood in My Eye.* Baltimore: Black Classic Press, 1990.

———. *Soledad Brother: The Prison Writings of George Jackson.* New York: Coward-McCann, 1970.

Jones, Charles E., ed. *The Black Panther Party [Reconsidered].* Baltimore: Black Classic Press, 1998.

Major, Reginald. *A Panther Is a Black Cat.* New York: William Morrow, 1971.

Marine, Gene. *The Black Panthers.* New York: New American Library, 1969.

New Black Panther Party for Self-Defense: www.newblackpanther.com.

New Panther Vanguard Movement: www.globalpanther.org.

Newton, Huey P. *To Die for the People: The Writings of Huey P. Newton.* New York: Random House, 1972.

———. *Revolutionary Suicide.* New York: Harcourt, Brace and Jovanovich, 1973.

———. "War against the Panthers: A Study of Repression in America." PhD diss., University of California-Santa Cruz, 1980.

Olsen, Jack. *Last Man Standing: The Tragedy and Triumph of Geronimo Pratt.* New York: Doubleday, 2000.

O'Reilly, Kenneth. *"Racial Matters": The FBI's Secret File on Black America, 1960–1972.* New York: The Free Press, 1989.

Rucker, Madalynn C., and JoNina M. Abron. "Comrade Sisters: Two Women of the Black Panther Party." In *Unrelated Kin: Race and Gender in Women's Personal Narratives,* edited by Gwendolyn Etter Lewis and Michele Foster. New York: Routledge, 1996.

Seale, Bobby. *Seize the Time: The Story of the Black Panther Party and Huey P. Newton.* New York: Random House, 1970.

———. *A Lonely Rage: The Autobiography of Bobby Seale.* New York: Times Books, 1978.

Shakur, Assata. *Assata: An Autobiography.* Westport, CT: Lawrence Hill & Co., 1987.

Tannenbaum, Robert, and Philip Rosenberg. *Badge of the Assassin.* New York: Dorison House, 1979.

U.S. Senate. Select Committee to Study Governmental Operations. *Supplementary Detailed Staff Reports on Intelligence Activities and the Rights of Americans, Book III.* Washington, DC: U.S. Government Printing Office, 1976.

Both Sides Now Remembered: Or, The Once and Future Journal

ELIHU EDELSON

Part 1: The Original Historical Version from 1990

Both Sides Now (*BSN*) barely made the sixties. The first issue was dated November 29, 1969. Its banner headline reflected one of the Movement's main concerns of the moment: "Paul McCartney Dead!" Two more issues managed to get squeezed in before the end of the decade.

BSN's original base, Jacksonville, Florida, was not the most fertile ground for an underground paper at the turn of the seventies. The city was ruled like a feudal fiefdom by a local machine that included the Florida Publishing Company, a monopoly that put out both the morning and evening papers. FPC, in turn, was owned by the Florida East Coast Railroad. Three nearby military bases contributed to the ultraconservative atmosphere. The St. Johns River and the intersection of Interstates 10 and 75 cut the community into pieces. Jacksonville University, a private institution, was far from a hotbed of student activism. In fact, its name appeared on a list of five hundred CIA-connected institutions circulated by the Yippies.

The New Leftists could be counted on the fingers of one hand—a RYM (Revolutionary Youth Movement) Maoist and his wife, a couple of Trots (Trotskyites), and a few ACLU/Unitarian/Democrat-type liberals. A handful of blacks sporting berets and leather jackets put together a local version of the Black Panthers under the name Florida Black Front. Some good rock bands—like the Allman Brothers and Lynyrd Skynyrd—were to come out of Jax, but they had to make their names in Atlanta.

So it is not surprising that, like many other events of the time, the counterculture came belatedly to Jacksonville. The Haight-Ashbury scene had already passed its peak by the time people were getting hassled for long hair in Jax. The heads—as potheads and acidheads called themselves—had set up crash pads where people could come down gently from bad acid trips, but the cops kept harassing them. The deep Southeast had a well-established and exemplary underground paper in Atlanta's *Great Speckled Bird*, and the Jacksonville hippies wanted a publication like that as a voice for their concerns.

The Jacksonville hippies were always more an aggregation of people with related lifestyles than a coherent community. Because none of them had any journalistic experience, they went, naively, to an editor of the morning establishment paper, the *Florida Times-Union*, for advice.

This is the point in the story of *Both Sides Now* where I got sucked in. I was an art teacher in the public school system at the time, but I also wrote a weekly column of art criticism as a stringer for the evening paper, the *Jacksonville Journal.*

The counterculture had only recently entered my consciousness, as I began to pick up on the messages being communicated by rock groups like the Doors, Jefferson Airplane, and Steppenwolf. My wife, Joan, and I were introduced to a speed freak who had done light shows for the Allman Brothers before they moved to Macon, Georgia, and he put me up to using my press credentials to get passes for the First Atlanta Pop Festival, with him as my photographer. I wrote a glowing review of the counterculture scene I saw there.

So when the hippies went to that editor, he referred them to me. I didn't know beans about the nuts and bolts of putting together a paper, but the husband of one of my art teacher colleagues was into small-scale tabloid publishing, and he taught us the basics. The first issues of *BSN* were hacked out on a number of manual typewriters, with lots of hand lettering.

Despite the lead story about Paul McCartney, *BSN*'s first issue had a variety of serious material, including an antiwar sermon by the local Unitarian minister, reviews of *Easy Rider* and *Alice's Restaurant* (by me), a drug rap interview with the vice-squad honcho, and items appealing to men from the naval bases who wore long-hair wigs when on shore leave. *BSN* was distributed from a combination wig and head shop.

BSN came out every two weeks for several issues into 1970 before entropy began to set in. At first it was driven by high energy and a sense of wonder as we saw our typewriter-pounding, cutting, and pasting transformed by the miracle of offset lithography into a real publication. We tackled a variety of current issues: the Charles Manson case, Bob Dylan's stylistic changes, high school dress codes, student rights, the draft, pollution of the St. Johns River, the emerging women's movement, the Chicago 8 trial, the first Earth Day (scorned by the same Establishment that embraced it in 1990), and the killings at Kent State and Jackson State. Street poets saw their verses in print, decorated by elaborate drawings. Local culture was viewed from the underside of society.

But after a while, the staff got into some strange trips. We held tedious discussions on how to fairly divide the proceeds among the collective staff, though the paper barely broke even. Much of our income depended on street sales by vendors, who were often harassed by the police and occasionally disappeared with their bit of money. Staffers had a variety of odd jobs, but sometimes we had to "pass the hat" to pay the printing bill. In the longer run, it became apparent to the dreamers that putting out a paper was mostly shitwork with very little glamour. The round-the-clock grinds every two weeks before press time were getting everyone down, and staff attrition began to set in.

In June 1970, after nine issues, the operation screeched to a halt. The situation had been essentially anarchic—not so much because we were deliberately attempting to fashion a structurally organized microcosm of an anarchistic state, but because we were disorganized. A core group with various friends came together in somebody's apartment a couple of days before press time and put the assembled material into camera-ready format. Nevertheless, the group as a whole was not particularly political.

On the other hand, I—the former card-carrying ACLU member—was becoming radicalized by the information coming in from exchange underground papers, Liberation News Service dispatches, and other publications like *Ramparts*. As was true with so many other activists around the country, I was disillusioned by revelations of the U.S. political system as evidenced by the Indochina War, sabotage of peace and justice movements, frame-up trials of activists, gratuitous violence against protesters—not only at Kent State but everywhere—government alliances with organized crime, cover-ups of assassinations, and manipulation of the electoral process (Watergate).

So, as the other staff members began to drift away, I became more intense in my involvement because of my own growing awareness of a noticeable dialectic between two cultures—one oriented toward life and freedom, the other characterized by death and violence. This dialectic was analyzed in writing on the popular level by Abbie Hoffman and the underground press in general, and on the academic level by authors like Theodore Roszak, in *The Making of a Counterculture.*

The original founder of *BSN*, Larry Hanson, was a true hippie. He looked like the conventional Jesus pictures, and wore a long white robe without affectation. After getting *BSN* started, he opened a head shop and was duly hassled by the police. Once he was pushed around by a cop at a Krystal diner just for the way he dressed. The staff and friends picketed the place for about a week and told the story in *BSN.*

Eventually, however, the harassment became so unbearable that Larry moved away and out of our lives. Although he was too beset by personal problems to put much energy into *BSN* toward the end anyhow, his benign presence was sorely missed by those who knew him.

Ultimately, I was the only one left of the original staff. Almost single-handedly, aided by some contributed material and reprints, I put together an anniversary issue in December 1970. A liberal Lutheran minister had given me an antique VariTyper strike-on typesetter before issue number 9, and I did most of the typing after that. The small, news-size type allowed much more material to be included in the same number of pages. In much the same manner, I was able to put together two issues in 1971: number 11 in April and number 12 (a 24-page monster) for August/September.

A 1972 attempt to bring in new people and diminish my role ended in a fiasco. I believed there should be input from others besides myself, and also wished that the workload could again be shared by more people. Through a Movement "bulletin board" ad, Joan and I imported a couple from Ithaca, New York. In those days, a lot of activists were willing to work for subsistence pay. We provided room and board plus a little spending money. The man was competent at artwork and layout, and both were handy in general. At the same time, some new volunteers materialized, and it looked as though an actual staff was coming together. Two issues were put out in quick succession: number 13 for February/March and number 14 for March/April. Then a series of events led to rapid deterioration.

A cartoon the Ithaca man did for *BSN* number 14 should have given me a clue. It showed a bewhiskered man with a big nose wearing a black cloak and beanie while brandishing a rolled-up *BSN*, standing next to a toady-looking little *BSN* paperboy. Joan pointed out to me that there was a decided anti-Semitic stereotype in the way the man was drawn. Despite two requests for revision, only slight improvement was made. Tired of nagging, I let the cartoon go through, for which I'm sorry. In retrospect, the drawing suggests Dickens's Fagin, who exploits little boys to do his dirty work.

The final straw came when the Ithaca couple and the new volunteers decided to use the little bit of money *BSN* had to put out a big newsprint poster instead of another issue. I was trying hard not to be the big decision maker at that time and was not involved in this idea.

Seeing that this crew was not likely to get *BSN* back on track, Joan and I angrily demanded the return of its number-one asset: the old VariTyper, which we had lent to the volunteers. (I later acquired a rebuilt IBM Executive with small type that I used for most of the copy, and toward the end I added a late model VariTyper.) So I had that and the *BSN* name and nothing else. The staff dissipated, and the Ithaca folks went on to other pastures. I still wonder if they were screwups or provocateurs.[1]

Over the remainder of the decade, I put out one or two issues a year as time and finances allowed, with occasional help from friends. A rundown of the frequency of the remaining issues will give some idea of what it was like. Without any help, I was able to put out one more issue later in 1972. It was called "War without Honor" and was largely intended for distribution at the Republican Convention in Miami, as part of the protests against Nixon's prolonging of the war. Unfortunately, issues like that come off as downers and do not help to attract new readers. The count of issues for the remaining years of the decade went like this: 1973 (1), 1974 (3), 1975 (2), 1976 (2), 1977 (1), 1978 (0), 1979 (1), 1980 (1).

Part of the irregularity was due to the fact that most of the funding came out of my own pocket, with a little income from store sales, ads, and subscriptions. Street sales were a thing of the past, so *BSN* had to rely more on the mails. The economics of tabloid printing were peculiar. Most of the expense went into making the negatives and setting up the big web presses. Printing 1,000 papers cost only a little more than printing 500, and 2,000 cost just a little more than that. So I would have 2,000 printed and give the majority away with enclosed subscription pitches.

In 1975 I got a bulk-rate mailing permit, and in 1976 I got a nonprofit incorporation under the name Free People Inc. This last move was to end any question of anyone making money off the deal, but mostly it was made so that I could get the lowest mailing rates, which were less than four cents a copy back then. However, it took about two years of wrangling with the Postal Service to get the permit, because Free People was not tax-exempt. All in all, one might look upon *BSN* as a somewhat expensive hobby during this period.

Publication was suspended in 1980 when Joan and I, in an attempt to de-urbanize, moved to Texas and shifted all our resources into homesteading. We're largely out of touch with Jax now, but from what I gather, new peace activists have gotten together, mainly to protest the Trident submarine base just across the Georgia border—which *BSN* had warned about before it was built.

Both Sides Now put out a total of twenty-six issues. Minimal as that might be, some of the events, considerations, and concerns that were involved are of retrospective interest. One amusing irony was how much attention the FBI gave to such an ineffectual once- or twice-a-year effort—I guess they had to show J. Edgar Hoover they were doing their bit to stamp out dissent.

For instance, I was informed by associates that agents had questioned them about my sex life, presumably to get some dirt to use against me—as it turned out they had done on Martin Luther King Jr., and others also. (There was no dirt to find.) They apparently tried to have me lose my teaching job by putting the school administration up to pulling a surprise evaluation of me that no other faculty member went through. No reasons were given.

The biggest farce, however, was to have a stooge start a rival paper called *Climax!*, which even subscribed to Liberation News Service. It lured away potential staffers—but no actual ones, since I was by then the only staffer—with offers of salaries. *Climax!* lasted for two issues,

US ISSN 0006-8233

FREE PEOPLE PRESENT THE NEW

BOTH SIDES NOW

NUMBER 16 – AUGUST 1973   PUBLISHED BY FREE PEOPLE IN JACKSONVILLE, FLORIDA   LOCAL 20¢ – ELSEWHERE 25¢

A TYPICAL CASE OF AMERICAN BLIND JUSTICE.

DOES WATERGATE MEAN MURDER?

To Impeach or Not

Lettuce & Grape Boycotts

After Wounded Knee

Reviews

Inflation Komix

WATERGATE & GAINESVILLE 8

The celebrated Gainesville 8 trial is the government's attempt at justifying Watergate, according to Peter Mahoney, who is one of the 8.

"It seems that one of the principal reasons for the whole thing was an attempt to embarrass the Democrats. We see it now as being part of the whole political espionage campaign that the Nixon Administration was putting on and a direct attempt to justify the whole Watergate thing," Mahoney said in a recent LNS interview.

The Gainesville 8 are seven members of the Vietnam Veterans Against the War/Winter Soldier Organization (VVAW/WSO) and one supporter. They are charged with conspiracy to incite riot at last year's Republican Convention. (See background story on Page 3.)

Numerous times during the Watergate hearings, various members of the bugging team (particularly McCord), the Committee to Re-Elect the President, and government officials have justified their actions—including bugging, surveillance, and informers—by saying that they expected violence at the Republican Convention. The only organization they mentioned by name was VVAW/WSO. The trial has been called by many observers, "the last gasp chance for a justification of Watergate."

Pete Mahoney sees many widespread connections between the Gainesville 8 trial and Watergate. He stated that he believes part of the Republicans' original planned political espionage was to create violence at the Democratic Convention.

"That violence was going to be blamed on VVAW and other groups. Then we were going to be indicted," Pete charges.

Once the Republicans got caught at Watergate they had to change their original plan.

But they needed a justification for the break-in so they said, "These people were going to be violent at the Republican Convention. Let's indict them for that," according to Pete.

He also claims that many of the same characters involved in Watergate "are involved in our thing."

"There's Alfred Baldwin who was caught at Watergate monitoring the bug. But that was a secondary job. He had been specifically hired by the FBI to infiltrate the VVAW, but after getting caught he never got a chance to carry out his primary mission.

"Another person who appears both places is Robert Mardian—head of the Internal Security Division of the Justice Department. The whole Internal Security Division seems to be very much involved in all of the dirty tricks and the espionage things of the Nixon Administration. And they're the people who brought the indictment

In other developments, in what was termed as the "most incredible withdrawal of First Amendment rights," Judge Winston Arnow, presiding over the Gainesville 8 trial, has put a gag rule on practically everything any of the defendants, lawyers, or almost everybody active in the trial can say about the case.

"They want to keep the trial a secret from everybody," said one lawyer who heard about the gag rule which Arnow imposed on July 12.

The judge's unprecedented action came as no surprise to Pete Mahoney, since Arnow has used tactics prejudicial to the defense in the past.

"He tried to move the trial from Gainesville where it was originally scheduled to Pensacola which is his home town. Pensacola also happens to be about 90% retired military, so a trial in Pensacola would beat about the same as a court-martial—because those were the type of people we would have had on the jury," the veteran claims.

This gag rule means that if any defendant, lawyer, or "person acting for them"—presumably the defense committee or perhaps anyone from VVAW/WSO—is quoted in a newspaper anywhere in the U.S. saying anything about the case which is not from the record, they can be held in contempt. If a newspaper, for example, says "one of the defendants," the reporters can be called in and forced to say who told them, under penalty of going to jail if they refuse. CBS was fined for broadcasting sketches made from memory.

Furthermore, there will be no photographing, interviewing on tape or for radio and TV or sketching in the courtroom "or in its environs," which Arnow defines as the interior of the entire courthouse. CBS was fined for broadcasting sketches made from memory.

Arnow also banned any demonstrations, marches, rallies, vigils, picketing or parades within two blocks of the courthouse. He had previously moved the trial date up two weeks, apparently to interfere with the plans of demonstrators who had arranged summer vacation time to coincide with the start of the trial.

The VVAW/WSO, which is appealing his order, went ahead with plans for five days of demonstrations at the beginning of the trial on July 31.

Although the government has had singular lack of success in prosecuting conspiracy cases, and although this case rests on weak grounds (preposterous charges, dubious sources of information), the prosecution is obviously out for blood in this one. It is part of the administration's extensive effort to crush all dissent regarding its military efforts in Indochina. For no one speaks on the war with more authority than the men who fought there

DIRTY TRICKS COME TO JAX

On April 22 the Duval County Vietnam Veterans Against the War/Winter Soldier Organization chapter scheduled a showing of the film "Winter Soldier" at the University of North Florida campus. Before the showing could take place, the film was stolen from the home of its owner, local VVAW/WSO coordinator, Tony Siddell.

This movie documents the testimony of honorably discharged Vietnam veterans on U.S. war crimes they had witnessed in Indochina. The testimony was given at the Winter Soldier Investigation held by VVAW from January 31 to February 2, 1971, in Detroit. (A full page story on Winter Soldier may be found in BSN No. 15, p. 12)

Another showing was scheduled on May 24, with Scott Camil of the Gainesville 8 bringing a print in person. Interestingly, the only local paper to give full coverage to the theft and second showing was Free People's Penny Press (No. S-5).

Meanwhile, what became of the stolen film? Somehow, at the pre-trial hearings on the Gainesville 8 case in Pensacola it came out that the F.B.I. had the film. When an allegation was made that Gene Thrasher, who had posed as an enthusiastic member of VVAW, was the most likely suspect, the F.B.I. admitted that Thrasher had not stolen the film but had acquired it from David Williams and then turned it over to the F.B.I. (Siddell had not been formally notified of the recovery of his film.) The F.B.I. also admitted that Thrasher was not an agent but had done work for them before.

At the pre-trial hearings where all this came out, Siddell was cited for contempt of court for an alleged threat against Thrasher. It looked as though the victim of a crime was going to be treated as the criminal, but the citation did not stick and was later dropped.

An interesting footnote we can add is that three years ago Thrasher attempted to start a rival paper to Both Sides Now, called Climax. It folded after two issues.

All of which leaves a number of interesting questions: Why was the Winter Soldier film stolen in the first place? Why would an F.B.I. informer want to start an underground paper? Who is trying to keep the people of Jacksonville from learning the truth about the Indochina War and government policies? Is it legal for an arm of the law to receive stolen goods and not return them to the owner? Will the alleged burglar be prosecuted?

FIGURE 1: Cover of *Both Sides Now* issue 16 (August 1973): Watergate issue, with a front-page story also on the trial of the Gainesville 8. Courtesy *Both Sides Now*.

largely by publishing LNS reprints. Maybe the FBI realized it was a stupid waste of money and dropped it.

I didn't realize what the game was till it developed that the stooge was doing some dirty work for the FBI during the Gainesville 8 trial. The Gainesville 8 were a group of Vietnam Veterans Against the War (VVAW) leaders who were framed by the government to keep them from organizing demonstrations at the 1972 Republican Convention in Miami. As reported in *BSN* number 16 (August 1973; see figure 1), a Jax Vietnam vet had acquired a print of the *Winter Soldier* film and was bringing Scott Camil, one of the Gainesville 8 and a prominent figure in the film, to show it at the University of Northern Florida. After a visit to the vet's home by the person who started *Climax!*, the reel disappeared. It later turned up in the hands of the FBI people who were working on the Gainesville 8 trial. Eventually it was returned and shown at the university to a very small audience—another case of the FBI going to a lot of ineffectual bother trying to hamper dissent.[2] The FBI must have squandered millions on such trivial pursuits, and is probably still doing so.

BSN's shift from collective to autocratic management exemplifies polarities that have existed in alternative journalism from the beginning. Paul Krassner's one-man iconoclastic journal, *The Realist*, is generally acknowledged as the ancestor of the underground press. The true undergrounds that followed usually struggled with various forms of staff collectives. While these dealt broadly with Movement concerns, the one-person alternatives tended to take a more personal and personalist turn. Some of my favorite personal journals have been the *Little Free Press* (anarchistic), Irv Thomas's *Black Bart Brigade* (originally for middle-aged dropouts),[3] and *Heretic's Journal* (synthesis of radical politics and spirituality). The most substantial and enduring has been Sy Safransky's "magazine of ideas," *The Sun*, a professional-looking production that has attracted some of the best writers around. Although a staff is listed, one gets the impression that Safransky decides what the contents will be. *Little Free Press* is the only other one of these that is still around.[4] Unknown to each other at first, the *Heretic's Journal* and *BSN* were striving for a similar synthesis—an interesting synchronicity. Other current favorites include Tris Coffin's *Washington Spectator* and Mark Satin's *New Options*.[5]

In retrospect, *BSN*'s history is a frustrating one with respect to some good concepts that I did not have the means, support, or business sense to develop properly. At first I tried to keep up the general Movement interest approach of the alternative press. In issue number 18 (June 1974) a sensational tabloid-style (*Enquirer*) treatment was given to the late Mae Brussel's analysis of the Symbionese Liberation Army—the dubious "revolutionary" group that kidnapped Patty Hearst. Brussel, a noted conspiracy investigator, believed that the SLA was fabricated by the government to discredit bona fide radical groups, which are usually nonviolent.

I still believe a nationally distributed underground-type paper is desirable, in addition to ones of local interest, just as *Time* and *Newsweek* augment the daily papers. The nearest paper to that type today is *In These Times*, with its comprehensive coverage of national and international news, as well as some fine cultural criticism.[6]

BSN number 22 (May 1976) was a last effort to attract a local audience and support. That issue featured reprints of exposés of Jacksonville politics that had appeared in major national publications—*Rolling Stone* and *Columbia Journalism Review*.

Unfortunately, the response was virtually nil. As I indicated earlier, Jax was "from nowhere" to start with politically; by the mid-seventies, interest in the Movement was down everywhere.

So *BSN* number 23 (September 1976) took up the idea of a modest national tabloid with several features on "the greatest Bicentennial scandals": the growing gap between super-rich and poor, Pentagon gluttony, the skyrocketing cost of nuclear power, government harassment of the American Indian Movement (AIM), Watergate criminals making bucks on books, the news blackout of alternative Bicentennial activities, cheating at West Point, D.C. sex scandals. . . . Under the front-page logo of that issue was the characterization "An Alternative Paper and Digest." Since many of *BSN*'s features were reprints, I believed that some kind of alternative *Reader's Digest* would be a good idea. Eric Utne later proved my idea to be correct with his highly successful magazine, *Utne Reader*, whose contents include reprints from other alternative publications.

Getting back to *Rolling Stone* for a moment: Though it has featured a lot of good journalism, I have general contempt for the publication because of its deliberate co-optation and under-mining of the underground press. *RS* developed a distinctive format that had an underground look, only slicker. It avoided taking really radical positions (though later it got into some good muckraking). This made it more attractive as an advertising vehicle for the big record labels, which subsequently placed virtually no ads in the true undergrounds—a serious setback for many shoestring operations.

My reasons for contempt are perfectly exemplified by a coffee-table-size book *RS* put out on the sixties that covered every sixties topic from Abbie Hoffman to Twiggy except the underground press. Not one word. The nonperson treatment.

With *BSN* number 24 (April 1977), *BSN* was given a final editorial turn. I had been interested in esoteric spirituality, or metaphysics, long before my involvement in the Movement, but I had put that interest aside under the pressure of all the causes that had emerged in the sixties and early seventies. Around 1976–1977, I read the writings of William Irwin Thompson, and Paul Hawken's account of the Findhorn community.

Thompson, a cultural historian, taught at MIT, York University, and the University of Toronto. After a visit to Findhorn, he dropped out of academe and founded the Lindisfarne Association, a sort of leading-edge think tank.

Findhorn is an intentional community in northern Scotland that developed under direct spiritual guidance. Humans cooperating with nature achieved miraculous results in an organic garden grown in sandy beach soil. Cooperation, rather than competition, brought out the potential in the varied individuals who gravitated toward this place. These people were given to understand that Findhorn was a working model of what life in the New Age could be like.

Inspired by these literary works, and aware now that the Age of Aquarius was indeed dawning, I turned *BSN* into a New Age publication.

Still, I was not prepared to give up my Movement concerns. Indeed, the editorial direction of *BSN* was toward a synthesis of radical politics and New Age spirituality. *BSN* number 24 reprinted a *Berkeley Barb* essay by Louise Billotte entitled "Can the Left Find Room for Spirituality?" along with my response, which appeared in the *Barb* under the heading "The Movement Has a Strong Spiritual Core." This exchange was reprinted in turn by the Alternative Press Syndicate magazine *Alternative Review*.

Billotte, who said she was studying Tibetan Buddhism at the time, started out by observing that "there definitely is a conflict between politics and spirituality, one whose roots are deep and complex." She was specifically referring to the Left's longstanding suspicion of religion, which Marx had called "the opium of the people." In response to this suspicion, she stated, "What so many people on the Left seem unwilling to accept is the fact that RELIGION IS A FACT OF HUMAN CONSCIOUSNESS." If there was to be progress toward an ideal society, she added, the Left had to come to terms with the need for spiritual content. At the same time, spiritual people needed to become aware of the economic factors that were determining the kind of world we live in.

My point was to reinforce Billotte's theme and inject another viewpoint. I stated that the term "the Left" "has a tendency to narrow our definitive base" and noted a preference for "the Movement" as a name to summarize the broad spectrum of forces striving for a new society. I pointed out that many Movement groups and individuals were spiritually oriented, such as the American Friends Service Committee (AFSC), the Berrigans, and others. The counterculture itself had a definite spiritual side—sometimes lumped in with "cultural" as opposed to political—as seen in people like poet Allen Ginsberg; John Wilcock, a founder of the underground press; and Robert Anton Wilson, a fairly well-known countercultural writer, devotee of Aleister Crowley and Timothy Leary (neither of whom I care for), and student of the occult and conspiracy theories. In closing, I made a pitch for a spiritual/political synthesis to rejuvenate the Movement, which was noticeably foundering by 1977, when our exchange of articles took place.

I should mention that *BSN*'s New Age turn was strongly foreshadowed two years earlier in *BSN* number 20 (late February 1975), which carried the headline "Special Prophecy Issue 1975–2000." *BSN* had just received a review copy of *California Superquake: 1975–77*, by Paul James, who made a convincing case for the possibility that a quake of unprecedented magnitude was likely to take place within that time frame. Taking James seriously, I wrote a full-page review of his book, accompanied by a three-page article on the national karma that might have brought on such a catastrophe, and what the rest of the century might be like if it really did come about. The term "New Age" was used several times in that feature. Of course, James's timing was way off, but there are still many indications that drastic natural cataclysms will accompany the end of the old order—possibly before the end of this century.[7]

BSN number 20 also saw the debut of Michael Dorian as the one and only volunteer staffer for five issues. Michael had tapped into the heady mixture of spiritual currents that were swirling around at that time, and he was a very talented pen-and-ink artist. For that issue, he contributed and edited a 2⅔-page feature on neopaganism that was generously sprinkled with his imaginative spot drawings. Michael had major input on *BSN* number 21, called "Earth Issue," with a cover, an editorial on planetary consciousness, and a feature on the chakras. His last major contribution was a beautiful reinterpretation of a tarot card for the cover of *BSN* number 25.

With that issue, *BSN* started billing itself as "An Alternative Journal of Aquarian/New Age Transformations." The contents were a mixture of New Age material, Movement thinking, and editorializing. Of New Age interest were an article on "The Dialectics of Astrology" by Martha Gold from *Liberation* magazine, and a long interview with Dr. Andrija Puharich on New Age children. On the Movement side were articles on "Overcoming Oppression" and "Tools for Empowerment" from the Movement for a New Society. I contributed two editorials. One, on death trips, commented on the remarkable number of notable people who died in 1977, including Elvis Presley, Bing Crosby, Groucho and Gummo Marx, Joan Crawford, Zero Mostel, Ethel Waters, Charlie Chaplin, Leopold Stokowski, Loren Eiseley, Wernher von Braun, Robert

Lowell, E. F. Schumacker, and Ralph Borsodi, among others. The other editorial remarked on how we have let celebrities take the place of heroes.

Also in that issue were a short biography of Peter Maurin (cofounder with Dorothy Day of the Catholic Worker Movement) and a full page of his "Easy Essays." A parable by Irv Thomas of *Black Bart Brigade* dramatized the meaning of true freedom. An experimental feature was the inclusion of an insert called *Alternative Research Newsletter*, which was produced in Canada.

The one piece I most regret having published also appeared in *BSN* number 25. It was a photocopy of a communiqué, purportedly from a Jonestown victim, which had been sent to a number of Movement and New Age groups and publications. At the time, I was not alert to certain indicators that would have identified this as a Far Right hoax. Fortunately, I had asked conspiracy investigator John Judge for feedback on the communiqué, and he sent a full-page response. In his first paragraph, he observed that the missive smacked of the U.S. Labor Party (Lyndon LaRouche) and Liberty Lobby, then proceeded to offer proof that Jonestown was a major mind-control experiment conducted by fascistic elements in our government.

The last issue of *BSN* (number 26, May 1980) featured a shift in format I had desired for some time—from tabloid to half-tabloid newsprint magazine. There is a tendency to associate the tabloid format with scandal sheets ranging from the *New York Daily News* to the *National Enquirer*, and the underground press acquired some of that stigma, due largely to uncensored language, sexual frankness, raunchy comix, and spicy classified ads. Even standard newspapers are considered to be transient publications. Magazines, on the other hand, automatically command more respect, and are often considered worth saving. *The Nation* and the *Texas Observer* are good examples of quality newsprint magazines.

BSN had been leaning more and more toward magazine-type content, and readers were encouraged to save their copies. Frequent references were made to articles in back issues.

Magazine format also had technical advantages. Pages are much easier to lay out. Reprints often came from publications with the same page size, so it was simpler to have a good photocopy made than to type the whole article over. Between reprints and original material, a new issue could be put together much more quickly and efficiently.

BSN number 26 came out at the beginning of the Iran hostage crisis and featured related concerns of the moment: Russian intervention in Afghanistan, talk of reinstituting the draft, and the possibility of war with Iran. Though the themes were essentially political, the responses (all reprints except the introductory editorial) were mostly from mainstream religious quarters: Protestant, Catholic, and Jewish. Authors included William Stringfellow, Richard Barnet, Arthur Waskow, Dave Dellinger, Jim Wallis, Charles A. Kimball, David McReynolds, and Rarihokwats.

A major theme of the issue was to recall that the Iran crisis could be traced back to 1953, when a CIA-run coup ousted the existing parliamentary government and reestablished a monarchy under the late shah. The shah's police state gave rise to the anti-U.S. sentiment that persists to the present. When the hostages were taken, the righteous U.S. response would have been to apologize to the new revolutionary government of Iran for past injuries, and show some genuine repentance. This response might have resulted in a much faster release of the hostages, but, of course, nation-states never say they're sorry. My editorial introduction to the issue contributed a New Age element by observing that unholy government decisions will inevitably result in bad karma somewhere down the line.

When *BSN* started, the youth movement was saying not to trust anyone over thirty, and

I was over forty—forty-four, to be exact. Max Scherr was even older when he founded the *Berkeley Barb.* Art Kunkin was thirty-six when he founded the *Los Angeles Free Press.* When the "kids" pooped out and left me holding the bag, why didn't I quit, too? I believe it's because some of us are truth freaks. We can't stand living in an Orwellian world of lies, distortions, doublethink, secrecy, cover-ups, and whitewashes. A need to communicate the truth becomes an obsession—an addiction, like having a monkey on your back. Some of the more notable truth freaks of our time include Noam Chomsky, George Seldes, and I. F. Stone. Even after a lapse of ten years, my monkey is still there. Though many good alternative publications exist, some bases still are not covered.

I believe that the international Green movement that started taking shape at the turn of the eighties has a potential for developing the spiritual/political synthesis that *BSN* and others were seeking. In their 1984 book *Green Politics*, Fritjof Capra and Charlene Spretnak noted that leading founders of the German Greens—Petra Kelly and Rudolf Bahro—insisted that a spiritual element was essential to the Green movement. However, Greens, who come from a Left background, may not be inclined to agree. The conflict that Billotte had observed several years earlier was now reappearing in a new context. In the United States, social ecologist/anarchist Murray Bookchin has shown hostility toward any New Age elements that appear in the Green movement. Those who think like this fear that metaphysical speculation will divert attention from the economic roots of social and ecological problems. On the other hand are those, like Spretnak, who believe that a change of consciousness is essential to the making of a new society.

A literary forum is much needed here to discuss such ideas. New Age magazines seldom venture into the spiritual implications of world events, and even the *Utne Reader*—whose founder, Eric Utne, was one of the founders of *New Age Journal*—has limits to its metaphysical adventurousness. In short, there's room for a New Age/Green publication in the current alternative scene—an idea toward which *BSN* was groping over ten years ago, before there was a Green movement.

The term "New Age" has been so commercialized, trivialized, misused, abused, and vilified that it has almost lost any semantic value. It has been applied to humanistic therapies, soporific music, bizarre cults, and new concepts in physics, economics, medicine, and a wide range of subjects. Most often forgotten in all the confusion is the meaning of the word "age."

An age is a specific time frame, and the New Age concept is based on astrological reckoning wherein our solar system is in a changing relationship to the constellations of the zodiac about every 2,160 years. Historic times cover only three ages: Taurus, Aries, and Pisces (now in its waning years). The New Age, as we have heard in the popular song and elsewhere, is the Age of Aquarius. While some journalists look on the New Age as a fad soon destined for the dustbin of history, the fact is that the Age of Aquarius will not really begin till the next century.[8] Ages do not end and start abruptly. There is a transition period like a segue as one fades out and the next makes its entrance. If we look at our times in this light, we can observe the entropy of the Old Order in political upheavals, economic instability, wars and rumors of war, plagues, famines, earthquakes, and climate changes. At the same time, we see seeds of the new order in ecological awareness, feminism, pacifism, new approaches to healing, and a fusion of old and new religious traditions. Spirituality is the unifying core behind the bewildering changes we are seeing all around us, and if we do not comprehend this, we will not be able to understand these changes.

The function of *BSN*, as I saw it, was (or is) to read the "signs of the times" and interpret them in terms of the major shift from one age to another. I always liked the name "Both Sides Now" because of its many ambiguities. In this case, it conveys the idea of a bridge between the old and the new. The role of such a publication is essentially prophetic.

From the foregoing, it may be seen that the Green movement is an appropriate politic for the New Age. When the German Greens formed a party, they rested their platform on four pillars: ecology, social responsibility, grassroots democracy, and nonviolence. Capra and Spretnak discerned other implied pillars, including decentralism, feminism, and spirituality. Hence, I feel comfortable about identifying *BSN* with the Green movement, as long as it sticks to first principles.

At the same time, *BSN* should remain an independent voice, not connected to any factions or personalities in the Movement. The maverick role allows one to venture into territories that are too far out for the more "respectable" journals.

At the time this is being written, I am engaged in an informal investigation of the anti–New Age movement. Over the past decade, there has been a growing body of books, articles, workshops, audio tapes, and TV broadcasts bent on discrediting the movement, which has been characterized as everything from a fascist plan for world domination to an anti-Christian heresy conjured up by Satan himself. Investigating this phenomenon takes one into a twilight zone of the paranoid style, conspiracy theories, Satanism, cults, skeptics, and spiritual counterfeits. Most of this flak comes from the fundamentalist/Pentecostal axis, which has close ties to the Far Right in politics, but there are also salvos from skeptical humanists. Hardly anyone is picking up on all this because so few political/spiritual minds are around.

My original idea was to put out an occasional newsletter, to be called *The Tejas Light*, whenever enough research material came together. This idea quickly led to the thought that, if one were to get back into publishing, why not revive *BSN* itself to cover the broader range of interests already indicated, with *TTL* serving as a department to cover the investigative material?[9] Perhaps, by the time this essay appears in print, *BSN* could be reborn like the mythical phoenix. . . .

Part 2: The Resurrection
THE REST OF THE STORY

Part 1 of this story is as it appeared in the original edition of *Voices from the Underground*. In fact, *BSN* did make its comeback in August 1991 with a cover-story analysis of the Gulf War entitled "More Lost Than Won: A War in Retrospect." But in order to move forward, it might be well to backtrack and fill a significant gap in the lives of those behind *Both Sides Now*. While I was teaching and publishing, Joan, who was an RN, was becoming seriously involved in the feminist health movement. Her presentation of a self-help workshop was vividly described in "The Hidden Malpractice" (1978) by Gena Corea. Few today remember that abortion rights were mainly championed by liberal clergy. When abortion was legalized in New York, Clergy Consultation Service opened a counseling center and helped women to make the trip north, when appropriate. The director was a Protestant minister. Joan served on the board and was a counselor herself.

A group of feminists in Gainesville were not pleased at there being a male-led program, and they wished to go beyond having a single-issue facility. They wanted a general health center. Since Feminist Women's Health Centers existed on the West Coast, Joan was recruited to visit one and learn the nuts and bolts of setting one up. She returned to join the board of the Gainesville Women's Health Center and become its first director.

After a time, one of the black women on the staff became pregnant and, complaining about the way she was treated by some of the racist male interns at the University of Florida medical school, asked the GWHC staff to assist her at a home birth. None of them, including Joan, had specific obstetric experience, but they knew that almost all healthy women were at very low risk. Of course the birth went swimmingly. Word got out, and soon two more couples requested home births. This led Joan to recommend that GWHC establish a separate birth center, but the board balked at expanding so early in the game.

To Joan, women having a decisive role in the birth process was as important as anything else, and she returned to Jax, determined to do something about it. We were considering where to set up shop when Joan had a flash on her trip to Tallahassee to incorporate the future Alternative Birth Center (ABC) of Jacksonville. It was the first free-standing birth center in the Southeast. (The GWHC later did establish one of its own, with Joan as consultant.) We were living in a huge brick Victorian house in a neighborhood that had seen much better times. It had two main floors, a two-room attic where *BSN* was produced, and a large basement (former servants' quarters and kitchen), which was an apartment in itself. There were fireplaces in the rooms, plus central heat from radiators. So the flash was: Why not have the birth center in our own home? Our older son, Joe, was married and already moved out. Daughters Chaia and Sarah were in the work force and could take care of themselves. Our younger son, Ellic, was finishing high school, so he stayed and occupied a small bedroom in the basement, where Joan and I settled in the rest of the space, installing a large water bed.

The building itself had deteriorated during the Depression, and during World War II had been converted into a rooming house. With the help of the neighboring gay community, it was restored to its former glory. Two bedrooms on the second floor were furnished with antique beds to serve as birth rooms. Before we were open for business, an Australian midwife married to an American learned of us from the Gainesville center and employed Joan as her own midwife. Then Joe's wife, Anna, decided she wanted a home birth, and she gave birth to our first grandchild, Rachael, on the first-floor parlor sofa. We were in business. (Joan was later to deliver Rachael's daughter, Shannon, in Jax.)

Satisfying as that was, toward the end of the 1970s we were feeling burnout from a number of stresses. Ellic had moved to Houston, so there were just the two of us. Looking for a less urbanized setting, a series of circumstances led to our acquiring acreage near Tyler, Texas, and establishing a homestead there late in 1979. Before our leaving Jax, a few women requested home births, and Joan realized we didn't need to open another center, with all the work involved. From then on she practiced home-birthing under the name Midwife Service of East Texas. At first we rented offices in town, but later we acquired a small trailer for an office on our land.

Though she did part-time nursing when funds were scarce, midwifery remained Joan's primary vocation to the end. Less than a week after assisting a delivery, she suffered a stroke on October 26, 1999, leaving half her body completely paralyzed. Rehabilitation efforts were of no avail. Not wanting to be a useless burden, Joan summoned her indomitable will and departed from this world via a heart attack around midnight, January 30/31, 2000.

If the above appears to be a digression, well, it is, but it is also to show that underground publishing was but one facet of a larger alternative movement to change America, as well as to pay homage to Joan's part in it. She was recently listed in "Feminists Who Changed America, 1963–1975," published by the University of Illinois Press, 2006. Those included were called the "second wave" of feminism.

THE RETURN OF *BSN*

Part 2 of this account began with a note that *BSN* finally made a comeback after a lapse of about eleven years. The motivation was President George H. W. Bush's troop buildup, leading up to the First Gulf War. The old tabloid format was impractical, but another option had become available. The husband of one of Joan's clients was in the business of rebuilding photocopiers, and he bartered a huge ledger-sized Sharp for the birthing. Its primary purpose was for producing charts for the birth clients, but now I also had my own "press." The old typesetters had the sit-ups after more than a decade of idleness, but they produced readable if funky copy. However, the war was over in the blink of an eye, and Bush crowed that he had beaten the "Vietnam Syndrome"—which referred to the buildup of an antiwar movement that previously had taken several years to coalesce.

Nevertheless, I wanted to get the word out on what was wrong with the war, and so went ahead to produce *BSN* number 27, "More Lost Than Won," in letter-size format in August of 1991. Ten pages (five sheets of paper) were the most that would go on a first class stamp, so that became the standard size for an issue.

In 1992 Dr. Helen Caldicott gave a stirring talk locally on the looming environmental crisis. A pamphlet version of her subject was in print, and with good old-fashioned cutting and pasting it was reformatted as the sole content of *BSN* number 28, with the headline "Saving the Planet."

By 1993 the "Satanic panic" mentioned earlier was beginning to be seen for the bummer it was, and I was able to pull together enough related articles to add up to the first *BSN* double issue, numbers 29–30, in February, with 20 pages. Later that year, the Branch Davidian tragedy near Waco made big news, and think pieces on it occupied number 31.

Number 32 (1994) saw a return to New Age interests with a focus on Barbara Marx Hubbard's interpretation of the Book of Revelation. But another issue (number 33) did not appear till October 1997. Like number 31, it was devoted to think pieces on the consciousness of events—in this case the deaths of celebrities Elvis Presley and Princess Diana. In 1998, two essays on the Great Seal of the U.S. from the old *BSN* were brought together in one issue, numbers 34–35. In 1999 only one double issue appeared. You will recall that Joan was stricken later that year. At the time I was also doing a brief three and a half year stint as one-man art department for Jarvis Christian College, a United Negro College Fund school near Hawkins, Texas. After Joan's death I produced issue number 38, which commented on her passing and all the fuss over Y2K, among other matters. It was to be the last single issue.

In the summer of the same year, numbers 39–40 came out, featuring the synthesis of spirituality I had been contemplating for so many years. It is notable for my review of three transformational novels by Dana Redfield, who had also written about her experiences as an ET contactee. Dana, who lived in Moab, Utah, became a close e-mail friend until her death in early 2007. Subsequent issues of *BSN* carried tributes to her, as well as some of her writing and artwork. Being a "font freak," I was able to provide special typography for her unpublished book on the mystique of the alphabet.

Another long-distance friendship has been with poet Joan Thomas of Phoenix, who was the widow of Ammon Hennacy, a noted anarchist-pacifist who for a time was associated with Dorothy Day's Catholic Worker Movement. We became pen pals shortly after the move to Texas when I ordered Ammon's autobiography from her, and after Joan's death our relationship became warmer. I recruited Joey (as her friends call her) to be the *BSN* poetry editor; she also contributes occasional essays.

After 2000 I was striving to get *BSN* out more frequently, with the goal of becoming a quarterly. It was quite a struggle. (Remember that these are all double issues.) There were two in 2001, one in 2002 (on 9/11), two in 2003, and three in 2004. The year 2005 finally saw the attainment of quarterly frequency, and it has been maintained ever since. As this is written late in 2007, *BSN* has seen the appearance of issue numbers 79–80.

The intention here is not to review every issue since *BSN*'s revival, but rather to tell how it came to make a comeback, and what topics were in the air at that time. More recently *BSN* has been seeing current events from a New Age and peacemaker's perspective, and looking beyond them into the future. A most insightful example was issue 45–46, *BSN*'s response to 9/11 in which it was shown that the rush to war (cheered on by the straight press) was not an appropriate response and could result in a *1984*-type authoritarian regime at home.

More recent issues focused on increasing signs of a coming New Age. It always seemed ironic that mass society was preoccupied with the negativity of war and the triviality of celebrity consciousness while significant phenomena were taking place, as well as new thinking on where we were headed. The main phenomena were UFO sightings, the overnight appearance of crop circles in different parts of the world, and the birthing of precocious children called "Indigos." (Note that this had been anticipated years before in *BSN* number 25.) A major phenomenon has been channeling—psychic downloading of information from nonphysical beings. There is a wealth of print and electronic information on this. It is clear that the human race is evolving and is not alone in the universe; others are watching and communicating with us. But the so-called "world leaders" muddle on, clueless and oblivious to all this.

Another major concern has been all the buzz about the year 2012. Ellic turned me on to the writings of Carl Johan Calleman, who has made a good case for the year 2011. In any event, we are coming to the end of a long age (or "world" as Native Americans call it) of over 5,000 years, after which we will be in an entirely new ball game that we can't begin to envision, except that it should be better than the nightmarish one we're in now. As this is written, the world is entering a 360-day dark night (most of 2008), according to Calleman, which will likely see the collapse of many systems—ecological, economic, and political. After that, the world should be reorganizing toward the new dawn of 2011. We are living in interesting times.

Technical Update

Over this revival period, *BSN* also made technical progress. As of issue 33, I had acquired a hand-me-down computer, but much of the issue was still photocopied from other sources

BOTH SIDES NOW

Back to our Roots

NO. 93-94   A JOURNAL OF LIGHTWORKING, PEACEMAKING, & CONSCIOUSNESS $2.50

Darkness and Scattered Light

ON THE MOVE

The headline, taken from the title of a 1978 book by William Irwin Thompson, is very appropriate for the times we have been going through. On the dark side we have seen wars, ecological crisis, economic collapse, false religion, political irrelevance, and other signs of the end of an era. On the other hand there have always been among us lightworkers who have held fast to the vision of a better world and have been striving for its fulfillment in word and deed. That fulfillment has been referred to as a New Age.

Both Sides Now (BSN) has been following this movement since the late 1970s. Issue No. 24 (April 1977) had the first appearance of its current logo, a cover illustration with a new version of the tarot card "The Sun," and the text: SPECIAL ISSUE - THE DAWN OF A NEW AGE AND A NEW BOTH SIDES NOW. There was a boom in New Age phenomena back then, following the counter-cultural one of the 1960s and early 1970s. Unfortunately, too much of it became cultish, leaving a bad taste as some cults became too insular or controlling, while some cult leaders had messy personal lives, to put it mildly. Such phenomena were not authentically New Age in the first place, since the concept is essentially anarchic.

As this issue developed, the idea of getting back to our own New Age roots emerged. Since the New Age—or Age of Aquarius—is on the horizon, there is no good reason why we should not be using the term freely and openly, reclaiming it from the dustbin to which some had relegated it. Speaking personally as editor, my own New Age consciousness began with reading "There is a River" by Thomas Sugrue, the first biography of Edgar Cayce, a most remarkable psychic. I was just out of college at the time and the book had recently been published. Up to that time, I was a sort of humanist, but the book presented such overwhelming evidence of other dimensions via psychic phenomena that my worldview was completely turned around. Many others have had a similar experience from reading this book.

Once the "doors of perception" have been opened, synchronicities start to happen, and related information started coming my way. Most particularly, other books

that attracted my attention contributed to my developing worldview. Cayce had already referred to a coming New Age, but "The Magic of Findhorn" by Paul Hawken told that the New Age was already happening in prototype form at a remote village in northern Scotland. In this issue there is a reprint of an article on Cayce that first appeared in the 1970s, and one on Findhorn which was originally published in the "old" BSN from around the same time. Other significant influences have been "The Tarot" by Paul Foster Case and "A Course in Miracles"—all of which illuminated the existence of other dimensions and pointed the way to much more profound spiritual understandings. A main motivation for publishing BSN is the sharing of such insights as they come to us.

FIGURE 2: Cover of *Both Sides Now* issue 93/94 (third quarter 2009). Courtesy *Both Sides Now.*

and pasted up. Subsequent issues were completely typeset on the computer, but spaces were left for the graphics, which were pasted in for photocopying. The old Sharp wore out and replacement parts could not be found, so it was ultimately replaced by a versatile Canon NP1020. It had a large bed that allowed one to reduce copy from tabloid to letter size. It too suffered from overwork, which forced me to realize that with the help of a scanner I could integrate graphics and produce an issue directly from computer to printer. At present I'm using a fine Compaq computer and a Hewlett Packard Laser Jet 1018 printer plus HP scanner (see figure 2).

Another step forward was the acquisition of a Web site, www.bothsidesnow.info, where people could learn about *BSN*. It was set up by son Ellic, who maintains it and serves as tech support from his present base in Birmingham.

NOTES

1. We learned that the couple soon split up. As I recall, she became a Jesus freak while he returned to Ithaca and did notable work in developing the local barter currency called Ithaca Money. Still, his use of an anti-Semitic stereotype was unforgivable. (However, we New Agers are supposed to be forgiving.)

2. The film *Winter Soldier* was reissued on DVD in 2007 and I was finally able to acquire a disc and watch it at leisure, as well as share it with others.

3. Irv is still at it, now putting out a zine, *Irv's Scrapbook*, on the Internet, as well as irregular letters to his mailing list between issues.

4. *The Sun* is going strong and winning awards for excellence. *Little Free Press* died with its publisher years ago.

5. The *Washington Spectator* now has Lou Dubose at the helm. Satin went on to develop a *Radical Middle* concept with Web site, but that has been discontinued.

6. *In These Times* went from tabloid to magazine format, joining other fine left-leaning publications like *The Progressive* and *The Nation*. The Internet explosion has brought with it some fine underground journalism. My favorites include Truthout, TomDispatch, Truthdig, and Alternet. The underground press, meanwhile, has morphed into the zine scene, a motley assortment of small-scale homemade publications with an extreme variety of formats, contents, and quality. Technically, *BSN* is a zine. The best source of information on this phenomenon is *Zine World: A Reader's Guide to the Underground Press*, PO Box 330156, Murfreesboro, TN 37133-0156, and its Web site www.undergroundpress.org.

7. That prediction was premature. See Note 8.

8. Based on the writings of outstanding astrologer Dane Rudhyar, I originally thought his calculation of 2062 C.E. was the turning point for the New Age, but Calleman's calculation of 2011, based on his interpretation of a Mayan calendar, now seems to make sense, although most other "experts" prefer the year 2012; 2062, exactly fifty years after 2012, is still likely to be a milestone, since the transition may not happen overnight.

9. The *TTL* concept was dropped after a short time as the "Satanic panic" subsided.

It Aint Me Babe: From Feminist Radicals to Radical Feminists

BONNIE EISENBERG, WITH HELP FROM LAURA X,
TRINA ROBBINS, STARR GOODE, AND ALTA

The Summer That Changed My Life

The 1960s was a tumultuous time in Berkeley, California, where the spark of student rebellion in the U.S. was born with the nonviolent free speech movement (FSM) in 1964. As the Vietnam War escalated and students faced the threat of being drafted, the U.C. Berkeley campus and surrounding residential communities became the site of numerous major student protests, which Ronald Reagan used to catapult himself to stardom as governor in the 1966 election. Protesters disrupted classes and confronted the police during marches and demonstrations, starting with Stop the Draft Week (1967). Next came the Third World Liberation Front Strike for Ethnic Studies, where the police first used tear gas (December 1968 to February 1969), and resistance to the Vietnam War continued. By the spring of 1969, Governor Reagan was "fed up" with student dissent, and sex, drugs, and rock-and-roll lifestyles. He was determined to On Sunday, April 20, 1969, an innocuous group of students and local counterculture activists turned a university-owned vacant block into a park by laying sod, planting trees, and building children's play structures. They were met three weeks later with an astounding show of force called in by Reagan. With little warning, at 4:45 in the morning of Thursday, May 15, the park and an eight-block area around it were cleared by over 250 highway patrol and Berkeley police. That morning a tall chainlink fence was erected.

When a rally was called on campus to protest the destruction of People's Park, authorities greeted the protestors with shotguns and teargas. One bystander, a student from another college, James Rector, was mortally wounded by Alameda County Sheriff's deputies who were shooting at people on rooftops of stores near campus; he died four days later. Another bystander who was on the rooftop of the Telegraph Repertory Cinema with Rector, Alan Blanchard, an artist and carpenter for the Cinema, was blinded for life; he killed himself two years later. Scores of people were shot with birdshot and beaten, and thousands on campus and in the surrounding community, including children and patients in the campus hospital, suffered the agonizing effects of tear gas on that day, which became known as Bloody Thursday, May 15.

That evening, Reagan declared martial law in Berkeley and sent in the National Guard with fixed bayonets facing forward to clear the streets. Two days later, they herded anybody in the downtown area, including shoppers, into parking lots and arrested more than five hundred people. On Tuesday, May 20, helicopters sprayed tear gas over the campus and trapped students who had assembled there for the memorial for James Rector.

I was one of those who felt the tear gas that week and saw my community turned into a war zone by the presence, on street corners throughout the city, of National Guard troops, who added insult to injury by bivouacking in People's Park. When the Independent Socialist Club (ISC), of which I had been a member for two years, offered to send me to Boston for the summer to participate in a printing apprenticeship program at the New England Free Press (NEFP), I was happy to leave town. Their motivation was that I would learn to use a printing press so they could print more revolutionary tracts to distribute to the masses. As I didn't have any other plans for the summer, and had only one more semester of college left before me, I was ready for an adventure.

The New England Free Press was well known on the left for printing, in pamphlet form, radical articles that had appeared in magazines and underground newspapers, and distributing them to campuses and organizations around the country. Only two months before, in April 1969, they had been the organizing center of the student strike at Harvard that was a response to the administration's use of force against antiwar student protesters occupying University Hall. They were the publishers the next year of *Women and Their Bodies*, the 136-page pamphlet that later evolved into *Our Bodies, Ourselves*, the women's health bible of the early feminist movement. I learned all aspects of printing, from typesetting and publication layout to running the presses and bindery.

At NEFP, I met some pretty incredible people—including Hester Butterfield, who introduced me to the women's liberation "small group," and Tim Moriarty, who was my primary teacher there—who had dedicated their lives to changing the world through the printed word. Watching the staff work on their projects, I learned that it was not all that difficult to create your own newspaper. The motto of the NEFP was "Freedom of the press belongs to those who own their own press," an idea that they adapted from the well-known quote of journalist A. J. Liebling: "Freedom of the press is guaranteed only to those who own one." I took that as my motto as well.

At this time, an important educational vehicle of the newly emerging women's movement was the "consciousness-raising" (CR) group, which had been developed in New York Radical Women and formulated by Kathie Sarachild for distribution in her paper "Program for Feminist Consciousness-Raising" at the 1968 Chicago Women's Liberation Conference. A CR group was a small group of women who met regularly to discuss their upbringing, attitudes, relationships, workplace experiences, aspirations, and other issues that we had in common as women, to help us understand the societal forces, restrictive ideology, and limitations we faced in everyday life. We learned that many of the "problems" we experienced as individuals (such as being sexually harassed at work, or having husbands who constantly put us down) were actually shared by many women, and that they weren't strictly "personal problems." I joined my first CR group while in Boston that summer and began to understand the meaning of the phrase "The personal is political," as put forth by Carol Hanisch in a paper by that name the previous March:

So the reason I participate in these meetings is not to solve any personal problem. One of the first things we discover in these groups is that personal problems are political problems. There are no personal solutions at this time. There is only collective action for a collective solution.

"Political" was used here in the broad sense of the word as having to do with power relationships, not the narrow sense of electoral politics.

I also got a theoretical education on women's oppression and the necessity for a separate women's movement by attending lectures by two of the leading voices of the women's movement in the Northeast, Roxanne Dunbar and Dana Densmore, who had founded a group known as Cell 16 in Boston, and published a journal called *No More Fun and Games*. Roxanne was a radical, committed to liberation movements, but she understood—like the leaders of the nineteenth-century women's movement when they left the antislavery movement to organize for women's rights—the need for women to organize as women, for our own liberation from oppressive roles and relationships, before we could be effective participants in antiwar or civil rights struggles.

Organizing in Berkeley

When I returned to Berkeley at the end of the summer, I was ready to take on an active role in Berkeley Women's Liberation. However, being in the leadership of that organization put me in conflict with the Independent Socialists who fancied themselves Trotskyist, and therefore preferred to act as the leftist agitation within larger political groups, not as the leadership. I was forced to choose between remaining in that group and my active role in women's liberation. Needless to say, I chose the latter. There were probably twenty to thirty women who actively participated in meetings of Berkeley Women's Liberation in the fall of 1969. Much of our meeting time was taken up by various male-dominated groups asking us to help them with whatever it was they were doing. I don't recall them ever coming to ask if they could help us.

Being a trained printer, I wasted no time finding others to help me start a women's liberation newspaper. I found a pilot Head Start teacher and aspiring film critic, Laura X, a socialist feminist with friends in ISC. The former Laura Murra had taken her name, Laura X, on September 17, 1969, to parallel for women Malcolm X's protest that black people had to carry their slave owners' names and study white males' history because their names and histories had been stolen from them. In the case of women, she added, their individual histories disappear when they get married and their surnames are changed.

At the time, Laura X had been writing for various papers and the women's liberation journal *Tooth and Nail*. She was a veteran of the peace, civil rights, free speech, educational reform, antiwar, anti-nuke, Farm Workers, Native American, and ecology movements, as well as an active supporter of struggles against anti-Semitism and for Puerto Rican independence, starting when she trained in graduate school at the University of Puerto Rico for Head Start. As an alumna that spring, she had taught "Women and Film," the first women's studies course at UCB, where she brought in Native American women to show their documentaries and tell their stories. To celebrate May Day 1969, she had organized the event that showed *Salt of the Earth* to break the blacklist against the film that many consider the most important women's liberation film of all time. (It also was one of the first hundred American films saved by the Library of Congress in 1996.)

Two months before the *Salt of the Earth* showing, on March 8, the first public street demonstration for International Women's Day in the United States since 1947 had taken place in Berkeley, due to Laura's initiative in working with Berkeley Women's Liberation through Phyllis Mandel (see appendix 1). As a result of the national and international publicity, people from forty countries began to send Laura materials, which became the International Women's History Archive of our movement. From April to December 1969, Laura published a women's liberation newsletter called *SPAZM*, the only national women's liberation newsletter during that period. In addition to her expertise and movement connections, Laura provided seed money, her mailing list, and a subscription to Liberation News Service. She also exchanged subscriptions with many women's journals and other radical papers, which were already beginning to receive irate letters from women about the way the fledgling movement was being covered (or not being covered, as was more often the case), including the insulting male chauvinist remarks that were driving women out of the male-dominated movement—what Flo Kennedy called the "StagNation."

We planned to begin publishing in mid-January 1970.

One day in late fall, I was sitting around with my friends Sue Klein and Peggy White, both of whom were soon to become a part of the newspaper staff, and we were looking at the schedule of classes for Berkeley's winter trimester. Peggy noticed that the self-defense classes were only offered for men. We decided this was a good issue to organize around. We designed and printed a flier telling women who were interested in signing up for self-defense classes to come to the men's gym at a specified day and time to register. We passed out the fliers at the women's liberation meeting and to all those waiting in line to sign up for women's phys. ed. classes. We didn't really know what would happen, but we figured it would be a good photo op and opening story for our newspaper, which was at that point still unnamed. Well, we got that, and much more.

About sixty women showed up on January 7, 1970, and, of course, we were barred entry into the men's gym. We formed a march and began protesting. The protest went on for several days—initially at preregistration, then the next day when the self-defense class held its first meeting, and then the following day with a rally. I remember speaking at the rally on the steps of the administration building, Sproul Hall (under an assumed name, as I had just graduated and was therefore considered an "outside agitator" and banned from speaking). Then we marched around campus banging on pots and pans. We ended up sitting in at the chancellor's office and made the evening news. That evening news clip, with Berkeley Women's Liberation martial artist Phyllis Mandel, was immortalized in the film *Berkeley in the 60's*. Yippie and martial artist Judy Gumbo made the cover of *Berkeley Tribe* with an article, and the photograph of Laura X glaring at Vice-Chancellor Johnson made the *Chronicle* with the caption "Hell hath no fury like a woman scorned." Our demands for women's self-defense classes were not met, but the women's liberation movement in Berkeley had made a stunning statement.

Ruth Rosen, now a famous historian of the women's movement and author of *The World Split Open: How the Modern Women's Movement Changed America*, took a great picture of the

IT AINT ME BABE

TO SUBSUME ME IN YOUR SHADOW~TO COME EACH TIME YOU CALL~A LOVER FOR YOUR LIFE AND NOTHING MORE

| vol.1 no.1 | BERKELEY WOMEN'S LIBERATION | Jan 15 15¢ |

Sisters have united in Berkeley to defend our right to be treated as human beings. We want the right to defend ourselves, an end to discrimination in hiring and admissions, birth control and abortion information, adequate child care facilities, and courses about our history. During the past week we began a struggle for these demands, among others. We would like to share our experiences with you.

Winter Quarter 1970. We peruse the schedule of classes. There is a new P.E. section-particularly important to us-Karate 1. We believe that the university is finally offering a much needed class in self-defense. However, the pre-enrollment listings reveal that Karate 1 is for men only!

ON JANUARY 7, 60 WOMEN MET AT HARMON GYM TO PRE-ENROLL FOR KARATE AND TO CHALLENGE THE SEXIST PRACTICES OF THE UNIVERSITY. THEY MARCHED TO THE MEN'S LOCKER ROOM (WHERE PRE-ENROLLMENT WAS TAKING PLACE) CHANTING "SELF DEFENSE FOR WOMEN NOW!" THE P.E. DEPARTMENT NOT ONLY REFUSED TO LET THEM PRE-ENROLL BUT CALLED IN THE COPS WHO THREATENED THE WOMEN WITH ARREST.

We were outraged at this blatant denial of our rights and decided to return for the first class session the following day. In the leaflet we passed out on Thursday we tried to explain the importance of self-defense as it relates to the daily oppression of women throughout society.

SELF DEFENSE FOR WOMEN

THURSDAY 1:00 A LARGE GROUP OF WOMEN GATHERED AT HARMON GYM FOR THE FIRST MEETING OF KARATE 1. THEY WERE BLOCKED FROM ENTERING THE CLASS BY A NUMBER OF COPS. THE WOMEN CHANTED, SANG AND REPEATEDLY DEMANDED ENTRANCE TO THE CLASS. THE COPS' THREATS TO PICK UP INDIVIDUAL WOMEN LATER WITH WARRANTS DID NOT INTIMIDATE THE GROUP. THE WOMEN REMAINED AT THE GYM UNTIL KARATE 1 WAS DISMISSED AND THEN MARCHED TO THE OFFICE OF CHANCELLOR HEYNS TO PRESENT A LIST OF DEMANDS TO THE UNIVERSITY.

continued page 4-5

photo: Ruth

The ever increasing rate of traditional crimes against women has prompted women's magazines and newspapers to issue warnings and offer advice to their female readers. We are warned not to go out unaccompanied after dark, but if we must venture out alone, we are advised to carry alarms, mace, nailfiles, to avoid enticing clothing, and of course if attacked--scream, so some passing man will come to our rescue.

The crimes against women are the most blatant expression of the pervasive attitude of men towards women. While some of us have not experienced the extreme, all of us have been subjected to the more "harmless" forms--being handled, whistled at, pinched, hooted at. You don't treat an equal human being like that. Any female not under the protection of a male is "free game". If she's a private property, then she's public property.

We have depended on males to protect us too long. The right to protect is also the right to oppress. It is time that all females learn to defend themselves.

Males are taught to take care of themselves while growing up. Females are systematically denied this right. Our culture does not allow women to develop strength. Girls are not supposed to do physical things. The result is that women are pitifully weak. The psychological consequences are of even greater significance. Women feel they should be weak, that they need a man to protect them.

Women's physical weakness and its psychological consequences can only be overcome through developing their bodies. Of the various forms of self-defense, karate enables you to become consciously aware of your physical potential by teaching you to mobilize your whole body. Only when we have gained the self confidence that comes through developing our physical potential and exercising it, will we be able to gain any individual mobility.

It is a basic and immediate necessity that all women be given access to self defense instruction. It is not an individual problem. WE DEMAND THAT SELF DEFENSE INSTRUCTION BE PROVIDED BY THE UNIVERSITY, BY TOWNS, SCHOOLS, BUSINESSES, WELFARE DEPARTMENTS--ALL INSTITUTIONS WHICH HAVE DIRECT CONTROL OVER WOMEN'S LIVES.

FIGURE 1: Cover of It Aint Me Babe volume 1, number 1 (January 15, 1970), featuring a review of a women's demonstration demanding the right to enroll in a Berkeley self-defense class, with accompanying photo by Ruth Rosen. Courtesy Bonnie Eisenberg. The name came from the song by Bob Dylan. Lyrics were changed only slightly for the masthead, from the original: "To gather flowers constantly, and to come each time you call, a lover for your life and nothing more. It ain't me, babe," to: "To subsume me in your shadow, to come each time you call, a lover for your life and nothing more . . . it aint me babe." Courtesy Bonnie Eisenberg.

demonstration, which we featured on the front cover of the first edition of our newspaper, along with a report on that demonstration on the Berkeley campus (see figure 1). Other features in that first issue were a detailed list of our demands—which included daycare on campus, equal employment opportunity and pay for female faculty members, and self-defense classes for women—and an article about the importance of women being able to defend themselves and learning the relationship between "protection" and "domination." A long editorial about the oppression of women within the nuclear family was our opening statement of the necessity for a women's liberation movement.

> Adult society in America is based on a psychological unit of two and there is some question whether the system could survive if this were not the case. It is the women whose job it is to cushion the worst effects of an inhuman system by providing love and support for the male who is constantly threatened by the deadly competition of other males and the emasculating crush of the boss within the rigid hierarchical structures which control the economy. This is true no matter what niche the man occupies in that structure, although the compensations of power over underlings increase as one goes up the ladder. Male-dominated man needs a woman to dominate as an additional compensation for his loss of autonomy. This means that although the woman needs to escape the boredom, isolation, subjugation and drudgery of the nuclear family, it is obvious that men will be loath to give up the psychological benefits of their domination of women. Hence male backlash appears as women begin to assert themselves and begin to fight for control of their lives. (See appendix 2 for full text of the editorial.)

Peggy, Starr Goode, and I had moved into a house together in December 1969. Peggy and Starr had met in a consciousness-raising group earlier in the year. The house became a commune for running the paper. We laid out the paper on the dining room table. Peggy, Starr, and I functioned as the editors of the paper in the beginning, deciding the content and the look of the paper. One memorable night, just before the first issue was to go to the printer, the three of us were frantically brainstorming for a name for the paper. After considering many other options, we came up with *It Aint Me Babe*, from a Bob Dylan song title we dug up at the last minute. We only had to change the words of his song a little bit for our masthead, "To subsume me in your shadow, to come each time you call, a lover for your life and nothing more . . . it aint me babe."

We printed probably 1,000 copies of that first issue and sold them for 15 cents apiece, mostly in the Bay Area. I didn't know it at the time, but "the *Babe*," as we affectionately called it, was the first national newspaper of the emerging women's liberation movement in the United States.

About eight or ten of us worked on the paper at the beginning, as I recall. Peggy and Starr worked on the paper for its entire run, and wrote many articles. I did not do a lot of writing for the paper, other than a women's history article in the March issue and an article or two that I coauthored with Peggy and Starr. The staff members wrote some of the articles, while other Bay Area feminists, including Joan Jordan, Lynn O'Connor ("Male Dominance, the Nitty Gritty of Oppression"), and Susan Griffin ("Single or Schizoid"), wrote others. Susan Griffin is one of the major writers of our generation. She brought Harriet Tubman to the women's liberation movement with her poem "I like to think of Harriet Tubman," which we published in issue 14 (September 17–October 1, 1970). We also looked up to living black women like poets Nikki Giovanni and Beulah Richardson. Nikki Giovanni's "My Poem" was finally published in book form in *The Collected Poetry of Nikki Giovanni: 1968–1998* (HarperCollins, 2003), but it appeared first in issue 13 (September 4–17, 1970). Beulah Richardson's "A Black Woman Speaks . . . of White Womanhood, of White Supremacy, of Peace . . ." graced the back cover of our inaugural issue. When *A Black Woman Speaks*, the documentary about her life, appeared at the Mill Valley Film Festival in 2005, the festival guide described her poetry performances as "visionary, radical words which have brought audiences to their feet and which triggered an FBI investigation during the 1950s and 60s." Acting under her stage name of Beah Richards, she received the Academy Award nomination for her portrayal as Sidney Poitier's mother in the 1968 groundbreaking film *Guess Who's Coming to Dinner.*

Our articles covered a wide geographical and cross-cultural range of subjects, including violence against women, sexual politics, and abortion. We printed letters from Montreal to Seattle to Venice, including one from a transsexual at a time when transsexual people writing openly was unusual, and another from a high-schooler. The article "La Chicana: Let's Build a New Life" achieved renown for Enriqueta Longeaux y Vasquez when it was published in *El Grito del Norte* in November 1969, but we published it first, in our premier issue.

One major piece, "Anatomy of an Abortion," published in issue 11 (August 6–20, 1970), blew the whistle on a Berkeley gynecologist for sexually abusing a patient. The woman's friend wrote the article after she also was treated horribly by him. Her first-person testimony, along with her bold naming of the doctor, was a watershed moment. Other topics included antiwar work, race issues, child care, and employment discrimination. (The landmark U.S. Court of Appeals victory, which desegregated the *San Francisco Chronicle* "help wanted" ads, raised great hopes in 1969 for ending employment discrimination everywhere.) Unfortunately our use of first names only, or total anonymity in bylines, has obscured the identity of most of the authors (though we know now that "You've Come a Long Way Baby: Women's Magazines, 1860–1960," an article that concluded that "the fundamental assumptions about being female had not changed in a century in women's magazines," was the first graduate-school research paper of Ruth Rosen, who signed it at the time only as Ruth).

We were hungry to learn about history and culture and saw their power for our movement. In that spirit, we printed James Oppenheim's 1912 poem "Bread and Roses," which was very meaningful at the time, although no one knew who wrote it and Mimi Fariña's 1974 music had not been written for it yet—we knew it as sung to Beethoven's "Symphony No. 9 Ode to Joy," or the way the early women's liberation movement leader Meredith Tax, from the group Bread and Roses, did it to the original 1912 music by Caroline Kohlsaat. In issue 10 (July 23–August 5, 1970) we published "Metamorphosis into Bureaucrat," with the famous ending, "I wonce was a woman" (with the "w" included in "wonce"). The poem was circulating anonymously at the time and only later was discovered to have been written by Marge Piercy, one of our movement's most powerful poets and novelists. Another poem in that same issue was by Canadian poet Margaret Atwood, who was just beginning her career as a novelist. Her untitled poem, about energy-draining lovers, began with the line "You are the sun in reverse. . . ."

We loved poetry. We published the works of women from the past, like Dorothy Parker

("The Lady's Reward"), and some who had recently passed, like Sylvia Plath, whose poem "Every Woman Loves a Fascist" really affected us, as did her suicide and that of Marilyn Monroe, the subject of a piece called "How Society Suicided Norma Jean," by Gina and Shelly. One of our reviews expressed for so many of us the agony we felt over the attempted suicide of the son of the woman in Doris Lessing's "Golden Notebook" because he represented our generation with no future. It has been a joy to see how far our contributors have gone: Starr, songwriter Judy Busch, Susan Griffin, Hilary Ayer Fowler, Laurel Burch, Alta, Marsha Hudson, Donna Mandelblatt, Jennie Orvino-Sorcic, and Lyn Lifshin, among others.

Any extra space was filled with reprints from other women's publications, such as

- Film review of *Battle of Algiers*—from *Twin Cities Female Liberation Newsletter* (by the way, they hated it!);
- "Good Health for Poor People"—Chicago Women's Liberation newsletter;
- "Beauty Queen or Human Being"—*Pedestal* from Vancouver;
- "Redstockings Manifesto" from New York, parts of the Redstockings West Manifesto from San Francisco, and "Brainwashing and Women" by a Redstockings sister elsewhere;
- "Lesbianism" and "Subversion in the Women's Movement: What Is to Be Done"—Martha Shelley;
- "Lesbians and Bogeywomen"—Gay Women's Liberation from Berkeley and San Francisco;
- "If That's All There Is"—Del Martin;
- Excerpts from "The Politics of Housework or Man Meets the Joy of Being a Woman"—Pat Mainardi;
- "There was an Young Woman who Swallowed a Line" and excerpts from "Woman and Her Mind: A Story of Everyday Life"—Meredith Tax (note: the actual title of her song says "swallowed a lie," but we misnamed it. The "swallowed a line" usage is part of her song); and
- "Playboy after the Dark Ages"—Claudia Dreifus.

Another important reprint, from a male-dominated publication, was "Protective Legislation," by Vilma Sanchez.

A Movement Apart

During the first few months, a lot of the articles focused on elements of our relationships with men. In March, in addition to our usual numbered issue, we published what we called a "Special Supplement." One article in that issue, "Beat the Pecking Order," studied the connection between state, corporate, and "private" violence in our lives. The article, cowritten by the female leader of the People's Park protest, Wendy Schlesinger, and Judy Busch, laid out the "pecking order" of society. As they described it, the ruling elite, only 2 percent of society, controls 70 percent of the wealth and power. They use their power to repress their underlings, who, to combat this abuse, oppress their underlings, on through the largely male labor class, who have no one working under them, so they go home and oppress and abuse their wives. This pecking-order system is the enemy keeping all these people except the elite miserable, the authors concluded. Therefore, women should revolt against the whole system, which, if it is "beat," will free everyone. "We have nothing but misery to lose and everything to gain." Other pieces in that issue included Betty Ryan's "Do Visions of Helicopters Dance in Your Head?," Susan Levy's (Susan Griffin's) "The History of Helicopters in My Life," and an article by the Women's Liberation Childcare Collective that pointed out that police helicopters were being funded instead of child-care centers in Berkeley.

As time went on, the focus changed to larger social issues, and the relationship between feminists and the male-dominated Left. In issue 5 we published Robin Morgan's classic "Good Bye to All That" (reprinted from *The Rat*), a vehement manifesto of why feminists were leaving the male-dominated Left to form our own organizations and to work for our own liberation. Issue number 5 also contained an editorial about the need for a women's movement independent of the male-dominated Left and capable of handling diversity of opinion:

> Our woman's movement must be completely independent of the male dominated left at this time. We must create a structure that suits the kind of organizing we must do and a program that will speak to the needs and interests of all women.
>
> The analysis that we develop will necessarily be different from that of the male dominated left for as women we are treated very differently by this society. Our understanding of our oppression, and analysis of its origin, its magnitude and the means necessary for overthrowing it, must come from our own experience as women. Because we do not all have the same experience, because we come from different backgrounds, are of different ages, etc., the analysis that we women develop may vary. Such differences must not be allowed to degenerate into factionalism. This will inevitably be the case if we try to maintain women's liberation as a mass umbrella organization.
>
> Women across the country have found that room for ideological differences must be structured into the woman's movement. We must keep in mind that we are a movement, not an organization.

Besides the numerous women's liberation groups emerging in many college towns and cities across the country, there was another, very different wing of the women's movement operating on a whole other level. This other wing included the National Organization for Women and leaders such as Betty Friedan, who were working within the establishment power structure to get discriminatory laws changed, and to force businesses, government, and educational institutions to be more open to women's participation. Today it is hard for many to believe that only forty years ago, many colleges did not admit women or had limited quotas, that the work force was highly sex-segregated, that married women could not get credit or purchase a home in their own name, and that there were only a handful of women in elective office anywhere in the country.[1] Moreover, while corporations had been ruled "legal persons" in 1886 (in *Santa Clara County v. Southern Pacific Railroad Company*), women would have to wait until 1971 (*Reed v. Reed*). This wing of the movement sought to address these issues from within the establishment structures, all the while reassuring liberal males that they were merely seeking equal rights as citizens and did not consider men to be the enemy of women.

Those of us who came to the women's movement from the radical Left saw the issue not as civil rights but as much larger, a position that was delineated in issue 5. We did not define males as the "enemy," but we did see men as the "culprits," that segment of the human race responsible for both personal violence and warfare; for the oppression of large groups of people, including all women and children; for the corporate greed that left millions in poverty for the benefit of a few; and for the degradation of the planet, our mother earth. We encouraged women to withdraw from male-dominated organizations and institutions, to become "woman-identified" in order to establish an authentic "women's culture" and ourselves as strong, independent individuals.

The term "woman-identified woman" — and "male-identified woman" — appeared first in a paper of the same name that was handed out by a group called Lavender Action on the Friday evening of the Second Congress to Unite Women, held in New York City the first weekend of May 1970. According to the paper, "Woman-Identified Woman (WIW) referred to the kind of consciousness, the kind of bonding among women that would be required for transforming our male supremacist society." The article was signed by lead author and integrator Artemis March, Ellen Shumsky, Cynthia Funk, Rita Mae Brown, Lois Hart, and Barbara Goldstone. Their names were followed by the phrase "with other RadicaLesbians." This paper introduced that term (with the shared L) as well and, along with the Lavender Menace action, launched the lesbian-feminist movement.

Issue 5 featured a cover drawing by our own staff cartoonist Trina Robbins of a feminist "Bride of Frankenstein" emerging from the lab of male leftists (see figure2). An editorial addressed the issue of women's culture, and the articles reflected various aspects of this emerging concept:

> Because women have needs on so many levels, there are many levels to women's libera-
> tion. We are a political movement, a social movement, an economic movement and a
> cultural movement all at once. . . . We see the development of women's culture as an
> essential part of the liberation struggle. The creation of a cultural ideology is a form of
> work; we have accepted male products in this area for too long. We find that when the
> cultural values and definitions that one accepts have been created by others, they bear
> down on the soul as an externally imposed presence. Any ideology must be controlled
> by the people who live with its tenets.
>
> The cultures which surround us today in America, whose tenets we have internalized,
> have all been created by men. It is extremely oppressive for us to function in a culture
> where ideals are male oriented and definitions are male controlled. Our alternative is clear;
> we must develop a new culture, new images of ourselves and of the forces surrounding us.

To this end, Starr and Peggy wrote many articles together, such as "What Are You Afraid of in the Dark?" and "Witch Dreams," which analyzed the origins of patriarchy and the male fear of female power, and regarded the medieval witches as our subversive sisters. These articles explored the concepts of wholeness and equality versus a hierarchy of power based on domination. Perhaps their strongest collaboration was a science-fiction story about the Bene OE, a cosmic order of witch/priestesses who were out to save the universe from being infected by "domenerge," the dominator energy that destroys everything it touches. Loosely based on the then-popular *Dune* series by Frank Herbert, and illustrated by Trina, the priestesses must restore balance to the world. They must remove the deadly obstruction

FIGURE 2: Cover of *It Aint Me Babe* volume 1, number 5 (April 7, 1970), featuring a feminist "Bride of Frankenstein" emerging from a lab of male leftists. Courtesy Trina Robbins.

of male domination so that energy can flow naturally again. For guidance on how to solve this problem, they turn to their traditions. The women gather in a circle for the magic of ritual, and then they take psychedelic drugs. The priestesses partake of magic blue crystals so that they may hear the ageless wisdom of their ancient sisters. In light of the flowering of women's circles in the 1980s and the feminist spirituality of the goddess movement that emerged, we were ahead of our time.

Peggy and Starr once organized a demonstration in front of a local radio station in San Francisco, as the "Red W.I.T.C.H.s," in protest of the station's sexist broadcasts, and we also demonstrated on campus. The name Red W.I.T.C.H.s claimed the radical stance of the times and our connection to persecuted women of power from the past (W.I.T.C.H. was "Women's International Terrorist Conspiracy from Hell"). *Babe* also printed the "W.I.T.C.H." Manifesto from the New York W.I.T.C.H., and "W.I.T.C.H. Power" by Jean Tepperman, and these were instant classics.

As a graphic symbol of the end of male dominance, Starr and I built a large papier-mâché penis painted with an American-flag motif, which we put in a small trash can. Our photographer took many pictures, and then ended up shooting it among her own trash cans. We ran the picture on the cover of issue 8, which appeared in the summer of 1970, as a demonstration of our frustration with the American male power and violence we saw playing out in the Vietnam War (see figure 3). That picture caused a huge sensation. Not only was it picked up and run on the cover of Atlanta's underground paper the *Great Speckled Bird*, but it was also mentioned by Herb Caen, a popular *San Francisco Chronicle* columnist. More importantly, he gave out the address of the paper, which helped our circulation grow considerably. Although no documentation remains of what our press run was at any point, I would guess our circulation was up to around 3,000 by the end of the summer. The increase was felt not only locally but outside the Bay Area as well after we started mailing subscriptions bulk-rate in June.

Reverberating Influence

Although we were based in Berkeley, we considered the *Babe* to be a national newspaper because we had several hundred subscribers throughout California and across the country. These papers found their way into the hands of eager feminists and were passed around. The paper only lasted a year, but it had a major impact on the women's movement because of some of the issues we discussed and our belief that the personal is political.

For example, when a local artist was raped hitchhiking home to Marin County from her first women's liberation meeting in Berkeley, she went to Laura's small home, which also was a refuge at the time for women fleeing their abusers. There she decided to publish her story in the *Babe*. Laura taped her testimony, which included an analysis of the power relationships involved; male attitudes toward women as sex objects; criticism of the local police handling of her case, which was basically an outright dismissal because she had been hitchhiking and therefore "asking for it"; and her boyfriend's response: "Two of them? You must have been nice and slippery." The article was featured in issue 10 (July 23, 1970) under the title "Anatomy of a Rape." Two other articles on rape appeared in that same issue ("Disarm Rapists" and "Fight"), and another one appeared three issues later (September 4, 1970), about a retaliatory action taken against a rapist by the Women's Anti-Rape Squad. In the events leading up to

FIGURE 3: *It Aint Me Babe's* graphic symbol of the end of male dominance, from the cover of volume 1, number 8 (June 11–July 1, 1970). Courtesy Bonnie Eisenberg.

that action, a bridegroom had raped a go-go dancer at his bachelor party after his friends forced her into the bedroom, doused her with wine, and stole her payment. The Anti-Rape Squad then plastered the guests' cars with leaflets that named names.

These articles led to a national dialogue about rape. The first classic piece on rape to appear in the U.S. media was written by our very own Susan Griffin, whose "Rape: The All American Crime" was published in the September 1971 issue of the national leftist magazine *Ramparts*. "And if the professional rapist is to be separated from the average dominant heterosexual [male]," she wrote, "it may be mainly a quantitative difference."

The *Babe* articles, thanks to *Babe* reader Diane Crothers, were read with great interest by members of a consciousness-raising group in New York City including Susan Brownmiller, who describes in her autobiography, *In Our Time: Memoir of a Revolution*, how this first-person testimony and the Squad's political actions inspired the speakout in New York on January 24, 1971, that inspired the entire anti-rape movement. Susan's best-known contribution to that movement, which she began writing that year and finally published in 1975, was her classic book *Against Our Will: Men, Women, and Rape*, a thorough historical analysis of how rape has been used to terrorize women in almost every civilization since the beginning of time. *Against Our Will* helped define the issue for feminists as well as for the larger society: "[Rape] is nothing more or less than a conscious process of intimidation by which all men keep all women in a state of fear."

Looking back today, it is almost unbelievable how callously rape was handled by the police and other authorities in those days. The victim was routinely victimized again by the

FIGURE 4: Centerfold collage by Laura X and Lynn O'Connor, showing the many faces of dominance exemplified by President Nixon and monkeys on one side, and women in

the charming smile
a gesture of
submission

dejection and depression are
submission

and the most

s
u
b
m
i
s
s
i
v
e

gesture   is   presenting

a beautiful submissive grin

or if we must, the direct stare
modified by hair and make-up,
the threat transformed to
"sexiness"

without an army close behind
gestures of dominance are
meaningless and still we
discover with horror that

wo men

Male supremacy is a mal-adaptive system
that has led our species to create a dangerous world of death-trap highways, inhuman prisons, endless wars, and poisonous
air, land and water. Male behavior is over-
specialized; it has lost its capacity to
adapt to environmental changes. The system
must change if we are to survive. And women
must be the agents of change. It rests on
us to overthrow male supremacy. Power must
be removed from men and placed in the hands
of all women, who with their flexibility and
capacity to adapt will use it to reorganize
society in a way that allows the human animal to live in non-destructive interaction
with the earth and all its inhabitants.

our
gestures of
struggle
are met
with
policemen
and jail.

our most

serious expression met with jeers and
laughter, poverty, abandonment, death

and

burning flames
that live on
through our
painful history

Lynn Ellen o'Connor

It Ain't Me Babe, June 11 - July1, 1970

submissive poses on the other. From *It Aint Me Babe* volume 1, number 8 (June 11–July 1, 1970). Courtesy Bonnie Eisenberg.

courts if she dared press charges. She was considered to have been "asking for it" if she was out alone after dark, was wearing anything more provocative than a nun's habit, was sexually active with others, or knew the perpetrator. Her sexual history could be raised in court, but the rapist's criminal history could not. It took many years and the dedicated work of women in communities across the nation before the laws and police practices were changed to treat rape as the violent crime it is.

Uniquely "*Babe*"

This was Berkeley in its heyday, so you can imagine there was a fair amount of drug use among some of us on the staff. Many creative discussions occurred while high on LSD or pot, which may have given the *Babe* its unique political outlook.

Another feature that made the *Babe* unique was Laura X, a woman whose perspective and energy was, and remains, light years beyond what is normal for most humans, even though she didn't do drugs. From the beginning she was given a page or two for her amazing features, called "Laura's Labyrinth," dubbed a "pointed political pastiche." She also did film criticism and announcements of upcoming events, including media events, especially on KPFA, the listener-sponsored mother of Pacifica Radio. She helped me with the "Women's Almanac" and major articles that we published first, including Beulah Richardson's 1951 poem "A Black Woman Speaks" (discussed above), after Laura's friend, writer James Baldwin, introduced the two women. In issue 8 she got together with early evolutionary psychologist Lynn O'Connor for a two-page spread showing Nixon with various facial expressions juxtaposed with monkeys with similar expressions, other animals in submissive poses, and women in similar poses (see figure 4). In another of her pages she reproduced many newspaper articles about women who had killed their abusive husbands. No editorial comment was necessary. She wanted people to understand women's anger and the reasons they were forced to defend themselves, while continuing her commitment to nonviolence, which began during her days as a CORE picket captain at the top of the sixties. Laura chose the term Tyrannosaurus Rex to head an article about "tyranny over the mind of woman" in which she quoted the "Declaration of Sentiments" by Elizabeth Cady Stanton; a similar quote from Eleanor Marx, one of Karl's daughters; and Abigail Adams saying to her husband John, "All men would be tyrants if they could."

But what was most uniquely "*Babe*" was our sense of humor. The first few issues featured comic strips from Jules Feiffer and *Miss Peach* by Mel Lazarus. In issues 3 and 4 we reprinted a humorous argument for our liberation by biochemist and prolific writer Isaac Asimov, "Uncertain, Coy, and Hard to Please" from *Fantasy and Science Fiction* (February 1969), in which he explains the origins and absurdities of the male-female relationship. What made his explanation brilliant was how he showed that men put women down for being manipulative when it is the men who create the conditions of our slavery. He named it! He called our oppression slavery, explaining that being oppressed as slaves, unable to work as equals, caused the need to be manipulative.

> This is not to say that a clever woman, even in Stone Age times, might not have managed to wheedle and cajole a man into letting her have her own way. And we all know this is certainly true nowadays, but wheedling and cajoling are slave weapons. If you, Proud

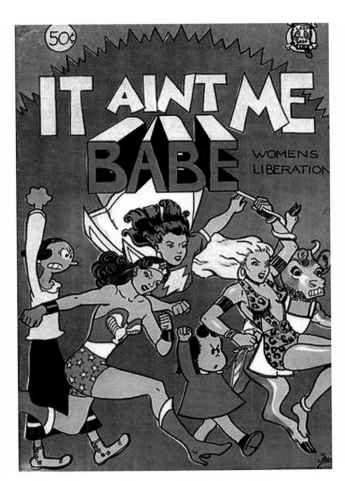

FIGURE 5: Cover of *It Aint Me Babe Comix*, the first "women's" comic book in the underground comic world. Courtesy Trina Robbins.

Reader, are a man and don't see this, I would suggest you try to wheedle and cajole your boss into giving you a raise, or wheedle and cajole a friend into letting you have your own way, and see what happens to your self-respect.

A few months later, we received a postcard from Isaac Asimov himself. Someone had passed the paper on to him. He admonished us for jeopardizing his copyright by publishing his article in a non-copyrighted paper, but his tone did not seem angry. I suppose he may have been a little flattered that the radical feminists liked his story. For us, it was important to have a male ally at all, and especially one of that stature and so early on.

Then the Goddess sent feminist cartoonist Trina Robbins to us (see appendix 3). In issue 4 we began featuring an original comic strip on the back page, *Belinda Berkeley*, drawn by Trina, depicting the trials and tribulations of a young feminist trying to keep her dignity while living with a chauvinist boyfriend and working a dehumanizing job. Trina's contribution to the paper was enormous; not only did she produce the ongoing comic strip, which appeared seven times between issues 4 and 11, she also created several stunning covers and numerous article illustrations. Later that year, Trina brought several other women cartoonists together and published *It Aint Me Babe Comix*, featuring several original strips, plus a story with several well-known cartoon characters, including Petunia Pig, Wonder Woman, and Olive Oyl, having a consciousness-raising session (see figure 5). It was the first "women's" comic book in the underground comix world. I don't know how I ended up leaving Berkeley without one; we had thousands in our basement at Harwood House (most of which got ruined when the basement flooded after a heavy rain). It is quite the collector's item today, and I recently was able to purchase one on eBay.

The house we lived in when we published the first issue of the *Babe* in 1970 had a small basement, and in the basement I had a small printing press. On that press I printed Pam Allen's *Free Space* booklet on consciousness-raising groups and a series of pamphlets on various women's issues, which we sold through the *Babe* and on campus. I called it the Women's Liberation Basement Press. It was under that name that *It Aint Me Babe Comix* was published. The staff of the *Babe* sometimes referred to itself in print as the Women's Liberation Basement Press collective.

By the summer of that year, we were forced to move because we were being harassed — I presumed by a neighbor, either because he was politically motivated or he just didn't like three women living together in the neighborhood. Starr and I moved to Harwood House, a feminist commune started by Rosalie Prosser and Alta. According to Rosalie, Harwood House was an emotional refuge for many women over its two- to three-year herstory. Besides Alta, Starr, and me, residents included two single mothers, two children (a boy and a girl), students, working women, and a French woman looking for an all-female environment for her pending birth (with her husband's blessing and understanding). Rosalie helped with the mailings of the *Babe*, but was never involved in the writing and production. However, it was she who coined the grafitto "Disarm Rapists," which started out as a flip comment, but with an immediately obvious deeper meaning, and then became the title of one of the landmark articles that spurred the anti-rape movement. Like the best comments, first you laugh and then you think.

Alta also had a printing press and was printing her own and other feminist poets' works under the name of Shameless Hussy Press. (I always loved that name!) The *Babe* followed us to Harwood House, and Alta became a contributing staff member. After she published the first edition of Ntozake Shange's *For Colored Girls Who Have Considered Suicide When the Rainbow Is Enuf*, most of the books from Shameless Hussy Press were printed by professional printers. But for a while there, both the *Babe* and Shameless Hussy Press came out of Harwood House.

Structural Integrity

The *Babe* was self-supporting after the first few issues, on subscriptions and local sales. It was relatively inexpensive to print a few thousand copies of a 16- or 20-page tabloid, and a lot could be fit into those pages. We saw the *Babe* as a vehicle for communication, education, and consciousness raising, and as a stimulus for conversation. In the beginning, we were not very professional. Headlines were sometimes hand-lettered, columns were sometimes crooked, language was rambling, full of radical jargon and slang, but the basics I had learned at the New England Free Press served us well, and the look of the paper improved greatly as time went on, especially after Trina Robbins joined the staff. A group of us would get together to do the layout on the floor of various staff members' houses. We borrowed graphics from other underground papers, and they from us. Local artists and photographers contributed their work. It was truly an "underground" paper. Besides the printed pages, it had no physical existence other than the list of subscribers and a small bank account.

I usually handled the national news section, "Sisters in Struggle," and served as the business manager, such as it was. I knew how to lay out a newspaper, and we soon learned how to do bulk mailings. I handled the bank account, the mailing list, and our relationship with the post office. A friend who worked in the sociology department on campus would let us in at night to use their typewriters to type up the articles. We were always so careful to leave no trace of our having been there.

We sold the paper at political rallies (of which there were many in those days), on campus, and through local bookstores in Berkeley and San Francisco. We also had a national circulation of paid subscribers, and we traded subscriptions with many other papers. The later issues were 20 to 24 pages, and we always seemed to have enough money to cover the cost of printing and postage, but the staff received no compensation for our time, which was considerable.

Throughout that year, we struggled to define our political analysis of women's oppression, and to resolve organizational issues and the various issues (gay/straight, middle class/working class, socialist/anarchist) that separated us. Many of the early staff members of the *Babe* were students or graduates of U.C. Berkeley, which probably means we were mostly middle class. Many of us had been involved with leftist groups of one kind or another. Our initial analysis of women's oppression, as printed in the first edition, which was dated January 15, 1970, reflected a Marxist ideology that the oppression of women was a result of oppression of the working class by the ruling class, and that the nuclear family was the main purveyor of that oppression. That analysis changed fairly quickly within our group to a belief that the oppression of women was the original male power trip, and that the oppression of race and class, or of one nation by another, developed from that model.

We did not demonstrate much of an awareness of our own bias as middle-class women or heterosexual women in the early editions. As more lesbians joined the staff, we became more woman-identified in general. We focused less on nuclear-family issues and more on issues of violence against women in all its forms. As conflict emerged with the male-identified, socialist-identified women controlling Berkeley Women's Liberation, we came to see the primacy of women's oppression and the need for a separate movement for women's liberation, rather than women's oppression as an issue of the socialist agenda.

An article titled "It Aint Me Babe: A Struggle for Identity," published in issue 11 (August 6, 1970), reviews the changing staff structure of the paper over the first eight months of our existence and our evolving self-definition.

It begins by noting our early efforts to keep editorial decisions "open":

For the first two issues, we called open meetings for women in the community to look over all articles that had been submitted and collectively decide on the content of the paper. This was a disastrous failure. The meetings took about seven hours and the layout crew would end up throwing out half of the material that was selected (there would not be enough room.) The meetings were simply too large. We felt that the haggling discussions over moot points in various articles were a drain of time and energy.

We weren't the only ones who felt that way. By the third issue, only six or seven women remained on the editorial board. In the name of efficiency, we declared the board "closed" in mid-March.

But efficiency wasn't our only issue.

> About that time the *Babe* began to deviate noticeably from the "line" of the women then in control of Berkeley Women's Liberation (they were Maoists, RYM [Revolutionary Youth Movement] II socialists [one section of the split in Students for a Democratic Society]; we were feminists). Around the time of International Women's Day (March 8) there was a major split in Berkeley WL; the leftists' approach had become so different from the feminists' approach that women felt it was impossible for the two to work in the same organization. Many of us were becoming disillusioned with the idea of organizations at all. In our editorial in issue 4, *Babe* stressed that "women's liberation was a movement, not an organization."
>
> Then we faced our first crisis. Angered at our editorial and at the first strip of Belinda Berkeley (which was a critique of the RYM-sponsored San Francisco International Women's Day rally), the leftists in Berkeley called a meeting with the *Babe* editorial board, demanding that we allow two of them to be on the board. We refused, claiming that the *Babe* had been started as an independent feminist newspaper, that we were not the organ of Berkeley Women's Liberation, and that we were within our rights closing the board, particularly to women with a radically different approach to women's liberation. We felt that "feminists" and "leftists" could each accomplish the most by working independently. We suggested to these women that they start their own paper.

Fortunately they agreed and left us alone, but they never did start their own paper. Meanwhile, our editorial board continued to dwindle in size as members left for personal reasons or because they were just too busy with other work. By issue 9, only three or four women were making all of the editorial decisions.

> So with issue 10 we revolutionized our structure. Our new structure, in accordance with the feminist anarchist beliefs of the staff, is designed to encourage maximum autonomy in each staff member. As anarchists, autonomy is our definition of liberation—it means functioning at a maximum energy level, with no energy blocks. Autonomy for each individual means an absence of power relationship or leader-follower patterns. Everyone contributes their utmost . . . to the paper, giving the collective the highest possible sum total of creativity available to us.

What this meant in practice was that each collective member was given full editorial control of one page. In this role, she was responsible for creating the material and getting it typed and laid out. In addition, we made five pages available for articles from women in the local community or from out of town. These free pages were "womanned" on a rotating basis by members of the collective.

The article concluded:

We realize that the highest form of autonomy can only exist in a group. (Individuals can operate at the highest energy level by working cooperatively in groups.) Amerika is an individualist society that teaches us that things are done best by individuals. We, on the other hand, believe that cooperative groups can do things far better than individuals. Thus the autonomy of each of us is best developed collectively, as a group. This means that we are working not only to achieve autonomy ourselves but to achieve it for our other sisters in the collective.

Defining ourselves in this manner has been a process and it is far from completed. At this point, the membership of our collective is tentative and uncertain. This article is the last statement of the *Babe* editorial board. As of now we are dissolving ourselves, we are members of the *Babe* collective, and nothing more. However, one of our major ideas has been that a collective, if it is to successfully maximize the autonomy and energy output of its members, must be an affinity group—i.e. it must be composed of women who are strongly attracted to each other on many levels, with similar basic orientations. We felt that the Christian and hippie ideals of loving everyone equally were a shuck, that people were not attracted to each other equally and that people could function best on the basis of real felt attractions. An affinity group collective would be a group of people with these kinds of feelings for each other, a group of people who could interact with a minimum of energy hang-ups (i.e. people not vampirizing each other—draining each other's energy, or trying to be "leaders" for other people—destroying others' energy). We do not have such a group at present but we are growing and changing. If the paper looks motley and un-unified it is because each page is the expression of a different woman. Long Live the Anarchist-feminist struggle.

This "Philosophy of Autonomy" met a major crisis with the very next issue (12, August 21, 1970) when one of our contributing "collective members" submitted a page that was absolutely unacceptable to the rest of us (or at least to most of the rest of us). For several issues, a group of women in San Francisco, most of whom were members of Redstockings West, had contributed a page that they called "The Women's Page." The group included revolutionary feminists who were mostly from middle-class, highly educated, liberal backgrounds, with access to financial support, along with a strong cadre of working-class women. Women who had to work as administrative assistants, or who were otherwise part of the clerical work force, were unable to undo the visible trappings of male supremacy without risking losing their jobs. They were often the sole support of their young children, and they simply didn't have the freedom to change their outward appearance. Feeling left out of the types of activities common to the early feminist movement (like, for example, no longer shaving their legs or underarms) sponsored by the young women's liberation movement, they were calling out for an end to classism in the women's movement.

The basic theme of the Women's Page was that working-class women felt invisible, disrespected, and often excluded from the left-oriented women's movement, which was also influenced by the "sexual-freedom culture." Issue 11 contained several letters to the editor critical of the Women's Page. Despite disagreements, the Women's Page submitted for issue 12 a political piece titled "Women as Prison Guards." They described in some detail various behaviors—carried out by women—that they believed rendered them silent and invisible at the larger women's liberation meetings. They likened the situation to that in which some prisoners get jobs working against their own people, as "prison guards" literally. In retrospect, we understood what they were after; they were trying to broaden the women's movement to include working-class women, who they felt were the essential people to lead a revolution of women, to change the economy and culture.

Unfortunately, at that time, we had low consciousness around class issues, and little understanding of class dynamics, and so we felt personally attacked by the Women's Page. Also perhaps unfortunate here, the writing on the Women's Page was heavily influenced by the rhetoric of Valerie Solanas—a virulently anti-male anarchist best known for her *S.C.U.M. Manifesto* and for shooting Andy Warhol—and the Black Panther Party, and reflected that heavy-handed edge that was difficult for us to even listen to. We just didn't get it; their position escaped us entirely. And they were confrontational and unable to listen to us as well. I understand now that they did not mean to attack middle-class women as privileged, they only wanted working-class women to be welcomed into the movement, but that was how it came across to us. We refused to include it in the paper. There is a blank page in issue 12 where the Women's Page was to go; on other pages we ran several short pieces explaining the conflict and how we felt about it. As a result of this conflict, Laura X, one of the founding members of the collective, left the paper. Herself a member of Redstockings West and the Women's Page staff, she felt our rejection of the Women's Page was censorship.

An interesting side note from Lynn O'Connor and Debbie Chase (personal communication, 2010): While the Women's Page evoked fury in Berkeley, it was mightily welcomed in Minneapolis, where the young women's liberation movement was inadvertently expressing implicit homophobia, driving away lesbian women. Upon reading the Women's Page, the gay contingent in Minneapolis contacted the Women's Page staff, saying that the paper was speaking for them, not only as working women, but as gay women, and they formed a strong alliance.

The *Babe* staff continued its search for affinity for several more months. Articles and stories that we published during that time were no less important to the women's liberation movement than those that had appeared in earlier issues. For instance, thanks to the backing of the now fifty-year-old San Francisco Mime Troupe, we printed their play *Independent Female, or, A Man Has His Pride*, written by feminist playwright Joan Holden, in the last three issues of the year (15–17). Unfortunately, those were our last three issues before disbanding at the end of the year. Trina remembers feeling alienated as a heterosexual woman and left the staff in December. I moved in with my boyfriend across the bay at the end of December, and Starr recalls that the remaining group's energy dissipated.

There was one more issue in April of 1971, but the energy could not be sustained.

Where Did We Go from Here?

I left Berkeley at the end of 1970. A year or two later, I helped start another feminist paper in Marin County, California, called the *Marin Women's News Journal*, a locally focused feminist monthly that covered a wide range of topics. We had several contributing artists and a consistent staff of about twelve, several of whom are still close friends. In 1981, while working as projects director for the Sonoma County Commission on the Status of Women, I started *Sonoma County Women's Voices*, which was conceived as a communication vehicle for the flourishing women's community in Sonoma County. At that time, there was a women's café, a bookstore, a clinic, an annual art festival, a readers' theatre focusing on issues of lesbian alcohol abuse, and the annual Women's History Week celebration (which eventually went national and became National Women's History Month). We established a nonprofit organization that served as an umbrella organization for the paper, the readers' theatre, and the history project. I was managing editor for *Women's Voices* for four years, and then left the paper when I began working full time at the National Women's History Project (NWHP). *Women's Voices* continued publication for over twenty years.

I worked for the National Women's History Project—which initiated and now promotes the celebration of National Women's History Month and offers a mail-order catalog of women's history materials—for close to fifteen years. I was both education and publications director, which included researching, writing, and publishing women's history materials: curriculum materials for all ages, posters, biographies, several tabloids on various aspects of women's history; teaching women's history to educators across the country; and producing seven women's history videos. The NWHP continues to offer most of those materials through their website at www.nwhp.org. My early training at New England Free Press has served me well throughout my career and enabled me to contribute greatly to the growth of the women's liberation and women's history movements.

Laura X continued her archival work with the Women's History Research Center (WHRC) until 1974, collecting just about everything being written about women's liberation and the women's movement. Her archives were then processed into microfilm and promoted first by outside companies, then by WHRC staff. They are now available through over 450 universities and libraries in fourteen countries. When WHRC folded in 1989 and gave the microfilms to the National Women's History Project in Santa Rosa, I reconnected with Laura and helped arrange for their distribution through NWHP (see appendix 1).

From 1976 to 1978, Laura ran a successful campaign to save San Francisco's big band radio station KMPX, which was a showcase for women's musical talents from the 1920s to 1952. The next year, in 1979, she developed the National Clearinghouse on Marital and Date Rape, and led the successful campaign in California to make marital rape a crime. She continued campaigning state by state, until the fifty-state victory in 1993 to remove the special exemption from rape prosecution that husbands and dates had enjoyed everywhere in the United States. Her name and its symbolic connection to slavery was a galvanizer for people joining her campaign, because the basis for the exemption was the legal ownership of women.

In recent decades she has been active in the disability-rights, environmental-health, and healthy-homes movements. Her numerous lifetime commendations include an Emma Lazarus Award for carrying the torch for Jewish Women's History (although she is not Jewish), a "Woman of Achievement" award from *Mademoiselle* magazine, a World Congress on Victimology award for Innovative Programs and Services, and recognition by the American Library Association, former surgeon general Everett Koop, Governor Deukmajian of California, and the National Coalition Against Domestic Violence.

Starr Goode went on to work in the feminist spirituality movement and to become a professor of literature at Santa Monica (California) College. Recent publications include "The

Fable of the Invisible Women," in *The Rule of Mars: Readings on the Origins, History, and Impact of Patriarchy*; and "The Sheela na gigs," the cover story of *Irish Journal of Feminist Studies* 4, no. 2 (2002). She is a winner of the David L. Kubal Memorial Essay Prize, and a recipient of the Henri Coulette Memorial Poetry Award from the Academy of American Poets. She has been profiled for her work as a cultural commentator in the *LA Weekly*, the *Los Angeles Times*, and the *Wall Street Journal*. She produced and moderated the first cable series on the Goddess called *The Goddess in Art*.

Alta moved back to the suburbs of the East Bay and continued to develop Shameless Hussy Press for the next twenty years. She published early works by Susan Griffin, Ntozake Shange, Pat Parker, Mary Mackey, Mitsuye Yamada, Judith Arcana, and many other major feminist authors, which enabled those authors to gain a wider audience and bigger publishers down the line. She specialized in great books that others would not publish. Alta's beautifully rendered scenes of real life that she depicted in her poems for *Babe* were talked about constantly during the *Babe*'s brief existence; readers anticipated each issue wondering what Alta was going to say in her poems, which were so often talked about because of their impact and the courage they gave us ("Surely a woman has been here before me"). After the *Babe* folded, Alta continued writing poetry and has had fourteen books published. She taught women's poetry through U.C. Berkeley Extension in the mid-1970s and currently has a gallery in Berkeley called Alta Galleria. She says she still has scars on her face from the tear gas, although she was not on campus, but in her own backyard at the time of the People's Park protests.

After being treated badly in both underground and mainstream comix as a cartoonist, Trina Robbins eventually gave up cartooning and became a writer. She continues in that field today, specializing in forgotten women cartoonists from the early twentieth century. Her collection of original comic art by women, probably the world's largest, has been shown all over Europe—including in Spain, Portugal, Germany, and Austria—as well as New York and San Francisco. In December 2009 she took her exhibit to Japan. She has also scripted numerous graphic novels, mostly about and/or for girls, and written about superheroines, comics for and by girls and women, and non-comic-related women's history like dark goddesses, Irish women, and women who kill. Her latest book is a history of the Golden Age of Chinese nightclubs in San Francisco's Chinatown.

NOTE

1. An excellent book on the changes brought about by the second wave of the women's movement is *When Everything Changed*, by Gail Collins.

WOMEN OF THE RUSSIAN REVOLUTION INSPIRE ANOTHER REVOLUTION: LAURA X AND THE WOMEN'S HISTORY ARCHIVES
(by Laura X)

I'll start with the strike that was inspired by Russian women in 1917, the discovery of which inspired me to help organize a demonstration in Berkeley for International Women's Day (IWD) on March 8, 1969, and to begin to build the idea of Women's History Month around March 8. Our Women's History Library, which maintained the International Women's History Archive of our movement from 1968–74, took a quantum leap forward from the national publicity as a result of that Berkeley demonstration. There had been no such demonstration for IWD in the United States since 1947. By the next year, 1970, there were women's liberation events in thirty cities around the world for March 8.

Back in late 1968, I saw the 1929 Soviet film *The End of St. Petersburg*, by Pudovkin. The women's demonstration in St. Petersburg on February 23, 1917, for "bread, peace, and land" is clearly the spark that ignited the strike for the Putilov factory workers. Their strike toppled the rule of the czars within four days of the women's protest. What was not known, partly due to the confusion of the use of another calendar system by the Eastern Church, is that February 23 was March 8 on the Western calendar, and the Bolshevik women who organized the demonstration, over the protests of their male comrades, were celebrating International Women's Day, which had been declared seven years earlier.

Although by 1969 I had considered myself a socialist for thirteen years, had been immersed in Left politics in New York and Berkeley, and had been to the Soviet Union twice to celebrate the fiftieth anniversary in 1967, I still did not learn until late 1968 that International Women's Day was based on a U.S. event on March 8, 1908. It had been celebrated big time in the socialist countries around the world, but by 1969 in the USSR it had deteriorated into something like Mother's Day in the U.S., where women are given flowers, and the day was ignored here.

In November 1968, I called for U.S. celebrations of IWD in a review of *The End of St. Petersburg* for the U.C. Berkeley newspaper, *The Daily Cal*. I had just been told by Noel Ignatin, a socialist active in Chicago, about the Russian women inspiring the 1917 strike by demanding an end to World War I as well as bread and land. He also told me that the Socialist International meeting in Copenhagen in 1910 had declared March 8 International Working Women's Day in a motion made by Clara Zetkin, a German Communist, and seconded by Lenin, the Russian Bolshevik (majority) party leader whose triumphant return from exile was made possible by the so-called February Revolution of 1917—the one begun by women on March 8 on the Western calendar. I believe his source was Isaac Deutscher's *The Unfinished Revolution: Russia, 1917–1967*.

But what really ignited me was that once again, American history had been stolen from us. I had just recently been angry about discovering that May Day, the enormous international socialist event on May 1, commemorated the Haymarket Square massacre of the workers in Chicago struggling for an eight-hour day in 1881. Noel told me that the resolution for International Women's Day in 1910 was commemorating a demonstration in

New York in 1908 of garment workers who were demanding an end to sweatshops and to child labor, and also the right to vote.

The part about the vote intrigued me because women on the Left in the late sixties were being hooted down and dismissed as bourgeois whenever we demanded our rights as women—indeed as human beings—in 1969. And leftist men were perpetuating the myth that no one in the working class wanted any women's rights, including the right to vote. I had been collecting mimeographed manifestos and letters to the editors of the leftist press about many such outrages by men in the antiwar and civil rights movements for six months or more in order to try to recapture my sanity after being battered and nearly killed by my own comrade and lover. (He had been a child prodigy violinist and was by then a revolutionary poet. We met demonstrating in Puerto Rico against the U.S. invasion of Santo Domingo. The grief over the loss of that relationship and my fright over how it ended seemed insurmountable until I discovered the rising up of women in all the movements of the sixties.)

In January/February 1969 I was invited to a little party of sociology professors to show the mimeos and pamphlets to Pauline Bart, who was considering teaching a women's studies course, the first at U.C. Berkeley. As we were being introduced, everyone's favorite male radical professor—David Matza—whose courage had been demonstrated on the Third World Strike picket lines on campus, overheard us, and, before I could speak, told Pauline not to bother teaching such a course, because there was not enough about women to fill a quarter course. That betrayal knocked me into the orbit of the pure fury of those heady days. In three days I pestered friends everywhere and pulled together a list of one thousand women in world history, politics, the arts and sciences. I had had the immense privilege of going to girls' schools and a women's college. It was only in my last year in college, at U.C. Berkeley, that I discovered that not everybody knew that women could do everything! I nailed the list to Prof. Matza's door (in homage to Luther) and went in search of a local women's liberation group.

Bill Mandel had a show on the Soviet Union on Pacifica Radio, which I had started listening to in 1960 in New York, though it originated from Pacifica's mother station in Berkeley. He regularly read from the Soviet press on International Women's Day. His daughter Phyllis, a long-time activist, took me to the Berkeley Women's Liberation group, which then organized the first street demonstration for International Women's Day since 1947 in the U.S. Many of us dressed up as women in history from my list. I was a cross between Alexandra Kollontai, the Bolshevik feminist, and Isadora Duncan, the American woman who lived for a time in Russia and transformed the world of dance away from the confines of the ballet.

Liberation News Service picked up the story from a San Francisco paper about our parade in Berkeley and its sources from my list. This caused people from this and many other countries to send me everything imaginable about women in history, some of them about their own family members. People also came to visit from around the country, and to volunteer. About 10,000 copies of the list, by now called the HERSTORY SYNOPSIS, were sold within a few short years. Some 5,000 people have volunteered here.

We put out the only national women's liberation newsletter from April through December 1969, *SPAZM* (the Sophia Perovskaya and Andrei Zhelyabov Memorial Society for Peoples' Freedom through Women's Liberation). Sophia and Andrei were lovers. She was the sixteen-year-old daughter of the governor of St. Petersburg, and the two of them assassinated the czar in 1881. I was not comfortable about assassinations as a political tactic, having just lived through several in the sixties: Kennedy, Evers, Malcolm X, King, and Kennedy. But I liked the part about the comrade-lovers, and the rebellious adolescent daughter of a powerful man. The name was also in the style of rock groups, but the last part of it fully embodied my philosophy for people's freedom, which I still hold today.)

Before January 1970 I connected with other women who wanted to do a paper, too—so *It Aint Me Babe* was born, the first newspaper of the U.S. women's liberation movement. (Women from *off our backs* in Washington, DC, called me to pick my brain for their name—which ended up being a combination of the quote from the Grimke sisters about getting our brothers off our necks, and revulsion at the quote attributed to Stokely Carmichael about the position of women in SNCC being prone and silent. Their paper came out only a few weeks later and is still publishing, now in magazine format.)

There were many other firsts from the Women's History Library—the anthology *Masculine/Feminine* in 1969 with all the great manifestos; *Women's Songbook*, which I compiled with songwriter Judy Busch, who gathered the songs during her travels around the country; *Female Artists Past and Present*; *Films by/and/or about Women Internationally, Past and Present*; *Bibliography on Rape*; and *Women and Religion Bibliography*. Most lasting is the microfilm of the records of our movement, which includes nearly one million documents. The microfilm set is comprised of Herstory, Women and Law, and Women's Health/Mental Health, and is available through Gale Publishing Primary Source Media division (www.gale.cengage.com), who distribute it for the National Women's History Project in Santa Rosa, California (707-636-2888; nwhp@aol.com; www.nwhp.org).

The folks at National Women's History Project are the people who carry on the ideas we had at the beginning of our library beyond our wildest dreams, including getting Congress to declare March as Women's History Month. They also put up the fabulous Web site for all the celebrations that were held in 1998 to celebrate the 150th anniversary of the women's rights movement in the United States: www.legacy98.org. They have designed and published National Women's History Month posters since 1978, distribute a Women's History Resource Catalog, and have a fabulous Web site: www.nwhp.org.

This article appeared originally in *Sojourner* (May 1998) and may be found at http://ncmdr.org/whm98.html.

It is adapted here courtesy of Laura X.

APPENDIX 2

EDITORIAL FROM FIRST ISSUE

Resistance from male dominated society is to be expected as the movement for women's liberation grows in strength and influence. That this should take the form of a male backlash is as unavoidable as the white backlash that followed the emergence of black liberation forces.

Male backlash is a reactionary phenomenon based on the sort of fear which everywhere divides oppressed peoples, preventing the recognition of their common interests. The expression "castrating bitch" is often heard, but is it in fact women who are responsible for male feelings of impotence or is it the established power structure which frustrates the desires of both men and women for self-expression and control over their lives?

Adult society in America is based on a psychological unit of two and there is some question whether the system could survive if this were not the case. It is the women whose job it is to cushion the worst effects of an inhumane system by providing love and support for the male who is constantly threatened by the deadly competition of other males and the emasculating crush of the boss within the rigid hierarchical structures which control the economy. This is true no matter what niche the man occupies in that structure, although the compensations of power over underlings increase as one goes up the ladder. Male-dominated man needs a woman to dominate as an additional compensation for his loss of autonomy. This means that although the woman needs to escape the boredom, isolation, subjugation and drudgery of the nuclear family, it is obvious that men will be loath to give up the psychological benefits of their domination of women. Hence male backlash appears as women begin to assert themselves and begin to fight for control of their lives.

But such reactionary defense of the very basis of subjugation—the nuclear family, which suppresses the potential of the woman, socialized the children and ties the man through indebtedness and family responsibility to the very system that oppresses him—must be firmly resisted and exposed for the evil that it is. Men cannot achieve permanent social, economic and cultural revolution while ignoring three-fourths of society, the women and children. Nor can women expect to find a solution to their problems and miseries inside the narrow confines of the individual home and family.

If society is to be radically changed, the whole fabric of social relations must be changed. Women have minds and creative powers to be developed, not just housemaid's knees, wombs and nipples. Those who advocate that women stay in the home neglect the fact that children need more for their development than just one bored and harried woman's love and care. They need exposure to many adults and other children, experiences outside the home to expand their minds and develop the kind of individual autonomy and emotional strength that will enable them to resist domination and be free of the need to dominate. Girls must be allowed to develop freely without the sex-typing and suppression of their vital energies which makes them passive beings instead of enabling them to live full human lives. Only then will the society based on competition, violence, subjugation of the people and destruction of human values be annihilated forever. Men and women and their children must join their strengths and intelligence to recreate and renew the earth.

It Aint Me Babe 1, no. 1 (January 15, 1970): 2.

APPENDIX 3

FEMINISTS DO HAVE A SENSE OF HUMOR: THE FIRST WOMEN'S COMIX (by Trina Robbins)

It was earlyish 1970, and I, an idealistic (and pregnant) underground cartoonist, arrived in San Francisco from New York, thinking I was coming to the underground comix mecca. I quickly discovered that it was indeed an underground comix mecca, but only if you were a guy. The male underground cartoonists invited each other into each other's books and to each other's parties, but ignored me. It didn't help that I had recently become a feminist and the guys were terrified of feminism. Then somebody showed me the first issue of *It Aint Me Babe*—I couldn't believe it! A feminist underground newspaper! (By the way, in defense of underground newspapers, I need to add that the local underground papers were all very nice to me, not at all like the guys in underground comix, and that once every three weeks I was taking the bus into Berkeley to draw cartoons and do layouts for the *Berkeley Tribe*, for which I was paid the grand sum of $20, just because someone needed my art and I needed to be needed—and that later that year both the *San Francisco Good Times* and the *Berkeley Barb* invited me to draw comix for them, and I picked the *Good Times* simply because they were in San Francisco, so I wouldn't have to take the bus into Berkeley again.)

Anyway, back to *Babe*; I immediately phoned them and volunteered my services. Peggy and Bonnie met me in Golden Gate Park, at a Be-In; I was wearing a "Super Sister" T-shirt that I had designed—there was only one ever made, and I still have it! They invited me into the paper, and I gratefully accepted. Thereafter, I again was taking the bus into Berkeley periodically, on paste-up nights, but I was also contributing a comic to the back pages and drawing covers for the front pages. I remember one antiwar cover I drew that got a lot of negative feedback; it showed a Vietnamese woman lying down about to be symbolically raped by an American bomb. Readers complained that she was lying passively while being raped; they didn't get it that she was supposed to be DEAD! When my daughter was born, I did a cover just for her, showing a woman and a baby with the words "This girl child is born free." I also drew a back cover that started a kind of mini-movement; it was a portrait of Angela Davis saying, "Sister, you are welcome in this house" (see figure 1). The idea was to put it into your window. Soon other people were making posters like that, too, for their windows.

My comix, on the other hand, were none too subtle propaganda, the continued hapless plight of Belinda Berkeley, who works a wretched office job to support a pig of a husband who hopes to write the Great American Porn Novel (see figure 2). They were kind of based on my real-life situation: a sexist "old man" who was drawing misogynistic underground

FIGURE 1: Back cover window poster of Angela Davis from *It Aint Me Babe* volume 1, number 12 (August 21, 1970). The poster was intended to show support for former University of California professor and black power activist Angela Davis, who was a fugitive from the law at that time. Courtesy Trina Robbins.

FIGURE 2: Belinda Berkeley made her debut in *It Aint Me Babe* volume 1, number 4 (March 15, 1970) as a young secretary supporting her husband's effort to write the Great American novel. In the next six installments, readers watch her consciousness grow as she resists her sexist boss, questions her sexist husband, has a nightmare, hosts her liberated friend for dinner, goes to a women's liberation meeting, walks to work in a miniskirt, quits her job, and encounters members of a women's terrorist group. Volume 1, number 11 (August 6, 1970) ends with the promise of "Exciting adventures coming soon!" Unfortunately, that was Belinda's last appearance in *It Aint Me Babe*. Courtesy Trina Robbins.

comix and living off my welfare. Then I got the idea to do something I could never have done without the moral support of the *Babe* staff: an entire feminist comic book.

The Print Mint, a Berkeley-based comix publisher, expressed interest; they had already published my comix in their comix anthology, *Yellow Dog.* (Again, I have to add that it wasn't the comix publishers who excluded me; they were in the business to sell good comix, and they didn't care if the art was by a man or a woman, so they published me. It was only the male underground cartoonists themselves who treated me as if I were invisible—and, I think, who hoped I WAS invisible!) It wasn't easy finding women to contribute, but I wrote to two women in New York who I knew drew comix, and included Willy Mendes, who at that time was the only other woman in San Francisco besides me who was drawing comix (and who was also feeling left out by the guys). I got two beautiful pages by socialist cartoonist Lisa Lyons, and four terrific pages by a Point Richmond woman, Michelle Brand; and the entire *Babe* collective worked together to produce a four-page comic in which all the female comic characters finally rebel and join together against their oppressing male characters. My cover echoed that theme, with Olive Oyl, Wonder Woman, Little Lulu, Sheena, Queen of the Jungle, and Elsie the Borden Cow all marching together, fists raised, looking pissed-off.

Print Mint didn't publish the comic after all. Instead, after hearing that a new publisher, Last Gasp, which had so far published an ecology comic, was looking for a "women's liberation" comic, I phoned the publisher, Ron Turner, and told him I had an entire "women's liberation" comic put together. He came right over and handed me a check for $1,000, which in those days was an enormous amount of money! I'll always remember what Ron did for me and always be grateful to him for it. Later, when the guys from the Print Mint asked me why I hadn't given the book to them, I answered truthfully that Ron had come right over with a check. We were so in demand!

Working with the *Babe* women, and especially putting out that comic—which really started the entire women's comix movement—worked magic on my self-esteem, which was in rags from the way I was being treated by the guys, and kept me going—and I haven't stopped since!

About the Authors

Steve Abbott, a poet, writer, and faculty member at Columbus State Community College, is active in union work, community organizing, and literary events. He dedicates this chapter to the memory of Libby Gregory (d. 1991) and Steve Conliff (d. 2006).

JoNina M. Abron was the last editor of *The Black Panther Intercommunal News Service* and a member of the Black Panther Party for nine years. She is the former managing editor of *Black Scholar* magazine, and associate professor emerita of communication at Western Michigan University, Kalamazoo, where she taught journalism from 1990 to 2003. A news correspondent at the 2001 UN World Conference Against Racism in Durban, South Africa, Abron was also a delegate at the conference's meeting of nongovernmental organizations. With her husband, veteran black activist Lorenzo Ervin, Abron lives in Nashville, Tennessee, where she is a member of Power to the People, a black social-justice group, and has been a part-time journalism instructor at Tennessee State and Fisk universities.

Ginny Z. Berson was one of the founders of *The Furies*. She cofounded Olivia Records, which she left in 1980. Without realizing it, she has made a career in public radio, working in a variety of positions at KPFA and Pacifica Radio—director of women's programming, program director, senior producer of live national programs—and, since 1998, with the National Federation of Community Broadcasters. Her passions include women, justice, writing, radio, and scuba diving.

Susan Brownmiller is a feminist historian and the author of *Against Our Will: Men, Women and Rape* and *In Our Time: Memoir of a Revolution*.

Charlotte Bunch is now executive director for the Center for Women's Global Leadership at Rutgers University, New Brunswick, NJ.

David Doggett is a medical research analyst in the Evidence-Based Practice Center at Johns Hopkins University School of Medicine in Baltimore. He grew up in Mississippi, where he was involved in the civil rights movement in the sixties. He was the Mississippi organizer for the Southern Student Organizing Committee (SSOC) and a founder of *The Kudzu* in 1968. After leaving Mississippi in 1972, he was a freelance photographer in various places in the Southeast. He lived for two years in Nashville, where he did construction work and played bluegrass and country music (dobro and pedal steel guitar). In 1975 he went back to school to study biology at the University of Tennessee. He received a PhD in molecular biology from the University of Southern California in Los Angeles and then lived in Boston and Philadelphia. He has four children, and is still a part-time musician playing rockabilly and blues on pedal steel and sax.

Elihu Edelson is an artist, calligrapher, writer, and teacher. He was listed as a critic in *Who's Who in American Art, 1976* and *1980*. He remains *Both Sides Now*'s factotum.

Bonnie Eisenberg is a lifelong feminist activist who organized and published women's newspapers in three different communities from 1970 to 1984. She then became publications director for the National Women's History Project, where she published dozens of posters, biographies, curriculum materials, and speeches on women's history. She also coproduced seven women's history videos, including a music video titled *A Fine and Long Tradition*. She is now retired and living in New Mexico.

Ed Felien: After writing this piece in 1990, Felien writes, he was "almost overcome with the intoxicating comfort of nostalgia." When Bush the First invaded Kuwait a few months later, he was anxious to spring into action. He started a weekly neighborhood newspaper, *Southside Pride*, and delivered it door to door in two neighborhoods in South Minneapolis. Since then it has grown to twenty-five neighborhoods and is published in three editions each month. It can be found on the Web at www.southsidepride.com. In it, Felien continues to rail against the government. In recent months he defended his congressman, Keith Ellison, for comparing Bush the Second to Hitler and showed he didn't go far enough; he also supported the Morelos Club's attempt to place a statue of Emiliano Zapata in a local park.

Pablo "Yorúba" Guzmán is a reporter for WCBS-TV/Channel 2 in New York.

Harry W. Haines teaches in the Communication Department at Trinity University in San Antonio, Texas. He is a communication researcher who writes about film and television portrayals of the Vietnam War and veterans. He was drafted in 1969 and took part in the GI Resistance to the War in Vietnam. He has taught a course on the history and media representations of the Vietnam War for twenty years.

Patrick Halley was a playwright, dramatist, and cab driver from Detroit who wrote and produced *Werewolf of Grosse Pointe*, *The Canary House*, and numerous articles, skits, and irate "letters to the editor." He wrote extensively for the *Fifth Estate* and was a legend of the Detroit streets, known as Pat "the Rat" and "the troubadour of the Cass Corridor." He took his own life on November 16, 2007.

Bob Hippler was a member of the *Fifth Estate* from 1970–1974. He is a longtime activist for peace, feminism, and gay rights. He went to one of the first demonstrations against the Vietnam War (Washington, DC, 1965). He also attended the first national gay rights demonstration (Washington, DC, 1979). He has been a member of the American Federation of Teachers and the UNITE/H.E.R.E. union, and was a member of the Service Employees International Union for six years.

Peter Jensen has been an activist for peace and freedom since 1960. In addition to teaching English at Linn Benton Community College in Albany, Oregon, he has published three books of poems: *This Book Is Not a Mask for Tear Gas* (1970); *When Waves Sprout Birds: Twenty Years of Poetry (1965–1985)*; and *Confluence* (with David Johnson and Erik Muller, 1991); and a book on Shakespeare's sonnets.

Paul Krehbiel became a union auto-parts factory worker in 1968 in Buffalo, New York, and was a founder of the progressive rank-and-file workers' newspaper *New Age*. He has been an elected union steward and local union president, a full-time union representative, and national union editor of the *Furniture Workers Press*. He is the author of *Shades of Justice* (2008), available at autumnleafpress.com.

James Lewes got his PhD from the University of Iowa in 2000. His doctoral thesis, *Protest and Survive: An Analysis of the Influence and Effect of GI-produced Underground Newspapers on the United States Armed Forces during the Vietnam War*, was published by the Praeger imprint of the Greenwood Press in 2003. From 2004 to 2007 he worked as a researcher and Web designer for the film *Sir! No Sir!* His principal contribution to this project was the creation of an archive that is the largest repository of Vietnam-era GI movement materials on the Internet. From 2007 through 2009 he edited the blog *Military Lies*, which he modeled after the news packets distributed by the GI Press Service from 1969 to 1971. Currently, he is engaged in a race against time to digitize all surviving copies of GI newspapers before the poor quality of the paper used to produce them crumbles to dust.

Trina Robbins retired from cartooning in the early 1990s and became a full-time writer and herstorian, the acknowledged expert on early-twentieth-century women cartoonists. Along with her histories of women cartoonists, women's and girls' comics, and superheroines, she has chronicled the histories of Irish women, dark goddesses, and women who kill. She also scripts graphic novels, including the ongoing adventures of her flying teenage heroine, GoGirl!

Charley Shively is currently a member of the *Fag Rag* collective. He is the author of three books on Walt Whitman, and numerous poems.

Ken Wachsberger is a long-time author and editor and is the founder and publisher of Azenphony Press. He has been a member of the National Writers Union for over a quarter century and is a former national officer. He is the editor of the four-volume Voices from the Underground series, of which this book is the third volume. His first book, the cult classic *Beercans on the Side of the Road: The Story of Henry the Hitchhiker*, is available at www.azenphonypress.com.

Tim Wong recently retired as a planning analyst for the state of Wisconsin, concentrating on health-care access for the uninsured, cost containment, welfare reform, and a variety of other assignments over thirty years. He is still active in advocating for transportation alternatives (to the automobile) in Madison, particularly transit and bicycling. He also owns a mail-order stamp business known as No Limits Stamps.

Laura X is an original member of *It Aint Me Babe.* She is the founder and director of the former National Clearinghouse on Marital and Date Rape, and the Women's History Research Center.

Index

A

Abbey, Edward, 88

Abbott, Steve (pseud. Houston Fearless; Dennis Menimen; [Free] Lance Ryder), xii, 306–24, 328; "Poem for the Fifth Anniversary of the Columbus Tenants Union," 324

a'Bout Face, 45nn8–9

Aboveground, xvii, 1–14, 17, 19; financial support for, 4; harassment of printer by FBI, 8; ideological split between factions, 10; legacy of, 10, 12; political factions involved, 2–4

Abron, Joe, 356, 358, 361

Abron, JoNina M., xii, 335, 357–58, 361

Acme Steel Company, Chicago, Ill., 217

Aerospaced, 18

Against Our Will: Men, Women, and Rape (Brownmiller), xv, 397

Age of Aquarius, 378, 384n8

Agnew, Spiro, 75, 311

Airco-Speer, Niagara Falls, N.Y., 214

Akwesasne Notes, 293

Albizu Campos, Pedro, 235–36

Alice's Restaurant (film), 370

All Ready on the Left, 16, 19

Allen, Pam: *Free Space* (booklet on CR groups), 402

Allende, Salvador, 211, 212

Allied and Technical Workers Union, 200

Allied Chemical and Dye Corporation, Buffalo, N.Y., 198–99

Allman Brothers, 128, 369, 370

Ally, The, 12–13, 17, 26

Alta: *It Aint Me Babe,* xvi, 392; Shameless Hussy Press, 402, 408

Alternative Birth Center, Jacksonville, Fla., 380

alternative economic institutions, Madison, Wisc., 155

alternative journalism, Madison, Wisc., 153, 156, 160

Alternative Press Conference, Boulder, Colo. (1973), 162

Alternative Research Newsletter, 377

Alternative Review, 375

Amato, Nino, 160

Amazon Quarterly (Oakland), 99

American Indian Movement (AIM), 75, 181

American Odyssey, The (Conot), 49

American Servicemen's Union (ASU), 2, 26–27

Amsterdam News, 235

anarchists, types of, 175

And Beautiful, 156

Anderson, Larry, 103, 105

Andrle, Fred, 310

Angelo, Jude, 307, 324

Ann Arbor Sun, 293

Another Country (Baldwin), 81

anti-draft demonstrations, 256–57

antiwar demonstrations, 154, 155

Arbus, Diane, 184

Arcana, Judith, 408

Armies of the Night (Mailer), 60

Army Math Research Center, University of Wisconsin, Madison, Wisc., 154, 155, 265

Army of Ex-Lovers: My Life at the Gay Community News, An (Hoffman), 119

Arnold, Jeff, 310

Arvin, Newton, 98

Asimov, Isaac, 400–401

Atkinson, Ti-Grace, 81

Attitude Check, 17

Atton, Chris, xvi

Atwood, Margaret, 391

AUGUR, 290–96; campaigns for quality-of-life issues, 292; "The Airwar & Then . . . More War!" (Jensen), 298–301

Austin, Richard, 58

Avakian, Bob, 164

Avatar, 98

Axelrod, Beverly, 346

Ayers, Bill, xvi

B

Bad Attitude, 101

Bad Moon Rising, 156

Bahro, Rudolf, 378

Baker Orange student newspaper, Baker University, Baldwin, Kan., 357

Baldwin, James: *Another Country*, 81; *Go Tell It on the Mountain*, 81

Baraka, Amari: *Preface to a 20-Volume Suicide Note*, 81

Barbedette, Giles: translation of "The Simplest of Pleasures [Suicide]" (Foucault), 112

Barnet, Richard, 377

Bart, Pauline, 410

Battle of Algiers (film), 392

Battlefront, 45n10

Behind the State Capitol (Wieners), 118

Bennett, Alan, 129

Beoddy, James, 324

Berkeley Barb, 129, 375, 378, 413

Berkeley in the 60's (film), 388

Berkeley Tribe, 293, 388, 413

Berkeley Women's Liberation group, 387, 388, 403, 410; split with *It Aint Me Babe*, 404

Berrigan, Ted, 316

Berry, Millard, 64, 74, 86, 87, 88

Berson, Ginny Z., 271–81; "The Dentist," 288; "The Furies," 281–83

Bethlehem Steel, Lackawanna, N.Y., 218–20

Betz, Cheryl, 306, 307, 311, 321, 328

Bibliography on Rape, 411

Big Fat, 63

Billotte, Louise: "Can the Left Find Room for Spirituality?," 375–76

Binger, James, 260–61

Bingham, Stephen, 336

Bird, Suzie, 312, 328

Biren, Joan (pseud. JEB), 271, 275

Black and Red Press, 82, 88

Black Bart Brigade (personal journal) (Thomas), 374, 377

Black Guerrilla Family, 336, 338

black liberation movement, U.S., 342–43

Black Muslims. *See* Nation of Islam

Black Panther, The, 235, 239, 293. *See also Black Panther Community News Service, The; Black Panther Intercommunal News Service, The* (BPINS)

Black Panther Black Community News Service, The, 365

Black Panther Community News Service, The, 342–56; BPP statement protesting the Mulford Bill (excerpt), 342; changes in editorial staff, 349–50; Executive Mandate #1 protesting Mulford bill, 341–42; Executive Mandate #2 drafting Stokely Carmichael into BPP (excerpt), 345–46; memorial issue, publication of, 364; name change to *The Black Panther Intercommunal News Service*, 352; under scrutiny of Committee on Internal Security (U.S. House of Representatives), 350

Black Panther Intercommunal News Service, The

(BPINS), xii, 352–56, 358–63; name change from *The Black Panther Community News Service,* 352

Black Panther Manifesto, 262

Black Panther Militia, Milwaukee, Wisc., 364

Black Panther Newspaper Committee, 363–64

Black Panther Party (BPP), 56–57, 58, 234, 267, 269, 305, 318, 406; assassination of party members by U.S. Treasury Department, 267; Bobby Seale as cofounder, 336, 338, 365; and Chicago Young Lords Organization, 239; formation of, 338–41; free speech movement, 350; Huey P. Newton as cofounder, 335, 338, 365; legacy of, 365; men as comrade brothers, 335; merger with SNCC, 344, 348; Minneapolis chapter, 267; murder of Alprentice Carter, 352; murder of Fred Hampton, 305, 343; murder of John Huggins, 352; murder of Mark Clark, 343; Ten Point Platform and Program, 336, 338–40; women as comrade sisters, 335

Black Panther Party (Reconsidered), The (Jones), 365

Black Panther Party for Self-Defense, 338

Black Panther: The Revolutionary Art of Emory Douglas (Durant), 348

Black Panthers' Revolutionary Constitutional Convention, 99, 103

Black Woman Speaks, A (film), 391

"Black Woman Speaks, A" (poem) (Richardson), 391

Bloody Thursday, Berkeley, Calif. (May 15, 1969), 385–86

Bobby Seale Brigade, 155

Body Politic (Toronto), 99

Bond, Julian, 255

Bond, The, xi, 17, 26–27

Bookchin, Murray, 378

bookstores, gay: Glad Day Bookstore, Boston, 107; Oscar Wilde Memorial Bookstore, New York City, 116

Boston Gay Review, 97, 117–18

Boston Lesbian and Gay Pride March (June 18, 1977), 109–10

Both Sides Now, 370–79, 381–84; anniversary issue, December 1970, 371; change in focus to New Age journalism, 375, 376; and the Green movement, 378–79; irregularity of issues, 372; Ithaca couple as staff members, 371–72, 384n1

Boyer, Richard O.: *Labor's Untold Story,* 194

Boyland, Bill, 322, 324

Bragg Briefs, 15

Branch Davidian tragedy, Waco, Tex., 381

"Bread and Roses" (poem) (Oppenheim), 391

Brotherhood of Sleeping Car Porters, 255

Brower, David, 181

Brown, Benjamin, 126

Brown, Elaine, 358, 359, 364; Black Panther Party leader, 335, 336; and Los Angeles BPP chapter, 352, 354; "Responding to Radical Racism: David Horowitz Barely Remembered," 363

Brown, H. Rap, 234, 244

Brown, Rita Mae: and *The Furies,* 270, 275–79; and *The Ladder,* 279; "Woman-Identified-Woman" (Lavender Action), 270, 394

Browning, Darrell, 327

Brownmiller, Susan, xv; *In Our Time: Memoir of a Revolution,* xvi, 397; *Against Our Will: Men, Women, and Rape,* xv, 397

Brubaker, Bob (pseud. Panda Bear), 175, 180–81, 183

Buffalo Draft Resistance Union (BDRU), 192

Bugle-American, 318–19

Bunch, Charlotte, 272–75, 277; and D.C. Women's Liberation, 270; *Lesbianism and the Women's Movement,* 283, 287; "Lesbians in Revolt: Male Supremacy Quakes and Quivers," 272, 283–87

Burch, Laurel, 392

Burger Boy Food-o-Rama (BBF) riots, Columbus, Ohio, 306, 311

Burroughs, William, 98, 118; *Naked Lunch,* 81

Busch, Judy, 392; *Women's Songbook,* 411

Bush, George H. W., 89

Butterfield, Hester, 386

C

Cady, Beth, 68

Caen, Herb, 396

Caldicott, Helen, 381

California Superquake: 1975–77 (James), 376, 384n7

Call, The, 156

Callahan, Frank, 172

Calleman, Carl Johan, 382

Callison, William, 26

Cambodia, 325; invasion of by U.S., 1970, 155, 193, 260, 294; Pol Pot-guided mass murders, 183

"Can the Left Find Room for Spirituality?" (Billotte), 375–76

Cantrell, Burton, 314

Capra, Fritjof, 379; *Green Politics: The Global Promise,* 378

Capriotti, Jimmy "Cap," 131

Caprow, Rick, 164–67

Captain America (comic book), 262

Carl (Allied Chemical strike leader), 198–99, 203–4

Carleton College, Northfield, Minn., 154

Carmichael, Stokely (pseud. Kwame Tour), 234, 411; Cleaver attack on Carmichael's "Black Power" philosophy, 349; "drafted" into BPP, 344–46; and James Meredith march (Spring 1966), 124

Carpenter, Cassell, 129, 133

Carson, Barbara, 65, 66, 67, 74

Carter, Alprentice "Bunchy," 352

Carter, Jimmy, 185

Cassell, Mike, 129

Castro, Fidel, 62, 348

Catch-22 (Heller), 303

Catholic Worker Movement, 52, 377, 382

Cavanagh, Jerome, 53

Cell 16, Boston, 387

Chase, Debbie, 406

Chavez, Cesar, 70

chemically-enhanced fruit, 197

Chicago 7/Chicago 8 conspiracy trial, 257, 271, 370

Chicago Seed, 260, 264

Chicago Women's Liberation Conference (1968), 386

Chicago Women's Liberation newsletter, 392

Chile: overthrow of pro-worker government by U.S.-backed military generals, 212; workers and socialism, 211–12, 214

Chisholm, Margaret, 308

Chomsky, Noam, 378

Christopher, Judy, 308, 312, 321, 323

Church Committee Report on COINTELPRO, 343, 352, 354

City Lights bookstore, 81, 117

Clark, Ed, 127, 137, 138, 151

Clark, Mark, 343

class in the U.S., analysis of, 275

Cleage, Albert, 49

Cleaver, Eldridge, 346, 350, 354; editor of *The Black Panther,* 344; in exile in Algeria, 348; *Soul on Ice,* 344

Cleaver, Kathleen (née Neal), 348, 364

Climax!, 372

Clover (writer for *Fag Rag*), 101

Cockrel, Ken, 57

Cockrel, Sheila Murphy, 52

Cocteau, Jean: *The White Paper,* 97

Coffin, Tris: *Washington Spectator,* 374, 384n5

Cohn, Jack, 144

Cohodas, Steve, 326

COINTELPRO. *See* FBI Counterintelligence Program (COINTELPRO)

Cold Steel, 193–94

Cole, Don, 146–48, 151

Collected Poetry of Nikki Giovanni: 1968–1998, The (Giovanni), 391

College Press Service, 154

Columbia Journalism Review, 374

Columbus Free Press, xii, 303, 304, 306–20; change in name to *Columbus Freepress,* 320; drug use among staffers, 318–20; legacy of, 331–33; as a "new" paper following demise of *Columbus Freepress,* 328–31; OSU Gay Liberation Front, participation of, 307; women's issue, 309

Columbus Freepress, 320–28; harassment by police and right-wing groups, 323; name change from *Columbus Free Press*, 320; struggle with male-female relationships, 320–21

Come Out (New York), 99

Come Out! (play) (Katz), 116

Commemoration Committee for the Black Panther Party, 363

Commemorator, The, 363

Committee of Returned [Peace Corps] Volunteers, 269

Committee of Small Magazine Editors and Publishers (COSMEP), 117

Communist Party (American): power struggle with PL in SDS, 138–39; takeover of SSOC's Nashville office, 138

Communist Party (China), 74

Community Union, Columbus, Ohio, 314–15, 316

Community Union, Madison, Wisc., 168–69, 178, 179

Complaints and Disorders: The Sexual Politics of Sickness (English and Ehrenreich), 68

Conant, Ralph W.: *Prospects for Revolution*, 48–49

Coney Island of the Mind, A (Ferlinghetti), 81

Congress of Industrial Organizations (CIO), 69

Congress of Racial Equality (CORE), 342

Conliff, Steve (pseud. Leon Karg; Leon Yipsky): and *Columbus Free Press*, 310, 314, 316; and *Columbus Freepress*, 320, 323, 324; founder of *Purple Berries*, 305, 308; "pieing" Ohio Governor James Rhodes, 328, 330

Connections, 156

Conot, Robert: *The American Odyssey*, 49

consciousness-raising (CR) groups, 101, 269, 386, 390, 397, 402

"Constructing the List of GI Papers" (Lewes), 28–45

Cooney, Jimmy, 256

Coordinating Council of Literary Magazines (CCLM), 117

Corydon (Gide), 97

Count Down, 184

Crawford, Bryce, 68

Creem (rock magazine), 54

Croal, George, 168

Crockett, George, 58

Crothers, Diane, 397

Culp, Pat, 322

Cuscuria, Amy. *See* Quigley, John

D

Daily Cardinal, The, 173

Danky, Jim, 160, 173–74

Darrow, Clarence, 49

Davis, Angela, 67, 81, 308, 316, 413

Davis, Phil, 164, 172

Davis, Rennie, 80

Day, Dorothy, 52, 377

D.C. Women's Liberation movement, 269, 270

de Beauvoir, Simone: *Must We Burn Sade?*, 98

de Sade, Marquis, 263

Debs, Eugene V., 52, 214

Deevey, Sharon, 271, 275

Dellinger, Dave, 377

Democratic National Convention, Chicago, Ill. (1968), 60

Dennison, Earlene. *See* Rothman, Earlene

Densmore, Dana, 387

Detroit, Mich.: Belle Isle Be-In, 1967, 55; black activism, emergence of, 56–58; blues music scene, 73; changing sexual mores, 53; diversity of religious and ethnic population, 51–52; emergence of gay and lesbian community, 54; Plum Street as "Detroit's Art Community," 53; political climate, 1880s–1960s, 51–52; race riots, 1967, 55, 256; social and cultural climate, 1960s, 48–49

Detroit: I Do Mind Dying (Georgakis and Surkin), 73

Detroit Lives (Mast), 52

Detroit Police Officers Association, 48

Detroit Police STRESS unit, 59, 74

Devlin, Bernadette, 215–16

Dharma Bums, The (Kerouac), 81

Diana Press, 281

Dickie (*Hundred Flowers* staff member), 260

Diggers, 126–27

Dillaway, Diana: *Power Failure*, 220

Dionysius (film), 54

DiPrima, Diane, 90; *Revolutionary Letters,* 81

Dobkin, Alix, 274

Dock of the Bay, The, 256

Doggett, David, 122, 123, 124, 129–50; *The Mocking-bird,* 125

Dohrn, Bernadine, 139

Donaldson, Ivanhoe, 255

Doors, 370

Dorian, Michael, 376

Douglas, Emory, 335, 344, 346, 347, 358

Douglass, Frederick, 234

Dowell, Denzil, 343–44

Doyle, Roger, 306, 320

Dr. Huey P. Newton Foundation, 365

Dr. Ross, 73

Dreifus, Claudia, 392

Drenning, Vicki, 186

"driveaway" pickup trucks, 188n2

drugs, psychedelic, 143–44

Drumgo, Fleeta, 337

Du Bois, David, 354–56, 358, 359

Du Bois, Shirley Graham, 359

Du Bois, W.E.B., 234

Du Bois clubs, 255

Dunbar, Roxanne, 387; "The Movement and the Working Class," 275

DuPont: Behind the Nylon Curtain (Zilg), 205

DuPont Chemical, Niagara Falls, N.Y.: 1970 workers' strike, 204–6; and racism, 206–7; supplier of war material to Nazi Germany, 205

Durant, Sam: *Black Panther: The Revolutionary Art of Emory Douglas,* 348

Duren, Kwaku, 364

Dylan, Bob, 294

E

Earth First!, 88, 89

Earth First Journal, 88

Easy Rider (film), 370

Eberly, David, 108

Eckleberry, Dick, 307

ecocide, 290

Edelson, Elihu, 370–79, 381–84

Edelson, Ellic, 380, 382, 384

Edelson, Joan, 379–80

Edge City community center, Jackson, Miss., 144, 149

Ehrenreich, Barbara: *Complaints and Disorders: The Sexual Politics of Sickness,* 68

Eisenberg, Bonnie, xvi, 386, 388, 390–406; and National Women's History Project, 407; organizer for Berkeley Women's Liberation group, 387; *Women's Songbook,* 411

Electric Battlefield devices, 299, 300

Electric Kool-Aid Acid Test, The (Wolfe), 144, 303

Ellsberg, Daniel, 64, 72

Empire City, The (Goodman), 81

End of St. Petersburg, The (Pudovkin), 409

English, Dierdre: *Complaints and Disorders: The Sexual Politics of Sickness,* 68

Erwin, Adeline Comer, 357

Erwin, J. Otis, 357

Estrada, Liz. *See* Morris, Mimi

Eugene, Oreg.: demonstrations in, 290; history of cooperatives in, 293

Eugene Thirteen, 294

Evans, Arthur: *Witchcraft and the Gay Counterculture,* 118

Evergreen Review, 98

"Exiles' Kingdom" (Shively), 98–99

Exorcism of the Straight Man Demon (Shurin), 107–8

Eyes Right, 45n11

F

Fag Rag, 97–120; *Boston Gay Review,* relationship with, 117; "Boston GLF's 10-Point Demands Presented to the Democratic Convention in Miami Beach, July 1972," 103–4; conflict between "professional" and "amateur" staff members, 110–12; creation of new gay community, call for, 102; division between gay men and lesbians, 100–101; and *Gay Community News,* relationship with, 119; and Good Gay Poets group, 108; government grants for, 117; prisoner writings, publication of, 118–20; problems with printers and distribution, 115–16; publication and page layout issues, 112–15; and *Street Sheet,* publication of, 105

Fakiranand, Mahatma, 80

Farber, Jerry: *Student as Nigger,* 64

Fariña, Mimi, 391

Farinella, Salvatore, 108; *San Francisco Experience,* 118

Father Knows Best (television program), 304

FBI Counterintelligence Program (COINTELPRO), 311, 342–43; BPP, operations against, 350–52, 354, 357; Church Committee Report, 343; and informer-provocateurs, 145, 151, 311; targets of, 342–43

Fearless, Houston. *See* Abbott, Steve

Featherston, Steve, 168, 174

Feiffer, Jules, 400

Fein, Leonard, 61

Felien, Ed, 257, 260, 267

Fellner, Michael, 159, 160

Felong, Cindy, 65, 66, 67, 68, 74

Female Artists Past and Present, 411

feminist health movement, 380

feminist press publications: *The Furies,* xii, xvi, 272–87; *It Aint Me Babe,* xii, xvi, 390–406, 411–12; *off our backs,* xvi, 269, 271, 280, 293, 411; rise of, xii

"Feminists Do Have a Sense of Humor: The First Women's Comix" (Robbins), 412–15

Ferlinghetti, Lawrence, 81, 117; *A Coney Island of the Mind,* 81; *Unfair Arguments with Existence,* 81

Fife, Darlene, 131

Fifth Estate, xi, 47–96; black activism in Detroit, coverage of, 56–59, 74; 40th anniversary issue, 90; gay community in Detroit, coverage of, 84; labor movement in Detroit, coverage of, 68–70, 86–87; legacy of, 94–96; Roots of the Underground series, 80–81; staff editorial (February 1, 1969), 63–64; White Panther Party, influence of, 50; Winter Soldier Investigation, coverage of, 72; Women's Issue (March 8, 1971), 66–67;

youth revolt (1969–1975), coverage of, 64–65

Fifth Estate Coffeehouse, Los Angeles, Calif., 47

Films by and/or about Women Internationally, Past and Present, 411

Findhorn community, Moray, Scotland, 375

Fireman, Ken, 59, 62, 74, 75

First Amendment, 45n12

First Atlanta Pop Festival, 370

Fish, Norma Jean. *See* Gregory, Libby

Fitzhugh, Chuck, 131

Flaming Creatures (film), 54

Fletcher, Richard, 80

Florida Black Front, 369

Flower, Marilyn, 326, 327

Flynn, Elizabeth Gurley, 67

Focus, 325

Fonda, Jane, 15

For Colored Girls Who Have Considered Suicide When the Rainbow Is Enuf (Shange), 402

Forbidden City: The Golden Age of Chinese Nightclubs (Robbins), 408

Forcade, Tom, 148

Foreman, Dave, 88

Fort Polk Puke, The, 18

Foucault, Michel: "The Simplest of Pleasures [Suicide]," 112

Four-Year Bummer, A, 18

Fowler, Hilary Ayer, 392

France, Chuck, 185, 186

Frank, Miriam, 84

Franklin, Alan, 59, 86–88

Franklin, Aretha, 52

Franklin, C. L., 52

Frazier, Greg, 308

Free For All, 161–75; Bob Avakian speech, reaction to, 164–65; and drift towards anarchist philosophy, 164–65; evolution of staff into a collective, 169; "On the Road to Fascism" (Wong), 163; philosophical split among staff, 167–73, 179–80, 188n3; post-split, 174–75; split of assets, 172–73; "Wong Truth Conspiracy" (Wong), 163–64

Free People Inc., 372

Free Southern Student (newsletter), 123

Free Space (booklet on CR groups) (Allen), 402

Free University, Jackson, Miss., 127–28

Free University Cosmic Kosmic, 304

Freedom Information Service, 124, 126, 147

Freedom of Information Act, 150

Frey, John, 347

Friedan, Betty, 270, 278, 393

Friedman, Jerry, 316

Friends of Resistors Inside the Military (FRITM), 45n7

FTA (Fort Knox), 18

FTA Show (variety program), 15

Fultz, Michael, 359

Fund for a Feminist Majority, 278

Funk, Cynthia: "Woman-Identified-Woman" (Lavender Action), 394

Furies, The, xii, xvi, 99, 272–81; "The Dentist" (Berson), 288; discussion of themes of, 271–78; "The Furies" (Berson), 281–83; lesbianism as a political choice, 274; "Lesbians in Revolt: Male Supremacy Quakes and Quivers" (Bunch), 272, 283–87

Furies, The (lesbian feminist collective), 269, 270–71, 279, 281–82

Furniture Workers Press, 228

G

Gainesville 8 trial, 374

Gainesville Women's Health Center, Gainesville, Fla., 380

Gardner, Fred, 15

Gardner, Tom, 127, 138

Garland, Teresa, 76

Garry, Charles, 361

Garvey, Marcus, 234

Gay Activist Alliance, Ohio State University, 310, 312

gay community, divisions within, 100–102

Gay Community Center (Detroit), 84

Gay Community News (Boston): Lesbian/Gay Prisoner Project, 119; relationship with *Fag Rag,* 106–7, 119

Gay Lesbian Advocates and Defenders (GLAD),
108

Gay Liberation Front (GLF): consciousness-awareness and study groups, 101

Gay Liberator, 54, 99

Gay Male Liberation collective, 104–5

Gay Sunshine (Berkeley/San Francisco), 99

Gay Women's Liberation, 392

Gazette (Lincoln), 162

Georgakis, Dan: *Detroit: I Do Mind Dying,* 73

German Greens, 378; pillars of, 379

GI coffeehouses as centers of dissident political activity, 15

GI News and Discussion Bulletin, 26, 44n2

GI Press Project, xviii

GI Press Service, 27

GI Resistance (cultural revolution), 14

GI Resistance: Military Undergrounds during the Vietnam War, The (Haines), 14–28

GI underground press publications: *Aboveground,* 1–10; *The Ally,* 12–13; difficulty in maintaining continuity, 14; GI newspapers with notes, list of, 29–32; with local distribution, list of, 20–26; with national or international distribution, list of, 26–28; news workers, obstacles faced by, 28; newspaper titles, list of, 32–41; pamphlets and project reports, 41–44; wordplay using military commands and slang in titles, 16–18

GI Underground Press: Two Case Studies of Alternative Military Newspapers (Haines), 14

Gide, André: *Corydon,* 97

Gigline, 17

Ginsberg, Allen, 55, 74, 91, 98, 303, 307; "Howl" (poem), 81, 304; "Kaddish" (poem), 81

Ginzburg, Ralph, 316

Giorno, John, 118

Giovanni, Nikki: *The Collected Poetry of Nikki Giovanni: 1968–1998,* 391

GIs Are Fighting, 45n13

GIs United, 15

Glad Day Bookstore, 107

GLF publications: *Amazon Quarterly* (Oakland), 99; *Body Politic* (Toronto), 99; *Boston Gay Review,* 97; *Come Out* (New York), 99; *The*

Furies (Washington, DC), 99; *Gay Liberator* (Detroit), 99; *Gay Sunshine* (Berkeley/San Francisco), 99

globalism vs. labor solidarity, 226–28

Glover, Danny, 348

Go Tell It on the Mountain (Baldwin), 81

Goldstone, Barbara: "Woman-Identified-Woman" (Lavender Action), 394

Gomez, Mauricio, 241, 242

Gonzalez, Juan, 235

"Good Bye to All That" (Morgan), 393

Good Gay Poets group, 119; members of, 107–8; NEA grant for, 118; relationship with *Fag Rag*, 108

Good Times, 257, 307

Goode, Starr, xvi, 390, 392, 394, 396, 402; and feminist spirituality movement, 407–8

Goodman, Jeff, 60, 75, 83, 85–86

Goodman, Paul: *The Empire City*, 81; *Growing Up Absurd*, 81; *People or Personnel*, 81

Gordon, Dexter, 185

Gotkin, Alan, 62

Graff, Alison "Sunny" (pseud. Frieda P. Pole), 320, 321, 323, 324–25

Grahn, Judy, 275

Grant, John, 59, 88

Grapes of Wrath (Steinbeck), 303

Grateful Dead, 52

Great Speckled Bird, 68, 128, 293, 369, 396

Green Machine, 18

Green movement, international, 378

Green Politics: The Global Promise (Capra and Spretnak), 378

Greene, Felix: *Vietnam! Vietnam!*, 191

Greenfield, Freddie, 108; *Were You Always a Criminal?*, 119

Greenpeace, 89

Gregory, 304

Gregory, Libby (pseud. Norma Jean Fish), 308, 310, 321, 322, 323, 327, 330

Gribbs, Roman, 58–59

Griffin, Susan (pseud. Susan Levy), 392, 393, 408; "Rape: The All-American Crime" (from *Ramparts*), 397; "Single or Schizoid," 390–91

Grimshaw, Gary, 51

Growing Up Absurd (Goodman), 81

Guardian, 253, 326

Guevara, Che, 264

Guitar Army (Sinclair), 50

Gumbo, Judy, 388

Guzmán, Pablo "Yorúba," xii, 234, 242–53

Guzman, Paul, 235

H

Haines, Harry W., xi, xvii, 1–2, 4, 7–8, 10; *The GI Resistance: Military Undergrounds during the Vietnam War*, 14–28; *The GI Underground Press: Two Case Studies of Alternative Military Newspapers* (Department of Communication, University of Utah), 14

Hair (Revived), 44–45n3

Hall, Radclyffe: *Well of Loneliness*, 97

Halley, Patrick: "Looking for Utopia," 90–96; "pieing" Guru Maharaj Ji, xi, 77–78, 80, 91–93

Hamill, Larry, 324

Hamlet, Ed, 140

Hampton, Fred, 58, 239, 343

Hansberry, Lorraine, 81

Hanson, Larry, 371

"Hard Times" conferences, 168

Harris, Helaine, 271

Hart, Lois: "Woman-Identified-Woman" (Lavender Action), 394

Harvest Quarterly, The, 160

Hatcher, Richard, 255

Hathaway, Susan, 271

Hawken, Paul, 375

Hayden, Tom, xvi, 156

Hayes, James R., 19, 26; *The War within a War: Dissent in the Military with an Emphasis on Vietnam*, 14

Head, Bob, 131

Heanes, Herbert, 347

Heller, Joseph: *Catch-22*, 303

Helm, Cheryl, 311

Hendrix, Jimi, 65, 265

Hennacy, Ammon, 382

herbicides: in Eugene, Oreg., effects of spraying of, 291–92; in Southeast Asia, effects of spraying of, 290

Heretic's Journal (personal journal), 374

Herron, Bobby, 350

HERSTORY SYNOPSIS, 410

heterosexuality, definition of, 274–75

Hewitt, Raymond "Masai," 235, 348–49

Hillegas, Jill, 124, 147

Hilliard, David, 354, 364, 365; BPP chief of staff for Eldridge Cleaver, 348; and COINTEL-PRO, 351; leader of BPP, 335; meeting with Stokely Carmichael in Algiers, 349

hippie movement in Mississippi, 125

Hippler, Bob, xi, xii; and *Fifth Estate*, 63, 68, 74, 75, 81, 84; and march on Chrysler's Warren Tank Plant, 71; senior editor of the *Michigan Daily*, 60, 91

Hiser, Jim, 326

Hoedads, 293

Hoeper, Jo, 327

Hoffman, Abbie, 74, 126–27, 309, 371; *Revolution for the Hell of It*, 303

Hoffman, Amy: *An Army of Ex-Lovers: My Life at the Gay Community News*, 119

Holden, Joan: *Independent Female, or, A Man Has His Pride* (play), 406

Holm, Nancy, 65

Home Front (GI coffeehouse, Colorado Springs, Colo.), 1, 2, 3, 4, 10

homosexual publications. *See also* GLF publications: censorship of, 97–98; early history of, 97; *Fag Rag*, 97; Fag Rag Books, 97; Good Gay Poets books, 97; *Lavender Vision*, 97; *OUTLOOK* (Berkeley), 116; *Street Sheet*, 97

Honeywell Corporation, 260

Hooka, 319

Hooker, John Lee, 73; *The Motor City's Burnin'* (song), 55

Hoover, Gayle, 326

Hoover, J. Edgar: and Black Panther Party, actions against, 338, 350

Horowitz, David, 363

House Un-American Activities Committee (HUAC), 75

How the Other Half Lives (Riis), 303

Howard, Elbert "Big Man," 349–50

Howard, Mike, 306

Howl (Ginsberg), 81, 304

Hubbard, Barbara Marx, 381

Hubert, Claude, 352, 354

Hudson, Marsha, 392

Huggins, Ericka, 335, 352, 354

Huggins, John, 352

Hundred Flowers, 260–68; Black Panther Party issue, 267; "Hundred Flowers' 'Declaration of Independence: Update'", 261; "Revolutionary Cultural Terrorists," 263; Women's Liberation issue, 264

Hunt, Carolina. *See* Lehman, Alice

Hunt, John, 306

Hutton, Bobby, 348

I

I Ching, 303

Ichord, Richard H., 350

In Our Time: Memoir of a Revolution (Brownmiller), xvi, 397

In These Times, 374, 384n6

Independent Female, or, A Man Has His Pride (play) (Holden), 406

Indochina Coalition, 312, 316

Industrial Workers of the World (IWW), 171, 293

Inner City Voice, 57

Insurgent, 187

Intercommunal Youth Institute, Oakland, Calif., 354, 358

Internal Security Committee, U.S. House of Representatives: *Annual Report for the Year 1972*, 14, 15

International Socialists, 68

International Women's Day (March 8, 1969), 388, 404, 409, 410

Isthmus, 167

It Aint Me Babe, xii, xv–xvii, 390–406, 411; dissolution of editorial board, 404–5; "Editorial

from First Issue," 411–12; evolving self-
definition, 403; major split with Berkeley
Women's Liberation group, 404; Women's
Page, 405–6
It Aint Me Comix (Robbins), 401–2
It's About Time, 365
Ivanny, Sonia, 246

J

Jackson, George: and Black Guerrilla Family, 336;
murder of, 310, 336–38; *Soledad Brother: The
Prison Letters of George Jackson,* 338
Jackson, Jesse, 58
Jackson, Scoop, 181
Jackson State College: student shootings by
police, 64, 141, 155, 305, 370
Jackson State Prison, Mich., 70
Jacksonville, Fla.: hippie community, 369; New
Left, 370
Jacobs, Jim, 83
Jager, Duane, 330–31
Jam-Cin. *See* Neiburger, Colin
James, Paul: *California Superquake: 1975–77,* 376,
384n7
James Meredith March from Memphis, Tenn. to
Jackson, Miss. (Spring 1966), 124
James White Review, 117–18
Jamrock, Greg, 184
Jaschik, Mike, 310
JEB. *See* Biren, Joan
Jefferson Airplane, 52, 370
Jenkins, Bobo, 73
Jennings, William "Billy X," 365
Jensen, Peter: and *AUGUR,* 290–96
Jesus, 263
Johnson, David, 337
Johnson, James, 57
Johnson, Lyndon, 61
Johnston, Art, 59
Johnston, Jill, 99–100
Jones, Charles E.: *The Black Panther Party (Recon-
sidered),* 365
Jones, Frank, 349

Jones, Jim, 361
Jones, LeRoi: *Preface to a 20-Volume Suicide Note,*
81
Jonestown, Guyana, 361–62
Jonestown: The Life and Death of Peoples Temple
(film), 361
Jordan, Joan, 390
Joyce, Frank, 62, 73

K

Kafka, Franz: *The Trial,* 303
Kaleidoscope (Madison), 153, 156, 157–58
Kaleidoscope (Milwaukee), 156
Karenga, Maulana, 352
Karg, Leon. *See* Conliff, Steve
Kathleen Cleaver Community Information Cen-
ter, Minneapolis, 267
Katz, Jonathan Ned: *Come Out!* (play), 116
Kauflin, Cathy, 81–82
Kaufman, Michael, 163–72, 174–75
Keating, Stephen, 260
Keep on Trucking, 48, 59, 67, 75, 77
Kelly, Petra, 378
Kennedy, Flo, 388
Kennedy, Jane, 67
Kennedy, Jim, 48, 59, 72–73
Kennedy, John F., 52
Kennedy, Mike, 129
Kent State University student shootings: reported
in various underground papers, 64, 141, 155,
193, 260, 305, 311, 370
Kerouac, Jack: *The Dharma Bums,* 81; *On the
Road,* 81, 304
Kerry, John, 14, 72
Kesey, Ken: *One Flew over the Cuckoo's Nest,* 293;
Sometimes a Great Notion, 293
Khomeini, Ayatollah, 185
Kimball, Charles A., 377
King, Martin Luther, Jr., 52, 255, 303, 342, 348,
357
King Street Trolley, 158
Klein, Sue, 388
Klonsky, Mike, 136–37, 139

Knops, Mark, 156, 158, 159

Knot, The, 45n4

Korea Free Press, 45n14

Kramer, Barry, 54

Krassner, Paul, 65, 81, 374

Krehbiel, Paul, xvii, 189–225, 228

Ku Klux Klan rallies, 328

Kucinich, Dennis, xv

Kudzu, The, 121–50; article on COINTELPRO activities in Alabama, 145; closure of, 149–50; Edge City community center, 144, 149; Jackson police raid, October 26, 1970, 146; Mississippi Youth Jubilees, 141; and surveillance by FBI, 145

Kunkin, Art, 47, 378

Kwant, Pete, 75

L

labor solidarity vs. globalism, 226–28

Labor's Untold Story (Morais and Boyer), 194

Lacy, Fred, 137

Ladder, The, 279

Lane, Mark, 72

LaPorta, John, 108

Larkin, Doug, 76

LaRouche, Lyndon, xi; and National Caucus of Labor Committees, 76, 181

LaRue, Bunny, 101

Last Incursion, The, 17

Last Picture Show, The (film), 277

Last Poets, 244

Laura X, xvi–xvii, 387–88, 400, 406; and National Clearinghouse on Marital and Date Rape, 407; publisher for *SPAZM,* 388; "Women of the Russian Revolution Inspire Another Revolution: Laura X and the Women's History Archives," 409–11; and Women's History Research Center, 407

Lavender Action: "Woman-Identified-Woman," 394

Lavender Menace (New York City), 279

Lavender Vision, 97, 104; as an all-lesbian publication, 99

Lazarus, Mel, 400

League of Revolutionary Black Workers, 56–58

Leary, Timothy, 55

Leave It to Beaver (television program), 304

Leaves of Grass (Whitman), 97

LeGuin, Ursula K., 90

Lehman, Alice (pseud. Carolina Hunt), 308, 310, 321, 323

Lennon, John, 74, 326

Lerman, Rob, 164, 165, 187

Lesbian Nation, 99

lesbian-feminist movement, 394

lesbian-feminist politics, development of, 283–87

Lesbian/Gay Prisoner Project, Michigan, 119

Lesbianism and the Women's Movement (Myron and Bunch), 283, 287

Lessing, Doris, 392

Levertov, Denise, 303

Levy, Susan. *See* Griffin, Susan

Lewes, James, xvii–xviii; "Constructing the List of GI Papers," 28–45

Lewis, Joan, 348

Lewis, John L., 69

Lewis, Raymond, 349

Liberation News Service, 370; article about first street demonstration for International Women's Day, 410; creation of, 293; and Harvey Wasserman, 331; national articles for *Free Press* (Columbus), 330; national articles for *The Carletonian,* 154; national articles for *The Kutzu,* 131; *Palante,* support for, 253; report on local draft board restrictions on drafting writers from underground papers, 134; reports on FBI informant/provocateurs, 316; reprint of drawing from *Hundred Flowers,* 260; subscription to by *Climax!,* 372; subscription to by *SPAZM,* 388

Life of Brian, The (film), 312

Lifshin, Lyn, 392

Lindisfarne Association, 375

Links, 156

Little Free Press (personal journal), 374

Livesay, Jeff, 129

Lobsinger, Donald, 71

Long, Everett, 129
Longeaux y Vasquez, Enriqueta, 391
"Looking for Utopia" (Halley), 90–96
Los Angeles Free Press, 47, 378
Louisiana Weekly, 129
Luciano, Felipe, 235, 244, 246
Lynyrd Skynyrd, 369

M

Machel, Samora, 348
Mackey, Mary, 408
Madison, Wisc.: alternative economic institu-
    tions, 155–56; alternative newspapers, 156,
    158–87; Mifflin community, 154–55
Madison Free Press, 156
Maharaj Ji, Guru, xi; and Divine Light Mission,
    92; "pied" by Patrick Halley, 77–78, 80, 91–93
Mailer, Norman, 53; *Armies of the Night*, 60
Mainardi, Pat, 392
Makamson, Lee, 123, 125, 146
Making of a Counterculture, The (Roszak), 371
Malcolm X, 234, 303
male-identified woman, 394
Mandel, Phyllis, 388, 410
Mandelblatt, Donna, 392
Manson, Charlie, 263
Manson murders, 304
March, Artemis: "Woman-Identified-Woman"
    (Lavender Action), 394
March on Washington, DC (1963), 52
Marin Women's News Journal, 406
Marine Blues, 18
Maristany, Hiram, 240–41, 242
Marks, Norma Ovshinsky, 47
Martin, Del, 392
Martin, John, 67
Martinez, José "Cha-Cha," 239, 242, 246
Masculine/Feminine, 411
Masel, Ben (Zippie), 181
mass media, U.S., during Vietnam War era, 193
Mast, Robert: *Detroit Lives*, 52
Mathews, Teddy, 101
Mathiak, Lucy, 165

Matilaba, 348
Mattachine Society, 98
Matthews, Connie, 351
Matza, David, 410
Maurin, Peter, 377
May Day Demonstration, Washington, DC (1971),
    72
Mayer, Mark, 76
McCain, John, 14
McCall, Cheryl, 59
McCarthy, Eugene, 257
McCarthy, Joe, 2
McCartney, Paul, 370
McCoy, Chuck, 310
McDonald, Country Joe, xviii
McDowell, Fred, 144
McFarland, Patti, 327
McGee, Michael, 364
McGovern presidential campaign, 74
McHale, Howard, 305
McNamara, Mike, 144
McNamara, Robert, 48
McPherson, Scott (pseud. Polar Bear), 175, 176,
    180–81, 183
McReynolds, David, 377
Medvecky, Nick, 61, 64
Melendez, Mickey, 235, 241, 244
Menimen, Dennis. *See* Abbott, Steve
Meredith, James, 124
Merton, Thomas, 52
Michaels, Aaron, 364
Michel, Gregg: *Struggle for a Better South: The
    Southern Student Organizing Committee,
    1964–1969*, 139, 140
Michigan Daily (University of Michigan), 60
Midwife Service of East Texas, 380
Miernik, John, 310, 311, 316; as informer-
    provocateur, 323
Mifflin alternative community, Madison, Wisc.,
    154–55, 160
Mijo (writer for *Fag Rag*), 101
Military Research Network (MRN), 300
Miller, Henry, 256
Miller, Patrick, 326

Millsaps College, Jackson, Miss., 123, 125–28

Minh, Ho Chi, 62, 257

Minnesota 8 trial, 267

Mirodias, Maurice, 65

Misra, Jupteswar, 80

Mississippi Youth Jubilees, Mt. Beulah, Miss., 141

Mitch Ryder and the Detroit Wheels, 52

Mitzel, John, 113, 115, 116

Mockingbird, The (Doggett), 125

Molk, Steve, 330

Molly Maguires, 215

Monroe, Marilyn, 392

Moore, Bob, 59, 60, 75, 83

Moore, Ralph, 365

Moore, Sebastian, 132

Moore, Tom, 308

Morais, Herbert J.: *Labor's Untold Story,* 194

Moratorium demonstration, Washington, DC (1969), 64

Morgan, Robin: "Good Bye to All That," 393

Moriarty, Tim, 386

Morris, Evan, 310, 326

Morris, Mimi (pseud. Liz Estrada; Angela Motorman), 308, 316, 319, 321, 323, 326

Morrison, Norman, 48

Morse, Wayne, 293

Mother of Voices, The, 257

Motor City Five, 52

Motor City Labor League (Detroit), 164

Motor City's Burnin',' The (song) (Hooker), 55

Motorman, Angela. *See* Morris, Mimi

Movement for a Democratic Military, 19

Muhammad, Khallid, 364

Muhammad Speaks, 253, 350, 351

Mulford, Don, 341

Mulford Act (California), 341–42

Murfin, Patrick, 184

Murra, Laura. *See* Laura X

Murrow, Edward R., 2

Must We Burn Sade? (de Beauvoir), 98

Myron, Nancy, 271, 276; *Lesbianism and the Women's Movement,* 283, 287

N

Naked Lunch (Burroughs), 81

Napier, Sam, 347–48, 351

Nation of Islam, 52, 342, 350, 351, 364

National Caucus of Labor Committees (NCLC), 181; and Operation Mop Up, 76

National Clearinghouse on Marital and Date Rape, 407

National Endowment for the Arts (NEA) grants, 117–18

National Liberation Front (NLF) of South Vietnam, 289, 312

National Man Boy Love Association (NAMBLA), 108

National Organization for Women, 89, 393

National Unemployed and Welfare Rights Organization (NUWRO), 76

National Welfare Rights Organization (NWRO), 269

National Writers Union, xvii

Nationalist Party of Puerto Rico, 235

Neal, Kathleen, 344. *See also* Cleaver, Kathleen

Neiburger, Colin (pseud. Jam-Cin; Colinda Tomato), 312, 316, 320, 323

Neiswonger, Michael, 74, 75, 81, 83–84, 91

Nelson, Ancher, 264

Nelson, Stanley: *Jonestown: The Life and Death of Peoples Temple* (film), 361

Neruda, Pablo, 303

New Age, 378–79, 381, 382, 384n8

New Age, 195–225; all-women's issue, 222, 224–25; coverage of labor issues, 200–202, 204–7, 208, 210, 211–12, 214, 215, 216; exposure of racism in the workforce, 216–17; goals of, 196; legacy of, 226–28

New Age Journal, 378

New Alliance Party, 76

New Black Panther Party for Self-Defense, Dallas, Tex., 364; publisher of *The Black Panther Black Community News Service,* 365

New Left, 61, 62, 128, 129, 370

New Left Convention, Chicago, Ill. (Summer 1967), 255–56

New Options (personal journal) (Satin), 374,

384n5

New Panther Vanguard Movement, Los Angeles, Calif., 364; publisher of "new" *The Black Panther Intercommunal News Service,* 365

New Solidarity (National Caucus of Labor Committees), 181–82

New Year's Gang of Madison: and Army Math Research Center bombing, 155, 156, 265

New York Gay Pride March, New York City (June 1971), 116

New York Radical Lesbians, 271

New York Radical Women, 386

Newman, Fred, 76

Newton, Frederika, 365

Newton, Gwen, 358

Newton, Huey P., 265, 350, 361; cofounder of the Black Panther Party, 335, 338, 365; exile to Cuba following murder charges in Oakland, 358–59; funeral, 335–36; jailed for murder of white police officer, 347; murder by Tyrone Robinson, 338; "On the Defection of Eldridge Cleaver from the Black Panther Party and the Defection of the Black Panther Party from the Black Community," 351–52; *War Against the Panthers: A Study of Repression in America,* 342, 363

Newton, Mike, 291

Nhat Hanh, Thich: *Vietnam: Lotus in a Sea of Fire,* 208

Nichols, John, 74

Niebuhr, Reinhold, 52

Niggas, 235

Nin, Anaïs, 256

Nixon, Julie, 256

Nixon, Richard M.: Cambodia, invasion of, 155, 193; election of, 60; Hanoi and Haiphong, bombing of, 294; negative endorsement of Du Bois clubs, 255; reelection of, 74; and troop withdrawal from South Vietnam, 161; Vietnamization of South Vietnamese Army, 10; and Watergate scandal, 75, 269

No Limits, 175–87; excerpts from "Thus Spoke the Collective," 179–80; response to *Free For All* split, 177–80; "Who We Are," 176; "Wong Truth Conspiracy" (Wong), 181

No More Fun and Games, 387

NOLA Express, 131

Nonprofit Service Corporation (NPSC), 15

NOW, 278

O

Oakland, Calif.: police brutality against black communities, 341

Oakland Concerned Citizens for Urban Renewal, 359

Obama, Barack, xiv, xv, 187–88

Ochs, Phil, 74

O'Connor, Lynn, 406; "Male Dominance, the Nitty Gritty of Oppression," 390

off our backs, xvi, 269, 271, 280, 293, 411

Oglesby, Carl, 156

Ohio Prisoners Labor Union (OPLU), 316

Oil, Chemical, and Atomic Workers Union, 214

Old Left, 61

Old Mole, 113

Olson, McKinley: *Unacceptable Risk,* 181

On the Road (Kerouac), 81, 304

One Flew over the Cuckoo's Nest (Kesey), 293

One Magazine, 98

O'Neal, William, 343

One-String Sam, 73

Ono, Yoko, 74, 326

Open City, 63, 67

Oppenheim, James: "Bread and Roses" (poem), 391

Ortiz, Juan "Fi," 246

Orvino-Sorcic, Jennie, 392

Oscar Wilde Memorial Bookstore, New York City, 116

Oscar's Underground Ghetto Press, 156

Other Side, The, 45n15

Out Out Damn Faggot (play), 105

OUTLOOK (Berkeley), 116

Ovshinsky, Harvey: and *Fifth Estate,* 47–50, 51, 53, 56; resignation from *Fifth Estate,* 62–63

Ovshinsky, Stan, 47

P

Pabón, Diego, 245

Pacific Counseling Service, 19

Palante (newspaper for Young Lords Party), xii, 236, 251, 253

Palante (radio show), 253

Panda Bear. *See* Brubaker, Bob

Panther (film), 364

Parker, Dorothy, 391–92

Parker, Pat, 275, 408

Partisan Review, 117

Patchen, Kenneth, 303

Pedestal, 392

Peltz, Bill, 127; and Southern Media, 128, 131

"Pentagon Papers, The," 72

People Against Racism, 62

People into Sabotaging Surveillance (PISS), 294

People or Personnel (Goodman), 81

People Yes, The, 304–5, 307

People's Bicentennial Commission, 165

People's Dispatch, 162

People's Office, Madison, Wisc., 157, 160

People's Park demonstration, Berkeley, Calif. (May 15, 1969), 385–86

People's Temple, San Francisco, Calif., 361

Perez, David, 239, 244

Perez, Richie, 251

Perlman, Fredy, 82, 88

Perlman, Lorraine, 88

personal news journals: *Black Bart Brigade* (Thomas), 374, 384n3; *Heretic's Journal,* 374; *Little Free Press,* 374; *New Options* (Saun), 374, 384n5; *The Realist* (Krassner), 374; *Washington Spectator* (Coffin), 374, 384n5

Peterson, Tasha, 271, 276

Phillips, William, 117

Phoenix (Madison), 187

Phoenix, The, 256

Piercy, Marge, 303, 391; *Small Changes,* 68

Pinell, Hugo, 337

Plafkin, Sol, 62

Plain Rapper, 17

Plath, Sylvia, 392

Polar Bear. *See* McPherson, Scott

Pole, Frieda P. *See* Graff, Alison "Sunny"

police informants: John Miernik, 323; Steve Featherton, 168

police/COINTELPRO agent: William O'Neal, 343

political lesbianism, 272–75

Postman, Neil: *Teaching as a Subversive Activity,* 307

Power Failure (Dillaway), 220

Prairie Fire (Weather Underground), 168

Prairie Fire Organizing Committee, 326

Preface to a 20-Volume Suicide Note (Jones), 81

Problem in Greek Ethics, A (Symonds), 97

Progressive Action Caucus of the United Glass and Ceramic Workers, 220–21, 229–31

Progressive Labor Party, 126, 312; campaign for SDS to break ties with SSOC, 135, 137; power struggle with Communist Party in SDS, 138–39

Prospects for Revolution (Conant), 48–49

Prosser, Rosalie, 402

Pryor, Richard, 234–35

Psst!, 156

Pudovkin: *The End of St. Petersburg,* 409

Puerto Rican activist groups, New York City, 239–41, 242

Puerto Rican independence, support for, 326

Puerto Ricans, militant history of, 235–36

Puharich, Andrija, 376

Purple Berries, 305–6, 307, 308

Pyongyang Times (North Korea), 181–82

Python, Monty: *The Life of Brian* (film), 312

Q

Quest: A Feminist Quarterly, 281

Quicksilver Times, 316

Quigley, John (pseud. Amy Cuscuria; Vanya; E. Victor), 310, 312, 320, 323, 326, 327, 331; report on the Kampuchea, Cambodia Killing Fields, 330

Quimby, Bill, 306, 307, 308, 310, 311

Quimby, Sandi, 306, 308, 310

R

Rackham, Earlene. *See* Earlene Rothman

Radical Education Project, Ann Arbor, Mich., 63

RadicaLesbians, 394

"Radio with a View," WMBR 88.1 FM (Boston, Mass.), xiii

Ragazine, 325

Rainbow Coalition, 58, 76

Rainbow Lobby, 76

Ramparts, 344, 363, 370, 397

Rarihokwats, 377

Rasputin, 263

Rastillini, Eddie, 118

Rat, 129, 248, 253, 393

Ravitz, Mel, 78

Reagan, Ronald, xiii, 118, 185, 263, 385

Real Great Society (RGS), 241

Realist, The, 81, 374

Red Book Prison Project, 119

Redfield, Dana, 381–82

Redstockings West, 392, 405, 406

Reeves, Tom, 107, 108

Reid, Coletta, 271, 276, 277, 280

religious cults, rise of, 77, 80, 92

Renaissance, 305

Republic of New Africa, 58; gun battle with Jackson vice squad, 148–49

Republican National Convention, Miami Beach, Fla. (August 1972), 318

Revolution for the Hell of It (Hoffman), 303

Revolutionary Action Movement, 342

Revolutionary Anarchist Alliance, 184

Revolutionary Letters (DiPrima), 81

Revolutionary Movement, 342

Revolutionary People's Constitutional Convention, 307

Revolutionary Student Brigade, 165

Revolutionary Union, 164

Revolutionary Youth Movement, 369

Rhodes, James, 328, 330

Ricciardo, Paul, 306, 307

Richards, Beah (actress): *Guess Who's Coming to Dinner* (film), 391

Richardson, Beulah (pseud. Beah Richards), 391;

"A Black Woman Speaks" (poem), 391; *A Black Woman Speaks* (documentary film), 391

Riddle, Dave: and *Fifth Estate*, 61, 64–65, 74–75, 77, 79, 83; letter to the editor of *Fifth Estate*, 87; and march on Chrysler's Warren Tank Plant, 71; and Radical Education Project (Ann Arbor), 63

Riegle, Mike, 118, 119; translation of "The Simplest of Pleasures [Suicide]" (Foucault), 112

Rifkin, Jeremy, 165

Right On Post, 17

Riis, Jacob: *How the Other Half Lives*, 303

River, Charles, 108

Rivera, Geraldo, 241–42

Road, The, 44n1

Robbins, Trina, xvi–xvii, 394, 408; creator of *Belinda Berkeley* comic strip, 401, 413; "Feminists Do Have a Sense of Humor: The First Women's Comix," 412–15; *Forbidden City: The Golden Age of Chinese Nightclubs*, 408; *It Aint Me Babe Comix*, 401–2

Roberts, Tom: and *Aboveground*, 1–4, 8, 10, 13, 17; death of, 14

Robinson, Tyrone, 338

Roehm, Bob, 330

Rogers, Doug, 129

Rogers, Lynn, 129

Roldan, Julio, 242

Role, Roxanne, 326

Rolling Stone, 133, 374, 375

Roselyn (folk singer), 73

Rosen, Ruth: *The World Split Open: How the Modern Women's Movement Changed America*, 388; "You've Come a Long Way Baby: Women's Magazines, 1860–1960," 391

Roszak, Theodore: *The Making of a Counterculture*, 371

Rothman, Earlene (pseud. Earlene Dennison; Earlene Rackham), 327, 330

Rothman, Steve, 327

Rowe, Bill, 71

Rucker, Madalynn C., 365

Rudd, Mark, 137, 139, 145

Rusk, Bill, 144, 149

Russell, Harold, 351
Ryan, Betty, 393
Ryan, Leo, 361
Ryder, [Free] Lance. *See* Abbott, Steve

S

Sacco, Ferdinando, 216
Sacstrated, 18
Safransky, Sy: *The Sun,* 374, 384n4
Salcetti, Marianne, 322
Salt of the Earth (film), 388
Samphan, Khieu, 183
San Francisco Chronicle, 388, 396
San Francisco Experience (Farinella), 118
San Francisco Good Times, 413
San Francisco Mime Troupe, 296, 406
San Francisco Oracle, 260
San Quentin 6 trial, 337–38
Sanchez, Ken, 114
Sanchez, Vilma, 392
Sanders, Bernie, xv
Santeria, 235
Sarachild, Kathie, 386
Sarber, Margaret, 312, 316, 328
Satin, Mark, 374, 384n5
Savio, Mario, 154
Schafer, Len, 74, 76, 81, 83–84
Scheer, Robert, 255
Scherr, Max, 378
Schlesinger, Wendy, 392
Schoenfeld, Eugene, 54–55
Schrieber, Ron, 108
Schwartz, Nomi, 164, 165, 170
Schwing, Lee, 271
Score, Herb, 162
Scott, Ron, 365
S.C.U.M. Manifesto (Solanas), 65, 406
Seale, Bobby, 350, 358; benefit concert for John
    Sinclair, attendance at, 74; *Black Panther: The
    Revolutionary Art of Emory Douglas,* essays
    in, 348; cofounder of the Black Panther
    Party, 155, 335, 336, 338, 355, 365; leader
    of protest against California's Mulford Bill,

341–42
Second Congress to Unite Women (May 1970),
    394
Second Front, 45n5
Seldes, George, 378
Selective Service System, 134–35
Senate Subcommittee to Investigate the Admin-
    istration of the Internal Security Act and
    Other Internal Security Laws: *Organized Sub-
    version in the U.S. Armed Forces* (September
    25, 1975), 14
Service Employees International Union, 70
Shakedown, 17
Shameless Hussy Press: *For Colored Girls Who
    Have Considered Suicide When the Rainbow
    Is Enuf* (Shange), 402; Judith Arcana, early
    works of, 408; Mary Mackey, early works of,
    408; Mitsuye Yamada, early works of, 408;
    Ntozake Shange, early works of, 408; Pat
    Parker, early works of, 408; Susan Griffin,
    early works of, 408
Shange, Ntozake, 408; *For Colored Girls Who Have
    Considered Suicide When the Rainbow Is Enuf,*
    402
Shelley, Martha, 392
Shively, Charley, 106–20; "Browning Evergreen
    32" (poem), 98; "Exiles' Kingdom" (poem),
    98–99; "Millennium" (poem), 120
Short Times, 17
Shumsky, Ellen: "Women-Identified-Woman"
    (Lavender Action), 394
Shurin, Aaron: *Exorcism of the Straight Man
    Demon,* 107–8
Sick Slip, 45n16
sickle cell anemia, 356
Sierra Club, 89
Silkwood, Karen, 185
Silverthorne, Maya, 101
Simpson, David, 136
Sinclair, John: Artist's Workshop (Detroit),
    49–50; benefit concert for, 74; and *Fifth
    Estate,* 51; *Guitar Army,* 50; and Motor City
    Five rock group, 52; and *Warren-Forest Sun,*
    54; and White Panther Party, 62

Sinclair, Leni, 51

Skinner, Louis, 149

Skinner, Sandra, 322

Skinner, Stephen, 323

Small Changes (Piercy), 68

Smart magazine, 363

Smith, Clark, 12

Smith, David Emerson, 108

Smith, Donna, 326

Smith, Jack: *Flaming Creatures* (film), 54

Snyder, Gary, 91

socialism in Chile, 212, 214

Socialist Workers Party, 61–62

Sociedad de Albizu Campos, New York City, 234

Society for Cutting Up Men (S.C.U.M.), 65

Soglin, Paul, 155, 160, 162

Solanas, Valerie: *S.C.U.M. Manifesto*, 65, 406

Soledad Brother: The Prison Letters of George Jackson (Jackson), 338

Sometimes a Great Notion (Kesey), 293

Sonoma County Women's Voices, 407

Sophia Perovskaya and Andrei Zhelyabov Memorial Society for Peoples' Freedom through Women's Liberation (SPAZM): published by Laura X, 388, 410–11

South End (Wayne State University), 57, 61, 75, 88; name change from *Wayne State Daily Collegian*, 59; and relationship with *Fifth Estate*, 59–60

South Vietnam, 191, 318; fall of Saigon, 325; Tet Offensive, 61; U.S. companies, comparison of U.S. and Vietnam workers, 208–10; withdrawal of U.S. troops from, 161

Southern Christian Leadership Conference (SCLC), 255, 342

Southern Exposure, 139

Southern nationalism, 135–36

Southern Student Organizing Committee (SSOC), 123–24; disintegration of, 121, 137–38

Spain, Johnny, 336

SPAZM: published by Laura X, 388, 410–11

Spock, Benjamin, 256

Spoerl, Steve, 183–85, 186, 187; "Cambodia Goes to Pot," 183

Spretnak, Charlene, 379; *Green Politics: The Global Promise*, 378

Standard Mirror Company, South Buffalo, N.Y., 196; working conditions, 189–90, 228–29

Stapp, Andrew, 27

Stearns, Roger, 116

steelworker strikes, 217, 218–20

Steffes, Bob, 182

Steichen, Edward, 98

Steinbeck, John: *Grapes of Wrath*, 303

Steinem, Gloria, 81, 278

Steppenwolf, 370

Stern, Marc, xiii

Sterrett, Sandy, 322

Sterrett, Stephen, 323

Stiner, George, 352, 354

Stiner, Larry, 352, 354

Stocker, Curt, 12; and *Aboveground*, 1–4, 8, 10, 13, 17; interrogation of Harry Haines about Stocker's activities, 7

Stone, I. F., 378

Stone, Merlin: *When God Was a Woman*, 303

Stone, Peggy, 129

Stonewall Rebellion, New York City (June 27, 1969), 65, 97, 98–99

Strategic Hamlet, 17

Street Sheet, 97, 105

Strike Support Coalition, 76

Stringfellow, William, 377

Struggle for a Better South: The Southern Student Organizing Committee, 1964–1969 (Michel), 139, 140

Stryker, David, 113

Student as Nigger (Farber), 64

Student Homophile League, Boston, Mass., 99

Student Mobilization to End the War, 27

Student Nonviolent Coordinating Committee (SNCC), 124, 255, 342; merger with Black Panther Party, 344

student shootings, reports in various underground papers: Jackson State University, 64, 141, 155, 305, 370; Kent State University, 64, 141, 155, 193, 260, 305, 311, 370

Students for a Democratic Society (SDS), 123;

campaign to eliminate ROTC programs from college campuses, 192; Days of Rage protest, Chicago, Ill. (Fall 1969), 155; in Mississippi, disintegration of, 121, 139; national convention, Chicago, Ill. (June 1969), 65; national convention, Clear Lake, Iowa (1966), 124–25; Ohio State University chapter, 304; Port Huron Statement (1962), 52; University of Buffalo chapter, 192; University of Oregon chapter, 290; University of Wisconsin chapter newsletter, 156; Weatherman group, 2, 139

Sun, The (personal journal) (Safransky), 374, 384n4

Surkin, Marvin: *Detroit: I Do Mind Dying,* 73

Sutherland, Donald, 15

Sweet, Ossian, 49

Sydney, Sylvia, 101

Sydney FTA, 45n17

Symonds, John Addington: *A Problem in Greek Ethics,* 97

T

Tackwood, Louis, 338

Take Over, 158–60, 188n1

Talamentez, Luis, 337

Tate, Willie, 337

Tax, Meredith, 391, 392

Teaching as a Subversive Activity (Postman), 307

Teamsters Union, 70

Teemer, Mark, 348

Tejas Light, The, 379, 384n9

10-point 5 arts magazine, 296–97

Thomas, Irv, 384n3; *Black Bart Brigade,* 374, 377

Thomas, Joan, 382

Thompson, William Irwin, 375

Time magazine socialism exposé, 181–82

Tomato, Colinda. *See* Neiburger, Colin

Tooth and Nail, 387

Torres, José "Chegui," 242

Tour, Kwame. *See* Carmichael, Stokely

Trial, The (Kafka), 303

Trotskyist Socialist Workers Party, 51–52

Tubman, Harriet, 234, 390–91

Turner, Nat, 234

Twin Cities Female Liberation Newsletter, 392

U

UFO (first GI coffeehouse, Columbia, SC), 15

Ultimate Weapon, The, 17

Unacceptable Risk (Olson), 181

underground papers, Madison: reunion for veterans of (1989), 160

underground press: after demise of SDS and SSOC, 148; *The Bond,* xi; factors that gave rise to, 303–4; *Fifth Estate,* xi; formation of syndicate, 293; *Free Press* (Columbus), xii

Underground Press Syndicate: conference, Boulder, Colo. (1973), 162; network of counterculture newspapers and magazines, 131, 148, 293, 307, 315, 316

Underground Underdog, 156

Unfair Arguments with Existence (Ferlinghetti), 81

Unicorn, The, 128

United Auto Workers, 48; national convention, Atlantic City, N.J. (1972), 69; strikes, 201, 214

United Electrical Workers Union (UE), 194, 228

United Farmworkers, 70, 359

United Furniture Workers of America, 228

United Glass and Ceramic Workers union: Progressive Action Caucus, 220–21, 229–31

United Slaves (US), 352, 354

United States Servicemen's Fund (USSF), 1, 4, 15

University of Buffalo, Buffalo, N.Y.: shootings of student strikers, 193

University of Wisconsin Business School, Madison, Wisc., 154

Urbas, Sue, 312, 328

U.S. House of Representatives: Committee on Internal Security, 350

USS Enterprise, 19

USS Forrestal, 18

Utne, Eric, 375, 378

Utne Reader, 375, 378